Lecture Notes in Computer Science 3108

Commenced Publication in 1973
Founding and Former Series Editors:
Gerhard Goos, Juris Hartmanis, and Jan van Leeuwen

T0181467

Huaxiong Wang   Josef Pieprzyk
Vijay Varadharajan (Eds.)

Information Security and Privacy

9th Australasian Conference, ACISP 2004
Sydney, Australia, July 13-15, 2004
Proceedings

 Springer

Volume Editors

Huaxiong Wang
Josef Pieprzyk
Vijay Varadharajan
Macquarie University
Department of Computing
Sydney, NSW 2109, Australia
E-mail: {hwang,josef,vijay}@ics.mq.edu.au

Library of Congress Control Number: 2004108445

CR Subject Classification (1998): E.3, K.6.5, D.4.6, C.2, E.4, F.2.1, K.4.1

ISSN 0302-9743
ISBN 3-540-22379-7 Springer-Verlag Berlin Heidelberg New York

Springer-Verlag is a part of Springer Science+Business Media

springeronline.com

© Springer-Verlag Berlin Heidelberg 2004
Printed in Germany

Typesetting: Camera-ready by author, data conversion by PTP-Berlin, Protago-TeX-Production GmbH
Printed on acid-free paper   SPIN: 11019282   06/3142   5 4 3 2 1 0

Preface

The 9th Australasian Conference on Information Security and Privacy (ACISP 2004) was held in Sydney, 13–15 July, 2004. The conference was sponsored by the Centre for Advanced Computing – Algorithms and Cryptography (ACAC), Information and Networked Security Systems Research (INSS), Macquarie University and the Australian Computer Society.

The aims of the conference are to bring together researchers and practitioners working in areas of information security and privacy from universities, industry and government sectors. The conference program covered a range of aspects including cryptography, cryptanalysis, systems and network security.

The program committee accepted 41 papers from 195 submissions. The reviewing process took six weeks and each paper was carefully evaluated by at least three members of the program committee. We appreciate the hard work of the members of the program committee and external referees who gave many hours of their valuable time.

Of the accepted papers, there were nine from Korea, six from Australia, five each from Japan and the USA, three each from China and Singapore, two each from Canada and Switzerland, and one each from Belgium, France, Germany, Taiwan, The Netherlands and the UK. All the authors, whether or not their papers were accepted, made valued contributions to the conference.

In addition to the contributed papers, Dr Arjen Lenstra gave an invited talk, entitled *Likely and Unlikely Progress in Factoring*.

This year the program committee introduced the Best Student Paper Award. The winner of the prize for the Best Student Paper was Yan-Cheng Chang from Harvard University for his paper *Single Database Private Information Retrieval with Logarithmic Communication*.

We would like to thank all the people involved in organizing this conference. In particular we would like to thank members of the organizing committee for their time and efforts, Andrina Brennan, Vijayakrishnan Pasupathinathan, Hartono Kurnio, Cecily Lenton, and members from ACAC and INSS.

July 2004

Huaxiong Wang
Josef Pieprzyk
Vijay Varadharajan

Australasian Conference on Information Security and Privacy
ACISP 2004

Sponsored by
Centre for Advanced Computing – Algorithms and Cryptography (ACAC)
Information and Networked Security Systems Research (INSS)
Macquarie University
Australian Computer Society

General Chair:

Vijay Varadharajan   *Macquarie University, Australia*

Program Chairs:

Josef Pieprzyk   *Macquarie University, Australia*
Huaxiong Wang   *Macquarie University, Australia*

Program Committee

Feng Bao   *Institute for Infocomm Research, Singapore*
Lynn Batten   *Deakin University, Australia*
Colin Boyd   *QUT, Australia*
Nicolas Courtois   *Axalto Smart Cards, France*
Ed Dawson   *QUT, Australia*
Yvo Desmedt   *Florida State University, USA*
Cunsheng Ding   *Hong Kong University of Sci. & Tech., China*
Dieter Gollmann   *Technical University of Hamburg, Germany*
Goichiro Hanaoka   *University of Tokyo, Japan*
Thomas Johansson   *Lund University, Sweden*
Kwangjo Kim   *ICU, Korea*
Kaoru Kurosawa   *Ibaraki Univ., Japan*
Kwok-Yan Lam   *Tsinghua University, China*
Keith Martin   *Royal Holloway, UK*
Yi Mu   *University of Wollongong, Australia*
Christine O'Keefe   *CSIRO, Australia*
David Pointcheval   *CNRS, France*
Leonid Reyzin   *Boston University, USA*
Greg Rose   *Qualcomm, Australia*
Rei Safavi-Naini   *University of Wollongong, Australia*
Palash Sarkar   *Indian Statistical Institute, India*
Jennifer Seberry   *University of Wollongong, Australia*

Igor Shparlinski   *Macquarie University, Australia*
Doug Stinson   *University of Waterloo, Canada*
Hung-Min Sun   *National Tsinghua University, Taiwan*
Serge Vaudenay   *EPFL, Switzerland*
Chaoping Xing   *National University of Singapore, Singapore*

External Referees

Mehdi-Laurent Akkar	Matt Henricksen	Miyako Ohkubo
Kazumaro Aoki	Shoichi Hirose	Yasuhiro Ohtaki
Tomoyuki Asano	Yvonne Hitchcock	Wakaha Ogata
Paul Ashley	Chiou-Ting Hsu	Michael Paddon
Nuttapong Attrapadung	Min-Shiang Hwang	Doug Palmer
Roberto Avanzi	Gene Itkis	Jacques Patarin
Gildas Avoine	Toshiya Itoh	Kenny Paterson
Thomas Baigneres	Tetsu Iwata	Kun Peng
Emmanuel Bresson	Marc Joye	Krzysztof Pietrzak
Dario Catalano	Pascal Junod	Angela Piper
Sanjit Chatterjee	Byoungcheon Lee	Jason Reid
Chien-Ning Chen	Yan-Xia Lin	Ryuichi Sakai
Ling-Hwei Chen	Der-Chyuan Lou	Renate Scheidler
Xiaofeng Chen	Chi-Jen Lu	Nichoas Sheppard
Bo-Chao Cheng	Stefan Lucks	SeongHan Shin
Chi-Hung Chi	Phil MacKenzie	Leonie Simpson
Joo Yeon Cho	Subhamoy Maitra	Hong-Wei Sun
Siu-Leung Chung	Cecile Malinaud	Willy Susilo
Andrew Clark	Tal Malkin	Isamu Teranishi
Scott Contini	Wenbo Mao	Dong To
Don Coppersmith	Thomas Martin	Woei-Jiunn Tsaur
Yang Cui	Tatsuyuki Matsushita	Din-Chang Tseng
Tanmoy Kanti Das	Toshihiro Matsuo	Takeyuki Uehara
Alex Dent	Luke Mcaven	David Wagner
Christophe Doche	Robert McNerney	Chih-Hung Wang
Ratna Dutta	Tom Messerges	William Whyte
Chun-I Fan	Pradeep Kumar Mishra	Hongjun Wu
Serge Fehr	Chris Mitchell	Tzong-Chen Wu
Ernest Foo	Jean Monnerat	Sung-Ming Yen
Pierre-Alain Fouque	Joern Mueller-Quade	Lu Yi
Jun Furukawa	James Muir	Takuya Yoshida
Rosario Gennaro	Seiji Munetoh	Ming Yung
Juanma Gonzalez-Nieto	Sean Murphy	Moti Yung
Louis Goubin	Anderson Nascimento	Fangguo Zhang
Zhi Guo	Lan Ngyuen	Rui Zhang
Philip Hawkes	Phong Nguyen	Xi-Bin Zhao
Martin Hell	Philippe Oechslin	

Table of Contents

Cryptanalysis (II)

Digital Signatures (I)

Cryptosystems (I)

Security Management

Access Control and Authorisation

Cryptosystems (II)

Cryptanalysis (III)

Author Index

Multi-service Oriented Broadcast Encryption

Shaoquan Jiang and Guang Gong

Department of Electrical and Computer Engineering
University of Waterloo
Waterloo, Ontario N2L 3G1, CANADA
{jiangshq, ggong}@calliope.uwaterloo.ca

Abstract. Multi-service oriented broadcast encryption is a mechanism that allows a center to securely distribute multiple services to its authorized users. In this paper, we suggest a framework called $\mathcal{M}$ framework from the subset cover method [12] using RSA exponentiation technique. In this framework, each user's secret storage is independent of the number of services. Service subscriptions and service providing can be efficiently processed. The service unsubscriptions are dealt scalably. A small number of service unsubscriptions can be handled without key updating while the number of such users reaches a threshold, a rekeying algorithm is proposed to update the user's service memberships *explicitly*. We formalize and prove the framework is dynamically secure under the random oracle model. We realize our framework with a scheme based on complete subtree method.

1 Introduction

Broadcast encryption is a mechanism that allows one party to securely distribute his data to privileged users. This mechanism has important applications in Pay-TV, stock quotes and online database, etc. After the work by Fiat and Naor in 1993 [9], it has been extensively studied in the literature, for example, schemes for stateless receivers [1,12], public key based schemes [2,6,14] and rekeying schemes [16,15,4,10].

In this paper, we consider the multi-service oriented broadcast encryption (MOBE), which is explained as follows. Suppose that a broadcast center (BC) wants to distribute multiple services to a set of users such that each user is allowed to access a specific service if and only if he has subscribed to it. Here the security concerns are traitor tracing, service unsubscriptions, etc. A possible solution is to associate each service with a distinct system (in a single service setting). The main problem here is that a user's secret storage is proportional to the number of his subscribed services.

1.1 Related Work

MOBE problem is related to flexible access control by Chick and Tavares [5], where each user is assigned a master key using RSA exponentiation technique

H. Wang et al. (Eds.): ACISP 2004, LNCS 3108, pp. 1–11, 2004.

that allows him to access his subscribed services. However, users get an identical key set if they subscribe the same services. Thus, it is impossible to distinguish such users. Consequently, traitor tracing and service unsubscriptions are not achievable.

Narayanan, et al. [13] considered a multi-service notion called practical Pay-TV scheme. They proposed three schemes. The third one is the most interesting scheme which is secure and has traceability. However, their scheme is only suitable for application with a small number of services since the user key size is linear in the number of subscribed services. Furthermore, their service unsubscription utilizes a unicast channel. It follows that it is not suitable for applications with a large number of users or applications with frequent membership updating. The second scheme claimed the collusion can not compute the secret associated with service i. But we show that this is incorrect in the full paper [11].

1.2   Contribution

In this paper, we propose a framework called $\mathcal{M}$ framework for MOBE problem. We first achieve the multi-service functionality from the subset cover method [12] (in the single service setting) using RSA exponentiation technique. But this is not sufficient since it might become less efficient(e.g., the message overhead grows large; it increases management burdens; revoked IDs can not be reused) when unsubscription is frequent, due to lack of a rekeying mechanism. We thus propose a multi-service rekeying algorithm by extending a rekeying framework [7,10]. In the obtained full framework, user key size in $\mathcal{M}$ is independent of the number of services. Subscription and new service providing are handled without involving unintended users. Furthermore, service unsubscription is handled scalably, which makes the system flexible. To gain a better understanding of this framework, we realize it by an efficient scheme $\mathcal{M}_{cs}$, which is based on a complete subtree method [12]. Finally, in order to evaluate the security of our framework, we formalize a notion of *dynamic security*. It captures threats from an adaptive adversary that might issue queries such as subscription, rekeying, corruption and new service providing. We show that $\mathcal{M}$ framework is secure under such a *severe* attack. Our proof is in the random oracle model.

This paper is organized as follows. In Section 2, we introduce our $\mathcal{M}$ framework and show their features. In Sections 3, we present a realization of $\mathcal{M}$ framework, from complete subtree method. In Section 4, we formalize and prove the dynamic security of $\mathcal{M}$ framework.

2   A Framework for Multi-service Oriented Broadcast Encryption

In this section, we introduce our $\mathcal{M}$ framework for MOBE problem and show some advantages of this framework.

2.1   Description of $\mathcal{M}$ Framework

Let U be the set of all possible users; BC be the broadcast center; w be the number of services BC provides. BC wants to provide services $\{1, \cdots, w\}$ with a controlled access right.

Preprocessing Phase

1. BC chooses a RSA composite $N = pq$ and w primes $p_1, p_2, \cdots, p_w$, where p, q are two large primes. Then he makes $N, p_1, \cdots, p_w$ public and keeps p, q secret.
2. BC defines a collection of subsets of U: $S_1, S_2, \cdots, S_z$, where z is polynomially bounded. For security reason, we require that $\{u\}$ is contained in the collection for all $u \in U$. Then BC associates S_i with a secret number $k_i, i = 1, \cdots, z$.
3. BC defines $Q = \prod_{i=1}^{w} p_i$. Let $\{1, 2, \cdots, w\}$ be the set of services currently available, $B(u)$ be the set of services user u has subscribed, $Z(u) = \prod_{i \in B(u)} p_i$, and $K(u) = \{k_i^{Q/Z(u)} \pmod{N} | u \in S_i, i = 1, \cdots, z\}$.

Note that without a special mention in this paper we always assume that the exponentiation is carried out over modular N.

Join Phase.   When a new person asks for join, BC first finds a free ID $u \in U$ and assigns $K(u)$ and a random subscription key c_u to this person. Here c_u is only for subscription use and remains unchanged as long as he is in the system. We denote this person simply by u when the context is clear.

Broadcast Phase. Let U_i be the set of all the users that subscribe service i. When BC wants to broadcast message M of service i to all users in $U_i \backslash R_i$, for some $R_i \subseteq U_i$, he first finds a set cover $S_{i_1}, S_{i_2}, \cdots, S_{i_m}$ for $U \backslash R_i$, i.e., $S_{i_1} \cup S_{i_2} \cup \cdots \cup S_{i_m} = U \backslash R_i$. He then forms the ciphertext as

$$\mathcal{H}_i(R_i, M) := \langle i_1, \cdots, i_m, E_{sk_{i_1,i}}(k), \cdots, E_{sk_{i_m,i}}(k), F_k(M) \rangle, \qquad (1)$$

where $sk_{i_j,i} = f(k_{i_j}^{Q/p_i})$, E and F are two encryption algorithms (usually E has a higher security than F), $f : Z_N^* \rightarrow \{0,1\}^L$ is a public hash function where L is the key size of E.

Decryption Phase. When receiving $\mathcal{H}_i(R_i, M)$, a user u in $U_i \backslash R_i (\subseteq U \backslash R_i)$ first finds j such that $u \in S_{i_j}$. Since u has $k_{i_j}^{Q/Z(u)}$, he can compute $sk_{i_j,i}$ and obtain message M.

Subscribing More Services. We now show that it is convenient for an existing user u to subscribe more services. Suppose u wants to add service j to $B(u)$. He first updates $B(u)$ to $B'(u) = B(u) \cup \{j\}$, $Z(u)$ to $Z'(u) = Z(u) \times p_j$.

BC then provides a key set $\{k_i^{Q/p_j} | u \in S_i, i = 1, \cdots, z\}$ to u encrypted under the subscription key c_u. When u gets this key set, he can update $K(u)$ to $K'(u) := \{k_i^{Q/z'(u)} | u \in S_i, i = 1, \cdots, z\}$ as follows. He finds integers a, b using the Euclidean algorithm such that $p_j a + bZ(u) = 1$ and then computes

$$(k_i^{Q/Z(u)})^a (k_i^{Q/p_j})^b = k_i^{aQ/Z(u) + bQ/p_j} = k_i^{\frac{Q}{Z'(u)}(p_j a + Z(u)b)} = k_i^{Q/Z'(u)}.$$

It is clear that $K'(u)$ is the current key set for user u. For simplicity, we still denote the updated parameters as $K(u), B(u), Z(u)$, respectively.

Service Unsubscription. Some users R'_i may quit service i at some moment. The main concern is to prevent them from access to it again after their leave. If the size of R'_i is small, this can be handled without updating other users' secret information. Specifically, in the broadcast phase, BC can use a set R_i containing R'_i as the excluding set. However, as mentioned in the introduction, when the size of R'_i grows large, this method is inefficient. In our method, we propose an extension of a rekeying algorithm [7] to *explicitly* update users' service memberships, see the rekeying phase.

Providing New Services. We show that it is convenient for BC to provide a new service $(w + 1)$. To do this, BC first finds a prime number p_{w+1} and updates Q to $Q' = Q \times p_{w+1}$. Then he computes $q_{w+1} = p_{w+1}^{-1} \pmod{\phi(N)}$, where $\phi(\cdot)$ is the Euler function. For each k_i, he computes $k'_i := k_i^{q_{w+1}}$. For an existing user u, his secret key information keeps invariant since $k'^{Q'/Z(u)}_i = k_i^{Q/Z(u)}$. If u wants to subscribes service $(w + 1)$, BC provides p_{w+1} and $\{k'^{Q'/p_{w+1}}_i | u \in S_i, i = 1, \cdots, z\}$ to him, encrypted under c_u. Then u updates $B(u), Z(u), K(u)$.

As a summary, providing a service does not affect an existing user's activity or even he does not need to know about this new service. On the other hand, subscribing this new service is as easy as subscribing an existing service.

Rekeying Phase. When the size of the set R_i for quitting a certain service i grows large, the system will become inefficient. Thus it is desired to permanently update users' service memberships. Let $\Delta : U \to \{1, \cdots, w\}$ be a function such that $\Delta(u)$ is the set of services that u will quit in this rekeying event. Note that revoking an illegal user is looked as quitting all the services. Now we extend a rekeying algorithm in [7] to the multi-service setting. We remark that the rekeying algorithm in [7] is an extension of that in [10]. Let R be the set of users that will quit at least one service. Then for a given pair (R, Δ), we can *simultaneously* update every user's key information (for all possible services). In order to present the algorithm in a clear way, we introduce some notations.

Definition 1. *Define $C(k_i)$ to be the minimal subset of $\{k_1, \cdots, k_z\}$ containing k_i such that generation process for elements in $C(k_i)$ shares no random bits with generation process for elements in $\{k_1, \cdots, k_z\} \backslash C(k_i)$.*

Since k_t^{Q/p_j} needs updating if and only if k_t needs updating, we only need to determine the exact subset of $\{k_1, \cdots, k_z\}$ that needs updating. In fact we have the following lemma. The proof can be found in the full paper [11].

Lemma 1. *1. $C(k_i)$ and $C(k_j)$ are either disjoint or identical.*
2. Let R be the set of users that will quit at least one service, then the exact subset of $\{k_1, \cdots, k_z\}$ that need updating is $\cup_{i:S_i \cap R \neq \emptyset} C(k_i)$.

From this lemma, we see that the exact subset G to be updated is only dependent on R instead of (R, Δ). For future easy presentation reason, we would like to use the exact subcollection whose corresponding keys need updating. And denote this subcollection as $D(R)$. I.e., $D(R) := \{S_i : k_i \in G\}$.

Definition 2. *Let $S_1, \cdots, S_z$ be the subsets defined in the preprocessing phase. We say that S_i has a level l if there exists a chain of length l for S_i :*

$$S_{i_1} \subset S_{i_2} \subset \cdots \subset S_{i_{l-1}} \subset S_i, \qquad (2)$$

where $i_1, i_2, \cdots, i_{l-1}, i$ are distinct; and there is no such a chain of length $l+1$. We use $\subset$ to represent "proper subset".

Definition 3. *For two subsets S_i and S_j with $S_i \subset S_j$, if there exists no S_t such that $S_i \subset S_t \subset S_j$, then we say S_i is a child of S_j.*

Let L be the maximal level for subsets $S_1, \cdots, S_z$. Our rekeying algorithm is described as Table 1.

The figure 1 graphically demonstrates this rekeying process. In this figure $R = \{u_1, u_2, u_4, u_5\}$ (note that subsets not involved in the rekeying event are omitted in the graph). And u_1, u_4 will quit service j while u_2 and u_5 are still legal users for it. Thus u_2(resp. u_5) decrypts the ciphertext in the box and gets the key $k_2'^{Q/p_j}$ (resp. $k_5'^{Q/p_j}$). Then he uses this key for further updating.

The following lemma shows the completeness of the rekeying algorithm.

Lemma 2. *Any new service key $k_i'^{Q/p_j}$ is received by his designated users.*

2.2   Performance

Now we discuss some performance of our framework. Other parameters, e.g., broadcast overhead, rekeying complexity, can be clear only in a specific construction.

User Storage. From the key assignment, we know that user private storage is at most $|K(u)| + 1$[1] thus is independent of the number of services. On the other hand, an efficient representation of primes could be achieved by a generation

---

[1] Note the actual storage might be smaller than this(e.g., a construction based Asano method [1]). We omit in the current version due to the presentation complexity.

Table 1. Rekeying Algorithm

1. BC first updates $B(u), Z(u)$ for all $u \in R$, where R is the set of users that will quit one or more services according to Δ. For simplicity, we still use symbols $B(u), Z(u)$ after updating. Note that revoking an illegal user is considered as a case that he quits all the services.
2. Determine $D(R)$.
3. For each service $j = 1, \cdots, w$, do the following:
   For each set $S_i \in D(R)$ at level 1 do
       Let $S_i = \{u\}$. Send $E_{sk_{i,j}}(k_i^{\square Q/p_j})$ to u if $j \in B(u)$ where $sk_{i,j} = f(k_i^{Q/p_j})$.
   For $l = 2, \cdots, L$ do
   For each set $S_i \in D(R)$ at level l do
       For each child S_t of S_i, broadcast $E_{sk'_{t,j}}(k_i^{\square Q/p_j})$ to all users in S_t if at least one user in S_t is privileged for service j. Here $sk_{t,j}^\square = f(k_t^{\square Q/p_j})$, where $k_t^\square = k_t$ if it is not updated; otherwise, it is the updated value.

program. Thus the corresponding memory can be regarded as negligible. Thus, our framework has an important gain over the method using an indecent system for each service, especially when the number of services is large.

Flexible Subscription/Unsubscription. In our method, subscription has no interference with other users. Service unsubscription is scalable. A small number of service unsubscriptions can be treated without key updating while if such a number reaches a threshold, rekeying algorithm can update user key set explicitly. Such a scalability indeed avoids inefficiency problems occurred in a stateless scheme when unsubscriptions are frequent (e.g., incremental management burden, reduced capacity of users).

Traitor Tracing. Traitor tracing is an algorithm for finding illegal users who help build a pirate decoder with their secret keys. Naor et al. [12] presented a subset tracing algorithm to locate the traitors in logarithmic time if the system is secure and satisfies a bifurcation property. In our system, we can apply their algorithm for each service. Notice that the bifurcation is a property of the set collection $S_1, \cdots, S_z$. Thus, an efficient tracing procedure in their single setting implies an efficient one in our multi-service setting. If we suppose the encryption algorithms in the broadcast phase are ideal, then violation of the security of this tracing procedure implies that the capability for traitors to compute a service key which they are not entitled to. However, in our system a dynamic security guarantees that adversary has only a negligible success probability. Thus, a dynamic security implies the security of the tracing algorithm.

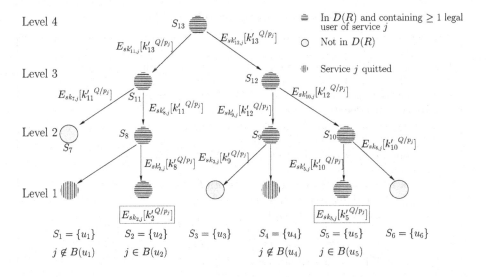

Fig. 1. A Small Example for Rekeying Process

3 $\mathcal{M}_{cs}$ Scheme

Complete Subtree (CS) broadcast encryption scheme for stateless receivers was proposed by Naor, et al. [12], which is a single service oriented scheme. Specifically, BC first builds a complete binary tree TR. Let its nodes be $v_1, \cdots, v_{2n-1}$ in width first order. Let the leaves $v_n, \cdots, v_{2n-1}$ represent users $u_1, \cdots u_n$. Then, he puts a random key k_i at each node v_i. A user's secret key set is composed of the keys on the path from the root to this user inclusive.

If we let S_i be the users rooted at node v_i, the multi-service scheme $\mathcal{M}_{cs}$ can be obtained from the above CS method as follow. Assume that $N, p_1, \cdots, p_w, B(u), Z(u)$ and Q are defined as in the framework. For ID u, $K(u) = \{k_i^{Q/Z(u)} | u \in S_i, i = 1, \cdots, z\}$. Message broadcast, decryption, User joining, Subscribing more services, service unsubscriptions and providing new services can be done as specified in $\mathcal{M}$ framework. Next we present our rekeying algorithm.

Rekeying Algorithm. It is clear that the maximal level among that of subsets $S_1, \cdots, S_{2n-1}$ is $L = 1 + \log n$. Since the fact that S_i has level l is equivalent to say v_i at depth $L - l$. Suppose that the users in R have one or more services to quit. Note that a different user can quite arbitrary services of his choice. Our rekeying algorithm can handle the service quitting for all R *simultaneously*, see Table 2. This algorithm actually is an extension of [10] to the multi-service setting. We remark that in the single service setting, the algorithm for one user quitting was proposed in [3,16].

Table 2. Rekeying Algorithm for $\mathcal{M}_{cs}$

---

1. BC updates $B(u), Z(u)$ for all $u \in R$ (but we still use these symbols for simplicity). Then he finds $Steiner(R)$ (i.e., the smallest subtree in TR that includes R and the root) and for each $v_i \in Steiner(R)$ he updates k_i to a random number $k_i^{\square}$ of the same length.
2. For service $j = 1, \cdots, w$ do the following:
    (i) For each $v \in Steiner(R)$ at depth $L - 1$ do
         Suppose $S_i = \{v\}$. BC sends $E_{sk_{i,j}}(k_i^{\square Q/p_j})$ to v if $j \in B(v)$.
    (ii) For $l = L - 2, \cdots, 0$ do
         For each node $v_i \in Steiner(R)$ at depth l,
             BC updates k_i to a random key $k_i^{\square}$;
             For each child v_b of v_i, he
             sends $E_{sk'_{b,j}}(k_i^{\square Q/p_j})$ to all users rooted at v_b if $\exists$ a privileged user; where
             $sk_{b,j}^{\square} = f(k_b^{\square Q/p_j})$ and $k_b^{\square}$ is the current associated random number for v_b if it is updated; otherwise, $k_b^{\square} = k_b$.

3.1   Performance

Now we briefly summarize the performance of $\mathcal{M}_{cs}$. The following parameters are of main concerns: (1) user secret storage, (2) the message overhead in the broadcast phase, i.e. the number of the cover sets used there, and (3) the number of rekeying ciphertexts, representing the computational complexity at the server and the number of times to use a broadcast channel. In $\mathcal{M}_{cs}$, a user only needs to store $1 + \log n$ secret keys in $K(u)$. Additionally, he should store $p_1, \cdots, p_w, N$ and $B(u)$ (as before, when w is large, primes p_i's can be represented by a generation program). The message overhead in the broadcast phase is $r \log(n/r)$, where $r = |R_i|$. The number of rekeying ciphertexts is upperbounded by $rw \log(n/r)$) for $r = |R|$. This can be easily proved by induction. Notice r for R or R_i is always less than a threshold. Thus, these two parameters can always be controlled small. Furthermore, the traceability property inherits from that of the original CS method, due to its dynamic security (see security section).

4   Security

In this section, we investigate the security of our $\mathcal{M}$ framework. We only consider the security threats from the dynamic feature of key assignments. We first give a primitive notion of key computational infeasibility property, which is similar to the notion of key indistinguishability [12]. Then we formalize an adversary model for $\mathcal{M}$ framework and analyze the *dynamic security* of $\mathcal{M}$ framework under the random oracle model.

Definition 4. *Let $\mathcal{A}$ be any probabilistic polynomial time (PPT) adversary against the (static) key assignment of $\mathcal{M}$ scheme. And let $\{p_1, \cdots, p_\nu\}$ be the set of primes currently used to define the service keys. Let k_t be the key associated with $S_t, t = 1, \cdots, z$. $\mathcal{A}$ first chooses a pair (i, j). Then he receives all k_t for $S_t \not\subseteq S_i$ and all $k_r^{p_j}$ for all $S_r \subseteq S_i$. The $\mathcal{M}$ scheme is said to satisfy* key computational infeasibility (KCI) property *if the success probability of $\mathcal{A}$ is negligible.*

We are now ready to formalize an adversary model to $\mathcal{M}$ framework, for which the KCI property is not affected by the dynamic feature of key assignments. In other words, we consider that $\mathcal{A}$ can issue four types of queries: corrupting existing users, providing new services, subscribing more services, running the rekeying algorithm. As a response, the ciphertexts in case of the last two events will be provided to the adversary. Upon corruption, the corrupted user's secret key set as well as his subscription key will be provided to adversary. After interaction with the challenger for a while, he announces to attack on a specific service key. He then tries to compute the target. The $\mathcal{M}$ scheme is said to be *dynamically secure* if the success probability of $\mathcal{A}$ is negligible. Formally,

Definition 5. *Let $\mathcal{A}$ be a PPT adversary against $\mathcal{M}$ scheme. We let $u \in U$ always represent the user who is currently using it. $\mathcal{A}$ first choose (i, j) as his target. Then $\mathcal{A}$ can issue the following queries.*

1. *He can request to provide a new service. As a response, the challenger will choose a new prime p_{w+1} and then update k_r to $k_r' = k_r^{q_{w+1}}$, where $q_{w+1} = p_{w+1}^{-1} \pmod{\phi(N)}$ and w is the number of existing services. Then he provides p_{w+1} to $\mathcal{A}$.*
2. *He can ask to subscribe a new service J on behalf of some user u. As a response, $\mathcal{A}$ will receive the ciphertext $E_{c_u}(\{k_r^{Q/p_J} : u \in S_r, r = 1, \cdots, z\})$.*
3. *He can ask to execute the rekeying algorithm on (R, Δ) of his choice, where $\Delta : R \to \{1, \cdots, w\}$ is a function such that $\Delta(u)$ is the set of services that u will quit in this query. As a response, he will receive all the ciphertexts in this rekeying event.*
4. *He can ask to corrupt a user u. As a response, $\mathcal{A}$ will receive $K(u)$ as well as c_u.*

After interaction with the challenger for a while, $\mathcal{A}$ can announce to attack as long as no user in S_i, who is privileged for service j, is corrupted at the present time. $\mathcal{M}$ scheme is said to be dynamically secure *if the success probability for $\mathcal{A}$ to compute k_i^{Q/p_j} is only negligible.*

Remark 1. Two clarifications follow here.

1. When adversary announces to attack, we require that currently corrupted persons should not be privileged for service j. This is reasonable since such a person directly has k_i^{Q/p_j}. Obviously, success by this does not imply the weakness of the system. On the other hand, we stress that we indeed allow a

user to be corrupted at some earlier time but later purged from the system (recall that revoking a user is looked as quitting all the services).

2. We require the adversary to select his target pair (i, j) before his interaction. This has the same power as an adversary who chooses his target adaptively. The reason is that a non-adaptive adversary always can correctly guess the target pair of an adaptive adversary with non-negligible probability.

By the above security model, we have the following theorem. The proof can be found in the full paper [11].

Theorem 1. *Assume that E is semantically secure against chosen plaintext attack (IND-CPA). Let $f()$ be a random oracle. For any i, $C(k_i)$ is distributed exactly the same as $\{k_j^a | k_j \in C(k_i)\}, i = 1, \cdots, z$, where a is coprime with $\phi(N)$. If the (static) key assignment of $\mathcal{M}$ satisfies KCI property, then it is* dynamically secure.

Based on Theorem 1, we can easily conclude the security of $\mathcal{M}_{cs}$.

Corollary 1. *If k_i is uniformly random in Z_N^*, $i = 1, \cdots, z$, and E is secure against CPA attack, then $\mathcal{M}_{cs}$ is dynamically secure.*

Acknowledgements. The authors would like to thank anonymous referees for instructive comments. Shaoquan Jiang would like to thank Huaxiong Wang for encouragement.

References

1. T. Asano, A Revocation Scheme with Minimal Storage at Receivers, *Advanced in Cryptology-Asiancrypt'02*, Y. Zheng (Ed.), LNCS 2501, Springer-verlag, 2002, pp. 433-450.
2. D. Boneh and M. K. Franklin, An Efficient Public Key Traitor Tracing Scheme, *Advances in Cryptology-CRYPTO'99*, M. J. Wiener (ed.), LNCS 1666, Springer-verlag, 1999, pp. 338-353.
3. R. Canetti, J. A. Garay, G. Itkis, D. Micciancio, M. Naor and B. Pinkas, Multicast Security: A Taxonomy and Some Efficient Constructions, *IEEE INFOCOM'99*, 21-25, March 1999, New York, Vol. 2, 708-716
4. R. Canetti, T. Malkin and K. Nissim, Efficient Communication-Storage Tradeoffs for Multicast Encryption, *Advances in Cryptology-EUROCRYPT'99*, J. Stern (Ed.), LNCS 1592, Springer-verlag, 1999, pp. 459-474.
5. Gerald C. Chick, Stafford E. Tavares, Flexible Access Control with Master Keys, *Advances in Cryptology-CRYPTO'89*, G. Brassard (Ed.), LNCS 435, 1990, Springer-verlag, 316-322.
6. Y. Dodis and N. Fazio, Public Key Trace and Revoke Scheme Secure against Adaptive Chosen Ciphertext Attack, *Public Key Cryptography 2003*, Y. Desmedt (Ed.), LNCS 2567, Springer-verlag, 2002, pp. 100-115.
7. S. Jiang and G. Gong, Hybrid Broadcast Encryption and Security Analysis, Available at http://eprint.iacr.org/2003/241.

8. Yong Ho Hwang, Chong Hee Kim, Pil Joong Lee, An Efficient Revocation Scheme with Minimal Message Length for Stateless Receivers, *ACISP 2003*, 377-386.
9. A. Fiat and M. Naor, Broadcast Encryption, *Advances in Cryptology-CRYPTO'93*, D. Stinson (Ed.), LNCS 773, Springer-verlag, 1994, pp. 480-491.
10. Hartono Kurnio, Reihaneh Safavi-Naini, Huaxiong Wang, A Secure Re-keying Scheme with Key Recovery Property, ACISP 2002, L. M. Batten et al. (Eds.), LNCS 2384, Springer-Verlag, 2002, pp. 40-55.
11. Shaoquan Jiang and Guang Gong, Multi-service Oriented Broadcast Encryption, Available at http://calliope.uwaterloo.ca/~jiangshq
12. D. Naor, M. Naor and J. Lotspiech, Revocation and Tracing Schemes for Stateless Receivers, *Advances in Cryptology-Crypto'01*, J. Kilian (Ed.), LNCS 2139, Springer-verlag, 2001, pp. 41-62.
13. Arvind Narayanan, C. Pandu Rangan, Kwangjo Kim, Practical Pay TV Schemes. *ACISP 2003*, 192-203.
14. W. Tzeng and Z. Tzeng, A Public-Key Traitor Tracing Scheme with Revocation Using Dynamic Shares, *Public Key Cryptography 2001*, K. Kim (ed.), LNCS 1992, Springer-verlag, 2001, pp. 207-224.
15. D. M. Wallner, E. J. Harder and R. C. Agee, Key Management for Multicast: Issues and Architectures, Internet Request for Comments 2627, June, 1999. Available: ftp.ietf.org/rfc/rfc2627.txt
16. Chung Kei Wong, Mohamed G. Gouda, Simon S. Lam, Secure Group Communication Using Key Graphs, *Sigcomm'98*.

Secure and Insecure Modifications of the Subset Difference Broadcast Encryption Scheme

Tomoyuki Asano

Sony Corporation
6-7-35 Kitashinagawa, Shinagawa-ku, Tokyo 141-0001, Japan
tomo@arch.sony.co.jp

Abstract. In ACISP 2003, Hwang et al. proposed a broadcast encryption scheme, which is a modification of the Subset Difference (SD) method. In this paper we present how their scheme can be broached in a way a collusion of two receivers can obtain other receivers' keys which are not given to any of the colluding receivers. We also propose a new method using trapdoor one-way permutations to reduce the storage overhead in the SD and Layered SD methods. This new method eliminates $\log N$ labels from receivers' storage, where N is the total number of receivers. The method requires few public values and little computational overhead.

1 Introduction

Broadcast encryption schemes, introduced by Berkovits [4] and Fiat et al. [6] independently, enable a sender to distribute secret information securely to a group of receivers excluding specified *revoked receivers* over a broadcast channel. There are some important criteria to evaluate this technology: the upper bound of the number of broadcast ciphertexts (the communication overhead), the number of keys each receiver stores (the storage overhead), and the computational overhead at a receiver. Note that administrators and broadcasters usually have much greater memory and computing resources than receivers.

Wallner et al. [14] and Wong et al. [15] proposed efficient methods for key distribution, using a logical key-tree structure. In these methods receivers update the keys they store, however giving receivers the mechanism to change their keys increases the production cost and might also weaken their security. Hence, methods which allow receivers without the ability to change their keys are preferred for many applications. Such receivers are called *stateless receivers*.

The notion of stateless receivers was introduced by Naor et al. [10], who also proposed two efficient methods using a binary key-tree structure. The Complete Subtree (CS) method is a direct application of the structure proposed in [14] and [15] for stateless receivers. The communication and storage overhead in CS are $r \log (N/r)$ and $\log N + 1$, respectively, where N and r denote the total number of receivers in the scheme and the number of revoked receivers, respectively. The second method proposed in [10], the Subset Difference (SD) method, improves the subset algorithm and the key assignment mechanism of CS using a pseudo-random sequence generator. Its communication, storage and computational overhead are $2r - 1$, $\frac{1}{2} \log^2 N + \frac{1}{2} \log N + 1$ and $O(\log N)$, respectively.

H. Wang et al. (Eds.): ACISP 2004, LNCS 3108, pp. 12–23, 2004.

Table 1. The properties of the original SD and Basic LSD methods, the modifications proposed in [2] and in this paper. N, r and M denote the total number of receivers, the number of revoked receivers and the modulus of RSA, respectively. †The computational overhead in the original methods is $\log N$ applications of a pseudo-random generator

SD	Original [10]	SD-MK [2]	This paper
# ciphertexts	$2r - 1$	$\leftarrow$	$\leftarrow$
# labels	$\frac{1}{2}\log^2 N + \frac{1}{2}\log N + 1$	$\frac{1}{2}\log^2 N - \frac{1}{2}\log N + 1$	$\leftarrow$
Comp. overhead	$O\left(\log N\right)^\dagger$	$O\left(\max\{\log^5 N, \log^2 N \log^2 M\}\right)$	$O\left(\log N \log^2 M\right)$
# public values	–	$O\left(N\right)$	$O\left(1\right)$
Basic LSD	Original [7]	BLSD-MK [2]	This paper
# ciphertexts	$4r - 2$	$\leftarrow$	$\leftarrow$
# labels	$\log^{3/2} N + 1$	$\log^{3/2} N - \log N + 1$	$\leftarrow$
Comp. overhead	$O\left(\log N\right)^\dagger$	$O\left(\max\{\log^5 N, \log^2 N \log^2 M\}\right)$	$O\left(\log N \log^2 M\right)$
# public values	–	$O\left(N\right)$	$O\left(1\right)$

Halevy et al. [7] introduced the concept of a layer in order to reduce the storage overhead of SD, and proposed the Layered Subset Difference (LSD) method. The basic version of LSD, the Basic LSD (BLSD) method, reduces the number of labels a receiver stores to $\log^{3/2} N + 1$, while maintaining the communication and computational overhead in $O\left(r\right)$ and $O\left(\log N\right)$, respectively. The general version, the General LSD (GLSD) method, reduces the number of labels to $O\left(\log^{1+\epsilon} N\right)$ in exchange for an increase in the communication overhead by a constant factor, where ϵ is an arbitrary positive number.

Asano [1] modified CS using an a-ary tree and the master-key technique [5], where a is an arbitrary integer satisfying $a > 1$. One of Asano's methods reduces the storage overhead and the communication overhead to one key and to $\frac{r \log(N/r)}{\log a} + r$, respectively, in exchange for an increase in the computational overhead to $O\left(\frac{2^a \log^5 N}{\log a}\right)$. The master-key technique is also applied to SD and LSD in order to eliminate $\log N$ labels from receivers' storage [2].

1.1   Our Contribution

In ACISP 2003, Hwang, Kim and Lee [8] proposed a method for broadcast encryption schemes. We call it the HKL method and write it as HKL. It modifies the subset algorithm and key assignment mechanism of SD. However, it is insecure against a collusion of two receivers, as we show in this paper.

Then we propose a new method to modify SD and LSD. Recently, Nojima et al. [12] and Ogata et al. [13] independently modified CS using trapdoor one-way permutations based on RSA cryptosystem and reduced the number of node keys a receiver stores to one. We apply their concept to SD and LSD.

Table 1 summarizes the properties (the number of broadcast ciphertexts, the number of labels a receiver stores, the computational overhead at a receiver, and the total number of public values in the method) of the original SD, BLSD and their modifications using the master-key technique proposed in [2] (which are denoted by SD-MK and BLSD-MK, respectively), and modifications proposed in this paper. Our modifications, as well as SD-MK and BLSD-MK, eliminate log N labels from receivers' storage in SD and BLSD while maintaining the same communication complexity. Although SD-MK and BLSD-MK use $O(N)$ public values, ours use only a constant number of public values. The computational overhead at receivers in our modifications is smaller compared with these methods. Similar to the modification proposed in [2], our method also eliminates log N labels from receivers' storage in GLSD.

Attrapadung et al. [3] generalized the key generation mechanism of SD and LSD with pseudo-random sequence generators and eliminated $\log N - x_u$ labels from the storage of receiver u ($1 \leq u \leq N-1$) in SD (thus the number of labels in their modification becomes $\frac{1}{2}\log^2 N - \frac{1}{2}\log N + x_u + 1$), and $\log N - x_u - y_u$ in BLSD, where $x_u = \max\{k : 2^k | u\}$ and $y_u = |\{j : 1 \leq j \leq \log N, \sqrt{\log N} \nmid j, 2^j - 2^{\lfloor \frac{j}{\sqrt{\log N}} \rfloor \sqrt{\log N}} + 1 \leq u \bmod 2^j \leq 2^j - 1\}|$. The advantage of our method is the number of labels which can be eliminated — ours eliminates log N labels from the storage of all receivers.

Notations. We call the entity which manages the broadcast encryption scheme *Trusted Center* (TC). TC defines a binary tree with N leaves and assigns a receiver to each leaf, where N is the total number of receivers and for simplicity we assume it is a power of 2. Let $path_m$ be the path from the root to a leaf to which receiver u_m is assigned. In order to represent relationships of nodes, let $P(i)$, $S(i)$, $LC(i)$ and $RC(i)$ denote the parent, sibling, left-child and right-child node of node i, respectively. The base of "log" is 2, throughout this paper.

2   The SD Method

Since both HKL and our method are based on SD, we will briefly explain SD. Subset $S_{i,j}$ used in SD is specified by two nodes, i and j, and defined as $S_{i,j} = S_i \setminus S_j$, where S_i and S_j are sets of receivers assigned to the leaves of a subtree rooted at i and its descendant j, respectively. In this arrangement, any combination of unrevoked receivers can be covered by a disjoint union of at most $2r-1$ subsets. Hence the number of broadcast ciphertexts is at most $2r-1$.

SD uses pseudo-random sequence generator $G : \{0,1\}^C \mapsto \{0,1\}^{3C}$, and the concept of *label* $LABEL_{i,j}$ for subset $S_{i,j}$ in order to derive the corresponding subset key and other labels. Let $G_L(s)$, $G_M(s)$ and $G_R(s)$ denote the left, middle and right third of the output of G on seed s, respectively. For each internal node i, TC chooses element $s_i \in \{0,1\}^C$ and sets $LABEL_{i,LC(i)} = G_L(s_i)$ and $LABEL_{i,RC(i)} = G_R(s_i)$. Labels corresponding to subsets $S_{i,LC(j)}$ and $S_{i,RC(j)}$ are generated in the same way: $LABEL_{i,LC(j)} = G_L(LABEL_{i,j})$ and $LABEL_{i,RC(j)} = G_R(LABEL_{i,j})$, respectively, where i is an ancestor of j. TC generates the labels $LABEL_{i,j}$ for all subsets $S_{i,j}$ by repeating this process. Subset key $SK_{i,j}$ of subset $S_{i,j}$ is defined as $SK_{i,j} = G_M(LABEL_{i,j})$.

Receiver u_m is given labels $LABEL_{i,j}$ such that i is a node on $path_m$ and j is a descendant of i just hanging off $path_m$. The number of labels a receiver stores (including one for the case of no revocation) is $\frac{1}{2}\log^2 N + \frac{1}{2}\log N + 1$.

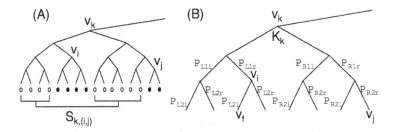

Fig. 1. (A) An example of a subset, (B) Assignment of primes in HKL

3   The HKL Method

In HKL, a subset is defined in a similar way as in SD but using three nodes — v_k, v_i and v_j — as $S_{k,(i,j)} = S_k \setminus (S_i \cup S_j)$, where v_k is the least common ancestor of v_i and v_j, and v_k is located at level 2 or higher. Figure 1 (A) shows an example of a subset. In addition, HKL defines three special subsets: subset S_{ALL} consisting of all receivers in the scheme, subset S_{LH} consisting of receivers assigned to leaves on the left half of the tree, and subset S_{RH} consisting of receivers on the right half.

TC chooses two large primes and publishes their product M. It uniformly chooses K_k $(\in \mathbb{Z}_M^*)$ for each node v_k located at level 2 or higher. It also publishes one-way hash function H, and $4(\log N - 1)$ primes $\{P_{XYZ} : \gcd(P_{XYZ}, \phi(M)) = 1, X \in \{L, R\}, Y \in \{1, \dots, \log N - 1\}, Z \in \{l, r\}\}$. Prime P_{XYZ} corresponds to an edge from node v_w to its child node, where v_w is located on the X side (namely, L: *left* or R: *right*) half at the level of depth Y in a subtree rooted at v_k, and the child node is on the Z side (namely, l: *left* or r: *right*) of v_w. Figure 1 (B) shows the correspondence between node v_k and primes P_{XYZ}. For example, prime P_{L1r} corresponds to an edge from the left child of v_k (this is v_w in the above description) to its right child (i. e. v_i).

Subset key $SK_{k,(i,j)}$ of subset $S_{k,(i,j)}$ is calculated from its index $I_{k,(i,j)}$ as $SK_{k,(i,j)} = H\left(I_{k,(i,j)}\right)$. Here, the index is defined as $I_{k,(i,j)} = K_k^{D_{k,(i,j)}} \bmod M$, where $D_{k,(i,j)}$ is a product of the primes corresponding to the edges on two paths: from v_k to v_i and from v_k to v_j. For example, we have $D_{k,(i,j)} = P_{L1r}P_{R1r}P_{R2r}$ and $I_{k,(i,j)} = K_k^{P_{L1r}P_{R1r}P_{R2r}} \bmod M$ for three nodes v_k, v_i and v_j in Fig. 1 (B).

In this arrangement, index $I_{k,(i',j')}$ and subset key $SK_{k,(i',j')}$ are easily computed from index $I_{k,(i,j)}$, where node $v_{i'}$ equals to v_i or its descendant, and $v_{j'}$ equals to v_j or its descendant. Let us look at another node v_f in Fig. 1 (B), which is the left child of v_i. For subset $S_{k,(f,j)}$, we have $D_{k,(f,j)} = P_{L1r}P_{L2l}P_{R1r}P_{R2r}$ and $I_{k,(f,j)} = K_k^{P_{L1r}P_{L2l}P_{R1r}P_{R2r}} \bmod M$. If a receiver has index $I_{k,(i,j)}$, it can derive index $I_{k,(f,j)}$ as $I_{k,(f,j)} = I_{k,(i,j)}^{D_{k,(f,j)}/D_{k,(i,j)}} \bmod M = I_{k,(i,j)}^{P_{L2l}} \bmod M$, and compute the corresponding subset key as $SK_{k,(f,j)} = H\left(I_{k,(f,j)}\right)$.

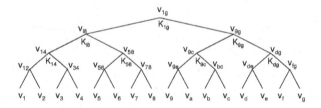

Fig. 2. The structure of HKL

Receiver u_m is given indices $I_{k,(i,j)}$ such that: (1) node v_k is located on $path_m$ at level 2 or higher, (2) node v_i is a child node of v_k just hanging off $path_m$, and (3) node v_j, just hanging off $path_m$, is a child node of another node v_t, where v_t is a descendant of v_k and located on $path_m$. The receiver stores $\frac{1}{2}\log^2 N - \frac{1}{2}\log N$ indices and two keys for special subsets.

Example. An example construction with $N = 16$ given in [8] is depicted in Fig. 2. Receiver u_m ($m = 1, \ldots, 9, a, \ldots, g$) assigned to leaf v_m is given the following secret indices and keys. Note that node v_{xy} in the figure denotes the root of a minimum subtree containing all leaves from v_x to v_y, and K_{xy} is an element in $\mathbb{Z}_M^*$ chosen for node v_{xy}. SK_{ALL}, SK_{LH} and SK_{RH} denote the subset keys of subsets S_{ALL}, S_{LH} and S_{RH}, respectively. We omit "mod M" for simplicity.

u_m u_m's indices and keys

u_1 K_{1g}^{PL1r}, $K_{1g}^{PL1l\,PL2r}$, $K_{1g}^{PL1l\,PL2l\,PL3r}$, K_{18}^{PL1r}, $K_{18}^{PL1l\,PL2r}$, K_{14}^{PL1r}, SK_{LH}, SK_{ALL}

u_2 K_{1g}^{PL1r}, $K_{1g}^{PL1l\,PL2r}$, $K_{1g}^{PL1l\,PL2l\,PL3l}$, K_{18}^{PL1r}, $K_{18}^{PL1l\,PL2l}$, K_{14}^{PL1l}, SK_{LH}, SK_{ALL}

u_3 K_{1g}^{PL1r}, $K_{1g}^{PL1l\,PL2l}$, $K_{1g}^{PL1l\,PL2r\,PL3r}$, K_{18}^{PL1l}, $K_{18}^{PL1r\,PL2r}$, K_{14}^{PR1r}, SK_{LH}, SK_{ALL}

$\vdots$ $\vdots$

u_g K_{1g}^{PR1l}, $K_{1g}^{PR1r\,PR2l}$, $K_{1g}^{PR1r\,PR2r\,PR3l}$, K_{9g}^{PR1l}, $K_{9g}^{PR1r\,PR2l}$, K_{dg}^{PR1l}, SK_{RH}, SK_{ALL}

3.1   The Attack

In this section we present a concrete attack on the above example construction of HKL. This attack uses the secret indices possessed by two receivers, and derives indices and subset keys which have not been given to any of the colluding receivers.

Suppose that two receivers u_1 and u_g in the example collude with each other. In other words, attacker $\mathcal{Z}$ knows the indices given to these receivers. We focus on u_1's $I_{1g,(58,9g)} = K_{1g}^{PL1r} \bmod M$, and u_g's $I_{1g,(18,9c)} = K_{1g}^{PR1l} \bmod M$. Since P_{L1r} and P_{R1l} are different public primes, $\mathcal{Z}$ can compute integers α and β, such that $\alpha P_{L1r} + \beta P_{R1l} = 1$, using the extended Euclid's algorithm [9]. Running time of the algorithm is $O\left(\log P_{L1r} \log P_{R1l}\right)$. Here, either α or β

must be positive, and the other must be negative. $\mathcal{Z}$ computes K_{1g} as follows: If $\alpha < 0$ then $K_{1g} = \left(I_{1g,(58,9g)}^{-1}\right)^{-\alpha} \left(I_{1g,(18,9c)}\right)^{\beta} \bmod M$, otherwise $K_{1g} = \left(I_{1g,(58,9g)}\right)^{\alpha} \left(I_{1g,(18,9c)}^{-1}\right)^{-\beta} \bmod M$. Note that $\mathcal{Z}$ can use the extended Euclid's algorithm in order to compute the inverse of $I_{1g,(58,9g)}$ or $I_{1g,(18,9c)}$. Now, using K_{1g} and public primes, $\mathcal{Z}$ can compute any index $I_{k,(i,j)}$, such that $v_k = v_{1g}$. Moreover, it is also easy to compute subset key $SK_{k,(i,j)}$ from index $I_{k,(i,j)}$.

It should be noted that other pairs of indices are also useful for this attack. For example, if $\mathcal{Z}$ uses u_1's $K_{18}^{P_{L1}r} \bmod M$ and u_3's $K_{18}^{P_{L1}l} \bmod M$, the attacker can obtain K_{18} and compute any index $I_{k,(i,j)}$, such that $v_k = v_{18}$. There are pairs of receivers such that one of the pair has $K_k^{D_\gamma} \bmod M$ and the other has $K_k^{D_\delta} \bmod M$, where $\gcd(D_\gamma, D_\delta) = D_\zeta$. Using these indices, one can obtain $K_k^{D_\zeta} \bmod M$ and compute any index $K_k^{D_\eta} \bmod M$ such that $D_\zeta \mid D_\eta$. The problem with HKL is that such index $K_k^{D_\eta} \bmod M$ is used as a secret of other receivers.

4   The Proposed Method

Asano [2] has reported some facts about SD. One is that receivers belonging to subset $S_{i,j}$ also belong to subset $S_{P(i),S(i)}$. Another is that there are two cases in which a label is obtained by a receiver: label $LABEL_{i,j}$ is (case I) directly given to the receiver, or (case II) derived from another label using generator G by the receiver. However, there only exists case I for *special labels* $LABEL_{i,j}$, such that i is the parent of j. The third fact is that each receiver stores $\log N$ special labels. We apply the mechanism proposed by Nojima et al. [12] and Ogata et al. [13] to these special labels in SD to reduce the storage overhead.

4.1   Setup

1. TC defines a rooted full binary tree with N leaves. Each node is numbered l ($l = 1, 2, \ldots, 2N - 1$) where the root is 1 and other nodes are numbered with breadth first order. Receiver u_m ($m = 1, 2, \ldots, N$) is assigned to each leaf in the tree. For each internal node i ($i = 1, 2, \ldots, N - 1$), TC defines subsets $S_{i,j} = S_i \setminus S_j$, such that j is a descendant of i, in the same way as in SD. Let $SS_{i,k}$ denote a *special subset* such that i is the parent of k among all subsets. Note that each k ($k = 2, 3, \ldots, 2N - 1$) appears exactly once in representations of all special subsets $SS_{i,k}$. TC also defines subset $S_{1,\phi}$ including all receivers for the case where there are no revocations.

2. TC selects parameters of RSA, i.e. modulus M and exponents e and d, and publishes M and e. It also publishes pseudo-random sequence generator G : $\{0,1\}^C \mapsto \{0,1\}^{3C}$ and pairwise independent hash functions $H_1 : \{0,1\}^{|M|} \mapsto \{0,1\}^C$ and $H_2 : \{0,1\}^* \mapsto \{0,1\}^{|M|}$, where C is the key size of an algorithm for encryption of secret information. TC generates x_k ($k = 1, \ldots, 2N - 1$) as

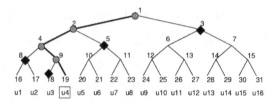

Fig. 3. A binary tree and receivers

follows. It chooses a random value $x_1 \in \mathbb{Z}_M^*$ and computes values from x_2 to x_{2N-1} as $x_k = \left(x_{\lfloor k/2 \rfloor} + H_2\left(k\right)\right)^d \bmod M$. Then TC defines *intermediate labels* $IL_{1,\phi}$ for subset $S_{1,\phi}$, and $IL_{i,k}$ for special subsets $SS_{i,k}$. It sets $IL_{1,\phi} = x_1$ and $IL_{P(k),S(k)} = x_k$ for $k = 2, \ldots, 2N - 1$. Note that the latter is also denoted as $IL_{k,2k} = x_{2k+1}$ and $IL_{k,2k+1} = x_{2k}$ for $k = 1, \ldots, N - 1$. Labels of these subsets are defined as $LABEL_{1,\phi} = H_1\left(IL_{1,\phi}\right)$ and $LABEL_{i,k} = H_1\left(IL_{i,k}\right)$.

3. Using generator G and special labels $LABEL_{i,k}$, TC generates all labels $LABEL_{i,j}$ for all subsets $S_{i,j}$. This process is the same as in SD.

4. For receiver u_m, TC tentatively selects labels which are given to u_m in SD, except for label $LABEL_{1,\phi}$. These are labels $LABEL_{i,j}$ such that i is located on $path_m$ and j is its descendant just hanging off $path_m$. Among these selected labels, TC gives non-special labels to u_m. In addition, TC gives u_m intermediate label $IL_{P(n),S(n)}$, where n is a leaf to which u_m is assigned.

Example. Figure 3 depicts a binary tree with $N = 16$. In SD, receiver u_4 assigned to leaf 19 stores eleven labels: $LABEL_{1,\phi}$ and $LABEL_{i,j}$ such that $(i,j) = \{(1,3), (1,5), (1,8), (1,18), (2,5), (2,8), (2,18), (4,8), (4,18), (9,18)\}$. In our method, receiver u_4 stores intermediate label $IL_{9,18}$ and six labels: $LABEL_{1,5}$, $LABEL_{1,8}$, $LABEL_{1,18}$, $LABEL_{2,8}$, $LABEL_{2,18}$ and $LABEL_{4,18}$.

4.2   Broadcasting

The way to transmit secret information I is the same as in SD. Namely, TC finds an appropriate disjoint union of subsets which includes all unrevoked receivers but no revoked ones, encrypts I with each of the corresponding subset keys, and broadcasts the ciphertexts. The way to derive subset key $SK_{i,j}$ from label $LABEL_{i,j}$ is also the same as in SD, i. e. $SK_{i,j} = G_M\left(LABEL_{i,j}\right)$.

4.3   Decryption

An unrevoked receiver belongs to a subset corresponding to the subset key used for encryption in the broadcasting phase. The way for the receiver to find an appropriate ciphertext to decrypt is the same as in SD. After finding the ciphertext, the receiver derives the corresponding subset key $SK_{i,j}$ from its intermediate label or another label as follows, then decrypts the ciphertext.

Receiver u_m checks that node j for subset $S_{i,j}$ corresponding to subset key $SK_{i,j}$ used for the ciphertext is either (a) a descendant of node k (including the case $j = k$) such that u_m stores label $LABEL_{i,k}$, or (b) a descendant of node k (including the case $j = k$) such that subset $S_{i,k}$ is a special subset and the corresponding special label $LABEL_{i,k}$ can be derived from its intermediate label $IL_{P(n),S(n)}$ (in other words, j is equal to k or its descendant where k is the child node of i and not located on $path_m$). If no receivers are revoked and subset key $SK_{1,\phi}$ is used, it is case (b). If the situation is case (b), u_m derives intermediate label $IL_{i,k}$ from intermediate label $IL_{P(n),S(n)}$ it possesses as follows. If $i = P(n)$ and $j = k = S(n)$, it already has $IL_{i,k}$. Otherwise, u_m computes intermediate label $IL_{P(P(n)),S(P(n))}$ as $IL_{P(P(n)),S(P(n))} = \left(\left(IL_{P(n),S(n)} \right)^e - H_2(n) \right) \bmod M$. By repeating this operation, u_m can compute any intermediate label corresponding to a special subset to which it belongs. Namely, $IL_{P(P(t)),S(P(t))} = \left(\left(IL_{P(t),S(t)} \right)^e - H_2(t) \right) \bmod M$, where t is a node on $path_m$. Intermediate label $IL_{1,\phi}$ is also derived from $IL_{1,2}$ or $IL_{1,3}$ as $IL_{1,\phi} = \left((IL_{1,2})^e - H_2(3) \right) \bmod M = \left((IL_{1,3})^e - H_2(2) \right) \bmod M$. After obtaining $IL_{i,k}$, it derives the corresponding label as $LABEL_{i,k} = H_1(IL_{i,k})$.

The remaining process is common to both cases (a) and (b), and it is the same as in the original SD: the receiver applies generator G to label $LABEL_{i,k}$ at most $\log N$ times to obtain $LABEL_{i,j}$, then derives subset key $SK_{i,j} = G_M(LABEL_{i,j})$ for decryption of the ciphertext.

5   Discussion

5.1   Security

The subset keys in our method are generated in three steps: (Step 1) special label $LABEL_{i,k}$ for special subset $SS_{i,k}$ is generated using the mechanism based on trapdoor one-way permutations, (Step 2) label $LABEL_{i,j}$ for non-special subset $S_{i,j}$ is derived from the special label with generator G, then (Step 3) subset key $SK_{i,j}$ is computed from label $LABEL_{i,j}$ using G.

The mechanism for derivation of special labels was proposed by Nojima et al. [12] and Ogata et al. [13] independently. They used this mechanism for node keys in CS. Nojima et al. demonstrated the intractability of node keys in their method, under the assumption that RSA is secure. Namely, if there exists polynomial-time algorithm $\mathcal{A}$ that outputs a node key which is not known to any of the colluding revoked receivers, given all node keys known to the coalition with probability $P_{\mathcal{A}}$, we can construct poly-time algorithm $\mathcal{B}$ that computes $x^d \bmod M$ for any x with probability $P_{\mathcal{B}} \geq \frac{2}{N} P_{\mathcal{A}}$. Ogata et al. constructed a similar scheme without using hash function H_2, and showed that the security of their scheme is still equivalent to RSA. These analyses show that it is difficult for any coalition of receivers to obtain intermediate label $IL_{i,k}$ corresponding to special subset $SS_{i,k}$ to which no receivers in the coalition belong. Special label $LABEL_{i,k}$ is derived from the intermediate label as $LABEL_{i,k} = H_1(IL_{i,k})$.

Since the output of H_1 is pairwise independent, it is also difficult for any coalition with no receivers belonging to $SS_{i,k}$ to obtain $LABEL_{i,k}$.

Since the process in Steps 2 and 3 is the same as in SD, the discussion of the security of SD given in [10] is applicable to these steps. The combination of this and the above discussions shows the intractability of subset keys in our method. To conclude, we say that our method is secure against any coalition of revoked receivers if RSA is secure.

5.2   Communication Overhead

Since our method adopts the same way for sending secret information as SD, the communication overhead is also the same. Namely, the upper bound of the number of ciphertexts is $2r - 1$, where r is the number of revoked receivers.

5.3   Storage and Computational Overhead

We first consider the size of the receiver's secure memory for storing labels. Recall that the number of labels a receiver stores is $\frac{1}{2}\log^2 N + \frac{1}{2}\log N + 1$ in SD. $\log N$ of them are special labels and another label is $LABEL_{1,\phi}$. In our method, a receiver drives these $\log N + 1$ labels from an intermediate label. Therefore the total number of labels and the intermediate label a receiver stores becomes $\frac{1}{2}\log^2 N - \frac{1}{2}\log N + 1$. Since the derivation mechanism is based on RSA, the size of the intermediate label is the size of a secure RSA modulus. Recall that SD-MK denotes the modification of SD proposed in [2], using the master-key technique. If we consider an example with the same parameters as in [2], i.e. $N = 2^{25}$, $|LABEL_{i,j}| = C = 128$ bits and $|IL_{i,j}| = |M| = 1024$ bits, then the size of the secure memory of the receiver in our method is about 5.5% smaller than in SD, and it is the same reduction rate as SD-MK. However, the computational or non-secret storage overhead in ours is far smaller, as discussed below.

SD-MK uses $2N - 1$ primes as public information in total, and each receiver needs the unique combination of $\log N + 1$ primes. Receivers must store them (which increases the non-secret storage overhead) or generate them by calculation (which increases the computational overhead). On the other hand, our method uses only one public exponent e. It reduces the non-secret storage or computational overhead significantly compared with SD-MK.

Next, let us study the computational overhead. In order to derive a special label from an intermediate label, the receiver in our method performs at most $\log N$ executions of modular exponentiation with index e. Similar to usual RSA applications, we can use a special value for e which reduces the computational cost. We estimate the cost for an evaluation of modular exponentiation at $O\left(\log^2 M\right)$. After deriving the targeted intermediate label, the receiver feeds the intermediate label into pairwise independent hash function H_1. It has been reported in [11] that the computational overhead for an evaluation of such a function is much smaller than modular exponentiation, thus we ignore it. In total, the computational overhead of the receiver in our method is $O\left(\log N \log^2 M\right)$.

Here we consider SD-MK. It has been reported in [2] that the computational overhead for the generation of primes for a receiver in SD-MK is $O\left(\log^5 N\right)$.

Even if the receiver stores these primes in order to avoid generating them, it still needs $O\left(\log^2 N \log^2 M\right)$ computation for derivation of the subset key. Hence, our method is much more efficient than SD-MK by at least a factor of $\log N$.

Note that the receiver must derive a special label only in case (b) in the decryption phase. In addition, in either case (a) or (b), the receiver must compute the subset key from the derived special label or the non-special label it stores using generator G at most $\log N$ times, which is also necessary in SD and SD-MK.

6   Modification of the Layered Subset Difference Method

6.1   The Basic LSD Method

Suppose that $\log^{1/2} N$ is an integer. BLSD defines the level of the root and every level of depth $l \log^{1/2} N$ for $l = 1, 2, \ldots, \log^{1/2} N$ as special. It also defines the collection of levels between (and including) adjacent special levels as a layer.

Subset $S_{i,j}$ defined in BLSD satisfies at least one of the following additional conditions: both i and j belong to the same layer, or i is located at a special level. Namely, BLSD adopts stricter conditions for subsets than SD. It reduces the number of labels a receiver stores. It has been reported in [2] that the number of labels for a receiver in BLSD is $\log^{3/2} N + 1$.

Consider two nodes i and j such that j is a descendant of i but do not satisfy either of the above two conditions. Although subset $S_{i,j}$ is defined in SD, it is not defined in BLSD and must be represented using two defined subsets as $S_{i,j} = S_{i,k} \cup S_{k,j}$, where k is the first node on the path from i to j which is located at a special level. As a result, the communication overhead of BLSD becomes at most twice that of SD.

6.2   Modification of the Basic LSD Method

Our modification of SD adopts the mechanism using trapdoor one-way permutations in order to derive $\log N + 1$ labels from an intermediate label, which can be applied directly to BLSD. We avoid giving a detailed construction of our modification of BLSD, since it is almost same as the modification of SD. Recall that SD and BLSD differ only in the conditions for subsets. This relationship is also applicable to our modifications of these methods.

Let us consider the example tree illustrated in Fig. 3 again. There exist three special levels: the level of the root, nodes 4 to 7, and the leaves. In the original BLSD, receiver u_4 stores nine labels: $LABEL_{1,\phi}$ and eight labels $LABEL_{i,j}$ such that $(i, j) = \{(1, 3), (1, 5), (1, 8), (1, 18), (2, 5), (4, 8), (4, 18), (9, 18)\}$. On the other hand, receiver u_4 in our method stores only four labels ($LABEL_{1,5}$, $LABEL_{1,8}$, $LABEL_{1,18}$ and $LABEL_{4,18}$) and intermediate label $IL_{9,18}$.

It has been reported in [2] that the number of special labels the receiver stores in BLSD is $\log N$. In our modification, the receiver can derive these special labels and label $LABEL_{1,\phi}$ from its intermediate label. Therefore, the total number of labels and the intermediate label for the receiver becomes $\log^{3/2} N - \log N + 1$, which is eliminated by $\log N$ from BLSD. If we consider the same parameters again, i.e. $N = 2^{25}$, $|LABEL_{i,j}| = C = 128$ bits and $|IL_{i,j}| = |M| = 1024$ bits, then the total size of labels a receiver stores is 14% smaller than that in BLSD. While this reduction rate is the same as in the modification of BLSD proposed in [2] based on the master-key technique, the advantage of our method is the non-secret storage and computational overhead, as noted in Section 5.3.

Our modification only changes the mechanism for generation of labels and it does not affect the communication overhead. The discussions of the security and the storage and computational overhead in our modification of SD given in Section 5 are directly applicable not only to the modification of BLSD but also to the modification of GLSD which will be presented in Section 6.4.

6.3   The General LSD Method

GLSD uses several kinds of special levels and stricter conditions for subsets than BLSD. Halevy et al. [7] have provided the following explanation. The path from the root to a leaf in a tree is considered as a line graph. A node in the graph, which corresponds to a node in the tree, is represented by its distance from the root, expressed as a d digit number in base $b = O\left(\log^{1/d} N\right)$. For example, the root in the tree is represented by $0 \dots 00$, and its child node is $0 \dots 01$, etc.

Subset $S_{i,j}$ in BLSD satisfies the following condition: if node i in the graph is represented as a d digit number in base b by $\overrightarrow{x} a \overrightarrow{0}$ then node j must be represented either by $\overline{x + 1} \overrightarrow{0}$ or by any number $\overrightarrow{x} a' \overrightarrow{y}$, where a is the rightmost nonzero digit, $\overrightarrow{x}$ is a sequence of arbitrary digits, $\overrightarrow{0}$ is a sequence of zeroes, $a' \geq a$, and $\overrightarrow{y}$ is an arbitrary sequence of digits of the same length as $\overrightarrow{0}$. Note that the number of trailing zeroes in the representation of node i determines how special it is. j of defined subset $S_{i,j}$ can be any node from $i + 1$ to the first node which is even more special than i, inclusive.

Any subset in SD can be represented as a disjoint union of at most d subsets in GLSD. Thus the communication overhead of GLSD is d times larger than that of SD. As we enlarge parameter d, the number of labels a receiver stores decreases, and finally it becomes $O\left(\log^{1+\epsilon} N\right)$, where $\epsilon > 0$ is an arbitrary value.

6.4   Modification of the General LSD Method

We can apply the same mechanism to GLSD in order to reduce the number of labels a receiver stores, as we have already done to SD and BLSD. Note that the difference between BLSD and GLSD is only the condition for defined subsets. Therefore we omit a detailed description of our modification of GLSD in order to avoid redundancy. We just say that it is constructed with the same mechanism for deriving special labels from an intermediate label.

As reported in [2], the receiver in GLSD stores the same number of special labels as SD and BLSD, i.e. $\log N$. Our modification eliminates these $\log N$ special labels and label $LABEL_{1,\phi}$ from the receiver's storage in exchange for an addition of the intermediate label. Recall that the receiver stores $O\left(\log^{1+\epsilon} N\right)$ labels in GLSD, where ϵ is an arbitrary positive value. Therefore, this reduction can be very significant. This reduction rate is the same as the modification of

GLSD proposed in [2], however our method is more efficient with regard to the non-secret storage and computational overhead, as discussed in Section 5.

References

1. T. Asano, "A Revocation Scheme with Minimal Storage at Receivers," Advances in Cryptology - Asiacrypt 2002, LNCS 2501, Springer, pp. 433-450, 2002.
2. T. Asano, "Reducing Storage at Receivers in SD and LSD Broadcast Encryption Schemes," Information Security Applications, 4th International Workshop, WISA 2003, LNCS 2908, Springer, pp. 317-332, 2004.
3. N. Attrapadung, K. Kobara, and H. Imai, "Sequential Key Derivation Patterns for Broadcast Encryption and Key Predistribution Schemes," Advances in Cryptology - Asiacrypt 2003, LNCS 2894, Springer, pp. 374-391, 2003.
4. S. Berkovits, "How to Broadcast a Secret," Advances in Cryptology - Eurocrypt '91, LNCS 547, Springer, pp. 535-541, 1991.
5. G. C. Chick and S. E. Tavares, "Flexible Access Control with Master Keys," Advances in Cryptology - Crypto '89, LNCS 435, Springer, pp. 316-322, 1990.
6. A. Fiat and M. Naor, "Broadcast Encryption," Advances in Cryptology - Crypto '93, LNCS 773, Springer, pp. 480-491, 1994.
7. D. Halevy and A. Shamir, "The LSD Broadcast Encryption Scheme," Advances in Cryptology - Crypto 2002, LNCS 2442, Springer, pp. 47-60, 2002.
8. Y. H. Hwang, C. H. Kim and P. J. Lee, "An Efficient Revocation Scheme with Minimal Message Length for Stateless Receivers," Information Security and Privacy, 8th Australasian Conference, ACISP 2003, LNCS 2727, Springer, pp. 377-386, 2003.
9. A. J. Menezes, P. C. van Oorschot and S. A. Vanstone, "Handbook of Applied Cryptography," CRC Press, 1997.
10. D. Naor, M. Naor and J. Lotspiech, "Revocation and Tracing Schemes for Stateless Receivers," Advances in Cryptology - Crypto 2001, LNCS 2139, Springer, pp. 41-62, 2001.
11. M. Naor and O. Reingold, "Number-Theoretic Constructions of Efficient Pseudo-Random Functions," Proceedings of 38th IEEE Symposium on Foundations of Computer Science, pp. 458-467, 1997.
12. R. Nojima and Y. Kaji, "Efficient Tree-based Key Management Using One-way Functions," (in Japanese), Proceedings of the 2004 Symposium on Cryptography and Information Security, pp. 189-194, 2004.
13. W. Ogata, T. Hiza and D. V. Quang, "Efficient Tree Based Key management based on RSA function," (in Japanese), Proceedings of the 2004 Symposium on Cryptography and Information Security, pp. 195-199, 2004.
14. D. Wallner, E. Harder and R. Agee, "Key Management for Multicast: Issues and Architectures," IETF Network Working Group, Request for Comments: 2627, available from ftp://ftp.ietf.org/rfc/rfc2627.txt, 1999.
15. C. K. Wong, M. Gouda and S. S. Lam, "Secure Group Communications Using Key Graphs," Proceedings of ACM SIGCOMM '98, 1998.

Linear Code Implies Public-Key Traitor Tracing
with *Revocation*

Vu Dong Tô and Reihaneh Safavi-Naini

School of Information Technology & Computer Science,
University of Wollongong, NSW 2522, Australia

Abstract. It was shown in [K. Kurosawa et al., Proc. PKC'02, LNCS 2274, pp. 172–187, 2002] that a public-key (k, n)-traitor tracing scheme, called linear-coded Kurosawa–Desmedt scheme, can be derived from an $[n, u, d]$-linear code such that $d \geq 2k + 1$. In this paper, we show that the linear-coded Kurosawa–Desmedt scheme can be modified to allow revocation of users, that is to show a revocation scheme can be derived from a linear code. The overhead of the modified scheme is very efficient: there is no extra user secret key storage, the public encryption key size remains the same, and the ciphertext size is of length $O(k)$. We prove the modified scheme is semantically secure against a passive adversary. Since the Boneh–Franklin scheme is proved to be equivalent to a slight modification of the corrected Kurosawa-Desmedt scheme, we show that we can also modify the Boneh–Franklin scheme to provide user revocation capability for this scheme. We also look at the problem of permanent removing a traitor in the Boneh-Franklin and prove some negative results.

1 Introduction

Digital content distribution is an important application of global networking. In such an application, data suppliers want their digital content to be available to authorized users only. The number of authorized users is large enough so that broadcasting data is much more efficient than establishing a secure channel between the data supplier and each individual authorized user.

In a public-key (k, n)-traitor tracing scheme, there are n users, each holds a secret decryption key (or a decoder device). The encryption key is made public and the data supplier can use this public key to encrypt the digital content and broadcast the corresponding ciphertext. Authorized users, using their secret decryption keys, should be able to decrypt the broadcast messages. If a coalition of up to k users collude to form a pirate decryption device, upon capturing this pirate device, the system uses tracing algorithm to identify at least one of the colluders.

Kurosawa–Desmedt [12] and Boneh–Franklin [2] proposed public key traitor tracing schemes based on the difficulty of decision Diffie–Hellman problem. To avoid linear attack [18,2], the Kurosawa–Desmedt scheme is modified to become the corrected Kurosawa–Desmedt scheme. It is an important property that the

H. Wang et al. (Eds.): ACISP 2004, LNCS 3108, pp. 24–35, 2004.

corrected Kurosawa–Desmedt scheme can be generalized to use any linear code. It is shown that a public-key (k, n)-traitor tracing scheme, called linear-coded Kurosawa–Desmedt scheme [13], can be derived from an $[n, u, d]$-linear code such that $d \geq 2k+1$ and the Boneh–Franklin scheme is equivalent to the linear-coded Kurosawa–Desmedt scheme where Reed–Solomon code is used.

In both Kurosawa–Desmedt and Boneh–Franklin schemes, broadcast data can be decrypted by all legitimate users and it is not possible to target the data to a subgroup of users. Trace and revoke schemes [1,7,16,22,21,17,20,5,6,19,11] have the extra property that users can be revoked and so the broadcast targeted to a subgroup of users. In schemes [1,7,16,22,21] the encryption key is secret so it only supports one data provider. The scheme [5] by Dodis et al is the first trace and revoke scheme that has CCA2 security. The scheme [11] by Kim et al is a modification of Dodis scheme, it has CCA2 security and the ciphertext size is half that of Dodis's scheme. Most of public-key revocation schemes are polynomial based that make use of the Shamir's secret sharing technique, in which there is a correspondence between the secret key held by each user with a value of the polynomial at a specific point; and when a user is revoked, the information of the polynomial value corresponds to the revoked user is broadcasted in the ciphertext.

In this paper, we show that the linear-coded Kurosawa–Desmedt and the Boneh–Franklin schemes can be modified to have user revocation capability. It is interesting that in modifying these schemes we do not introduce any more complexity in the key generation process. Users will keep exactly the same secret keys as the original schemes. The public encryption key in the linear-coded Kurosawa–Desmedt remains the same as it is in the modified scheme. For the Boneh–Franklin scheme, only one more group element is added into the public encryption key. The ciphertext size is as efficient as other revoke schemes [17, 20,11,19,6]. For a tracing threshold k, our modified schemes can afford up to $2k-1$ user revocation and the ciphertext consists of $2k$ field elements and $2k+2$ group elements. We also prove the semantic security for our proposed revocation schemes.

Dodis et al. [6] introduced the notion of *scalable* system. A broadcast system is *server-side scalable* if any party can broadcast messages, this can be accomplished by using public key approach. A broadcast system is *client-side scalable* if it supports increasing number *add-user* and *remove-user* operations. Our proposed revocation schemes are server-side scalable but not client-side scalable since they cannot remove more than $2k$ users. The only known scalable scheme is the Dodis et al. scheme [6]. In this paper, we look at the possibility of repeatedly permanent-removing users by modifying only the public key and public parts of users keys. If it is possible to do so then we would have a client-side scalable scheme. Unfortunately, we prove that it is not possible, at least, for the Boneh–Franklin scheme. We consider the first case when we remove a user by modifying only the public encryption key so that the decryption key of the removed user become invalid in the new encryption-decryption system, however, the remained non-removed users should have their decryption keys remain valid.

We show that it is impossible to do so. The second case we consider is to remove a user by modifying the public encryption key and the public parts of users keys (which are the rows of the public matrix). We show that it is also impossible to do so in this case.

The rest of the paper is organized as follows. In section 2, we give a model of traitor tracing scheme. The Boneh–Franklin scheme, the corrected Kurosawa–Desmedt and the linear-coded Kurosawa–Desmedt schemes are reviewed in section 3. In section 4, we present revocation functionality for these three schemes. In section 5, we look at the problem of permanently removing a user in the Boneh–Franklin scheme and prove some negative results.

2   Preliminaries

An $[n, u, d]$-linear code is a linear code contains n codewords, dimension u and the minimum Hamming distance d. The parity check matrix for an $[n, u, d]$-linear code is a matrix of size $(n - u) \times n$ and any $d - 1$ columns vectors are linear independent. The notation $\cdot$ denotes the inner product of two vectors.

Let $q > n$ be a prime number. Let G_q be a group of prime order q. The Decision Diffie–Hellman problem in G_q is to determine whether $w = uv$ given g, g^u, g^v, g^w where g is chosen random from G_q and u, v, w are chosen random from Z_q.

2.1   Model of Traitor Tracing

A (k, n)-traitor tracing scheme with revocation has four components.

Key Generation: given a security input 1^ℓ, the key generation procedure outputs an encryption key PK and n user decryption keys SK_1, ..., SK_n. The encryption key PK is made public so any data supplier can use it to broadcast data. Decryption key SK_i is given to the user i to keep secretly.

Encryption: taken as input a message M, the encryption key PK and a revoked set of users R, the encryption procedure $\mathcal{E}$ outputs the corresponding ciphertext $C = \mathcal{E}_{PK}(R, M)$. If the scheme do not support revocation (for instance, the linear-coded Kurosawa–Desmedt scheme and the Boneh–Franklin scheme) then R is always an empty set.

Decryption: taken as input a ciphertext $C = \mathcal{E}_{PK}(R, M)$ and a decryption key SK_i, the decryption procedure $\mathcal{D}$ outputs the message M if $i \notin R$.

Traitor Tracing: if up to k users collude to form a pirate decryption box then upon capturing this pirate device, the traitor tracing procedure can identify at least one of the colluders. It is assumed that the pirate decryption box is resettable to the initial state.

There are two types of tracing: *open-box* tracing and *black-box* tracing. In *open-box* tracing, it is assumed that the pirate box can be opened and the pirate keys inside the box can be obtained. In *black-box* tracing, the tracing algorithm cannot open the decoder box and access the stored keys. However it can make *queries* and see the responses. That is, it can send encrypted contents to the box and see the outputs of the box.

3   Previous Public-Key Traitor Tracing Schemes

In this section, we look at three public-key traitor tracing schemes: the Boneh–Franklin (BF) scheme [2], the linear-coded Kurosawa–Desmedt (LC-KD') scheme and the corrected Kurosawa–Desmedt (corrected KD) scheme [13].

3.1   Boneh–Franklin Scheme

Below is the description of the Boneh–Franklin traitor tracing scheme for n users and collusion threshold k.

Key Generation: Let G_q be a group of order prime q and g be a group generator. It is assumed that the Decision Diffie-Hellman problem in G_q is hard.

Let A be the following $(n - 2k) \times n$ matrix

$$
A = \begin{pmatrix}
1 & 1 & 1 & \cdots & 1 \\
1 & 2 & 3 & \cdots & n \\
1^2 & 2^2 & 3^2 & \cdots & n^2 \\
1^3 & 2^3 & 3^3 & \cdots & n^3 \\
\vdots & & & & \vdots \\
1^{n-2k-1} & 2^{n-2k-1} & 3^{n-2k-1} & \cdots & n^{n-2k-1}
\end{pmatrix} .
$$

Since A has full rank, the equation $Ax = 0$ has a nullspace of dimension $2k$. Let Γ be an $n \times 2k$ matrix whose columns are $2k$ independent solutions $x_1, \ldots, x_{2k}$ of $Ax = 0$. Let $\gamma^{(1)}, \gamma^{(2)}, \ldots, \gamma^{(n)}$ denote the n row vectors of Γ, each of length $2k$. The matrix Γ is made public.

Choose random $b = (b_1, \ldots, b_{2k}) \in \mathbf{Z}_q^{2k}$. Let $\Gamma \cdot b = e = (e_1, \ldots, e_n)$. Let $h_1 = g^{b_1}, \ldots, h_{2k} = g^{b_{2k}}$. Choose random $r_1, \ldots, r_{2k}$ in $\mathbf{Z}_q$ and let $y = h_1^{r_1} \ldots h_{2k}^{r_{2k}}$. We have $y = g^a$ with $a = b_1 r_1 + \ldots + b_{2k} r_{2k}$. (It is commented in [13] that, it is redundant to store system secret values $r_1, \ldots, r_{2k}$. Instead, we can just choose a random a and let $y = g^a$.)

Public encryption key is $PK = (y, h_1, \ldots, h_{2k})$.

Note that the matrix Γ is made public.

User secret decryption keys. For each $1 \le i \le n$, let $v_i = a/e_i$. Decryption key for user i is the vector $\theta^{(i)} = v_i \gamma^{(i)}$. This decryption key can be thought of as two-part key. The first part is the row vector $\gamma^{(i)}$ of the public matrix Γ. User i only needs to keep the second part v_i secret.

Discrete Log (DL) Representation. A vector $\theta = (\theta_1, \theta_2, \ldots, \theta_{2k}) \in \mathbf{Z}_q^{2k}$ satisfying

$$
y = h_1^{\theta_1} h_2^{\theta_2} \ldots h_{2k}^{\theta_{2k}} \tag{1}
$$

is called a DL-representation of the DL-element y with respect to the DL-base $h_1, \ldots, h_{2k}$. The condition (1) is equivalent to

$$
a = \theta \cdot b = \theta_1 b_1 + \ldots + \theta_{2k} b_{2k} . \tag{2}
$$

We note that the decryption key for user i, $\theta^{(i)} = v_i \gamma^{(i)} \in \mathbf{Z}_q^{2k}$, is a scalar multiple of the ith row vector $\gamma^{(i)}$ of the matrix Γ. It is also a DL-representation of y with respect to $h_1, \ldots, h_{2k}$ since, $\theta^{(i)} \cdot b = v_i (\gamma^{(i)} \cdot b) = v_i e_i = a$.

Encryption: a message $M \in G_q$ is encrypted as

$$\langle My^r, h_1^r, h_2^r, \ldots, h_{2k}^r \rangle$$

where r is randomly chosen in $\mathbf{Z}_q$.

Decryption: Any DL-representation $\boldsymbol{\theta} \in \mathbf{Z}_q^{2k}$ of y with respect to $h_1, \ldots, h_{2k}$ can be used to decrypt

$$M = \frac{My^r}{(h_1^r)^{\theta_1}(h_2^r)^{\theta_2} \ldots (h_{2k}^r)^{\theta_{2k}}} \ .$$

Decryption key of each user is a DL-representation so they can use it to decrypt the ciphertext.

Traitor tracing: a collusion of c users can generate a pirate key from their c keys $\boldsymbol{\theta}^{(u_1)}, \ldots, \boldsymbol{\theta}^{(u_c)}$ as follows

$$\boldsymbol{\theta}_{pirate} = \mu_1\,\boldsymbol{\theta}^{(u_1)} + \ldots + \mu_c\,\boldsymbol{\theta}^{(u_c)}, \quad \text{where } \mu_1 + \ldots + \mu_c = 1 \ .$$

The pirate key $\boldsymbol{\theta}_{pirate}$ is called a convex combination of the colluders' keys $\boldsymbol{\theta}^{(u_1)}$, $\ldots, \boldsymbol{\theta}^{(u_c)}$. It is easy to verify that $\boldsymbol{\theta}_{pirate}$ is a DL-representation of y with respect to $h_1, \ldots, h_{2k}$. Since $\boldsymbol{\theta}^{(u_i)}$ is a scalar multiple of $\boldsymbol{\gamma}^{(u_i)}$, the pirate key $\boldsymbol{\theta}_{pirate}$ is a linear combination of $\boldsymbol{\gamma}^{(u_1)}, \ldots, \boldsymbol{\gamma}^{(u_c)}$. The BF tracing algorithm bases on this fact. It uses the Berlekamp's algorithm to identify *all* of the colluders $u_1, \ldots, u_c$. In Berlekamp's algorithm, given a linear combination of $\boldsymbol{\gamma}^{(u_1)}, \ldots, \boldsymbol{\gamma}^{(u_c)}$ as input, it outputs all the indices $u_1, \ldots, u_c$.

3.2   Linear-Coded Kurosawa–Desmedt (LC-KD') Scheme

Below is the description of the LC-KD' scheme for n users and collusion threshold k.

Key Generation: Let G_q be a group of order prime q and g be a group generator. It is assumed that the Decision Diffie-Hellman problem in G_q is hard.

Let $\mathcal{C}$ be an $[n, u, d]$-linear code over Z_q whose distance $d \geq 2k + 1$. Let $m = n - u$, we have $m \geq d - 1 \geq 2k$. (In the corrected KD scheme, it is chosen that $m = d - 1 = 2k$.) Let H be the parity check matrix for $\mathcal{C}$. Let $\Gamma = H^T$ then Γ is a matrix of size $n \times m$. Let $\boldsymbol{\gamma}^{(1)}, \boldsymbol{\gamma}^{(2)}, \ldots, \boldsymbol{\gamma}^{(n)}$ denote the n row vectors of Γ, each of length $m \geq 2k$. Any $(d - 1)$ rows of Γ are linear independent.

Choose random $\boldsymbol{b} = (b_1, \ldots, b_m) \in \mathbf{Z}_q^m$ such that $\boldsymbol{\gamma}^{(i)} \cdot \boldsymbol{b} \neq 0$ for $i = 1, \ldots, n$. Let $h_1 = g^{b_1}, \ldots, h_m = g^{b_m}$, and $\Gamma \cdot \boldsymbol{b} = \boldsymbol{e} = (e_1, \ldots, e_n)$. Then $e_i = \boldsymbol{\gamma}^{(i)} \cdot \boldsymbol{b} \neq 0$.
Public encryption key is $PK = (g, h_1, \ldots, h_m)$.
Note that the matrix Γ is made public.
User secret decryption keys. The decryption key for user i is e_i.
Encryption: a message $M \in G_q$ is encrypted as

$$\langle Mg^r, h_1^r, h_2^r, \ldots, h_m^r \rangle$$

where r is randomly chosen in $\mathbf{Z}_q$.

Decryption: Each user i uses the ith row of Γ, $\gamma^{(i)}$, and his secret e_i to decrypt as follows

$$M = \frac{M\, g^r}{\left[(h_1^r)^{\gamma_1^{(i)}} \cdots (h_m^r)^{\gamma_m^{(i)}} \right]^{1/e_i}} \quad .$$

3.3 The Corrected Kurosawa–Desmedt Scheme

The corrected KD scheme chooses an $[n, n - 2k, 2k + 1]$-Reed Solomon code. The matrix Γ in this case has size $n \times 2k$ and the ith row vector of Γ is $\gamma^{(i)} = (1, i, i^2, \ldots, i^{2k-1})$. Let $f(x) = b_1 + b_2 x + \ldots + b_{2k} x^{2k-1}$ then in the matrix equation $\Gamma \cdot b = e = (e_1, \ldots, e_n)$ we have $e_i = \gamma^{(i)} \cdot b = f(i)$. Thus, the secret key for user i is the polynomial value $e_i = f(i)$.

Encryption: a message $M \in G_q$ is encrypted as

$$\langle g^r, M\, h_1^r, h_2^r, \ldots, h_{2k}^r \rangle$$

where r is randomly chosen in $\mathbf{Z}_q$.

Decryption: Each user i uses the secret key $e_i = f(i)$ to decrypt as follows

$$M = \frac{(M\, h_1^r)(h_2^r)^i (h_3^r)^{i^2} \cdots (h_{2k}^r)^{i^{2k-1}}}{(g^r)^{f(i)}} \quad .$$

4 Modified Schemes with Revocation

In this section, we show that revocation schemes can be derived from linear codes. We propose revocation technique for the three schemes: the linear-coded Kurosawa–Desmedt scheme, the corrected Kurosawa–Desmedt scheme and the Boneh–Franklin scheme. The advantage of the proposed schemes is that no user secret keys needed to change. There is no changes in public encryption keys, except in the BF scheme, a single group element is added to the public key. The security is provable (semantic security against passive adversary). The proposed revocation schemes are threshold schemes, up to $2k - 1$ users can be revoked where k denotes the collusion threshold. Broadcast ciphertexts contain $2k$ field elements and $2k + 2$ group elements which is as efficient as other revocation schemes such as Naor–Pinkas [17], Tzeng–Tzeng [20], Tô et al [19], and Kim et al [11].

4.1 LC-KD' with Revocation

Revocation: Let R be a subset of $\{1, \ldots, n\}$ such that $1 \le |R| < 2k$. R represents the set of revoked users. Choose $\boldsymbol{\beta} = (\beta_1, \ldots, \beta_m)$, such that in the equation $\Gamma \cdot \boldsymbol{\beta} = \boldsymbol{\epsilon} = (\epsilon_1, \ldots, \epsilon_n)$, we have $\epsilon_i = 0$ if and only if $i \in R$. This can be done because any $2k$ rows of Γ are linear independent.

Let $\eta_1 = g^{\beta_1}, \ldots, \eta_m = g^{\beta_m}$.

A message $M \in G_q$ is encrypted as

$$\langle\, g^{r_1}, M\, g^{r_2}, \beta_1, \ldots, \beta_m, h_1^{r_1}\eta_1^{r_2}, \ldots, h_m^{r_1}\eta_m^{r_2}\,\rangle$$

where r_1, r_2 are random numbers in Z_q.

Decryption. User i first calculates $\epsilon_i = \boldsymbol{\gamma}^{(i)} \cdot \boldsymbol{\beta}$. If $\epsilon_i = 0$ then i is revoked. Otherwise, $i \notin R$, and user i can use secret value e_i and the vector $\boldsymbol{\gamma}^{(i)}$ of the public matrix Γ to decrypt

$$(M\, g_1^{r_2})\left(\frac{(g^{r_1})^{e_i}}{(h_1^{r_1}\eta_1^{r_2})^{\gamma_1^{(i)}} \ldots (h_{2k}^{r_1}\eta_{2k}^{r_2})^{\gamma_{2k}^{(i)}}}\right)^{1/\epsilon_i} = M\ .$$

4.2   The Corrected Kurosawa–Desmedt Scheme

If $R = \{i_1, \ldots, i_c\}$, $1 \le c < 2k$, is the revoked user set then in the revocation procedure we need to find a vector $\boldsymbol{\beta} = (\beta_1, \ldots, \beta_{2k})$ such that in the equation $\Gamma \cdot \boldsymbol{\beta} = \boldsymbol{\epsilon} = (\epsilon_1, \ldots, \epsilon_n)$ we have $\epsilon_i = 0$ if and only if $i \in R$. Consider the polynomial $g(x) = \beta_1 + \beta_2\, x + \ldots + \beta_{2k}\, x^{2k-1}$ formed by the vector $\boldsymbol{\beta}$. We have $\epsilon_i = \boldsymbol{\gamma}^{(i)} \cdot \boldsymbol{\beta} = g(i)$. Thus $g(i) = 0$ if and only if $i \in R$. That means $g(x)$ can be written as $g(x) = (x - i_1)\ldots(x - i_c)z(x)$ where z is a polynomial of degree up to $2k - c$ whose roots are not in the set $U = \{1, \ldots, n\}$. In particular, if the number of revoked user is $2k$ then $z(x)$ is a non-zero number in $\mathbf{Z}_q$.

In summary, for the corrected KD scheme, the revocation procedure is as follows.

Revocation. Let $R = \{i_1, \ldots, i_c\}$, $1 \le c < 2k$, be the revoked user set. Choose a random polynomial $z(x)$ of degree up to $2k - c$ such that $z(i) \ne 0$ for all $i = 1, \ldots, n$. Let $g(x) = (x - i_1)\ldots(x - i_c)z(x) = \beta_1 + \beta_2\, x + \ldots + \beta_{2k}\, x^{2k-1}$. Let $\eta_1 = g^{\beta_1}$, $\ldots$, $\eta_{2k} = g^{\beta_{2k}}$.

A message $M \in G_q$ is encrypted as

$$\langle\, g^{r_1}, M\, g^{r_2}, \beta_1, \ldots, \beta_{2k}, h_1^{r_1}\eta_1^{r_2}, \ldots, h_{2k}^{r_1}\eta_{2k}^{r_2}\,\rangle$$

where r_1, r_2 are random numbers in Z_q.

Decryption. User i first calculates $\epsilon_i = g(i) = \beta_1 + \beta_2\, i + \ldots + \beta_{2k}\, i^{2k-1}$. If $g(i) = 0$ then i is revoked. For $i \notin R$, $\epsilon_i = g(i) = (i - i_1)\ldots(i - i_c)z(i) \ne 0$. User i then uses secret value $e_i = f(i)$ to decrypt

$$(M\, g_1^{r_2})\left(\frac{(g^{r_1})^{f(i)}}{(h_1^{r_1}\eta_1^{r_2})(h_2^{r_1}\eta_2^{r_2})^i (h_3^{r_1}\eta_3^{r_2})^{i^2} \ldots (h_{2k}^{r_1}\eta_{2k}^{r_2})^{i^{2k-1}}}\right)^{1/g(i)} = M\ .$$

4.3   BF with Revocation

For the BF scheme, the public encryption key is slightly changed. A single group element is added to the encryption key.

The new encryption key is $PK' = (g_1, y, h_1, \ldots, h_{2k})$.

The added element g_1 is an arbitrary generator of G_q, indeed, we can choose $g_1 = g$.

Revocation. Let R be a subset of $\{1, \ldots, n\}$ such that $1 \leq |R| < 2k$. R represents the set of revoked users. Choose $\beta = (\beta_1, \ldots, \beta_{2k})$, such that in the equation $\Gamma \cdot \beta = \epsilon = (\epsilon_1, \ldots, \epsilon_n)$, we have $\epsilon_i = 0$ if and only if $i \in R$. This can be done because any $2k$ rows of Γ are linear independent.

Let $\eta_1 = g_1^{\beta_1}, \ldots, \eta_{2k} = g_1^{\beta_{2k}}$.

A message $M \in G_q$ is encrypted as

$$\langle\, y^{r_1}, M\, g_1^{r_2}, \beta_1, \ldots, \beta_{2k}, h_1^{r_1} \eta_1^{r_2}, \ldots, h_{2k}^{r_1} \eta_{2k}^{r_2} \,\rangle$$

where r_1, r_2 are random numbers in $\mathbf{Z}_q$.

Decryption. User i first calculates $\epsilon_i = \gamma^{(i)} \cdot \beta$. If $\epsilon_i = 0$ then i is revoked. Otherwise, $i \notin R$, user i can use his decryption key $\theta^{(i)} = v_i \gamma^{(i)}$ to decrypt

$$(M\, g_1^{r_2}) \left(\frac{y^{r_1}}{(h_1^{r_1} \eta_1^{r_2})^{\theta_1^{(i)}} \cdots (h_{2k}^{r_1} \eta_{2k}^{r_2})^{\theta_{2k}^{(i)}}} \right)^{1/(v_i \epsilon_i)} = M \ .$$

4.4   Semantic Security for Revocation

We show that the proposed revocation schemes are semantically secure against a passive adversary who controls up to $2k - 1$ users assuming the difficulty of the DDH problem in the group G_q. We give a security proof for the linear-coded Kurosawa–Desmedt (LC-KD') scheme. The proof can be easily adjusted for other schemes.

Model of Adversary. The following game models an *Adversary* $\mathcal{A}$ who controls up to $2k - 1$ users and an *Oracle* who represents the revocation scheme.

1. Adversary adaptively chooses a set $\mathcal{A}_{\text{users}}$ of up to $2k-1$ users that it controls.
2. Given $\mathcal{A}_{\text{users}}$, for a given security parameter λ, the Oracle runs the key generation procedure and gives the Adversary the public encryption key together with all secret keys of the users in $\mathcal{A}_{\text{users}}$ under the control of the Adversary.
3. The Adversary then produces two challenge messages M_0 and M_1 and gives them to the Oracle.
4. The Oracle selects a random bit $r \in \{0, 1\}$ and gives the Adversary back the ciphertext of M_r encrypted with the revoked set $R = \mathcal{A}_{\text{users}}$.
5. The Adversary output a bit r'.

The advantage of the adversary $\mathcal{A}$ is defined as $Adv_{\mathcal{A}}(\lambda) = |Pr(r = r') - 1/2|$. We say that the revocation scheme is semantically secure if $Adv_{\mathcal{A}}(\lambda)$ is negligible.

Theorem 1 states that the linear-coded Kurosawa–Desmedt revocation scheme is semantically secure, the proof is given in the full version of the paper.

Theorem 1. *The LC-KD' revocation scheme is semantically secure against a collusion of up to $2k - 1$ revoked users assuming the difficulty of the DDH problem.*

5   Permanent User Removal

In a revocation scheme, we can remove a traitor permanently by always including the traitor in the revoked user set. However, in a threshold revocation scheme such as our proposed schemes, the number of revoked users is limited so we cannot use it to remove many traitors. Dodis et al. [6] define a scheme to be *scalable* if any party can broadcast messages using public key (*server-side scalable*) and if it supports increasing number of *add-user* and *remove-user* operations (*client-side scalable*).

Our proposed revocation schemes are server-side scalable but not client-side scalable since they cannot remove more than $2k - 1$ users. The only known scalable scheme is the Dodis et al. scheme [6]. In this scheme, everytime after removing v users, it allows legitimate users update their secret keys. So the time line is divided into many "windows", and in each window, v users are removed. To calculate new secret key, legitimate users need to use their old secret key together with a single update information broadcasted by the system administrator. The only problem with this scheme is, in each key update time, the same update information is used for all users. Even a revoked user, if by any chance he has this update information, he can use it to update his key to a valid key in the new session. Therefore, as emphasized in their paper, the Dodis et al. scheme is only secure against *window adversary*. That is, it is secure against up to a threshold of v revoked users who are *subsequently revoked in the same window*. This make the scheme vulnerable under the collusion of as small as two revoked users who are revoked in two different windows. It remains as an open problem to design a scalable scheme that is secure against a collusion of a threshold number of arbitrary revoked users.

In this section, we look at the possibility of repeatedly removing permanently users by modifying only the public key and public parts of users keys. If it is possible to do so then we would have a scalable scheme. Unfortunately, we prove that it is not possible, at least, for the BF scheme. Section 5.1 considers the case when we remove a user by modifying only the public encryption key. Section 5.2 considers the case when we remove a user by modifying the public encryption key and the public parts of users keys (which are the rows of the public matrix).

5.1   Modifying Public Key, Keeping User Keys Unchanged

Consider the Boneh–Franklin scheme. Let $y = g^a$, $h_1 = g^{b_1}$, $h_2 = g^{b_2}$, ..., $h_{2k} = g^{b_{2k}}$ be the current public encryption key. The user decryption key is $\boldsymbol{\theta}^{(i)} = v_i \boldsymbol{\gamma}^{(i)}$.

For simplicity, assume now we want to remove user n. We want to change the public encryption key become $y' = g^{a'}$, $h_1' = g^{b_1'}$, $h_2' = g^{b_2'}$, ..., $h_{2k}' = g^{b_{2k}'}$.

For each $i = 1, \ldots, n-1$, in order to have user i remained valid, the decryption key $\boldsymbol{\theta}^{(i)} = v_i \boldsymbol{\gamma}^{(i)}$ must be a DL-representation of the new DL-element y' with respect to the new DL-base $h_1', \ldots, h_{2k}'$. Therefore,

$$a' = \boldsymbol{\theta}^{(i)} \cdot \boldsymbol{b}' = v_i(\boldsymbol{\gamma}^{(i)} \cdot \boldsymbol{b}'), \quad \forall i = 1, \ldots, n-1 \ .$$

We want the decryption key of the removed user n, $\boldsymbol{\theta}^{(n)} = v_n \, \boldsymbol{\gamma}^{(n)}$, to become invalid. That is, the vector $\boldsymbol{\theta}^{(n)}$ is not a DL-representation of the new DL-element y' with respect to the new DL-base $h'_1, h'_2, \ldots, h'_{2k}$:

$$\boldsymbol{\theta}^{(n)} \cdot \boldsymbol{b}' = v_n(\boldsymbol{\gamma}^{(n)} \cdot \boldsymbol{b}') \neq a' \ .$$

We will prove that this cannot be achieved.

Theorem 2. *Let A be a full rank matrix of size $(n - 2k) \times n$ and let Γ be an $n \times 2k$ matrix whose columns are $2k$ linear independent solutions of the equation $Ax = 0$. Let $\boldsymbol{\gamma}^{(1)}, \ldots, \boldsymbol{\gamma}^{(n)}$ denote the n row vectors of Γ.*

If for some vectors $\boldsymbol{b}$, $\boldsymbol{b}'$ of length $2k$, and some non-zero numbers a, a', v_1, $v_2, \ldots, v_n$ we have $v_1(\boldsymbol{\gamma}^{(1)} \cdot \boldsymbol{b}) = v_2(\boldsymbol{\gamma}^{(2)} \cdot \boldsymbol{b}) = \ldots = v_n(\boldsymbol{\gamma}^{(n)} \cdot \boldsymbol{b}) = a$ and $v_1(\boldsymbol{\gamma}^{(1)} \cdot \boldsymbol{b}') = v_2(\boldsymbol{\gamma}^{(2)} \cdot \boldsymbol{b}') = \ldots = v_{n-1}(\boldsymbol{\gamma}^{(n-1)} \cdot \boldsymbol{b}') = a'$, then it holds that $v_n(\boldsymbol{\gamma}^{(n)} \cdot \boldsymbol{b}') = a'$.

From Theorem 2, we can see that the secret key of user n, $\boldsymbol{\theta}^{(n)}$, remains valid for the new decryption with the new public encryption key.

We have proved in this section that it is impossible to remove a user by changing only the public encryption key and keeping all user secret keys fixed. In the next section, we will see a method by Silja Mäki to remove an user by changing public encryption key together with the matrix Γ.

5.2   Silja Mäki's Attempt: Changing Public Key Together with Public Parts of User Keys

In BF scheme, the user decryption key $\boldsymbol{\theta}^{(i)} = v_i \, \boldsymbol{\gamma}^{(i)}$ can be viewed as two parts. The secret part v_i is kept by the user and the public part $\boldsymbol{\gamma}^{(i)}$ is kept by the system. Mäki's [14] idea is to keep the secret part v_i unchanged while the public part of the key, $\boldsymbol{\gamma}^{(i)}$, is changing whenever the system wants to remove a colluder.

Below is a summary of Mäki's modification to BF

1. Replace $\boldsymbol{b} = (b_1, b_2, \ldots, b_{2k})$ with $\boldsymbol{b}' = (b'_1, b'_2, \ldots, b'_{2k})$, that is, replace $h_1 = g^{b_1}, \ldots, h_{2k} = g^{b_{2k}}$ by $h'_1 = g^{b'_1}, \ldots, h'_{2k} = g^{b'_{2k}}$.
2. Replace the matrix Γ with the new matrix Γ' whose $2k$ columns vectors also are $2k$ linear independent solutions of the equation $Ax = 0$. Denote the n row vectors of Γ' by $\boldsymbol{\gamma}^{(1)\prime}, \boldsymbol{\gamma}^{(2)\prime}, \ldots, \boldsymbol{\gamma}^{(n)\prime}$. Matrix Γ' is chosen so that the vector $\boldsymbol{\theta}^{(i)\prime} = v_i \boldsymbol{\gamma}^{(i)\prime}$ is a DL-representation of y with respect to the new DL-base $h'_1, h'_2, \ldots, h'_{2k}$. In the other words, the row vectors $\boldsymbol{\gamma}^{(i)\prime}$ must satisfy $\boldsymbol{\theta}^{(i)\prime} \cdot \boldsymbol{b}' = v_i(\boldsymbol{\gamma}^{(i)\prime} \cdot \boldsymbol{b}') = a$.
3. Make the first $n - 1$ row vectors $\boldsymbol{\gamma}^{(1)\prime}, \boldsymbol{\gamma}^{(2)\prime}, \ldots, \boldsymbol{\gamma}^{(n-1)\prime}$ of the matrix Γ' public so that each user i, $1 \le i \le n - 1$, can use the corresponding new vector with his secret key v_i to form the new decryption key $\boldsymbol{\theta}^{(i)\prime} = v_i \boldsymbol{\gamma}^{(i)\prime}$ for the future decryption.
4. The last row vector $\boldsymbol{\gamma}^{(n)\prime}$ of the matrix Γ' is kept secret so that the removed user n cannot form the decryption key.
5. Since $A\Gamma' = 0$, the tracing remains the same.

However, Mäki also presented a successful attack, in which the removed user n by looking at the matrix Γ and the first $n-1$ rows of matrix Γ' can calculate the last row $\gamma^{(n)\prime}$ of Γ'. Therefore, the removed user can obtain the new decryption key for himself.

We can eliminate this attack by choosing the matrix Γ' so that even the user n can calculate the last row vector $\gamma^{(n)\prime}$ but he cannot use it to form the decryption key. That is $\gamma^{(n)\prime}$ must be chosen so that the vector $\theta^{(n)\prime} = v_n\,\gamma^{(n)\prime}$ is not a DL-representation of y with respect to the new DL-base $h'_1, h'_2, \ldots, h'_{2k}$. Or equivalently, $\theta^{(n)\prime} \cdot b' = v_i(\cdot\gamma^{(n)\prime} \cdot b') \neq a$. However, we will prove that this cannot be done.

Theorem 3. *Let A be a full rank matrix of size $(n - 2k) \times n$ and let Γ, Γ' be two $n \times 2k$ matrices both of whose $2k$ columns are linear independent solutions of the equation $Ax = 0$. Let $\gamma^{(1)}, \ldots, \gamma^{(n)}$ and $\gamma^{(1)\prime}, \ldots, \gamma^{(n)\prime}$ respectively denote row vectors of Γ and Γ'.*

If for some vectors b, b' of length $2k$, and some non-zero numbers a, a', v_1, v_2, $\ldots$, v_n we have $v_1(\gamma^{(1)} \cdot b) = v_2(\gamma^{(2)} \cdot b) = \ldots = v_n(\gamma^{(n)} \cdot b) = a$ and $v_1(\gamma^{(1)\prime} \cdot b') = v_2(\gamma^{(2)\prime} \cdot b') = \ldots = v_{n-1}(\gamma^{(n-1)\prime} \cdot b') = a'$, then it holds that $v_n(\gamma^{(n)\prime} \cdot b') = a'$.

From Theorem 3, if for all i, $1 \leq i \leq n - 1$, user i can combine the new vector $\gamma^{(i)\prime}$ with v_i to get the new decryption key $\theta^{(i)\prime} = v_i\,\gamma^{(i)\prime}$ then the last vector $\gamma^{(n)\prime}$ also makes a valid decryption key $\theta^{(n)\prime} = v_n\,\gamma^{(n)\prime}$. Since $A\Gamma' = 0$ and $n - 1$ row vectors of Γ' is publicly known, the removed user n can calculate the last row $\gamma^{(n)\prime}$ and hence obtain the valid decryption key $\theta^{(n)\prime}$.

6   Conclusion

In this paper, we have shown that from an $[n, u, d]$-linear code such that $d \geq 2k + 1$, it is possible to construct a public-key (k, n)-traitor tracing scheme with *revocation*. We demonstrate this technique for three schemes: the Boneh–Franklin scheme, the corrected Kurosawa–Desmedt scheme and the linear-coded Kurosawa–Desmedt scheme. The security of our proposed revocation schemes is provable (semantic security against passive adversary). It seems that CCA2 security can be also achieved if we use Cramer and Shoup approach [4] to modify our schemes.

We also look at the problem of permanently removing a user to make the system scalable. We prove that it is impossible to obtain a *remove-user* procedure for the Boneh–Franklin scheme where all the secret part of user keys are kept unchanged and only the public encryption key and the public part of user keys are allowed to modified. Dodis et al [6] is the only known scalable scheme, however it is only secure against "window adversary", which is not a strong model. It remains as an open problem to design a public key traitor tracing with revocation which is fully scalable.

References

1. T. Asano, *A revocation scheme with minimal storage at receivers*, AsiaCrypt'02, LNCS 2501, 433–450, 2002.
2. D. Boneh and M. Franklin, *An Efficient Public Key Traitor Tracing Scheme*, Crypto'99, LNCS 1666, 338–353, 1999.
3. D. Boneh and J. Shaw, *Collusion-Secure Fingerprinting for Digital Data*, IEEE Transactions on Information Theory, **44** (1998), 1897–1905.
4. R. Cramer and V. Shoup, *A Practical Public Key Cryptosystem Provable Secure Against Adaptive Chosen Ciphertext Attack*, Crypto'98, LNCS 1462, 13–25, 1998.
5. Y. Dodis and N. Fazio, *Public Key Trace and Revoke Scheme Secure against Adaptive Chosen Ciphertext Attack*, PKC'03, LNCS 2567, 100–115, 2003.
6. Y. Dodis, N. Fazio, A. Kiayias and M. Yung, *Scalable Public-Key Tracing and Revoking*, Principles of Distributed Computing (PODC), July 2003.
7. D. Halevy and A. Shamir, *The LSD broadcast encryption scheme*, Crypto'02, LNCS 2442, 47–60, 2002.
8. A. Kiayias and M. Yung, *Self Protecting Pirates and Black-Box Traitor Tracing*, Crypto'01, LNCS 2139, 63–79, 2001.
9. A. Kiayias and M. Yung, *On Crafty Pirates and Foxy Tracers*, SP-DRM'01, LNCS 2320, 22–39, 2001.
10. A. Kiayias and M. Yung, *Traitor Tracing with Constant Transmission Rate*, EuroCrypt'02, LNCS 2332, 450–465, 2002.
11. C.H. Kim, Y.H. Hwang and P.J. Lee, *An Efficient Public Key Trace and Revoke Scheme Secure against Adaptive Chosen Ciphertext Attack*, AsiaCrypt'03, LNCS 2894, 359–373, 2003.
12. K. Kurosawa and Y. Desmedt, *Optimum Traitor Tracing and Asymmetric Schemes with Arbiter*, EuroCrypt'98, LNCS 1403, 145–157, 1998.
13. K. Kurosawa and T. Yoshida, *Linear Code Implies Public-Key Traitor Tracing*, PKC'02, LNCS 2274, 172–187, 2002.
14. S. Mäki, *On Long-Lived Public-Key Traitor Tracing: First Steps,* Tik-110.501 Seminar on Network Security (2000), Helsinki University of Technology.
15. S. Mitsunari, R. Sakai and M. Kasahara, *A New Traitor Tracing*, IEICE Trans. Fundamentals, Vol. E85-A, No. 2, Feb 2002.
16. D. Naor, M. Naor and J. Lotspiech, *Revocation and Tracing Schemes for Stateless Receivers*, Crypto'01, LNCS 2139, 41–62, 2001.
17. M. Naor and B. Pinkas, *Efficient Trace and Revoke Schemes*, Financial Cryptography'00, LNCS 1962, 1–20, 2001.
18. D.R. Stinson and R. Wei, *Key Preassigned Traceability Schemes for Broadcast Encryption*, SAC'98, LNCS 1556, 144–156, 1998.
19. V.D. Tô, R. Safavi-Naini and F. Zhang, *New Traitor Tracing Schemes Using Bilinear Map*, ACM DRM'03, 67–76, 2003.
20. W. Tzeng and Z. Tzeng, *A Public-Key Traitor Tracing Scheme with Revocation Using Dynamic Shares*, PKC'01, LNCS 1992, 207–224, 2001.
21. D.M. Wallner, E.J. Harder, and R.C. Agee, *Key Management for Multicast: Issues and Architectures*, IETF Network Working Group, RFC 2627, 1999.
22. C.K. Wong, M. Gouda and S. Lam, *Secure Group Communications Using Key Graphs*, ACM SIGCOMM'98, 68–79, 1998.

TTS Without Revocation Capability Secure Against CCA2*

Chong Hee Kim[1], Yong Ho Hwang[2], and Pil Joong Lee[3]

[1] Samsung Electronics Co., LTD, Korea
chonghee.kim@samsung.com
[2] IS Lab., Dept. of Electronic and Electrical Eng., POSTECH, Korea
yhhwang@oberon.postech.ac.kr
[3] IS Lab., Dept. of Electronic and Electrical Eng., POSTECH
(on leave at KT Research Center), Korea
pjl@postech.ac.kr

Abstract. A traitor tracing scheme (TTS) deters traitors from giving away their secret keys to decrypt the transmitted data by enabling the system manager to trace at least one of the traitors who participated in the construction of a pirate decoder after confiscating it. In an asymmetric scheme, the system manager is also under suspicion, so the system manager must convince a judge of the implication of the traitors. Recently, Kiayias and Yung proposed an asymmetric public key traitor tracing scheme [13]. However, their scheme does not provide CCA2 security even if a single user is a traitor. That is, their scheme is secure against *adaptive chosen ciphertext (CCA2) attack* only when there is *no* traitor. In this paper, we first introduce the security notion against CCA2 attack in a *traitor tracing scheme with no revocation capability*. This notion is somewhat different from the traditional security notion against CCA2 attack in a two-party encryption scheme [5]. To the best of our knowledge, no security notion against CCA2 attack in a traitor tracing scheme with no revocation capability has been presented. In addition, we modify the Kiayias and Yung's scheme to achieve security against CCA2 attack under the decision Diffie-Hellman assumption and the collision-resistant hash function assumption.

1 Introduction

A traitor tracing scheme (TTS) is a variant of a broadcast encryption scheme [9]. In a broadcast encryption scheme, the system manager broadcasts encrypted data to users and only legitimate users can decrypt transmitted data. However, if some of legitimate users leak information of their secret keys (we call these users *traitors*) and make a pirate decoder that can decrypt transmitted data, then the system is broken. A TTS is an alternative solution to this problem. In a

---

* This research was supported by University IT Research Center Project and the Brain Korea 21 Project.

H. Wang et al. (Eds.): ACISP 2004, LNCS 3108, pp. 36–49, 2004.

TTS, the system manager can trace at least one of the traitors who participated in the construction of a pirate decoder after confiscation of the pirate decoder.

After the advent of the TTS by Chor et al. [4], many variants have been investigated. We can divide TTS into two categories. One is a scheme that uses a secret key and coding approach [3,4,10,17,19,20,21] and the other uses a public key [2,11,22,14]. In the secret key scheme, the keys in a pirate decoder can be identified by combinatorial methods. In the public key approach, the size of the enabling block is independent of the number of users. In addition, the public key TTS enables the system manager to prepare a public key that allows all content providers to broadcast data to users.

In TTS, users share all secret keys with the system manager. Therefore, non-repudiation cannot be offered. That is, a malicious system manager can implicate an innocent user in the construction of a pirate decoder, and users can always deny their implication in the construction of a pirate decoder and claim that it was the malicious system manager. A solution to this problem is an *asymmetric* TTS, which was first introduced by Pfitzmann and Waidner [19, 20]. In an asymmetric TTS, the system manager does not know the entire secret key of the user.

An *asymmetric public key* TTS was presented in [15,23]. These schemes used an *oblivious polynomial evaluation* (OPE) protocol [18] to achieve an asymmetric property. An OPE protocol involves two parties, the sender S who possesses a secret polynomial $P \in Z_q[x]$, and the receiver R who possesses a secret value $\alpha \in Z_q$. An OPE protocol allows R to compute $P(\alpha)$ in such a way that:

- S cannot extract any non-trivial information about α.
- R cannot extract any information about the polynomial P, other than what can trivially be extracted from $P(\alpha)$.

Recently, Kiayias and Yung showed weakness of [15,23] and proposed a new scheme (we call it the KY scheme) [13]. They used the idea of the use of the OPE protocol as in [15,23], especially a *malleable* OPE protocol [13], to achieve an asymmetric property and the idea of [2] to construct a tracing algorithm. They also claimed that: *"We remark that semantic security against a chosen ciphertext security can be achieved also, following the techniques of [5], as it was demonstrated in [2]"*. However, their claim is correct *if and only if* there is *no* traitor. If there is even a single traitor, then semantic security cannot be achieved.

There is a notion of security against CCA2 attack in a two-party encryption scheme [5,6]. Recently, Dodis and Fazio [7] and Kim et al. [12] proposed the notion of security against CCA2 attack in a multi-party encryption scheme, especially a *revocation scheme*. In the revocation scheme, there are a sender and multiple receivers. In the notion of security against CCA2 attack in the revocation scheme, the advantage of an attacker is negligible even if he can obtain the secret keys of revoked users [12]. We cannot directly apply this security notion to the traitor tracing scheme without revocation capability, because if an attacker obtains the secret keys of traitors, he can decrypt all transmitted data and win the game.

Our results. We first introduce the security notion against CCA2 attack in a traitor tracing scheme with *no revocation capability*. We show that the KY scheme does not provide the semantic security even if a single user is a traitor. We modify the KY scheme to achieve security against an *adaptive chosen ciphertext (CCA2) attack* under the decision Diffie-Hellman assumption and the collision-resistant hash function assumption.

Remark. Recently, Dodis and Fazio [7] and Kim *et al.* [12] proposed a public key trace and revocation scheme against a CCA2 attack. Their schemes provide semantic security in a *symmetric* case and are based on [22] scheme. We remark that Dodis and Fazio's scheme and Kim *et al.*'s scheme are revocation schemes and no CCA2 schemes were known in an *asymmetric* public key TTS with *no revocation capability*. Our achievement is not trivial, as we have to resolve some difficulties inherent in the asymmetric setting and no revocation property.

2   Preliminaries

In this section, we review the decision Diffie-Hellman (DDH) assumption and public key encryption schemes secure against CCA2 attack.

The Decision Diffie-Hellman Assumption. Let G be a group of large prime order q, and consider the following two distributions:

- the distribution **R** of random quadruples $(g_1, g_2, u_1, u_2) \in G^4$,
- the distribution **D** of quadruples $(g_1, g_2, u_1, u_2) \in G^4$, where g_1, g_2 are random, and $u_1 = g_1^r$ and $u_2 = g_2^r$ for random $r \in Z_q$.

The decision Diffie-Hellman (DDH) assumption is that it is computationally hard to distinguish these two distributions. That is, we consider an algorithm that should output 0 or 1, given a quadruple coming from one of the two distributions. Then the difference between the probability that it outputs a 1 given an input from **R**, and the probability that it outputs a 1 given an input from **D** is negligible.

Our scheme is based on the modified Cramer-Shoup (M-CS) scheme [16]. The M-CS scheme is a variant of the Cramer-Shoup (CS) scheme [5]. We briefly review these schemes.

The Cramer-Shoup scheme. Given a security parameter 1^λ, the secret key is (x_1, x_2, y_1, y_2, z) and the public key is $(p, q, g_1, g_2, c, d, h, H)$ where p is a λ-bit prime, g_1, g_2 are generators of G(a subgroup of Z_p^* of a large prime order q), function H is a hash function chosen from a collision-resistant hash function family, $x_1, x_2, y_1, y_2, z \overset{R}{\leftarrow} Z_q$, $c = g_1^{x_1} g_2^{x_2}$, $d = g_1^{y_1} g_2^{y_2}$, and $h = g_1^z$.

Given a message $m \in G$, the encryption algorithm runs as follows. First, it chooses $r \overset{R}{\leftarrow} Z_q$ and computes $u_1 = g_1^r, u_2 = g_2^r, e = h^r m, \alpha = H(u_1, u_2, e), v = c^r d^{r\alpha}$. The ciphertext is (u_1, u_2, e, v). Given a ciphertext, the decryption algorithm runs as follows. First, it computes $v' = u_1^{x_1 + y_1 \alpha} \cdot u_2^{x_2 + y_2 \alpha}$. Next, it performs a validity check. If $v \neq v'$, then it outputs an error message, denoted '$\perp$'; otherwise, it outputs $m = \frac{e}{u_1^z}$. The security of this scheme against CCA2 is proven, based on DDH assumption, in [5].

The Modified Cramer-Shoup scheme. Canetti and Goldwasser slightly modified the above CS scheme as follows, without losing in security [16]. If the decryption algorithm finds $v \neq v'$, instead of outputting '$\perp$' it outputs a random value in G. In a sense, the modified scheme is even "more secure" since the adversary is not notified by the decryption algorithm whether a ciphertext is valid.

Now that the decryption algorithm does not explicitly check validity, given (u_1, u_2, e, v) it outputs $(\frac{e}{u_1^z}) \cdot (\frac{v'}{v})^s$ instead, where v' is computed as in the CS scheme and $s \overset{R}{\leftarrow} Z_q$. Note that the decryption algorithm is now randomized. To ascertain the validity of this modification, notice that if $v = v'$ then $(\frac{v}{v'})^s = 1$ for all s, and the correct value is outputted. If $v \neq v'$, then the decryption algorithm outputs a uniformly distributed value in G, independent of m. The security of M-CS scheme against CCA2 is proven, based on the DDH assumption, in [16].

3   Asymmetric Public Key Traitor Tracing Scheme

We define the model of an asymmetric public key traitor tracing scheme and security notion against adaptive chosen ciphertext attack in an asymmetric public key traitor tracing scheme. In an *asymmetric public key traitor tracing scheme* **A-PK-TTS**, a session key s is encrypted and broadcasted with the symmetric encryption of the "actual" message. Generally, the encryption of s is called the *enabling block*.

3.1   Asymmetric Public Key Traitor Tracing Scheme

An *asymmetric public key traitor tracing scheme* **A-PK-TTS** involves 4 entities (a system manager, content providers, users, and a judge) and consists of a 6-tuple of poly-time algorithms (**KeyGen, Reg, Enc, Dec, Tracing, Trial**). A *system manager* generates system parameters and registers a new user and traces traitors. *Content providers* send an encrypted message to users given a public key *PK*. A *judge* verifies whether users accused by the system manager have been implicated in the construction of a pirate decoder. A traitor tracing scheme is called $t - resistant$ if the scheme can reveal at least one traitor on the confiscation of a pirate decoder that was constructed by up to t traitors.

- **KeyGen**, *the key generation algorithm, is a probabilistic algorithm used by the system manager to set up all the parameters of the scheme.* **KeyGen** takes as input a security parameter 1^λ and generates the public key PK and the master secret key SK_{TTS}.

- **Reg**, *the registration algorithm, is a probabilistic algorithm used between the system manager and a new user to compute the secret initialization data needed to construct a new decoder each time a new user subscribes to the system.* **Reg** is a critical component in the context of asymmetric schemes: on the one hand, a new user should commit to his key in a non-repudiation manner; on the other hand, the system manager should be oblivious to a portion of the subscriber key (to prevent a malicious system manager from implicating an innocent user). We denote the set of all registered users as $|\mathcal{U}|$

- **Enc**, *the encryption algorithm, is a probabilistic algorithm used to encapsulate a given session key s within an enabling block T.* **Enc** takes as input the public key PK and the session key s, and returns the enabling block T.

- **Dec**, *the decryption algorithm, is a deterministic algorithm that takes as input the secret key SK_i of user i and the enabling block T and returns the session key s that was encapsulated within T if user i was a legitimate user when T was constructed, or the special symbol "$\perp$".*

- **Tracing**, *the traitor tracing algorithm, is a deterministic algorithm used by the system manager that takes as input a pirate decoder and returns at least one identity of the traitors that participated in the construction of the decoder by revealing his key.* **Tracing** outputs non-repudiable information that can be verified in a trial by a judge.

- **Trial**, *the trial algorithm, is a deterministic algorithm used by a judge that takes as input non-repudiable information provided by the system manager and outputs whether a user accused by the system manger is guilty or not.*

Definition 1 (asymmetric public key traitor tracing scheme). *We say that a public key traitor tracing scheme is asymmetric if it satisfies:*

i) **frameproof**: *an honest user cannot be framed even in the presence of arbitrary collusions, including the system manager;*

ii) **direct non-repudiation**: *in a trial, the system manager has enough evidence to convince any judge without participation by the accused users.*

3.2   Adaptive Chosen Ciphertext Security in an Asymmetric Traitor Tracing Scheme

In a CCA2 model of a two-party encryption scheme[5], in order to obtain a *non-malleable* ciphertext, an additional "tag" message is added to each encrypted message so that it can be verified before proceeding with "actual" decryption. To make a "tag" message, each user receives *additional secret keys* (these keys are regarded as *partial key information* of the user's total secret keys). In addition an attacker can query an encryption oracle and a decryption oracle.

In a traitor tracing scheme, there are many receivers. Therefore, we have to pay more attention to construct a CCA2 secure scheme, because some receivers can expose *partial key information* for "tag" message without being traced back to himself. Only with this *partial key information* an attacker cannot decrypt the ciphertext itself, but break the CCA2 security by making the ciphertext *malleable*.

Therefore, a new security model against CCA2 attack in which an adversary has more ability than that of a two-party encryption CCA2 model is required. In our model, a legitimate user who wants to break the security of the TTS by leaking partial information of his secret key without revealing the identity of himself, is also included to a traitor.

To explain such attacker, we define a new oracle, called Acquisition, as follows.

- Acquisition(i): This oracle receives as input the index i of the user, and computes $SK_i \leftarrow$ **A-PK-TTS.Reg**(SK_{TTS}, i). Then the oracle outputs partial secret information, SK_i^*, for the "tag" message.

In our model, an adversary queries to the Acquisition oracle instead of the Corrupt oracle.

In Section 4.1, we will show an example of how an attacker with partial key information can break CCA2 security in a traditional model.

Formal Model. An adversary $\mathcal{A}$ in an *adaptive chosen ciphertext attack* (CCA2) is a probabilistic, poly-time *oracle query* machine. The attack game is defined in terms of an interactive computation between the adversary and its *environment*. We describe the attack game used to define the security against CCA2; that is, we define the environment in which $\mathcal{A}$ runs. We assume that the input to $\mathcal{A}$ is 1^λ for some λ.

Stage 1: The adversary queries a key generation oracle. The key generation oracle computes $(PK, SK_{TTS}) \leftarrow$ **A-PK-TTS.KeyGen**(1^λ) and responds with PK.

Stage 2: The adversary enters the *partial key acquisition stage*, where he is given oracle access to the *partial key acquisition oracle* Acquisition($\cdot$). This oracle can be called adaptively for at most t times. We note that the adversary cannot decrypt the ciphertext itself only with partial secret keys.

Stage 3: The adversary submits two session keys s_0, s_1 to an encryption oracle. On input s_0, s_1, the encryption oracle computes: $\sigma \xleftarrow{R} \{0, 1\}$; $T^* \leftarrow$ **A-PK-TTS.Enc**(PK, s_σ) and responds with the "target" enabling block T^*.

Stage 4: The adversary continues to make calls to the decryption oracle, subject only to the restriction that a submitted enabling block T is not identical to T^*.

Stage 5: The adversary outputs $\sigma^* \in \{0, 1\}$.

We define the advantage of $\mathcal{A}$ as $Adv_{TTS,\mathcal{A}}^{CCA2}(\lambda) = |Pr(\sigma^* = \sigma) - \frac{1}{2}|$.

Definition 1 *(t-resiliency against CCA2 of an asymmetric public key traitor tracing scheme).*
*We say that an asymmetric public key traitor tracing scheme **A-PK-TTS** is t-resilient against CCA2 attack if for all probabilistic, poly-time oracle query machines $\mathcal{A}$, the function $Adv_{TTS,\mathcal{A}}^{CCA2}(\lambda)$ grows negligibly in λ.*

4   The KY Schemes

In this section, we describe the KY scheme [13] suggested by Kiayias and Yung. They assume that every user u possesses a digital signature mechanism $\mathbf{sign}_u$ that allows him to sign messages. The signature of user u on a message M will be denoted by $\mathbf{sign}_u(M)$.

Key generation algorithm: KeyGen selects a random generator $g \in G$, where G is a group of order q in which q is a large prime such that $2q = p - 1$, and p is a large prime. It selects one random polynomial $Q_1(x) = a_0 + a_1 x + \ldots + a_{2t}x^{2t}$ over Z_q and a random $b \in Z_q$ and outputs (PK, SK_{TTS}), where $PK = < y, h_0, h_1, \ldots, h_{2t}, h' > = < g^{a_0}, g, g^{-a_1}, \ldots, g^{-a_{2t}}, g^{-b} >$, $SK_{TTS} = < Q(x, y) >$, and $Q(x, y) = Q_1(x) + by$.

Registration algorithm: Reg is executed between the system manager and a new user. The goal of the registration algorithm is to allow the user to compute a point $< i, \alpha_i, Q(i, \alpha_i) >$ of the bivariate polynomial Q so that i is randomly selected by the system manager, and $\alpha_i = \alpha_i^C + \alpha_i^R$, where α_i^C is a value selected and committed by the user, and the value α_i^R is randomly selected by the system manager. The commitment of the user to the value α_i^C will be of the form $< C_i = g^{\alpha_i^C}, \mathbf{sign}_i(C_i) >$. The registration algorithm can be implemented by employing an instantiation of a malleable OPE [13] over a committed value. The user's secret key is $SK_i = < \delta_0, \delta_1, \delta_2, \ldots, \delta_{2t}, \delta' > = < Q(i, \alpha_i), i, i^2, \ldots, i^{2t}, \alpha_i >$.

Encryption algorithm: Any content provider can send an encrypted message to users through an insecure channel using an encryption algorithm. The encryption algorithm receives as input the public key PK, the session key s, and finally it outputs T. It proceeds as follows:

$$T = < sy^r, h_0^r, h_1^r, \ldots, h_{2t}^r, (h')^r > .$$

Where r is randomly selected by a content provider

Decryption algorithm: Given an enabling block $T = \; < G, \; G_0, \; G_1, \; ..., \; G_{2t}, \; G' >$ and $SK_i = \; < \delta_0, \; \delta_1, \; \delta_2, \; ..., \; \delta_{2t}, \; \delta' >$, to recover the session key, a user i can proceed as follows:

$$Dec(i, T) = \frac{G}{(G')^{\delta'}(G_0)^{\delta_0} \prod_{j=1}^{2t}(G_j)^{\delta_j}}$$

$$= \frac{s \cdot y^r}{(h'^r)^{\delta'}(h_0^r)^{\delta_0} \prod_{j=1}^{2t}(h_j^r)^{ij}}$$

$$= \frac{s \cdot (g^{a_0})^r}{(g^{-br})^{\alpha_i} \{ g^{rQ(i,\alpha_i)} g^{-ra_1 i} ... g^{-ra_{2t} i^{2t}} \}}$$

$$= \frac{s \cdot (g^{a_0})^r}{(g^{-br})^{\alpha_i} \{ g^{r \{Q_1(i) + b\alpha_i\}} g^{-ra_1 i} ... g^{-ra_{2t} i^{2t}} \}}$$

$$= \frac{s \cdot (g^{a_0})^r}{g^{rQ_1(i)} g^{-ra_1 i} ... g^{-ra_{2t} i^{2t}}}$$

$$= \frac{s \cdot (g^{a_0})^r}{g^{ra_0}}$$

$$= s$$

Tracing and Trial: Due to space limitations we will omit the traitor tracing part and the trial part. For a detailed description, see [13].

4.1 Security Problem of the KY CCA2 Scheme

Kiayias and Yung claim that: "*We remark that semantic security against a chosen ciphertext security can be achieved also, following the techniques of [5], as it was demonstrated in [2]*". Their claim is correct *if and only if* there is no traitor. If they use a technique as in [2], the secret key for user i, SK_i, will be $< \delta_i, \; x_1, \; x_2, \; y_1, \; y_2 >$, where $\delta_i = \{ \delta_0^i, \; \delta_1^i, \; \delta_2^i, \; ..., \; \delta_{2t}^i, \; (\delta')^i \}$ and $< x_1, \; x_2, \; y_1, \; y_2 >$ are secret keys to make additional "tag" message so that it can be verified before proceeding with the actual decryption, as in the CS scheme [2]. Notice that all users share the same value $< x_1, \; x_2, \; y_1, \; y_2 >$ in their secret keys, although each user has a different value δ_i. Therefore, if a traitor user publishes the partial key $< x_1, \; x_2, \; y_1, \; y_2 >$ - it can be done without a fear of being traced -, then the KY scheme cannot be secure against CCA2 any longer. In our security model, an adversary can obtain the partial key $< x_1, \; x_2, \; y_1, \; y_2 >$ by only one **Acquisition** query. We note that the attacker only with the partial key cannot decrypt a ciphertext, but he can break the security against CCA2 by making the ciphertext *malleable*. Bellare *et al.*[1] proved that if any scheme is *malleable* against CCA2 then the scheme is not semantically secure against CCA2. Therefore, the semantic security of the KY scheme is also broken.

In the next section, we will show how to achieve security against CCA2 attack in the KY scheme when there are at most t traitors.

5 Proposed Scheme

In this section, we propose a new asymmetric public key traitor tracing scheme secure against adaptive chosen ciphertext attack. We omit the traitor tracing part and the trial part due to space limitations. They are the same as those of the KY scheme.

Key generation algorithm: KeyGen selects two random generators $g_1, g_2 \in G$ where G is a group of order q in which, q is a large prime such that $2q = p - 1$, and p is a large prime. It selects $x_1, x_2, y_1, y_2 \in Z_q$ and $2t$-degree polynomials $X_1(\xi)$, $X_2(\xi)$, $Y_1(\xi)$, $Y_2(\xi)$ over Z_q such that $X_1(0) = x_1$, $X_2(0) = x_2$, $Y_1(0) = y_1$, $Y_2(0) = y_2$. It also selects $2t$-degree polynomials $Z_1(\xi)$, $Z_2(\xi)$ over Z_q and computes $c = g_1^{x_1} g_2^{x_2}$, $d = g_1^{y_1} g_2^{y_2}$.

We represent $X_1(\xi)$, $X_2(\xi)$, $Y_1(\xi)$, $Y_2(\xi)$, $Z_1(\xi)$, and $Z_2(\xi)$ as follows :

$$
\begin{aligned}
X_1(\xi) &= a_{0,X_1} + a_{1,X_1}\xi + \cdots + a_{2t,X_1}\xi^{2t}, \\
X_2(\xi) &= a_{0,X_2} + a_{1,X_2}\xi + \cdots + a_{2t,X_2}\xi^{2t}, \\
Y_1(\xi) &= a_{0,Y_1} + a_{1,Y_1}\xi + \cdots + a_{2t,Y_1}\xi^{2t}, \\
Y_2(\xi) &= a_{0,Y_2} + a_{1,Y_2}\xi + \cdots + a_{2t,Y_2}\xi^{2t}, \\
Z_1(\xi) &= a_{0,Z_1} + a_{1,Z_1}\xi + \cdots + a_{2t,Z_1}\xi^{2t}, \\
Z_2(\xi) &= a_{0,Z_2} + a_{1,Z_2}\xi + \cdots + a_{2t,Z_2}\xi^{2t},
\end{aligned}
$$

Then, $a_{0,X_1} = x_1$, $a_{0,X_2} = x_2$, $a_{0,Y_1} = y_1$, and $a_{0,Y_2} = y_2$. It also selects a random $b \in Z_q$. Let $Q_1(x) = Z_1(x)$ and $Q_2(x, y) = Z_2(x) + by$. Finally, it outputs (PK, SK_{TTS}) as follows :

$PK = < p, q, g_1, g_2, c, d, x_{1,1}, \ldots, x_{1,2t}, x_{2,1}, \ldots, x_{2,2t},$

$\qquad y_{1,1}, \ldots, y_{1,2t}, y_{2,1}, \ldots, y_{2,2t}, h_0, h_1, \ldots, h_{2t}, h', H >$

$SK_{TTS} = < X_1(\xi), X_2(\xi), Y_1(\xi), Y_2(\xi), Z_1(\xi), Z_2(\xi) >.$

where

$$
\begin{aligned}
x_{1,1}, \ldots, x_{1,2t} &= g_1^{-a_{1,X_1}}, \ldots, g_1^{-a_{2t,X_1}} \\
x_{2,1}, \ldots, x_{2,2t} &= g_2^{-a_{1,X_2}}, \ldots, g_2^{-a_{2t,X_2}} \\
y_{1,1}, \ldots, y_{1,2t} &= g_1^{-a_{1,Y_1}}, \ldots, g_1^{-a_{2t,Y_1}} \\
y_{2,1}, \ldots, y_{2,2t} &= g_2^{-a_{1,Y_2}}, \ldots, g_2^{-a_{2t,Y_2}} \\
h_0 &= g_1^{a_{0,Z_1}} g_2^{a_{0,Z_2}} \\
h_j &= g_1^{-a_{j,Z_1}} g_2^{-a_{j,Z_2}}, \ j = 1, \ldots, 2t \\
h' &= g_2^{-b}
\end{aligned}
$$

Registration algorithm: Reg is executed between the system manager and a new user. The system manager randomly selects i and computes $Q_1(i)$, $X_1(i)$, $X_2(i)$, $Y_1(i)$, and $Y_2(i)$. These values are securely transmitted to the user. Then a point $Q_2(i, \alpha_i)$ is computed by the OPE protocol between the system manager and a user as the KY scheme. After the registration process, the user's secret key is $SK_i = < i, \alpha_i, Q_1(i), Q_2(i, \alpha_i), X_1(i), X_2(i), Y_1(i), Y_2(i) >$.

Encryption algorithm: Our scheme is based on the idea of the M-CS [16] scheme. The encryption algorithm receives as input the public key PK and the session key s. It proceeds as described in Table 1, and finally it outputs T.

Decryption algorithm: To recover the session key, a user i can proceed as in Table 1. We here verify that the output of the decryption algorithm is identical to the session key s as follows:

Table 1. Our proposed scheme

Encryption algorithm **Enc**(PK, s)	Decryption algorithm **Dec**(SK_i, T)
$E_1.\ r_1 \leftarrow_r Z_q$	$D_1.\ e \leftarrow H(S, u_1, u_2)$
$E_2.\ u_1 \leftarrow g_1^{r_1}$	$D_2.\ C_i \leftarrow u_1^{X_1(i)+Y_1(i)e} \cdot u_2^{X_2(i)+Y_2(i)e}$
$E_3.\ u_2 \leftarrow g_2^{r_1}$	$D_3.\ Q \leftarrow u_1^{Q_1(i)} \cdot u_2^{Q_2(i,\alpha_i)}$
$E_4.\ G_j \leftarrow (h_j x_{1,j} x_{2,j} y_{1,j} y_{2,j})^{r_1}, (j = 1,..,2t)$	$D_4.\ s \leftarrow \dfrac{S \cdot C}{C_i \cdot (G')^{\alpha_i} \cdot Q \cdot \prod_{j=1}^{2t}(G_j)^{i^j}}$
$E_5.\ G^{\blacksquare} \leftarrow (h^{\blacksquare})^{r_1}$	
$E_6.\ S \leftarrow s \cdot (h_0)^{r_1}$	
$E_7.\ e \leftarrow H(S, u_1, u_2)$	
$E_8.\ C \leftarrow c^{r_1} d^{r_1 e}$	
$E_9.\ T \leftarrow\ <S, u_1, u_2, C, G^{\blacksquare}, G_1, \ldots, G_{2t}>$	

$$\frac{S \cdot C}{C_i (G')^{\alpha_i} Q \prod_{j=1}^{2t}(G_j)^{i^j}}$$

$$= \frac{(sh_0^{r_1})(c^{r_1} d^{r_1 e})}{(u_1^{X_1(i)+Y_1(i)e} u_2^{X_2(i)+Y_2(i)e})(h'^{r_1})^{\alpha_i}(u_1^{Q_1(i)} u_2^{Q_2(i,\alpha_i)}) \prod_{j=1}^{2t}\{(h_j x_{1,j} x_{2,j} y_{1,j} y_{2,j})^{r_1}\}^{i^j}}$$

$$= \frac{(sh_0^{r_1})}{(h'^{r_1})^{\alpha_i}(u_1^{Q_1(i)} \cdot u_2^{Q_2(i,\alpha_i)}) \prod_{j=1}^{2t}(h_j^{r_1})^{i^j}}$$
$$\cdot \frac{(c^{r_1} d^{r_1 e})}{(u_1^{X_1(i)+Y_1(i)e} u_2^{X_2(i)+Y_2(i)e}) \prod_{j=1}^{2t}\{(x_{1,j} x_{2,j} y_{1,j} y_{2,j})^{r_1}\}^{i^j}}$$

$$= \frac{s(g_1^{a_0,Z_1} g_2^{a_0,Z_2})^{r_1}}{(g_2^{-br_1 \alpha_i})(g_1^{r_1 Z_1(i)} g_2^{r_1(Z_2(i)+b\alpha_i)}) \prod_{j=1}^{2t}(g_1^{-a_j,Z_1} g_2^{-a_j,Z_2})^{r_1}}$$
$$\cdot \frac{(g_1^{a_0,X_1} g_2^{a_0,X_2})^{r_1}(g_1^{a_0,Y_1} g_2^{a_0,Y_2})^{r_1 e}}{(g_1^{X_1(i)} g_1^{Y_1(i)e})^{r_1}(g_2^{X_2(i)} g_2^{Y_2(i)e})^{r_1} \prod_{j=1}^{2t}\{(g_1^{-a_j,X_1} g_2^{-a_j,X_2} g_1^{-a_j,Y_1} g_2^{-a_j,Y_2})^{r_1}\}^{i^j}}$$

$$= \frac{s(g_1^{a_0,Z_1} g_2^{a_0,Z_2})^{r_1}}{(g_1^{r_1 Z_1(i)} g_2^{r_1 Z_2(i)}) \prod_{j=1}^{2t}(g_1^{-a_j,Z_1} g_2^{-a_j,Z_2})^{r_1}}$$

$$= s$$

Security:

Theorem 1. *If the DDH problem is hard in G and H is chosen from a collision-resistant hash function family $\mathcal{F}$, then our scheme is t-resilient against the adaptive chosen ciphertext attack.*

Proof. Our overall strategy for the proof follows the structural approach in [6]. We shall define a sequence $\mathbf{G}_0, \mathbf{G}_1, \ldots, \mathbf{G}_l$ of modified attack games. Each of the games $\mathbf{G}_0, \mathbf{G}_1, \ldots, \mathbf{G}_l$ operates on the same underlying probability space. Specifically, the public key cryptosystem, the coin tosses **Coins** of $\mathcal{A}$, and the hidden bit σ take on identical values across all games, while some of the rules that define how the environment responds to oracle queries may differ from game to game. For any $1 \leq i \leq l$, we let T_i be the event that $\sigma = \sigma^*$ in the game $\mathbf{G}_i$. Our strategy is to show that for $1 \leq i \leq l$, the quantity $|Pr[T_{i-1}] - Pr[T_i]|$ is negligible. In addition, it will be evident from the definition of game $\mathbf{G}_l$ that $Pr[T_l] = \frac{1}{2}$, which will imply that $|Pr[T_0] - \frac{1}{2}|$ is negligible.

Before we start the game, we first state an advantage of the adversary obtained from `Acquisition` queries. In our scheme, the adversary can obtain partial secret information $SK_{i_1}^*, \ldots, SK_{i_t}^*$ of at most t users from the `Acquisition` oracle in **Stage 2**. Since partial secret information SK_i^* of user u_i for "tag" message are $X_1(i)$, $X_2(i)$, $Y_1(i)$, $Y_2(i)$, and $X_1(\cdot)$, $X_2(\cdot)$, $Y_1(\cdot)$, and $Y_2(\cdot)$ are $2t$-degree polynomials, the adversary cannot make the ciphertext malleable without revealing the identity of traitors from partial secret information of t traitors. In the consequence, the CCA2 security of our scheme is not broken.

In addition, we introduce the following simple but useful lemma in [6].

Lemma 1. *Let U_1, U_2, and F be the events defined on some probability space. Suppose that the event $U_1 \wedge \neg F$ occurs if and only if $U_2 \wedge \neg F$ occurs. Then $|Pr[U_1] - Pr[U_2]| \leq Pr[F]$.*

Game G_0: Let G_0 be the original attack game, let $\sigma^* \in \{0,1\}$ denote the output of $\mathcal{A}$, and let T_0 be the event that $\sigma = \sigma^*$ in G_0, so that $Adv_{Ourscheme,\mathcal{A}}^{CCA2}(\lambda) = |Pr[T_0] - \frac{1}{2}|$.

Game G_1: G_1 is identical to G_0, except that in G_1, steps E_4, E_5 and E_6 are replaced with the following:

$$E_4'.\ G_j' \leftarrow u_1^{-a_j,Z_1} u_2^{-a_j,Z_2} u_1^{-a_j,X_1} u_2^{-a_j,X_2} u_1^{-a_j,Y_1} u_2^{-a_j,Y_2},\ j = 1, \ldots, 2t$$
$$E_5'.\ C'' \leftarrow u_1^{-b}$$
$$E_6'.\ S' \leftarrow s \cdot (u_1^{a_0,Z_1} u_2^{a_0,Z_2})$$

The change we have made is purely conceptual, its purpose is to make explicit any functional dependency of the above quantities on u_1 and u_2. Cleary, it holds that $Pr[T_0] = Pr[T_1]$.

Game G_2: We again modify the encryption oracle, replacing steps E_1 and E_3 by

$$E_1'.\ r_1 \leftarrow_r Z_q, r_2 \leftarrow_r Z_q \backslash \{r_1\}$$
$$E_3'.\ u_2 \leftarrow g_2^{r_2}$$

Notice that, while in G_1 the values u_1 and u_2 are obtained using the same value r_1, in G_2 they are independent subject to $r_1 \neq r_2$. Therefore, any difference in behavior between G_1 and G_2 immediately yields a PPT algorithm $\mathcal{A}_1$ that is able to distinguish the DH tuples from totally random tuples with a non negligible advantage. That is, $|Pr[T_2] - Pr[T_1]| \leq \epsilon_1$ for some negligible ϵ_1.

Game G_3: In this game, we modify the decryption oracle in G_2 to obtain G_3 as follows(let $g_2 = g_1^w$):

$D_1.$ $e \leftarrow H(S, u_1, u_2)$

$D_2'.$ $C_i \leftarrow u_1^{X_1(i)+Y_1(i)e+(X_2(i)+Y_2(i)e)w}$

$D_{2-1}.$ if $(u_2 = u_1^w)$

$D_3'.$ then $Q_i \leftarrow u_1^{Q_1(i)+Q_2(i,\alpha_i)w}$

$D_4'.$ $s \leftarrow \dfrac{S \cdot C}{C_i(G')^{\alpha_i}Q\prod_{j=1}^{2t}(G_j)^{ij}}$

$D_5'.$ else return $\bot$

At this point, let R_3 be the event that the adversary $\mathcal{A}$ submits some decryption queries that are rejected in Step D_{2-1} in $\mathbf{G_3}$, but passed in $\mathbf{G_2}$. Note that if a query passes in D_{2-1} in $\mathbf{G_3}$, it would have also passed in $\mathbf{G_2}$. It is clear that $\mathbf{G_2}$ and $\mathbf{G_3}$ proceed identically until event R_3 occurs. In particular, the event $T_2 \wedge \neg R_3$ and $T_3 \wedge \neg R_3$ are identical. Therefore, by Lemma 1, we have

$$|Pr[T_3] - Pr[T_2]| \leq Pr[R_3]$$

and so it suffices to bound $Pr[R_3]$. To accomplish this we consider two more games, $\mathbf{G_4}$ and $\mathbf{G_5}$.

Game $\mathbf{G_4}$: This game is identical to $\mathbf{G_3}$, except for a change in Step E_6 as follows:

$$E_6'.k \leftarrow_r Z_q, S \leftarrow g_1^k$$

It is clear by construction that $Pr[T_4] = \frac{1}{2}$, since in $\mathbf{G_4}$, the variable σ is never used at all, and so the adversary's output is independent of σ.

Let R_4 be the event that some decryption queries that would have passed in $\mathbf{G_2}$, fail to pass in Step D_{2-1} in $\mathbf{G_4}$. Then we have the following facts.

Lemma 2. $Pr[T_4] = Pr[T_3]$ and $Pr[R_4] = Pr[R_3]$.

Our proofs are similar to those of [8,12] except for some variables and notations. The proof of Lemma 2 is shown in [8,12].

Game $\mathbf{G_5}$: This game is identical to $\mathbf{G_4}$, except for the following modification. In the decryption algorithm, we add the following *special rejection rule*, to prevent $\mathcal{A}$ from submitting an illegal enabling block to the decryption oracle once she has received her challenge T^*.

Special rejection rule: After the adversary $\mathcal{A}$ receives the challenge $T^* = (S^*, u_1^*, u_2^*, C^*, G'^*, G_1^*, \ldots, G_{2t}^*)$, the decryption oracle rejects any query $< i, T >$, with $T = (S, u_1, u_2, C, G', G_1, \ldots, G_{2t})$, such that $(S^*, u_1^*, u_2^*) \neq (S, u_1, u_2)$, but $e = e^*$, and it does so before executing the test in Step D_{2-1}.

To analyze this game, we define two events. Let C_5 be the event where the adversary $\mathcal{A}$ submits a decryption query that is rejected using the above special rejection rule, and R_5 the event where the adversary $\mathcal{A}$ submits some decryption query that would have passed in $\mathbf{G_2}$, but fails to pass in Step D_{2-1} in $\mathbf{G_5}$. Now it is clear that $\mathbf{G_4}$ and $\mathbf{G_5}$ proceed identically until event C_5 occurs. In particular, the event $R_4 \wedge \neg C_5$ and $R_5 \wedge \neg C_5$ are identical. Therefore, by Lemma 1, we have

$$|Pr[R_5] - Pr[R_4]| \le Pr[C_5].$$

At this point, if event C_5 occurs with non-negligible probability, we can construct a PPT algorithm $\mathcal{A}_2$ that breaks the collision resistance assumption with non-negligible probability. So, $|Pr[C_5]| \le \epsilon_2$ for some negligible ϵ_2.

Finally, we show that event R_5 occurs with negligible probability.

Lemma 3. $Pr[R_5] \le \frac{Q_{\mathcal{A}}(\lambda)}{q}$.

Where $Q_{\mathcal{A}}(\lambda)$ is an upper bound on the number of decryption queries made by the adversary $\mathcal{A}$. The proof of Lemma 3 is also shown in [8,12].

Finally, combining the intermediate results, we conclude that the adversary $\mathcal{A}$'s advantage is negligible:

$$Adv^{CCA2}_{Ourscheme,\mathcal{A}}(\lambda) \le \epsilon_1 + \epsilon_2 + \frac{Q_{\mathcal{A}}(\lambda)}{q}$$

$\square$

References

1. Mihir Bellare, Anand Desai, David Pointcheval and Phillip Rogaway, Relations Among Notions of Security for Public-Key Encryption Schemes, *CRYTO'98, LNCS V.1462*, pp.26-45, 1998.
2. D. Boneh and M. Franklin, An efficient public key traitor tracing scheme, *CRYTO'99, LNCS V.1666*, pp.338-353, 1999.
3. D. Boneh and J. Shaw, Collusion-secure fingerprinting for digital data, *IEEE Transaction on Information Theory 44(5)*, pp.1897-1905, 1998.
4. B. Chor, A. Fiat, and M. Naor, Tracing traitor, *CRYPTO'94, LNCS V.839*, pp.257-270, 1994.
5. R. Cramer and V. Shoup, A practical public key cryptosystem provably secure against adaptive chosen ciphertext attack, *CRYPTO'98, LNCS V.1462*, pp.13-25, 1998.
6. R. Cramer and V. Shoup, Design and analysis of practical public key encryption scheme secure against adaptive chosen ciphertext attack, *Manuscript*, 2001.
7. Y. Dodis and N. Fazio, Public key trace and revoke scheme secure against adaptive chosen ciphertext attac, *PKC'03*, pp.100-115, 2003.
8. Y. Dodis and N. Fazio, Public key trace and revoke scheme secure against adaptive chosen ciphertext attac, *Full version of [7]*
9. A. Fiat and M. Naor, Broadcast encryption, *CRYPTO'93, LNCS V.773* pp.480-491, 1993.
10. E. Gafni, J. Staddon, and Y. L. Yin, Efficient methods for integrating traceability and broadcast encryption, *CRYPTO'99, LNCS V.1666*, pp.372-287, 1999.
11. K. Kurosawa and Y. Desmedt, Optimum traitor tracing and asymmetric schemes, *EUROCRYPT'98, LNCS V.1403*, pp.145-157, 1998.
12. C. H. Kim, Y. H. Hwang, and P. J. Lee, An efficient public key trace and revoke scheme secure against adaptive chosen ciphertext attack, *ASIACRYPT'03, LNCS V.2894*, pp.359-373, 2003.

13. A. Kiayias and M. Yung, Breaking and repairing asymmetric public-key traitor tracing, *ACM workshop on digital rights management, LNCS V.2696*, 2002. available at http://www.cse.uconn.edu/~akiayias/pubs/asymvpp-f.pdf
14. A. Kiayias and M. Yung, Traitor tracing with constant transmission rate, *EUROCRYPT'02, LNCS V. 2332*, pp.450-465, 2002.
15. H. Komaki, Y. Watanabe, G. Hanaoka, and H. Imai, Efficient asymmetric self-enforcement scheme with public traceability, *PKC'01, LNCS V.1992*, pp.225-239, 2001.
16. R. Canetti and S. Goldwasser, An efficient threshold public key cryptosystem secure against adaptive chosen ciphertext attack, *EUROCRYPT'99, LNCS V.1592*, pp.90-106, 1999.
17. M. Naor and B. Pinkas, Threshold traitor tracing, *CRYPTO'98, LNCS V.1462*, pp.502-517, 1998.
18. M. Naor and B. Pinkas, Oblivious transfer and polynomial evaluation, *STOC'99,*, pp.245-254, 1999.
19. B. Pfitzmann, Trials of traced traitors, *Workshop on Information Hiding, LNCS V.1174*, pp.49-64, 1996.
20. B. Pfitzmann and M. Waidner, Asymmetric fingerprinting for large collusions, *ACM conference on Computer and Communication Security*, pp.151-160, 1997.
21. D. R. Stinson and R. Wei, Combinatorial properties and constructions of traceability schemes and frameproof codes, *SIAM Journal on Discrete Math 11(1)*, pp.41-53, 1998.
22. W. G. Tzeng and Z. J. Tzeng, A public-key tracing scheme with revocation using dynamic shares, *PKC'01, LNCS 1992*, pp.207-224, 2001.
23. Y. Watanabe, G. Hanaoka, and H. Imai, Efficient asymmetric public-key traitor tracing without trusted agents, *CT-RSA'01, LNCS V.2020*, pp.392-407, 2001.

Single Database Private Information Retrieval with Logarithmic Communication

Yan-Cheng Chang

Division of Engineering and Applied Sciences,
Harvard University,
Cambridge, MA 02138, USA
ycchang@eecs.harvard.edu

Abstract. We study the problem of single database private information retrieval, and present a solution with only logarithmic server-side communication complexity and a solution with only logarithmic user-side communication complexity. Previously the best result could only achieve polylogarithmic communication on each side, and was based on certain less well-studied assumptions in number theory [6]. On the contrary, our schemes are based on Paillier's cryptosystem [16], which along with its variants have drawn extensive studies in recent cryptographic researches [3,4,8,9], and have many important applications [7,8].
In fact, our schemes directly yield implementations for 1-out-of-N ℓ-bit string oblivious transfer with $O(\ell)$ sender-side communication (against semi-honest receivers and malicious senders). Note the sender-side communication complexity is independent of N, the constant hidden in the big-O notation is quite small, and ℓ is unrestricted. Moreover, we show a way to do communication balancing between the sender-side and the receiver-side, and show how to handle malicious receivers with small communication overheads.

1 Introduction

Single database private information retrieval (1dPIR) is a cryptographic protocol between a database server, who has an N-bit database x, and a user, who has an index $1 \leq i \leq N$, such that the user can learn the i-th bit of x without revealing his index while the database server can send less than N bits to the user (as otherwise the problem becomes trivial). In addition to its numerous applications [1], 1dPIR is a very strong cryptographic primitive in that it can be used to construct oblivious transfer [5], a cryptographic primitive that is known to be *complete* for secure computations [12]. Historically, the first 1dPIR scheme was proposed in [13], with its security based on the hardness of the quadratic residuosity problem and with superlogarithmic communication complexity. After that, in fact, only a few implementations of 1dPIR were discovered.

Specifically, a scheme with polylogarithmic communication was proposed in [6]; however, its security is based on certain less well-studied assumptions in number theory, i.e. the hardness of Φ-Hiding and the existence of Φ-Sampling.

H. Wang et al. (Eds.): ACISP 2004, LNCS 3108, pp. 50–61, 2004.
© Springer-Verlag Berlin Heidelberg 2004

Besides, the only known result is 1dPIR can be based on trapdoor permutations [14]. As the result of [14] is reduction-oriented, it requires more communication than the previous schemes.

In this paper, we present a 1dPIR scheme with only logarithmic server-side communication complexity and a 1dPIR scheme with only logarithmic user-side communication complexity, which break the polylogarithmic bounds given in [6]. Our schemes are based on the additive homomorphic properties of Paillier's cryptosystem [16], which is *semantically secure* under Composite Residuosity Assumption (CRA). CRA is a natural extension of the well-studied Quadratic Residuosity Assumption (QRA) stating that it is computationally intractable to decide whether a random element in $\mathbb{Z}_n^*$ has a square root modulo n, where n is a RSA modulus. And CRA states that it is computationally intractable to decide whether a random element in $\mathbb{Z}_{n^2}^*$ has an n-th root modulo n^2.

Because Paillier's cryptosystem along with its variants have drawn extensive studies in recent cryptographic researches [3,4,8,9] (just to cite a few), and have many important applications (e.g., the Cramer-Shoup CCA2 encryption scheme in the standard model [7] and the Damgård-Jurik electronic voting scheme [8]), we believe CRA could be a good candidate for hardness assumption.

Supposing the security parameter is $O(\log N)$ bits in length, we can use the following table to compare our results with other known 1dPIR schemes:[1] (Here $d \gg 1$, and ϵ can be any positive constant.)

Result	Server-side Comm.	User-side Comm.	Computational Assumption
[13]	$O(N^\epsilon)$	$O(N^\epsilon \log N)$	Quadratic Residuosity is hard
[6]	$O((\log N)^d)$	$O((\log N)^4)$	Φ-Hiding is hard,$\exists$ Φ-Sampling
[14]	$N(1 - \frac{1}{6N^\epsilon}) + O(N^{2\epsilon})$	$O(N^{2\epsilon})$	$\exists$ Trapdoor Permutations
Theorem 1	$O(\log N)$	$O(N^\epsilon \log N)$	Composite Residuosity is hard
Theorem 2	$2^{\log N - 1/\epsilon}$	$O(\log N)$	Composite Residuosity is hard

Clearly, our results are more efficient than all the previous solutions regarding the one-side communication complexity. In fact, our schemes can be directly used to implement 1-out-of-N ℓ-bit string oblivious transfer ($\binom{N}{1}\mathsf{OT}^\ell$), which is a cryptographic protocol between a sender, who has N ℓ-bit strings, and a receiver, who has an index $1 \leq i \leq N$, such that receiver can obtain the i-th string from sender without revealing his index and can learn nothing more. Our constructions for $\binom{N}{1}\mathsf{OT}^\ell$ only require $O(\ell)$ sender-side communication complexity, and are secure against semi-honest receivers and malicious senders. Note the sender-side communication complexity is independent of N, the constant hidden in big-O notation is quite small, and ℓ is unrestricted. Moreover, we show a natural way to do communication balancing between the sender-side and the receiver-side, and show a way to make our schemes secure against malicious receivers under CRA with only small communication overheads.

---

[1] Y. Ishai, E. Kushilevitz, and R. Ostrovsky discover a similar approach to build efficient 1dPIR protocols using Paillier's cryptosystem, and their approach can also achieve the same result as our Theorem 1. We are informed by E. Kushilevitz.

We organize the rest of this paper as follows. In section 2, we first define 1dPIR and $\binom{N}{1}\text{OT}^{\ell}$ and then introduce CRA as well as the nice properties of Paillier's cryptosystem. In section 3, we present several schemes for 1dPIR with different communication efficiency, and show how to use them to implement efficient schemes for $\binom{N}{1}\text{OT}^{\ell}$ with capability of doing communication balancing. In Section 4, finally, we consider the case of malicious receivers.

2   Preliminaries

For an integer $\ell \in \mathbb{N}$, let $[\ell]$ denote the set $\{1, 2, \cdots, \ell\}$. For an N-bit string x, let $x[i]_{i\in[N]}$ denote its i-th bit. A *semi-honest* player always follows the protocol properly with the exception that it keeps a record of all its intermediate computations [10]. On the other hand, we put no restriction on the behavior of a *malicious* player. We use the notation $a \overset{R}{\leftarrow} A$ to denote choosing an element a uniformly at random from the set A, and use PPT to denote *probabilistic polynomial time*. Also, we say a function is negligible in k if for any polynomial p there exists a k_0 such that for all $k > k_0$ we have $f(k) < 1/p(k)$. All logarithms in this paper have base 2.

Moreover, an encryption scheme is *semantically secure* if it hides all partial information of the input, or equivalently, if it is *polynomial time indistinguishable*, i.e. there is no adversary can find even two messages which encryptions he can distinguish between [11]. We state them formally as follows.

Definition 1. *A probabilistic encryption scheme $\mathcal{E}$ with security parameter k, input domain $\mathcal{M}(k)$ and randomness domain $\mathcal{R}(k)$ is said to be* semantically secure *if for any PPT algorithm A, any message $m \in \mathcal{M}(k)$ and any function h, there is PPT algorithm B such that the following value is negligible in k:*

$$|\mathbf{Pr}[A(1^k, c) = h(m)| \ r \overset{R}{\leftarrow} \mathcal{R}(k), \ c = \mathcal{E}(m, r)] - \mathbf{Pr}[B(1^k) = h(m)]|.$$

Definition 2. *A probabilistic encryption scheme $\mathcal{E}$ with security parameter k, input domain $\mathcal{M}(k)$ and randomness domain $\mathcal{R}(k)$ is said to be* polynomial time indistinguishable *if for any PPT algorithm A and any two messages $m_0, m_1 \in \mathcal{M}(k)$, the following value is negligible in k:*

$$|\mathbf{Pr}[A(1^k, m_0, m_1, c) = m_b| \ b \overset{R}{\leftarrow} \{0, 1\}, \ r \overset{R}{\leftarrow} \mathcal{R}(k), \ c = \mathcal{E}(m_b, r)] \ - \ 1/2|.$$

Lemma 1. *[11] A probabilistic encryption scheme is semantically secure if and only if it is polynomial time indistinguishable.*

2.1   Single Database Private Information Retrieval and Oblivious Transfer

In this section, we define 1dPIR and t-out-of-N ℓ-bit string oblivious transfer ($\binom{N}{t}\text{OT}^{\ell}$).

Definition 3. Single database private information retrieval (1dPIR) *is a proto-col between two players* Server, *who has an* N-*bit string* x, *and* User, *who has an index* $i \in [N]$, *that guarantees*

1. *Correctness: User can learn* $x[i]$ *and Server can send less than* N *bits to User, and*
2. *User's security: for any PPT algorithm* A *and any* $j \in [N]$, *the following value is negligible in the security parameter* k:

$$|\mathbf{Pr}[A(1^k, C_k(i)) = 1] - \mathbf{Pr}[A(1^k, C_k(j)) = 1]|,$$

where $C_k(y)$ *is the distribution of communication from User induced by an index* $y \in [N]$.

Definition 4. t-*out-of-*N ℓ-*bit string oblivious transfer* $\left(\binom{N}{t}OT^\ell\right)$ *is a protocol between two players* Sender, *who has* N ℓ-*bit strings* $x_1, x_2, \cdots, x_N$, *and* Receiver, *who has* t *indexes* $i_1, i_2, \cdots, i_t \in [N]$, *that guarantees*

1. *Correctness: User can learn* $x_{i_1}, x_{i_2}, \cdots, x_{i_t}$, *and*
2. *Receiver's security: for any PPT algorithm* A *and any* $j_1, j_2, \cdots, j_t \in [N]$, *the following value is negligible in the security parameter* k:

$$|\mathbf{Pr}[A(1^k, C_k(i_1, i_2, \cdots, i_t)) = 1] - \mathbf{Pr}[A(1^k, C_k(j_1, j_2, \cdots, j_t)) = 1]|,$$

where $C_k(y_1, y_2, \cdots, y_t)$ *is the distribution of communication from Receiver induced by indexes* $y_1, y_2, \cdots, y_t \in [N]$, *and*
3. *Sender's security: for any PPT algorithm* A *and any* $x_1', x_2', \cdots, x_N' \in \{0,1\}^\ell$ *such that* $x_{i_1}' = x_{i_1}, x_{i_2}' = x_{i_2}, \cdots, x_{i_t}' = x_{i_t}$, *the following value is negligible in the security parameter* k:

$$|\mathbf{Pr}[A(1^k, C_k(x_1, x_2, \cdots, x_N)) = 1] - \mathbf{Pr}[A(1^k, C_k(x_1', x_2', \cdots, x_N')) = 1]|,$$

where $C_k(z_1, z_2, \cdots, z_N)$ *is the distribution of communication from Sender induced by strings* $z_1, z_2, \cdots, z_N \in \{0,1\}^\ell$.

2.2   Composite Residuosity Assumption

Let $n = pq$ be a RSA modulus, i.e. product of two safe primes of the same length in bits. (A prime p is *safe* if it has the form of $2q + 1$ with q also a prime). Consider the multiplicative group $\mathbb{Z}_{n^2}^*$.

Definition 5. *An element* $z \in \mathbb{Z}_{n^2}^*$ *is said to be an* n-*th residue if there exists an element* $y \in \mathbb{Z}_{n^2}^*$ *such that* $z = y^n \bmod n^2$, *otherwise it is said to be an* n-*th non-residue.*

Note the problem to distinguish n-th residues from n-th non-residues, like the problem to decide quadratic residues and quadratic non-residues, is *random-self-reducible*, i.e. each instance of the problem is an average case [16]. Specifically, all instances of a random-self-reducible problem are either uniformly intractable or uniformly solvable in polynomial time [2].

Definition 6. *Composite Residuosity Assumption (CRA): If the factorization of n is unknown, there is no PPT distinguisher for n-th residues modulo n^2 [16].*[2]

Note due to the random-self-reducibility, the validity of CRA only depends on the choice of n [16].

2.3   Paillier's Cryptosystem

Let $n = pq$ be a RSA modulus, i.e. product of two safe primes of the same length in bits. Consider the multiplicative group $\mathbb{Z}^*_{n^2}$. Given any $g \in \mathbb{Z}^*_{n^2}$ whose order is a non-zero multiple of n (for example, $g = n + 1$), it can be shown that g induces a bijection [16]:

$$\mathcal{E}_g(a, b) = g^a b^n \bmod n^2.$$
$$(\mathbb{Z}_n \times \mathbb{Z}^*_n \to \mathbb{Z}^*_{n^2})$$

In other words, for every element $w \in \mathbb{Z}^*_{n^2}$, there exists a unique pair $(a, b) \in \mathbb{Z}_n \times \mathbb{Z}^*_n$ such that we have $w = g^a b^n \bmod n^2$, and vice versa. We know under CRA it is computationally intractable to compute a given only w, n and g, as otherwise we can decide the n-th residuosity of w. However, if we know the factorization of n, we can compute a using the following method [16]:

$$a = \mathcal{D}_g(w) = \frac{L(w^\lambda \bmod n^2)}{L(g^\lambda \bmod n^2)} \bmod n,$$

where $L(u) = (u - 1)/n$ for $u \in \mathbb{Z}^*_{n^2}$, and $\lambda = lcm(p - 1, q - 1)$.

Accordingly, Paillier defines a probabilistic public-key cryptosystem using $\mathcal{E}_g$ as the encryption scheme for any message $a \in \mathbb{Z}_n$ with randomness $b \in \mathbb{Z}^*_n$ [16]. Specifically, the public keys are n and g, the private key is the factorization of n, and $\mathcal{D}_g$ is the decryption scheme.

This cryptosystem has many nice properties. First, it is *additive homomorphic*. Note we have

- $\mathcal{D}_g(\mathcal{E}_g(m_0, r_0)\mathcal{E}_g(m_1, r_1)) = m_0 + m_1 \bmod n$, and
- $\mathcal{D}_g(\mathcal{E}_g(m_0, r_0)^c) = cm_0 \bmod n$.

Second, it is *semantically secure* under CRA [16]: assume $m_0, m_1 \in \mathbb{Z}_n$ are two known messages and the ciphertext c is either from m_0 or m_1; note c is from m_0 iff $cg^{-m_0} \bmod n^2$ is an n-th residue. In other words, any successful chosen plaintext attack can be used to decide the composite residuosity, and vice versa.

---

[2] In [16], this assumption is named Decisional Composite Residuosity Assumption (DCRA).

3 Cryptographic Schemes

3.1 A Basic Scheme

W.l.o.g. we assume $N = \ell^2$ for some $\ell \in \mathbb{N}$. Let $x(i,j)_{i,j\in[\ell]}$ denote the bit $x[(i-1)\ell+(j-1)+1]$, and let $x(i^*,j^*)$ be the bit User wants to learn. Specifically, we treat the database as a 2-hypercube. Also, let $I(t,t_0)$ be an indicating function such that $I(t,t_0) = 1$ iff $t = t_0$, otherwise $I(t,t_0) = 0$.

PIR ON 2-HYPERCUBE

- **Initializing:** User sends $\alpha_t = \mathcal{E}_g(I(t,i^*),r_t)$ and $\beta_t = \mathcal{E}_g(I(t,j^*),s_t)$ to Server for $t \in [\ell]$, where r_t and s_t are chosen uniformly at random from $\mathbb{Z}_n^*$.
- **Filtering:** Server computes $\sigma_i = \prod_{t\in[\ell]} (\beta_t)^{x(i,t)} \bmod n^2$ for $i \in [\ell]$.
- **Splitting-and-then-filtering:** Server splits each σ_i by computing $u_i, v_i \in \mathbb{Z}_n$ such that $\sigma_i = u_i n + v_i$, and then sends $u = \prod_{t\in[\ell]} (\alpha_t)^{u_t} \bmod n^2$ and $v = \prod_{t\in[\ell]} (\alpha_t)^{v_t} \bmod n^2$ to User.
- **Reconstructing:** User computes $x(i^*,j^*) = \mathcal{D}_g(\mathcal{D}_g(u)n + \mathcal{D}_g(v))$.

Lemma 2. *Under CRA,* PIR ON 2-HYPERCUBE *is a one-round implementation of* 1dPIR *with Server-side communication $2k$ bits and User-side communication $2kN^{\frac{1}{2}}$ bits, where $k = \lceil 2\log n \rceil$ is the security parameter.*

Proof. First, we prove the correctness of the scheme. Note each σ_i is equal to $\mathcal{E}_g(x(i,j^*),\tau_i)$ for some $\tau_i \in \mathbb{Z}_n^*$ since $\mathcal{E}_g$ is additive homomorphic. Similarly, $u = \mathcal{E}_g(u_{i^*},\tau_u)$ and $v = \mathcal{E}_g(v_{i^*},\tau_v)$ for some $\tau_u,\tau_v \in \mathbb{Z}_n^*$. Next, note $\mathcal{D}_g(u)n + \mathcal{D}_g(v) = u_{i^*}n + v_{i^*} = \sigma_{i^*} = \mathcal{E}_g(x(i^*,j^*),\tau_{i^*})$ for some $\tau_{i^*} \in \mathbb{Z}_n^*$. Consequently, $\mathcal{D}_g(\mathcal{D}_g(u)n + \mathcal{D}_g(v)) = x(i^*,j^*)$. On the other hand, both the Server-side and the User-side communication complexity can be easily verified.

Next, we prove User's security. Note the only communication sent from User to Server consists of $\{\alpha_t,\beta_t\}_{t\in[\ell]}$. Let $\{\alpha'_t,\beta'_t\}_{t\in[\ell]}$ be the communication induced by another $(i',j') \neq (i^*,j^*)$, $i',j' \in [\ell]$. Clearly, if Server can distinguish these two distributions, it must be the case that Server either can distinguish the distributions of $\{\alpha_t\}_{t\in[\ell]}$ and $\{\alpha'_t\}_{t\in[\ell]}$ or can distinguish the distributions of $\{\beta_t\}_{t\in[\ell]}$ and $\{\beta'_t\}_{t\in[\ell]}$. Suppose Server can distinguish the distributions of $\{\alpha_t\}_{t\in[\ell]}$ and $\{\alpha'_t\}_{t\in[\ell]}$, then by standard hybrid argument we know Server can distinguish the distributions of either $\alpha_{i^*} = \mathcal{E}_g(1,U_{\mathbb{Z}_n^*})$ and $\alpha'_{i^*} = \mathcal{E}_g(0,U_{\mathbb{Z}_n^*})$ or $\alpha_{i'} = \mathcal{E}_g(0,U_{\mathbb{Z}_n^*})$ and $\alpha'_{i'} = \mathcal{E}_g(1,U_{\mathbb{Z}_n^*})$, where $U_{\mathbb{Z}_n^*}$ is the uniform distribution over $\mathbb{Z}_n^*$, as the distributions of α_t and α'_t are identical for $t \in [\ell], t \neq i^*, i'$. Obviously, this implies Server can be used to break the polynomial time indistinguishability of $\mathcal{E}_g$, a contradiction. Since the same argument holds for the case of $\{\beta_t\}_{t\in[\ell]}$ and $\{\beta'_t\}_{t\in[\ell]}$, we finish the proof. $\square$

Lemma 3. *Under CRA,* PIR ON 2-HYPERCUBE *is actually an implementation of $\binom{N}{1}\mathrm{OT}^1$ against semi-honest Receiver and malicious Sender.*

Proof. Just call Server *Sender* and call User *Receiver*. Note Receiver's security is guaranteed even if Sender is malicious, since the protocol starts from Receiver and is one-round, i.e. Receiver's message is independent of Sender's behavior.

Next, note Sender's security is guaranteed if Receiver is semi-honest, as the messages u, v sent from Server to User do not depend on $x(i,j)_{i,j \in [\ell],(i,j) \neq (i^*,j^*)}$. On the other hand, the correctness can be easily verified.   □

3.2   Not Just a Bit

Let x' be an array of N entries with each entry containing a $\lfloor \log n \rfloor$-bit string. W.l.o.g., we use $x'[i]_{i \in N}$ to denote the $\lfloor \log n \rfloor$-bit string in the i-th entry of x', and similarly, we use $x'(i,j)$ to denote $x'[(i-1)\ell + (j-1) + 1]$ when N is assumed to be ℓ^2 for some $\ell \in \mathbb{N}$.

Now we make a small modification on our basic scheme: to replace $x(i,t)$ in the second step of the basic scheme by $x'(i,t)$. Clearly, as long as $x'(i^*,j^*) \in \mathbb{Z}_n$, it can be reconstructed in the final step of the modified scheme by the nature of Paillier's cryptosystem. So we have the following.

Corollary 1. *Under CRA, PIR* ON 2-HYPERCUBE *can be modified to implement $\binom{N}{1}OT^{\lfloor \log n \rfloor}$ against semi-honest Receiver and malicious Sender without increasing communication complexity.*

In fact, the above modification directly yields an implementation for $\binom{N}{1}OT^\ell$ for any $\ell > \lfloor \log n \rfloor$. Here the reason is Sender can split each ℓ-bit string into strings of $\lfloor \log n \rfloor$ bits, construct respective arrays, and compute the returning messages separately. Note the protocol is parallelly one-round, and there is no need of additional communication from Receiver since his message can be reused. Moreover, the Sender-side communication is bounded by $2k\lceil \ell / \lfloor \log n \rfloor \rceil = 2\lceil 2 \log n \rceil \lceil \ell / \lfloor \log n \rfloor \rceil$ bits.

Corollary 2. *Under CRA, PIR* ON 2-HYPERCUBE *can be modified to implement $\binom{N}{1}OT^\ell$ against semi-honest Receiver and malicious Sender with Sender-side communication $O(\ell)$ bits.*

3.3   A Scheme on c-Hypercube

Recall in the basic scheme we treat the database x as a 2-hypercube. Actually, we can treat the database as a c-hypercube for any integer constant $c > 2$. And by recursive calls, we can achieve communication balance between the Server-side and the User-side, depending on the choice of c.

Here for illustration, let us first consider the case $c = 3$, and w.l.o.g. assume $N = \ell^3$ for some $\ell \in \mathbb{N}$. Similarly, we use the notation $x(i,j,\kappa)_{i,j,\kappa \in [\ell]}$ to denote the bit $x[(i-1)\ell^2 + (j-1)\ell + (\kappa - 1) + 1]$, and let $x(i^*,j^*,\kappa^*)$ be the bit User wants to learn. Moreover, we keep the definition of $I(t,t_0)$.

PIR ON 3-HYPERCUBE

- **Initializing:** Server and User have to treat the 3-hypercube database x as ℓ 2-hypercube databases $x(1) = x(i,j,1)_{i,j\in[\ell]}$, $x(2) = x(i,j,2)_{i,j\in[\ell]}$, ..., $x(\ell) = x(i,j,\ell)_{i,j\in[\ell]}$, while User sends $\gamma_t = \mathcal{E}_g(I(t,\kappa^*),\tau_t)$ to Server for $t \in [\ell]$, where each τ_t is chosen uniformly at random from $\mathbb{Z}_n^*$.
- **Invoking:** User executes PIR ON 2-HYPERCUBE with Server on all $x(d)_{d\in[\ell]}$ in parallel yet omitting the **Reconstructing** step of PIR ON 2-HYPERCUBE and complying the following:
  - User's messages are the same in all executions, with his choice fixed to be (i^*, j^*). This says one copy is enough for all executions, and Server should reuse that copy (of $\{\alpha_t, \beta_t\}_{t\in[\ell]}$).
  - Server does not send to User the pair $(u(d), v(d))$, namely his returning message in PIR ON 2-HYPERCUBE with respect to $x(d)$, after computing it.
- **Splitting-and-then-filtering:** Server instead computes uu_d, uv_d, vu_d, $vv_d \in \mathbb{Z}_n$ such that $u(d) = (uu_d)n + uv_d$ and $v(d) = (vu_d)n + vv_d$, and then sends $uu = \prod_{d\in[\ell]} (\gamma_d)^{uu_d} \bmod n^2$, $uv = \prod_{d\in[\ell]} (\gamma_d)^{uv_d} \bmod n^2$, $vu = \prod_{d\in[\ell]} (\gamma_d)^{vu_d} \bmod n^2$ and $vv = \prod_{d\in[\ell]} (\gamma_d)^{vv_d} \bmod n^2$ to User.
- **Reconstructing:** User computes

$$x(i^*,j^*,\kappa^*) = \mathcal{D}_g(\mathcal{D}_g([\mathcal{D}_g(uu)n + \mathcal{D}_g(uv)])n + \mathcal{D}_g([\mathcal{D}_g(vu)n + \mathcal{D}_g(vv)])).$$

Lemma 4. *Under CRA,* PIR ON 3-HYPERCUBE *is a one-round implementation of* 1dPIR *with Server-side communication $4k$ bits and User-side communication $3kN^{\frac{1}{3}}$ bits, where $k = \lceil 2\log n \rceil$ is the security parameter.*

Proof. The protocol is one-round as User's sending of $\{\gamma_t\}_{t\in[\ell]}$ can be merged into the executions of PIR ON 2-HYPERCUBE. Next, note that $[\mathcal{D}_g(uu)n + \mathcal{D}_g(uv)] = (uu_{\kappa^*})n + uv_{\kappa^*} = u_{\kappa^*}$ and that $[\mathcal{D}_g(vu)n + \mathcal{D}_g(vv)] = (vu_{\kappa^*})n + vv_{\kappa^*} = v_{\kappa^*}$. So we have

$$\mathcal{D}_g(\mathcal{D}_g([\mathcal{D}_g(uu)n + \mathcal{D}_g(uv)])n + \mathcal{D}_g([\mathcal{D}_g(vu)n + \mathcal{D}_g(vv)]))$$
$$= \mathcal{D}_g(\mathcal{D}_g(u_{\kappa^*})n + \mathcal{D}_g(v_{\kappa^*}))$$
$$= x(i^*,j^*,\kappa^*).$$

On the other hand, the security follows directly the proof for PIR ON 2-HYPERCUBE, while the Server-side communication is straightforward. Finally, the User-side communication follows the fact that User just needs to send one copy of $\{\alpha_t, \beta_t\}_{t\in[\ell]}$, along with $\{\gamma_t\}_{t\in[\ell]}$, to Server. $\square$

In fact, the above scheme itself is a non-black-box reduction from PIR ON 3-HYPERCUBE to PIR ON 2-HYPERCUBE, and the same technique can be applied recursively.

Theorem 1. *Under CRA, We can construct* PIR ON c-HYPERCUBE, *a one-round implementation of* 1dPIR *with Server-side communication $2^{c-1}k$ bits and User-side communication $ckN^{\frac{1}{c}}$ bits for any integer constant $c > 3$, where $k = \lceil 2\log n \rceil$ is the security parameter.*

Proof. (SKETCH ONLY) We just give a high-level description of the claimed PIR ON c-HYPERCUBE, which invokes PIR ON $(c-1)$-HYPERCUBE as a sub-routine.

PIR ON c-HYPERCUBE
- **Initializing:** Server and User have to treat the c-hypercube database x as ℓ $(c-1)$-hypercube databases, while User sends the c-th dimensional encrypted indexes to Server.
- **Invoking:** User executes PIR ON $(c-1)$-HYPERCUBE with Server on those ℓ $(c-1)$-hypercube databases in parallel yet omitting the **Reconstructing** step of PIR ON $(c-1)$-HYPERCUBE and complying the following:
  - User's messages are the same in all executions and is in accordance with his choice. This says one copy is enough for all executions, and Server should reuse that copy.
  - Server does not send his returning messages in PIR ON $(c-1)$-HYPERCUBE to User after computing them.
- **Splitting-and-then-filtering:** Instead, Server splits the computed returning messages and filters them by multiplying the c-th dimensional encrypted indexes raised to the splits, and then sends the results to User.
- **Reconstructing:** User reconstructs the answer by recursive decryptions.

Here the security and the User-side communication can be easily verified, while the Server-side communication follows the recursive splitting.   □

Corollary 3. *Under CRA, PIR ON c-HYPERCUBE can be modified to implement $\binom{N}{1}OT^\ell$ against semi-honest Receiver and malicious Sender for any ℓ, while we can use the constant c as a parameter to do communication balancing between Sender and Receiver.*

Theorem 2. *Under CRA, PIR ON c-HYPERCUBE can be modified to implement 1dPIR with Server sending $2^{\log N - c}$ bits and User sending $4ck$ bits.*

Proof. Note the User-side communication in Theorem 1 can be improved to be $ck(2N/k)^{\frac{1}{c}}$ bits if Server divides the database into entries of $\lfloor \log n \rfloor \simeq k/2$ bits and lets User retrieve an entry at a time. Next, note Server can divide the database into sub-databases of $2^{2c-1}k$ bits and execute the improved scheme with User on each sub-database, with User's choice fixed in all executions.   □

4 Oblivious Transfers Against Malicious Players

We have shown how to implement $\binom{N}{1}OT^\ell$ against semi-honest Receiver using our 1dPIR schemes. Next, we will deal with the case of malicious Receiver. Our strategy is to employ the efficient transformation proposed in [15], which can transform any 1dPIR protocol against malicious Server on N-bit database into a communication-efficient $\binom{N}{1}OT^\ell$ protocol against malicious players for any ℓ. Note in addition to 1dPIR, the transformation requires $\log N$ executions of a $\binom{2}{1}OT^\rho$ protocol against malicious players, where ρ is the security parameter.

Since our 1dPIR schemes are secure against malicious Server, it suffices to design a $\binom{2}{1}\mathsf{OT}^\rho$ protocol secure against malicious players under CRA and plug them into the transformation. Note the $\log N$ executions of $\binom{2}{1}\mathsf{OT}^\rho$ will only yield small communication overheads.

Due to the structure behind CRA, it could be easier for us to first design a $\binom{4}{2}\mathsf{OT}^\rho$ protocol against malicious players and then use it to implement $\binom{2}{1}\mathsf{OT}^\rho$. We emphasize that the only zero-knowledge proof setup in our protocol is to prove n is valid (i.e. n is a product of two safe primes of the same length in bits), which is inevitable but can be done efficiently [17]. Besides, CRA is sufficient to guarantee the security of our protocol against malicious players.

Consider computations modulo n^2, where n is the product of two $(\rho+1)$-bit safe primes p and q. Assume Sender has four ρ-bit strings m_1, m_2, m_3, m_4, and Receiver has two choices $c_1, c_2 \in \{1, 2, 3, 4\}$ and wants to learn m_{c_1} and m_{c_2}. Here is the protocol for them to achieve this task in an oblivious way, with their security being guaranteed even if the other player is malicious.

2-OUT-OF-4 STRING OBLIVIOUS TRANSFER
- Receiver uses zero-knowledge proof to convince Sender that his public key n is a product of two safe primes p, q, and computes $a \in \mathbb{Z}_n$ such that $[a + c_1 = 0 \bmod p]$ and $[a + c_2 = 0 \bmod q]$.
- Let $g = n + 1$; Receiver sends $x = \mathcal{E}_g(a, r)$ to Sender, who then verifies $x \in \mathbb{Z}_{n^2}^*$.
- Sender computes the following with computations modulus n^2:

$$y_1 = r_1^n(xg^1)^{\alpha_1}g^{m_1}, \ y_2 = r_2^n(xg^2)^{\alpha_2}g^{m_2}, \ y_3 = r_3^n(xg^3)^{\alpha_3}g^{m_3}, \ y_4 = r_4^n(xg^4)^{\alpha_4}g^{m_4},$$

where r_1, r_2, r_3, r_4, (resp. $\alpha_1, \alpha_2, \alpha_3, \alpha_4$) are chosen uniformly at random from $\mathbb{Z}_n^*$ (resp. $\mathbb{Z}_n$).
- Sender sends y_1, y_2, y_3, y_4 to Receiver, who then compute

$$m_{c_1} = [\mathcal{D}_g(y_{c_1}) \bmod p], \ m_{c_2} = [\mathcal{D}_g(y_{c_2}) \bmod q].$$

Lemma 5. *Under CRA, for sufficiently large ρ, the above* 2-OUT-OF-4 STRING OBLIVIOUS TRANSFER *is an implementation of* $\binom{4}{2}\mathsf{OT}^\rho$ *against malicious players.*

Proof. First, we claim Receiver is secure against malicious Sender if Receiver follows the protocol. Clearly, this claim follows the facts that $x = \mathcal{E}_g(a, r)$ is the only message from Receiver, that $\mathcal{E}_g$ is semantically secure, and that the generation of x does not depend on Sender's behavior.

Next, we claim the correctness can be guaranteed if both players follow the protocol. Note Receiver has the following for $1 \le i \le 4$:

$$y_i = [(r^{\alpha_i}r_i)^n g^{\alpha_i(a+i)+m_i} \bmod n^2].$$

In fact, $y_i = [(\Delta_2)^n g^{\Delta_1} \bmod n^2]$, where $\Delta_1 = [\alpha_i(a+i) + m_i \bmod n]$ and $\Delta_2 = [(r^{\alpha_i}r_i) \bmod n]$, since $[g^n = (n+1)^n = 1 \bmod n^2]$ and $[x^n \bmod n^2] = [(x \bmod n)^n \bmod n^2]$ for $x \in \mathbb{N}$. Also, note $\Delta_1 \in \mathbb{Z}_n$ and $\Delta_2 \in \mathbb{Z}_n^*$ (since $r, r_i \in \mathbb{Z}_n^*$). In consequence, we have the following for $1 \le i \le 4$:

$$\mathcal{D}_g(y_i) = \Delta_1 = [\alpha_i(a+i) + m_i \bmod n].$$

So if Receiver follows the protocol, he certainly can obtain $[m_{c_1} \bmod p]$ and $[m_{c_2} \bmod q]$ since $[a+c_1 = 0 \bmod p]$ and $[a+c_2 = 0 \bmod q]$. Moreover, because m_{c_1} (resp. m_{c_2}) is strictly less than p (resp. q), we claim Receiver can learn the correct values for sure.

Last but most importantly, we have to prove Sender's security against a malicious Receiver, and we will prove that in any case at least two out of $\{y_1, y_2, y_3, y_4\}$ are random in Receiver' view. Recall Receiver has proven to Sender in a zero-knowledge manner that n is valid, i.e. n is a product of two ρ-bit safe primes. Conditioned on such validity of n, we obtain the following observations.

First, note that given any $c \in \mathbb{Z}_{n^2}^*$ and the factorization of n, one can always compute the corresponding $(a, r) \in (\mathbb{Z}_n, \mathbb{Z}_n^*)$ satisfying $[g^a r^n = c \bmod n^2]$ by the following:

$$a = \mathcal{D}_g(c), \quad c_* = cg^{-a}, \quad r = [c_*^{(n^{-1} \bmod \lambda)} \bmod n].$$

Recall such mapping is bijective (see Section 2). Next, note one can always decide whether a given value is in $\mathbb{Z}_{n^2}^*$ or not (by checking whether it is in $[n^2]$ and is relative prime to n). So we claim

- Receiver cannot send a message $\notin \mathbb{Z}_{n^2}^*$ as Sender can detect it easily, and thus
- Sender can be sure that the only message from Receiver is of the form $[g^a r^n \bmod n^2]$ for some $(a, r) \in (\mathbb{Z}_n, \mathbb{Z}_n^*)$ and that Receiver chooses and knows (a, r) directly or indirectly.

In other words, Receiver's malicious behavior is restricted within the choices of a and r.

Next, the following proof goes for any fixed a, r, and m_1, m_2, m_3, m_4. Note that at least two out of four successive integers are relative prime to n, so we know at least two elements of $\mathcal{A} = \{a_i | a_i = a + i \bmod n\}_{1 \le i \le 4}$ are in $\mathbb{Z}_n^*$ and thus have their own inverses. Assume $a_i \in \mathbb{Z}_n^*$ for some $1 \le i \le 4$. We claim y_i is uniformly distributed in Receiver's view, by the following observations:

- $y_i = [(\Delta_2)^n g^{\Delta_1} \bmod n^2]$, where $\Delta_1 = [\alpha_i a_i + m_i \bmod n]$ and $\Delta_2 = [(r^{\alpha_i} r_i) \bmod n]$.
- Δ_1 is uniformly distributed in $\mathbb{Z}_n$. (Because $a_i \in \mathbb{Z}_n^*$ and α_i is uniformly distributed in $\mathbb{Z}_n$, we know $[\alpha_i a_i \bmod n]$ is uniformly distributed in $\mathbb{Z}_n$, and so is Δ_1.)
- When Δ_1 is fixed, Δ_2 is uniformly distributed in $\mathbb{Z}_n^*$. (Since m_i and Δ_1 are fixed, so is $\alpha_i = (\Delta_1 - m_i)(a_i)^{-1}$; since $r \in \mathbb{Z}_n^*$ and r_i is uniformly distributed in $\mathbb{Z}_n^*$, we know Δ_2 is uniformly distributed in $\mathbb{Z}_n^*$.)
- $y_i = [(\Delta_2)^n g^{\Delta_1} \bmod n^2]$ is uniformly distributed in $\mathbb{Z}_{n^2}^*$ due to the bijective mapping.

Consequently, we claim at least two of $\{y_1, y_2, y_3, y_4\}$ are random in Receiver's view, and thus leak no information about the corresponding strings. Since y_1, y_2, y_3, y_4 are the only messages from Sender, we finish the proof of Sender's security against a malicious Receiver. □

Theorem 3. 2-OUT-OF-4 STRING OBLIVIOUS TRANSFER *can be directly used to implement* $\binom{2}{1}\mathsf{OT}^{\rho}$ *against malicious players.*

Proof. Assume Sender has two ρ-bit strings x_0, x_1, and Receiver has a choice $b \in \{0,1\}$ and wants to learn x_b. It suffices for Sender to choose two ρ-bit random strings σ_1, σ_2 and execute 2-OUT-OF-4 STRING OBLIVIOUS TRANSFER with Receiver using the following settings: $m_1 = x_1 \oplus \sigma_1, m_2 = \sigma_1, m_3 = x_2 \oplus \sigma_2, m_4 = \sigma_2, c_1 = 2b + 1, c_2 = 2b + 2$, where $\oplus$ means bitwise exclusive-or. □

As mentioned, we can plug the above $\binom{2}{1}\mathsf{OT}^{\rho}$ and our 1dPIR schemes into the transformation of [15] to obtain efficient $\binom{N}{1}\mathsf{OT}^{\ell}$ protocols against malicious players for any ℓ. We leave the complexity analysis in the full paper.

References

1. D. Asonov, "Private information retrieval: an overview and current trends," Manuscript, 2001.
2. M. Blum and S. Micali, "How to generate cryptographically strong sequences of pseudo-random bits," *SIAM Journal on Computing, 13(4)*: pp. 850–864, 1984.
3. D. Catalano, R. Gennaro, and N. H.-Graham, "Paillier's trapdoor function hides up to O(n) bits," *Journal of Cryptology, 15(4)*: pp. 251–269, 2002.
4. D. Catalano, R. Gennaro, N. H.-Graham, and P. Nguyen, "Paillier's cryptosystem revisited," *ACM Conference on Computer and Comm. Security 2001*, pp. 206–214.
5. G. Crescenzo, T. Malkin, and R. Ostrovsky, "Single database private information retrieval implies oblivious transfer," *Eurocrypt 2000*, pp. 122–138.
6. C. Cachin, S. Micali, and M. Stadler, "Computationally private information retrieval with polylogarithmic communication," *Eurocrypt'99*, pp. 402–414.
7. R. Cramer and V. Shoup, "Universal hash proofs and a paradigm for adaptive chosen ciphertext secure public-key encryption," *Eurocrypt 2002*, pp. 45–64.
8. I. Damgård and M. Jurik, "A generalisation, a simplification and some applications of Paillier's probabilistic public-key system," *PKC 2001*, pp. 119–136.
9. S. Galbraith, "Elliptic curve Paillier schemes," *Journal of Cryptology, 15(2)*: pp. 129–138, 2000.
10. O. Goldreich, "Secure multi-party computation," Manuscript, 1998.
11. S. Goldwasser and S. Micali, "Probabilistic encryption," *JCSS, 28(2)*: pp. 270–299, 1984.
12. J. Kilian, "Founding cryptography on oblivious transfer," *STOC'88*, pp. 20–31.
13. E. Kushilevitz and R. Ostrovsky, "Replication is not needed: single database, computationally-private information retrieval," *FOCS'97*, pp. 364–373.
14. E. Kushilevitz and R. Ostrovsky, "One-way trapdoor permutations are sufficient for non-trivial single-server private information retrieval," *Eurocrypt 2000*, pp. 104–121.
15. M. Naor and B. Pinkas, "Oblivious transfer and polynomial evaluation," *STOC'99*, pp. 245–254.
16. P. Paillier, "Public-key cryptosystems based on composite degree residuosity classes," *Eurocrypt'99*, pp. 223–238.
17. G. Poupard and J. Stern, "Short proofs of knowledge for factoring," *PKC 2000*, pp. 147–166.
18. M. Rabin, "How to exchange secrets by oblivious transfer," Tech. Memo TR-81, Aiken Computation Laboratory, Harvard University, 1981.

Information Theoretically Secure Oblivious Polynomial Evaluation: Model, Bounds, and Constructions

Goichiro Hanaoka[1], Hideki Imai[1], Joern Mueller-Quade[2],
Anderson C.A. Nascimento[1], Akira Otsuka[1], and Andreas Winter[3]

[1] Institute of Industrial Science, The University of Tokyo
4-6-1, Komaba, Meguro-ku, Tokyo, 153-8505 Japan
{hanaoka,imai,anderson,otsuka}@imailab.iis.u-tokyo.ac.jp
[2] Universitaet Karlsruhe, Institut fuer Algorithmen und Kognitive Systeme
Am Fasanengarten 5, 76128 Karlsruhe, Germany
muellerq@ira.uka.de
[3] School of Mathematics, University of Bristol
University Walk, Bristol BS8 1TW, U.K.
a.j.winter@bris.ac.uk

Abstract. We introduce an information theoretical model for oblivious polynomial evaluation relying on predistributed data, and prove very general lower bounds on the size of the predistributed data, as well as the size of the communications in any (one-round) protocol. We then show that these bounds are tight by exhibiting a scheme for oblivious polynomial evaluation achieveing all the lower bounds simultaneously. We also present a natural generalisation to oblivious linear function evaluation.

1 Introduction

Oblivious polynomial evaluation is a variant of oblivious function evaluation and was introduced in [5]. Like its little cousin oblivious transfer (OT), oblivious polynomial evaluation (OPE) is a very useful tool for achieving secure distributed computations.

Oblivious polynomial evaluation is a two-party protocol where a sender (Alice) inputs a polynomial over a finite field and a receiver (Bob) inputs a single point of the same finite field. At the end of the protocol, Alice receives nothing and Bob should receive the polynomial input by Alice, evaluated on the point chosen by him. The protocol is secure if Alice learns nothing on which point was chosen by Bob and Bob evaluates the polynomial input by Alice on at most one point.

Note that OPE can be understood as an execution of one-out-of-n OT where Alice's inputs are evaluations of her polynomial on n points while Bob chooses one of those evaluations.

Since its introduction in [5] OPE has been extensively studied. In [7] the problem of implementing OPE was efficiently reduced to that of achieving OT.

H. Wang et al. (Eds.): ACISP 2004, LNCS 3108, pp. 62–73, 2004.

Also, in [7] an information theoretical secure protocol for implementing OPE was proposed. The security of that protocol was based on trustiness of a third party which took an active role in the protocol execution.

In this paper, we analyze the problem of achieving information theoretical oblivious polynomial evaluation without using an active (on-line) trusted party. That is, we propose and solve the problem of implementing information theoretical secure OPE with the help of an off-line party which pre-distributes some data during a setup phase, the so-called commodity-based cryptography model [1].

We provide a model (sections 2 and 3), bounds for the amount of memory which is required from players taking part in the protocol (section 4) and a construction which achieves these bounds, thus showing their tightness (section 5).

Finally, we propose a more general protocol called oblivious linear functional evaluation (OLF), in section 6. In OLF Alice inputs a linear functional while Bob evaluates this linear functional on a vector of his choice. As a side result of our bounds, we prove the optimality of oblivious transfer protocols proposed by Rivest [6] and Beaver [1].

Commodities based cryptography. We propose protocols based on the so-called commodity cryptographic model. In [1], Beaver introduced a model, where players buy cryptographic primitives from "off-line" servers. These primitives can be used later on to implement general cryptographic protocols. The commodity based model was inspired in the internet architecture, which is usually based on the "client-server" paradigm. Once the primitives, or commodities as they are called by Beaver, are acquired, no further interactions between server and users are required. Therefore, the servers need not know the values which are computed by the players. Moreover, if several servers are available, they need not to be completely trusted, that is, the system is secure even if some servers collude with the users of the commodities and/or among themselves. Another interesting feature of Beaver's model is that no interaction among the servers is required.

In this contribution, we show that the use of off-lines servers provides very efficient and simple protocols for secure oblivious polynomial evaluation over a finite field.

Although this model was formalized just in [1], several independent works share the same flavor. We cite key-pre-distribution schemes [4], unconditionally secure bit commitments [6,2] and unconditionally secure digital signature schemes [3].

2   Preliminaries

Given a sample space (a set of events), a random variable X is a mapping from the sample space to a certain range $\mathcal{X}$ and it is characterized by its probability distribution P_X that assigns to every $x \in \mathcal{X}$ the probability $P_X(x)$ of the event that X takes on the value x.

Then entropy of a random variable is a measure of the uncertainty of a random variable X:

$$H(X) = -\sum_x P_X(x) \log_2 P_X(x)$$

assuming that $0 \log_2 0 = 0$. A very important property of the entropy function is

$$0 \le H(X) \le \log_2 |X|,$$

with equality iff X is uniformly distributed. In this way, and actually asymptotically in Shannon's information theory, $H(X)$ is the amount of space (in bits) needed to store X. We shall always in this paper use entropies to measure the (storage) size of data — which is sensible even nonasymptotically when the distribution of X is uniform over its range.

It is easy to extend this definitions to several random variables. For example, given three random variables XYZ with joint probability distribution P_{XYZ} we have

$$H(XYZ) = -\sum_{x,y,z} P_{XYZ}(x,y,z) \log_2 P_X(x,y,z)$$

Conditional entropy is another important concept in information theory. It is based on the definition of conditional probability. The conditional probability of the random variable X, given the event $Y = y$ is given by

$$P_{X|Y}(x,y) = P_{XY}(x,y)/P_Y(y),$$

when $P_Y(y) \ne 0$. The conditional entropy of X given that $Y = y$ is given by

$$H(X|Y=y) = -\sum_x P_{X|Y}(x,y) \log_2 P_{X|Y}(x|y).$$

When we average over Y we have the conditional entropy of X given Y,

$$H(X|Y) = \sum_{y \in Y : P_Y(y) \ne 0} H(X|Y=y)P_Y(y) = -\sum_{x,y} P_{XY}(x,y) \log_2 P_{X|Y}(x,y).$$

The conditional entropy of X given Y can be understood as the uncertainty of guessing the random variable X when Y is known. It is easy to show that additional knowledge cannot increase entropy:

$$0 \le H(X|Y) \le H(X),$$

with equality $H(X|Y) = H(X)$ iff X and Y are statistically independent, i.e. Y conveys no information on X.

Entropy obeys the chain rule

$$H(XY) = H(X) + H(Y|X).$$

The chain rule states that the entropy of XY is equal to the entropy of X plus the entropy of Y when X is given. This rule can be easily generalized to many variables,

$$H(X_1 X_2 \ldots X_n) = \sum_{p=1}^{n} H(X_p | X_1 \ldots X_{p-1}).$$

The mutual information and conditional mutual information are defined as

$$I(X:Y) = \sum_{x,y} P_{XY}(x,y) \log_2 \frac{P_{XY}(x,y)}{P_X(x) P_Y(y)},$$

$$I(X:Y|Z) = \sum_{z} P_Z(z) \sum_{x,y} P_{XY|Z}(x,y|z) \log_2 \frac{P_{XY|Z}(x,y|z)}{P_{X|Z}(x|z) P_{Y|Z}(y|z)}$$

$$= \sum_{x,z,y} P_{XYZ}(x,y,z) \log_2 \frac{P_{XYZ}(x,y,z,) P_Z(z)}{P_{XZ}(x,z) P_{YZ}(y,z)}.$$

From this definition we can prove the following equality:

$$I(X:Y) = H(X) - H(X|Y),$$

which means that the mutual information is the amount by which the uncertainty about X is reduced by learning Y. Similarly,

$$I(X:Y|Z) = I(X:YZ) - I(X:Z) = H(X|Z) - H(X|YZ).$$

3   Definitions

A two-party protocol consists of a program which describes a series of messages to be exchanged and local computations to be performed by the two parties. The protocol is said to halt if no more local computations or message exchanges are required. At the end of an execution of a protocol, each party emits an accept/reject message, depending on the messages he/she received and on the result of local computations.

As OPE can be seen as a particular case of one-out-of-n OT, we review the definitions of security for this protocol.

In an oblivious transfer protocol, there are two parties: a sender (Alice) and a receiver (Bob). The sender's inputs to the protocol consist of n elements of a finite field $\mathbf{F}_q$. We denote those inputs by U_i, $0 \le i < n$. The receiver's input is a single number $0 \le c < n$. At the end of the protocol Bob receives U_c as his output, while Alice receives nothing. The protocol is said to be correct, if for honest players, Bob receives his desired output and both players do not abort the protocol. It is said to be private if Alice has no information on Bob's choice and Bob learns information concerning at most one of Alice's inputs.

The protocol (for honest players) or more generally any strategy (in the case of cheaters) defines random variables for all the messages exchanged and results of computations performed during an execution of the protocol, depending on their mutual inputs. For the sake of simplicity, we use the same notation for outcomes of a random experiment and their random variables. Denote by $V_A(V_B)$ the random variable which represents all the information in possession of Alice (Bob) at the end of the protocol (including the results of all local computations, local random samplings, local inputs and messages exchanged). This information is also known as the *view of a player*. We denote an execution of a program G by players A and B on inputs x_A and x_B which generates the outcomes y_A and y_B by $G[A, B](x_A, x_B) = (y_A, y_B)$. A party receiving no output is represented by $y = \Delta$. For the following, we also assume distributions on the inputs $U_0, \ldots, U_{n-1}$ and c (most conveniently, uniform).

Definition 1. *A protocol* $G[A, B](x_A, x_B) = (y_A, y_B)$ *is an ϵ-correct implementation of a 1-out-of-n oblivious transfer protocol,* $\binom{n}{1} - OT$ *for short, if at the end of its execution for honest players Alice and Bob, we have that*

$$\Pr\{G[A, B]((U_0, U_1, \ldots, U_{n-1}), c) \neq (\Delta, U_c)\} \leq \epsilon$$

for any $U_i \in Z_q$, $0 \leq i < n$ and $0 \leq c < n$.
   It is ϵ-private for Bob if for any possible behavior of Alice,

$$I(V_A : C) \leq \epsilon$$

where $I(\cdot ; \cdot)$ is Shannon's mutual information, V_A is the random variable which represents Alice's view after the completion of the protocol and C is the random variable which represents Bob's input c (assuming uniform distribution).
   It is ϵ-private for Alice if for any possible behaviour of Bob, he can obtain information on at most one of the U_i. Formally, if there exists a random variable $\widehat{C}$ which is a function of his view V_B such that

$$I(U_0 U_1 \ldots U_{n-1} : \widehat{C}) \leq \epsilon,$$
$$I(U_0 U_1 \ldots U_{n-1} : V_B | \widehat{C} U_{\widehat{C}}) \leq \epsilon.$$

A protocol is said to be ϵ-private if it ϵ-private for both Alice and Bob.

A 1-out-of-n oblivious transfer protocol is said to be perfect if $\epsilon = 0$. From here on, we focus on perfect and round optimal protocols (in the case of OT, a protocol with one round, as non-interactive OT protocols can easily be proven to be impossible).

In an oblivious polynomial evaluation, Alice's inputs consists of evaluations of a polynomial $P(X) \in \mathbf{F}_q[X]$ (q a prime power) on the finite field $\mathbf{F}_q$; note that we identify P with its associated function $P : \mathbf{F}_q \longrightarrow \mathbf{F}_q$.

In our model we have three players: Alice, Bob and Ted. We assume the three players to be interconnected by private pairwise channels. Ted is a trusted center who pre-distributes some secret data to Alice and Bob during a setup phase, but does not take part in the protocol later on. Alice and Bob are malicious players who may deviate from the original protocol in an arbitrary way.

The protocol should consist of an initialization phase where Alice and Bob receive "commodities" from Ted and of a computation phase where Alice and Bob interact in order to perform an oblivious polynomial evaluation. We denote the data received by Alice and Bob by U_a and U_b. The domains where these data are taken from are denoted by $\mathfrak{U}_a$ and $\mathfrak{U}_b$ respectively.

The computation phase consists of Bob choosing his input to the protocol (a point $i \in \mathbf{F}_q$) and sending a message $e_i = t(U_b, i)$ where $t(\cdot)$ is a public known deterministic function. After receiving e_i, Alice computes $h = f(U_a, e_i, P(x))$, where $f(\cdot)$ is a public known deterministic function and $P(x) \in \mathbf{F}_q[X]$ is the polynomial which is her input to the protocol, and sends it to Bob. After receiving h from Alice, Bob extracts $P(i)$ out of h by using another public known function $w(\cdot)$ and his data i, U_b. Note that random variables can be easily defined for all the variables here specified as stated previously: $\mathbf{P}$, $\mathbf{i}$ and $(\mathbf{U}_a, \mathbf{U}_b)$ are then independent variables. We assume $\mathbf{i}$ to take positive probabilities on all $i \in \mathbf{F}_q$, for technical reasons, but $\mathbf{P}$ can have an arbitrary distribution subject to the constraint that $\mathbf{P}(i)$ and $\mathbf{P}(j)$ are independent for $i \neq j$.

Assuming a perfect, round optimal protocol like we specified above, the general security definitions stated in our previous definitions can be rewritten:

The protocol is *correct* if for Alice and Bob following the protocol, we have $P(i) = w(h, i, U_b)$, i.e.

$$H(\mathbf{P(i)}|\mathbf{iU}_b\mathbf{h}) = 0. \tag{1}$$

The protocol is said to be *(perfectly) private for Alice* if Bob does not learn anything about the polynomial input by Alice except for the value at most one point he has chosen, even if he actively deviates from the protocol. That is, for whatever Bob does, there is a random variable $\mathbf{j}$ (independent of $\mathbf{P}$), such that $H(\mathbf{j}|\mathbf{ehU}_b) = 0$ and

$$H(\mathbf{P}|\mathbf{U}_b\mathbf{eh}) \geq H(\mathbf{P}|\mathbf{jP(j)}|\mathbf{U}_b\mathbf{eh}) = H(\mathbf{P}|\mathbf{jP(j)}) \tag{2}$$

holds, and $\mathbf{j} = \mathbf{i}$ with equality above, if Bob follows the protocol. Note that in this case the right hand side simplifies to

$$H(\mathbf{P}|\mathbf{iP(i)}) = H(\mathbf{P}) - H(\mathbf{P(i)}|\mathbf{i}).$$

The protocol is *(perfectly) private for Bob* if Alice does not learn anything on Bob's input even if she actively cheats, that is

$$H(\mathbf{i}|\mathbf{U}_a\mathbf{ehP}) = H(\mathbf{i}). \tag{3}$$

4   Bounds

In this section we prove bounds for oblivious polynomial evaluation in the commodity based model as specified in the last section. The following propositions refer to scenarios in which the players follow the protocol (are "honest but curious").

It is natural to think that, in our scenario, if Bob is given access to Alice's secret data U_a, he should be able to break the secrecy condition completely, that is he should be able to learn all the information about Alice's input $P(X)$. We formally prove this fact in the next proposition.

Proposition 1. *Bob learns all the information on $P(x)$ if he is given access to Alice's secret data after completing a successful execution of oblivious polynomial evaluation. Mathematically, $H(\mathbf{P}|\mathbf{U}_a\mathbf{eh}) = 0$.*

Proof. Let $\mathbf{P} = P$. After one successful run of the protocol and after obtaining Alices's data, Bob can try to compute the function $h(\cdot)$ for all the possible inputs (polynomials) $P(x)$. The correct input will produce a view equal to the one obtained during the protocol execution. Furthermore, because the condition of privacy for Bob, eq. (3), states that

$$H(\mathbf{i}|\mathbf{ehU}_a\mathbf{P}) = H(\mathbf{i})$$

no two different polynomials should produce the same view, otherwise Alice would obtain knowledge on Bob's inputs (if two polynomials produce the same transcript, Bob's choice must be limited to the points where those polynomials coincide).

An equivalent result holds for Alice: if she is given access to Bob's input and the secret data he received from Ted, she is able to break the protocol's security condition for her completely.

Proposition 2. *Alice learns the point which was chosen by Bob if she is given access to the secret data he received from Ted: $H(\mathbf{i}|\mathbf{eU}_b) = 0$.*

Proof. First we note that as the functions $t(\cdot)$ and $f(\cdot)$ are deterministic, given a certain value U_b there should be no two points $i \neq j$ such that $t(U_b, i) = t(U_b, j)$ since that would imply that Bob could learn the evaluation of $P(x)$ on two different points. This however says that e and U_b together uniquely determine i, hence the result.

Remark 1. This proposition tells us that in eq. (2), privacy for Alice, we can add $\mathbf{i}$ to condition without making the equation wrong; at least, if Bob follows the protocol.

We now prove another auxiliary result: namely, that the messages exchanged are independent of Alice's and Bob's inputs P and i.

Proposition 3. *In a secure commodity based polynomial evaluation protocol, $I(\mathbf{Pi} : \mathbf{eh}) = 0$. In particular, $H(\mathbf{P}|\mathbf{eh}) = H(\mathbf{P})$.*

Proof. We start by rewriting the mutual information of interest:

$$
\begin{aligned}
I(\mathbf{P}i : \mathbf{eh}) &= I(\mathbf{P}i\mathbf{P}(i) : \mathbf{eh}) \\
&= I(i\mathbf{P}(i) : \mathbf{eh}) + I(\mathbf{P} : \mathbf{eh}|i\mathbf{P}(i)) \\
&= I(\mathbf{P}(i) : \mathbf{eh}|i) + I(i : \mathbf{eh}) + I(\mathbf{P} : \mathbf{eh}|i\mathbf{P}(i))
\end{aligned}
$$

The last two terms here are both 0, because of the conditions for privacy for Bob and for Alice, eqs. (3) and (2), which read $I(i : \mathbf{P}\mathbf{U}_a\mathbf{eh}) = 0$ and $I(\mathbf{P} : \mathbf{U}_b\mathbf{eh}|i\mathbf{P}(i)) = 0$. Hence we get

$$
I(\mathbf{P}i : \mathbf{eh}) = I(\mathbf{P}(i) : \mathbf{eh}|i).
$$

It remains to prove that the right hand side is 0. Assume this were not the case.

Intuitively, we get a contradiction because i is independent of $\mathbf{eh}$, so Bob could go through the protocol and after receiving $\mathbf{h}$ decide which value $P(j)$ he wants to obtain information about. Thus, he could not only learn his allotted $P(i)$ but also some more information, in violation of privacy for Alice.

The formal argument involves our technical condition on the distribution of $\mathbf{P}$, in section 3. Let $\mathbf{j} = \mathbf{i} + 1$; in this way also $\mathbf{j}$ takes on all values with positive probability, and the first part of our intuitive argument is valid: $I(\mathbf{P}(j) : \mathbf{eh}|j) > 0$, because $\mathbf{j}$ can be generated by Bob independently of $\mathbf{eh}$, just as $\mathbf{i}$. Now we can estimate

$$
\begin{aligned}
I(\mathbf{P}(j) : j) &< I(\mathbf{P}(j) : j) + I(\mathbf{P}(j) : \mathbf{eh}|j) \\
&= I(\mathbf{P}(j) : \mathbf{ehj}) \\
&\leq I(\mathbf{P}(j) : \mathbf{ehij}\mathbf{P}(i)) \\
&= I(\mathbf{P}(j) : \mathbf{ij}\mathbf{P}(i)) + I(\mathbf{P}(j) : \mathbf{eh}|\mathbf{ij}\mathbf{P}(i)) \\
&= I(j : \mathbf{P}(j)) + 0,
\end{aligned}
$$

a contradiction. We have only used standard identities and inequalities, except for the last line: there once more privacy for Alice, eq. (2) was brought to bear, and the independence of $\mathbf{P}(i)$ and j for $i \neq j$.

Hence our assumption was wrong, and the proposition is proved.

Now, we use the above propositions to prove a lower bound on the size of the data which is pre-distributed to Alice.

Theorem 1. *In any commodity based secure polynomial evaluation, the size of the data which is pre-distributed to Alice is as large as the size of the polynomial to be evaluated: $H(\mathbf{U}_a) \geq H(\mathbf{P})$.*

Proof. Consider $I(\mathbf{U}_a : \mathbf{P}|\mathbf{eh})$: on the one hand we can rewrite it

$$
\begin{aligned}
I(\mathbf{U}_a : \mathbf{P}|\mathbf{eh}) &= H(\mathbf{P}|\mathbf{eh}) - H(\mathbf{P}|\mathbf{eh}\mathbf{U}_a) \\
&= H(\mathbf{P}) - 0,
\end{aligned}
$$

by propositions 3 and 1. On the other hand,

$$
I(\mathbf{U}_a : \mathbf{P}|\mathbf{eh}) \leq H(\mathbf{U}_a|\mathbf{eh}) \leq U(\mathbf{U}_a),
$$

which, put together with our previous identity, proves the theorem.

Another auxiliary result is actually just a corollary of proposition 3:

Proposition 4. *In any commodity based secure polynomial evaluation protocol,* $H(\mathbf{iP(i)}|\mathbf{eh}) = H(\mathbf{iP(i)}) = H(\mathbf{i}) + H(\mathbf{P(i)}|\mathbf{i})$.

Proof. Proposition 3 states $I(\mathbf{Pi} : \mathbf{eh}) = 0$. By data processing, we thus have $I(\mathbf{P(i)} : \mathbf{eh}) = 0$, which is just a reformulation of the claim.

Here, we show a bound on the size of the data pre-distributed to Bob.

Theorem 2. *In any commodity based secure polynomial evaluation, the size of the data which is pre-distributed to Bob is bounded by the following expression: for any* $j \in \mathbf{F}_q$, $H(\mathbf{U}_b) \geq H(\mathbf{i}) + H(\mathbf{P(i)}|\mathbf{i})$.

Proof. Consider the following:

$$I(\mathbf{U}_b : \mathbf{P(i)i}|\mathbf{eh}) = H(\mathbf{P(i)i}|\mathbf{eh}) - H(\mathbf{P(i)i}|\mathbf{ehU}_b)$$
$$= H(\mathbf{i}) + H(\mathbf{P(i)}|\mathbf{i}) - 0$$

using proposition 4 for the first entropy term, and proposition 2 (plus correctness of the protocol) for the second: $\mathbf{i}$ is a function of $\mathbf{e}$ and $\mathbf{U}_b$, and all these data together determine the polynomial value $\mathbf{P(i)}$. On the other hand,

$$H(\mathbf{U}_b) \geq H(\mathbf{U}_b|\mathbf{eh}) \geq I(\mathbf{U}_b : \mathbf{P(i)i}|\mathbf{eh}),$$

and with the previous identity the claim is proved.

We end this section with bounds on the size of the messages which have to be exchanged between Alice and Bob.

Theorem 3. $H(\mathbf{e}) \geq H(\mathbf{i})$ *and* $H(\mathbf{h}) \geq H(\mathbf{P})$.

Proof. For the first one, use proposition 2 for the first step in the following chain and then independence of $\mathbf{i}$ and $\mathbf{U}_b$:

$$H(\mathbf{i}) = I(\mathbf{i} : \mathbf{eU}_b) = I(\mathbf{i} : \mathbf{U}_b) + I(\mathbf{i} : \mathbf{e}|\mathbf{U}_b)$$
$$= I(\mathbf{i} : \mathbf{e}|\mathbf{U}_b) \leq H(\mathbf{e}|\mathbf{U}_b) \leq I(\mathbf{e}).$$

For the second one, use proposition 1 for the first step in the following chain and then independence of $\mathbf{P}$ and $\mathbf{eU}_a$:

$$H(\mathbf{P}) = I(\mathbf{P} : \mathbf{ehU}_a) = I(\mathbf{P} : \mathbf{eU}_a) + I(\mathbf{P} : \mathbf{h}|\mathbf{eU}_a)$$
$$= I(\mathbf{P} : \mathbf{h}|\mathbf{eU}_a) \leq H(\mathbf{P}|\mathbf{eU}_a) \leq I(\mathbf{P}).$$

5   An Optimal Construction

In this section we present a construction based on polynomials over finite fields which matches the lower bounds we proved in the last section, thus proving their tightness. The intuition behind the protocol is that Ted distributes a random evaluation performed on a random polynomial to Alice and Bob during a setup phase. Later on, they will exchange messages to turn the random evaluation into the desired one. In the protocol below, capital letters denote variables, as opposed to particular values.

Protocol OPE
Setup Phase

- Ted selects at random a random polynomial $R(X) \in \mathbf{F}_q[X]$ of degree n and a random point $d \in \mathbf{F}_q$. Ted sends $R(X)$ to Alice and $d, g = R(d)$ to Bob.

Computing Phase (Alice's input: $P(X)$ of degree n; Bob's input: $x_0 \in \mathbf{F}_q$).

- Bob sends $e = x_0 - d$ to Alice.
- Alice computes $F(X) = P(X + e) + R(X)$ and sends it to Bob.
- Bob computes $F(d) - g = P(d + e) + R(d) - R(d) = P(x_0)$, the desired output.

Theorem 4. *The above stated protocol is a secure implementation of an oblivious polynomial evaluation protocol. Moreover, it is optimal regarding its space complexity*

Proof. Correctness is obvious from the protocol. To prove privacy for Bob, note that d is uniformly distributed and not known to Alice, thus $H(\mathbf{i}|U_a\mathbf{eh}) = H(\mathbf{i})$ holds. Privacy for Alice follows from the fact that every action of Bob's (sending an e) amounts to choosing an x_0. However, given x_0 and $P(x_0)$, he can evidently simulate his view of an execution of the above protocol: he simply chooses randomly d and g and a polynomial $F(X)$ such that $F(d) = P(x_0) + g$. Since this uses no further knowledge of P, the security condition eq. (2) is clear.

Finally, or theorems 1, 2 and 3, with uniform distribution over all inputs, show that indeed the size of the predistributed data as well as of the communicated data meet the lower bounds.

6   Oblivious Linear Functional Evaluation

Here we generalize the previous protocol to the case where Bob inputs $v \in V$ (vector space) and Alice inputs a linear functional $l \in V^*$ (the dual vector space of linear functionals on V). First, notice that evaluating a polynomial $P(x) = a_0 + a_1x + a_2x^2 + \ldots + a_nx^n$ on a point x is the same as evaluating the linear functional $l = (a_0, a_1, \ldots, a_n)$ (as a row vector) on the (column) vector $v = (1, x, x^2, \ldots, x^n)^T$. Thus OPE can be seen as a particular case of oblivious linear functional evaluation. This idea can be generalized to affine linear functionals, but we chose not to break the inherent beautiful symmetry via duality of the problem.

Protocol OLF
Setup Phase

- Ted gives a random affine linear function m to Alice and a random $w \in V$ and $c = m(w)$ to Bob.

Computing Phase (Alice's input: $l \in V^*$; Bobs input $v \in V$).

- Bob sends $d := v - w$ to Alice
- Alice sends the function $n := l + m + l(d)$ to Bob
- Bob computes $n(w) - c = l(w) + m(w) + l(v - w) - m(w) = l(v)$

Correctness is immediate. The security of our oblivious linear functional evaluation protocol can be proven in a way similar to our OPE protocol. All Alice learns is d which is completely random to her. Bob on the other hand can simulate his view of an execution of this protocol if he is given v and $l(v)$. (Notice that as in the OPE protocol, any action of Bob's — sending some d — is essentially the same as choosing a point v.) He just chooses w and c randomly and then an affine linear function n such that $n(w) = l(v) + c$.

7   Conclusions

In this paper we introduced and solved the problem of efficiently evaluating polynomials obliviously within the so-called commodity-based cryptography, as proposed by Beaver [1]. We proposed a model and then proved bounds on the amount of "commodities" which have to be pre-distributed by the trusted center, thus providing bounds for the amount of memory required by the players engaged in the protocol, as well as bounds on their communications.

Then, we proved the tightness of our bounds by showing an explicit construction which meets them.

Finally, we proposed a generalisation of oblivious polynomial evaluation: oblivious linear functional evaluation.

In the full version of this paper, we will generalize the results here presented to the case of multiple trusted centers. Also, we will show how to overcome the bounds here presented by assuming the existence of one-way functions. Note that one-way functions alone are not believed to provide us with the full power of oblivious transfer, since one-way trapdoor functions are believed to be a necessary and sufficient conditions for achieving OT (and thus OPE).

References

1. D. Beaver: Commodity-Based Cryptography (Extended Abstract). STOC 1997: 446-455, 1997.
2. C. Blundo, B. Masucci, D.R. Stinson, and R. Wei. Constructions and Bounds for Unconditionally Secure Non-Interactive Commitment Schemes. Designs, Codes, and Cryptography, Special Issue in Honour of Ron Mullin, 26(1-3): 97-110, 2002.
3. G. Hanaoka, J. Shikata, Y. Zheng, and H. Imai. Unconditionally Secure Digital Signature Schemes Admitting Transferability. ASIACRYPT 2000: 130-142, 2000.
4. T. Matsumoto and H. Imai. On the Key Predistribution Systems: A Practical Solution to the Key Distribution Problem. CRYPTO 1987: 185-193, 1988.
5. M. Naor and B. Pinkas. Oblivious transfer and polynomial evaluation. 31st STOC, pp. 245–254, 1999.
6. R.L. Rivest. Unconditionally Secure Commitment and Oblivious Transfer Schemes Using Concealing Channels and a Trusted Initializer. Preprint available from http://theory.lcs.mit.edu/~rivest/Rivest-commitment.pdf
7. Yan-Cheng Chang, Chi-Jen Lu: Oblivious Polynomial Evaluation and Oblivious Neural Learning. ASIACRYPT 2001: 369-384, 2001.

Optimistic Fair Exchange
Based on Publicly Verifiable Secret Sharing

Gildas Avoine and Serge Vaudenay

EPFL

http://lasecwww.epfl.ch

Abstract. In this paper we propose an optimistic two-party fair exchange protocol which does not rely on a centralized trusted third party. Instead, the fairness of the protocol relies on the honesty of part of the neighbor participants. This new concept, which is based on a generic verifiable secret sharing scheme, is particularly relevant in networks where centralized authority can neither be used on-line nor off-line.

1 Introduction

A two-party fair exchange protocol is a protocol in which two participants, an originator P_o and a recipient P_r, wish to exchange items m_o and m_r in a fair way, i.e. such that no party can gain any advantage by cheating. There are two major kinds of two-party fair exchange protocols: those which rely on a Trusted Third Party (TTP) to ensure the fairness of the protocol, and those which do not. Even and Yacobi proved however in 1980 [9] that it is impossible to ensure a perfect fairness between only two participants without using a TTP. Protocols without TTP (e.g. [3,5,7]) are therefore only able to ensure fairness in a gradual or probabilistic way. The probability of fairness increases with the number of messages which are exchanged between the two participants. This implies a communication complexity cost which is too important for most of the practical applications. Finally, these protocols usually require that the involved parties have roughly equivalent computational powers, an assumption which is difficult to guarantee when dealing with heterogeneous networks. The second category of protocols rely on the use of a TTP to guarantee the fairness of the protocol. In all protocols the TTP acts as a central authority. TTP can be *on-line*, i.e. it is required in every exchange, or *off-line* (e.g. [1,2,11,15]). In this latter case, Asokan, Schunter, and Waidner invented the notion of *optimistic protocol* [1], where TTP is required only in case of conflict among participants. Fairness is ensured in a deterministic way and with few exchanges, but items must be either revocable or generatable by the TTP. Unfortunately, many environments, such as mobile ad hoc networks (MANET), do not allow either the use of a centralized authority (even in an optimistic case) for topologic reason, nor the usage of gradual protocols, which generate huge communication overheads. It is therefore important to design protocols based on other concepts. We propose a protocol which relies on the honesty of some "neighbor participants": when the exchange

H. Wang et al. (Eds.): ACISP 2004, LNCS 3108, pp. 74–85, 2004.
© Springer-Verlag Berlin Heidelberg 2004

runs well, no communication overhead is required to any third party, but when a conflict occurs, neighbor participants are requested to restore fairness, by recovering the unreceived item. The recovery protocol relies on a publicly verifiable secret sharing scheme (PVSS). Indeed, a secret sharing scheme allows to share a secret among participants such that only certain subsets of participants can recover the secret. When the scheme is publicly verifiable, anybody is able to check whether the distributed shares are correct.

In what follows we define the protocol requirements, and the communication and security model. In Section 2, we recall briefly the verifiable secret sharing concept and describe such a practical protocol. We propose then our optimistic two-party fair exchange protocol based on a generic PVSS. A security analysis is finally provided in Section 4.

2 Communication and Security Model

2.1 Requirements

Several (different) definitions for the fair exchange are available in the literature; most of them are context-dependent. We use the following common definition.

Definition 1 (exchange protocol). *An exchange protocol between an originator P_o and a recipient P_r is a protocol in which P_o and P_r own some items m_o and m_r respectively and aim at exchanging them. We define the security properties as follows.*

1. **Completeness**: *when there is no malicious misbehavior, P_o gets m_r and P_r gets m_o at the end of the protocol.*
2. **Fairness**: *when at least one of the two participants follows the protocol, the exchange terminates so that either P_o gets m_r and P_r gets m_o (success termination), or P_o gets no information about m_r and P_r gets no information about m_o (failure termination).*
3. **Timeliness**: *the exchange eventually terminates.*
4. **Privacy**: *no other participant gets any information about m_o and m_r.*
5. **Optimism**: *no other participant is involved when P_o and P_r are honest.*

We say that the protocol is a fair exchange protocol when it is complete, fair, and timely.

According to this definition, we design in this paper an optimistic fair exchange protocol between two parties, that do not require centralized TTP, implies reasonably low communication overhead, and protects privacy.

2.2 Threat Model

We say that an active participant is *honest* if he follows the protocol; otherwise he is *dishonest*. Note that due to the communication assumptions (below), all messages from honest participants are eventually delivered. The fairness of the protocol is ensured when either P_o or P_r is dishonest. Note that we do not need to consider the case where both P_o and P_r are dishonest: in this case they obviously always have the ability to halt the exchange on an unfair termination. We now consider the passive participants' behaviors.

- $\mathcal{B}_1$: participants who honestly collaborate with both P_o and P_r.
- $\mathcal{B}_2$: participants who may harm P_o by colluding with P_r.
- $\mathcal{B}_3$: participants who may harm P_r by colluding with P_o.
- $\mathcal{B}_4$: participants who do not collaborate at all.

Note that $\mathcal{B}_1$, $\mathcal{B}_2$, $\mathcal{B}_3$, and $\mathcal{B}_4$ form a partition of the passive participants $\mathcal{P}$. We denote $b_i = |\mathcal{B}_i|$ where $1 \leq i \leq 4$. We assume that participants cannot move from one set to another, focusing on the "honesty status" at the time of the recovery protocol only.

2.3   Communication Model and Hypothesis

Definition 2 (secure channel). *A channel is said to be secure if it ensures confidentiality, integrity, authentication, sequentiality, and timeliness.*
Confidentiality *ensures that the message is kept secret from any third party.* Integrity *ensures that the message cannot be modified by any third party.* Authentication *ensures that no third party can insert a forged message in the channel.* Sequentiality *ensures that the sequence of messages received by one party is equal to the sequence of messages sent by the other party in the same ordering at some time.* Timeliness *ensures that a message inserted into the channel is eventually delivered.*

Remark 1. Sequentiality ensures that no messages are swapped, dropped, or replayed.

Definition 3 (environment). *We say that two entities P and P' are in the same environment if and only if P and P' are able to communicate through a secure channel. We let Env_P denote the set of all the entities which are in the same environment as P*

Remark 2. The relation $P' \in Env_P$ between P and P' is symmetric but not transitive due to the timeliness requirement.

Definition 4 (participant). *We say that an entity which is involved in the protocol, either during the exchange stage or the recovery stage, is a participant. Participants which are only involved in the recovery stage are said* passive; *otherwise they are said* active.

Remark 3. In an optimistic *two-party* fair exchange, only participants P_o and P_r are active.

Hypothesis 1. In what follows we assume that $P_r \in Env_{P_o}$; P_r knows a subset of passive participants $\mathcal{P}$ of $Env_{P_o} \cap Env_{P_r}$ and a constant $T_{\max} < +\infty$ such that messages from P_r to any participant in $\mathcal{P}$ are always delivered within a time delay less than $T_{\max}$; $b_1 > 0$; and P_o and P_r know some constant k such that $b_2 < k \leq b_2 + b_1$.
We give here two examples in order to illustrate this assumption.

Example 1. If P_o and P_r know that there is a majority of honest participants in the network i.e. $b_1 > \frac{n}{2}$ then we take $k = \left\lceil \frac{n}{2} \right\rceil$.

Example 2. If P_o knows that at least 40% of the network is honest with him (i.e. $b_1 + b_3 \geq \frac{2n}{5}$) and P_r knows that at least 70% of the network is honest with him (i.e. $b_1 + b_2 \geq \frac{7n}{10}$) then we can take k such that $\left\lfloor \frac{6n}{10} \right\rfloor < k \leq \left\lceil \frac{7n}{10} \right\rceil$. For instance, if $n = 100$, k is chosen such that $60 < k \leq 70$. We show in Section 3 that k is actually the threshold of the secret sharing.

3   Optimistic Two-Party Fair Exchange Protocol

In this section, we first recall the notion of publicly verifiable secret-sharing; then we give an optimistic two-party fair exchange protocol. The main idea consists of sharing items among n participants such as k participants are enough to recover these items in case of conflict. The constraints on k will be analyzed in Section 4.

3.1   Publicly Verifiable Secret Sharing

Secret sharing [4,13] allows to share a secret m among several participants such that only some specific subsets of participants can recover m by collusion. In the Shamir secret sharing scheme, there is a threshold k so that only subsets of at least k participants can reconstruct m. A drawback of the Shamir scheme is that participants cannot verify that the distributed shares effectively allow to recover the secret m. In other words, the basic secret sharing scheme assumes that the dealer is not malicious. *Verifiable* secret sharing [6,10,12,14] resists to a malicious dealer who sends wrong shares: each participant can indeed check his own share. In *Publicly* verifiable secret sharing [12,14], introduced by Stadler in 1996, anybody can perform this verification and not only the participants. Below we describe a model for non-interactive publicly verifiable secret sharing (PVSS).

Distribution stage. The dealer generates the shares m_i of m and then publishes the encrypted values $E_i(m_i)$ such that only the participant P_i is able to decrypt $E_i(m_i)$. The dealer also publishes an information Δ containing $\theta = \mathcal{W}(m)$ where $\mathcal{W}$ is a one-way function. This information allows to prove that the distributed shares are correct i.e. they allow to recover some m such that $\mathcal{W}(m) = \theta$.

Verification stage. Given the P_is' public keys, the $E_i(m_i)$s, Δ, and a verification algorithm, anybody can verify that the shares allow to recover some m such that $\mathcal{W}(m) = \theta$.

Reconstruction stage. The participants decrypt their share m_i from $E_i(m_i)$ and pool them in order to recover m.

3.2   A Practical Publicly Verifiable Secret Sharing Scheme

We describe in this section a practical publicly verifiable secret sharing scheme which has been proposed by Stadler in [14]. This scheme relies on both ElGamal's public key cryptosystem [8] and on the double discrete logarithms assumption [14]. Let p be a large prime number so that $q = (p-1)/2$ is also prime, and let $h \in (\mathbb{Z}/p\mathbb{Z})^*$ be an element of order q. Let G be a group of order p, and let g be a generator of G such that computing discrete logarithms to the base g is difficult. Let $m \in \mathbb{Z}/p\mathbb{Z}$ be the secret and let $\mathcal{W}(m) = g^m$. As in Shamir's scheme, we assume that a publicly known element $x_i \in \mathbb{Z}/p\mathbb{Z}$, $x_i \neq 0$, is assigned to each participant P_i. We assume also that each participant P_i owns a secret key $z_i \in \mathbb{Z}/q\mathbb{Z}$ and the corresponding public key $y_i = h^{z_i} \bmod p$.

Distribution stage. The dealer chooses random elements $a_j \in \mathbb{Z}/p\mathbb{Z}$ ($j = 1, ..., k-1$) and publishes the values $A_j = g^{a_j}$ ($j = 1, ..., k-1$) in Δ. Then he securely computes the share

$$m_i = m + \sum_{j=1}^{k-1} a_j x_i^j \quad \bmod p \tag{1}$$

for P_i and he publishes the value g^{m_i} in Δ ($1 \le i \le n$). He uses the ElGamal encryption: he chooses a random value $\alpha_i \in \mathbb{Z}/q\mathbb{Z}$, computes the pair

$$E_i(m_i) = (\sigma_i^1, \sigma_i^2) = (h^{\alpha_i}, m_i^{-1}.y_i^{\alpha_i}) \quad \bmod p$$

and publishes it in Δ ($1 \le i \le n$). The precise content of Δ is described below.

Verification stage. The first step of this procedure consists in verifying the consistency of the shares. Anybody is able to perform this step by checking whether $g^{m_i} = g^m . \prod_{j=1}^{k-1} A_j^{x_i^j}$, obtained by exponentiating (1), is satisfied in G (Note that Δ includes g^m, g^{m_i}, A_j).

The second step consists in verifying that the pairs (σ_i^1, σ_i^2) really encrypt the discrete logarithms of public elements g^{m_i}. This verification is based on the fact that the discrete logarithm of $\sigma_i^1 = h^{\alpha_i}$ to the base h equals the double discrete logarithm of $g^{m_i \sigma_i^2} = g^{(y_i^{\alpha_i})}$ to the bases g and y_i. One may give a zero-knowledge interactive verification procedure between the dealer and participants as described on Fig. 1; we describe here the non-interactive version which is obtained by simulating the verifier by a hash function. We assume that the dealer randomly picked some values $w_{i,\ell} \in \mathbb{Z}/q\mathbb{Z}$ ($1 \le \ell \le L$ where $L \approx 100$ from [14]) for each share m_i and computed:

$$\delta_{i,\ell} := h^{w_{i,\ell}} \bmod p$$

$$\gamma_{i,\ell} := g^{y_i^{w_{i,\ell}}}$$

$$r_{i,\ell} := w_{i,\ell} - c_{i,\ell} \alpha_i \bmod q$$

where $c_{i,\ell}$ denotes the ℓ-th bit of $c_i = \mathcal{H}(g^{m_i}\|\sigma_i^1\|\sigma_i^2\|\delta_{i,1}\|\gamma_{i,1}\|...\|\delta_{i,L}\|\gamma_{i,L})$ with $\mathcal{H}$ a hash function from $\{0,1\}^*$ to $\{0,1\}^L$. Participants have therefore to check whether $\delta_{i,\ell} = h^{r_{i,\ell}}\sigma_i^{1c_{i,\ell}}$ mod p and $\gamma_{i,\ell} = (g^{1-c_{i,\ell}}g^{m_i c_{i,\ell}}\sigma_i^2)^{y_i^{r_{i,\ell}}}$ for all ℓ.

Δ finally contains g^m, the g^{m_i}s, the $r_{i,\ell}$s, the $\delta_{i,\ell}$s, the $\gamma_{i,\ell}$s, and A_j.

Reconstruction stage. Each participant P_i decrypts his own share m_i by computing

$$m_i = \frac{(\sigma_i^1)^{z_i}}{\sigma_i^2} \quad \text{mod } p.$$

A subset of k participants can then recover m by using the Lagrange's interpolation formula.

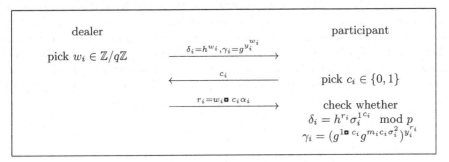

Fig. 1. Interactive verification procedure

3.3 Primitives

We define in this section some primitives which will be used in our protocol. These primitives are not related to a particular PVSS.

Signature. We consider P_o's authentication function S_o which, given a message m, outputs the signed version $m' = S_o(m)$ and the corresponding verification function V_o. Note that S_o is either a signature with message recovery or the concatenation of the message with the signature.

Item description. As is typically assumed in the literature, we suppose that P_o and P_r have committed to their items beforehand. We consider therefore that P_o and P_r established a legal agreement linking the authentic human-readable descriptions of the items with mathematical descriptions of these items $\text{descr}(m_o)$ and $\text{descr}(m_r)$. For instance, $\text{descr}(m) = \mathcal{W}(m) = g^m$. According to the fact that the authentic descriptions match the mathematical descriptions (a conflict at this layer can only be resolved by legal means), participants will be satisfied if they receive an item m which is consistent with its description $\text{descr}(m)$. To check that, we consider the public contract $\Omega = S_o(P_o\|P_r\|\mathrm{descr}(m_o)\|\mathrm{descr}(m_r)\|T)$, where T is the expiration date after what the exchange has to be considered as null and void.

Encryption. We consider P_i's encryption function E_i which, given a message m, outputs the encrypted message $m' = E_i(m)$ for P_i and the corresponding decryption function D_i such that, given an encrypted message m', outputs the plain message $m = D_i(m')$.

Verifiable secret sharing. We consider a publicly verifiable secret sharing scheme using the functions Share, Verify, and Recover. Given a message m and some participants P_i ($1 \le i \le n$), Share outputs the encrypted shares $E_1(m_1)$, ..., $E_n(m_n)$, and the proof Δ, as described in Section 3.2; given a list of encrypted shares, a list of participants, Δ, and $\mathrm{descr}(m)$, Verify outputs true if the shares allow any subset of k participants to recover m and false otherwise; given some shares m_{i_1}, ..., m_{i_k} and participants P_i ($i \in \{i_1, ..., i_k\}$), Recover outputs the message m.

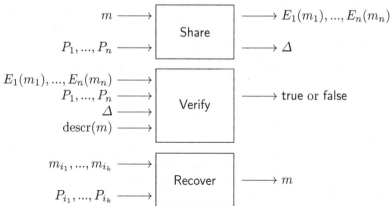

Verifiable encryption. We describe the CheckEnc function which is pretty similar to the Check function except that its input is $E_o(m)$ rather than m. This function is used by the *passive* participants. We will not detail this function for the sake of simplicity but it could come from a PVSS with a single participant. We only sketch the primitives related to CheckEnc:

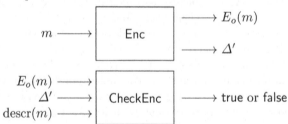

3.4 Description of the Protocols

Two participants P_o and P_r wish to exchange items m_o and m_r in a set of participants $\mathcal{P}$ such that $\mathcal{P} \subset Env_{P_o} \cap Env_{P_r}$ with $|\mathcal{P}| = n$. Note that for the sake of simplicity, we exclude P_o and P_r from $\mathcal{P}$, although it is not mandatory; so $\mathcal{P}$ contains only passive participants. Here are the exchange protocol and the recovery protocol.

Exchange protocol. The exchange protocol (Fig. 2) implies only the active participants, P_o and P_r, and consists in exchanging items m_o and m_r after a commitment step. This commitment gives to P_r the ability to restore fairness of the exchange, helped by the passive participants, in case of conflict with P_o.

- *Step 1:* P_o picks a random element a and computes b such that $m_o = a + b$. He computes $\mathsf{Share}(a, P_1, ..., P_n)$ and sends $E_1(a_1), ..., E_n(a_n), \Delta, \Omega, b$ to P_r.

- *Step 2:* P_r checks that $\mathsf{Verify}(E_1(a_1), ..., E_n(a_n), P_1, ..., P_n, \Delta, \mathsf{descr}(a))$ is true where $\mathsf{descr}(a)$ is deduced from $\mathsf{descr}(m_o)$ (extracted from Ω) and b, e.g. $g^a = g^m \times g^{-b}$; if the test succeeds then he sends m_r to P_o; otherwise he has just to wait until the expiration date T to give up the exchange.

- *Step 3:* P_o checks that m_r is correct running $\mathsf{Check}(m_r, \mathsf{descr}(m_r))$. If it is the case then P_o sends m_o to P_r. Otherwise, he has just to wait until the expiration date T in order to give up the exchange.

- *Step 4:* If P_r does not receive m_o or if $\mathsf{Check}(m_o, \mathsf{descr}(m_o))$ is false then he runs the recovery protocol.

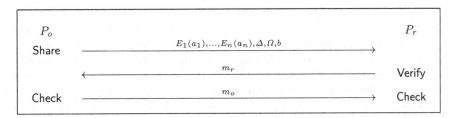

Fig. 2. Exchange protocol

Recovery protocol. The recovery protocol (Fig. 3) is started before $T - T_{\max}$ by the recipient, P_r, when he is injured, that is if the third message of the exchange, m_o, is wrong or missing.

- *Step 1:* P_r encrypts m_r for P_o and sends $E_i(a_i)$, $E_o(m_r)$, Δ', and Ω to P_i.

– *Step 2:* P_i computes $\mathsf{CheckEnc}(E_o(m_r), \mathrm{descr}(m_r), \Delta')$ where $\mathrm{descr}(m_r)$ is extracted from Ω; if the output is **true** and if the expiration date, contained in Ω, has not expired, P_i sends a_i to P_r and $E_o(m_r)$ to P_o.

– *Step 3:* after having received k shares, P_r runs $\mathsf{Recover}$. From a he computes $m_o = a + b$.

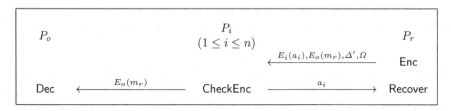

Fig. 3. Recovery protocol

Remark 4. In optimistic fair exchange protocols using TTP (e.g. [11]), the TTP is stateful: the TTP keeps in mind whether the **recovery** or **abort** protocol has already been performed. Due to our distributed architecture we cannot use this model here and we prefer using expiration dates.

4   Security Analysis

We prove in this section that our protocol is complete, fair, timely and respects the privacy property even in case of misbehaviors. We recall that the security parameter k, which is the threshold of the PVSS, is such that $b_2 < k \leq b_2 + b_1$. We defined in Section 2.2 the set of passive participants $\mathcal{B}_1$, $\mathcal{B}_2$, $\mathcal{B}_3$, and $\mathcal{B}_4$. We rewrite these definitions here according to our protocol defined in Section 3.4: $\mathcal{B}_1$: participants who honestly collaborate with both P_o and P_r; $\mathcal{B}_2$: participants P_i such that when P_r sends $E_i(a_i)$ to $P_i \in \mathcal{B}_2$, P_i decrypts $E_i(a_i)$ and sends a_i to P_r (even if the date is expired) but does not send m_r to P_o; $\mathcal{B}_3$: participants P_i such that when P_r sends $E_i(a_i)$ to $P_i \in \mathcal{B}_3$, P_i sends $E_o(m_r)$ to P_o (even if the date is expired) but does not decrypt $E_i(a_i)$ for P_r; $\mathcal{B}_4$: participants who do not collaborate at all. We denote M_1, M_2, and M_3 the three messages of the exchange protocol consisting respectively of $[E_1(a_1), ..., E_n(a_n), \Delta, \Omega, b]$, $[m_r]$, and $[m_o]$.

4.1   Completeness of the Protocol

Proving that the protocol is complete when P_o and P_r are honest is straightforward. In case of late discovery of M_3 due to communication protocol reasons, P_r runs the recovery protocol. Since $b_2 < k \leq b_2 + b_1$ we have at least k participants who will collaborate with P_r and at least one who will collaborate with P_o.

4.2   Fairness of the Protocol

We saw in the previous section that the protocol is fair if both active participants are honest. We explained furthermore in Section 2.2 that the case where both active participants are dishonest is not relevant.

P_o **is honest and** P_r **is dishonest.** Since P_o is honest, M_1 is correctly formed. On the other hand M_2 is wrong (or missing) otherwise both P_o and P_r would be honest. Here P_o can detect that M_2 is wrong using $\mathsf{Check}(m_r,\mathrm{descr}(m_r))$; therefore he does not transmit M_3 and waits for T. If P_r does not run the recovery protocol then nobody can obtain anything valuable on the expected items and the exchange is trivially fair. If P_r starts the recovery protocol after T then he cannot obtain m_o since $b_2 < k$. If P_r starts the recovery protocol before T (note that if he only contacts participants in $\mathcal{B}_2$ or $\mathcal{B}_4$ before T then we fall into the previous case) then P_o receives m_r from a passive participant either in $\mathcal{B}_1$ or $\mathcal{B}_3$; therefore the protocol is fair iff P_r can obtain m_o that is if and only if $b_1 + b_2 \geq k$.

P_o **is dishonest and** P_r **is honest.** Since P_o is dishonest, we consider the case where M_1 is wrong (or missing) and the case where M_1 is correct but M_3 is not (or missing). If M_1 is wrong (or missing), the exchange will die after T; indeed P_r can perform $\mathsf{Verify}(E_1(a_1), ..., E_n(a_n), P_1, ..., P_n, \Delta, \mathrm{descr}(a))$ and detects so that M_1 is wrong; he decides therefore not to disclose m_r. The exchange ends therefore on a trivially fair termination after T. Secondly, if M_1 is correct but M_3 is not (or missing): P_r can detect such a wrong M_3 using $\mathsf{Check}(m_o,\mathrm{descr}(m_o))$ and therefore start the recovery protocol. The fairness of the exchange relies thus on the ability of the passive participant to supply a to P_r, that is if and only if $b_1 + b_2 \geq k$. The fairness is so ensured since P_o has already received m_r in M_2.

4.3   Timeliness of the Protocol

Timeliness of the protocol is straightforward.

4.4   Privacy of the Protocol

Privacy of the protocol is straightforward. If the recovery protocol is not performed, then only information between P_o and P_r are exchanged and passive participants receive nothing. If the recovery protocol is used, then some participants receive shares of a_i. However, although k participants colluding can recover a, they cannot recover m_o since they do not know b. Obviously, they cannot discover m_r either. Privacy is here a great improvement with regard to previous optimistic fair exchange protocol where we usually assume that the trusted third party is able to regenerate expected items.

4.5   Complexity of the Protocol

When both P_o and P_r are honest, the complexity in terms of exchanged messages is very small since only the three messages of the exchange protocol are sent. When somebody misbehaves, the complexity obviously increases since the recovery procedure is performed. In the worst case, the n passive participants are contacted by P_r, each receives one message and sends at most two messages, so the complexity is only $O(3n)$ in terms of exchanged messages.

5 Conclusion

We proposed an optimistic two-party fair exchange protocol using publicly verifiable secret sharing. Our protocol is the first optimistic fair exchange protocol which does not rely on a centralized trusted third party. This concept is therefore particularly suitable for ad-hoc networks. We proved that our protocol ensures fairness and privacy even in quite dishonest environment and implies only low communication overheads. Our protocol works assuming that a majority of participants are honest or that only one is honest but we can estimate the number b_2 of participants who may harm P_o by colluding with P_r.

Acknowledgment. The work presented in this paper was supported (in part) by the National Competence Center in Research on Mobile Information and Communication Systems (NCCR-MICS), a center supported by the Swiss National Science Foundation under grant number 5005-67322.

References

1. N. Asokan, Matthias Schunter, and Michael Waidner. Optimistic protocols for fair exchange. In *Proceedings of 4th ACM Conference on Computer and Communications Security*, pages 7–17, Zurich, Switzerland, April 1997. ACM Press.
2. N. Asokan, Victor Shoup, and Michael Waidner. Asynchronous protocols for optimistic fair exchange. In *Proceedings of the IEEE Symposium on Research in Security and Privacy*, pages 86–99, Oakland, California, USA, May 1998. IEEE Computer Society Press.
3. Gildas Avoine and Serge Vaudenay. Fair exchange with guardian angels. In Kijoon Chae and Moti Yung, editors, *The 4th International Workshop on Information Security Applications – WISA 2003*, volume 2908 of *Lecture Notes in Computer Science*, pages 188–202, Jeju Island, Korea, August 2003. Springer-Verlag.
4. George Robert Blakley. Safeguarding cryptographic keys. In *National Computer Conference*, volume 48 of *American Federation of Information*, pages 313–317, 1979.
5. Ernest F. Brickell, David Chaum, Ivan B. Damgård, and Jeroen van de Graaf. Gradual and verifiable release of a secret. In Carl Pomerance, editor, *Advances in Cryptology – CRYPTO'87*, volume 293 of *Lecture Notes in Computer Science*, pages 156–166, Santa Barbara, CA, USA, August 1988. IACR, Springer-Verlag.
6. Benny Chor, Shafi Goldwasser, Silvio Micali, and Baruch Awerbuch. Verifiable secret sharing and achieving simultaneity in the presence of faults. In *Proceedings of the 26th IEEE Annual Symposium on Foundations of Computer Science – FOCS'85*, pages 383– 395, Portland, OR, USA, October 1985. IEEE.

7. Richard Cleve. Controlled gradual disclosure schemes for random bits and their applications. In Gilles Brassard, editor, *Advances in Cryptology – CRYPTO'89*, volume 435 of *Lecture Notes in Computer Science*, pages 573–588, Santa Barbara, California, USA, August 1990. IACR, Springer-Verlag.
8. Taher El Gamal. A public key cryptosystem and a signature scheme based on discrete logarithms. *IEEE Transactions on Information Theory*, 31(4):469–472, July 1985.
9. Shimon Even and Yacov Yacobi. Relations amoung public key signature systems. Technical Report 175, Computer Science Department, Technicon, Haifa, Israel, 1980.
10. Eiichiro Fujisaki and Tatsuaki Okamoto. A practical and provably secure scheme for publicly veriable secret sharing and its applications. In Nyberg Kaisa, editor, *Advances in Cryptology – EUROCRYPT'98*, volume 1403 of *Lecture Notes in Computer Science*, pages 32–46, Helsinki, Finland, May–June 1998. IACR, Springer-Verlag.
11. Olivier Markowitch and Shahrokh Saeednia. Optimistic fair exchange with transparent signature recovery. In *Financial Cryptography – FC'01*, Lecture Notes in Computer Science, Cayman Islands, February 2001. IFCA, Springer-Verlag.
12. Berry Schoenmakers. A simple publicly verifiable secret sharing scheme and its application to electronic voting. In Michael Wiener, editor, *Advances in Cryptology – CRYPTO'99*, volume 1666 of *Lecture Notes in Computer Science*, pages 148–164, Santa Barbara, California, USA, August 1999. IACR, Springer-Verlag.
13. Adi Shamir. How to share a secret. *Communications of the ACM*, 22(11):612–613, November 1979.
14. Markus Stadler. Publicly verifiable secret sharing. In Ueli Maurer, editor, *Advances in Cryptology – EUROCRYPT'96*, volume 1070 of *Lecture Notes in Computer Science*, pages 190–199, Saragossa, Spain, May 1996. IACR, Springer-Verlag.
15. Holger Vogt. Asynchronous optimistic fair exchange based on revocable items. In Rebecca N. Wright, editor, *Financial Cryptography – FC'03*, volume 2742 of *Lecture Notes in Computer Science*, Le Gosier, Guadeloupe, French West Indies, January 2003. IFCA, Springer-Verlag.

NGSCB: A Trusted Open System

Marcus Peinado, Yuqun Chen, Paul England, and John Manferdelli

Microsoft Corporation
Redmond, WA 98008
USA
{marcuspe,yuqunc,pengland,jmanfer}@microsoft.com

Abstract. We describe Microsoft's Next Generation Secure Computing Base (NGSCB). The system provides high assurance computing in a manner consistent with the commercial requirements of mass market systems. This poses a number of challenges and we describe the system architecture we have used to overcome them. We pay particular attention to reducing the trusted computing base to a small and manageable size. This includes operating the system without trusting the BIOS, most devices and device drivers and the bulk of the code of mass market operating systems. Furthermore, we seek to strengthen access control and network authentication in mass market systems by authenticating executable code at all system layers. We have implemented a prototype of the system and expect the full system to be mass deployed.

1 Introduction

A major challenge the computer industry is facing today is how to effectively protect the end users against a plethora of email viruses and network intrusions. An obvious solution is to make the desktop operating system and applications flawless and bug free. However, experience shows that this is an impractical goal. The reasons are threefold. Firstly, the rich functionality that users expect from mass-market operating systems makes them so large and complex that security bugs are nearly impossible to get rid off completely. Secondly, similar problems also apply to applications and device drivers. And finally, configuration and maintenance are non-trivial, such that users often misconfigure the system.

Security vulnerabilities exist largely due to software bugs. Some of these bugs are in the operating systems. Commercial operating systems have rapidly grown in size in order to provide ever richer user experiences. The use of advanced quality assurance methodology during the development process and rigorous testing can uncover and eliminate a large percentage of these bugs. However, a small number of software bugs will always remain. The problem is further compounded by the necessity to support an arbitrary number of devices in a consumer desktop operating system. A bug in a device driver may be exploited to subvert the system. Again, though stringent testing standards are successful at reducing the number of driver bugs, security vulnerabilities cannot be completely eliminated in complex device drivers.

These problems were recognized decades ago and led to the development of systems that focused on simplicity, correctness and security, rather than rich mass market functionality [5,25,11]. Despite their security merits, none of these systems was successful in

H. Wang et al. (Eds.): ACISP 2004, LNCS 3108, pp. 86–97, 2004.

the mass market, partly due to the fact that these systems were crafted for special-purpose, vertical market segments and hence lacked appeal to a broader user base. These highly specialized systems, no matter how secure they still are, would be even less appealing to today's users who have grown used to the rich experience on personal computers. What the user wants as a secure operating system is one that can provide the same rich functionality found on Windows, MacOS, and Linux as well as strong protection for a limited set of tasks that need such security guarantees (e.g. electronic banking).

In light of the virtual impossibility of providing ultimate security for a large mass market operating system, we opt to construct a safe execution environment that coexists with the mass-market operating system on a desktop – a tight security sanctuary on an otherwise bug-prone system. Such a platform would allow the user to run a few highly trusted applications without having to worry about interference from malicious applications, compromised operating systems, and subverted hardware devices. This alternative has a pragmatic attraction: The secure execution environment only has to support a few trusted applications. Its construction can therefore be highly specialized, reducing the code size by orders of magnitude, and lending itself to close scrutiny.

NGSCB, the Next-Generation Secure Computing Base (NGSCB) being developed by Microsoft, provides exactly this high-assurance runtime environment for trustworthy applications on a regular personal computer. This paper describes the NGSCB system architecture and some aspects of its implementation. Due to the page limit, we had to omit many details from this extended abstract. The full version of this paper is available at [16].

Section 2 lists the requirements under which the system was designed. Sections 3 and 4 describe how a safe execution environment and a mass market operating system can coexist on a single computer, with Section 3 summarizing existing approaches and their shortcomings and Section 4 providing a detailed description of our solution. Section 5 describes how a complete system can be configured. Section 6 discusses related work.

2   Requirements

NGSCB strives for a general-purpose, secure computing environment for running trusted applications. The task would be much simpler if we were to only concentrate on providing a set of application-specific hardware systems, for example a custom-designed terminal that allows secure, authenticated remote access by bank customers. This narrow approach may be suitable for a limited set of applications but would not meet the security demands of the majority of corporate customers and home users. From both the ergonomic and the economic point of view, it is safe to argue that most people would prefer a unified computing environment to an ever increasing number of home and office gadgets.

On such a system, security constraints must be devised to protect the trusted applications from the rest of the system, and to protect the interaction between the user and a trusted application, that between a trusted application and a remote service and that between a user and a remote service.

2.1   Security Requirements

More specifically, the execution environment must possess the following properties.

- No interference: The execution environment must provide a program that executes in it with the same underlying machine interface every time the program executes. The program must be isolated from external interference. A necessary condition is that a deterministic sequential program that does not access devices or persistent state should always reach the same result, irrespective of other programs that might have executed earlier or at the same time on the same machine.
- No observation: The computations and data of a program should not be observable by other entities, except for data the program chooses to reveal (e.g. through IPC).
- Trusted paths: A program should be able to receive data from a local input device (keyboard, mouse), such that only the program and the user of the input device share the data. Data integrity must be assured. A similar requirement applies to local output devices (video).
- Persistent storage: A program should be able to store data (e.g. cryptographic keys) persistently, such that the integrity and the confidentiality of the data are ensured.
- Communication: A program should be able to exchange data with another program, such that the integrity and the confidentiality of the data are ensured.
- Local authentication: A local user should be able to determine the identity of a program.
- Remote authentication: A program should be able to authenticate itself to a remote entity. For example, a corporate network administrator should be able to verify that all machines on his network are running the latest security patches and virus checker files.

Threat Model. The security properties listed above must hold in the presence of adversarial code (e.g. viruses) executing on the machine. We assume an adversary may execute his code not only in user mode but also in kernel (supervisor) mode. The adversarial code may also program certain devices (e.g. DMA controllers) to assist in the attack.

Our adversary model is significantly more powerful than common system security models. These models typically assume that adversarial application code may execute in user mode. Furthermore, they equate adversarial code executing in kernel mode with a complete breakdown of the system's security. Such assumptions are unrealistic, as the open architecture of personal computers entails the presence of a large number of often very complex device drivers, which are subject to different types of attacks by applications. Consequently, we chose a more powerful adversary model so as to avoid the unrealistic assumption that every single device driver is immune to such attacks.

Assurance. The system has to provide high assurance for its security features. Assurance is the confidence one has that a system will behave as specified [7,20]. Given some specified functionality for which high assurance is required, the *trusted computing base (TCB)* is defined as the collection of hardware and software components, on which this functionality depends. Based on vast empirical evidence and the current state of assurance methodology (formal methods, testing), it is generally believed that high assurance systems require a TCB that is small, simple and stable over time and centrally controlled and verified.

This paper focuses not on the assurance methodology,[1] but on the impact of the assurance requirement on system architecture. Several fundamental design choices described in this paper are the result of the need to keep the TCB small and simple, in order to make it 'assurable.' One such design decision, a salient feature of our system, is to exclude the mass market operating system and most device drivers from the TCB.

2.2 Commercial Requirements

In order to be commercially viable in a mass market environment, our system has to meet the following requirements:

– Open architecture: The system has to host a large class of hardware components and expose them to applications by means of device drivers. Many of the hardware components and peripherals of personal computers (CPU, chipset, graphics, storage, printers, imaging) are produced in different versions and with a variety of hardware interfaces by different vendors. This variety leads to a large number of hardware configurations, which increases continually as new devices become available. It leads to a similar number of software configurations, due to the fact that each new device requires an associated software driver. Our system has to operate in this very diverse hardware and software environment.
– No central authority: This requirement is closely related to the previous one. The system must not require a central authority (e.g. a certification authority) to 'approve' hardware or software before the system 'admits' it.
– Legacy support: The system must be compatible with existing mass market technology. That is, the system must be compatible with most existing peripheral devices and application programs. For example, most deployed PCI cards or USB devices should work in the new system. The system may only require very limited changes to core computer hardware (CPU, chipset) and operating system software. These changes must not lead to a significant increase in the production cost of platform hardware.
– Performance: The security-related features of the system must not deteriorate performance significantly (more than a few percent).

3 Existing Approaches and Problems

The security and assurance requirements call for a simple and constrained operating environment. In contrast, the commercial requirements call for the rich and diverse legacy operating environment of mass market personal computers. In particular, the latter must allow arbitrary devices to be attached to the system and support an open device driver model. The former has to exclude most device drivers, in order to be assurable.

The generic resolution to these conflicting requirements is to run two different operating systems in isolation on the same computer: one rich mass market operating system for all uses without special security requirements and one or more constrained operating

---

[1] We are using a combination of formal methods (specification, automatic verification) and rigorous testing.

systems that meet our security and assurance requirements. In this setting, it is of critical importance to protect these operating systems from each other. This task is performed by a third component: the isolation layer. Clearly, the isolation layer is part of the TCB, and it has to meet our assurance and security requirements.

Implementations of isolation layers that have been proposed in the past include microkernels [22], exokernels [9] and virtual machine monitors (VMM) [13]. In spite of their many merits, these systems fall short of addressing our requirements in several aspects. The rest of this section summarizes these deficiencies. Section 4 describes our isolation layer and how it solves these problems.

3.1   Assurance and Device Support

VMMs expose devices to their guest operating systems by *virtualizing* them. That is, a VMM intercepts a guest operating system's attempt to access a physical device and performs the *actual* device access on behalf of the guest, with possible modifications of the request and/or access-control checks. This allows the VMM to coordinate access requests from different guests and to share devices among them.

However, this approach requires a driver for each virtualized device to be part of the isolation layer (TCB). As described above, the set of devices that have to be supported in today's consumer environment is very large and diverse, and many device drivers are very complex. In this setting, any system that uses device virtualization for more than a very constrained collection of devices cannot meet the assurance requirement. This problem is exacerbated in the hosted VMM architecture (Type 2 VMM [24]), in which the VMM, rather than being a self-contained system with its own device drivers, executes within a host operating system and uses the device drivers of the latter. In the hosted VMM architecture, the TCB of the isolation layer is expanded to include even an entire operating system.

An alternative to device virtualization is to *export* devices to guest operating systems. The isolation layer controls only which guests can access a device. However, device accesses by guests are made directly to the device – without intervention by the isolation layer. Thus, the isolation layer does not have to include the device driver.

Unfortunately, this approach does not work on existing PC hardware. Mainstream personal computers give any DMA device unrestricted access to the full physical address space of the machine. Thus, a guest in control of a DMA device can circumvent any protection put in place by the isolation layer to protect guests from each other. It will have unrestricted access to most resources on the machine, including the parts of main memory that belong to the isolation layer or other guests.

In summary, any existing implementation of an isolation layer for mainstream personal computers suffers from at least one of the following problems: (1) It may severely restrict the set of devices that can be accessed on the machine. This solution does not meet our commercial requirements. (2) It may virtualize devices. This solution does not meet our assurance requirements. (3) It may export DMA devices. On existing PC hardware, this solution does not meet our security requirements.

3.2   Operating System Compatibility

There are two options regarding the interface between the isolation layer and its guests. VMMs try to expose the original hardware interface. This has the important benefit that existing off-the-shelf operating systems can be used as guests, but increases the complexity of the isolation layer. This increase in complexity is especially severe on PC hardware, since the instruction set of x86 CPUs is not virtualizable [23,24].

Other implementations of isolation layers (e.g. exokernel, microkernels) expose different interfaces, requiring new guest operating systems to be written [9] or existing operating systems to be modified [22,3]. These solutions, while possible in principle, are not appealing under our requirements, because of the development overhead they entail.

4   The Isolation Kernel

In light of the conflict between commercial and security requirements, we follow the approach outlined above of allowing several operating systems to execute on the same machine. Accesses by these operating systems to system resources (e.g. memory, devices) are controlled by an isolation layer. The operating system layer consists of copies of Windows or other operating systems and possibly instances of a smaller high assurance operating system. The hardware layer consists of standard hardware resources (CPU, RAM, MMU etc.) which are shared among the software components. Furthermore, the system contains a collection of devices and their device drivers.

This section describes the isolation layer and focuses on the design decisions we took to minimize its complexity. The isolation layer exposes the original hardware interface to all guests. In order to reflect the differences between our isolation layer and a regular VMM, we will call our isolation layer the *isolation kernel* for the rest of the paper.

4.1   CPU

We mentioned above that VMMs for the x86 CPU incur significant complexity due to the fact that the instruction set of the x86 is not virtualizable. For a virtualizable CPU instruction set, every instruction whose behavior depends on the ring in which it executes causes a trap into the most privileged ring [PG74]. The x86 CPU has four protection rings (ring 0 to 3). Existing operating system kernels typically execute in ring 0 (supervisor mode). Applications typically execute in ring 3 (user mode).

When a VMM is present, the VMM typically executes in the most privileged ring (ring 0 on the x86). Guest operating systems execute in a less privileged ring (ring 1 or ring 3). On a CPU with a virtualizable instruction set, the VMM can hide this ring change from the guest by appropriately reacting to all instruction traps it receives. However, the x86 instruction set contains 17 instructions that should trap, but do not [RI00], leaving the VMM with the complex task of identifying these instructions at runtime before they execute and compensating for their changed behavior.

In connection with NGSCB, upcoming versions of the x86 processor will introduce a new CPU mode that is strictly more privileged than the existing ring 0. Effectively, this amounts to a new ring -1. Our isolation kernel executes in this ring. Executing the isolation kernel in ring -1 allows us to execute guest operating systems in ring 0, thus avoiding the problems entailed by the fact that the x86 instruction set is not virtualizable.

4.2   Memory

A VMM has to partition the physical memory of the machine among multiple guests. That is, it must allow each guest to access some memory that no other guest can access. Furthermore, it has to reserve some memory for its own use. On most platforms, VMMs can use existing virtual memory hardware in CPUs and memory management units (MMUs) to enforce memory partitioning efficiently. Under virtual memory, instructions that execute on the CPU address memory through *virtual addresses*. Each virtual address is translated by the MMU into a *physical address*, which is used to access physical resources (RAM or memory mapped devices). The mapping is defined by software by means of editing – depending on the CPU type – either the translation-lookaside buffer (TLBs) or the page tables (on x86 processors).

Abstractly speaking, if a range of physical addresses is not in the image of the current mapping from virtual to physical addresses then this range of physical addresses is inaccessible unless the mapping is changed. Thus, by taking control of the data structures that control the virtual to physical mapping (page tables, TLBs), the VMM can confine the physical accesses a guest can make to any subset of the physical address space. The VMM can therefore partition the physical address space of the machine among its guests by controlling the virtual to physical mapping that is active for each guest. We use the well known shadow page table algorithm to implement this approach [21].

4.3   Devices

The isolation kernel does not support a general device driver model. It contains device-specific code for a very small collection of devices. This collection includes devices that are required in the configuration or operation of the isolation kernel and guest operating systems (e.g. disk, network card). The code to manage these devices is physically separated from the rest of the isolation kernel and executes as a guest.

All remaining devices, including most consumer peripherals (cameras, scanners, printers etc.) are assigned to and managed by guest operating systems. This obviates the need for driver code in the isolation kernel. The rest of this section describes these approaches in more detail and explains how we avoid the problems outlined in Section 3.

Exporting Non-essential Devices. On personal computer hardware, many devices are memory-mapped. That is, the control registers of a given device can be accessed by writing to or reading from certain physical addresses. The isolation kernel makes a device accessible to a guest by allowing the guest to map the control registers of the device into its virtual address space (cf. Sect. 4.2) – thus enabling the guest to read and write to these addresses. The isolation kernel controls which guest can access the device, but does not contain any device specific knowledge (device driver).

As mentioned above, on existing personal computer hardware, DMA devices have unrestricted access to the full physical address space. In this situation, a guest in control of a DMA device can circumvent the virtual memory based protections described in Sect. 4.2. In order to solve this problem, we have encouraged chipset manufacturers to change the hardware as follows.

Conceptually, we require an access control system [18]. In light of the need to minimize hardware cost and impact on performance, the system has to be very lightweight. We will begin by outlining the general concept and then discuss simplifications and implementation options.

Consider a set of resources (physical addresses), a set of subjects (software components or DMA devices) and a set of access modes (read, write). Given a state X of the system, the current access control policy is given by the function f that decides which access requests are allowed. More precisely, in state X, subject s should be allowed to access a resource r in mode a if and only if $f_X(r, s, a)$ is true.

Our general strategy is to store the DMA policy map f in main memory. The DMA policy is set by software (e.g. the isolation kernel) with write access to the memory region that stores f. The DMA policy map f is read and enforced by hardware: In the case where the protected resource is main memory, the memory controller or bus bridges can enforce the security policy. The policy will typically include the requirement that no DMA device under the control of a guest operating system has write access to the memory that stores f.

In the most general case, the isolation kernel could assign each DMA device read or write access rights to an arbitrary set of memory pages. In the other extreme, if all DMA devices are under the control of one guest operating system then it would be sufficient to allow the isolation kernel to deny all device access to a subset of main memory. A very simple concrete example of f, which is still useful, addresses resources at the granularity of pages and does not depend on subjects and access modes. This reduces the storage requirements for f to one bit per page and allows for very simple control logic in the memory controller: A page is inaccessible to all DMA devices if the bit is false. Otherwise, all DMA devices have read and write access to the page.

4.4   Access Control

The isolation kernel has to control access by guest operating systems to the resources under its control (e.g. memory, devices, IPC channels). The isolation kernel implements an access control system, in which programs (e.g. guest operating systems) – identified by an appropriately defined notion of code identity – can be security principals. The authentication of these programs can be rooted in hardware. We omit details due to the page limit. A description of the mechanisms employed can be found in [8] and [2]. Abadi [1] describes several applications.

4.5   Prototype Implementation

We have implemented a prototype of the system. The system runs on prototype hardware from various vendors. The isolation kernel comprises the isolation component that allows memory and devices to be assigned to a particular guest for its exclusive use. Furthermore, the isolation kernel prototype exposes interfaces that allow a guest to be booted, the system to be shut down and resources to be assigned to a different guest. The isolation kernel prototype consists of 2000 lines of C code, whose correctness has been verified with a theorem prover. Initial performance measurements on a regular PC (2.5 GHz Pentium 4) using standard benchmarks show that the impact of the isolation kernel on the performance of Windows XP is small. For example, the performance of Windows XP on the Winstone 2002 Content Creation benchmark [10] when hosted by our isolation kernel prototype comes within 5% of the native performance of Windows XP on the same benchmark. The prototype and the performance measurements are described in detail in [6].

5   System Overview

We are now ready to outline how the components and concepts described so far can be combined into a complete system. The missing piece are operating systems and applications that execute on the isolation kernel.

Possibly the most intuitive configuration would be to execute an existing mass market operating system along side and existing high assurance operating system, such as [14, 26]. The former provides access to most mass market devices and allows mass market applications to execute. The latter can be used for a reduced set of applications with special security needs (e.g. electronic banking).

Alternatively, the isolation kernel can host several instances of an existing mass market operating system, where some of these instances execute applications with special security needs. This configuration is similar to systems, such as [17].

Given sufficiently strong isolation between the VMs and appropriate security policies in the VMM, the need for high assurance in the operating system may be relaxed. For example, the VMM of [17] implemented mandatory access control for VMs running largely unmodified VMS. This approach is appealing for several reasons:

– The amount of code that requires high assurance is reduced. While the isolation kernel becomes somewhat more complex (see below), this added complexity does not amount to that of a full operating system.
– Being able to use a regular operating system simplifies application compatibility and provides more functionality to applications.

Clearly, reducing the assurance level of the operating system has implications for the rest of the system. If the isolation kernel implements mandatory access control (e.g. [4]), even corrupted operating systems are prevented from leaking information by the isolation kernel. However, in practice, it is extremely difficult to mitigate the covert channels of the PC platform to a meaningful level.

If the isolation kernel implements only discretionary access control, any application that can compromise the operating system can compromise all applications running in the same virtual machine. Even so, several useful configurations exist. For example, the problem disappears if each virtual machine can run exactly one application, and combinations of operating system and application cannot impersonate each other.

Implementing this approach requires the isolation kernel to make some devices available to the different VMs. The isolation kernel has two options for handling each device. It can (a) export it to a single VM or it can (b) virtualize it for all VMs. The main benefit of option (a) is reduced complexity in the isolation kernel. Given the device treatment described above, managing the keyboard, the mouse and the disk is sufficiently simple to let the isolation kernel virtualize these devices.

6   Related Work

Traditionally, high assurance systems have been built for settings (e.g. military) in which security concerns were paramount and existing mass market requirements were of little importance and not addressed. Examples include [5,11,17]. The SCOMP system [11] included hardware protections against DMA devices that allowed it to move the corresponding device drivers from the base layer to less critical parts of the system. [19, 15].

More recently, several monolithic secure operating systems, such as Eros [26] have been built for personal computers. SE/Linux [28] adds security features to a mass market operating system. None of these systems reconciles the conflict between the requirements of assurance (a manageable TCB) and those of the mass market (a large and complex set of device drivers as well as performance and functionality requirements on the operating system).

The Perseus system [22] uses a microkernel to host a modified version of Linux and 'secure applications'. The assurance problems posed by DMA device drivers in the base layer (microkernel) on open architectures are recognized in [22] but not solved. While [22] mentions the virtual address approach used by SCOMP, it dismisses it as unrealistic and instead assumes a small fixed set of simple hardware components, i.e. a closed hardware platform. Similar systems built by using regular VMMs [12] or Exokernels to host mass market and secure operating systems suffer from the same problem. In contrast, we have presented a solution that allows all DMA device drivers to be excluded from the TCB without violating safety or restricting the openness of the architecture.

Several recent papers [3,27] describe new VMMs or isolation kernels for PC hardware. In each case, simplifications of the VMM software and performance improvements are obtained by exposing a simplified virtual hardware interface to guest operating systems. While we have also described a modified VMM, our goals and our solutions differ from those of [3] and [27]. For example, neither system addresses the problem of supporting a large and diverse set of device drivers in a security setting. Xen [3] addresses the fact that the x86 CPU is not virtualizable by requiring modifications in guest operating systems. In contrast, we make use of hardware enhancements that make the x86 virtualizable and to which we have contributed.

7   Conclusions

We have described a system that reconciles the conflicting requirements of high assurance and the mass market. Our general approach has been to preserve the open architecture of mass market computers with its large and diverse hardware and software base and to build an execution environment that is isolated from it and requires only a far smaller trusted computing base. In particular, we have shown how device drivers can be excluded from the TCB in an open hardware environment and how memory can be protected efficiently from unauthorized CPU and device accesses. A common design choice has been to introduce simple hardware protections in order to exclude large bodies of code from the TCB. While working within the constraints of legacy personal computer hardware and software has been a challenge throughout the project, it is also a prerequisite for our main goal: bringing high-assurance computing to the broad mass market.

References

1. M. Abadi. Trusted computing, trusted third parties and verified communications. 2004.
2. M. Abadi and T. Wobber. A logical account of NGSCB. 2004.
3. P. Barham, B. Dragovic, K. Fraser, S. Hand, T. Harris, A. Ho, R. Neugebauer, I. Pratt, and A. Warfield. Xen and the art of virtualization. In *Proceedings of the 19th Symposium on Operating Systems Principles (SOSP'03)*, pages 164–177, 2003.
4. D. Bell and L. La Padula. Secure computer systems: Mathematical foundations and model. Technical Report M74-244, Mitre Corporation, 1975.
5. T. Berson and G. Barksdale. KSOS – a development methodology for a secure operating system. In *Proceedings of the 1979 AFIPS National Computer Conference*, pages 365–371, 1979.
6. Y. Chen, P. England, M. Peinado, and B. Willman. High assurance computing on open hardware architectures. Technical Report MSR-TR-2003-20, Microsoft Research, 2003.
7. DOD, Washington, DC. *Department of defense trusted computer system evaluation criteria*, December 1985. DOD 5200.28-STD.
8. P. England and M. Peinado. Authenticated operation of open computing devices. In *Information Security and Privacy – Proceedings of ACISP 2002*, pages 346–361, 2002.
9. D. Engler, M. F. Kaashoek, and J. O'Toole, Jr. Exokernel: An operating system architecture for application-level resource management. In *Proceedings of the 15th Symposium on Operating Systems Principles (15th SOSP'95), Operating Systems Review*, pages 251–266, 1995.
10. eTestingLab. Business Winstone 2002 and Multimedia Content Creation Winstone 2002, 2002. http://www.winstone.com.
11. L. Fraim. Scomp: A solution to the multilevel security problem. *IEEE Computer*, 16:26–34, 1983.
12. T. Garfinkel, B. Pfaff, J. Chow, M. Rosenblum, and D. Boneh. Terra: A virtual-machine based platform for trusted computing. In *Proceedings of the 19th Symposium on Operating Systems Principles (SOSP'03)*, 2003.
13. T. Garfinkel, M. Rosenblum, and D. Boneh. A broader vision of trusted computing. In *Proceedings of the 9th USENIX Workshop on Hot Topics in Operating Systems (HotOS-IX)*, 2003.
14. H. Härtig, M. Hohmuth, J. Liedtke, S. Schönberg, and J. Wolter. The performance of μ-kernel-based systems. In *Proceedings of the 16th Symposium on Operating Systems Principles (SOSP'97)*, 1997.
15. Hermann Härtig. Security architectures revisited, 2002.
16. http://research.microsoft.com/research/pubs/.
17. P. Karger, M. Zurko, D. Bonin, A. Mason, and C. Kahn. A restrospective on the VAX VMM security kernel. *IEEE Transactions on Software Engineering*, 17(11):1147–1165, November 1991.

18. B. Lampson. Protection. *ACM Operating Systems Review*, 8(1):18–24, 1974.
19. B. Leslie and G. Heiser. Towards untrusted device drivers. Technical Report UNSW-CSE-TR-0303, University of New South Wales, 2003.
20. NIST. *Common Criteria for Information Technology Security Evaluation*, version 2.1 edition, August 1999.
21. R. Parmelee, T. Peterson, C. Tillman, and D. Hatfield. Virtual storage and virtual machine concepts. *IBM Systems Journal*, 11(2):99–130, 1972.
22. B. Pfitzmann, J. Riordan, C. Stüble, M. Waidner, and A. Weber. The Perseus system architecture. Technical report, IBM Research Division, 2001.
23. G. Popek and R. Goldberg. Formal requirements for virtualizable third generation architectures. *Communications of the ACM*, 17(7):412–421, 1974.
24. J. Robin and C. Irvine. Analysis of the Intel Pentium's ability to support a secure virtual machine monitor. In *Proceedings of the 9th USENIX Security Symposium (SECURITY-00)*, pages 129–144. The USENIX Association, 2000.
25. R. Schell, T. Tao, and M. Heckman. Designing the GEMSOS security kernel for security and performance. In *Proceedings of the 8th DoD/NBS Computer Security Conference*, pages 108–119, 1985.
26. J. Shapiro, J. Smith, and D. Faber. EROS: a fast capability system. In *Proceedings of the 17th Symposium on Operating Systems Principles (SOSP-99)*, Operating Systems Review, pages 170–185. ACM Press, 1999.
27. A. Whitaker, M. Shaw, and S. Gribble. Scale and performance in the Denali isolation kernel. In *Proceedings of the 5th Symposium on Operating Systems Design and Implementation (OSDI'02)*, pages 195–209, 2002.
28. C. Wright, C. Cowan, S. Smalley, J. Morris, and G. Kroah-Hartman. Linux security modules: General security support in the Linux kernel. In *Proceedings of the 11th USENIX Security Symposium*, 2002.

The Biryukov-Demirci Attack on Reduced-Round Versions of IDEA and MESH Ciphers

Jorge Nakahara, Jr.[*], Bart Preneel, and Joos Vandewalle

Katholieke Universiteit Leuven, Dept. ESAT/SCD-COSIC, Belgium
jorge_nakahara@yahoo.com.br,
{bart.preneel,joos.vandewalle}@esat.kuleuven.ac.be

Abstract. This paper presents a dedicated known-plaintext attack on up to four rounds of the IDEA cipher, that trades-off a small number of known data blocks (114) for a larger time complexity (2^{114}). This attack is also applied to up to 2.5-round MESH block ciphers, but are not more effective than previously known attacks. An advantage of this attack compared to previous known-plaintext attacks on IDEA/MESH is that no assumptions on the key value are required. Chosen-plaintext and chosen-plaintext-adaptively-chosen-ciphertext attacks can reach the full 8.5-round IDEA, and up to 5.5-round MESH ciphers, but always under weak-key assumptions.

Keywords: Cryptanalysis, IDEA and MESH ciphers, known-plaintext attack.

1 Introduction

IDEA [14] is a block cipher operating on 64-bit blocks, using a 128-bit key and consisting of 8 rounds plus an output transformation (OT). This cipher evolved from the PES cipher [15]. The security of IDEA is based on the mixing of three group operations on 16-bit words: exclusive-or, denoted $\oplus$, addition in $\mathbb{Z}_{2^{16}}$, denoted $\boxplus$, and multiplication in $GF(2^{16} + 1)$, denoted $\odot$, with $0 \equiv 2^{16}$. MESH [13] is a family of block ciphers with variable block size (64, 96, or 128 bits), and that use the same group operations of IDEA. IDEA became widely known because it was embedded in the popular Pretty Good Privacy software package from Philip Zimmermann [9], for general purpose file encryption.

Table 1 lists previously known attacks on IDEA and compares them with the attacks described in this paper. Table 2 lists attacks [13] on the MESH ciphers and compares their complexities with the attacks described in this paper.

The motivation for this paper is an observation by A. Biryukov [2] that in the computational graph of IDEA the two middle 16-bit words in a block are only combined with subkeys or internal cipher data via two group operations,

---

[*] Sponsored by the Katholieke Universiteit Leuven, and partially by GOA project Mefisto 2000/06 of the Flemish Government.

H. Wang et al. (Eds.): ACISP 2004, LNCS 3108, pp. 98–109, 2004.

$\boxplus$ and $\oplus$, across the full cipher, and for any number of rounds. Thus, restricted to the least significant bit, their xor combination results in a linear trail with probability one. The first and fourth words in a block are combined only via $\oplus$ and $\odot$ across the full cipher. Notice that this property does not hold in PES [15], where all words in a block are combined across the cipher with all the three group operations.

This paper is organized as follows: Sect. 2 describes a known-plaintext attack on up to 4-round IDEA; Sect. 3 applies the same reasoning for up to 2-round MESH-64. The attacks on MESH-96 and MESH-128 are similar and also reach up to 2 rounds for each of them. Section 4 concludes the paper, comparing the attack complexities for reduced-round IDEA and MESH ciphers.

2   A Known-Plaintext Attack on Reduced-Round IDEA

The core of a round in IDEA and MESH ciphers is the MA-box or Multiplication-Addition box. It is composed of a series of multiplications and additions, alternated, and computed in a zig-zag order (Fig. 1). Let (n_i, q_i) and (r_i, s_i) denote the inputs and outputs to the i-th MA-box of IDEA, and (P_1, P_2, P_3, P_4), (C_1, C_2, C_3, C_4) be a plaintext and ciphertext after 8.5 rounds. If one tracks the value of the input and output of only the two middle words in a block, the results are:

$$((((((((P_2 \boxplus Z_2^{(1)}) \oplus r_1 \boxplus Z_3^{(2)}) \oplus s_2 \boxplus Z_2^{(3)}) \oplus r_3 \boxplus Z_3^{(4)}) \oplus s_4 \boxplus$$
$$Z_2^{(5)}) \oplus r_5 \boxplus Z_3^{(6)}) \oplus s_6 \boxplus Z_2^{(7)}) \oplus r_7 \boxplus Z_3^{(8)}) \oplus s_8 \boxplus Z_2^{(9)} = C_3, \qquad (1)$$

$$((((((((P_3 \boxplus Z_3^{(1)}) \oplus s_1 \boxplus Z_2^{(2)}) \oplus r_2 \boxplus Z_3^{(3)}) \oplus s_3 \boxplus Z_2^{(4)}) \oplus r_4 \boxplus$$
$$Z_3^{(5)}) \oplus s_5 \boxplus Z_2^{(6)}) \oplus r_6 \boxplus Z_3^{(7)}) \oplus s_7 \boxplus Z_2^{(8)}) \oplus r_8 \boxplus Z_2^{(9)} = C_2. \qquad (2)$$

Equations (1) and (2) still hold with probability one, if restricted only to the least significant bit (lsb_1):

$$\mathrm{lsb}_1(P_2 \oplus Z_2^{(1)} \oplus r_1 \oplus Z_3^{(2)} \oplus s_2 \oplus Z_2^{(3)} \oplus r_3 \oplus Z_3^{(4)} \oplus s_4 \oplus Z_2^{(5)} \oplus$$
$$r_5 \oplus Z_3^{(6)} \oplus s_6 \oplus Z_2^{(7)} \oplus r_7 \oplus Z_3^{(8)} \oplus s_8 \oplus Z_2^{(9)} \oplus C_3) = 0, \qquad (3)$$

$$\mathrm{lsb}_1(P_3 \oplus Z_3^{(1)} \oplus s_1 \oplus Z_2^{(2)} \oplus r_2 \oplus Z_3^{(3)} \oplus s_3 \oplus Z_2^{(4)} \oplus r_4 \oplus Z_3^{(5)} \oplus$$
$$s_5 \oplus Z_2^{(6)} \oplus r_6 \oplus Z_3^{(7)} \oplus s_7 \oplus Z_2^{(8)} \oplus r_8 \oplus Z_2^{(9)} \oplus C_2) = 0. \qquad (4)$$

If only the xor of the LSBs of r_i and s_i could be discovered, then two bits of information on the key, namely

$$\mathrm{lsb}_1(Z_2^{(1)} \oplus Z_3^{(2)} \oplus Z_2^{(3)} \oplus Z_3^{(4)} \oplus Z_2^{(5)} \oplus Z_3^{(6)} \oplus Z_2^{(7)} \oplus Z_3^{(8)} \oplus Z_3^{(9)}),$$

and

$$\mathrm{lsb}_1(Z_3^{(1)} \oplus Z_2^{(2)} \oplus Z_3^{(3)} \oplus Z_2^{(4)} \oplus Z_3^{(5)} \oplus Z_2^{(6)} \oplus Z_3^{(7)} \oplus Z_2^{(8)} \oplus Z_2^{(9)}),$$

could be derived for IDEA, and similarly for any number of rounds. The following analysis combines this observation by Biryukov, and the approach by Demirci in [7]. The analysis starts with 1.5-round IDEA (the first 1.5 rounds in Fig. 1).

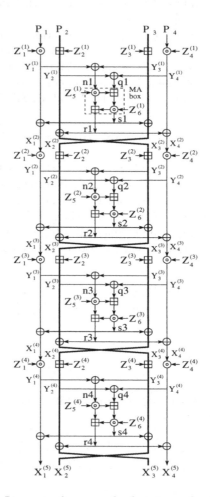

Fig. 1. Linear trails across the first 4 rounds of IDEA.

Let $(X_1^{(i)}, X_2^{(i)}, X_3^{(i)}, X_4^{(i)})$ denote the i-th round input, and $(Y_1^{(i)}, Y_2^{(i)}, Y_3^{(i)}, Y_4^{(i)})$ the output after the i-th key mixing. The value n_1 can be computed as follows:

$$n_1 = (P_1 \odot Z_1^{(1)}) \oplus (P_3 \boxplus Z_3^{(1)}) = (Y_1^{(2)} \odot (Z_1^{(2)})^{-1}) \oplus (Y_2^{(2)} \boxminus Z_2^{(2)}). \qquad (5)$$

Demirci's relation for the least significant bits of (r_1, s_1) is[1]:

$$\text{lsb}_1(r_1 \oplus s_1) = \text{lsb}_1(n_1 \odot Z_5^{(1)}). \tag{6}$$

Following the input and output of the two middle words in a block gives:

$$\text{lsb}_1(P_2 \oplus Z_2^{(1)} \oplus r_1 \oplus Z_3^{(2)}) = \text{lsb}_1(Y_3^{(2)}), \tag{7}$$

$$\text{lsb}_1(P_3 \oplus Z_3^{(1)} \oplus s_1 \oplus Z_2^{(2)}) = \text{lsb}_1(Y_2^{(2)}). \tag{8}$$

From the xor-combination of (6), (7) and (8):

$$\text{lsb}_1(Y_2^{(2)} \oplus Y_3^{(2)} \oplus Z_2^{(2)} \oplus Z_3^{(2)} \oplus P_2 \oplus Z_2^{(1)} \oplus P_3 \oplus Z_3^{(1)}) = \text{lsb}_1(n_1 \odot Z_5^{(1)}). \tag{9}$$

Expressions (5) and (9), plus the key overlapping property in the key schedule of IDEA provide the one-bit distinguisher (10), which allows to recover 49 bits of information on the key: $Z_5^{(1)}$, $Z_1^{(1)}$, $Z_3^{(1)}$, and $\text{lsb}_1(Z_2^{(2)} \oplus Z_3^{(2)} \oplus Z_2^{(1)} \oplus Z_3^{(1)})$, using only known plaintext/ciphertext data $(P_i, Y_i^{(2)})$, $1 \le i \le 4$:

$$\text{lsb}_1(Y_2^{(2)} \oplus Y_3^{(2)} \oplus Z_2^{(2)} \oplus Z_3^{(2)} \oplus P_2 \oplus Z_2^{(1)} \oplus P_3 \oplus Z_3^{(1)} \oplus$$
$$Z_5^{(1)} \odot ((P_1 \odot Z_1^{(1)}) \oplus (P_3 \boxplus Z_3^{(1)}))) = 0. \tag{10}$$

Expression (10) consists of nine $\oplus$, two $\odot$ and one $\boxplus$, equivalent[2] to 16 $\oplus$, or $16/30 = 8/15$ of the cost of 1.5-round IDEA. The attack recovers 49 bits of the key (numbered 0–15, 32–47, and the xor of bits numbered 31, 40 and 127) with about 49 known plaintext/ciphertext pairs, and time complexity about $\frac{8}{15} \cdot 2^{49} \approx 2^{48}$ 1.5-round IDEA computations. Note that it is a known-plaintext attack without any weak-key assumption.

An attack on 2.5-round IDEA (the first 2.5-rounds in Fig. 1) follows a similar procedure. Note that the xor of the LSBs of the input and output of the two middle words in a block gives:

$$\text{lsb}_1(P_2 \oplus Z_2^{(1)} \oplus r_1 \oplus Z_3^{(2)} \oplus s_2 \oplus Z_2^{(3)}) = \text{lsb}_1(Y_2^{(3)}), \tag{11}$$

$$\text{lsb}_1(P_3 \oplus Z_3^{(1)} \oplus s_1 \oplus Z_2^{(2)} \oplus r_2 \oplus Z_3^{(3)}) = \text{lsb}_1(Y_3^{(3)}). \tag{12}$$

Demirci's relation for one-round IDEA results in:

$$\text{lsb}_1(r_1 \oplus s_1) = \text{lsb}_1(Z_5^{(1)} \odot ((P_1 \odot Z_1^{(1)}) \oplus (P_3 \boxplus Z_3^{(1)}))), \tag{13}$$

---

[1] There are alternative relations such as $\text{lsb}(s_1 \odot (Z_6^{(i)})^{\boxdot 1}) = \text{lsb}(n_1 \odot Z_5^{(1)} \boxplus q_1)$, but it is dependent on both inputs and both subkeys, thus less attractive than (6).

[2] One $\odot$ costs about three times one $\boxplus$ or $\oplus$.

$$\mathrm{lsb}_1(r_2 \oplus s_2) = \mathrm{lsb}_1(Z_5^{(2)} \odot ((Y_1^{(3)} \odot (Z_1^{(3)})^{-1}) \oplus (Y_2^{(3)} \boxminus Z_2^{(3)}))). \tag{14}$$

Combining (11), (12), (13), and (14) gives a one-bit distinguisher that involves 90 user key bits (numbered 64–79, 0–15, 32–47, 57–72, 89–104, 105–120, and the exclusive-or of key bits numbered 31, 47, 40, 120, 8), according to the key schedule of IDEA:

$$\mathrm{lsb}_1(P_2 \oplus Z_2^{(1)} \oplus P_3 \oplus Z_3^{(1)} \oplus Z_3^{(2)} \oplus Z_2^{(3)} \oplus Y_2^{(3)} \oplus Z_2^{(2)} \oplus Z_3^{(3)} \oplus$$
$$Y_3^{(3)}) = \mathrm{lsb}_1(r_1 \oplus s_1) \oplus \mathrm{lsb}_1(r_2 \oplus s_2) = \mathrm{lsb}_1(Z_5^{(1)} \odot ((P_1 \odot Z_1^{(1)}) \oplus$$
$$(P_3 \boxminus Z_3^{(1)}))) \oplus \mathrm{lsb}_1(Z_5^{(2)} \odot ((Y_1^{(3)} \odot (Z_1^{(3)})^{-1}) \oplus (Y_2^{(3)} \boxminus Z_2^{(3)}))). \tag{15}$$

Expression (15) contains 12 $\oplus$, 4 $\odot$ and 2 $\boxminus$, equivalent to 26 $\oplus$ or 26/52 of the cost of 2.5-round IDEA. Expression (15) allows recovery of subkey bits $Z_5^{(1)}$, $Z_1^{(1)}$, $Z_3^{(1)}$, $Z_5^{(2)}$, $Z_1^{(3)}$, $Z_2^{(3)}$, and $\mathrm{lsb}_1(Z_2^{(1)} \oplus Z_3^{(1)} \oplus Z_3^{(2)} \oplus Z_2^{(3)} \oplus Z_2^{(2)} \oplus Z_3^{(3)})$, with about 90 known plaintexts, and $\frac{26}{52} \cdot 2^{90} = 2^{89}$ 2.5-round IDEA computations.

An attack on 3.5-round IDEA (the first 3.5 rounds in Fig. 1) uses the fact that the exclusive-or of the LSBs of the input and output of the two middle words in a block gives:

$$\mathrm{lsb}_1(P_2 \oplus Z_2^{(1)} \oplus r_1 \oplus Z_3^{(2)} \oplus s_2 \oplus Z_2^{(3)} \oplus r_3 \oplus Z_3^{(4)}) = \mathrm{lsb}_1(Y_3^{(4)}), \tag{16}$$

$$\mathrm{lsb}_1(P_3 \oplus Z_3^{(1)} \oplus s_1 \oplus Z_2^{(2)} \oplus r_2 \oplus Z_3^{(3)} \oplus s_3 \oplus Z_2^{(4)}) = \mathrm{lsb}_1(Y_2^{(4)}). \tag{17}$$

Combining (16) and (17) gives:

$$\mathrm{lsb}_1(P_2 \oplus Z_2^{(1)} \oplus Z_3^{(2)} \oplus Z_2^{(3)} \oplus Z_3^{(4)} \oplus P_3 \oplus Z_3^{(1)} \oplus Z_2^{(2)} \oplus Z_3^{(3)} \oplus$$
$$Z_2^{(4)} \oplus Y_3^{(4)} \oplus Y_2^{(4)}) = \mathrm{lsb}_1(r_1 \oplus s_1) \oplus \mathrm{lsb}_1(r_2 \oplus s_2) \oplus \mathrm{lsb}_1(r_3 \oplus s_3). \tag{18}$$

Using Demirci's relation for one-round IDEA, results in:

$$\mathrm{lsb}_1(r_2 \oplus s_2) = \mathrm{lsb}_1(Z_5^{(2)} \odot ((Y_1^{(3)} \odot (Z_1^{(3)})^{-1}) \oplus (Y_2^{(3)} \boxminus Z_2^{(3)}))) =$$
$$\mathrm{lsb}_1(Z_5^{(2)} \odot ((((Y_1^{(4)} \odot (Z_1^{(4)})^{-1} \oplus s_3) \odot (Z_1^{(3)})^{-1})) \oplus$$
$$((Y_3^{(4)} \boxminus Z_3^{(4)}) \oplus r_3 \boxminus Z_2^{(3)}))), \tag{19}$$

$$\mathrm{lsb}_1(r_3 \oplus s_3) = \mathrm{lsb}_1(Z_5^{(3)} \odot ((Y_1^{(4)} \odot (Z_1^{(4)})^{-1}) \oplus (Y_2^{(4)} \boxminus Z_2^{(4)}))). \tag{20}$$

For (19) the individual values of r_3 and s_3 are needed:

$$s_3 = (((Y_1^{(4)} \odot (Z_1^{(4)})^{-1}) \oplus (Y_2^{(4)} \boxminus Z_2^{(4)})) \odot Z_5^{(3)} \boxplus$$
$$((Y_3^{(4)} \boxminus Z_3^{(4)}) \oplus (Y_4^{(4)} \odot (Z_4^{(4)})^{-1})) \odot Z_6^{(3)}), \tag{21}$$

$$r_3 = s_3 \boxplus (((Y_1^{(4)} \odot (Z_1^{(4)})^{-1}) \oplus (Y_2^{(4)} \boxminus Z_2^{(4)})) \odot Z_5^{(3)}). \tag{22}$$

Combining (13), (18), (19), (20), (21) and (22) contains 14 $\odot$, 10 $\boxplus$ and 20 $\oplus$, which is equivalent to 72 $\oplus$. This combination gives a one-bit distinguisher to recover 112 key bits (numbered 0–17, 32–47, 50–127), according to the key schedule of IDEA, using about 112 known plaintexts, and $\frac{72}{74} \cdot 2^{112} \approx 2^{112}$ 3.5-round IDEA computations. The subkeys involved are $Z_5^{(1)}$, $Z_1^{(1)}$, $Z_3^{(1)}$, $Z_5^{(2)}$, $Z_1^{(3)}$, $Z_2^{(3)}$, $Z_1^{(4)}$, $Z_2^{(4)}$, $Z_5^{(3)}$, $Z_3^{(4)}$, $Z_4^{(4)}$, $Z_6^{(3)}$, and $\mathrm{lsb}_1(Z_2^{(1)} \oplus Z_3^{(2)} \oplus Z_2^{(3)} \oplus Z_3^{(4)} \oplus Z_3^{(1)} \oplus Z_2^{(2)} \oplus Z_3^{(3)} \oplus Z_2^{(4)})$.

An attack on the first 4 rounds of IDEA (Fig. 1) uses the fact that the exclusive-or of the LSBs of the input and output of the two middle words in a block gives:

$$\mathrm{lsb}_1(P_2 \oplus Z_2^{(1)} \oplus r_1 \oplus Z_3^{(2)} \oplus s_2 \oplus Z_2^{(3)} \oplus r_3 \oplus Z_3^{(4)} \oplus s_4) = \mathrm{lsb}_1(X_2^{(5)}), \quad (23)$$

$$\mathrm{lsb}_1(P_3 \oplus Z_3^{(1)} \oplus s_1 \oplus Z_2^{(2)} \oplus r_2 \oplus Z_3^{(3)} \oplus s_3 \oplus Z_2^{(4)} \oplus r_4) = \mathrm{lsb}_1(X_3^{(5)}). \quad (24)$$

Combining (23) and (24) results in:

$$\mathrm{lsb}_1(P_2 \oplus Z_2^{(1)} \oplus Z_3^{(2)} \oplus Z_2^{(3)} \oplus Z_3^{(4)} \oplus P_3 \oplus Z_3^{(1)} \oplus Z_2^{(2)} \oplus Z_3^{(3)} \oplus$$
$$Z_2^{(4)} \oplus X_3^{(5)} \oplus X_2^{(5)}) = \mathrm{lsb}_1(r_1 \oplus s_1) \oplus \mathrm{lsb}_1(r_2 \oplus s_2) \oplus$$
$$\mathrm{lsb}_1(r_3 \oplus s_3) \oplus \mathrm{lsb}_1(r_4 \oplus s_4). \quad (25)$$

Using Demirci's relation for one-round IDEA, results in:

$$\mathrm{lsb}_1(r_2 \oplus s_2) = \mathrm{lsb}_1(Z_5^{(2)} \odot ((P_1 \odot Z_1^{(1)} \oplus \qquad\qquad (26)$$
$$s_1) \odot Z_1^{(2)} \oplus (((P_2 \boxplus Z_2^{(1)}) \oplus r_1) \boxplus Z_3^{(2)}))),$$

$$\mathrm{lsb}_1(r_3 \oplus s_3) = \mathrm{lsb}_1(Z_5^{(3)} \odot ((Y_1^{(4)} \odot (Z_1^{(4)})^{-1}) \oplus (Y_2^{(4)} \boxminus Z_2^{(4)}))), \quad (27)$$

$$\mathrm{lsb}_1(r_4 \oplus s_4) = \mathrm{lsb}_1((X_1^{(5)} \oplus X_2^{(5)}) \odot Z_5^{(4)}). \quad (28)$$

For (27) the individual values of r_1 and s_1 are needed:

$$s_1 = (((P_1 \odot Z_1^{(1)}) \oplus (P_3 \boxplus Z_3^{(1)})) \odot Z_5^{(1)} \boxplus ((P_2 \boxplus Z_2^{(1)}) \oplus (P_4 \odot Z_4^{(1)}))) \odot Z_6^{(1)}, \quad (29)$$

$$r_1 = s_1 \boxplus ((P_1 \odot Z_1^{(1)}) \oplus (P_3 \boxplus Z_3^{(1)})) \odot Z_5^{(1)}. \quad (30)$$

For (27) the individual values of $Y_1^{(4)}$ and $Y_2^{(4)}$ are needed:

$$Y_1^{(4)} = X_1^{(5)} \oplus s_4 = X_1^{(5)} \oplus ((X_1^{(5)} \oplus X_2^{(5)}) \odot Z_5^{(4)} \boxplus (X_3^{(5)} \oplus X_4^{(5)})) \odot Z_6^{(4)}, \quad (31)$$

$$Y_2^{(4)} = X_3^{(5)} \oplus r_4 = X_3^{(5)} \oplus (s_4 \boxplus (X_1^{(5)} \oplus X_2^{(5)}) \odot Z_5^{(4)}). \tag{32}$$

Combining (13), (25), (27), (27), (28), (29), (30), (31), and (32) gives 17 $\odot$, 11 $\boxplus$ and 25 $\oplus$, which is equivalent to about 87 $\oplus$. This combination gives a one-bit distinguisher to recover 114 key bits (numbered 0-113 according to the key schedule of IDEA), requiring about 114 known plaintexts and $\frac{87}{88} \cdot 2^{114} \approx 2^{114}$ 4-round IDEA computations. The subkeys involved are $Z_1^{(1)}$, $Z_3^{(1)}$, $Z_5^{(1)}$, $Z_5^{(2)}$, $Z_1^{(2)}$, $Z_2^{(1)}$, $Z_3^{(2)}$, $Z_4^{(1)}$, $Z_6^{(1)}$, $Z_5^{(3)}$, $Z_1^{(4)}$, $Z_2^{(4)}$, $Z_5^{(4)}$, $Z_6^{(4)}$, and $\mathrm{lsb}_1(Z_2^{(1)} \oplus Z_3^{(2)} \oplus Z_2^{(3)} \oplus Z_3^{(4)} \oplus Z_3^{(1)} \oplus Z_2^{(2)} \oplus Z_3^{(3)} \oplus Z_2^{(4)})$.

An attack on the first 4.5 rounds would involve all 128 key bits and would therefore not be more efficient than an exhaustive key search.

3   The Biryukov-Demirci Attack on MESH-64

Similar attacks to the previous section can be applied to at most two rounds of MESH-64 [13], with an effort less than that of an exhaustive key search.

To attack 1.5-round MESH-64, there are two possible trails to follow in the graph of Fig. 2.

Consider first the trails involving the two middle words in a block:

$$\mathrm{lsb}_1(P_2 \oplus Z_2^{(1)} \oplus r_1) = \mathrm{lsb}_1(Y_3^{(2)} \odot (Z_3^{(2)})^{-1}), \tag{33}$$

$$\mathrm{lsb}_1(P_3 \oplus Z_3^{(1)} \oplus s_1) = \mathrm{lsb}_1(Y_2^{(2)} \odot (Z_2^{(2)})^{-1}). \tag{34}$$

Combining (33) and (34) results in:

$$\mathrm{lsb}_1(P_2 \oplus Z_2^{(1)} \oplus P_3 \oplus Z_3^{(1)} \oplus Y_3^{(2)} \odot (Z_3^{(2)})^{-1} \oplus Y_2^{(2)} \odot (Z_2^{(2)})^{-1}) = \mathrm{lsb}_1(r_1 \oplus s_1). \tag{35}$$

The right hand side of (35) can be represented as:

$$\begin{aligned} \mathrm{lsb}_1(r_1 \oplus s_1) = \quad & \mathrm{lsb}_1((((P_1 \odot Z_1^{(1)}) \oplus (P_3 \boxplus Z_3^{(1)})) \odot Z_5^{(1)} \boxplus \\ & ((P_2 \boxplus Z_2^{(1)}) \oplus (P_4 \odot Z_4^{(1)}))) \odot Z_6^{(1)}) \end{aligned} \tag{36}$$

$$\begin{aligned} = & \mathrm{lsb}_1((((Y_1^{(2)} - Z_1^{(2)}) \oplus (Y_2^{(2)} \odot (Z_2^{(2)})^{-1})) \odot Z_5^{(1)} \boxplus \\ & ((Y_3^{(2)} \odot (Z_3^{(2)})^{-1}) \oplus (Y_4^{(2)} \boxminus Z_4^{(2)}))) \odot Z_6^{(1)}). \end{aligned} \tag{37}$$

Expressions (35) and (36) involve 7 $\oplus$, 6 $\odot$ and 3 $\boxplus$, which is equivalent to 28 $\oplus$. These expressions provide a one-bit condition to recover 128 bits of information on the key: $Z_1^{(1)}$, $Z_2^{(1)}$, $Z_3^{(1)}$, $Z_4^{(1)}$, $Z_5^{(1)}$, $Z_6^{(1)}$, $Z_2^{(2)}$, and $Z_3^{(2)}$. According to the key schedule of MESH-64:

$$Z_2^{(2)} = (((Z_1^{(1)} \boxplus Z_2^{(1)}) \oplus Z_3^{(1)} \boxplus Z_6^{(1)}) \oplus Z_7^{(1)} \boxplus Z_1^{(2)}) \lll 7 \oplus c_8,$$

$$Z_3^{(2)} = (((Z_2^{(1)} \boxplus Z_3^{(1)}) \oplus Z_4^{(1)} \boxplus Z_7^{(1)}) \oplus Z_1^{(2)} \boxplus Z_2^{(2)}) \lll 7 \oplus c_9,$$

which implies that the values of $Z_2^{(2)}$, and $Z_3^{(2)}$ cannot be deduced from the other subkey words, namely there is no similar overlap property such as in IDEA,

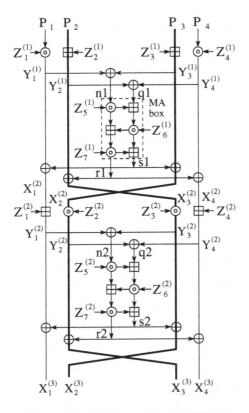

Fig. 2. The first 2 rounds of MESH-64.

to reduce the time complexity. The attack requires 128 known plaintexts and about $\frac{28}{34} \cdot 2^{128} \approx 2^{128}$ 1.5-round MESH-64 computations. Expressions (35) and (37) provide a one-bit condition to recover 128 bits of information on the key: $Z_1^{(1)}, Z_2^{(1)}, Z_3^{(1)}, Z_4^{(1)}, Z_5^{(1)}, Z_6^{(1)}, Z_3^{(2)}, Z_2^{(2)}$, with 128 known plaintexts and 2^{128} computations of (35) and (37).

Consider next the trails involving the first and fourth words in a block:

$$\mathrm{lsb}_1(P_1 \odot Z_1^{(1)} \oplus s_1) = \mathrm{lsb}_1(Y_1^{(2)} \oplus Z_1^{(2)}), \tag{38}$$

$$\mathrm{lsb}_1(P_4 \odot Z_4^{(1)} \oplus r_1) = \mathrm{lsb}_1(Y_4^{(2)} \oplus Z_4^{(2)}). \tag{39}$$

Combining (38) and (39) results in:

$$\mathrm{lsb}_1(P_1 \odot Z_1^{(1)} \oplus P_4 \odot Z_4^{(1)} \oplus Y_1^{(2)} \oplus Z_1^{(2)} \oplus Y_4^{(2)} \oplus Z_4^{(2)}) = \mathrm{lsb}_1(r_1 \oplus s_1). \tag{40}$$

The right hand side of (40) can be represented as (36) or (37). Expressions (40) and (36) provide a one-bit condition to recover 97 bits of information on the key: $Z_1^{(1)}, Z_2^{(1)}, Z_3^{(1)}, Z_4^{(1)}, Z_5^{(1)}, Z_6^{(1)}$, and $\mathrm{lsb}_1(Z_1^{(2)} \oplus Z_4^{(2)})$, with about 97 known plaintexts, and $\frac{28}{34} \cdot 2^{97} \approx 2^{97}$ 1.5-round MESH-64 computations.

Expressions (40) and (37) provide a one-bit condition to recover 128 bits of information on the key: $Z_1^{(1)}$, $Z_4^{(1)}$, $Z_5^{(1)}$, $Z_6^{(1)}$, $Z_1^{(2)}$, $Z_2^{(2)}$, $Z_3^{(2)}$, $Z_4^{(2)}$, with about 128 known plaintexts, and $\frac{28}{34} \cdot 2^{128} \approx 2^{128}$ 1.5-round MESH-64 computations.

To attack 2-round MESH-64, there are two possibilities in the graph of Fig. 2: consider first the trail involving the two middle words in a block:

$$\text{lsb}_1((P_2 \boxplus Z_2^{(1)} \oplus r_1) \odot Z_3^{(2)} \oplus s_2) = \text{lsb}_1(X_2^{(3)}), \tag{41}$$

$$\text{lsb}_1((P_3 \boxplus Z_3^{(1)} \oplus s_1) \odot Z_2^{(2)} \oplus r_2) = \text{lsb}_1(X_3^{(3)}). \tag{42}$$

Combining (41) and (42) results in:

$$\text{lsb}_1((P_2 \boxplus Z_2^{(1)} \oplus r_1) \odot Z_3^2 \oplus (P_3 \boxplus Z_3^{(1)} \oplus s_1) \odot Z_2^{(2)} \oplus X_2^{(3)} \oplus X_3^{(3)}) =$$
$$\text{lsb}_1(r_2 \oplus s_2). \tag{43}$$

The right hand side of (43) can be represented as:

$$\text{lsb}_1(r_2 \oplus s_2) = \text{lsb}_1(((X_1^{(3)} \oplus X_2^{(3)}) \odot Z_5^{(2)} \boxplus (X_3^{(3)} \oplus X_4^{(3)})) \odot Z_6^{(2)}). \tag{44}$$

For (43), the individual values of r_1 and s_1 are needed:

$$r_1 = (n_1 \odot Z_5^{(1)} \boxplus (n_1 \odot Z_5^{(1)} \boxplus q_1) \odot Z_6^{(1)}) \odot Z_7^{(1)}, \tag{45}$$

$$s_1 = r_1 \boxplus (n_1 \odot Z_5^{(1)} \boxplus q_1) \odot Z_6^{(1)}. \tag{46}$$

Combining (43), (44), (45) and (46) contains 10 $\odot$, 7 $\oplus$ and 7 $\boxplus$. This combination results in a one-bit condition to recover $Z_1^{(1)}$, $Z_2^{(1)}$, $Z_3^{(1)}$, $Z_4^{(1)}$, $Z_5^{(1)}$, $Z_6^{(1)}$, $Z_7^{(1)}$, $Z_2^{(2)}$, $Z_3^{(2)}$, $Z_5^{(2)}$, $Z_6^{(2)}$, which according to the key schedule of MESH-64, correspond to the full 128-bit user key. The effort is therefore not better than an exhausive key search.

Consider next the trails involving the first and fourth words in a block:

$$\text{lsb}_1(P_1 \odot Z_1^{(1)} \oplus s_1 \oplus Z_1^{(2)} \oplus s_2) = \text{lsb}_1(X_1^{(3)}), \tag{47}$$

$$\text{lsb}_1(P_4 \odot Z_4^{(1)} \oplus r_1 \oplus Z_4^{(2)} \oplus r_2) = \text{lsb}_1(X_4^{(3)}). \tag{48}$$

Combining (47) and (48) results in:

$$\text{lsb}_1(P_1 \odot Z_1^{(1)} \oplus Z_1^{(2)} \oplus X_1^{(3)} \oplus P_4 \odot Z_4^{(1)} \oplus Z_4^{(2)} \oplus X_4^{(3)}) =$$
$$\text{lsb}_1(r_1 \oplus s_1) \oplus \text{lsb}_1(r_2 \oplus s_2) =$$
$$\text{lsb}_1(((P_1 \odot Z_1^{(1)} \oplus (P_3 \boxplus Z_3^{(1)}) \odot Z_5^{(1)} \boxplus ((P_2 \boxplus Z_2^{(1)}) \oplus (P_4 \odot Z_4^{(1)}))) \odot$$
$$Z_6^{(1)}) \oplus \text{lsb}_1(((X_1^{(3)} \oplus X_2^{(3)}) \odot Z_5^2 \boxplus (X_3^{(3)} \oplus X_4^{(3)})) \odot Z_6^{(2)}). \tag{49}$$

Expression (49) contains 6 $\odot$, 4 $\boxplus$ and 5 $\oplus$, which is equivalent to 27 $\oplus$. This expression is a one-bit condition that allows to recover 128 bits of information on the key: $Z_1^{(1)}$, $Z_2^{(1)}$, $Z_3^{(1)}$, $Z_4^{(1)}$, $Z_5^{(1)}$, $Z_6^{(1)}$, $Z_5^{(2)}$, $Z_6^{(2)}$, with about 128 known plaintexts and $\frac{27}{52} \cdot 2^{128} \approx 2^{127}$ 2-round MESH-64 computations.

Similar attacks to the previous section can be applied on up to 2-round MESH-96 and 2-round MESH-128 [13], with an effort less than that of an exhaustive key search.

Table 1. Summary of attack complexities on IDEA.

Cipher	Attack	Source	#Rounds	Data	Memory	Time
IDEA	Biryukov-Demirci	this paper	1.5	49 KP	49	2^{48}
	Differential	[11]	2	2^{10} CP	2^{10}	2^{42}
	Demirci	[7]	2	23 CP	23	2^{64}
(8.5 rounds)	Square	[12]	2.5	2^{18} CP	2^{18}	2^{68}
	Demirci	[7]	2.5	55 CP	55	2^{81}
	Biryukov-Demirci	this paper	2.5	90 KP	90	2^{89}
	Differential	[11]	2.5	2^{10} CP	2^{10}	2^{106}
	Differential-Linear	[4]	3	2^{30} CP	2^{30}	2^{44}
	Demirci	[7]	3	71 CP	71	2^{71}
	Demirci	[7]	3	2^{33} CP	2^{33}	2^{82}
	Imposs. Differential	[1]	3.5	$2^{38.5}$ CP	2^{37}	2^{53}
	Truncated Differential	[5]	3.5	2^{56} CP	2^{32}	2^{67}
	Demirci	[7]	3.5	103 CP	103	2^{103}
	Biryukov-Demirci	this paper	3.5	112 KP	112	2^{112}
	Imposs. Differential	[1]	4	$2^{38.5}$CP	2^{37}	2^{70}
	Biryukov-Demirci	this paper	4	114 KP	114	2^{114}
	Demirci	[7]	4	2^{34} CP	2^{34}	2^{114}
	Imposs. Differential	[1]	4.5	2^{64} CP	2^{32}	2^{112}
	Meet-in-the-Middle	[8]	5	2^{24} CP	2^{58}	2^{126}

4   Conclusion

This paper presented a known-plaintext attack on reduced-round IDEA and MESH ciphers, combining an observation by A. Biryukov that there is a linear trail involving only the exclusive-or combination of the least significant bits of the two middle words in a block across the full cipher (Fig. 1); and an attack by Demirci in [8], in which a narrow linear trail exists across the MA-box of IDEA involving only one subkey and one input word (6).

The attacks in this paper were conducted such that the final complexity was always smaller than an exhaustive key search. Moreover, these attacks, together with the linear attack by Daemen *et al.* in [6], are the only attacks on IDEA and MESH ciphers that use exclusively known plaintext, but the former is not restricted to weak keys, as in the latter. The reason is that the linear trails exploited in this paper involve only the addition and exclusive-or operations, thus no multiplicative subkeys are directly involved. The use of weak keys would eventually lead to a smaller number of key bits to guess (in a key-recovery attack), but would not help extend the attack to more rounds.

The security of IDEA and MESH ciphers is not threatened since all of them have at least 8.5 rounds. But, these attacks somehow help corroborate the new design features of the MESH ciphers.

It is left as an open problem whether a redesign of the key schedule of IDEA would be enough to preclude our attack. Nonetheless, it can be noted that the redesigned key schedule of Daemen et al. in [6], which consisted of exclusive-oring

Table 2. Summary of attack complexities on MESH ciphers.

Cipher	Attack	#Rounds	Data	Memory	Time
MESH-64	**this paper**	1.5	97 KP	97	2^{97}
	Demirci	2	2^{21} CP	2^{16}	2^{47}
	this paper	2	128 KP	128	2^{127}
(8.5 rounds)	Square	2.5	$2^{50.5}$ CP	2^{16}	2^{76}
	Demirci	2.5	2^{21} CP	2^{16}	2^{111}
	Square	3	$2^{50.5}$ CP	2^{16}	2^{124}
	Imposs. Differential	3.5	$2^{39.5}$ CP	2^{61}	2^{64}
	Trunc. Differential	3.5	2^{64} CP	2^{32}	2^{78}
	Imposs. Differential	4	$2^{39.5}$ CP	2^{61}	2^{112}
	Trunc. Differential	4	2^{64} CP	2^{32}	2^{126}
	Linear	4.5	32 KP	32	2^{21}
	Boomerang	5.5	2^{10} CC/ACP	2^{10}	2^{10}
MESH-96	**this paper**	1.5	65 KP	65	$2^{64.3}$
	Demirci	2	2^{21} CP	2^{16}	2^{47}
	this paper	2	161 KP	161	$2^{160.3}$
(10.5 rounds)	Square	2.5	2^{50} CP	2^{16}	2^{96}
	Demirci	2.5	2^{21} CP	2^{16}	2^{143}
	Square	3	2^{50} CP	2^{16}	2^{144}
	Imposs. Differential	3.5	2^{56} CP	2^{93}	2^{96}
	Trunc. Differential	3.5	2^{96} CP	2^{64}	2^{109}
	Linear	4	32 KP	32	2^{53}
	Imposs. Differential	4	2^{56} CP	2^{93}	2^{144}
	Trunc. Differential	4	2^{96} CP	2^{64}	2^{157}
	Linear	4.5	32 KP	32	2^{149}
	Boomerang	5.5	2^{26} CC/ACP	2^{26}	2^{26}
MESH-128	**this paper**	1.5	1771 KP	177	$2^{177.3}$
	Demirci	2	$2^{37.6}$ CP	2^{32}	2^{79}
	this paper	2	225 KP	225	2^{225}
(12.5 rounds)	Square	2.5	2^{50} CP	2^{16}	2^{128}
	Demirci	2.5	$2^{37.6}$ CP	2^{32}	2^{143}
	Square	3	2^{50} CP	2^{16}	2^{192}
	Imposs. Differential	3.5	2^{65} CP	2^{157}	2^{128}
	Trunc. Differential	3.5	2^{128} CP	2^{64}	2^{142}
	Linear	4	32 KP	32	2^{69}
	Imposs. Differential	4	2^{65} CP	2^{157}	2^{192}
	Trunc. Differential	4	2^{128} CP	2^{64}	2^{206}
	Linear	4.5	32 KP	32	2^{197}
	Boomerang	5.5	2^{34} CC/ACP	2^{34}	2^{34}

a fixed constant (mask) to every 16-bit subkey word would not be enough, since the key overlapping property still holds underneath the masked subkeys.

Tables 1 and 2 compare the attack complexities for IDEA and MESH ciphers ("KP" means Known Plaintext, "CP" Chosen Plaintext, "CC/ACP" Chosen-Ciphertext Adaptively Chosen Plaintext).

The attack on 4-round IDEA has comparable complexity to that of Demirci *et al.*, but the former requires much less text and only known plaintext.

There are attacks on the full 8.5-round IDEA, such as linear cryptanalysis [6], differential-linear cryptanalysis [10], and boomerang attacks [3], but they all require the assumption of weak keys.

References

1. E. Biham, A. Biryukov, A. Shamir, "Miss-in-the-Middle Attacks on IDEA, Khufu and Khafre," 6th Fast Software Encryption Workshop, L.R. Knudsen, Ed., Springer-Verlag, LNCS 1636, 1999, 124–138.
2. A. Biryukov, personal communication, 2002.
3. A. Biryukov, J. Nakahara Jr, B. Preneel, J. Vandewalle, "New Weak-Key Classes of IDEA," ICICS 2002, R. Deng, S. Qing, F. Bao, J. Zhou, Eds., Springer-Verlag, LNCS 2513, Dec. 2002, 315–326.
4. J. Borst, "Differential-Linear Cryptanalysis of IDEA," ESAT Dept., COSIC group, Technical Report 96-2, 1996.
5. J. Borst, L.R. Knudsen, V. Rijmen, "Two Attacks on Reduced IDEA," Advances in Cryptology, Eurocrypt'97, W. Fumy, Ed., Springer-Verlag, LNCS 1233, 1997, 1–13.
6. J. Daemen, R. Govaerts, J. Vandewalle, "Weak Keys for IDEA," Advances in Cryptology, Crypto'93, D.R. Stinson, Ed., Springer-Verlag, LNCS 773, 1994, 224–231.
7. H. Demirci, "Square-like Attacks on Reduced Rounds of IDEA," 9th Selected Areas in Cryptography Workshop, SAC'02, K. Nyberg and H. Heys, Eds., Springer-Verlag, LNCS 2595, Aug. 2002, 147–159.
8. H. Demirci, E. Ture, A.A. Selcuk, "A New Meet-in-the-Middle Attack on the IDEA block cipher," 10th Selected Areas in Cryptography Workshop, SAC'03, M. Matsui and R. Zuccherato, Eds., Springer-Verlag, LNCS 3006, 2003.
9. S. Garfinkel, "PGP: Pretty Good Privacy," O'Reilly and Associates, 1994.
10. P.M. Hawkes, "Asymptotic Bounds on Differential Probabilities and an Analysis of the Block Cipher IDEA," The University of Queensland, St. Lucia, Australia, Dec. 1998.
11. W. Meier, "On the Security of the IDEA Block Cipher," Advances in Cryptology, Eurocrypt'93, T. Helleseth, Ed., Springer-Verlag, LNCS 765, 1994, 371–385.
12. J. Nakahara Jr, P.S.L.M. Barreto, B. Preneel, J. Vandewalle, H.Y. Kim, "Square attacks on reduced-round PES and IDEA Block Ciphers," 23rd Symp. on Info. Theory in the Benelux, B. Macq, J.-J. Quisquater, Eds., May 2002, 187–195.
13. J. Nakahara Jr, V. Rijmen, B. Preneel, J. Vandewalle, "The MESH Block Ciphers," The 4th International Workshop on Info. Security Applications, WISA 2003, K. Chae and M. Yung, Eds., Springer-Verlag, LNCS 2908, Aug. 2003, 458–473.
14. X. Lai, "On the Design and Security of Block Ciphers," ETH Series in Information Processing, J.L. Massey, Ed., vol. 1, 1995, Hartung-Gorre Verlag, Konstanz.
15. X. Lai, J.L. Massey, "A Proposal for a New Block Encryption Standard," Advances in Cryptology, Eurocrypt'90, I.B. Damgård, Ed., Springer-Verlag, LNCS 473, 1990, 389–404.

Differential-Linear Type Attacks on Reduced Rounds of SHACAL-2*

Yongsup Shin[1], Jongsung Kim[2], Guil Kim[2],
Seokhie Hong[2], and Sangjin Lee[2]

[1] Ministry of Information and Communications(MIC),
Seoul, Korea
{ysshin}@mic.go.kr
[2] Center for Information Security Technologies(CIST),
Korea University, Seoul, Korea
{joshep,okim912,hsh,sangjin}@cist.korea.ac.kr

Abstract. SHACAL-2 is a 256-bit block cipher with various key sizes based on the hash function SHA-2. Recently, it was recommended as one of the NESSIE selections. This paper presents differential-linear type attacks on SHACAL-2 with 512-bit keys up to 32 out of its 64 rounds. Our 32-round attack on the 512-bit keys variants is the best published attack on this cipher.

Keywords: Block Cipher, Differential-Linear Type Attacks, SHACAL-2

1 Introduction

SHACAL-2 [5] is a 256-bit block cipher which was suggested as a submission of the NESSIE (New European Schemes for Signatures, Integrity, and Encryption) project. Recently, SHACAL-2 was recommended as one of the NESSIE selections.

The best cryptanalytic result obtained on SHACAL-2 so far is the analysis of the impossible differential attack on 30-round SHACAL-2 [6]. The attack presented in [6] is based on 14-round distinguishers of which the last 3 rounds is a nonlinear relation.

In this paper we exploit the 3-round nonlinear relation presented in [6] to extend a 14-round truncated differential to a 17-round distinguisher. We use the extended 17-round distinguisher to devise an attack on 32-round SHACAL-2 with 512-bit keys, which is faster than exhaustive search. We also exploit the 3-round nonlinear relation to extend a 10-round square characteristic to a 13-round distinguisher. We use the extended 13-round distinguisher to devise an attack on 28-round SHACAL-2 with 512-bit keys, which is faster than exhaustive search. See Table 1 for a summary of our results.

* This work was supported (in part) by the Ministry of Information & Communications, Korea, under the information Technology Research Center (ITRC) Support Program.

H. Wang et al. (Eds.): ACISP 2004, LNCS 3108, pp. 110–122, 2004.
© Springer-Verlag Berlin Heidelberg 2004

This paper is organized as follows: Section 2 provides a description of SHACAL-2 and Section 3 presents several differential-linear type attacks which might be applied to other block ciphers. In Section 4 we present our differential-linear type attacks on SHACAL-2. Finally, Section 5 concludes the paper.

Table 1. Comparison of our results with the best previous attack on SHACAL-2.

Paper	Attack	Number of Rounds	Complexity Data / Time / Memory		
[6]	Impossible Differential	30	744CP / $2^{495.1}$ / $2^{14.5}$		
This paper	Differential-Linear Type	32	$2^{43.4}\text{CP}$ / $2^{504.2}$ / $2^{48.4}$		
		28	$463 \cdot 2^{32}\text{CP}$ / $2^{494.1}$ / $2^{45.9}$		

CP: Chosen Plaintexts, Time: Encryption units, Memory : Bytes of memory

2 Description of SHACAL-2

In [5] H. Handschuch and D. Naccache introduced the SHACAL-2 block cipher which is based on the compression function of the hash function SHA-2 [14]. It has a block size of 256 bits and supports a variable key length.

The encryption of the SHACAL-2 cipher is performed as follows. The 256-bit plaintext is divided into eight 32-bit words - A, B, C, D, E, F, G and H. We denote by X^i the value of word X before the ith round. According to this notation, the plaintext P is divided into $A^0, B^0, C^0, D^0, E^0, F^0$, G^0 and H^0. Since this cipher is composed of 64 rounds, the ciphertext is divided into $A^{64}, B^{64}, C^{64}, D^{64}, E^{64}, F^{64}, G^{64}$ and H^{64}. Following is the ith round of encryption.

$$T_1^{i+1} = H^i + \Sigma_1(E^i) + Ch(E^i, F^i, G^i) + K^i + W^i$$
$$T_2^{i+1} = \Sigma_0(A^i) + Maj(A^i, B^i, C^i)$$
$$H^{i+1} = G^i$$
$$G^{i+1} = F^i$$
$$F^{i+1} = E^i$$
$$E^{i+1} = D^i + T_1^{i+1}$$
$$D^{i+1} = C^i$$
$$C^{i+1} = B^i$$
$$B^{i+1} = A^i$$
$$A^{i+1} = T_1^{i+1} + T_2^{i+1}$$

for $i = 0, ..., 63$ where $+$ means the addition modulo 2^{32} of 32-bit words, W^i are the 32-bit round subkeys, and K^i are the 32-bit round constants which are different in each of the 64 rounds. The functions used in the above encryption process are defined as follows.

$$Ch(X, Y, Z) = (X \& Y) \oplus (\neg X \& Z)$$
$$Maj(X, Y, Z) = (X \& Y) \oplus (X \& Z) \oplus (Y \& Z)$$
$$\Sigma_0(X) = S_2(X) \oplus S_{13}(X) \oplus S_{22}(X)$$
$$\Sigma_1(X) = S_6(X) \oplus S_{11}(X) \oplus S_{25}(X)$$

where $\neg X$ means the complement of 32-bit word X and $S_i(X)$ means the right rotation of X by i bit positions.

The key schedule accepts a maximum 512-bit key and shorter keys than 512 bits are used by padding the key with zeros to a 512-bit string. In [5] it is strongly advised to use keys of at least 128 bits. Let the 512-bit key string be denoted $W = [W^0 || W^1 || \cdots || W^{15}]$. The key expansion of 512 bits W to 2048 bits is defined by

$$W^i = \sigma_1(W^{i \boxminus 2}) + W^{i \boxminus 7} + \sigma_0(W^{i \boxminus 15}) + W^{i \boxminus 16}, \ 16 \le i \le 63.$$
$$\sigma_0(x) = S_7(x) \oplus S_{18}(x) \oplus R_3(x)$$
$$\sigma_1(x) = S_{17}(x) \oplus S_{19}(x) \oplus R_{10}(x)$$

where $R_i(X)$ means the right shift of 32-bit word X by i bit positions.

3   Differential-Linear Type Attacks

In [10] Langford and Hellman showed that a differential attack and a linear attack can be combined together by a technique called differential-linear attack. The description of the differential-linear attack is as follows.

We use the notations Ω_P, Ω_T to present the input and output differences of the differential part, respectively and λ_P, λ_T, λ_K to present the input, output and subkey bit masks of the linear part, respectively. We assume that a block cipher E can be described as a cascade $E = E_1 \circ E_0$, such that for E_0 there exists a differential $\Omega_P \to \Omega_T$ with probability p, and for E_1 there exists a linear approximation $\lambda_P \to \lambda_T$ with probability $\frac{1}{2} + q$. Let P and P^* be a pair of plaintexts that satisfy $P \oplus P^* = \Omega_P$. Langford and Hellman [10] suggested to use a truncated differential $\Omega_P \to \Omega_T$ for E_0 with probability 1. This allows us to get the one bit equation $\lambda_P \cdot (E_0(P) \oplus E_0(P^*)) = a$ with probability 1 where $a = \lambda_P \cdot \Omega_T$. According to our assumption, we also have $\lambda_P \cdot E_0(P) \oplus \lambda_T \cdot E_1(E_0(P)) \oplus \lambda_K \cdot K = 0$ with probability $\frac{1}{2} + q$ and $\lambda_P \cdot E_0(P^*) \oplus \lambda_T \cdot E_1(E_0(P^*)) \oplus \lambda_K \cdot K = 0$ with probability $\frac{1}{2} + q$ where K is the subkey of the E_1 subcipher. Hence, using the piling up lemma presented in [12], we have the following equation

$$\lambda_T \cdot E_1(E_0(P)) \oplus \lambda_T \cdot E_1(E_0(P^*)) = a \tag{1}$$

with probability $\frac{1}{2} + 2q^2 (= \frac{1}{2} + 2^{2-1} \cdot q \cdot q)$. So the attack requires $O(q^{-4})$ chosen plaintext pairs.

In [2] Biham, Dunkelman and Keller enhanced the above technique into the cases where the probability of the differential part is smaller than 1. The description of the enhanced differential-linear attack is as follows.

In case the plaintext pair P and P^* satisfies the differential $\Omega_P \to \Omega_T$ (related to probability $p(\le 1)$), we get the one bit equation $\lambda_P \cdot (E_0(P) \oplus E_0(P^*)) = a$ with probability 1 where $a = \lambda_P \cdot \Omega_T$. In case the plaintext pair P and P^* does not satisfy the differential (related to probability $1 - p$), we assume that $\lambda_P \cdot (E_0(P) \oplus E_0(P^*))$ follows a random behavior. Thus, in the above two cases, we get the one bit equation $\lambda_P \cdot (E_0(P) \oplus E_0(P^*)) = a$ with probability $\frac{1}{2} + \frac{p}{2} (= p \cdot 1 + (1 - p) \cdot \frac{1}{2})$. Recall that the linear approximation satisfies that $\lambda_P \cdot E_0(P) \oplus \lambda_T \cdot E_1(E_0(P)) \oplus \lambda_K \cdot K = 0$ with probability $\frac{1}{2} + q$ and $\lambda_P \cdot E_0(P^*) \oplus \lambda_T \cdot E_1(E_0(P^*)) \oplus \lambda_K \cdot K = 0$ with probability $\frac{1}{2} + q$. Similarly, we use the piling up lemma to get one bit equation (1) with probability $\frac{1}{2} + 2pq^2 (= \frac{1}{2} + 2^{3-1} \cdot \frac{p}{2} \cdot q^2)$. The attack requires $O(p^{-2}q^{-4})$ chosen plaintext pairs. Especially, in case the probability of linear approximation is 1, it holds that $\lambda_T \cdot E_1(E_0(P)) \oplus \lambda_T \cdot E_1(E_0(P^*)) = a$ with probability $\frac{1}{2} + \frac{p}{2} (= \frac{1}{2} + 2^{3-1} \cdot \frac{p}{2} \cdot (\frac{1}{2})^2)$. This attack requires $O(p^{-2})$ chosen plaintext pairs.

We now introduce several possible differential-linear type attacks which are induced by the above techniques. The differential-linear attack can be extended to the cases where a set of plaintexts is used instead of a pair of plaintexts, i.e., the set of plaintexts in which some bits are composed of a saturated set[1] can be used in the attack. Assume that for the E_0 subcipher there exists a distinguisher whose input data consist of a set of 2^n plaintexts $P_i(i = 0, \ldots, 2^n - 1)$ in which some bits are formed of a saturated set. If this distinguisher has probability 1 and the output data of this distinguisher are associated with the bits of λ_P, then we can get the one bit equation $\lambda_P \cdot (\bigoplus_{i=0}^{2^n-1} E_0(P_i)) = 0$ with probability 1. According to our assumption, we also have $\lambda_P \cdot E_0(P_i) \oplus \lambda_T \cdot E_1(E_0(P_i)) \oplus \lambda_K \cdot K = 0$ with probability $\frac{1}{2} + q$ for each plaintext P_i. Hence, using the piling up lemma we have the following equation

$$\lambda_T \cdot \left(\bigoplus_{i=0}^{2^n-1} E_1(E_0(P_i)) \right) = 0$$

with probability $\frac{1}{2} + 2^{2^n-1}q^{2^n}$. This attack requires $O((2^{2^n-1}q^{2^n})^{-2})$ chosen plaintext sets. Thus, this attack can be efficiently applied to block ciphers when the value of q is very close to $1/2$ or equal to $1/2$. We call the distinguisher used in this attack the *square-linear distinguisher*.[2]

Furthermore, we can extend the above attacks to the cases where a nonlinear approximation is used instead of a linear approximation. If the probability of the nonlinear approximation which can be used in the attacks is larger than those of any linear approximations, the attack which uses such a nonlinear approximation may be efficiently applied to the underlying block cipher. We call the

---

[1] If every value in $\{0,1\}^w$ is found exactly once in the set, we call such a set "a saturated set".

[2] The square attack was introduced in [4]. This attack exploits a distinguisher whose input or output data consist of a set of plaintexts in which some bits are formed of a saturated set.

distinguishers used in these attacks the *differential-nonlinear distinguisher* and the *square-nonlinear distinguisher*, respectively.

4   Differential-Linear Type Attacks on SHACAL-2

In this Section we present differential-linear type attacks on reduced rounds of SHACAL-2. The following notations are used throughout this paper, where the right most bit is referred to as the 0-th bit, i.e., the least significant bit.

 - P : The 256-bit plaintext, i.e., $P = (A, \cdots, H)$ or $(A^0, \cdots, H^0)$.
 - P^r : The 256-bit input data of the rth round, i.e., $P^r = (A^r, \cdots, H^r)$.
 - x_i^r : The ith bit of X^r where $X^r \in \{A^r, B^r, \cdots, H^r, W^r, K^r\}$.
 - $t_{1,i}^r$: The ith bit of T_1^r.
 - $?$: An unknown value or a set of unknown values.
 - e_i : A 32-bit word that has $0's$ in all bit positions except for bit i.
 - $e_{i_1,\cdots,i_k}$: $e_{i_1} \oplus \cdots \oplus e_{i_k}$, denoted also e_M where $M = \{i_1, \cdots, i_k\}$.
 - $e_{i_1,\cdots,i_k,\sim}$: A 32-bit word that has $1's$ in the positions of bits $i_1, \cdots, i_k$, and unconcerned values in the positions of bits $(i_k + 1) \sim 31$, and $0's$ in the positions of the other bits where $i_1 < \cdots < i_k$. (The unconcerned value can be 0, 1 or an unknown value.)
 - z_i : A 32-bit word that has 0 in the position of bit i, and unconcerned values in the positions of the other bits.
 - CS (Constant Set) : A set containing a single value, repeated 2^{32} times.
 - PS (Permutation Set): A set containing all 2^{32} possible values once, in an arbitrary order.
 - $-PS$: A set containing all 2^{32} possible values once, in ordering $-x$ in case x is occurred in PS at the same round.
 - BS (Balanced Set) : A set containing 2^{32} elements with arbitrary values, but such that their sum (modulo 2^{32}) is zero. If this property only holds for the 0-th bit, we will denote BS_0.

All the attacks described in this Section exploit the 3-round nonlinear relation presented in [6]. The details of the 3-round nonlinear relation are as follows.

The value h_0^r can be represented as the output of nonlinear function $NF(A^{r+3}, B^{r+3}, \cdots, H^{r+3}, K^r, K^{r+1}, K^{r+2}, W^r, W^{r+1}, W^{r+2})$, denoted NF^{r+3}, where $0 \leq r \leq 61$.

$$h_0^r = c_0^{r+3} \oplus d_2^{r+3} \oplus d_{13}^{r+3} \oplus d_{22}^{r+3} \oplus (d_0^{r+3} \& (e_0^{r+3} \oplus t_{1,0}^{r+3})) \oplus (d_0^{r+3} \& (f_0^{r+3} \oplus t_{1,0}^{r+2}))$$
$$\oplus ((e_0^{r+3} \oplus t_{1,0}^{r+3}) \& (f_0^{r+3} \oplus t_{1,0}^{r+2})) \oplus h_6^{r+3} \oplus h_{11}^{r+3} \oplus h_{25}^{r+3}$$
$$\oplus (h_0^{r+3} \& h_0^{r+2}) \oplus ((\neg h_0^{r+3}) \& h_0^{r+1}) \oplus k_0^r \oplus w_0^r$$

The values h_0^{r+1}, $t_{1,0}^{r+2}$, h_0^{r+2} and $t_{1,0}^{r+3}$ in the above equation are represented as follows.

$$\begin{cases} h_0^{r+1} = t_{1,0}^{r+2} \oplus g_6^{r+3} \oplus g_{11}^{r+3} \oplus g_{25}^{r+3} \oplus (g_0^{r+3} \& h_0^{r+3}) \oplus ((\neg g_0^{r+3}) \& h_0^{r+2}) \oplus k_0^{r+1} \oplus w_0^{r+1} \\ \\ t_{1,0}^{r+2} = b_0^{r+3} \oplus c_2^{r+3} \oplus c_{13}^{r+3} \oplus c_{22}^{r+3} \oplus (c_0^{r+3} \& d_0^{r+3}) \oplus (c_0^{r+3} \& (e_0^{r+3} \oplus t_{1,0}^{r+3})) \oplus \\ \quad (d_0^{r+3} \& (e_0^{r+3} \oplus t_{1,0}^{r+3})) \\ \\ h_0^{r+2} = t_{1,0}^{r+3} \oplus f_6^{r+3} \oplus f_{11}^{r+3} \oplus f_{25}^{r+3} \oplus (f_0^{r+3} \& g_0^{r+3}) \oplus ((\neg f_0^{r+3}) \& h_0^{r+3}) \oplus k_0^{r+2} \oplus w_0^{r+2} \\ \\ t_{1,0}^{r+3} = a_0^{r+3} \oplus b_2^{r+3} \oplus b_{13}^{r+3} \oplus b_{22}^{r+3} \oplus (b_0^{r+3} \& c_0^{r+3}) \oplus (b_0^{r+3} \& d_0^{r+3}) \oplus (c_0^{r+3} \& d_0^{r+3}) \end{cases}$$

4.1   Attack on 32-Round SHACAL-2 Using a Differential-Nonlinear Distinguisher

Firstly, we describe how to construct a 14-round truncated differential and then concatenate the foregoing 3-round nonlinear relation to this differential. Secondly, we show how to exploit this 17-round differential-nonlinear distinguisher to attack 32-round SHACAL-2. Before constructing our 14-round truncated differential, we present two differential properties of SHACAL-2 which are used for computing the probability of the differential.

The first differential property of SHACAL-2 is derived from the use of both XOR and modular additions. Assume that $Z = X + Y$, $Z^* = X^* + Y^*$ where X, Y and X^*, Y^* be 32-bit random variables with uniform distribution. Then we have the following property.

- If $X \oplus X^* = e_j$ and $Y = Y^*$, then it holds $Z \oplus Z^* = e_{j,j+1,\cdots,j+k-1}$ with probability $1/2^k$ ($j < 31$, $k \geq 1$ and $j + k - 1 \leq 30$). Especially, in case $j = 31$, it holds $Z \oplus Z^* = e_{31}$ with probability 1.
- If $X \oplus X^* = e_j$ and $Y \oplus Y^* = e_j$, then it holds $Z \oplus Z^* = e_{j+1,\cdots,j+k-1}$ with probability $1/2^k$ ($j < 31$, $k \geq 1$ and $j + k - 1 \leq 30$). Especially, in case $j = 31$, it holds $Z \oplus Z^* = 0$ with probability 1.
- If $X \oplus X^* = e_{i,\sim}$, $Y \oplus Y^* = e_{j,\sim}$ and $i > j$, then it holds $Z \oplus Z^* = e_{j,\sim}$ (Note that if it holds $Z \oplus Z^* = e_{j,\sim}$, then it also holds $Z \oplus Z^* = z_k$ where $0 \leq k < j$).

The Second differential property of SHACAL-2 is derived from the functions Ch and Maj. These functions operate in the bit-by-bit manner, so each function can be regarded as a boolean function assigning from a 3-bit input to a 1-bit output. Table 2 shows the distribution of XOR differences through the Ch and Maj functions. The first three columns of Table 2 represent the eight possible differences in x, y, z. The next two columns indicate the differences in the outputs of each of the two functions. In the last two columns, a '0'(resp., '1') means that the difference will always be 0(resp., 1), and a '0/1' means that in half of the cases, the difference will be 0 and in the other half of the cases, the difference will be 1.

As stated in the previous paragraphs, a differential probability on SHACAL-2 is derived from either the use of both XOR and modular additions, or the

Table 2. The XOR differential distribution table of the Ch and Maj functions

x	y	z	Ch	Maj
0	0	0	0	0
0	0	1	0/1	0/1
0	1	0	0/1	0/1
1	0	0	0/1	0/1
0	1	1	1	0/1
1	0	1	0/1	0/1
1	1	0	0/1	0/1
1	1	1	0/1	1

functions Ch and Maj. However, in case a differential probability is derived from the functions Ch and Maj, we can control the differential probability over the first few rounds by fixing some bits of plaintext pairs. As an example, consider the Ch function. If an input difference of Ch is of the form $(0,0,1)$, then in half of the cases, the output difference is 0 and in the other half of the cases, the output difference is 1. However, if we choose two input values $(1,0,0)$ and $(1,0,1)$ whose difference is $(0,0,1)$, then the output difference of Ch is 0. It follows that if we fix some bits of two plaintexts of pairs, we can increase the differential probability derived from Ch by a factor of 2. In this way we can control a differential probability over the first few rounds by fixing some bits of two plaintexts of pairs.

From now on, we construct one trail of 14-round truncated differential from rounds r to $r + 13$. For the sake of clarity, we consider the case $r = 0$, which will be used in our attack. Let a plaintext pair $P = (A, B, C, D, E, F, G, H)$, $P^* = (A^*, B^*, C^*, D^*, E^*, F^*, G^*, H^*)$ has a difference $(0, 0, e_{M_1}, 0, 0, e_{31}, e_{M_2}, 0)$ where $M_1 = \{9, 18, 29\}$ and $M_2 = \{6, 9, 18, 20, 25, 29\}$, and assume that some bits of the P, P^* pair are fixed as depicted in Table 3. Then the least significant bit of output difference in the eighth word after 14 rounds, Δh_0^{14} is 0 with probability 2^{-22}. See Table 4 for more details of the trail. It is easy to check the probabilities depicted in Table 4 by using the two differential properties of SHACAL-2.

Table 3. Some fixed bits of the $P, P^\square$ pair

$A, A^\square$	$B, B^\square$	$E, E^\square$	$F, F^\square$	$G, G^\square$
$a_9 = a_9^\square = 0,$	$b_9 = b_9^\square = 0,$	$e_6 = e_6^\square = 1,$	$f_6 = f_6^\square = 0,$	$g_{31} = g_{31}^\square = 0$
$a_{18} = a_{18}^\square = 0,$	$b_{18} = b_{18}^\square = 0,$	$e_9 = e_9^\square = 1,$	$f_9 = f_9^\square = 0,$	
$a_{29} = a_{29}^\square = 0$	$b_{29} = b_{29}^\square = 0$	$e_{18} = e_{18}^\square = 1,$	$f_{18} = f_{18}^\square = 0,$	
$a_{31} = a_{31}^\square = 0$	$b_{31} = b_{31}^\square = 0$	$e_{20} = e_{20}^\square = 1,$	$f_{20} = f_{20}^\square = 0,$	
		$e_{25} = e_{25}^\square = 1,$	$f_{25} = f_{25}^\square = 0,$	
		$e_{29} = e_{29}^\square = 1$	$f_{29} = f_{29}^\square = 0$	
		$e_{31} = e_{31}^\square = 1$		

Table 4. A truncated differential trail for Rounds 0-13 of SHACAL-2 ($M_1 = \{9, 18, 29\}$, $M_2 = \{6, 9, 18, 20, 25, 29\}$, $M_3 = \{6, 9, 18, 20, 25\}$)

Round (r)	ΔA^r	ΔB^r	ΔC^r	ΔD^r	ΔE^r	ΔF^r	ΔG^r	ΔH^r	Prob.
Input ($r = 0$)	0	0	e_{M_1}	0	0	e_{31}	e_{M_2}	0	1
1	e_{31}	0	0	e_{M_1}	e_{31}	0	e_{31}	e_{M_2}	2^{-10}
2	0	e_{31}	0	0	0	e_{31}	0	e_{31}	2^{-2}
3	0	0	e_{31}	0	0	0	e_{31}	0	2^{-2}
4	0	0	0	e_{31}	0	0	0	e_{31}	1
5	e_{31}	0	0	0	0	0	0	0	2^{-4}
6	e_{M_1}	e_{31}	0	0	0	0	0	0	1
7	z_0	e_{M_1}	e_{31}	0	0	0	0	0	1
8	?	z_0	e_{M_1}	e_{31}	0	0	0	0	1
9	?	?	z_0	e_{M_1}	e_{31}	0	0	0	2^{-4}
10	?	?	?	z_0	$e_{M_3,\square}$	e_{31}	0	0	1
11	?	?	?	?	z_0	$e_{M_3,\square}$	e_{31}	0	1
12	?	?	?	?	?	z_0	$e_{M_3,\square}$	e_{31}	1
13	?	?	?	?	?	?	z_0	$e_{M_3,\square}$	1
Output ($r = 14$)	?	?	?	?	?	?	?	z_0	

Table 5. Possible ΔE^{10} values for the 14-round truncated differential trails with the respective probabilities

ΔE^{10}	Prob.	ΔE^{10}	Prob.	ΔE^{10}	Prob.
$e_{6,9,18,20,25,\square}$	2^{-22}	$e_{6,7,9,18,20,25,\square}$	2^{-23}	$e_{6,9,10,18,20,25,\square}$	2^{-23}
$e_{6,9,18,19,20,25,\square}$	2^{-23}	$e_{6,9,18,20,21,25,\square}$	2^{-23}	$e_{6,7,9,10,18,20,25,\square}$	2^{-24}
$e_{6,7,9,18,19,20,25,\square}$	2^{-24}	$e_{6,7,9,18,20,21,25,\square}$	2^{-24}	$e_{6,9,10,18,19,20,25,\square}$	2^{-24}
$e_{6,9,10,18,20,21,25,\square}$	2^{-24}	$e_{6,9,18,19,20,21,25,\square}$	2^{-24}	$e_{6,7,8,9,18,20,25,\square}$	2^{-24}
$e_{6,9,18,19,25,\square}$	2^{-24}	$e_{6,9,18,20,21,22,25,\square}$	2^{-24}		

Improvement of the probability: To combine a 14-round differential with the foregoing 3-round nonlinear relation, we need only the value Δh_0^{14} of this differential. Thus we can increase the above differential probability 2^{-22} taking into account a variety of truncated differential trails of which the values ΔH^{14} are of the form z_0. In order to improve the differential probability, we count over a variety of truncated differential trails which have the same first 9 rounds in the 14-round truncated differential trail described in Table 4. Table 5 presents some of these differential trails of which the values ΔH^{14} are of the form z_0. Based on these results we are able to increase the differential probability up to $2^{-18.7} (\approx 1 \cdot 2^{-22} + 4 \cdot 2^{-23} + 9 \cdot 2^{-24} + 16 \cdot 2^{-25} + 16 \cdot 2^{-26} + 42 \cdot 2^{-27} + 51 \cdot 2^{-28})$. Thus, we have a 14-round truncated differential (which includes a small portion of truncated differential trails) with a probability of approximately $2^{-18.7}$.

We use our 14-round truncated differential to build a distinguisher with a probability of $\frac{1}{2} + 2^{-19.7} (= 2^{-18.7} + \frac{1}{2} \cdot (1 - 2^{-18.7}))$. That is, if the plaintext pairs P, P^* have the $(0, 0, e_{M_1}, 0, 0, e_{31}, e_{M_2}, 0)$ difference and some bits of the pairs are fixed as depicted in Table 3, then it holds that $h_0^{14} = h_0^{*14}$ with a probability of $\frac{1}{2} + 2^{-19.7}$. This approximation assumes that the behavior of the remaining fraction of $1 - 2^{-18.7}$ of the pairs is taken with uniform distribution. In order to verify the probability $\frac{1}{2} + 2^{-19.7}$ we performed 10 simulations using 2^{34} plaintext pairs each (we used different random keys and different plaintext pairs in each of the simulations). While our estimation in the 2^{34} plaintext pairs is $2^{33} + 20170 (= 2^{34} \cdot (\frac{1}{2} + 2^{-19.7}))$, but we obtained the values $2^{33} + 153189, 2^{33} + 159168, 2^{33} + 161745, 2^{33} + 168761, 2^{33} + 173142, 2^{33} + 175476, 2^{33} + 177866, 2^{33} + 196441, 2^{33} + 197654, 2^{33} + 217151$ from our simulations. Our simulations show that the probability of the 14-round distinguisher is higher than our estimation $\frac{1}{2} + 2^{-19.7}$. This difference is due to the fact that our estimation only considers a small portion of truncated differential trails with high probabilities of which the values ΔH^{14} are of the form z_0. Thus, we conclude that the actual probability of our 14-round distinguisher is not less than $\frac{1}{2} + 2^{-19.7}$.

To this distinguisher we can concatenate the 3-round nonlinear relation with probability 1. Since given the P, P^* pairs it holds that $h_0^{14} = h_0^{*14}$ with a probability of approximately $\frac{1}{2} + 2^{-19.7}$, we have the following equation

$$NF^{17} = NF^{*17} \tag{2}$$

with a probability of approximately $\frac{1}{2} + 2^{-19.7}$. Thus, we have the 17-round differential-nonlinear distinguisher with a probability of approximately $\frac{1}{2} + 2^{-19.7}$.

We now present a method to use the 17-round distinguisher to find a master key of 32-round SHACAL-2. The attack procedure of 32-round SHACAL-2 is as follows.

1. Choose $2^{42.4} (= (2^3) \cdot (2^{-19.7})^{-2})$ plaintext pairs with the difference $(0, 0, e_{M_1}, 0, 0, e_{31}, e_{M_2}, 0)$ and the condition as depicted in Table 3. Request the corresponding ciphertext pairs for the plaintext pairs.
2. Guess a 463-bit key $W^{31}, W^{30}, \cdots, W^{20}, w_0^{19}, w_1^{19}, \cdots, w_{25}^{19}, w_0^{18}, w_1^{18}, \cdots, w_{25}^{18}, w_0^{17}, w_1^{17}, \cdots, w_{24}^{17}, w_0^{16}$, and w_0^{15}. (Note that it is sufficient to guess this 463-bit key for computing the value ΔNF^{17} from the ciphertext pairs of 32-round SHACAL-2. For more details, see [6].)
3. For each of the ciphertext pairs, do a partial decryption using the guessed key, and check Equation (2). If the number of satisfying Equation (2) is greater than or equal to $2^{41.4} + 2^{22}$, then keep the guessed key. Otherwise, go to Step 2.
4. For the suggested key, do an exhaustive search for the 49-bit remaining keys using trial encryption (For the suggested key, we use one or two known plaintext and ciphertext pairs for the trial encryption). If a 512-bit key is suggested, output the key as a master key of 32-round SHACAL-2. Otherwise, go to Step 2.

The data complexity of this attack is $2^{43.4}$ chosen plaintexts. The memory requirements of this attack is dominated by the memory for ciphertext pairs, so this attack requires about $2^{48.4} (= 2^{43.4} \cdot 32)$ memory bytes.

We now analyze the time complexity of this attack. The time complexity of Step 1 (the data collecting step) is $2^{43.4}$ 32-round SHACAL-2 encryptions, and the time complexity of Step 3 is $2^{504.2} (= \frac{1}{2} \cdot \frac{15}{32} \cdot 2^{43.4} \cdot 2^{463})$ 32-round SHACAL-2 encryptions on average (The factor $\frac{1}{2}$ means the average fraction of 462-bit keys which are tested in Step 3). In order to estimate the number of 462-bit keys which pass the test of Step 3, we use the following statistical method. For a wrong key the value NF^{17} according to each ciphertext behaves randomly. It implies that on the average half the ciphertext pairs satisfy $NF^{17} = NF^{*17}$ for a wrong key. Hence, in the case of a wrong key, the number of satisfying $NF^{17} = NF^{*17}$ is taken with a binomial random variable $X \sim Bin(2^{42.4}, \frac{1}{2})$. Since such a random variable can be approximated according to the normal distribution, i.e., $X \sim N(\mu, \sigma^2)$ where $\mu = 2^{41.4}$ and $\sigma^2 = 2^{40.4}$, equivalently $Z(= \frac{X-\mu}{\sigma}) \sim N(0,1)$, it is easy to see that $Pr[X \geq 2^{41.4} + 2^{22}] = Pr[Z \geq 3.5813] \approx 2^{-12.7}$. It follows that the number of 463-bit wrong keys[3] which pass the test of Step 3 is about $2^{449.7} (= \frac{1}{2} \cdot 2^{463} \cdot 2^{-12.7})$ on average. So, the time complexity of Step 4 is about $2^{498.7} (= 2^{449.7} \cdot 2^{49})$ 32-round SHACAL-2 encryptions, and thus the total time complexity of this attack is about $2^{504.2}$ 32-round SHACAL-2 encryptions.

Using the above analysis for the right key with $X \sim Bin(2^{42.4}, \frac{1}{2} + 2^{-19.7})$ we can check the probability that the right key passes the test of Step 3 is about 98%. Therefore, the success rate of this attack is about 98%.

Note: Our attack algorithm can be converted into the key ranking algorithm presented in [13]. That is, instead of keeping the keys whose counters are greater than or equal to $2^{41.4} + 2^{22}$ in Step 3, we can keep the $2^{450.3} (= 2^{463} \cdot 2^{-12.7})$ keys whose counters are greater than those of the other $(2^{462} - 2^{450.3})$ keys. Using the order statistics presented in [13] it is easy to see that the success rate of the key ranking algorithm is 98%, which is same with that of our attack algorithm. However, the key ranking algorithm requires a number of memory bytes for all possible 2^{463} keys.

4.2 Attack on 28-Round SHACAL-2 Using a Square-Nonlinear Distinguisher

In this subsection we describe a 13-round square-nonlinear distinguisher, and then exploit it to attack 28-round SHACAL-2.

In the similar way of the previous subsection, we design the 13-round square-nonlinear distinguisher of which the first 10 rounds are taken with a 10-round

---

[3] In fact, the number of the suggested keys in Step 3 is more than our estimation. Because some special wrong keys proposed in [6] produce a non-random value of ΔNF^{17}. However the number of such keys is less than 2^{83}. Thus, the expected number of wrong keys which are suggested in Step 3 is less than $2^{449.7} + 2^{83}$.

Table 6. A 10-round square characteristic used in our distinguisher

Round (r)	A	B	C	D	E	F	G	H
Input ($r = 0$)	**0**	**0**	PS	CS	**1**	CS	$-PS$	CS
1	CS	**0**	**0**	PS	CS	**1**	CS	$-PS$
2	PS	CS	**0**	**0**	CS	CS	**1**	CS
3	BS_0	PS	CS	**0**	CS	CS	CS	**1**
4	?	BS_0	PS	CS	CS	CS	CS	CS
5	?	?	BS_0	PS	CS	CS	CS	CS
6	?	?	?	BS_0	PS	CS	CS	CS
7	?	?	?	?	BS_0	PS	CS	CS
8	?	?	?	?	?	BS_0	PS	CS
9	?	?	?	?	?	?	BS_0	PS
Output ($r = 10$)	?	?	?	?	?	?	?	BS_0

square characteristic and the last 3 rounds are taken with the foregoing 3-round nonlinear relation. Given a well-chosen set of plaintexts we can get a property of the set of corresponding outputs after 10 rounds which is different from the case of a random permutation. That is, if we choose a set of 2^{32} plaintexts $P_i \in (\mathbf{0},\mathbf{0},PS,CS,\mathbf{1},CS,-PS,CS)$, $i = 0, \cdots, 2^{32} - 1$ where $\mathbf{0}$ and $\mathbf{1}$ represent constant sets composed of the 32-bit words 00000000_x and $ffffffff_x$, respectively, then the least significant bits of the eighth words after 10 rounds are balanced, i.e., $\bigoplus_{i=0}^{2^{32}-1} h_{i,0}^{10} = 0$. Table 6 shows this 10-round square characteristic with probability 1. As stated above, we concatenate the 3-round nonlinear relation to this characteristic, and thus we have the following equation

$$\bigoplus_{i=0}^{2^{32}-1} NF_i^{13} = 0 \tag{3}$$

with probability 1.

Using this property we can attack 28-round SHACAL-2. The attack procedure of 28-round SHACAL-2 is as follows.

1. Choose 463 plaintext sets whose forms are $(\mathbf{0},\mathbf{0},PS,CS,\mathbf{1},CS,-PS,CS)$. Request the corresponding ciphertext sets for the plaintext sets.
2. Guess a 463-bit key $W^{27}, W^{26}, \cdots, W^{16}, w_0^{15}, w_1^{15}, \cdots, w_{25}^{15}, w_0^{14}, w_1^{14}, \cdots, w_{25}^{14}, w_0^{13}, w_1^{13}, \cdots, w_{24}^{13}, w_0^{12}$ and w_0^{11}.
3. For each of the ciphertext sets, do a partial decryption using the guessed key, and if the ciphertext set does not satisfy Equation (3), then go to Step 2. If all the ciphertext sets satisfy Equation (3), then keep the guessed key.
4. For the suggested key, do an exhaustive search for the 49-bit remaining keys using trial encryption. If a 512-bit key is suggested, output the key as a master key of 28-round SHACAL-2. Otherwise, go to Step 2.

The data complexity of this attack is $463 \cdot 2^{32}$ chosen plaintexts, and the memory requirements are $2^{45.9}(= 463 \cdot 2^{32} \cdot 2^5)$ bytes. The time complexity of Step

1 (the data collecting step) is $463 \cdot 2^{32}$ 28-round SHACAL-2 encryptions, and the time complexity of Step 3 is $2^{494.1} (= \frac{1}{2} \cdot \frac{15}{28} \cdot (2^{463} \cdot 2^{32} + 2^{462} \cdot 2^{32} + \cdots + 2^1 \cdot 2^{32}))$ 28-round SHACAL-2 encryptions on average. Since the expectation of the suggested keys in Step 3 is about $1 (= 2^{463} \cdot 2^{-463})$, the time complexity of Step 4 is about 2^{49} 28-round SHACAL-2 encryptions. Thus, the total time complexity of this attack is about $2^{494.1}$ 28-round SHACAL-2 encryptions.

5   Conclusion

In this paper we presented some differential-linear type attacks on SHACAL-2. Using a differential-nonlinear distinguisher we can attack 32-round SHACAL-2 with a data complexity of $2^{43.4}$ chosen plaintexts and a time complexity of $2^{504.2}$ encryptions. This is the best published attack for this cipher. We can also attack 28-round SHACAL-2 with a data complexity of $463 \cdot 2^{32}$ chosen plaintexts and a time complexity of $2^{494.1}$ encryptions by using a square-nonlinear distinguisher.

In differential-linear type attacks, the use of a nonlinear approximation (resp., a square characteristic) may get an advantage over a linear approximation (resp., a differential characteristic). Although we do not know of any other concrete examples where the use of a nonlinear approximation or a square characteristic induces improved attacks, we expect that the possibility to apply differential-linear type attacks to any other block ciphers may be of interest.

References

1. E. Biham and A. Shamir, *Differential cryptanalysis of the full 16-round DES*, Advances in Cryptology - CRYPTO 1992, LNCS 740, pp. 487-496, Springer-Verlag, 1992.
2. E. Biham, O. Dunkelman and N. Keller, *Enhanced Differential-Linear Cryptanalysis*, Advances in Cryptology - ASIACRYPT 2002, LNCS 2501, pp. 254-266, Springer-Verlag, 2002.
3. E. Biham, O. Dunkelman and N. Keller, *Rectangle Attacks on 49-Round SHACAL-1*, FSE 2003, LNCS 2887, pp. 22-35, Springer-Verlag, 2003.
4. J. Daemen, L.R. Knudsen and V. Rijndael, *The block cipher Square*, FSE 1997, LNCS 1267, pp. 149-165, Springer-verlag, 1997.
5. H. Handschuh and D. Naccache, *SHACAL : A Family of Block Ciphers*, Submission to the NESSIE project, 2002.
6. S. Hong, J. Kim, G. Kim, J. Sung, C. Lee and S. Lee, *Impossible Differential Attack on 30-Round SHACAL-2*, INDOCRYT 2003, LNCS 2904, pp. 97-106, Springer-Verlag, 2003.
7. J. Kim, D. Moon, W. Lee, S. Hong, S. Lee and S. Jung, *Amplified Boomerang Attack against Reduced-Round SHACAL*, Advances in Cryptology - ASIACRYPT 2002, LNCS 2501, pp. 243-253, Springer-Verlag, 2002.
8. L.R. Knudsen, *Trucated and Higher Order Differentials*, FSE 1996, LNCS 1039, pp 196-211, Springer-Verlag, 1996.
9. L.R. Knudsen and D. Wagner, *Integral Cryptanalysis*, FSE 2002, LNCS 2365, pp 112-127, Springer-Verlag, 2002.

10. S.K. Langford and M.E. Hellman, *Differential-Linear Cryptanalysis*, Advances in Cryptology - CRYPTO 1994, LNCS 839, pp. 17-25, Springer-Verlag, 1994.
11. S. Lucks, *The Saturation Attack - a Bait for Twofish*, FSE 2001, LNCS 1039, pp. 189-203, Springer-Verlag, 2001.
12. M. Matsui, *Linear Cryptanalysis Method for DES Cipher*, Advances in Cryptology - EUROCRYPT 1993, LNCS 765, pp. 386-397, Springer-Verlag, 1994.
13. A.A. Selcuk, A. Bicak, *On Probability of Success in Linear and Differential Cryptanalysis*, SCN 2002, LNCS 2576, pp. 174-185, Springer-Verlag, 2002.
14. U.S. Department of Commerce.*FIPS 180-2*: Secure Hash Standard ,Federal Information Processing Standards Publication, N.I.S.T., August 2002.

The Related-Key Rectangle Attack –
Application to SHACAL-1*

Jongsung Kim[1], Guil Kim[1], Seokhie Hong[1],
Sangjin Lee[1], and Dowon Hong[2]

[1] Center for Information Security Technologies(CIST),
Korea University, Seoul, Korea
{joshep,okim912,hsh,sangjin}@cist.korea.ac.kr
[2] Information Security Technology Division, ETRI,
Taejon, Korea
dwhong@etri.re.kr

Abstract. The rectangle attack and the related-key attack on block ciphers are well-known to be very powerful. In this paper we combine the rectangle attack with the related-key attack. Using this combined attack we can attack the SHACAL-1 cipher with 512-bit keys up to 59 out of its 80 rounds. Our 59-round attack requires a data complexity of $2^{149.72}$ chosen plaintexts and a time complexity of $2^{498.30}$ encryptions, which is faster than exhaustive search.

Keywords: Block Ciphers, The Rectangle Attack, The Related-Key Attack, The Related-Key Rectangle Attack, SHACAL-1

1 Introduction

One of the most powerful known attacks on block ciphers is the differential attack [1] which was introduced by Biham and Shamir in 1990. This attack has been applied to many known block ciphers very efficiently. So algorithm designers have tried to make a block cipher secure against the differential attack. The differential attack has also been advanced variously - the truncated differential attack [14], the higher order differential attack [14], the impossible differential attack [3], the boomerang attack [16] and so on.

The boomerang attack [16] was introduced by Wagner in 1999. This attack requires chosen plaintext and adaptive chosen ciphertext queries, so it is considered harder to mount compared to chosen plaintext attacks. However, Kelsey, Kohno and Schneier showed in [12] that the boomerang attack can be converted into a chosen plaintext attack called the amplified boomerang attack. Later, the amplified boomerang attack was further developed by Biham, Dunkelman and Keller into a technique called the rectangle attack [4]. In the transition from the amplified boomerang attack to the rectangle attack, the probability of the distinguisher is improved.

* This work was supported by MOST research fund (M1-0326-08-0001).

H. Wang et al. (Eds.): ACISP 2004, LNCS 3108, pp. 123–136, 2004.
© Springer-Verlag Berlin Heidelberg 2004

Table 1. Comparison of our attacks with the previous ones

Type of Attack	Number of Rounds	Complexity Data / Time
Differential	30(0-29)	2^{110}CP / $2^{75.1}$[15]
	41(0-40)	2^{141}CP / 2^{491}[15]
Amp. Boomerang	47(0-46)	$2^{158.5}$CP / $2^{508.4}$[15]
Rectangle	47(0-46)	$2^{151.9}$CP / $2^{482.6}$[5]
	49(22-70)	$2^{151.9}$CP / $2^{508.5}$[5]
	49(29-77)	$2^{151.9}$CC / $2^{508.5}$[5]
Related-Key Rectangle	57(0-56)	$2^{154.75}$RK-CP / $2^{503.38}$ (New)
	59(0-58)	$2^{149.72}$RK-CP / $2^{498.30}$ (New)

CP: Chosen Plaintexts, RK-CP: Related-Key Chosen Plaintexts,
CC: Chosen Ciphertexts, Time: Encryption units

In 1994, Biham introduced the related-key attack [2] which allows the cryptanalyst to obtain plaintext and ciphertext pairs by using different, but related keys. This attack is based on the structure of the key scheduling algorithms. It is efficiently applied to block ciphers with weak key scheduling algorithms. After the related-key attack was introduced, the security of many known block ciphers against this attack has been evaluated [2,6,9,10,11,15].

In this paper we present the combination of rectangle and related-key attacks, called *the related-key rectangle attack*. This combined attack can share the features of both rectangle and related-key attacks.

In the related-key rectangle attack, there exist two types of distinguishers. The first type of distinguisher can be used in the attack which allows the cryptanalyst to choose plaintext pairs P and P^* under keys k and k^* respectively, where k and k^* be different, but related keys. On the other hand, the second type of distinguisher can be used in the attack which allows the cryptanalyst to choose plaintext pairs P and P' under a key k together with plaintext pairs P^* and P'^* under a key k^*. We call the above two types of distinguishers *the related-key rectangle distinguishers of TYPE 1 and TYPE 2*, respectively. We first describe the related-key rectangle attack in terms of these two types of distinguishers, and then demonstrate its use on reduced-round variants of the SHACAL-1 cipher.

SHACAL-1 is a 160-bit block cipher based on the hash standard SHA-1. SHACAL-1 was submitted to the NESSIE project and was among the primitives selected for the second phase of this project. However, it was not recommended as one of the NESSIE selections because of concerns about its key scheduling algorithm. The SHACAL-1 cipher has a key scheduling algorithm which is operated by the linear shift feedback register, so the subkeys are linearly dependent in the key. Moreover, it does not offer a large diffusion for all the expanded subkeys. Using these weaknesses of the key scheduling algorithm we construct a 46-round related-key rectangle distinguisher of TYPE 1 and a 48-round related-key rectangle distinguisher of TYPE 2. We exploit these distinguishers of TYPE

1 and 2 to devise attacks on 57 and 59-round SHACAL-1, respectively. See Table 1 for a summary of our results.

2   The Related-Key Rectangle Attack

This Section describes the related-key rectangle attack in terms of two types of distinguishers. Before describing this attack, we introduce some notations and assumptions which will be used throughout this paper.

Let a block cipher $E_k : \{0,1\}^n \to \{0,1\}^n$ (which can be also denoted $E : \{0,1\}^{|k|} \times \{0,1\}^n \to \{0,1\}^n$) be composed of a cascade $E_k = E_k^1 \circ E_k^0$ (which can be also denoted $E = E^1 \circ E^0$) where k is a master key of the E cipher. We assume that for E^0 there exist a differential $\alpha \to \beta$ with probability p and a related-key differential $\alpha \to \beta$ with probability p^* (i.e., $Pr[E_k^0(P) \oplus E_{k^*}^0(P^*) = \beta | P \oplus P^* = \alpha] = p^*$ where k and k^* be different, but related keys), and for E^1 there exist a differential $\gamma \to \delta$ with probability q and a related-key differential $\gamma \to \delta$ with probability q^* (i.e., $Pr[E_k^1(X) \oplus E_{k^*}^1(X^*) = \delta | X \oplus X^* = \gamma] = q^*$). As stated above, we denote by k and k^* different, but related keys.

The related-key rectangle distinguisher of TYPE 1 (The left of Fig. 1): Assume that P_i, P_j are encrypted under E_k and P_i^*, P_j^* are encrypted under E_{k^*} such that $P_i \oplus P_i^* = P_j \oplus P_j^* = \alpha$. We denote by X_i, X_i^*, X_j, X_j^* the encrypted values of P_i, P_i^*, P_j, P_j^* under E^0 respectively, and by C_i, C_i^*, C_j, C_j^* the encrypted values of X_i, X_i^*, X_j, X_j^* under E^1 respectively. We are interested in the cases where $X_i \oplus X_i^* = X_j \oplus X_j^* = \beta$ and $X_i \oplus X_j = \gamma$ (or $X_i \oplus X_j^* = \gamma$), as in these cases $X_i^* \oplus X_j^* = (X_i \oplus \beta) \oplus (X_j \oplus \beta) = \gamma$ (or $X_i^* \oplus X_j = (X_i \oplus \beta) \oplus (X_j^* \oplus \beta) = \gamma$) as well. If both the C_i, C_j pair and the C_i^*, C_j^* pair satisfy a δ difference (or both the C_i, C_j^* pair and the C_i^*, C_j pair satisfy a δ difference), a quartet satisfying all these differential conditions is called a right quartet. A description of such a quartet is shown in TYPE 1 of Fig. 1.

If we have m pairs with difference α where one plaintext of each pair is encrypted by using the key k and the other plaintext is encrypted by using the key k^*, then we have about mp^* pairs satisfying the related-key differential $\alpha \to \beta$ for E^0. The mp^* pairs generate about $\frac{(mp^*)^2}{2}$ quartets consisting of two such pairs. Assuming that the intermediate encryption values distribute uniformly over all possible values, we get $X_i \oplus X_j = \gamma$ with a probability of 2^{-n} and $X_i \oplus X_j^* = \gamma$ with a probability of 2^{-n}. In case we take into account the difference of the X_i, X_j pair, the differential $\gamma \to \delta$ with probability q is used in this distinguisher twice. On the other hand, in case we take into account the difference of the X_i, X_j^* pair, the related-key differential $\gamma \to \delta$ with probability q^* is used in this distinguisher twice. Therefore, the expected number of right quartets is about $m^2 \cdot 2^{-n-1} \cdot (p^*)^2 \cdot (q^2 + (q^*)^2) (= \frac{(mp^*)^2}{2} \cdot 2^{-n} \cdot (q^2 + (q^*)^2))$.

More generally, the related-key rectangle distinguisher of TYPE 1 exploits much more right quartets rather than the above two kinds of right quartets. That is, this distinguisher takes into account all the related-key differentials with input

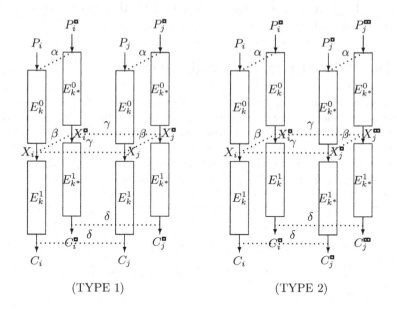

(TYPE 1)   (TYPE 2)

Fig. 1. Related-Key Rectangle Distinguishers

difference α through E^0, all the differentials and related-key differentials with output difference δ through E^1. Let the respective probabilities of the above differentials be denoted by $Pr^*[\alpha \to \beta']$, $Pr[\gamma' \to \delta]$, $Pr^*[\gamma'' \to \delta]$, and

$$\hat{p^*} = (\sum_{\beta'} Pr^{*2}[\alpha \to \beta'])^{\frac{1}{2}}, \ \hat{q} = (\sum_{\gamma'} Pr^2[\gamma' \to \delta])^{\frac{1}{2}}, \ \hat{q^*} = (\sum_{\gamma''} Pr^{*2}[\gamma'' \to \delta])^{\frac{1}{2}}.$$

Then the expected number of right quartets for this distinguisher is about

$$\sum_{\text{any } \beta',\gamma',\gamma''} \frac{(m \cdot Pr^*[\alpha \to \beta'])^2}{2} \cdot 2^{-n} \cdot (Pr^2[\gamma' \to \delta] + Pr^{*2}[\gamma'' \to \delta])$$

$$= m^2 \cdot 2^{-n-1} \cdot (\hat{p^*})^2 \cdot (\hat{q}^2 + (\hat{q^*})^2).$$

On the other hand, the expected number of right quartets for a random permutation is about $m^2 \cdot 2^{-2n} (\approx {}_mC_2 \cdot 2 \cdot 2^{-2n})$. Therefore, if $\hat{p^*} \cdot (\frac{1}{2} \cdot (\hat{q}^2 + (\hat{q^*})^2))^{1/2} > 2^{-n/2}$ and m is sufficiently large, we can distinguish between E and a random permutation.

In the related-key rectangle distinguisher of TYPE 1, we can use either differentials $\gamma' \to \delta$ (related to the probability $\hat{q}$) or related-key differentials $\gamma'' \to \delta$ (related to the probability $\hat{q^*}$). By using both of them, we increase the probability of a random permutation to succeed. However, if we take only the maximal one between $\hat{q}$ and $\hat{q}^*$, then the ratio of the expected number of right quartets between E and a random permutation is optimal. Assume that $\hat{q} \geq \hat{q}^*$ and the right quartets associated with $\hat{q}$ are only used in our distinguisher. Then the expected number of right quartets for the E cipher is about $m^2 \cdot 2^{-1} \cdot 2^{-n} \cdot (\hat{p}^* \cdot \hat{q})^2$. On the other hand, the expected number of right quartets for a random permutation is about $m^2 \cdot 2^{-1} \cdot 2^{-2n}$. Thus, $\hat{p}^* \cdot \hat{q} > 2^{-n/2}$ must hold for the related-key rectangle distinguisher to work. Note that it holds $\hat{p}^* \cdot \hat{q} \geq \hat{p}^* \cdot (\frac{1}{2} \cdot (\hat{q}^2 + (\hat{q}^*)^2))^{1/2}$ under the assumption $\hat{q} \geq \hat{q}^*$. Instead of $\hat{p}^* \cdot (\frac{1}{2} \cdot (\hat{q}^2 + (\hat{q}^*)^2))^{1/2}$, we will use the probability $\hat{p}^* \cdot \hat{q}$ to attack 57-round SHACAL-1.

The related-key rectangle distinguisher of TYPE 2 (The right of Fig. 1): Assume that P_i, P_i' are encrypted under E_k and $P_j^*, P_j'^*$ are encrypted under E_{k^*}. We denote by $X_i, X_i', X_j^*, X_j'^*$ the encrypted values of $P_i, P_i', P_j^*, P_j'^*$ under E^0 respectively, and by $C_i, C_i', C_j^*, C_j'^*$ the encrypted values of $X_i, X_i', X_j^*, X_j'^*$ under E^1 respectively. We are interested in the cases where $X_i \oplus X_i' = X_j^* \oplus X_j'^* = \beta$ and $X_i \oplus X_j^* = \gamma$ (or $X_i \oplus X_j'^* = \gamma$), as in these cases $X_i' \oplus X_j'^* = \gamma$ (or $X_i' \oplus X_j^* = \gamma$) as well. If both the C_i, C_j^* pair and the $C_i', C_j'^*$ pair satisfy a δ difference (or both the $C_i, C_j'^*$ pair and the C_i', C_j^* pair satisfy a δ difference), a quartet satisfying all these differential conditions is called a right quartet. A description of such a quartet is shown in TYPE 2 of Fig. 1.

If we have m_1 pairs (P_i, P_i') and m_2 pairs $(P_j^*, P_j'^*)$ with difference α, then we have about $m_1 \cdot p$ pairs together with $m_2 \cdot p$ pairs satisfying the differential $\alpha \rightarrow \beta$ for E^0. Assuming that the intermediate encryption values distribute uniformly over all possible values, we get $X_i \oplus X_j^* = \gamma$ with a probability of 2^{-n} and $X_i \oplus X_j'^* = \gamma$ with a probability of 2^{-n}. Since the probability that both pairs (X_i, X_j^*) and $(X_i', X_j'^*)$ (or both pairs $(X_i, X_j'^*)$ and (X_j^*, X_i')) are right pairs with respect to the related key differential $\gamma \rightarrow \delta$ for E^1 is $(q^*)^2$, the expected number of right quartets is about $m_1 \cdot m_2 \cdot 2^{-n+1} \cdot (p \cdot q^*)^2 (= (m_1 \cdot p) \cdot (m_2 \cdot p) \cdot 2^{-n} \cdot 2 \cdot (q^*)^2)$. Using the same method described in the previous paragraph (i.e., taking into account all possible right quartets), we can increase the expectation of right quartets up to $m_1 \cdot m_2 \cdot 2^{-n+1} \cdot (\hat{p} \cdot \hat{q}^*)^2$ where $\hat{p} = (\sum_{\beta'} Pr^2[\alpha \rightarrow \beta'])^{\frac{1}{2}}$. Since the expected number of right quartets for a random permutation is about $m_1 \cdot m_2 \cdot 2^{-2n+1}$, we can distinguish between E and a random permutation if $\hat{p} \cdot \hat{q}^* > 2^{-n/2}$ and m_1, m_2 are sufficiently large.

3   Description of SHACAL-1

SHACAL-1 [7] is a 160-bit block cipher with various key sizes. It is based on the compression function of the hash function SHA-1 introduced by NIST. SHACAL-1 is performed as follows.

1. Insert the 160-bit message $X(= X^1 \| X^2 \| X^3 \| X^4 \| X^5)$ where the 32-bit words X^i put in the 32-bit words, A^0, B^0, C^0, D^0, E^0 by

$$A^0 = X^1, \; B^0 = X^2, \; C^0 = X^3, \; D^0 = X^4, \; E^0 = X^5.$$

2. Encrypt the 32-bit words, A^0, B^0, C^0, D^0, E^0 in a total of 80 rounds. Encryption of the ith round is performed as follows.

$$A^{i+1} = W^i + ROTL_5(A^i) + f^i(B^i, C^i, D^i) + E^i + K^i$$
$$B^{i+1} = A^i$$
$$C^{i+1} = ROTL_{30}(B^i)$$
$$D^{i+1} = C^i$$
$$E^{i+1} = D^i$$

for $i = 0, \cdots, 79$, where $ROTL_j(X)$ represents rotation of the 32-bit word X to the left by j-bit positions, W^i are round subkeys, K^i are round constants, and

$$f^i(B, C, D) = f_{if} = (B\&C)|(\neg B\&D), \qquad\qquad (0 \le i \le 19)$$
$$f^i(B, C, D) = f_{xor} = B \oplus C \oplus D, \qquad (20 \le i \le 39, \ 60 \le i \le 79)$$
$$f^i(B, C, D) = f_{maj} = (B\&C)|(B\&D)|(C\&D), \qquad (40 \le i \le 59).$$

The ciphertext is composed of $A^{80}, B^{80}, C^{80}, D^{80}, E^{80}$.

The key schedule of SHACAL-1 takes a maximum 512-bit key and shorter keys may be used by padding the key with zeros to a 512-bit string. In [7] algorithm designers strongly advised to use keys of at least 128 bits. Let the 512-bit key string be denoted $W = [W^0||W^1||\cdots||W^{15}]$, where each W^i is a 32-bit word. The key expansion of 512 bits W to 2560 bits is defined by

$$W^i = ROTL_1(W^{i-3} \oplus W^{i-8} \oplus W^{i-14} \oplus W^{i-16}), \ \ (16 \le i \le 79)$$

4   Related-Key Rectangle Attack on 57-Round SHACAL-1

In this Section we describe a 46-round related-key rectangle distinguisher of SHACAL-1 and design our related-key rectangle attack on 57-round SHACAL-1 using this distinguisher.

4.1   A 46-Round Related-Key Rectangle Distinguisher of TYPE 1

As stated earlier, the key schedule of the SHACAL-1 cipher is operated by the linear shift feedback register. This key schedule allows us to control a difference of any consecutive 16-round key even though it is not the master key (i.e., if we set up a difference of any consecutive 16-round key, other 64-round key difference is determined by that of this 16-round key). In order to find a difference pattern of key which enables us to design a strong related-key rectangle distinguisher, we used a method of trial and error, and we could find a good difference pattern of key as depicted in Table 2. In Table 2 the notation e_i represents a 32-bit word that has zeros in all bit positions except for bit i, and the notation $e_{i_1,\cdots,i_k}$ represents a 32-bit word $e_{i_1} \oplus \cdots \oplus e_{i_k}$. The key differences depicted in Table 2 can be generated by the master key difference $\Delta W = (e_{31}, e_{31}, e_{31}, e_{31}, 0, e_{31}, 0, e_{31}, 0, 0, 0, 0, 0, 0, 0, e_{31})$. Note that the right most bit is referred to as the 0-th bit, i.e., the least significant bit.

Table 2. Key Differences Used for Attacking 57-Round SHACAL-1

i	ΔW^i	i	ΔW^i	i	ΔW^i	i	ΔW^i	i	ΔW^i	i	ΔW^i
0	e_{31}	10	0	20	0	30	0	40	e_3	50	$e_{3,7}$
1	e_{31}	11	0	21	0	31	e_0	41	e_4	51	e_5
2	e_{31}	12	0	22	0	32	e_1	42	0	52	e_7
3	e_{31}	13	0	23	0	33	0	43	$e_{1,3,4}$	53	e_8
4	0	14	0	24	0	34	e_1	44	e_5	54	0
5	e_{31}	15	e_{31}	25	0	35	e_2	45	$e_{2,3}$	55	$e_{3,5,7,8}$
6	0	16	0	26	0	36	0	46	e_5	56	e_9
7	e_{31}	17	0	27	0	37	$e_{2,3}$	47	$e_{1,2,6}$		
8	0	18	0	28	0	38	e_3	48	e_{31}		
9	0	19	0	29	e_0	39	e_1	49	$e_{3,5,6}$		

Table 3 shows a 33-round related-key differential characteristic $\alpha \to \beta$ with probability 2^{-47}, where $\alpha = (0, e_{8,22,1}, e_{1,15}, e_{10}, e_{5,31})$ and $\beta = (e_{1,5,15,30}, e_{10}, e_3, e_{30}, 0)$. This related-key differential characteristic requires plaintext pairs (P, P^*) with a 6-bit fixed value, i.e.,

$$b_{10} = b_{10}^* = 1, \; b_{15} = b_{15}^* = 0, \; c_8 = c_8^* = 0, \tag{1}$$
$$c_{10} = c_{10}^* = 0, \; d_8 = d_8^* = 0, \; d_{15} = d_{15}^* = 0.$$

where $P = (A, \cdots, H)$, $P^* = (A^*, \cdots, H^*)$ and x_i be the ith bit of 32-bit word X. Table 4 shows a 13-round differential characteristic $\gamma \to \delta$ with probability 2^{-26}, where $\gamma = (e_{1,3}, e_{1,8}, 0, e_{3,6,31}, e_{1,3,31})$ and $\delta = (e_{24,29}, e_{19}, e_{12}, e_7, e_2)$.

In order to obtain $\hat{p^*}$ (resp., $\hat{q}$) we should compute the probabilities of all the related-key differentials with input difference α through E^0 (resp., all the differentials with output difference δ through E^1). However, it is computationally infeasible to compute the probabilities of all these differentials. So we take into account as many differential characteristics as we can, i.e., we settle for counting over a wide variety of differential characteristics which have the same first 31 rounds (resp., the same last 11 rounds) in the 33-round related-key differential characteristic described in Table 3 (resp., the 13-round differential characteristic described in Table 4). Table 5 shows the number of counted differential characteristics according to their probabilities. As a result, we can increase a lower bound for $\hat{p^*}$ (resp., $\hat{q}$) up to $2^{-46.17}$ (resp., $2^{-25.08}$). Since the value $\hat{p^*} \cdot \hat{q} (\approx 2^{-71.75})$ is greater than 2^{-80}, this 46-round related-key rectangle distinguisher can distinguish between 46-round SHACAL-1 and a random permutation.

Table 3. The First Differential Characteristic Using a Related-Key

Round (i)	ΔA^i	ΔB^i	ΔC^i	ΔD^i	ΔE^i	ΔW^i	Prob.
0	0	$e_{8,22,1}$	$e_{1,15}$	e_{10}	$e_{5,31}$	e_{31}	
1	e_5	0	$e_{6,20,31}$	$e_{1,15}$	e_{10}	e_{31}	2^{-3}
2	0	e_5	0	$e_{6,20,31}$	$e_{1,15}$	e_{31}	2^{-6}
3	$e_{1,15}$	0	e_3	0	$e_{6,20,31}$	e_{31}	2^{-6}
4	0	$e_{1,15}$	0	e_3	0	0	2^{-3}
5	0	0	$e_{13,31}$	0	e_3	e_{31}	2^{-3}
6	e_3	0	0	$e_{13,31}$	0	0	2^{-3}
7	e_8	e_3	0	0	$e_{13,31}$	e_{31}	2^{-3}
8	0	e_8	e_1	0	0	0	2^{-2}
9	0	0	e_6	e_1	0	0	2^{-2}
10	0	0	0	e_6	e_1	0	2^{-2}
11	e_1	0	0	0	e_6	0	2^{-2}
12	0	e_1	0	0	0	0	2^{-1}
13	0	0	e_{31}	0	0	0	2^{-1}
14	0	0	0	e_{31}	0	0	2^{-1}
15	0	0	0	0	e_{31}	e_{31}	2^{-1}
16	0	0	0	0	0	0	1
$\vdots$	$\vdots$	$\vdots$	$\vdots$	$\vdots$	$\vdots$	$\vdots$	$\vdots$
28	0	0	0	0	0	0	1
29	0	0	0	0	0	e_0	1
30	e_0	0	0	0	0	0	2^{-1}
31	e_5	e_0	0	0	0	e_0	2^{-1}
32	e_{10}	e_5	e_{30}	0	0	e_1	2^{-2}
33	$e_{1,5,15,30}$	e_{10}	e_3	e_{30}	0		2^{-4}

Table 4. The Second Differential Characteristic

Round (i)	ΔA^i	ΔB^i	ΔC^i	ΔD^i	ΔE^i	ΔW^i	Prob.
33	$e_{1,3}$	$e_{1,8}$	0	$e_{3,6,31}$	$e_{1,3,31}$	0	
34	0	$e_{1,3}$	$e_{6,31}$	0	$e_{3,6,31}$	0	2^{-4}
35	e_1	0	$e_{1,31}$	$e_{6,31}$	0	0	2^{-3}
36	e_1	e_1	0	$e_{1,31}$	$e_{6,31}$	0	2^{-2}
37	0	e_1	e_{31}	0	$e_{1,31}$	0	2^{-1}
38	0	0	e_{31}	e_{31}	0	0	2^{-1}
39	0	0	0	e_{31}	e_{31}	0	1
40	0	0	0	0	e_{31}	0	1
41	e_{31}	0	0	0	0	0	1
42	e_4	e_{31}	0	0	0	0	2^{-1}
43	e_9	e_4	e_{29}	0	0	0	2^{-2}
44	e_{14}	e_9	e_2	e_{29}	0	0	2^{-3}
45	e_{19}	e_{14}	e_7	e_2	e_{29}	0	2^{-4}
46	$e_{24,29}$	e_{19}	e_{12}	e_7	e_2		2^{-5}

Table 5. Number of Differential Characteristics Used in the 46-Round Distinguisher

Probability ($p^{\square}$)	$2^{\square\,47}$	$2^{\square\,48}$	$2^{\square\,49}$	$2^{\square\,50}$	$2^{\square\,51}$	$\cdots$
Number of Characteristics	1	4	11	20	42	$\cdots$
Probability (q)	$2^{\square\,26}$	$2^{\square\,27}$	$2^{\square\,28}$	$2^{\square\,29}$	$2^{\square\,30}$	$\cdots$
Number of Characteristics	1	4	13	32	68	$\cdots$

4.2 Attack Procedure

We now present a method to exploit the 46-round related-key rectangle distinguisher to find a master key of 57-round SHACAL-1. The attack procedure of 57-round SHACAL-1 is performed as follows.

1. Prepare $\lceil 2^{153.75} \rceil$ plaintext pairs (P_i, P_i^*), $i = 0, 1, \cdots, \lceil 2^{153.75} \rceil - 1$ that have the α difference and the 6-bit condition in Eq. (1). (Note that each P_i is encrypted using a key k, and each P_i^* is encrypted using a key k^* where k and k^* have a difference as depicted in Table 2.) Encrypt all these plaintext pairs to get the $\lceil 2^{153.75} \rceil$ ciphertext pairs (C_i, C_i^*).
2. Guess a 352-bit subkey pair (sk, sk^*) for rounds $46 \sim 56$. This subkey pair has a difference for rounds $46 \sim 56$ depicted in Table 2.
3. For the guessed subkey pair (sk, sk^*), do the following:
   a) Decrypt C_i (resp., C_i^*) through rounds $56 \sim 46$ using the sk subkey (resp., the sk^* subkey), and denote the values we get by T_i (resp., T_i^*).
   b) Check that $T_{i_1} \oplus T_{i_2} = T_{i_1}^* \oplus T_{i_2}^* = \delta$ for all indexes i_1, i_2 such that $0 \le i_1 < i_2 \le \lceil 2^{153.75} \rceil - 1$. If the number of quartets $(T_{i_1}, T_{i_2}, T_{i_1}^*, T_{i_2}^*)$ passing the above δ test is greater than or equal to 6, then keep the guessed subkey pair. Otherwise, go to Step 2.
   c) For the suggested key, do an exhaustive search for the 160-bit remaining keys using trial encryption (For the suggested key, it is sufficient to use three known plaintext and ciphertext pairs for the trial encryption). If the 512-bit key is suggested, output the key as a master key of 57-round SHACAL-1. Otherwise, go to Step 2.

The data complexity of this attack is about $2^{154.75}$ related-key chosen plaintexts. The memory requirements of this attack is dominated by the memory for ciphertext pairs, so this attack requires about $2^{159.07} (= 2^{154.75} \cdot 20)$ memory bytes.

The time complexity of Step 1 (the data collection step) is $2^{154.75}$ 57-round SHACAL-1 encryptions and the time complexity of Step 3-(a) is $2^{503.38} (\approx 2^{154.75} \cdot 2^{352} \cdot \frac{1}{2} \cdot \frac{11}{57})$ 57-round SHACAL-1 encryptions on average (The factor $\frac{1}{2}$ means the average fraction of 352-bit subkey pairs which are used in Step 3-(a)). In Step 3-(b), each of all possible quartets must be compared to the δ difference twice. This can be done efficiently by using a hash table for storing and checking the δ difference. Moreover, in Step 3-(b), the probability that each wrong subkey pair produces at least 6 quartets passing the δ test is greater than or equal to 6 is about $2^{-90.50} (\approx \sum_{i=6}^{t} (_tC_i \cdot (2^{-160\cdot2})^i \cdot (1-2^{-160\cdot2})^{t-i}))$ where t is the value $\lceil 2^{306.50} \rceil$ which represents the number of all possible quartets (used in the above attack procedure) derived from the $\lceil 2^{153.75} \rceil$ plaintext pairs. It follows that the expected number of the suggested 352-bit subkey pairs in Step 3-(b) is $2^{260.50}(\approx 2^{352} \cdot \frac{1}{2} \cdot 2^{-90.50})$ on average, so the time complexity of Step 3-(c) is about $2^{420.50}(\approx 2^{260.50} \cdot 2^{160})$ 57-round SHACAL-1 encryptions. Thus, the time complexity of this attack is about $2^{503.38}(\approx 2^{154.75} + 2^{503.38} + 2^{420.50})$ 57-round SHACAL-1 encryptions.

Since this attack uses the forgoing 46-round related-key rectangle distinguisher with a probability of $(\hat{p^*} \cdot \hat{q})^2(\approx (2^{-71.75})^2)$, the expected number of quartets which pass the δ test for the right subkey pair is about $2^3(= {}_{2^{153.75}}C_2 \cdot 2^{-160} \cdot (2^{-71.75})^2)$. Thus, the success rate of this attack, i.e., the probability which the right subkey pair produces at least 6 quartets passing the δ test is about $0.80(\approx \sum_{i=6}^{t}({}_tC_i \cdot (2^{-160} \cdot (2^{-71.75})^2)^i \cdot (1 - 2^{-160} \cdot (2^{-71.75})^2)^{t-i}))$ where t is the value $\lceil 2^{306.50} \rceil$.

5   Related-Key Rectangle Attack on 59-Round SHACAL-1

In this Section we describe a 48-round related-key rectangle distinguisher of SHACAL-1 and design our related-key rectangle attack on 59-round SHACAL-1 using this distinguisher.

5.1   A 48-Round Related-Key Rectangle Distinguisher of TYPE 2

Using a similar way of subsection 4.1 we can construct two differential characteristics which support a 48-round related-key rectangle distinguisher of TYPE 2. Table 6 shows a 21-round differential characteristic $\alpha \to \beta$ with probability 2^{-40}, where $\alpha = (0, e_{22}, e_{15}, e_{10}, e_5)$ and $\beta = (e_{2,7,14,24,29}, e_{19}, e_{12}, e_7, e_2)$. Note that this differential characteristic is same with the one introduced in [15] except for some conditions of plaintext pairs, i.e., this differential characteristic requires plaintext pairs (P, P^*) with a 10-bit fixed value as follows.

$$a_{15} = a_{15}^* = 1, \ a_{20} = a_{20}^* = 0, \ b_{10} = b_{10}^* = 1,$$
$$b_{15} = b_{15}^* = 0, \ b_{17} = b_{17}^* = 0, \ c_{10} = c_{10}^* = 0, \qquad (2)$$
$$c_{20} = c_{20}^* = 0, \ c_{22} = c_{22}^* = 0, \ d_{15} = d_{15}^* = 0, d_{22} = d_{22}^* = 0.$$

Table 7 shows a 27-round related-key differential characteristic $\gamma \to \delta$ with probability 2^{-29}, where $\gamma = (e_{1,8}, 0, e_{3,6,31}, e_{1,3,31}, e_{3,13,31})$ and $\delta = (e_{6,20}, e_{1,15}, e_8, e_3, e_{30})$. In this differential the key differences depicted in Table 8 are used. These key differences can be generated by the master key difference $\Delta W = (0, e_{30}, e_{31}, e_{30,31}, e_{31}, e_{30,31}, e_{31}, e_{30,31}, e_{31}, e_{30}, e_{31}, e_{30,31}, e_{31}, e_{30}, e_{31}, e_{31})$.

In order to compute an approximate value (or a lower bound) of $\hat{p}$ (resp., $\hat{q^*}$) we use the counting method described in the previous section. Table 9 shows the number of counted differential characteristics according to their probabilities. (The counted number of differential characteristics related to the first 21-round

Table 6. The First Differential Characteristic

Round (i)	ΔA^i	ΔB^i	ΔC^i	ΔD^i	ΔE^i	ΔW^i	Prob.
0	0	e_{22}	e_{15}	e_{10}	e_5	0	
1	e_5	0	e_{20}	e_{15}	e_{10}	0	2^{-1}
2	0	e_5	0	e_{20}	e_{15}	0	2^{-1}
3	e_{15}	0	e_3	0	e_{20}	0	2^{-3}
4	0	e_{15}	0	e_3	0	0	2^{-2}
5	0	0	e_{13}	0	e_3	0	2^{-2}
6	e_3	0	0	e_{13}	0	0	2^{-2}
7	e_8	e_3	0	0	e_{13}	0	2^{-2}
8	0	e_8	e_1	0	0	0	2^{-2}
9	0	0	e_6	e_1	0	0	2^{-2}
10	0	0	0	e_6	e_1	0	2^{-2}
11	e_1	0	0	0	e_6	0	2^{-2}
12	0	e_1	0	0	0	0	2^{-1}
13	0	0	e_{31}	0	0	0	2^{-1}
14	0	0	0	e_{31}	0	0	2^{-1}
15	0	0	0	0	e_{31}	0	2^{-1}
16	e_{31}	0	0	0	0	0	1
17	e_4	e_{31}	0	0	0	0	2^{-1}
18	e_9	e_4	e_{29}	0	0	0	2^{-2}
19	e_{14}	e_9	e_2	e_{29}	0	0	2^{-3}
20	e_{19}	e_{14}	e_7	e_2	e_{29}	0	2^{-4}
21	$e_{2,7,14,24,29}$	e_{19}	e_{12}	e_7	e_2		2^{-5}

Table 7. The Second Differential Characteristic Using a Related-Key

Round (i)	ΔA^i	ΔB^i	ΔC^i	ΔD^i	ΔE^i	ΔW^i	Prob.
21	$e_{1,8}$	0	$e_{3,6,31}$	$e_{1,3,31}$	$e_{3,13,31}$	e_{31}	
22	$e_{1,3}$	$e_{1,8}$	0	$e_{3,6,31}$	$e_{1,3,31}$	0	2^{-4}
23	0	$e_{1,3}$	$e_{6,31}$	0	$e_{3,6,31}$	0	2^{-4}
24	e_1	0	$e_{1,31}$	$e_{6,31}$	0	0	2^{-3}
25	e_1	e_1	0	$e_{1,31}$	$e_{6,31}$	0	2^{-2}
26	0	e_1	e_{31}	0	$e_{1,31}$	0	2^{-1}
27	0	0	e_{31}	e_{31}	0	0	2^{-1}
28	0	0	0	e_{31}	e_{31}	0	1
29	0	0	0	0	e_{31}	e_{31}	1
30	0	0	0	0	0	0	1
$\vdots$	$\vdots$	$\vdots$	$\vdots$	$\vdots$	$\vdots$	$\vdots$	$\vdots$
42	0	0	0	0	0	0	1
43	0	0	0	0	0	e_0	1
44	e_0	0	0	0	0	0	2^{-1}
45	e_5	e_0	0	0	0	e_0	2^{-1}
46	e_{10}	e_5	e_{30}	0	0	e_1	2^{-3}
47	$e_{1,15}$	e_{10}	e_3	e_{30}	0	0	2^{-4}
48	$e_{6,20}$	$e_{1,15}$	e_8	e_3	e_{30}		2^{-5}

Table 8. Key Differences Used for Attacking 59-Round SHACAL-1

i	ΔW^i	i	ΔW^i	i	ΔW^i	i	ΔW^i	i	ΔW^i	i	ΔW^i
0	0	10	e_{31}	20	0	30	0	40	0	50	0
1	e_{30}	11	$e_{30,31}$	21	e_{31}	31	0	41	0	51	$e_{2,3}$
2	e_{31}	12	e_{31}	22	0	32	0	42	0	52	e_3
3	$e_{30,31}$	13	e_{30}	23	0	33	0	43	e_0	53	e_1
4	e_{31}	14	e_{31}	24	0	34	0	44	0	54	e_3
5	$e_{30,31}$	15	e_{31}	25	0	35	0	45	e_0	55	e_4
6	e_{31}	16	e_{31}	26	0	36	0	46	e_1	56	0
7	$e_{30,31}$	17	e_{31}	27	0	37	0	47	0	57	$e_{1,3,4}$
8	e_{31}	18	0	28	0	38	0	48	e_1	58	e_5
9	e_{30}	19	e_{31}	29	e_{31}	39	0	49	e_2		

differential characteristic was already presented in [5].) As a result, we can increase a lower bound for $\hat{p}$ (resp., $\hat{q^*}$) up to $2^{-38.64}$ (resp., $2^{-28.08}$). Since the value $\hat{p} \cdot \hat{q^*} (\approx 2^{-66.72})$ is greater than 2^{-80}, this 48-round related-key rectangle distinguisher can distinguish between 48-round SHACAL-1 and a random permutation.

Table 9. Number of Differential Characteristics Used in the 48-Round Distinguisher

Probability (p) [5]	2^{-40}	2^{-41}	2^{-42}	2^{-43}	2^{-44}	$\cdots$
Number of Characteristics [5]	1	7	24	73	182	$\cdots$
Probability (q^*)	2^{-29}	2^{-30}	2^{-31}	2^{-32}	2^{-33}	$\cdots$
Number of Characteristics	1	4	13	32	68	$\cdots$

5.2   Attack Procedure

This subsection presents a method to exploit the 48-round related-key rectangle distinguisher to find a master key of 59-round SHACAL-1. The attack procedure of 59-round SHACAL-1 is performed as follows.

1. Prepare $\lceil 2^{147.72} \rceil$ plaintext pairs (P_i, P_i') and the same amount of the plaintext pairs $(P_j^*, P_j'^*)$, $i, j = 0, 1, \cdots, \lceil 2^{147.72} \rceil - 1$ that have the α difference and the 10-bit condition in Eq. (2). (Note that all P_i and P_i' are encrypted using a key k, and all P_j^* and $P_j'^*$ are encrypted using a key k^* where k and k^* have a difference as depicted in Table 8.) Encrypt all these plaintext pairs (P_i, P_i') and $(P_j^*, P_j'^*)$ to get the corresponding ciphertext pairs (C_i, C_i') and $(C_j^*, C_j'^*)$, respectively.
2. Guess a 352-bit subkey pair (sk, sk^*) for rounds $48 \sim 58$. This subkey pair has a difference for rounds $48 \sim 58$ depicted in Table 8
3. For the guessed subkey pair (sk, sk^*), do the following:
   a) Decrypt C_i, C_i' (resp., $C_j^*, C_j'^*$) through rounds $58 \sim 48$ using the sk subkey (resp., the sk^* subkey), and denote the values we get by T_i, T_i' (resp., $T_j^*, T_j'^*$).

b) Check that $T_{i_1} \oplus T_{i_2}^* = T_{i_1}' \oplus T_{i_2}'^* = \delta$ or $T_{i_1} \oplus T_{i_2}'^* = T_{i_1}' \oplus T_{i_2}^* = \delta$ for all indexes i_1, i_2 such that $0 \le i_1 < i_2 \le \lceil 2^{147.72} \rceil - 1$. If the number of quartets $(T_{i_1}, T_{i_2}^*, T_{i_1}', T_{i_2}'^*)$ passing the above δ test is greater than or equal to 6, then keep the guessed subkey pair. Otherwise, go to Step 2.

c) For the suggested key, do an exhaustive search for the 160-bit remaining keys using trial encryption (For the suggested key, it is sufficient to use three known plaintext and ciphertext pairs for the trial encryption). If the 512-bit key is suggested, output the key as a master key of 59-round SHACAL-1. Otherwise, go to Step 2.

The data complexity of this attack is about $2^{149.72}$ related-key chosen plaintexts. The memory requirements of this attack is dominated by the memory for ciphertext pairs, so this attack requires about $2^{154.05} (= 2^{149.72} \cdot 20)$ memory bytes.

The time complexity of Step 1 (the data collection step) is $2^{149.72}$ 59-round SHACAL-1 encryptions and the time complexity of Step 3-(a) is $2^{498.30} (\approx 2^{149.72} \cdot 2^{352} \cdot \frac{1}{2} \cdot \frac{11}{59})$ 59-round SHACAL-1 encryptions on average. As stated in the previous attack, we can efficiently perform the δ test of Step 3-(b) by using a hash table. In Step 3-(b), the probability that each wrong subkey pair produces at least 6 quartets passing the δ test is greater than or equal to 6 is about $2^{-150.85} (\approx \sum_{i=6}^{t} ({}_t C_i \cdot (2^{-160 \cdot 2})^i \cdot (1 - 2^{-160 \cdot 2})^{t-i}))$ where t is the value $\lceil 2^{296.44} \rceil$ which represents the number of all possible quartets (used in the above attack procedure) derived from the two $2^{147.72}$ plaintext pairs. It follows that the expected number of the suggested 352-bit subkey pairs in Step 3-(b) is $2^{200.15} (\approx 2^{352} \cdot \frac{1}{2} \cdot 2^{-150.85})$ on average, so the time complexity of Step 3-(c) is about $2^{360.15} (\approx 2^{200.15} \cdot 2^{160})$ 59-round SHACAL-1 encryptions. Thus, the time complexity of this attack is about $2^{498.30} (\approx 2^{149.72} + 2^{498.30} + 2^{360.15})$ 59-round SHACAL-1 encryptions.

Since this attack uses the forgoing 48-round related-key rectangle distinguisher with a probability of $(\hat{p} \cdot \hat{q}^*)^2 (\approx (2^{-66.72})^2)$, the expected number of quartets which pass the δ test for the right subkey pair is about $2^3 (= (2^{147.72})^2 \cdot 2^{-159} \cdot (2^{-66.72})^2)$. Thus, the success rate of this attack, i.e., the probability which the right subkey pair produces at least 6 quartets passing the δ test is about $0.80 (\approx \sum_{i=6}^{t} ({}_t C_i \cdot (2^{-159} \cdot 2^{-66.72})^2)^i \cdot (1 - 2^{-159} \cdot (2^{-66.72})^2)^{t-i}))$ where t is the value $\lceil 2^{296.44} \rceil$.

6   Conclusion

The rectangle attack and the related-key attack are well-known to be very powerful. We have combined these two techniques, and have shown that it is efficiently applied to SHACAL-1 up to 59 rounds out of its 80 rounds. Using the weakness of the key schedule we have attacked 59-round SHACAL-1 with a data complexity of $2^{149.72}$ chosen plaintexts and a time complexity of $2^{498.30}$ encryptions.

Even though this combined attack is not generally applicable in block ciphers whose key schedules are secure, we believe it to be an important tool for both cryptanalysts and key-schedule designers.

References

1. E. Biham and A. Shamir, *Differential Cryptanalysis of DES-like Cryptosystems*, Advances in Cryptology, CRYPTO'90, LNCS 537, pp.2-21, Springer-Verlag, 1990.
2. E. Biham, *New Types of Cryptanalytic Attacks Using Related Keys*, Journal of Crytology, v. 7, n. 4, pp.229-246, 1994.
3. E. Biham, A. Biryukov and A. Shamir, *Cryptanalysis of skipjack reduced to 31 rounds using impossible differentials*, Advances in Cryptology, EUROCRYPT'99, LNCS 1592, pp.12-23, Springer-Verlag, 1999.
4. E. Biham, O. Dunkelman and N. Keller, *The Rectangle Attack - Rectangling the Serpent*, Advances in Cryptology, EUROCRYPT'01, LNCS 2045, pp.340-357, Springer-Verlag, 2001.
5. E. Biham, O. Dunkelman and N. Keller, *Rectangle Attacks on 49-Round SHACAL-1*, FSE'03, LNCS 2887, pp.22-35, Springer-Verlag, 2003.
6. M. Blunden and A. Escott, *Related Key Attacks on Reduced Round KASUMI*, FSE'01, LNCS 2355, pp.277-285, Springer-Verlag, 2001.
7. H. Handschuh and D. Naccache, *SHACAL*, preproceedings of NESSIE first workshop, Leuven, 2000.
8. S. Hong, J. Kim, G. Kim, J. Sung, C. Lee and S. Lee, *Impossible Differential Attack on 30-Round SHACAL-2*, INDOCRYPT'03, LNCS 2904, pp.97-106, Springer-Verlag, 2003.
9. G. Jakimoski and Y. Desmedt, *Related-Key Differential Cryptanalysis of 192-bit Key AES Variants*, SAC'03, To appear.
10. J. Kelsey, B. Schneier and D. Wagner, *Key Schedule Cryptanalysis of IDEA, G-DES, GOST, SAFER, and Triple-DES*, Advances in Cryptology, CRYPTO'96, LNCS 1109, pp.237-251, Springer-Verlag, 1996.
11. J. Kelsey, B. Schneir and D. Wagner, *Related-Key Cryptanalysis of 3-WAY, Biham-DES, CAST, DES-X, NewDES, RC2, and TEA*, ICICS'97, LNCS 1334, pp.233-246, Springer-Verlag, 1997.
12. J. Kelsey, T. Kohno and B. Schneier, *Amplified Boomerang Attacks Against Reduced-Round MARS and Serpent*, FSE'01, LNCS 1978, pp.75-93, Springer-Verlag, 2001.
13. J. Kim, D. Moon, W. Lee, S. Hong, S. Lee and S. Jung, *Amplified Boomerang Attack against Reduced-Round SHACAL*, Advances in Cryptology, ASIACRYPT 2002, LNCS 2501, pp.243-253, Springer-Verlag, 2002.
14. L.R. Knudsen, *Trucated and Higher Order Differentials*, FSE'96, LNCS 1039, pp.196-211, Springer-Verlag, 1996.
15. Y. Ko, S. Hong, W. Lee, S. Lee and J. Kang, *Related Key Differential Attacks on 26 Rounds of XTEA and Full Rounds of GOST*, FSE 2004, To appear.
16. D. Wagner, *The Boomerang Attack*, FSE'99, LNCS 1636, pp.156-170, Springer-Verlag, 1999.

Related Key Differential Cryptanalysis of Full-Round SPECTR-H64 and CIKS-1*

Youngdai Ko, Changhoon Lee, Seokhie Hong, and Sangjin Lee

Center for Information Security Technologies (CIST),
Korea University, Anam Dong, Sungbuk Gu, Seoul, Korea
{koyd, crypto77, hsh, sangjin}@cist.korea.ac.kr

Abstract. In this paper we show an attack on full-round SPECTR H64 and CIKS-1 using related key differential characteristic, which are based on data-dependent rotation with simple key schedule. To find partial 35-bit subkeys of SPECTR-H64 it needs about 2^{23} data and 2^{16} encryptions with an expected success probability 95.8%. As for CIKS-1, 2^4 data and 2^{33} encryptions are requried to find the final round key of it with an expected success probability 80%.

Keywords: SPECTR-H64, CIKS-1, Related Key differential attack, Data-dependent rotation

1 Introduction

CIKS-1 [6] and SPECTR-H64 [2] are 64 bit block ciphers with 256 key bits. They use only simple operations such as data dependent operation, exculsive-or, cyclic rotation, and simple nonlinear operation with simple key schedule. Hence above two algorithms are efficient for hardware so they are suitable for many network applications requiring high speed encryption in the case of frequent change of keys [7].

Data dependent operations such as $P_{n/m}$-box used in CIKS-1 and SPECTR-H64 have a weakness that Hamming weight is preserved. That is to say, $Hw(X) = Hw(P_{n/m}(X))$. Here with this weakness and simple key schedule, we will show an attack on full round SPECTR-H64 and full round CIKS-1 using related key differential characteristic [3]. To begin with we introduce a full 12-round related key differential characteristic of SPECTR-H64 with a probability of 2^{-17} and then show that how to recover the 30-bit subkeys used in the final round function and transformation FT of SPECTR-H64. This attack requires about 2^{23} plaintexts and 2^{16} encryption times with an expected success rate 95.8%. With similar methods, we suggest a related key differential attack on full-round CIKS-1. This attack allows us to recover the 32-bit final round key of CIKS-1 with an expected success rate 80% and requires about 2^4 plaintext pairs and 2^{33} encryption times.

* This work was supported (in part) by the Ministry of Information & Communications, Korea, under the Information Technology Research Center (ITRC) Support Program.

H. Wang et al. (Eds.): ACISP 2004, LNCS 3108, pp. 137–148, 2004.
© Springer-Verlag Berlin Heidelberg 2004

2   Preliminaries

2.1   Notations

Throughout this paper, the following notations will be used. Note that bits will be numbered from left to right, starting at bit 1. For example, the right most bit of a n-bit binary string P is p_n, while the leftmost bit is p_1, i.e., $P = (p_1, p_2, \cdots, p_n)$.

- $P_{lo} = (p_1, p_2, \cdots, p_{\frac{n}{2}})$, $P_{hi} = (p_{\frac{n}{2}+1}, p_{\frac{n}{2}+2}, \cdots, p_n)$
- e_i and d_i : a 32-bit and 80-bit binary strings in which the i-th bit is one and the others are zero, respectively
- $Hw(A)$: the Hamming weight of any binary string A
- $\otimes, |, \lll (\ggg)$: a bitwise-AND, a concatenation operation, a left (right) cyclic rotation

2.2   CP-Boxes

CP-box is used to perform data-dependent permutations (DDP). Such CP-box can be constructed as a superposition of the standard elementary $P_{2/1}$-boxes shown in Fig. 1(b). $P_{2/1}$-box is controlled by one bit v. In SPECTR-H64, if $v = 1$, it swaps two input bits otherwise (if $v = 0$), does not. On contrast, in CIKS-1, it swaps two input bits, if $v = 0$, otherwise ($v = 1$) the bits are not swapped. That is, the output bits of CP-box are the rearrangement of input bits by the control vector V. So, we can easily observe the following properties of $P_{2/1}$-box.

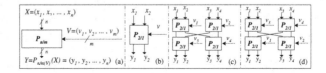

Fig. 1. CP-boxes : (a) $P_{n/m}$, (b) $P_{2/1}$, (c) $P_{4/4}$, (b) $P_{4/4}^{\square \, 1}$

Property 1. $P_{2/1(0)}(x_1, x_2) = P_{2/1(1)}(x_1, x_2)$ with a probability of 2^{-1}.

The equation in the above *Property* 1 holds only when $x_1 = x_2$. *Property* 1 is also expanded into the following properties.

Property 2. Let V and V' be m-bit control vectors for $P_{n/m}$-box and assume $V \oplus V' = d_i$ ($1 \leq i \leq m$), then $P_{n/m(V)}(X) = P_{n/m(V')}(X)$ with a probability of 2^{-1} where $X \in \{0, 1\}^n$.

Property 3. Let $Y = P_{n/m(V)}(X)$ and $Y' = P_{n/m(V)}(X')$. Then $Hw(X \oplus X') = Hw(Y \oplus Y')$

Also, we can easily check that *Property* 2 and 3 are holded in their inverses.

3 Related Key Differential Attack on Full-Round SPECTR-H64

3.1 Description of SPECTR-H64

Encryption Procedure. SPECTR-H64 is a 12-round block cipher using 64-bit block size and 256-bit key size. The algorithm is designed as the following sequences (See Fig. 2);

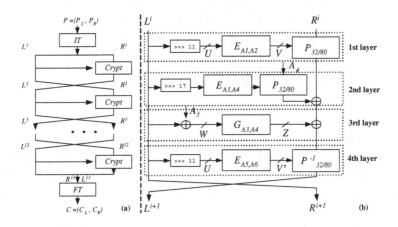

Fig. 2. (a). Encryption Scheme and (b) Round function $Crypt$

- IT and FT functions are simple transformations constructed by 32 parallel $P_{2/1}$-boxes.
- Round function $Crypt$ is composed of CP-boxes ($P_{32/80}$ and $P_{32/80}^{-1}$), extension box E, non-linear function G and some simple operations.
  - Let $V = (V_1 \mid V_2 \mid V_3 \mid V_4 \mid V_5)$, where $V \in \{0,1\}^{80}$, $X \in \{0,1\}^{32}$. Then $Y = P_{32/80(V)}^{-1}(X) = P_{32/80}^{-1}(X, V)$ is computed as like Fig. 3. $P_{32/80}$ is an inverse permutation of $P_{32/80}^{-1}$.

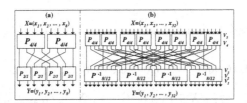

Fig. 3. Structure of the (a)$P_{8/12}^{-1}$-box and (b)$P_{32/80}^{-1}$-box

− E function extends a 32-bit input value U to a 80-bit control vector for the $P_{32/80}$ or $P_{32/80}^{-1}$-box using subkeys A and B. For example, in the 4-th layer of $Crypt$, $V' = (V_1'|V_2'|V_3'|V_4'|V_5') = E(U,A,B) = E_{(A,B)}(U)$ is computed by Table 1. In Table 1, i' denotes $u_i \oplus a_i$ and j'' denotes $u_j \oplus b_j$ where $A_5 = A = (a_1, \cdots, a_{32})$, $A_6 = B = (b_1, \cdots, b_{32})$, $U = (u_1, \cdots, u_{32})$ and $V_k' \in \{0,1\}^{16} (1 \le k \le 5)$.

Table 1. 80-bit control vectors and corresponding positions for $P_{32/80}^{\square -1}$-box

$P'_{32/80}$																
V'_5	10'	11'	12'	13'	14'	15'	16'	9'	2'	3'	4'	5'	6'	7	8'	1'	$(U \oplus A)_{lo}$
V'_4	14"	15"	16"	9"	10"	11"	12"	13"	6"	7"	8"	1"	2"	3"	4"	5"	$(U \oplus B)_{lo}$
Fixed permutation layer																
V'_3	30"	31"	32"	25"	26"	27"	28"	29"	22"	23"	24"	17"	18"	19"	20"	21"	$(U \oplus B)_{hi}$
V'_2	26'	27'	28'	29'	30'	31'	32'	25'	18'	19'	20'	21'	22'	23'	24'	17'	$(U \oplus A)_{hi}$
V'_1	17	18	19	20	21	22	23	24	25	26	27	28	29	30	31	32	U_{hi}

− G function is the only non-linear part of SPECTR-H64. Let $Z = G(W,A,B) = G_{(A,B)}(W)$, where $W = (w_1, \cdots, w_{32})$ is a 32-bit input value of G, and A and B are 32-bit subkeys. Then Z is computed as follows;

$$Z = W_0 \oplus W_1 \oplus (W_2 \otimes A) \oplus (W_2 \otimes W_5 \otimes B) \oplus (W_3 \otimes W_5) \oplus (W_4 \otimes B),$$

where $W_0 = W$, $W_1 = (1, w_1, \cdots, w_{31})$, $\cdots$, $W_5 = (1, 1, 1, 1, 1, w_1, \ldots, w_{27})$.

Key Schedule. Key schedule of SPECTR-H64 is very simple. The 256-bit master key K is split into eight 32-bit blocks $K_1, \cdots, K_8$, i.e., $K = (K_1, \cdots, K_8)$ and each round function directly uses six of them. In Fig. 2, $A = (A_1, A_2, A_3, A_4, A_5, A_6)$ denotes each round key sequence, where $A_j \in \{0,1\}^{32}$ $(1 \le j \le 6)$.

3.2   Properties of SPECTR-H64

Property 4. If we consider the input difference of FT as $0^{32} \mid e_i$ $(1 \le i \le 32)$, then the output difference of it is $0^{32} \mid e_j$ $(1 \le j \le 32)$ by *Property.* 3. Also, we can easily observe that if j is an odd integer then i is j or $j + 1$, and if j is an even integer then i is $j - 1$ or j.

Property 5. $E_{(A,B)}(U) \oplus E_{(A \oplus e_{32}, B)}(U) = d_{23}$, $E_{(A,B)}(U) \oplus E_{(A, B \oplus e_{32})}(U) = d_{35}$.

Property 6. Let A, B, and X be elements of $\{0,1\}^{32}$. Then

$$G_{(A,B)}(X) = G_{(A \oplus e_{32}, B)}(X \oplus e_{32}) \text{ or } G_{(A,B)}(X) \oplus G_{(A \oplus e_{32}, B)}(X \oplus e_{32}) = e_{32}.$$

Similarly, $G_{(A,B)}(X) = G_{(A, B \oplus e_{32})}(X)$ or $G_{(A,B)}(X) \oplus G_{(A, B \oplus e_{32})}(X) = e_{32}$.

For a $P_{8/12}^{-1}$-box[1], let (α,α') and (β,β') be the input and output pair of a $P_{8/12}^{-1}$-box respectively, where $\alpha, \alpha', \beta, \beta' \in \{0,1\}^8$. Then, we already know that $Hw(\alpha \oplus \alpha')=Hw(\beta \oplus \beta')$ under the same control vector by *Property* 3. In addition, we remark the following important property of $P_{8/12}^{-1}$-box. Let γ_i be a 8-bit binary strings in which the i-th bit is one and the others are zero, where $1 \leq i \leq 8$.

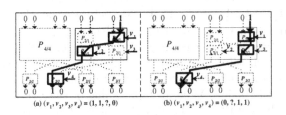

(a) $(v_1, v_2, v_3, v_4) = (1, 1, ?, 0)$ (b) $(v_1, v_2, v_3, v_4) = (0, ?, 1, 1)$

Fig. 4. An example of possible routes of the difference in $P_{8/12}^{\square\,1}$-box, when $i=8$ and $j=3$

Property 7. Suppose $\alpha \oplus \alpha' = \gamma_i$ and $\beta \oplus \beta' = \gamma_j$ and $1 \leq i,j \leq 8$. If i and j are known to us, then we can determine the two possible routes from i to j via 3 elements ($P_{2/1}$-boxes). That is, if we know i and j then we can also expect the corresponding two control vectors of 3 bits. Furthermore, if $i \in \{1,2,3,4\}$ then $j \in \{1,2,5,6\}$, otherwise ($i \in \{5,6,7,8\}$) $j \in \{3,4,7,8\}$ due to the structure of $P_{8/12}^{-1}$-box.

For example, if $i = 8$ and $j = 3$, then the corresponding control vector of 3 bits is whether $(v_1, v_2, v_3, v_4)=(1, 1, ?, 0)$ or $(v_1, v_2, v_3, v_4)=(0, ?, 1, 1)$, where $? \in \{0,1\}$. In Fig. 4, the bold line denotes the stream of the right most bit which has a difference and the dotted line represents the propagation of bits which have zero difference. *Property 7* is naturally expanded as follows.

Property 8. Let $X \oplus X' = e_i$ and $Y \oplus Y' = e_j$ under the same control vector V, where $Y = P_{32/80(V)}^{-1}(X)$, $Y' = P_{32/80(V)}^{-1}(X')$ and $1 \leq i,j \leq 32$. If we know i and j, then we can expect the corresponding two control vectors of possible routes from i to j.[2]

3.3 Related Key Differential Characteristic of Round Function *Crypt*

We consider the situation that two identical input values of *Crypt* change into two identical output values under two different round keys with a relation. Let

---

[1] Here, we consider the $P_{8/12}^{\square\,1}$-box as a inner component of $P_{32/80}^{\square\,1}$-box (see Fig. 1).

[2] In our attack scenario, we only consider the input difference of $P_{32/80}^{\square\,1}$-box as e_{32}, i.e., $i=32$. Then, due to the structure of $P_{32/80}^{\square\,1}$-box, the possible j is $4k$ or $4k-1$ where $1 \leq k \leq 8$.

two related round keys of $Crypt$ be $A=(A_1, A_2, A_3, A_4, A_5, A_6)$ and $A'=(A_1',$ $A_2', A_3', A_4', A_5', A_6')$ satisfying the following condition

$$A \oplus A' \in \{(e_{32},0,0,0,0,0),(0,e_{32},0,0,0,0),(0,0,e_{32},0,0,0)$$
$$,(0,0,0,e_{32},0,0),(0,0,0,0,e_{32},0),(0,0,0,0,0,e_{32})\}.$$

We call the subkey sequence pair A_j and A_j' with a relation $A_j \oplus A_j' = e_{32}$ 'the related subkey pair' and shortly denote it as (A_j,A_j'), where $1\leq j\leq6$. Notice that (A_1,A_1'), (A_2,A_2'), (A_5,A_5') and (A_6,A_6') are only used in $P_{32/80}$ or $P_{32/80}^{-1}$-box, and (A_3,A_3') and (A_4,A_4') are used in both $P_{32/80}$-box and nonlinear function G. With such observations, according to the position j of the related subkey pair (A_j,A_j'), we classify them into four cases represented in $C1$, $C2$, $C3$ and $C4$ as below. For convenience sake, we separate round function $Crypt$ into four layers (see Fig. 2 (b)). Let X be an input value of the i-th layer, and O_i and O_i' be output values of the i-th layer under the related subkey pair A_j and A_j' respectively, where $1\leq i\leq4$.

$C1$. $A_1 \oplus A_1' = e_{32}$ or $A_2 \oplus A_2' = e_{32}$
This case means that the related subkey pair (A_1,A_1') or (A_2,A_2') is only used to form 80-bit control vectors of the extension box E for a $P_{32/80}$-box in the 1-st layer.

By $Property$ 5 and $Property$ 2, if the input difference of the 1-st layer is zero then the output difference of it is zero with a probability of 2^{-1}.
Probability of $C1$: 2^{-1}

$C2$. $A_3 \oplus A_3' = e_{32}$
This case means that the related subkey pair (A_3,A_3') (1) is used to form 80-bit control vectors of the extension box E for a $P_{32/80}$-box in the 2-nd layer. (A_3,A_3') also (2) affects the input values of G in the 3-rd layer. The situation of the 3-rd layer are shortly described as follows :

$$O_3 = G_{(A_3,A_4)}(X \oplus A_3), \quad O_3' = G_{(A_3\oplus e_{32},A_4)}(X \oplus A_3 \oplus e_{32}).$$

(1) By $Property$ 5 and $Property$ 2, if the input difference of the 2-nd layer is zero then the output difference of it is zero with a probability of 2^{-1}.
(2) By $Property$ 6, if the input difference of the 3-rd layer is e_{32}, then the output difference of it is zero with a probability of 2^{-1}.
Probability of $C2$: 2^{-2}

$C3$. $A_4 \oplus A_4' = e_{32}$
In this case, the related subkey pair (A_4, A_4') (1) is used to form 80-bit control vectors of the extension box E for a $P_{32/80}$-box in the 2-nd layer and (2) is the input value of the $P_{32/80}$-box in the 2-nd layer, i.e., the input difference of the $P_{32/80}$-box is e_{32} in the 2-nd layer. Also, it (3) participate the operation of G as a key in the 3-rd layer. Note that by $Property$ 5, the control vectors for the $P_{32/80}$-box in the 2-nd layer are only differ in the

35-th bit position.Since we consider zero output difference for the $P_{2/1}$-box corresponding to control vectors v_{35} and $v_{35} \oplus 1$ in our related key differential characteristic, the input difference e_{32} of the $P_{32/80}$-box is independent of these control vectors in the 2-nd layer.

(1) In the 2-nd layer, if the input difference of the $P_{2/1}$-box corresponding to control vectors v_{35} and $v_{35} \oplus 1$ is zero, then the output difference of it is zero with a probability of 2^{-1} by *Property* 1.

(2) In the 2-nd layer, let the difference of two control vectors V and V' for the $P_{32/80}$-box be $\Delta V = (\Delta v_1, \Delta v_2, \cdots, \Delta v_{80})$, then ΔV is all zero except the 35-th bit position by *Property* 5, i.e., if

$$V = E_{(A_3, A_4)}(U) \text{ and } V' = E_{(A_3, A_4 \oplus e_{32})}(U), \text{ then } V \oplus V' = d_{35},$$

where $U = X \ggg 11$. We especially concentrate on the fact that the differences $\Delta v_{16}, \Delta v_{32}, \Delta v_{48}, \Delta v_{64}$, and Δv_{80} are all zero. Then, due to the structure of a $P_{32/80}$-box and *Property* 3, we can easily observe that the input difference e_{32} does not change after the $P_{32/80}$-box in the 2-nd layer with a probability of 2^{-5}, i.e., $O_2 \oplus O_2' = e_{32}$ with a probability of 2^{-5}.

(3) By *Property* 6, if the input difference of the 3-rd layer is zero then the output difference of it is e_{32} with a probability of 2^{-1}, i.e., if

$$O_3 = G_{A_3, A_4}(X \oplus A_3) \text{ and } O_3' = G_{A_3, A_4 \oplus e_{32}}(X \oplus A_3), \text{ then } O_3 \oplus O_3' = e_{32}$$

with a probability of 2^{-1}.

If all of the conditions (1), (2) and (3) are satisfied, then the output difference of round function is zero. That is, if the input difference is zero then the output difference is also zero under $C3$ with a probability of 2^{-7}.

Probability of $C3 : 2^{-7}$

C4. $A_5 \oplus A_5' = e_{32}$ or $A_6 \oplus A_6' = e_{32}$
This case is almost similar to $C1$.

Probability of $C4 : 2^{-1}$

3.4   Full-Round Attack on SPECTR-H64

Full-round related key differential characteristic. We can construct various full-round related key differential characteristic using four cases in Section 3.3.Here we present one of them in order to attack on full-round SPECTR-H64. First, we consider the respective encryption of a plaintext $P = (P_L, P_R)$ under the following two related keys K and K' :

$$K = (K_1, K_2, K_3, K_4, K_5, K_6, K_7, K_8) \text{ and}$$
$$K' = (K_1, K_2, K_3, K_4, K_5 \oplus e_{32}, K_6, K_7, K_8).$$

That is, the related subkey pair is $(K_5, K_5 \oplus e_{32})$ used in our attack. Then, we can easily construct a full-round related key differential characteristic with a probability of 2^{-17} represented in Table. 2. Note that the related subkey pair $(K_5, K_5 \oplus e_{32})$ is not used in the 1-st, 5-th and 9-th round by key schedule of SPECTR-H64. As a result, if we request ciphertexts $C = (C_L, C_R)$ of P under

Table 2. A full-round related key differential characteristic of SPECTR-H64

Round	1	2	3	4	5	6	7	8	9	10	11	12
Case	·	$C4$	$C1$	$C2$	·	$C4$	$C1$	$C3$	·	$C4$	$C1$	$C3$
Probability	1	2^{-1}	2^{-1}	2^{-2}	1	2^{-1}	2^{-1}	2^{-7}	1	2^{-1}	2^{-1}	2^{-2}

key K and $C' = (C'_L, C'_R)$ of P under key K', then C and C' also have the identical value, i.e., $C \oplus C' = 0$ with a probability of 2^{-17}. However, in order to recover the subkeys associated with the last round and FT, we actually consider another full-round related key differential characteristic. We call it Ψ. Ψ is equal to the full-round related key differential characteristic mentioned above except the output difference of the 3-rd layer, in the last round function. More precisely, we consider the output difference of the 3-rd layer as e_{32}, not zero in the last round function, i.e., the input difference of the $P^{-1}_{32/80}$-box in the last round function is e_{32} in Ψ. In addition, according to *Property.* 6, the probability that the output difference of G will be e_{32}, is also 2^{-1} when the input difference of the 3-rd layer is zero. In other words, Ψ is another full-round related key differential characteristic such that if the input difference of plaintext pair is zero, then the difference of ciphertext pair is $(0, e_i)$ under related keys K and K' with a probability of 2^{-17}.

Key recovery attack on full-round SPECTR-H64. Now, we describe how to recover the subkeys used in the final round and FT using Ψ. We consider 2^{23} plaintexts P_i for the success probability 95.8%, where $1 \le i \le 2^{23}$. Let C_i and C'_i be the ciphertexts of a plaintext P_i under the above keys K and K' respectively.

For each pair C_i, C'_i satisfying $C_i \oplus C'_i = (0, e_{j'})$ let $k_{e_{j'}}$ be a value of K_2 related to the difference $e_{j'}$ in FT and $k^{FT}_{j_1}, \cdots, k^{FT}_{j_6}$ be a possible value of '$K_2.P$ in FT'. '$K_2.P$ in FT' means the bit position of K_2 affecting $U \lll 11$ in FT. Refer to Table 3. If we guess $k_{e_{j'}}$, then we can get the output difference e_j of $P^{-1}_{32/80}$-box in the final round. Therefore, for e_j two possible C.V. values are determined by *Property* 8. Here, C.V. denotes a control vector and we let $b_{j_1}, \cdots, b_{j_6}$ be the C.V. value. Also, if we guess $k^{FT}_{j_1}, \cdots, k^{FT}_{j_6}$, then we can obtain $u_{j_1}, \cdots, u_{j_6}$ from C_i or C'_i where $u_{j_1}, \cdots, u_{j_6}$ be a possible value at the position $U.P$ in Table 3. $U.P$ means the bit position of U relevant to C.V..

Let $k^{A_5}_{j_1}, \cdots, k^{A_5}_{j_4}$ and $k^{A_6}_{j_1}, k^{A_6}_{j_2}$ be a possible values of $A_5.P$ and $A_6.P$, respectively. $A_5.P$ ($A_6.P$) denotes the bit position of K_1 (K_2) affecting C.V. as A_5 (A_6). Then, using Table 1, if we check that $k^{A_5}_{j_1} \oplus u_{j_1} = b_{j_1}, k^{A_5}_{j_1} \oplus u_{j_2} = b_{j_2}, k^{A_6}_{j_2} \oplus u_{j_3} = b_{j_3}, k^{A_5}_{j_2} \oplus u_{j_4} = b_{j_4}, u_{j_6} = b_{j_6}$ or $k^{A_5}_{j_1} \oplus u_{j_1} = b_{j_1}, k^{A_6}_{j_1} \oplus u_{j_2} = b_{j_2}, k^{A_6}_{j_2} \oplus u_{j_3} = b_{j_3}, k^{A_5}_{j_3} \oplus u_{j_5} = b_{j_5}, u_{j_6} = b_{j_6}$, there only remain four possible values of $k^{A_5}_{j_1}, \cdots, k^{A_5}_{j_4}, k^{A_6}_{j_1}, k^{A_6}_{j_2}$ among all 2^6 values. We call this procedure finding four possible values for $k^{A_5}_{j_1}, \cdots, k^{A_5}_{j_4}, k^{A_6}_{j_1}, k^{A_6}_{j_2}$ with the above guessing value of $k_{j_1}^{FT}, \cdots, k_{j_6}^{FT}, k_{e_{j'}}$ 'Find procedure', and denote it $Find(C_i, C_i')$. For convenience, let $k_{j_1}, \cdots, k_{j_7}$ be the value for $k_{j_1}^{FT}, \cdots, k_{j_6}^{FT}, k_{e_{j'}}$ and $k_{j_1}', \cdots, k_{j_6}'$ be the value for $k_{j_1}^{A_5}, \cdots, k_{j_4}^{A_5}, k_{j_1}^{A_6}, k_{j_2}^{A_6}$. '$k_1, k_2, \cdots, k_{13} \in Find(C_i, C_i')$' means that $k_1, k_2, \cdots, k_{13}$ is a possible value for $k_{j_1}, \cdots, k_{j_7}, k_{j_1}', \cdots, k_{j_6}'$ for given (C_i, C_i'). Let $x_1, \cdots, x_n$ be a binary string then $Bi(x_1, \cdots, x_n)$ denotes the number $x_1 * 2^0 + \cdots + x_n * 2^{n-1}$. Algorithm 1 describes how to recover partial 30 bits subkey of K_1 and K_2.

Assumption : The attacker knows that $K \oplus K' = (0, 0, 0, 0, e_{32}, 0, 0, 0,)$

Input : $(P_1, C_1), (P_1, C_1'), \cdots (P_{2^{23}}, C_{2^{23}}), (P_{2^{23}}, C_{2^{23}}')$

Output: 9-bit partial key of K_1 and 21-bit partial key of K_2

$\cdot \mathcal{D}_3, \mathcal{D}_4, \cdots, \mathcal{D}_{31}, \mathcal{D}_{32}$: empty set, $K[j][Bi(k_1, k_2, \cdots, k_{13})] = 0$

   where $j \in \{3, 4, 7, 8, \cdots, 31, 32\}$

1. For each i $(1 \leq i \leq 2^{23})$

   If $C_i \oplus C_i' = (0, e_j)$, for some j

   $\mathcal{D}_j = \mathcal{D}_j \cup \{(C_i, C_i')\}$

2. For each $(C_i, C_i') \in \mathcal{D}_j$

   Compute $Find(C_i, C_i')$

   2.1 For all $(k_1, k_2, \cdots, k_{13}) \in Find(C_i, C_i')$

      $K[j][Bi(k_1, k_2, \cdots, k_{13})] += 1$

   2.2 If a $K[j][Bi(k_1, k_2, \cdots, k_{13})] \geq 16$, output it

---

Algorithm 1: Related key differential attack on full-round SPECTR-H64.

Table 3. Partial table of C.V. position and C.V. value for each e_j when the input difference of $P_{32/80}^{\blacksquare 1}$-box is e_{32} ($? \in \{0, 1\}$)

e_j	C.V. position	C.V.value	U.P	$U \lll 11.P$	$K_2.P$ in FT	$A_5.P$	$A_6.P$
e_3	80,63,36,19,20,2	1,1,1,1,?,0 / 1,1,0,?,1,1	1,4,25,28,29,18	22,25,14,17,18,7	11,13,7,9,9,4	1,28,29	4,25
e_4	80,63,36,19,20,2	1,1,1,1,?,1 / 1,1,0,?,1,0	1,4,25,28,29,18	22,25,14,17,18,7	11,13,7,9,9,4	1,28,29	4,25
e_7	80,63,36,19,20,4	1,1,1,0,?,0 / 1,1,0,?,0,1	1,4,25,28,29,20	22,25,14,17,18,9	11,13,7,9,9,5	1,28,29	4,25
e_8	80,63,36,19,20,4	1,1,1,0,?,1 / 1,1,0,?,0,0	1,4,25,28,29,20	22,25,14,17,18,9	11,13,7,9,9,5	1,28,29	4,25
e_{11}	80,63,40,23,24,6	1,0,1,1,?,0 / 1,0,0,?,1,1	1,4,29,32,25,22	22,25,18,21,14,11	11,13,9,11,7,6	1,32,25	4,29
e_{12}	80,63,40,23,24,6	1,0,1,1,?,1 / 1,0,0,?,1,0	1,4,29,32,25,22	22,25,18,21,14,11	11,13,9,11,7,6	1,32,25	4,29
e_{15}	80,63,40,23,24,8	1,0,1,0,?,0 / 1,0,0,?,0,1	1,4,29,32,25,24	22,25,18,21,14,13	11,13,9,11,7,7	1,32,25	4,29
e_{16}	80,63,40,23,24,8	1,0,1,0,?,1 / 1,0,0,?,0,0	1,4,29,32,25,24	22,25,18,21,14,13	11,13,9,11,7,7	1,32,25	4,29

4   Related Key Differential Attack on Full-Round CIKS-1

In this section we briefly introduce a description of the block cipher CIKS-1 and how to construct a 7-round related key differential characteristic with a probability of 2^{-2}. Then we present a related key differential attack on full-round CIKS-1.

146   Y. Ko et al.

4.1   Description of CIKS-1

CIKS-1 is a 64-bit iterated block cipher with a 256-bit key size and the number of 8 rounds. One round encryption of CIKS-1 is composed of CP-box permutations ($P_{32/48}$, $P_{32/80}$), fixed permutations ($\prod_1$, $\prod_2$), rotations by 7bits ($\ggg 7$), one exclusive-or operation, and 16 parallel modulo 2^2 additions denoted by a single operation " $+ ... +$ " as shown on Fig. 5. For more details, see [6].

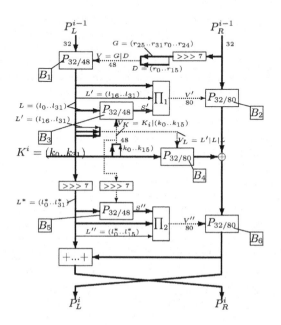

Fig. 5. The ith-round transformation with internal key scheduling

The Key schedule of CIKS-1 is based on CP-boxes and contained in each round transformation. To begin with, the master key K is divided into eight 32-bit subkeys as like $K = (K_1, ..., K_8)$ and then each of subkeys is inserted into each round transformation with internal key scheduling. Here we say that K_i is a input key of the ith round, where $1 \le i \le 8$.

4.2   Related Key Differential Attack on Full-Round CIKS-1

In this subsection, we attack on full-round CIKS-1 using a 7-round related key differential characteristic with a probability of 2^{-2}. First of all, in order to construct a 7-round related key differential characteristic, we consider the following two related keys K and K';

$$K = (K_1, \ldots, K_7, K_8) \text{ and } K' = (K_1, \ldots, K_7 \oplus e_{32}, K_8)$$

Then we request the encryption of the identical plaintext $P = (P_L, P_R)$ under K and K', respectively. We know that these two keys generate the same round keys for the first 6 rounds from the key schedule of CIKS-1. Thus the output difference of the 6th round is also zero with a probability of 1 because the input difference of the plaintexts is zero. This is what is called a 6-round related key differential characteristic with a probability of 1. Since there is a difference of the related round key pair, e_{32} in the 7th round, we must perceive that this difference directly affects the only B_3, B_4, B_5 boxes in round transformation of the 7th round (See Fig. 5). So, we can know the following facts from properties mentioned in Section 2.2.

1. The output difference of the B_3 box in the 7th round is zero with a probability of $1/2$ by the *property* 2.
2. The output difference of the B_5 box in the 7th round is zero with a probability of $1/2$ by the *property* 2.
3. Since the hamming weight of the input difference of B_4 is 1, the hamming weight of the output difference of it in 7th round is also 1 by *property* 3.

These facts allow us to construct the desired 7-round distinguisher. That is, they give us the following additional information;

- The output difference of the B_2 box in the 7th round is zero by the above fact 1.
- The hamming weight of the output difference of the B_6-box in the 7th round is 1 by the above facts 2 and 3.
- The hamming weight of the output difference of 16 parallel modulo 2^2 additions(" $+ \ldots +$ ") in the 7th round is equal to 1 or 2 because there can be generated the carry in performing modulo 2^2 addition.

Thus, by the above information, the hamming weight of the output difference of the 7th round is 2 or 3 with a probability of 2^{-2} because the hammming weight of the left output difference (respectively, the right output difference) of the 7th round is 1 or 2 (respectively, 1). This means one (7th)-round related key differential characteristic. Combining a 6-round related key differential characteristic with a probability of 1 with the 7th round related key differential characteristic with a probability of 2^{-2}, we can construct the desired 7-round related key differential characteristic with a probability of 2^{-2}. We have simulated whether this characteristic satisfies with a probability of 2^{-2} using 2^4 random plaintexts and 2^{20} random related key pairs and then we confirmed that the related key pairs satisfying this characteristic presented about 6.8 right pairs on average. So, we are convinced that our characteristic has the better probability than 2^{-2}.

We now attack on full-round CIKS-1 using the above 7-round related key differential characteristic with a probability of 2^{-2}. This attack is 1R related key differential attack in order to retrieve the 8th round key. The procedure of this attack is as follows;

1. Choose 2^4 plaintexts P^i, $i = 0, ..., 2^4 - 1$ and encrypt the plaintexts under $K = (K_1, \ldots, K_7, K_8)$ and $K' = (K_1, \ldots, K_7 \oplus e_{32}, K_8)$, respectively to get 2^4 ciphertext pairs, C^i and C'^i, of P under K and K' respectively.
2. Initialize an array of 2^{32} counters corresponding to the possible 8th round key K_8.

3. For each of 32-bit guessing key value K_8^i do the following;
   a) Decrypt the 2^4 ciphertext pairs, C^i and C''^i through the 8th round transformation and denoted 2^4 output pairs of the 7th round which we get through the decryption process by C_7^i and $C_7''^i$.
   b) Compute the difference $\triangle^i = C_7^i \oplus C_7''^i$ and Check whether the Hamming weight for each of $\triangle^i$ is 2 or 3. If so, increase the corresponding counter by 1.
4. Check all counters and output the round key whose counter is than or equal to 3.

The data complexity of the above algorithm is 2^4 chosen plaintexts and the time complexity of it is about 2^{33} $(= (1/8) \cdot 2^4 \cdot 2^{32})$ encryptions for an expected success probability 80%.

5   Conclusion

In this paper, we have shown related key differential attacks on full-round SPECTR-H64 and CIKS-1 which are very efficient algorithms for the applications of many network requiring high speed encryption. These are the best known attacks and can be implemented clearly in range of today's computing power. Our results show that the simple key schedule should be avoided in order to prevent such simple related key attacks.

References

1. N. D. Goots, B. V. Izotov, A. A. Moldovyan, and N. A. Moldovyan, "Fast Ciphers for Cheap Hardware : Differential Analysis of SPECTR-H64", *MMM-ACNS'03*, volume 2776 of *Lecture Notes of Computer Science*, Springer-Verlag, 2003, pp. 449-452.
2. N. D. Goots, A. A. Moldovyan, N. A. Moldovyan, "Fast Encryption ALgorithm Spectr-H64", *MMM-ACNS'01*, volume 2052 of *Lecture Notes of Computer Science*, Springer-Verlag, 2001, pp. 275-286.
3. J. Kelsey, B. Schneier, and D. Wagner, "Key Schedule Cryptanalysis of IDEA, G-DES, GOST, SAFER, and Triple-DES", *Advances in Cryptology - CRYPTO '96*, volume 1109 of *Lecture Notes of Computer Science*, Springer-Verlag, 1996, pp. 237-251.
4. Y. Ko, D. Hong, S. Hong, S. Lee, and J. Lim, "Linear Cryptanalysis on SPECTR-H64 with Higher Order Differential Property", *MMM-ACNS03*, volume 2776 of *Lecture Notes of Computer Science*, Springer-Verlag, 2003, pp. 298-307.
5. C. Lee, D. Hong, S. Lee, S. Lee, H. Yang, and J. Lim, "A Chosen Plaintext Linear Attack on Block Cipher CIKS-1", *The 4th International Conference, ICICS 2002*, volume 2513 of *Lecture Notes of Computer Science*, Springer-Verlag, 2002, pp. 456-468.
6. A. A. Moldovyan and N. A. Moldovyan, "A cipher Based on Data-Dependent Permutations", *Journal of Cryptology*, volume 15, no. 1 (2002), pp. 61-72
7. N. Sklavos, A. A. Moldovyan, and O. Koufopavlou, "Encryption and Data Dependent Permutations : Implementation Cost and Performance Evaluation", *MMM-ACNS'03*, volume 2776 of *Lecture Notes of Computer Science*, Springer-Verlag, 2003, pp. 337-348.

The Security of Cryptosystems Based on Class Semigroups of Imaginary Quadratic Non-maximal Orders

Michael J. Jacobson, Jr.*

Centre for Applied Cryptographic Research, University of Calgary,
2500 University Drive NW, Calgary, Alberta, Canada, T2N 1N4
jacobs@cpsc.ucalgary.ca

Abstract. In 2003, Kim and Moon [8] proposed two public-key cryptosystems based on arithmetic in the class semigroup of an imaginary non-maximal quadratic order. The authors argue that there is no known subexponential algorithm for solving the discrete logarithm problem in the class semigroup, and that as a result, their cryptosystems achieve a higher level of security as compared to those based on the class group. In this paper, we show that well-known structural properties of the class semigroup render these crytosystems insecure, and that any cryptosystems based on the class semigroup are unlikely to provide any more security than those using the class group.

1 Introduction

Since Diffie and Hellman's proposal of a key exchange system based on arithmetic in the multiplicative group of a finite field, other finite abelian groups have been used for numerous applications in public-key cryptography. The security of these schemes relies on the intractability of the discrete logarithm problem in the group. Generic algorithms for computing discrete logarithms have exponential complexity and work in any finite abelian group, but in most cases additional algebraic properties lead to index-calculus algorithms with subexponential complexity. As a result, larger parameters are required to provide equivalent levels of security, resulting in less efficient cryptosystems.

In an effort to find alternative mathematical bases for public-key cryptography, attention has been focused recently on other algebraic structures. By not using a finite abelian group, the hope is that stronger security can be achieved as the rich structure leading in many cases to subexponential algorithms for solving the discrete logarithm problem is absent.

Kim and Moon [8] propose to use the class semigroup of an imaginary non-maximal quadratic order to achieve this goal. The ideal class group (a finite abelian group) of an imaginary quadratic order, both maximal and non-maximal, has been used as the basis for a number of cryptosystems (see for example [2,10,

---

* The author is supported in part by NSERC of Canada.

H. Wang et al. (Eds.): ACISP 2004, LNCS 3108, pp. 149–156, 2004.

6]), and it has been shown that the associated discrete logarithm problem has subexponential complexity [5]. In contrast, little is known about computational problems in the class semigroup of an imaginary non-maximal quadratic order. Kim and Moon postulate that because the underlying algebraic structure is no longer a finite abelian group (it is instead a finite semigroup), computing discrete logarithms will have at best exponential complexity.

Unfortunately, the class semigroup considered by Kim and Moon is in fact a special type of semigroup called a Clifford semigroup [11] that has more structure than an arbitrary semigroup. In this paper, we recall the properties of Clifford semigroups and demonstrate that the cryptosystems proposed in [8] are insecure. In addition, we show that any cryptosystem based on arithmetic in the class semigroup of an imaginary non-maximal quadratic order is unlikely to provide more security than those based on the ideal class group itself.

2 Class Semigroups of Imaginary Quadratic Non-maximal Orders

The basic notions of imaginary quadratic orders can be found in [1,3]. For a more comprehensive treatment of the relationship between maximal and non-maximal orders we refer to [4,9].

Let $\Delta \equiv 0, 1 \pmod 4$ be a negative integer whose absolute value is not a square. The quadratic order of discriminant Δ is defined to be

$$\mathcal{O}_\Delta = \mathbb{Z} + \omega \mathbb{Z} \ ,$$

where

$$\omega = \begin{cases} \sqrt{\frac{\Delta}{4}}, & \text{if } \Delta \equiv 0 \pmod 4 \ , \\ \frac{1+\sqrt{\Delta}}{2}, & \text{if } \Delta \equiv 1 \pmod 4 \ . \end{cases}$$

If Δ_1 (or $\Delta_1/4$ if $\Delta_1 \equiv 0 \pmod 4$) is square-free, then $\mathcal{O}_{\Delta_1}$ is the *maximal order* of the quadratic number field $\mathbb{Q}(\sqrt{\Delta_1})$ and Δ_1 is called a fundamental discriminant. The *non-maximal order* of conductor $f > 1$ with non-fundamental discriminant $\Delta_f = \Delta_1 f^2$ is denoted by $\mathcal{O}_{\Delta_f}$. We omit the subscripts to reference arbitrary (fundamental or non-fundamental) discriminants. Because $\mathbb{Q}(\sqrt{\Delta_1}) = \mathbb{Q}(\sqrt{\Delta_f})$ we also omit the subscripts to reference the number field $\mathbb{Q}(\sqrt{\Delta})$.

The standard representation of a fractional $\mathcal{O}_\Delta$-ideal is

$$\mathfrak{a} = q \left(\mathbb{Z} + \frac{b + \sqrt{\Delta}}{2a} \mathbb{Z} \right) = q(a, b) \ ,$$

where $q \in \mathbb{Q}_{>0}, a \in \mathbb{Z}_{>0}, c = (b^2 - \Delta)/(4a) \in \mathbb{Z}$, and $-a < b \leq a$. The norm of this ideal is $N(\mathfrak{a}) = aq^2$. An ideal is called primitive if $q = 1$. The standard representation of a primitive ideal boils down to (a, b). A primitive ideal is called *reduced* if $|b| \leq a \leq c$ and $b \geq 0$ if $a = c$.

The product $\mathfrak{ab}$ of ideals $\mathfrak{a}$ and $\mathfrak{b}$ can be computed in polynomial time. An ideal $\mathfrak{a}$ is said to be invertible if there exists another ideal $\mathfrak{b}$ such that $\mathfrak{ab} = \mathcal{O}_\Delta$, and $\mathfrak{a}$ is invertible if and only if $\gcd(a, b, c) = 1$. The group of invertible $\mathcal{O}_\Delta$-ideals is denoted by $\mathcal{I}_\Delta$. Two ideals $\mathfrak{a}, \mathfrak{b}$ are said to be equivalent if there is a $\gamma \in \mathbb{Q}(\sqrt{\Delta})$, such that $\mathfrak{a} = \gamma\mathfrak{b}$. This equivalence relation is denoted by $\mathfrak{a} \sim \mathfrak{b}$. The set of principal $\mathcal{O}_\Delta$-ideals, i.e., those ideals which are equivalent to $\mathcal{O}_\Delta$, is denoted by $\mathcal{P}_\Delta$. The factor group $\mathcal{I}_\Delta/\mathcal{P}_\Delta$ is called the *class group* of $\mathcal{O}_\Delta$, denoted by $Cl(\Delta)$. The group elements are equivalence classes (the equivalence class of $\mathfrak{a}$ is denoted by $[\mathfrak{a}]$), and the neutral element is the class of ideals equivalent to $\mathcal{O}_\Delta$. Each equivalence class can be represented uniquely by a reduced ideal. Efficient algorithms for the group operation (multiplication and reduction of ideals) can be found in [7]. $Cl(\Delta)$ is a finite abelian group, and its order is called the *class number* of $\mathcal{O}_\Delta$, denoted by $h(\Delta)$.

Note that the class group $Cl(\Delta)$ is defined in terms of the invertible ideals of $\mathcal{O}_\Delta$. Similar definitions hold if all ideals, including non-invertible ideals are considered. Let $\mathcal{F}_{\Delta_f}$ denote the set of all non-zero ideals of a non-maximal order $\mathcal{O}_{\Delta_f}$. Because $\mathcal{F}_{\Delta_f}$ contains non-invertible ideals, it is not a group. The set of principal ideals $\mathcal{P}_{\Delta_f}$ is a subgroup of $\mathcal{F}_{\Delta_f}$ and the finite quotient semigroup $\mathcal{F}_{\Delta_f}/\mathcal{P}_{\Delta_f}$, denoted by $Cl_s(\Delta_f)$, is called the *class semigroup* of $\mathcal{O}_{\Delta_f}$.

2.1   The Structure of the Class Semigroup

In [11], the authors describe the structure of the class semigroup of an order in a number field. In particular, they prove that if the order is quadratic, then the class semigroup $Cl_s(\Delta_f)$ is a Clifford semigroup and has a particularly rich algebraic structure. There are a number of equivalent definitions of a Clifford semigroup (for example, see [11]); for our purposes, the important characteristic is that $Cl_s(\Delta_f)$ is a semilattice of groups and thus has the following properties:

1. $Cl_s(\Delta_f)$ is a disjoint union of groups G_k, where $k \in \mathcal{E}$ and $\mathcal{E}$ is a semilattice,
2. If $h, k \in \mathcal{E}$ and $k \leq h$ in the partial order defined on the semilattice $\mathcal{E}$, there exists a *bonding homomorphism* $\phi_{hk} : G_h \mapsto G_k$.

The semilattice $\mathcal{E}$ consists of all the idempotents of $Cl_s(\Delta_f)$, namely, the equivalence classes of ideals $\mathfrak{e}$ for which $\mathfrak{e}^2 \sim \mathfrak{e}$.

Proposition 2.1 ([11], Proposition 13). *The idempotents of $Cl_s(\Delta_f)$ are the equivalence classes of ideals of the form $\mathfrak{e} = (k, b_k)$ where $k \in \mathbb{Z}$ divides the conductor f.*

Thus, each idempotent $[\mathfrak{e}]$ corresponds to a unique divisor k of f. The partial order on the semilattice $\mathcal{E}$ is given by $[\mathfrak{e}] \leq [\mathfrak{h}]$ for $\mathfrak{e} = (k, b_k)$ and $\mathfrak{h} = (h, b_h)$ with $k, h \mid f$ if and only if $h \mid k$, or equivalently $\mathfrak{e}\mathfrak{h} \sim \mathfrak{e}$.

The idempotents of $Cl_s(\Delta_f)$ are in one-to-one correspondence with the subgroups G_k. Given k and $\mathfrak{e} = (k, b_k)$, the subgroup G_k corresponding to the idempotent $[\mathfrak{e}]$ is defined as:

$$G_k = \{[\mathfrak{a}] \in Cl_s(\Delta_f) : \mathfrak{a}\mathfrak{e} \sim \mathfrak{a} \text{ and } \exists [\mathfrak{b}] \in Cl_s(\Delta_f) \text{ such that } \mathfrak{ab} \sim \mathfrak{e}\} .$$

Notice that $G_1 = Cl(\Delta_f)$, as the idempotent corresponding to 1 is simply the equivalence class containing the order $\mathcal{O}_{\Delta_f}$ itself, and as a result, G_1 contains all the equivalence classes of invertible ideals in $\mathcal{O}_{\Delta_f}$.

For $[\mathfrak{h}], [\mathfrak{k}] \in \mathcal{E}$, if $[\mathfrak{k}] \leq [\mathfrak{h}]$ (i.e., $\mathfrak{h} = (h, b_k)$ and $\mathfrak{k} = (k, b_k)$ with $h, k \mid f$ and $h \mid k$) then the bonding homomorphism $\phi_{hk} : G_h \mapsto G_k$ is given by $[\mathfrak{a}] \mapsto [\mathfrak{a}\mathfrak{k}]$. Furthermore, in the case of $Cl_s(\Delta_f)$, the bonding homomorphisms are all surjective. In particular, we will need the following proposition:

Proposition 2.2. *For any $k > 1$ dividing f, there is a surjective homomorphism $\phi_k : Cl(\Delta_f) \mapsto G_k$ given by $[\mathfrak{a}] \mapsto [\mathfrak{a}\mathfrak{k}]$.*

Proof. We have $G_1 = Cl(\Delta_f)$. Because $1 \mid k$, we have $k \leq 1$ in the partial order defined on the corresponding idempotents, and the result follows.

Finally, the following proposition provides an easy criterion for determining whether two ideal equivalence classes lie in the same subgroup G_k :

Proposition 2.3. *Given ideals $\mathfrak{a} = (a_1, b_1)$ and $\mathfrak{b} = (a_2, b_2)$ of a non-maximal order $\mathcal{O}_{\Delta_f}$, $[\mathfrak{a}], [\mathfrak{b}] \in G_k$ if and only if $k = \gcd(a_1, b_1, c_1) = \gcd(a_2, b_2, c_2)$ where $c_1 = (\Delta_f - b_1^2)/4a_1$ and $c_2 = (\Delta_f - b_2^2)/4a_2$.*

Proof. Follows easily from Proposition 14 of [11].

3   Security of the Kim-Moon Cryptosystems

In [8], Kim and Moon propose two cryptosystems based on arithmetic in the class semigroup of an imaginary non-maximal quadratic order. The first is a variation of the Diffie-Hellman key exchange protocol using arithmetic in the class semigroup and the second is a straight-forward adaptation of this protocol to an El Gamal-type encryption protocol. As is the case with standard Diffie-Hellman key exchange and El Gamal encryption, the security considerations are essentially the same for both protocols, so we confine our attention to the key exchange protocol.

The key exchange protocol proceeds as described in [8]. The public system parameters are first selected:

- a non-fundamental discriminant $\Delta_f = \Delta_1 f^2$
- a *non-invertible* ideal $\mathfrak{a} = (a, b)$ of $\mathcal{O}_{\Delta_f}$.

Alice and Bob agree on the secret key k as follows:

1. Alice selects a random integer x, computes the reduced ideal $\mathfrak{b} \sim \mathfrak{a}^x$, and sends $\mathfrak{b}$ to Bob.
2. Bob selects a random integer y, computes the reduced ideal $\mathfrak{c} \sim \mathfrak{a}^y$, and sends $\mathfrak{c}$ to Alice.
3. Alice computes the reduced ideal $\mathfrak{k}_A = (a_1, b_1) \sim \mathfrak{c}^x$ and Bob computes the reduced ideal $\mathfrak{k}_B = (a_2, b_2) \sim \mathfrak{b}^y$. As pointed out in [8], we have $\mathfrak{k}_A \sim \mathfrak{k}_B$ and the shared key k is taken to be $k = \gcd(a_1, b_1, c_1) = \gcd(a_2, b_2, c_2)$, where $c_1 = (\Delta_f - b_1^2)/4a_1$ and $c_2 = (\Delta_f - b_2^2)/4a_2$.

The authors claim that the security of this protocol relies on the intractability of solving the discrete logarithm problem in the class semigroup of $\mathcal{O}_{\Delta_f}$; given $[\mathfrak{a}], [\mathfrak{b}] \in Cl_s(\Delta_f)$, compute $x \in \mathbb{Z}$ such that $\mathfrak{b} \sim \mathfrak{a}^x$. Indeed, as in the general Diffie-Hellman setting, by solving an instance of this discrete logarithm problem, an adversary can recover either x or y and thus compute the shared key. The authors argue further that the usual index-calculus algorithms for computing discrete logarithms in the ideal class group do not apply to the semigroup case, due to the non-invertibility of ideals in the semigroup setting (and hence lack of unique factorization). The conclusion is that there is no efficient algorithm to solve this discrete logarithm problem, and that as a result, their cryptosystem should be able to use smaller parameters than those based on the ideal class group.

However, the first immediate problem with this cryptosystem is that the set of possible keys is too small. In fact, given a choice of the non-invertible ideal $\mathfrak{a} = (a, b)$, only one value of the key will ever be obtained, namely $k = \gcd(a, b, c)$ where $c = (\Delta_f - b^2)/4a$. Furthermore, knowledge of the public parameter $\mathfrak{a}$ allows one to easily compute k and thus no secrecy is provided whatsoever. This mistake is most likely due to an error propagated from [11] (Remark, p.387) is which the authors state that two ideals $\mathfrak{a} = (a_1, b_1)$ and $\mathfrak{b} = (a_2, b_2)$ are equivalent if and only if $\gcd(a_1, b_1, c_1) = \gcd(a_2, b_2, c_2)$. This remark is false — an easy counterexample is the case in which both ideals are invertible and thus the gcds are both 1. Clearly, it is possible to have two invertible ideals that are not equivalent.

What the authors of [11] likely meant is that $\gcd(a_1, b_1, c_1) = \gcd(a_2, b_2, c_2)$ if and only if the equivalence classes of the corresponding ideals are in the same subgroup G_k (stated as Proposition 2.3 above). The implication of this for the Kim-Moon cryptosystem is that the usual Diffie-Hellman key exchange protocol is being executed in the finite abelian group G_k (a subgroup of the class semigroup) where $k = \gcd(a, b, c)$. Thus, all the ideals generated during the execution of the protocol lie in the same subgroup G_k, and in particular, the gcd of the coefficients of each of these ideals is k.

4   Suitability of Class Semigroups for Public-Key Cryptography

While the observation that the cryptosystems in [8] take place in a finite abelian group G_k exposes their main flaw, it also leads to an easy fix. Every equivalence class in G_k is represented uniquely by a reduced ideal. Thus, at the end of the protocol $\mathfrak{k}_A = \mathfrak{k}_B$, and we can take $k = a_1 = a_2$ for the shared key, exactly as in the Diffie-Hellman analogue in the full class group [2]. In short, the protocol is nothing more than the usual Diffie-Hellman key exchange protocol in the finite abelian group G_k.

The remaining question is whether cryptography in a subgroup G_k of $Cl_s(\Delta_f)$ offers any additional security to cryptography in the ideal class group $Cl(\Delta_f)$. Clearly the security is based on the difficulty of computing discrete logarithms in

G_k : given $\mathfrak{a}$, $\mathfrak{b}$ with $[\mathfrak{a}], [\mathfrak{b}] \in G_k$, find $x \in \mathbb{Z}$ such that $\mathfrak{b} \sim \mathfrak{a}^x$. Generic algorithms for computing discrete logarithms in finite abelian groups certainly apply. These algorithms will perform no worse than in $Cl(\Delta_f)$, because $|G_k| \leq |Cl(\Delta_f)|$ due to the fact that there is a surjective homomorphism from $Cl(\Delta_f)$ to G_k (Proposition 2.2). As pointed out in [8], index-calculus algorithms are unlikely to work directly in G_k.

However, the fact that the class semigroup is a Clifford semigroup provides us with an attack on the revised cryptosystem. In this case, the existence of a surjective homomorphism between $Cl(\Delta_f)$ and G_k allows us to reduce the problem of computing discrete logarithms in G_k to that in $Cl(\Delta_f)$, which is known to have running time subexponential in $\log|\Delta_f|$.

To compute a discrete logarithm in G_k, we need to find preimages of $[\mathfrak{a}]$ and $[\mathfrak{b}]$ under ϕ_k — invertible ideals $\mathfrak{A}$ and $\mathfrak{B}$ such that $\phi_k([\mathfrak{A}]) = [\mathfrak{a}]$ and $\phi_k([\mathfrak{B}]) = [\mathfrak{b}]$. If there exists $y \in \mathbb{Z}$ such that $\mathfrak{A} \sim \mathfrak{B}^y$ in $G_1 = Cl(\Delta_f)$, then because ϕ_k is a homomorphism $\mathfrak{a} = \mathfrak{b}^y$, i.e., y is also a solution of the discrete logarithm problem in G_k. Theorem 16 of [11] describes an algorithm for computing the required preimages given only a representative of an ideal class in G_k and k.

In general, $|G_k| < |Cl(\Delta_f)|$ meaning that the preimages $\mathfrak{A}$ and $\mathfrak{B}$ are not unique. It is thus possible that $\mathfrak{A}$ does not have a discrete logarithm with respect to $\mathfrak{B}$. The procedure for computing preimages under ϕ_k can be randomized by changing the representative of the ideal equivalence class. If the first choice of preimages does not yield the discrete logarithm, the process is simply repeated until it is found.

Computing discrete logarithms in $Cl_s(\Delta_f)$ is therefore no harder than computing discrete logarithms in $Cl(\Delta_f)$. Unfortunately, the situation is even worse for cryptographic applications based on $Cl_s(\Delta_f)$. In [6] an algorithm is described that, given the factorization of Δ_f, allows one to reduce the problem of computing discrete logarithms in $Cl(\Delta_f)$ to discrete logarithms in the class group of the corresponding maximal order $Cl(\Delta_1)$ and a small number of finite fields corresponding to the prime divisors of the conductor. These problems are significantly easier in practice; in fact, the main result of [6] is to use this reduction as the basis of a non-interactive ID-based cryptosystem for which a key generation center uses the secret knowledge of the factorization of Δ_f to compute discrete logarithms. In the case of cryptosystems in $G_k \subseteq Cl_s(\Delta_f)$, the public non-invertible ideal $\mathfrak{a}$ trivially reveals a factor of Δ_f. In the usual cryptographic case where f is prime, this provides everyone with enough information to compute discrete logarithms using the reduction of [6]. Thus, cryptosystems in class semigroups using non-invertible ideals offer less security than their counterparts in the class group, because the discrete logarithm problem can be easily reduced to computing discrete logarithms in the much smaller class group of the maximal order and finite fields without having to spend additional computational effort factoring Δ_f.

5   Open Problems

Although we have shown that the Kim-Moon cryptosystems are insecure and that cryptography in the class semigroup of an imaginary non-maximal quadratic order likely does not offer any additional security to cryptosystems using the class group, there are a number of open problems related to computational aspects of class semigroups that remain to be addressed.

1. Given $h(\Delta_f)$ and k, a divisor of the conductor f, what is the size of the group G_k? Can k be chosen such that G_k is not significantly smaller than $|Cl(\Delta_f)|$? Knowledge of $|G_k|$ and thus $|\ker(\phi_k)|$ is required in order to analyze determine the expected number of preimages that have to be computed before the discrete logarithm problem in G_k can be solved.
2. Is there a better algorithm for reducing the discrete logarithm problem in G_k to $Cl(\Delta_f)$? In particular, can preimages under ϕ_k of the two ideal equivalence classes in G_k for which the discrete logarithm exists in $Cl(\Delta_f)$ be chosen deterministically?
3. Is it possible to reduce the discrete logarithm problem in G_k directly to the class group of the maximal order $Cl(\Delta_1)$?

The bottom line is that the main problem with the cryptosystems proposed by Kim and Moon is that they do not exploit the full structure of the class semigroup. Both systems instead rely on arithmetic in a subgroup, opening the door to attacks based on the algebraic structure of groups. It is an open problem whether cryptosystems can be developed using the class semigroup that avoid this shortcoming. This, as well as the problems mentioned above, are the subject of on-going research.

References

1. Z.I. Borevich and I.R. Shafarevich, *Number theory*, Academic Press, New York, 1966.
2. J. Buchmann and H.C. Williams, *A key-exchange system based on imaginary quadratic fields*, Journal of Cryptology **1** (1988), 107–118.
3. H. Cohen, *A course in computational algebraic number theory*, Springer-Verlag, Berlin, 1993.
4. D.A. Cox, *Primes of the form $x^2 + ny^2$*, John Wiley & Sons, New York, 1989.
5. J.L. Hafner and K.S. McCurley, *A rigorous subexponential algorithm for computation of class groups*, J. Amer. Math. Soc. **2** (1989), 837–850.
6. D. Hühnlein, M.J. Jacobson, Jr., and D. Weber, *Towards practical non-interactive public-key cryptosystems using non-maximal imaginary quadratic orders*, Designs, Codes and Cryptography **30** (2003), no. 3, 281–299.
7. M.J. Jacobson, Jr. and A.J. van der Poorten, *Computational aspects of NUCOMP*, Algorithmic Number Theory - ANTS-V (Sydney, Australia), Lecture Notes in Computer Science, vol. 2369, Springer-Verlag, Berlin, 2002, pp. 120–133.
8. H. Kim and S. Moon, *Public-key cryptosystems based on class semigroups of imaginary quadratic non-maximal orders*, ACISP 2003, Lecture Notes in Computer Science, vol. 2727, 2003, pp. 488–497.

9. J. Neukirch, *Algebraische zahlentheorie*, Springer, Berlin, 1992.
10. S. Paulus and T. Takagi, *A new public-key cryptosystem over a quadratic order with quadratic decryption time*, Journal of Cryptology **13** (2000), 263–272.
11. P. Zanardo and U. Zannier, *The class semigroup of orders in number fields*, Math. Proc. Camb. Phil. Soc. **115** (1994), 379–391.

Analysis of a Conference Scheme Under Active and Passive Attacks

Feng Bao

Institute for Infocomm Research
21 Heng Mui Keng Terrace
Singapore 119613
baofeng@i2r.a-star.edu.sg

Abstract. Dynamic participation is a feature of the secure conference schemes that allows new conferees to join and the old conferees to leave. The conferees who have left should not be able to decrypt the secure conference communication anymore. A secure conference scheme with dynamic participation was proposed in [2] and later it was modified with the self-encryption mechanism in [4] for a better performance. In this paper we analyze both the original scheme and the modified version. We show that both of them are subject to the active and passive attacks presented in this paper. Our active attack works in the way that a colluding group of attackers can still obtain the conference key even after they all leave the conference. The passive attack does not need any attacker to ever participate in the conference. The conference key can be compromised with a large probability as long as the number of conferees is large.

1 Introduction

A secure digital conference scheme allows a group of people to communicate securely. Due to the mobility of the conferees, the group is dynamically changed from time to time. Dynamic participation is a key feature of the secure conference schemes that allows new conferees to join and the old conferees to leave. The confidentiality of the conference communication must be achieved among the current conferees. The conferees who have left should not be able to participate in the secure conference communication anymore, i.e., they should not have the updated secret key. This is the basic security requirement for dynamic participation; otherwise, dynamic participation makes no sense. The requirement is important in real applications, for example when current conference group has different commercial interests from the previous one. In fact, the studies on dynamic participation mainly focus on how to satisfy that requirement efficiently.

A secure conference scheme with dynamic participation was proposed in [2], which is an improved version of [1] that has no dynamic participation feature. Later it was pointed out that the scheme in [2] has a security weakness due to an attack presented in [3]. A counter measure against the attack was also

H. Wang et al. (Eds.): ACISP 2004, LNCS 3108, pp. 157–163, 2004.

proposed in [3] to secure the scheme. In [4], the scheme is further improved with the self-encryption mechanism for a better performance. The requirement of a public key cryptosystem in the scheme [2] is removed. The improved version in [4] exploits only a symmetric key cryptosystem.

In this paper we propose two more powerful attacks that breaks both the original scheme and the improved scheme. The countermeasure of [3] cannot resist our attacks.

The first attack is conducted by a group of colluding conferees. They first set up a conference session and discover NC's (network center) session secret by an active attack, i.e., selecting special session secrets for themselves. After that they invite other people to join while they gradually leave the conference. Finally the conference is going on with a completely different group of people without any of the attackers. However, the attackers still keep the NC's session secret and are able to decrypt the conference communication. In other words, the conference key update is transparent to the attackers.

The second attack works conditionally when the number of the conferees is large. The attack is successful with a probability which grows with the number of the conferees. The probability is close to 1 when there are over several thousand conferees. The attack is passive since the attacker is not necessarily to join the conference. What he needs to do is just to intercept the communication and conducts some computation. We also want to emphasize that the situation of several thousand conferees is possible in some real applications. Hence the attack is quite practical.

The paper is organized as follows. The description of the schemes [2] and [4] and the attack in [3] is presented in Section 2. The active colluding attack is presented in Section 3. The passive attack is presented in Section 4. Section 5 concludes the paper.

2   Description of the Schemes

2.1   The Scheme of [2]

The parties involved in the scheme [2] include a network center NC and m users. Each user U_i with identity ID_i has a personal terminal T_i, for $i = 1, 2, ..., m$. The NC has a RSA public key (e, n) and shares a secret s_i with U_i, where $s_i = f(ID_i)$ and f is a secret one-way function known only by NC. Without the loss of generality, we suppose that U_1 is the initiator of the conference. The scheme is as follows.

Step 1. T_1 randomly chooses 256-bit numbers r_{11}, r_{12} and sets $r_1 = r_{11} + r_{12}$.
Step 2. T_1 sends $C_1 = (t_1||s_1||r_{11}||r_{12}||ID_i, i = 1, ..., m)^e \bmod n$ to NC.
Step 3. NC decrypts C_1 and checks time t_1 and $s_1 = f(ID_1)$. Then NC calls the other conferees.
Step 4. T_i, $i = 2, ..., m$, randomly chooses 256-bit numbers r_{i1}, r_{i2} and sets $r_i = r_{i1} + r_{i2}$, which has 257 bits.

Step 5. T_i sends $C_i = (t_i||s_i||r_{i1}||r_{i2}||ID_i)^e \bmod n$ to NC, where t_i is T_i's timestamp.

Step 6. NC decrypts C_i and checks the validity of t_i and s_i, and computes $r_i = r_{i1} + r_{i2}$.

Step 7. NC chooses nonzero random numbers CK and r_0, where CK is the secret conference key smaller than 2^{256}. NC then computes public information $PI = CK + lcm(r_0, r_1, ..., r_m)$ and $PA = E_{CK}(ID_{NC})$, where lcm is the least common multiple and E is a symmetric key encryption algorithm.

Step 8. NC broadcasts PI and PA.

Step 9. T_i obtains $CK = PI \bmod r_i$ and verifies $PA = E_{CK}(ID_{NC})$.

The secret conference key is obtained by all the conferees.

Dynamic Participation

Case 1: When U_{m+1} joins the conference, the procedure of obtaining CK for U_{m+1} is the same as in steps 4 - 9, except that NC sends $CK + r_{m+1}$ to U_{m+1}.

Case 2: When U_j quits the conference, NC chooses a new secret conference key CK' and broadcasts PI' and t'. $PI' = CK' + lcm(r_i'$, for $i \neq j)$ where $r_i' = r_i + t'$ and t' is the current date and time, for $i = 0, 1, ..., j-1, j+1, ..., m$.

2.2   The Scheme of [4]

The parties involved in the scheme of [4] are the same as in [2], i.e., a network center NC and m users. Each user U_i with identity ID_i has a personal terminal T_i, for $i = 1, 2, ..., m$. But the NC has no RSA public key. NC still shares a secret s_i with U_i, where $s_i = f(ID_i)$ and f is a secret one-way function known only by NC. The scheme is as follows.

Step 1. T_1 randomly chooses 256-bit numbers r_{11}, r_{12} and sets $r_1 = r_{11} + r_{12}$.

Step 2. T_1 sends ID_1 and $C_1 = E_{s_1}(t_1||s_1||r_{11}||r_{12}||ID_i, i = 1, ..., m)$ to NC.

Step 3. NC decrypts C_1 and checks time t_1 and $s_1 = f(ID_1)$. Then NC calls the other conferees.

Step 4. T_i, $i = 2, ..., m$, randomly chooses 256-bit numbers r_{i1}, r_{i2} and sets 257-bit number $r_i = r_{i1} + r_{i2}$.

Step 5. T_i sends ID_i and $C_i = E_{s_i}(t_i||s_i||r_{i1}||r_{i2}||ID_i)$ to NC, where t_i is T_i's timestamp.

Step 6. NC decrypts C_i and checks the validity of t_i and s_i, and computes $r_i = r_{i1} + r_{i2}$.

Step 7. NC chooses nonzero random numbers CK and r_0, where CK is the secret conference key. NC then computes public information $PI = CK + lcm(r_0, r_1, ..., r_m)$ and $PA = E_{CK}(ID_{NC})$, where lcm is the least common multiple and E is a symmetric key encryption algorithm.

Step 8. NC broadcasts PI and PA.

Step 9. T_i obtains $CK = PI \bmod r_i$ and verifies $PA = E_{CK}(ID_{NC})$.

The dynamic participation remains the same as in [2]. The difference is at the removal of the public key cryptsystem. The public key encryption of M $PK_{NC}(ID_i||s_i||M)$ is replaced with the symmetric key encryption of M, $E_{s_i}(s_i||M)$ and ID_i in plaintext. In the former case, s_i is only for authentication while in the latter case s_i is used for both encryption and authentication. The upside of the modified scheme is to get rid of the public key encryption. The downside is that ID_i must be sent in plaintext. It is argued in [4] that the exposure of ID is not a serious problem in real applications.

2.3   Attack and Countermeasure in [3]

The attack in [3] is toward the *Case 1* where $CK + r_{m+1}$ is sent to U_{m+1}. Since all the conferees have CK, they can easily compute r_{m+1}. Even after some of them quit the conference, they can still compute the new conference key by $CK' = PI' \bmod (r_{m+1} + t')$.

The counter measure proposed in [3] is to replace $CK + r_{m+1}$ with $CK + k_{m+1}r_{m+1}$ where k_{m+1} is a random number. In this case, r_{m+1} cannot be discovered.

Actually the attack can be resisted by a secure channel between NC and U_{m+1}, which can be easily realized by encryption with key r_{m+1}, e.g., to replace $CK + r_{m+1}$ with $E_{r_{m+1}}(CK)$.

3   Active Colluding Attack

Our attack is very different from the one in [3]. Instead of attacking the *Case 1* (adding new conferees) , we attack the *Case 2* where old conferees leave conference. Our attack works well even if the secure channel is adopted in *Case 1*.

Let $U_1, U_2, ..., U_m$ be colluding parties. They follow the scheme to establish a conference session, but they do not choose r_{i1}, r_{i2} randomly. Instead, they choose prime numbers r_i's first and then split each r_i into $r_i = r_{i1} + r_{i2}$ randomly. The other steps are exactly the same as the scheme [2]. In the last step, they obtain CK. Since $lcm(r_0, r_1, ..., r_m) = PI - CK$, they obtain $lcm(r_0, r_1, ..., r_m)$. With great probability, the random r_0 is co-prime with $r_1, r_2, ..., r_m$ since they are 257-bit prime numbers. Therefore, r_0 is detected.

Later the conference is growing with new conferees joining. The attackers quit the conference gradually. Finally, the conference is among a completely different group of participants without any of the attackers. However, the attackers can still obtain the conference key CK' in *Case 2* by $CK' = PI' \bmod (r_0 + t')$ since $PI' = CK' + lcm(r_i + t', i = 0, 1, ...)$.

That is, the attackers who have left the conference can still listen to all the secret communications of the conference that are not supposed to be disclosed to them.

Situation Without r_0

In the above attack, r_0 is the loophole of the scheme. If r_0 is removed from the scheme, the attack still works, but in a little bit different way. The attackers will invite a victim conferee U_{m+1} to participate in the conference at first. They collude to obtain the victim's session secret r_{m+1} in a similar way as obtaining r_0. Then the attackers quit the conference. As long as U_{m+1} is still in the conference, the attackers can get the secret conference key.

Normal Size of PI

The advantage of the schemes is at the small size of PI. With the increasing of m, the difference between $|lcm(r_i, i = 0, 1, ...m)|$ and $\sum_{i=0}^{m} |r_i|$ is getting larger, which reduces the broadcasting burden. In our attack, the PI is larger than normal (for random r_i's) since r_i's are all prime numbers. This can be easily avoided by choosing each r_i a product of several prime numbers and letting different r_i's have some common prime factors. In such way, the size of PI can be controlled as the attackers' will and be the same as the normal situation. The prime factors should be large enough such that the probability of a randomly chosen number is co-prime with them is large.

4   Passive Attack

The passive attack can be done by a single attacker, who is not necessarily to participate in the conference. All he has to do is to intercept the PI or PI'. Considering that the number of conferees may not be large at the conference setup stage, the attack is more feasible at the conferees leaving stage *Case 2* when the number of conferees already grows large enough.

Suppose PI' is intercepted by the attacker and the number of conferees m is large at present. $PI' = CK' + lcm(r_i',$ for $i = 1, 2, ..., m)$ where $r_i' = r_i + t'$ and t' is the current date and time, for $i = 0, 1, ..., m$. Here we suppose the PI' is for the U_{m+1} leaving the conference. CK' is the new conference key for $U_1, U_2, ..., U_m$ only.

What the attacker needs to do is to find a factor P of $lcm(r_i',$ for $i = 1, 2, ..., m)$ such that P is larger than CK'. Then $CK' = PI' \bmod P$. For the parameter size given in the schemes, we need to find a 257-bit P such that $P | lcm(r_i',$ for $i = 1, 2, ..., m)$. Next we show that this P can be taken as the product of all the prime numbers smaller than 200. There are totally 46 primes from 2 to 199. Their product has more than 257 bits. Since the r_i's are randomly chosen, the probability that P divides $lcm(r_i',$ for $i = 1, 2, ..., m)$ becomes large when m is large enough.

So the attack itself is very simple: Set $P = \prod_{prime \le 200} prime$ and compute $CK' = PI' \bmod P$. The relationship between the successful probability and m is studied as follows.

Probability Analysis

Denote the first k primes in natural number by $p_1, p_2, ..., p_k$ where $p_1 < p_2 < ... < p_k$ and $P = \prod_{j=1}^{k} p_j$. The probability that r_i' does not have factor p_j is $1 - 1/p_j$ (note that $r_i' = r_i + t'$ is a random number). Since r_i''s (for $i = 1, 2, ..., m$) are independent, the probability that $lcm(r_i',$ for $i = 1, 2, ..., m)$ has factor p_j is $1 - (1 - 1/p_j)^m$. The probability that $lcm(r_i',$ for $i = 1, 2, ..., m)$ has factor P is

$$\prod_{j=1}^{k} (1 - (1 - \frac{1}{p_j})^m) > (1 - (1 - \frac{1}{p_k})^m)^k$$

since $p_1 < p_2 < ... < p_k$. Because $(1 - 1/n)^n < 1/e < 1/2$, we have

$$(1 - (1 - \frac{1}{p_k})^m)^k > (1 - \frac{1}{2^{m/p_k}})^k \qquad (1)$$

The prime numbers smaller than 200 are shown in Table 1. The product of these primes is lager than 2^{256}.

Table 1. Prime numbers and their binary length.

prime	2	3	5	7	11	13	17	19	23	29	31	37
length	2	2	3	3	4	4	5	5	5	5	5	6
prime	41	43	47	53	59	61	67	71	73	79	83	89
length	6	6	6	6	6	6	7	7	7	7	7	7
prime	97	101	103	107	109	113	127	131	137	139	149	151
length	7	7	7	7	7	7	7	8	8	8	8	8
prime	157	163	167	173	179	181	191	193	197	199		
length	8	8	8	8	8	8	8	8	8	8		

We substitute $k = 46$ and $p_k = 199$ into (1). The probability that $lcm(r_i',$ for $i = 1, 2, ..., m)$ has factor P is larger than

$$(1 - \frac{1}{2^{\frac{m}{199}}})^{46}.$$

Table 2 shows the probabilities for different m. We want to emphasize that the shown probabilities are a very loose lower bound. The actual probabilities can be larger if we take tight computation, which is not the focus of this paper.

Our result shows that the method exploiting $lcm(r_i',$ for $i = 1, 2, ..., m)$ in [1], [2] and [4] could lead to disaster when the number of conference participants is large, although it was taken as the advantage of reducing communication complexity.

Table 2. The probabilities that $lcm(r_i^a,$ for $i = 1, 2, ..., m)$ has factor P.

m	1000	1200	1400	1600	1800	2000	3000	4000
prob	0.1	0.28	0.64	0.82	0.91	0.955	0.997	0.9999

The attack can be improved in two ways. First, the P need not be the product of the first k primes. It could be a number like $2^7 3^4 5^3 \cdots$. Our analysis is valid as long as $p_1, p_2, ..., p_k$ are relatively prime. Secondly, the P has less than 257 bits. The attack works well as long as the P's number of bits is close to 257. The attacker can compute $CK \bmod P$ first, then find out other bits of CK by brute force search. This is because $PA = E_{CK}(ID_{NC})$ is broadcast.

5 Conclusion

In this paper we present a security analysis to the teleconference scheme in [2] and its modified version in [4]. Our analysis shows that both schemes are insecure.

Acknowledgements. I would like to thank the anonymous reviewers for their valuable comments and correction of several English errors in the earlier version of this paper.

References

1. M. S. Hwang and W. P. Yang, "Conference key distribution protocols for digital mobile communication network", IEEE J. Selected Areas Commun., vol 13, pp. 416-420, Feb. 1995.
2. M. S. Hwang, "Dynamic participation in a secure conference scheme for mobile communication", IEEE Transactions on Vehicular Technology, Vol. 48, pp. 1469-1474, Spet 1999.
3. S. L. Ng, "Comments on dynamic participation in a secure conference scheme for mobile communications", IEEE Transactions on Vehicular Technology, Vol. 50, pp. 334-335, Jan 2001.
4. K. F. Hwang and C. C. Chang, "A self-encryption mechanism for authentication of roaming and teleconference services", IEEE Trans. on Wireless Communications, vol. 2, no. 2, pp. 400-407, March, 2003.

Cryptanalysis of Two Password-Authenticated Key Exchange Protocols

Zhiguo Wan[1,3] and Shuhong Wang[2,3]

[1] School of Computing, National University of Singapore, Singapore 117543
wanzhigu@comp.nus.edu.sg
[2] School of Mathematical Sciences, Peking University, P.R. China 100871
wshong@math.pku.edu.cn
[3] Institute for Infocomm Research (I2R), Singapore 119613
{zhiguo,stushw}@i2r.a-star.edu.sg

Abstract. Password-Authenticated Key Exchange (PAKE) protocols enable two or more parties to use human-memorable passwords for authentication and key exchange. Since the human-memorable passwords are vulnerable to off-line dictionary attacks, PAKE protocols should be very carefully designed to resist dictionary attacks. However, designing PAKE protocols against dictionary attacks proved to be quite tricky. In this paper, we analyze two PAKE protocols and show that they are subject to dictionary attacks. The analyzed protocols are EPA which was proposed in ACISP 2003 and AMP which is a contribution for P1363. Our attack is based on the small factors of the order of a large group $\mathbb{Z}_p^*$ (i.e., the DLP of subgroup attack), by which the secret password can be fully discovered. We intend to emphasize that our attack is valid since the protocols neither select secure parameter p nor check the order of received values for achieving good efficiency.

1 Introduction

Using human-memorable passwords in authentication and key exchange protocols is very natural for people because these weak passwords are easy to remember. But these passwords are susceptible to dictionary attacks or password-guessing attacks since the password space is too small. This interesting problem on how to achieve authentication and key exchange using only a human-memorable password is first introduced by Bellovin and Merritt [4], and they also provided a password-authenticated key exchange (PAKE) protocol named Encrypted Key Exchange (EKE) protocol, and the augmented encrypted key exchange protocol in [5], which is an improvement of the EKE protocol. After that, a number of password-authenticated key exchange (PAKE) protocols are proposed in the literature [6,7,8,9,10,11,12,16,17,25] and these protocols require different computation and communication workloads. Among these protocols, the EPA protocol [8] and the AMP protocol [10,11,12] are relatively simple and efficient in communication and computation. Unfortunately, we find that both protocols are susceptible to our attack which can recover the secret password completely under reasonable parameter assumptions.

H. Wang et al. (Eds.): ACISP 2004, LNCS 3108, pp. 164–175, 2004.

Our attack is based on small factors of the order of the large group whose prime order subgroup is used in the two protocols. Many discrete log-based schemes are working in a prime order subgroup of a larger group because of the advantages of setting protocol in a prime order subgroup. For example, they use a subgroup $\mathbb{G}_{p,q}$ of $\mathbb{Z}_p^*$ with prime order q. For these schemes, choosing parameters p, q and checking the protocol variables are crucial to the security of the protocols [1]. If the parameter p is not particularly chosen, $p - 1$ will likely have many small factors much less than q, or $p - 1$ is smooth. In this case the schemes which do not take precautions can be vulnerable to some attacks [13, 20] as originally pointed out by van Oorschot and Wiener [23].

Similar to the attacks in [13] and [20], our attack against EPA and AMP exploits the same security flaw in choosing security parameters. The EPA protocol is insecure since it does not select secure protocol parameter p. It does not check the validity (the order) of the received numbers, otherwise the claimed good efficiency does not exist. It is the same for the final version of AMP protocol [12] which is flexible in allowing any form of a prime p. Our attack employs Pohlig-Hellman decomposition, Pollard's methods and dictionary attacks to recover the secret password.

The remainder of the paper is organized as follows. In the next section some background and related work on PAKE protocols and the attack against DL-based protocols are presented. After that, the EPA and AMP protocols are illustrated and discussed, and then we show how our attack can be applied on these protocols to disclose the secret password. Finally, we present the counter measures to such attacks and our concluding remarks.

2 Background and Related Work

2.1 PAKE Protocols and Attacks Against Them

The security protocols using low entropy passwords for authentication and key exchange, known as the PAKE protocols, have gained extensive attention and research interests until now. Moreover, the IEEE P1363 Standard Working Group is engaged in standardization on password-based public-key cryptographic protocols. Currently, the working group is studying the PAKE protocols SPEKE [9], SRP [25], PAK [17,16] and AMP [10,11,12]. Besides these protocols, there are a number of PAKE protocols proposed in the literature. For the PAKE protocols, the most crucial point is their resistance to off-line dictionary attacks (or password guessing attacks). Unfortunately, there have been many attacks against various PAKE protocols in the literature, which in turn shows that these PAKE protocols fail to fulfill the basic requirement.

Patel [19] has used some basic results from number theory to apply dictionary attacks on all versions of EKE protocols [4], including RSA-EKE, DH-EKE, and ElGamal-EKE. To break these EKE protocols, the attacker only needs the ability of the so-called *querying attacker* whose only capability is to initiate sessions with a legitimate party. As stated in Patel's paper, the RSA-EKE can be attacked no matter what parameters of RSA are chosen, while the DH-EKE and the ElGamal-EKE can only be compromised if the security parameters (p and g) are not verified.

The Open Key Exchange (OKE) protocol is an RSA-based PAKE protocol proposed by Lucks [14]. In his paper, Lucks proposed two versions of OKE protocols: a generic OKE protocol and a protected OKE protocol which has improved security. Although the OKE protocols are claimed to have proof of security, MacKenzie et al. [15] showed that both protocols are actually insecure. As discussed by MacKenzie, by choosing security parameters e and N judiciously, the adversary can mount a dictionary attack to discover the secret password.

The PAKE protocol proposed by Zhu et al. [26] is specially designed for imbalanced wireless networks. The advantage of this protocol is that one (the mobile node) of the two parties is very lightly computation burdened, which is desirable for mobile nodes in wireless networks. However, as pointed out by Bao [2], the security of this protocol relies on the length of the second party's identity, but not the size of RSA modulo n. As a result, this PAKE protocol is insecure if the length of the identity is short, which is highly possible in practice.

The PAKE protocols mentioned above are vulnerable to various attacks because security parameters of the protocols are not carefully chosen or verified. In fact, choosing secure parameters and verifying them in the protocols are extremely important for PAKE protocols. Since the security parameters are not carefully chosen and verified in EPA and AMP, our attack against them can be applied to discover the password successfully.

2.2   Attacks Against Discrete Log Problem Based Protocols

Many cryptographic protocols proposed in the literature, such as ElGamal signature and Diffie-Hellman key exchange, are based on the Discrete Logarithm Problem (DLP). The security of these protocols relies on the hardness of the underlying discrete logarithm problem. But a number of attacks against these kinds of protocols suggest that the security is closely related to the prime p of these protocols, and considerable care should be taken in the choice of parameter p in the protocols. Specifically, not only should the prime p be large enough, but also it should have a secure structure, which means $(p-1)/2$ should only have large prime factors.

A divide-and-conquer algorithm for discrete logarithms, combining Pollard's lambda method with a partial Pohlig-Hellman decomposition, is first noted by van Oorschot and Wiener [23]. This algorithm can partially or completely recover secret exponents, and it can be even more dangerous when combined with protocol attacks. It is accomplished by combining Pohlig-Hellman decomposition with Pollard's methods as well as Chinese Remainder Theorem.

Pohlig-Hellman decomposition [21] can break the discrete logarithm problem over $\mathbb{Z}_p^*$ into a number of small such sub-problems defined over small order subgroups of $\mathbb{Z}_p^*$. Subsequently, these sub-problems can be solved using Pollard's rho and lambda methods [22], and at last the original discrete logarithm problem can be settled by combining the solutions of the sub-problems using Chinese Remainder Theorem.

Consider the discrete logarithm problem $y = g^x \bmod p$ defined over $\mathbb{Z}_p^*$, where $p - 1 = \prod_{i=1}^{n} q_i$ (q_i prime and $q_i < q_{i+1}$). Define an appropriate bound B which depends on the computational resources available, then $p - 1$ is B-smooth if $q_i < B, i = 1, 2, \ldots, n$. Usually the bound B is much smaller than $\sqrt{q} \approx 2^{80}$. Suppose there is $r < n$ such that each q_i ($i = 1, 2, \ldots, r$) is B-smooth, then each sub-problems of the original problem takes the following form: $y_i = y^{(p-1)/q_i} = g_i^x \bmod p$ ($i = 1, 2, \ldots, r$), where $g_i = g^{(p-1)/q_i}$. Note that in each sub-problem, g_i has the order of q_i. For these sub-problems, each can be solved by Pollard's rho method in $O(\sqrt{q_i})$ time, yielding $x = x_i \bmod q_i$. Then by combining all the results, the logarithm x can be obtained as $x \bmod \prod_{i=1}^{r} q_i$ using the Chinese Remainder Theorem. Generally, if $p - 1 = q\omega$ where ω is B-smooth with regard to a bound B, then an attacker can recover the secret exponent modulo ω.

Lim and Lee [13] employ Pohlig-Hellman decomposition and Pollard's methods to attack on discrete logarithm based schemes working in a prime order subgroup. Their key recovery attack, which is also called direct low order attack, can disclose partial or complete secret key of a victim in a reasonable time for many DL-based schemes. Pavlovski and Boyd [20] further extend the attack to the cases where the group order can be either prime, composite, or unknown. The group signature schemes and electronic cash schemes discussed in their paper are insecure because these schemes work in a large group $\mathbb{Z}_p^*$ which may have small order elements.

In our attack against the EPA and the AMP protocol, we also exploit the flaw that the large group $\mathbb{Z}_p^*$ used in both protocols may have many small order elements, which leads to the complete disclosure of the secret password.

3   The EPA Protocols

The EPA protocol [8] proposed by Hwang, Yum and Lee is a password-authenticated key exchange protocol which needs only 3 passes and less exponentiation computation than other PAKE protocols. Based on an asymmetric model with the client obtaining a memorable password while the server holding a corresponding password file, EPA is claimed to be secure against off-line dictionary attacks and resilient to server compromise.

Setup of EPA. The EPA protocol involves two entities, the client and the server. A multiplicative group $\mathbb{Z}_p^*$ and its prime-order subgroup $\mathbb{G}_{p,q}$, where $p = qr + 1$, are used in EPA. The hardness of the Decision Diffie-Hellman problem is assumed. Before any transaction occurs, the client and the server share the parameters p, q, g and f, where g and f are two generators of the group $\mathbb{G}_{p,q}$. the client chooses a memorable password π and the server keeps the client's identity C with verifier $\pi_s = (V_1, V_2)$ where

$$V_1 = f^{v_1}, v_1 = h_1(C, \pi); V_2 = g^{v_2}, v_2 = h_2(C, \pi).$$

Here $h_1, \cdots, h_5$ are hash functions defined from $\{0,1\}^* \rightarrow \{0,1\}^k$.

Note that g, f are selected so that their discrete logarithmic relation cannot be found, the prime q is sufficiently large to resist Pohlig-Hellman decomposition and the various index-calculus methods [21,22,23]. In this paper, all the exponentiations are computed mod p, we will omit "mod p" in the remainder of this paper where it is clear from the context.

Description of EPA. Then the EPA protocol runs as follows:

1. The client computes $v_1 = h_1(C, \pi), v_2 = h_2(C, \pi)$. She chooses a random number $x \in_R Z_q$ where $x \neq -v_2 \mod q$. After the client computes $X = g^x f^{v_1}$, she sends (C, X) to the server.
2. After the server receives (C, X), he chooses a random number $y \in_R Z_q$ and then computes $X' = \frac{X}{V_1} = g^x, Y = (X'V_2)^y = g^{(x+v_2)y}$. The master key from which the session key is derived can be obtained as $K_S = (X')^y = g^{xy}$. After the server computes $H_S = h_3(K_S || X)$, he sends (Y, H_S) to the client.
3. After the client receives (Y, H_S), she computes $w = x(x + v_2)^{-1} \mod q$ and the master key $K_C = Y^w = g^{xy}$. The client computes $H'_S = h_3(K_C || X)$ with H_S. If H'_S is equal to H_S, the client regards the server as a valid server who knows π_S and accepts the master key K_C. The client computes $H_C = h_4(Y || K_C)$ and the session key $K = h_5(C, K_C)$. The client sends H_C to the server.
4. After the server receives H_C, he computes $H'_C = h_4(Y || K_S)$. The server compares H'_C with H_C. If H'_C is equal to H_C, the server regards the client as a valid user who knows π and accepts the master key K_S. The server computes the session key $K = h_5(C, K_S)$.

At the end, a common session key K is derived by the client and the server. The compete protocol is presented in Fig.1.

Note that from the setup of EPA, when the server's password file π_S is compromised, an adversary can find the client's secret key π by mounting a dictionary attack. Based on EPA, Hwang *et al.* [8] construct EPA+ using a modified amplified password file to resist the dictionary attack in case of server's password file compromise. EPA+ and EPA are different in the setup on the server's side, and our attack can be applied on EPA+ without any change since the attacker only needs to impersonate the client.

4   Attacks Against EPA

The EPA protocols is working in a prime order subgroup $\mathbb{G}_{p,q}$ of the multiplicative group $\mathbb{Z}_p^*$, where p is a prime and $p = qr + 1$. Normally, because the prime modulo p is selected randomly, it is of high probability that r may have a number of small prime factors besides 2. As discussed by van Oorschot and Wiener [23], if the adversary has computation power to compute discrete logarithms in cyclic groups of order up to 2^s, then one expects about s bits of an exponent x are

$$Client[C, \pi] \qquad\qquad Server[C, V_1, V_2]$$

$$v_1 = h_1(C, \pi), v_2 = h_2(C, \pi)$$
$$x \in_R \mathbb{Z}_q$$
$$X = g^x f^{v_1}$$

$$\xrightarrow{\quad C, X \quad}$$

$$y \in_R \mathbb{Z}_q$$
$$X' = \frac{X}{V_1}$$
$$Y = (X'V_2)^y$$
$$K_S = (X')^y$$

$$w = x(x + v_2)^{-1} \bmod q \qquad \xleftarrow{\quad Y, H_S \quad} \qquad H_S = h_3(K_S \| X)$$
$$K_C = Y^w$$
$$H'_S = h_3(K_C \| X)$$
$$\text{Test } H'_S \overset{?}{=} H_S$$
$$H_C = h_4(Y \| K_C) \qquad \xrightarrow{\quad H_C \quad} \qquad H'_C = h_4(Y \| K_S)$$
$$K = h_5(C, K_C) \qquad\qquad\qquad \text{Test } H'_C \overset{?}{=} H_C$$
$$K = h_5(C, K_S)$$

Fig. 1. The EPA Protocol

leaked by the p. And this leads to complete revealing of x if $\log x < s$. Usually the p is 1024-bit long and the exponent is 160-bit long, in this case the success rate of finding the 160-bit exponent is about 32% if an adversary is capable of 2^{40} multiplications mod p as indicated in [23]. As a result, complete disclosure of the exponent is highly possible according to the smoothness of random $p - 1$.

Our attack which is composed of three steps focuses on the first two passes of EPA and the server's random number $y \in_R \mathbb{Z}_q$. In the first step of our attack, the attacker masquerading the client substitutes the first message (C, X) with (C, X^*) where $ord(X^*) = \omega$ with $\omega | p - 1$ and ω being smooth with regard to a bound B. After receiving the message (Y, H_S) from the server, the attacker can use Pohlig-Hellman decomposition and Pollard's methods to recover y in the second step of our attack. And therefore the value of V_2/V_1 can be obtained. At last, the attacker can mount a dictionary attack against the V_2/V_1 to obtain the secret password.

Step 1: In the first step of our attack, we exploit the danger for one to apply its secret on an unknown received number. We consider an adversary who sends with the client's id C a specially chosen $X^* \in \mathbb{Z}_p^*$ of order ω instead of $X = g^x f^{v_1}$ ordered q. Depend on the structure of $p - 1$ and the computational capability of the adversary, the adversary chooses the ω such that ω is B-smooth for a bound B and $\omega > q$. As a result, he can receive Y from the second message with the form that $Y = (X'V_2)^y = (X^* \cdot \frac{V_2}{V_1})^y$ unless the server checks that $X^q \overset{?}{=} 1 \bmod p$ and stops with failure.

Obviously, our attack can be avoided by simply adding a new checking of the number X. But this check will cost the computation efficiency since it needs one more exponentiation. This is the reason why there are still so many schemes omitting such an authentication even though there are several papers pointing out the importance of checking public parameters and protocol variables [1,3,13, 20,23,24].

Step 2: The second step of our attack can recover the secret random number y chosen by the server. Upon receipt of $Y = (X^* \cdot \frac{V_2}{V_1})^y$ sent from the server, the attacker can use Pohlig-Hellman decomposition and Pollard's methods to recover y. Note that $V_1 = f^{v_1}$ and $V_2 = g^{v_2}$ are both in the subgroup $\mathbb{G}_{p,q}$, by raising Y to the qth power, one can get

$$Y^q = [(X^* \cdot \frac{V_2}{V_1})^y]^q = (X^*)^{yq}(\frac{V_2}{V_1})^{yq} = ((X^*)^q)^y = \alpha^y, \tag{1}$$

where α is a primitive ωth root of unity in $\mathbb{Z}_p^*$, for q is coprime to ω. Since $ord(\alpha) = ord(X^*) = \omega$, we can follow Pohlig-Hellman decomposition and Pollard's methods to obtain $y_0 = y \bmod \omega$. Note that $y \in \mathbb{Z}_q$, so we can claim that $y_0 = y$.

Step 3: In the last step of our attack, we can disclose user's password in EPA(EPA+) by mounting an off-line dictionary attack against the low-entropy password. Recall that Y has the form $Y = (X^* \cdot \frac{V_2}{V_1})^y$, where X^* is chosen by the adversary. Previously we have disclosed the server's random secret y. So we have

$$Y \cdot (X^*)^{-y} = (V_2/V_1)^y \in \mathbb{G}_{p,q}$$

since $V_1 = f^{v_1}, V_2 = g^{v_2}$ are both in group $\mathbb{G}_{p,q}$. By Euclid's algorithm one can compute y^{-1} such that $y \cdot y^{-1} \equiv 1 \bmod q$, hence we have

$$\frac{V_2}{V_1} = (Y \cdot (X^*)^{-y})^{y^{-1}} = \frac{g^{h_2(C,\pi)}}{f^{h_1(C,\pi)}}. \tag{2}$$

It is clear that by checking equation (2) with a dictionary attack, the adversary can easily recover password π.

5   The AMP Protocols

Similar to the EPA protocol, the AMP protocols proposed by Kwon [10,11,12] are based on the amplified password proof idea with the server storing the amplified verifiers in the amplified password file while the client holding the password. AMP is the most efficient PAKE protocol among the related protocols for fewest exponentiations are required in the protocol. And the security of AMP is proved in the random oracle model.

In the original proposal of AMP, the author emphasizes using a secure prime modulus p such that $(p-1)/2q$ is also prime or each prime factor of $(p-1)/2q$ is comparable to q, or a safe prime modulus p such that $p = 2q + 1$ [10]. However, in the latest versions of AMP [12], the author states that the final versions of AMP are flexible in allowing any form of a prime p. In fact, it is this flexibility on choice of primes that leads to the insecurity of AMP.

In this section, we demonstrate that the similar attack against EPA can break AMP to recover the password. Here we only present the description of AMP and the attack against it, since the AMP2 and AMP3 protocols also can be compromised by the similar attack strategy with little change.

Setup of AMP. The AMP protocol also involves two parties, the client and the server. Before the protocol, the client and the server agree on a large group $\mathbb{Z}_p^*$, its prime order subgroup $\mathbb{G}_{p,q}$, and a generator g of $\mathbb{G}_{p,q}$. In the final versions of AMP, $p = qr + 1$ where r is co-prime to q and hence r may have a number of small prime factors. The client has a secret memorable password π, and the server holds the corresponding transformed-password $\pi_S = (V_1, v_2)$, where

$$V_1 = g^{v_1}, v_1 = h_0(C, \pi); v_2 = h_1(C, \pi).$$

Here $h_0, \cdots, h_6$ are one-way hash functions and C is the id of the client.

Description of AMP. The complete AMP protocol is a four-pass protocol as depicted in Fig. 2.

1. The client computes $X = g^x \bmod p$ by choosing $x \in_R \mathbb{Z}_q$ and sends (C, X) to the server.
2. On receiving message 1, the server chooses $y \in_R \mathbb{Z}_q^*$ and computes $e_1 = h_2(C, S, X)$, where S is the id of the server. Then the server calculates $Y = (X^{e_1} V_1)^y$ and sends Y to the client. Note $Y = (X^{e_1} V_1)^y = (g^{x e_1} g^{v_1})^y$.
3. While waiting for message 2, the client computes $v_1 = h_0(C, \pi)$ and $e_1 = h_2(C, S, X)$. After receiving message 2, the client computes $e_2 = h_3(C, S, X, Y)$, $w = (xe_1 + v_1)^{-1}(x + e_2) \bmod q$, $K_C = Y^w \bmod p$, and $H_C = h_4(C, S, X, Y, K_C)$. Then H_C is sent to the server. Note that $K_C = Y^w = (g^{(xe_1 + v_1)y})^w = g^{(x + e_2)y}$.
4. While waiting for message 3, the server computes $e_2 = h_3(C, S, X, Y), K_S = (Xg^{e_2})^y$, and $H'_C = h_4(C, S, X, Y, K_S)$. On receipt of message 3, the server verifies the received H_C against H'_C, and computes $H_S = h_5(C, S, X, Y, K_S)$ if verification if successful. Then the server sends H_S to the client, and a session key K is derived as $h_6(C, S, X, Y, K_S)$. Note that $K_S = (Xg^{e_2})^y = g^{(x + e_2)y}$.
5. While waiting for message 4, the client computes $v_2 = h_1(C, \pi)$ and $H'_S = h_5(C, S, X, Y, K_C, v_2)$. After receiving message 4, the client verifies H_S against H'_S, if they match then the client can derive the session key $K = h_6(C, S, X, Y, K_C)$.

Client$[C, \pi]$ Server$[C, V_1, v_2]$
                                                          $\langle V_1 = g^{v_1} \bmod p, v_2 = h_1(C, \pi)\rangle$

$x \in_R \mathbb{Z}_q^*$
$X = g^x \bmod p$

$\xrightarrow{\quad C, X \quad}$

$v_1 = h_0(C, \pi)$ $y \in_R \mathbb{Z}_p^*$
$e_1 = h_2(C, S, X)$ $e_1 = h_2(C, S, X)$
                                                          $Y = (X^{e_1} V_1)^y \bmod p$

$\xleftarrow{\quad Y \quad}$

$e_2 = h_3(C, S, X, Y)$ $e_2 = h_3(C, S, X, Y)$
$w = (xe_1 + v_1)^{-1}(x + e_2) \bmod q$
$K_C = Y^w \bmod p$ $K_S = (Xg^{e_2})^y \bmod p$
$H_C = h_4(C, S, X, Y, K_C)$ $H_C' = h_4(C, S, X, Y, K_S)$

$\xrightarrow{\quad H_C \quad}$

$v_2 = h_1(C, \pi)$ abort if $H_C \neq H_C'$
$H_S' = h_5(C, S, X, Y, K_C, v_2)$ $H_S = h_5(C, S, X, Y, K_S, v_2)$

$\xleftarrow{\quad H_S \quad}$

abort if $H_S \neq H_S'$
$K = h_6(C, S, X, Y, K_C)$ $K = h_6(C, S, X, Y, K_S)$

Fig. 2. The AMP Protocol

The difference between the final version of AMP protocol and the previous AMP protocol is that v_2 is injected into H_S and H_S'. By doing this, the author argues that the authenticity of server can strongly be confirmed when p is neither a secure prime nor a safe prime. But the author ignores the potential threat of X which could be sent by an adversary, and this results in the failure of the protocol.

6   Attack Against AMP

The final version of AMP protocol has the same design flaw as EPA, and therefore the similar attack can applied on AMP to recover the secret password. Employing the similar strategy, the attack against AMP also focuses on the first two passes of the protocol, and it is also composed of three steps described as follows.

Step 1: The attacker impersonates the client and sends the id C and a specially composed X^* to the server. Different from the choice of X in the attack against EPA, the choice of X^* has a more stringent restriction. Besides that $X^* \in \mathbb{Z}_P^*$ where $ord(X^*) = \omega > q$ where ω is B-smooth for a computation bound B, it is further required that $\frac{\omega}{gcd(\omega, e_1)} > q$ where $e_1 = h_2(C, S, X^*)$. This is possible at a high probability under the assumption that the output of h_2 is uniformly distributed[1].

---

[1] If e_1 is a prime between B and q, then it is only required that $\omega > q$ because ω is B-smooth and hence $gcd(\omega, e_1) = 1$. The probability of e_1 being a prime between B

Step 2: As a result of last step, the server will return $Y = ((X^*)^{e_1} \cdot V_1)^y$ to the attacker. The attacker then employs the same technique to recover the secret exponent y as used in the attack against EPA. Note that $V_1 = g^{v_1}$ is in the subgroup of $\mathbb{Z}_q^*$ ordered q, by raising Y to the qth power, we can obtain

$$Y^q = [((X^*)^{e_1} \cdot V_1)^y]^q = ((X^*)^{q \cdot e_1})^y = \alpha^y, \tag{3}$$

where $e_1 = h_2(C, S, X^*)$ and $\alpha = (X^*)^{q \cdot e_1}$. It is easy to know that $ord(\alpha) = \frac{\omega}{gcd(\omega, e_1)} > q$ because X^* is selected for this purpose. Then the attacker follows Pohlig-Hellman decomposition and Pollard's methods to recover $y_0 = y \mod \frac{\omega}{gcd(\omega, e_1)}$. Since $y \in \mathbb{Z}_q$ and $\frac{\omega}{gcd(\omega, e_1)} > q$, we claim that $y_0 = y$.

Step 3: At last, the attacker can mount a dictionary attack against Y to recover the password π on the basis of last step. With the knowledge of y, the attacker can easily obtain Y as follows:

$$V_1 = [Y \cdot (X^*)^{-e_1 \cdot y}]^{y^{-1}} = g^{h_0(C, \pi)}. \tag{4}$$

Then a dictionary attack against equation (4) can yield the secret password π.

7   Counter Measures Against Attacks for EPA and AMP

The fundamental reason underlying the vulnerability of the EPA and AMP protocols is that one party applies its secret random number on an unknown received number. Moreover, the protocol parameter p is not a safe prime or secure primes, and protocol variables (X in EPA and AMP) are not checked whether they are within the valid subgroup.

Two straightforward counter measures can enable the protocols to be immune to our attack mentioned above. The first counter measure is very simple. It is sufficient for each party to add one check to counter our attack. That is to say, the server checks $X^q \stackrel{?}{=} 1 \mod p$ and stops with failure if they are not equal or continue if it passes this check; later, the client checks $Y^q \stackrel{?}{=} 1 \mod p$.

The drawback of checking variables is the loss of computation efficiency, since the improvement needs two more exponentiations. It increases the number of total exponentiations in EPA and AMP by 2, and hence deprives them of their advantage in computation.

The second counter measure can avoid the computational inefficiency resulted from the first one. It is to choose a safe prime or a secure prime as the protocol parameter p. A prime p is a safe prime only if $p = 2q + 1$ where q is prime. Also

and q is $\left(\frac{q}{\ln q} - \frac{B}{\ln B}\right)/q$, and this probability is about $\frac{1}{\ln q} \approx \frac{1}{160 \cdot \ln 2} \approx 0.01$ since $B < \sqrt{q} \approx 2^{80}$. Furthermore, the probability of $\frac{\omega}{gcd(\omega, e_1)} > q$ will be much larger than 0.01 for an $X^\square$ ordered ω. Hence it is expected that the desirable $X^\square$ can be found after much less than 100 tries.

the parameter p can be chosen such that $p = 2qp_1 + 1$ where p_1 is prime, or $p = 2qp_1p_2 \ldots p_n + 1$ where p_i's are primes comparable to q. How to generate primes with this form is presented in [13]. In this case, our attack will fail since the success of our attack relies on the fact that the protocol parameter $p - 1$ has many small factors, while the efficiency of the protocol remains.

8   Conclusion

In this paper, we presented an effective attack on the PAKE protocols EPA and AMP which work in a large prime order subgroup of a larger group. This attack is based on the assumption that the larger group has a subgroup of smooth order. Using Pohlig-Hellman decomposition, we deduce the discrete logarithm on the large prime order subgroup to several sub-problems on small order subgroups and expose the server's random number, and then apply an off-line dictionary attack to find out the client's password. The vulnerability of these two protocols results from the server's applying its random secret exponent on an unknown number which may be malicious. Then we present the counter measures to the attack. One measure is to check variables before proceeding, and the other is to use a secure prime or a safe prime p as the parameter of the protocols.

Our attack again shows that PAKE protocols are more vulnerable than other types of protocols because of their intrinsic characteristic. Therefore careful precautions should be taken to prevent potential attacks.

Acknowledgments. The authors would like to thank the anonymous reviewers for their valuable suggestions and Feng Bao for his insightful remarks and helpful discussion.

References

1. R. Anderson and S. Vaudenay, Minding Your p's and q's, *Advaces in Cryptology - ASIACRYPT'96*, LNCS 963, pages 236-247, Springer-Verlag, 1995.
2. F. Bao, Security Analysis of a Password Authenticated Key Exchange Protocol, *Proceedings of ISC 2003*, 2003.
3. D. Bleichenbacher, Generating ElGamal Signatures without Knowing the Secret, *Advances in Cryptology - EUROCRYPT'96*, LNCS 1070, pages 10-18, Springer-Verlag, 1996.
4. S. Bellovin and M. Merritt, Encrypted Key Exchange: Password-based Protocols Secure Against Dictionary Attacks, *Proceedings of IEEE Symposium on Security and Privacy*, pages 72-84, 1992.
5. S. Bellovin and M. Merritt, Augumented Encrypted Key Exchange: A Password-based Protocol Secure Against Dictionary Attacks and Password File Compromise. *Proceedings of CCS'93*, pages 244-250, 1993.
6. V. Boyko, P. MacKenzie, and S. Patel, Provably-secure Password Anthentiation and Key Exchange Using Diffie-Hellman. *EUROCRYPT 2000*, pages 156-171.
7. L. Gong, Optimal Authentication Protocols Resistant to Password Guessing Attacks. *8th IEEE Computer Security Foundations Workshop*, pages 24-29, 1995.

8. Y. H. Hwang, D. H. Yum, and P. J. Lee, EPA: An Efficient Password-Based Protocol for Authenticated Key Exchange, *ACISP 2003*, LNCS 2727, Springer-Verlag Berlin Heidelberg 2003, pages 452-463, 2003.

9. D. Jablon, Strong Password-Only Authenticated Key Exchange, *ACM Computer Communications Review*, vol.26, no.5, 1996.

10. T. Kwon, Authentication and Key Agreement via Memorable Password, *Proceedings of the ISOC NDSS Symposium*, 2001.

11. T. Kwon, Summary of AMP, Contribution for the P1363 standard, available at *http://grouper.ieee.org/groups/1363/passwdPK/contributions/ampsummary.pdf*, August 2003.

12. T. Kwon, Addendum to Summary of AMP, Contribution for the P1363 standard, available at *http://grouper.ieee.org/groups/1363/passwdPK/contributions/ ampsummary2.pdf*, November 2003.

13. C. H. Lim and P. J. Lee, A Key Recovery Attack on Discrete Log-based Schemes Using a Prime Order Subgroup, *Burton S. Kaliski Jr(Ed.), Advances in Cryptology - CRYPTO '97*, LNCS 1294, Springer-Verlag, pages 249-263, 1997.

14. S. Lucks, Open Key Exchange: How to Defeat Dictionary Attacks Without Encrypting Public Keys, *Proceedings of Security Protocols Workshop*, LNCS 1361, pages 79-90, Springer-Verlag, 1997.

15. P. MacKenzie, S. Patel, and R. Swaminathan, Password-Authenticated Key Exchange Based on RSA, *Proceedings of AsiaCrypt 2000*, pages 599-613, LNCS, Springer-Verlag, 2000.

16. P. MacKenzie, The PAK Suite: Protocols for Password-Authenticated Key Exchange, *Submission to IEEE P1363.2*, April 2002.

17. P. MacKenzie, More Efficient Password-Authenticated Key Exchange, *Progress in Cryptology – CT-RSA 2001*, pages 361-377, 2001.

18. W. Mao and C.H.Lim, Cryptanalysis in Prime Order Subgroups of $\mathbb{Z}_n^\bullet$, *Advances in Cryptology-ASIACRYPT'98*, LNCS 1514, Spinger-Verlag, 1998, pp.214-226.

19. S. Patel, Number Theoretic Attacks on Secure Password Schemes, *Proceedings of IEEE Symposium on Research in Security and Privacy*, pages 236-247, 1997.

20. C. Pavlovski and C. Boyd, Attacks Based on Small Factors in Various Group Structures, *ACISP 2001*, LNCS 2119, pages 36-50, 2001.

21. S. Pohlig and M. Hellman, An Improved Algorithm for Computing Logarithms over GF(p) and Its Cryptographic Significance, *IEEE Transactions on Information Theory*, vol 24, no 1, pages 106-110, 1978.

22. J. M.Pollard, Monte Carlo Methods for Index Computation (mod p), *Math. Comp.*, 32(143), pages 918-924, 1978.

23. P. C. van Oorschot and M. Wiener, On Diffie-Hellman Key Agreement with Short Exponents, *EUROCRYPT'96* LNCS 1070, pages 332-343, 1996.

24. S. Vaudenay, Hidden Collisions on DSS, *Advances in Cryptology - CRYPTO'96*, LNCS 1109, pages 83-88, Springer-Verlag, 1996.

25. T. Wu, Secure Remote Password Protocol, *ISOC Network and Distributed System Security Symposium*, 1998.

26. F. Zhu, D. S. Wong, A. H. Chan, and R. Ye, Password authenticated key exchange based on RSA for imbalanced wireless networks, *Proceedings of ISC 2002*, LNCS 2433, pp. 150-161, Springer-Verlag, 2002.

Analysis and Improvement of Micali's Fair Contract Signing Protocol

Feng Bao, Guilin Wang, Jianying Zhou, and Huafei Zhu

Institute for Infocomm Research
21 Heng Mui Keng Terrace, Singapore 119613
http://www.i2r.a-star.edu.sg/icsd/
{baofeng,glwang,jyzhou,huafei}@i2r.a-star.edu.sg

Abstract. In PODC 2003, Micali presented a fair electronic exchange protocol for contract signing with an invisible trusted party [17]. The protocol was filed as a US patent No 5666420 in 1997 [16]. In the protocol, two mutually distrusted parties exchange their commitments to a contract in a fair way such that either each of them can obtain the other's commitment, or neither of them does. The protocol is optimistic in the sense that the trusted party need not be involved in the protocol unless a dispute occurs. In this paper, we show that Micali's protocol cannot achieve the claimed fairness. In resolving a dispute, the trusted party may face a dilemma situation that no matter what it does, one of the exchanging parties can succeed in cheating. In other words, there is always a party who can get the other's commitment without the other party obtaining his. We further propose a revised version of contract signing protocol that preserves fairness while remaining optimistic.

1 Introduction

Contract signing is a particular form of fair exchange, in which two or more parties exchange commitments to a contract in a way that either all the parties are bound to the contract, or none does. Research on fair contract signing dates back to the work by Even and Yacobi [9] who proved that fairness is impossible in a deterministic two-party contract signing protocol.

Early efforts are mainly focused on contract signing schemes with *computational fairness* (e.g., [6,8,14]): Both parties exchange their commitments/secrets "bit-by-bit". If one party stops prematurely, both parties have about the same fraction of the peer's secret, which means they can complete the contract off-line by investing about the same amount of computing work.

The major advantage of this approach is that no third party is involved in contract signing. However, as pointed out in [4], this approach is unsatisfactory in real life. Suppose two parties are signing a house-sale contract. If the protocol stops prematurely, the seller cannot be sure whether the buyer will try to complete the contract (by a deadline), and vice versa. Obviously, such a non-deterministic status is favorable to a party with stronger computing power,

H. Wang et al. (Eds.): ACISP 2004, LNCS 3108, pp. 176–187, 2004.

which may conditionally force another party to enter into the contract by its own interest.

A more realistic approach for contract signing is to make *optimistic* use of a trusted third party, where the trusted third party is invoked only if one of the participants misbehaves. In [4], probabilistic fair contract signing is achieved by gradual increase of privilege. However, there is a non-negligible probability of uncertainty (but linearly small with increased number of rounds) on the status of a contract being signed. Other optimistic fair contract signing protocols are based on fair exchange of digital signatures [1,12,18]. The major advantages include improvements on fairness, timeliness, and communication overheads.

As an extension of two-party contract signing scenario, some multi-party contract signing protocols have also been proposed in the literature [2,10,13].

In PODC 2003, Micali presented a fair electronic exchange protocol for contract signing with an invisible trusted party [17]. This two-party contract signing protocol was filed as a US patent No 5666420 in 1997 [16]. The protocol allows two mutually distrusted parties to exchange their commitments to a contract in a fair way. The protocol is optimistic in the sense that the trusted party need not be involved in the protocol unless a dispute occurs.

In this paper, we show that Micali's fair contract signing protocol cannot achieve the claimed fairness. In resolving a dispute, the trusted party may face a dilemma situation that no matter what it does, one of the exchanging parties can succeed in cheating. In other words, there is always a party who can get the other's commitment without the other party obtaining his. We identify the cause that leads to the attacks, and further propose a revised version of contract signing protocol that preserves fairness while remaining optimistic. Like Micali's work, our protocol is a generic scheme since any secure digital signature scheme and most of secure encryption algorithms can be used to implement it. Compared with the existing protocols, our protocol is very efficient since only several basic cryptographic operations are required.

The rest of the paper is organized as follows. In Section 2, we give a brief description of Micali's fair contract signing protocol. In Section 3, we demonstrate detailed attacks against Micali's protocol. In Section 4, we propose a revised version of fair contract signing protocol. Section 5 concludes the paper.

2   Micali's Protocol ECS1

Micali presented a fair contract signing protocol in [17]. Here we give a brief description of his protocol ECS1.

Each user in the system has a unique identifier. We denote Alice's identifier by A, Bob's by B, and invisible trusted party by TP. We assume that Alice, Bob and the trusted party TP can all sign messages using a digital signature scheme non-existentially forgeable by an adaptive chosen message attack as defined by Goldwasser, Micali and Rivest [15]. Party X's signature on a message M is denoted by $SIG_X(M)$, and we assume, for convenience, that M is always retrievable from $SIG_X(M)$. We assume that Alice, Bob and TP can also encrypt messages by means of a public-key encryption algorithm secure against adaptive chosen ciphertext attack (i.e., CCA2 secure) as defined by Dolev, Dwork and Naor [7]. The encryption of a message M with party X's public key is denoted by $E_X(M)$. (For simplicity, we assume that messages are encrypted directly with a public-key algorithm. But, according to standard practice, we could first encrypt a message M conveniently with some key K, and then encrypt K with a public-key algorithm.) Such ciphertexts are necessarily generated probabilistically, because we want the encryption algorithm to be so secure, and we shall write $E_X^R(M)$ whenever we want to emphasize the random string R actually utilized in encryption. We also explicitly assume (as it is generally true) that, given the right secret key, not only is M computable from such ciphertexts, but R as well.

Assume that Alice and Bob have already negotiated a would-be contract C and now wish to execute it fairly. Then, Alice chooses a random and thus unpredictable message M, and uses TP's public encryption key to compute a value $Z = E_{TP}(A, B, M)$ as if she wanted to send M to Bob. Alice is committed to C if Bob has both (1) her own signature on (C, Z) and (2) M. Bob is committed to C if Alice has both (1') his own signature on (C, Z) and (2') his own signature on Z. Neither party is committed if the other gets only one of the two values he/she wants.

We now review Micali's protocol ECS1 as follows [17].

A1: Alice chooses a random message M, computes $Z = E_{TP}(A, B, M)$ and sends Bob $SIG_A(C, Z)$.

B1: Upon receiving Z, Bob returns $SIG_B(C, Z)$ and $SIG_B(Z)$.

A2: If Alice receives both properly signed quantities from Bob, she sends M in the clear to Bob.

B2: If Bob receives a string M such that encrypting A, B and M with TP's public key yields the value Z received in Step B1, then he halts: the contract's signing protocol has been successfully completed. Else, he sends the invisible TP the originally received value Z, $SIG_B(C, Z)$ and $SIG_B(Z)$, indicating that Alice is the first signatory and he is the second.

TP1: If Bob's signature of (C, Z) and Z are both correct, the invisible TP decrypts Z with its own secret key. If the result is a triplet consisting of A, B, and a string M, then TP (i) sends Alice $SIG_B(C, Z)$ and $SIG_B(Z)$, and (ii) sends M to Bob.

Micali further claimed that ECS1 is a fair contract signing protocol with an invisible TP by the following argument:

Indeed, if Bob never performs Step B1, then he is not committed to C, but neither is Alice, because Bob only has received $SIG_A(C, Z)$, and has no way of learning M. However, if Bob performs Step B1, then he is committed to C, but Alice too will be so committed: either because she will honestly send M to Bob, or because Bob will get M from the invisible TP. Again, if Bob tries to cheat bypassing Step B1 and accessing directly the invisible TP to learn M, then Alice will get $SIG_B(C, Z)$ and $SIG_B(Z)$

from the invisible TP, because the invisible TP will not help Bob at all unless it first receives both signatures, and because once it decrypts Z to find M, it will also discover that Alice is the first signatory, and thus that she is entitled to $SIG_B(C, Z)$ and $SIG_B(Z)$.

3   Security Analysis of Micali's Protocol ECS1

This section presents a security analysis of Micali's electronic contract signing protocol ECS1 [16,17]. First of all, when Bob requests dispute resolution from TP, he is only required to provide $SIG_B(C, Z)$ and $SIG_B(Z)$ (including C and Z by the assumptions) to TP. We remark that such information is not sufficient, since obviously $SIG_A(C, Z)$ should be sent too. Otherwise, the following trivial attack can be mounted.

Upon receiving Alice's signature $SIG_A(C, Z)$, dishonest Bob prepares another contract C', which may be a meaningless or disadvantageous contract for Alice. After that, to get the value of M, Bob sends $SIG_B(C', Z)$ and $SIG_B(Z)$ to TP. Since these two signatures are indeed valid and Z has the desired structure, according to the protocol specification, TP forwards $SIG_B(C', Z)$ and $SIG_B(Z)$ to Alice, and M to Bob. The result is that Bob gets Alice's commitment on contract C, while Alice only obtains Bob's commitment on another contract C' selected by Bob.

Based on this observation, in later discussion it is assumed that to get M from TP, Bob is also required to provide $SIG_A(C, Z)$ (together with $SIG_B(C, Z)$ and $SIG_B(Z)$). Our results in this section show that Micali's fair contract signing protocol is actually *unfair*.

3.1   Bob's Commitment

Here, we demonstrate an attack that exploits the definition of Bob's commitment. According to Micali's definition, the responder Bob's commitment on contract C consists of his signatures on messages (C, Z) and Z, i.e., $SIG_B(C, Z)$ and $SIG_B(Z)$. In other words, to validate Bob's commitment a third party is not supposed to check the specific structure of Z, i.e., whether $Z \equiv E_{TP}(A, B, M)$ for some string M. Based on this observation, attack 1 is identified and illustrated in Figure 1. In this attack, dishonest Alice always gets Bob's commitment to contract C but Bob cannot get Alice's commitment.

Attack 1. To initiate this attack, dishonest Alice first selects a random number Z (with proper length), and then sends her signature $SIG_A(C, Z)$ to Bob. Since $SIG_A(C, Z)$ is indeed Alice's valid signature, honest Bob returns Alice his commitment, i.e., $SIG_B(C, Z)$ and $SIG_B(Z)$. At this point, Alice halts the protocol permanently because she has obtained Bob's commitment on contract C successfully. However, even TP cannot find a string M such that $Z = E_{TP}(A, B, M)$ except a negligible probability, since Z is a random number. This implies that Bob cannot get Alice's commitment to contract C.

Goal: Dishonest Alice gets Bob's commitment to contract C.

Alice: Dishonest Initiator   Bob: Honest Responder

Choose random Z.   (1) $\xrightarrow{\quad SIG_A(C,Z) \quad}$

(2) $\xleftarrow{SIG_B(C,Z), SIG_B(Z)}$ Send (2) *iff* (1) is valid.

(3) $\xrightarrow{\quad Nothing \quad}$

Fig. 1. Attack 1.

An intuitive method to avoid this attack is to redefine Bob's commitment to contract C as a triplet $(SIG_B(C,Z), SIG_B(Z), M)$, where $Z \equiv E_{TP}(A,B,M)$. That is, compared with Micali's original definition, to convince a third party that Bob has committed to contract C, Alice is required to provide not only $(SIG_B(C,Z), SIG_B(Z))$ but also a string M that satisfies $Z \equiv E_{TP}(A,B,M)$. Unfortunately, further discussion will reveal such countermeasure is also not sufficient to secure the protocol.

3.2   TP's Dilemma

In literatures [16,17], Micali did not describe what TP is supposed to do if it receives a value Z that does not match the cipher of desired (A,B,M), even though $SIG_A(C,Z)$, $SIG_B(C,Z)$ and $SIG_B(Z)$ are valid signatures. In other words, TP is not given a dispute resolution policy when $D_{TP}(Z) \neq (A,B,M)$ for any M. Here we demonstrate two attacks that make TP in a dilemma to resolve such disputes: No matter what it does, one of the exchanging parties has advantage over the other. More specifically, one party can always get the other party's commitment while the other party cannot.

TP's Dilemma: If $SIG_A(C,Z)$, $SIG_B(C,Z)$ and $SIG_B(Z)$ are valid but $D_{TP}(Z) \neq (A,B,M)$, i.e., the first two components of $D_{TP}(Z)$ are not the identities of Alice and Bob, respectively, TP must decide whether to resolve the dispute. Essentially, it has only the following two choices of dispute resolution policy:

- *Policy 1*: TP rejects Bob's request, and sends nothing (or only error messages) to Bob (and related parties).
- *Policy 2*: TP forwards M to Bob, and $(SIG_B(C,Z), SIG_B(Z))$ to Alice (and related parties).

In the following part, we show that policy 1 is unfair for Bob, while policy 2 unfair for Alice. Note that policy 1 is employed by many fair exchange protocols. However, if TP uses it to resolve disputes, dishonest Alice can mount attack 2 as illuminated in Figure 2. In attack 2, dishonest Alice (maybe colluding with A') can get Bob's commitment on contract C such that Bob cannot obtain her (or their) commitment on contract C. We explain details as follows.

Goal: Dishonest Alice (colluding with $A^{\square}$) gets Bob's commitment to contract C.

Alice: (dishonest) Initiator   Bob: Responder

Choose M and prepare

$Z^{\square} = E_{TP}(A^{\square}, B, M)$.   (1) $\xrightarrow{\quad SIG_A(C, Z^{\square}) \quad}$

(2) $\xleftarrow{\quad SIG_B(C, Z^{\square}), SIG_B(Z^{\square}) \quad}$ Send (2) iff (1) is valid.

(3) $\xrightarrow{\quad Nothing \quad}$

Fig. 2. Attack 2.

Attack 2. Alice first properly chooses a random message M, and then dishonestly prepares $Z' = E_{TP}(A', B, M)$. After that, in message flow (1), she sends Bob her signature on message (C, Z'). Upon receiving $SIG_A(C, Z')$, Bob checks whether it is indeed Alice's signature on message (C, Z'). Since this is the fact, according to the protocol specification, in message flow (2) Bob returns Alice his commitment to contract C, i.e., $SIG_B(C, Z')$ and $SIG_B(Z')$. After obtaining Bob's commitment to contract C, dishonest Alice permanently halts the protocol execution, i.e., does not send back M to Bob in message flow (3).

Since the victim Bob only gets Alice's signature $SIG_A(C, Z')$, he will ask for help from TP. For this end, he sends $SIG_A(C, Z')$, $SIG_B(C, Z')$ and $SIG_B(Z')$ to TP. TP decrypts Z' and gets $D_{TP}(Z') = (A', B, M) \neq (A, B, M)$, so it finds the format of Z' is incorrect. Due to the predefined dispute resolution policy (policy 1), TP ignores this resolution request and sends nothing (or only error message) to Bob. The result is that Alice (and her colluding parter A') obtains B's commitment to contract C, i.e., $SIG_B(C, Z')$ and $SIG_B(Z')$, but Bob does not get Alice's commitment to contract C. Therefore, in this situation Micali's protocol is unfair to the responder.

Remark 1. We want to further emphasize that in the above attack TP could not simply identify Alice as a cheater just due to the fact $D_{TP}(Z') = (A', B, M) \neq (A, B, M)$. Otherwise, Bob can mount an attack to frame Alice as follows. Consider a situation where the protocol is initiated by dishonest Bob and responded by honest Alice. In such a case, Bob dishonestly prepares $Z' = E_{TP}(A', B, M)$ instead of $E_{TP}(B, A, M)$, and sends $SIG_B(C, Z')$ to Alice. Then, honest Alice sends her signatures $SIG_A(C, Z')$ and $SIG_A(Z')$ to Bob, since she is the responder now. By pretending as the responder of a protocol instance, Bob sends $SIG_A(C, Z'), SIG_B(C, Z'), SIG_B(Z')$ to TP as a request for dispute resolution. The result is that TP finds $D_{TP}(Z') = (A', B, M) \neq (A, B, M)$, and then honest Alice will be mistakenly identified as a cheater.

Remark 2. Note that attack 2 is valid even if Bob's commitment to contract C is redefined as above, i.e., a triplet $(SIG_B(C, Z), SIG_B(Z), M)$ where $Z \equiv E_{TP}(A, B, M)$. The reason is that $(SIG_B(C, Z'), SIG_B(Z'), M)$, what Alice obtained via attack 2, can be viewed as Bob's commitment to contract C

(with user A') due to the fact $Z' \equiv E_{TP}(A', B, M)$. However, if it is assumed that the identities of A and B are embedded in contract C, attack 2 will be invalid since A' is not embedded in C. This assumption is reasonable, since the involved parties' names are almost always included clearly in real-world contracts. But the fact is that such assumption is not specified in [16,17].

In the situation where policy 2 is used by TP, Bob colluding with Alice can cheat another user A' by mounting attack 3, which is illuminated in Figure 3 and explained in detail as follows.

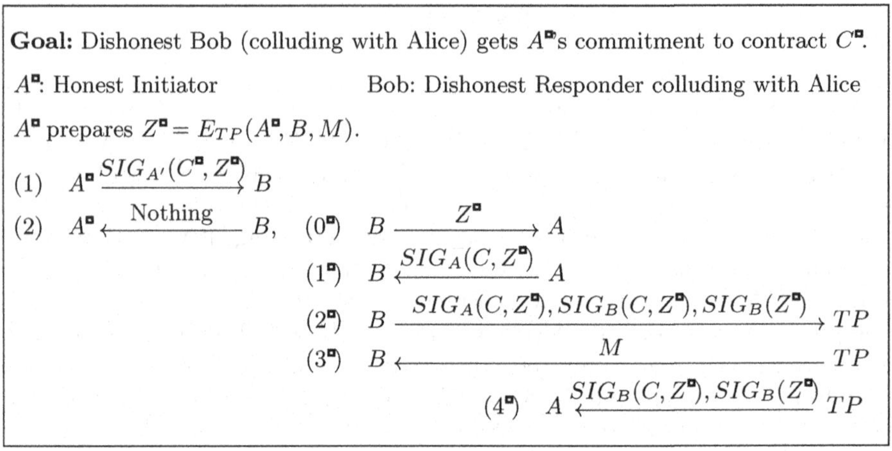

Goal: Dishonest Bob (colluding with Alice) gets $A^{\square}$s commitment to contract $C^{\square}$.

$A^{\square}$: Honest Initiator   Bob: Dishonest Responder colluding with Alice

$A^{\square}$ prepares $Z^{\square} = E_{TP}(A^{\square}, B, M)$.

(1) $A^{\square} \xrightarrow{SIG_{A'}(C^{\square}, Z^{\square})} B$

(2) $A^{\square} \xleftarrow{\quad Nothing \quad} B$,   (0$^{\square}$) $B \xrightarrow{\quad Z^{\square} \quad} A$

(1$^{\square}$) $B \xleftarrow{SIG_A(C, Z^{\square})} A$

(2$^{\square}$) $B \xrightarrow{SIG_A(C, Z^{\square}), SIG_B(C, Z^{\square}), SIG_B(Z^{\square})} TP$

(3$^{\square}$) $B \xleftarrow{\quad\quad\quad M \quad\quad\quad} TP$

(4$^{\square}$) $A \xleftarrow{SIG_B(C, Z^{\square}), SIG_B(Z^{\square})} TP$

Fig. 3. Attack 3.

Attack 3. In this attack, we assume that honest user A' and dishonest Bob run the contract signing protocol to exchange their commitments to contract C'. However, Bob colluding with Alice wants to get A''s commitment but does not release his commitment to A'. At the first, A' honestly selects a random string M and prepares $Z' = E_{TP}(A', B, M)$. Then A''s signature $SIG_{A'}(C', Z')$ is sent to Bob. Upon receiving $SIG_{A'}(C', Z')$, Bob intentionally terminates the protocol execution with A'. To start a new instance of protocol execution with his friend Alice, Bob sends Alice Z'. After that, Alice returns $SIG_A(C, Z')$ to Bob in message flow $(1')$, where C is another contract agreed between Alice and Bob previously. Then, to get the value of M, Bob sends $SIG_A(C, Z')$, $SIG_B(C, Z')$ and $SIG_B(Z')$ to TP as if he is a victim. Subsequently, TP finds those signatures are valid but $D_{TP}(Z') = (A', B, M) \neq (A, B, M)$. According policy 2, TP sends M to Bob and $(SIG_B(C, Z'), SIG_B(Z'))$ to Alice (and A'). The result is that with the help of Alice, Bob gets A''s commitment to contract C', i.e., $(SIG_{A'}(C', Z'), M)$ where $Z' = E_{TP}(A', B, M)$, while honest user A' does not obtain Bob's commitment to contract C' at the same time. (A' may get Bob's commitment to contract C, i.e., $(SIG_B(C, Z'), SIG_B(Z'))$, but C is different from C'.) Therefore, in this situation Micali's protocol is unfair for the initiator.

Remark 3. The essence of attack 3 is that Bob exploits TP as an oracle to get the value of M. In addition, we remark that our attack 3 is also valid even if we assume that the identities of involved parties are embedded in contracts because Bob indeed gets A''s signature on contract C' and the string M.

From the above discussion, we know that in attack 2 and attack 3, the transcripts sent by Bob to TP are the same, i.e., $SIG_A(C, Z')$, $SIG_B(C, Z')$ and $SIG_B(Z')$, where $D_{TP}(Z) = (A', B, M) \neq (A, B, M)$. Therefore, it is indistinguishable for TP whether attack 2 or attack 3 was mounted. In other words, based on those information, TP cannot identify who is the cheater: the initiator or the responder. Consequently, we showed that the invisible trusted party has to face a dilemma in some situation of resolving disputes.

4   Revised Protocol

To avoid the above weaknesses in Micali's scheme, we propose a revised contract signing protocol in this section. At the same time, security discussion is also provided to show that our protocol is fair.

4.1   Protocol Description

In our protocol, we use almost the same notation as in [17] (described in Section 2), but change the definition of commitment to a contract and the format of Z. More specifically, we also assume that $SIG_A(\cdot)$ and $SIG_B(\cdot)$ are secure signing algorithms of Alice and Bob, respectively, and $(E_{TP}(\cdot), D_{TP}(\cdot))$ is the trusted party TP's CCA-2 secure encryption/decryption algorithm pair. To emphasize a random number R is utilized to encrypt message M, we write $c = E_{TP}^R(M)$. Note that with the pair (M, R), anybody can verify whether a string c is the ciphertext of M encrypted under TP's public key. We also explicitly assume (as it is generally true) that, from the ciphertext c, TP can recover not only M but also R. For simplicity, we denote this fact as $(M, R) = D_{TP}(c)$. For example, this requirement is satisfied by the OAEP series of encryption schemes [3,11,19], but not by the Cramer-Shoup cryptosystems [5]. In addition, a one-way hash function $H(\cdot)$ is introduced to reduce the size of Z.

Alice's and Bob's commitments to a contract C are re-defined as follows:

- **The initiator Alice's commitment to a contract** C is defined as a triplet $(SIG_A(A, B, TP, C, Z), M, R)$, where $Z = E_{TP}^R(A, B, H(C), M)$.
- **The responder Bob's commitment to a contract** C is defined as a triplet $(SIG_B(A, B, TP, C, Z), M, R)$, where $Z = E_{TP}^R(A, B, H(C), M)$.

We say Alice is committed to C *if and only if* Bob obtains Alice's signature on message (A, B, TP, C, Z) and a pair (M, R) such that $Z = E_{TP}^R(A, B, H(C), M)$. Similarly, Bob is committed to C *if and only if* Alice obtains Bob's signature on message (A, B, TP, C, Z) and a pair (M, R) such that $Z = E_{TP}^R(A, B, H(C), M)$. Therefore, different from Micali's definition, the commitments of the initiator and responder are symmetric in our protocol.

As depicted in Figure 4, our protocol is so simple that only three messages are exchanged in normal case.

Alice: Initiator   Bob: Responder

Choose M, R and prepare

$Z = E_{TP}^R(A, B, H(C), M)$. (1) $\xrightarrow{\quad SIG_A(A, B, TP, C, Z) \quad}$

                                     Return message flow (2) *iff*

(2) $\xleftarrow{\quad SIG_B(A, B, TP, C, Z) \quad}$ message follow (1) is valid.

Send message flow (3) *iff*

message follow (2) is valid. (3) $\xrightarrow{\quad\quad M, R \quad\quad}$

Fig. 4. Revised Protocol.

Revised Protocol

Step 1. Alice selects a random pair (M, R) (with proper lengths), and then prepares an encrypted message Z by using the public known encryption algorithm E_{TP}, i.e., she computes $Z = E_{TP}^R(A, B, H(C), M)$. After that, Alice calculates and sends her signature $SIG_A(A, B, TP, C, Z)$ to Bob as message flow (1).

Step 2. Upon receiving this message, the responder Bob checks whether its content is *exactly* Alice's signature on the message (A, B, TP, C, Z). (Recall that we have assumed the message (A, B, TP, C, Z) can be recovered from $SIG_A(A, B, TP, C, Z)$.) If this is true, he computes and returns Alice his signature $SIG_B(A, B, TP, C, Z)$. Otherwise, he halts.

Step 3. When Alice gets the message follow (2), she checks whether it is Bob's signature on message (A, B, TP, C, Z). If this is the case, she reveals the pair (M, R) to Bob; otherwise, she stops.

When Bob receives the random pair (M, R), he checks whether $Z \equiv E_{TP}^R(A, B, H(C), M)$. If this equality holds, Bob has obtained Alice's commitment to contract C, i.e., $(SIG_A(A, B, TP, C, Z), M, R)$, where $Z = E_{TP}^R(A, B, H(C), M)$. Otherwise, if Bob does not receive (M, R) or only receives incorrect (M, R), he requests dispute resolution from the trusted party TP as follows.

Resolution request. Bob sends the signatures $SIG_A(A, B, TP, C, Z)$ and $SIG_B(A, B, TP, C, Z)$ to TP.

Resolution by TP. TP checks whether the two messages sent by Bob are Alice's and Bob's signatures on message (A, B, TP, C, Z), respectively. If this is not the fact, TP stops. Otherwise, TP decrypts Z and checks whether the decrypted plaintext matches the expected values of $(A, B, H(C), *, *)$, i.e., $D_{TP}(Z) =?(A, B, H(C), *, *)$. If this checking goes through, TP returns $(SIG_B(A, B, TP, C, Z), M, R)$ and $(SIG_A(A, B, TP, C, Z), M, R)$ to Alice and Bob, respectively. Otherwise, if TP finds the content of Z is not the expected, it stops or just sends an error message to Bob.

4.2   Security Discussion

One can check the completeness of our protocol directly. So, we only analyze the fairness of our protocol. We classified our discussion into two cases: (1) Alice is honest, but Bob is cheating; and (2) Bob is honest, but Alice is cheating.

Case 1. *Alice is honest, but Bob is cheating.* This implies that Alice sends a correct signature $SIG_A(A, B, TP, C, Z)$ to Bob, where $Z = E^R_{TP}(A, B, H(C), M)$ for some random pair (M, R). Upon receiving $SIG_A(A, B, TP, C, Z)$, dishonest Bob wants to get the value of (M, R) but does not release his signature $SIG_B(A, B, TP, C, Z)$ to Alice. According to the specifications and assumptions of our protocol, only two entities have the power for releasing (M, R), i.e., Alice who selected (M, R) and TP who can decrypt Z by using it's private decryption key. Of course, Bob cannot select Alice as the helper. Otherwise, he has to send Alice $SIG_B(A, B, TP, C, Z)$, which is contradictory to his goal. Therefore, the only choice left is to get help from TP. Again, Bob cannot send $SIG_A(A, B, TP, C, Z)$ and $SIG_B(A, B, TP, C, Z)$ to TP. Otherwise, TP will find those two signatures are valid and the structure of Z is correct, and then sends $(SIG_B(A, B, TP, C, Z), M, R)$ to Alice (though Bob will also get the value of (M, R)).

Furthermore, Bob cannot get (M, R) from TP by colluding with other parties. The reason is that Z is bound with $SIG_A(A, B, TP, C, Z)$ and $SIG_B(A, B, TP, C, Z)$ together, and TP is required to check whether $Z \equiv E^R_{TP}(A, B, H(C), M)$. For example, if Bob colludes with A', he might send $SIG_{A'}(A', B, TP, C, Z)$ and $SIG_B(A', B, TP, C, Z)$ to TP. Then TP will find, although $SIG_{A'}(A', B, TP, C, Z)$ and $SIG_B(A', B, TP, C, Z)$ are two valid signatures of A' and Bob, A' does not appear as an element of $D_{TP}(Z)$. According to the specification of our protocol, TP does not reveal (M, R) to Bob.

Case 2. *Bob is honest, but Alice is cheating.* Alice may cheats in step (1) and/or step (3). If Alice only cheats in step (3), she cannot take advantage over Bob. We explain the reasons as follows. First of all, this means that Alice properly selected a random pair (M, R), computed $Z = E^R_{TP}(A, B, H(C), M)$ and sent $SIG_A(A, B, TP, C, Z)$ to Bob. Since $SIG_A(A, B, TP, C, Z)$ is Alice's valid signature, Bob honestly returns his signature $SIG_B(A, B, TP, C, Z)$ to Alice. Upon receiving $SIG_B(A, B, TP, C, Z)$, however, Alice does not reveal or only reveals an incorrect (M, R) to Bob. In this situation, according to the specification of our protocol, Bob can get the value of (M, R) by requesting dispute resolution from TP, since he has obtained Alice's valid signature $SIG_A(A, B, TP, C, Z)$ and Z is in the correct format (though he is not sure about this).

On the other hand, if Alice dishonestly performs in step (1), which implies and only implies that Z is not in the correct format, we show she cannot take advantage too. When Bob receives $SIG_A(A, B, TP, C, Z)$, he checks and knows that it is Alice's valid signature on the message (A, B, TP, C, Z), and then honestly returns his signature $SIG_B(A, B, TP, C, Z)$ to Alice (although he does not know Alice prepared an incorrect Z). After getting $SIG_B(A, B, TP, C, Z)$, Alice may halt. However, according to our definition of commitments, $SIG_B(A, B, TP, C, Z)$ is not Bob's commitment to C since Alice cannot provide a correct pair (M, R) such that $Z \equiv E_{TP}^R(A, B, H(C), M)$. Remember that Z is prepared by Alice in an incorrect format.

Based on the above analysis, we conclude that our protocol achieves fair contract signing.

5   Conclusion

Contract signing is an important application in electronic commerce, and has attracted many research interests. A practical and efficient approach for fair contract signing is using an invisible trusted third party. Micali presented an optimized fair contract signing protocol at PODC 2003, which was filed in a US patent in 1997. In this paper, we demonstrated that Micali's protocol cannot achieve the claimed fairness. We further proposed a revised contract signing protocol that preserves fairness while remaining optimistic.

Acknowledgements. The authors would like to thank anonymous referees for their very helpful suggestions on the improvement of this paper.

References

1. N. Asokan, V. Shoup, and M. Waidner. *Asynchronous protocols for optimistic fair exchange.* 1998 IEEE Symposium on Security and Privacy, pages 86-99, 1998.
2. B. Baum-Waidner. *Optimistic asynchronous multi-party contract signing with reduced number of rounds.* ICALP'01, LNCS 2076, pages 898-911, Springer, 2001.
3. M. Bellare and P. Rogaway. *Optimal asymmetric encryption - How to encrypt with RSA.* Eurocrypt'94, LNCS 950, pages 92-111, Springer, 1994.
4. M. Ben-Or, O. Goldreich, S. Micali, and R. L. Rivest. *A fair protocol for signing contracts.* IEEE Transactions on Information Theory, 36(1): 40-46, 1990.
5. R. Cramer and V. Shoup. *A practical public key cryptosystem provably secure against adaptive chosen ciphertext attack.* Crypto'98, LNCS 1462, pages 13-25, Springer, 1998.
6. I. B. Damgård. *Practical and provably secure release of a secret and exchange of signatures.* Journal of Cryptology, 8(4): 201-222, 1995.
7. D. Dolev, D. Dwork, and N. Naor. *Non-meallleable cryptography.* 1992 IEEE Symposium on Foundations of Computer Science, 1992.
8. S. Even, O. Goldreich, and A. Lempel. *A randomized protocol for signing contracts.* Communications of the ACM, 28(6):637-647, 1985.
9. S. Even and Y. Yacobi. *Relations among public key signature schemes.* Technical Report 175, Computer Science Dept., Technion, Israel, 1980.

10. J. L. Ferrer-Gomila, M. Payeras-Capella, and L. Huguet-Rotger. *Efficient optimistic n-party contract signing protocol.* 2001 Information Security Conference, LNCS 2200, pages 394-407, Springer, 2001.
11. E. Fujisaki, T. Okamoto, D. Pointcheval, and J. Stern. *RSA-OAEP is secure under the RSA assumption.* Crypto'01, LNCS 2139, pages 260-274, Springer, 2001.
12. J. Garay, M. Jakobsson, and P. MacKenzie. *Abuse-free optimistic contract signing.* Crypto'99, LNCS 1666, pages 449-466, Sprnger, 1999.
13. J. Garay and P. MacKenzie. *Abuse-free multi-party contract signing.* 1999 International Symposium on Distributed Computing, LNCS 1693, pages 151-165, Springer, 1999.
14. O. Goldreich. *A simple protocol for signing contracts.* Crypto'83, pages 133-136, Plenum Press, 1984.
15. S. Goldwasser, S. Micali, and R. Rivest. *A digital signature scheme secure against adaptive chosen-message attack.* SIAM Journal of Computing, 17(2):281-308, 1988.
16. S. Micali. *Simultaneous electronic transactions.* US Patent No. 5666420, September 1997.
17. S. Micali. *Simple and fast optimistic protocols for fair electronic exchange.* 2003 ACM Symposium on Principles of Distributed Computing, pages 12-19, 2003.
18. B. Pfitzmann, M. Schunter, and M. Waidner. *Optimal efficiency of optimistic contract signing.* 1998 ACM Symposium on Principles of Distributed Computing, pages 113-122, 1998.
19. V. Shoup. *OAEP reconsidered.* Journal of Cryptology, 15(4): 223-249, 2002.

Digital Signature Schemes with Domain Parameters

Serge Vaudenay

EPFL
http://lasecwww.epfl.ch/

Abstract. Digital signature schemes often use domain parameters such as prime numbers or elliptic curves. They can be subject to security threats when they are not treated like public keys. In this paper we formalize the notion of "signature scheme with domain parameter" together with a new adversarial model: the "domain parameter shifting attack". We take ECDSA as a case study. We make a domain parameter shifting attack against ECDSA: an attacker can impersonate a honest signer either by trying to modify the subgroup generator G or, when using point compression representation, by trying to modify the elliptic curve a and b domain parameters. We further propose to fix this ECDSA issue.

1 Introduction

Following pioneer work by Merkle [17], Diffie-Hellman [8], and Rivest-Shamir-Adleman [19], a formal framework for public-key digital signature schemes was proposed. These schemes are used in order to transform an insecure communication channel into a channel which guarantees authentication, provided that an extra authenticating channel can be used for setting up the system. Typically, one uses an authenticating channel in order to transmit a public key. The public key is associated to a secret one. Then, the digital signature algorithm can provide authentication of a document by typically proving that the document has been signed by a process which possesses the secret key. (See Fig. 1.)

Authenticating public keys for a signature scheme is an odd problem since it already needs signatures from a Certification Authority (CA). This requires that the CA public key is initially authenticated by an alternate mean. This "root authentication" is more expensive and critical.

Digital signature algorithms e.g. DSA often rely on domain parameters. DSA [2,4,6] follows a long dynasty of ElGamal schemes [9,10,11,20,21]. It relies on some primes p, q and a q-ordered subgroup of $\mathbf{Z}_p^*$ generated by some g residue. An extra seed is used in order to convince that p and q were randomly generated, thus to make users trust their safety. Domain parameters consist of a (p, q, g, seed) quadruplet. ECDSA [3,6], a variant of DSA, relies on some finite field $\mathbf{F}_q$, some elliptic curve C over $\mathbf{F}_q$ defined by some $a, b \in \mathbf{F}_q$, some prime number n and some n-ordered subgroup of C generated by a point G. Domain parameters consist of a $(q, \text{representation}, a, b, n, G, \text{seed})$ tuple.

H. Wang et al. (Eds.): ACISP 2004, LNCS 3108, pp. 188–199, 2004.

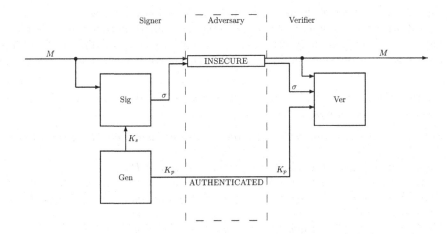

Fig. 1. Digital Signature Scheme.

Typically, making public-private key pairs in RSA [19] is much more expensive than signing or verifying. In DSA [6], the expensive computation for key generation factorizes in making common domain parameters. Then, making key pairs is inexpensive. Indeed, the *raison d'être* of domain parameters is essentially in being set up and validated once for all, e.g. in a ad-hoc network.

Domain parameters face to several security problems.

- They should be authenticated. This means that alternate authentication means have to be used.
- They should be trusted. End users should be protected against malicious choice of domain parameters. This point is particularly relevant in the case of ECDSA since seldom end users master elliptic curve techniques. (Fortunately, ECDSA can rely on some well established standardization bodies like SECG[1] which provide lists of standard elliptic curves.)

In this paper we propose a definition of "digital signature scheme with domain parameters" (DSSDP) in Sect. 2 and security requirements in Sect. 2.2. For our case study, we rephrase the ECDSA specifications in these settings in Sect. 3.1. We first review in Sect. 3.2 a known domain parameter issue from [24] and the proposed fix. We show that the fix is not enough by describing some new attacks in Sect. 3.3 and Sect. 3.4. We finally propose to update ECDSA.

2   Digital Signature Schemes with Domain Parameters

2.1   Definition

Digital signature schemes are traditionally defined as a set of three algorithms: key generation, signature, and verification algorithms. This definition does not

---

[1] http://www.secg.org

capture the notion of domain parameters. As a matter of fact, many current digital schemes use domain parameters as an intuitive notion which should be quite clear from context even though it was not properly formalized. We address this issue by proposing the following definition. We believe that it reflects the common intuition.

Definition 1. *A digital signature scheme with domain parameter (DSSDP) is a set of five algorithms.*

SetUp(t): *an algorithm which generates a domain parameter P using a security parameter t.*
Val(t, P): *an algorithm which verifies the validity of P.*
Gen(t, P): *an algorithm which generates public-secret key pairs (K_p, K_s).*
Sig(t, P, K_s, M): *an algorithm which produces a signature σ on a digital document M.*
Ver(t, P, K_p, M, σ): *an algorithm which verifies signed-documents.*[2]

Val and Ver are deterministic predicates. SetUp, Gen, and Sig are probabilistic algorithms, hence they output random values. **Completeness** *is achieved by the following properties.*

1. *For any t, if we let $P \leftarrow \text{SetUp}(t)$, then the $\text{Val}(t, P)$ predicate holds with probability 1.*
2. *For any t and M, if we let $P \leftarrow \text{SetUp}(t)$, $(K_p, K_s) \leftarrow \text{Gen}(t, P)$ and $\sigma \leftarrow \text{Sig}(t, P, K_s, M)$, then the $\text{Ver}(t, P, K_p, M, \sigma)$ predicate holds with probability 1.*

Here, the left arrow notation, e.g. in $P \leftarrow \text{SetUp}(t)$ means that P is random following the distribution generated by the SetUp probabilistic algorithm.

For simplicity reasons we assume that there is a canonical way to extract t from P so there is no need for having t as a parameter for Gen, Sig and Ver. We still need to verify that P is consistent with a chosen t in Val though.

The usage of this scheme is as depicted on Fig. 2.

Set up. Everyone agrees on a security parameter t. Some central service first generates $P \leftarrow \text{SetUp}(t)$ and broadcasts it.
Public key authentication. The signer checks that $\text{Val}(t, P)$ holds and generates $(K_p, K_s) \leftarrow \text{Gen}(P)$. She then sends K_p to the verifiers in an authenticated way (e.g. using a certificate obtained from a Certificate Authority).
Signature. To sign M, the signer computes $\sigma \leftarrow \text{Sig}(P, K_s, M)$ and sends M, σ to the verifier. The verifier checks that $\text{Val}(t, P)$ and $\text{Ver}(P, K_p, M, \sigma)$ hold.

We emphasize that we do not assume that broadcasting P is secure nor that the P issuer is trusted. In particular the signer and the verifier may receive different domain parameters due to malicious broadcast.

Other studies like Menezes-Smart [16] define a signature scheme with an additional algorithm: a public key validation scheme which is important when considering multi-user settings. We omit it in this paper.

---

[2] Signature schemes with message recovery do not take M as an input but rather produce it as an output. We do not consider it in this paper for simplicity reasons.

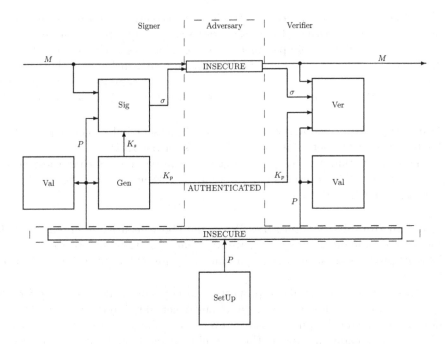

Fig. 2. Digital Signature Scheme with Domain Parameters.

2.2 Security Requirements

Here we formulate the security requirements on DSSDP.

Resistance to existential forgery. An adversary is given P, K_p, access to the $\text{Sig}(P, K_s, .)$ oracle, and aims at forging a (M, σ) pair such that $\text{Ver}(P, K_p, M, \sigma)$ holds without querying the oracle with M. We say that the signature scheme is (B_t, ε_t)-secure if for any t and any adversary of complexity bounded by B_t, we have $\Pr[\text{success}; P \leftarrow \text{SetUp}(t), (K_p, K_s) \leftarrow \text{Gen}(P)] \leq \varepsilon_t$.

This was proposed by Goldwasser, Micali and Rivest [12,13] as the strongest security requirement. Menezes and Smart proposed to extend it in a multi-user setting [16]. Here, an alternate goal for the adversary is to output (M, σ) and (K_p', K_s') such that both $\text{Ver}(P, K_p, M, \sigma)$ and $\text{Ver}(P, K_p', M, \sigma)$ hold and that (K_p', K_s') is a valid key pair. In this case, the adversary is allowed to query M to the $\text{Sig}(P, K_s, .)$ oracle. This is called a "key substitution attack".

Domain parameter integrity. The definition is the same, but for the goal of the adversary which is now to forge a (P', M, σ) triplet such that $P \neq P'$, $\text{Val}(t, P')$ and $\text{Ver}(P', K_p, M, \sigma)$ hold without querying the oracle with M.

We call this condition "domain parameter integrity" since it makes clear that when the verifier checks that $\text{Val}(t, P)$ and $\text{Ver}(P, K_p, M, \sigma)$ hold then his P is the same domain parameter than the one of the signer. Hence K_p is bound to P.

This condition may look strange. Actually, it becomes mandatory when we do not want to rely on trusting the P issuer or when P is not strongly authenticated.

Note that if the domain parameter P is considered as a part of the public key K_p, then this security requirement is already implicitly included in the Menezes-Smart one. [16] mentions this fact (Remark 5(ii)) but completely omits it in the analysis. (Otherwise our results from Sect. 3 would contradict their Theorem 9.)

Domain parameter consistency. For any t, the set of all P such that $\text{Val}(t, P)$ holds is exactly the set of all possible outputs for $\text{SetUp}(t)$.

This means that Val accepts no more domain parameters than those generated by SetUp. This prevents e.g. from having n domain parameters which are not prime numbers in ECDSA.

Trust in domain parameters. When the above security requirements hold for a fixed domain parameter P, we say that P is trusted. We say that the DSSDP provides trust in domain parameters if any P for which $\text{Val}(t, P)$ holds is trusted.

This means that the above properties do not only hold *on average* for any random domain parameter which was honestly generated, but for *any* acceptable domain parameter. Its purpose is to prevent from unknown attacks by malicious selection of domain parameters (like e.g. hiding trapdoors in an elliptic curve).

Abuse of trust in domain parameter may happen. As a famous example we mention the Bleichenbacher attack [7] against the ElGamal signature in which domain parameters p and g are chosen such that signatures are easy to forge.

Finally we formulate the following security definition. The adversary model is depicted on Fig. 3.

Definition 2. *Given a DSSDP as in Def. 1, we consider adversaries which are given P, K_p, access to the $\text{Sig}(P, K_s, .)$ oracle, and which aim at forging a (P', M, σ) triplet such that $\text{Val}(t, P')$ and $\text{Ver}(P', K_p, M, \sigma)$ hold without querying the oracle with M. When $P' \neq P$ we call it a "domain parameter shifting attack". We say that the signature scheme is (B_t, ε_t)-secure if for any t, any adversary of complexity bounded by B_t, and any P such that $\text{Val}(t, P)$, we have $\Pr[\text{success}; (K_p, K_s) \leftarrow \text{Gen}(P)] \leq \varepsilon_t$.*

2.3   Reduction to Traditional Signature Schemes

Obviously, traditional digital signature schemes are also DSSDP in which the domain parameter is void. Conversely, we can easily transform the DSSDP into a classical digital signature scheme as follows.

Gen'(t): run $P \leftarrow \text{SetUp}(t)$ and $(K_p, K_s) \leftarrow \text{Gen}(P)$, set $K'_p = (P, K_p)$, $K'_s = (P, K_s)$ and output (K'_p, K'_s).
Sig'(K'_s, M): same as $\text{Sig}(P, K_s, M)$.
Ver'(K'_p, M, σ): check that $\text{Val}(t, P)$ and $\text{Ver}(P, K_p, M, \sigma)$ hold.

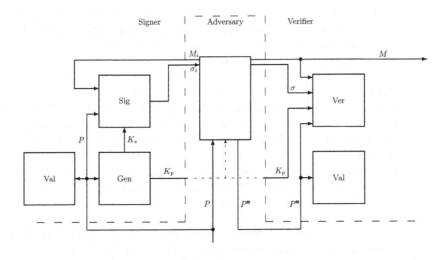

Fig. 3. Adversary for a Digital Signature Scheme with Domain Parameters.

Here P becomes a part of the public key. This is a typical situation in client-server communications: servers send their (P, K_p) pair in a X.509 [14] certificate. This works provided that inclusion of domain parameters in the certificate is mandatory. This is not the case in [14] which suggests that domain parameters can be transmitted "by other means". In this paper we concentrate on using DSSDP with common domain parameters e.g. in ad-hoc networks, which excludes treating domain parameters as part of public keys.

3 ECDSA

3.1 Definition

We summarize the ECDSA with notations from ANSI X9.62 [3][3] in our format. We use the hash function SHA-1 [5] which we denote H.

SetUp(t): do as follows. The security parameter t specifies the field size and type (either a field of characteristic two, or a large prime field).
1. Choose the finite field $\mathbf{F}_q$ according to t.
2. Either select a standard elliptic curve or use the following scheme.
   - Prime field case: pseudo-randomly generate a string c from a seed and translate it into a field element. Pick field elements a and b such that $a^3/b^2 \equiv c \pmod{q}$ and consider the curve $y^2 = x^3 + ax + b$ over $\mathbf{F}_q$. Note that the j-invariant of the curve is $j = 6912\frac{c}{4c+27}$.

---

[3] The only difference with [3] is that $\mathbf{F}_q$ denotes the finite field even when q is prime, instead of $\mathbf{F}_p$.

- Characteristic two case: pseudo-randomly generate a string c from a seed, translate it into a field element and call it b. Pick a field element a and consider the curve $y^2 + xy = x^3 + ax^2 + b$ over $\mathbf{F}_q$. Note that the j-invariant of the curve is $j = \frac{1}{b}$.

3. For q prime, check that $4a^3 + 27b^2 \bmod q \neq 0$. For q a power of two, check that $b \neq 0$. If this is not the case, go back to Step 2.
4. Count the number of points in the elliptic curve and isolate a prime factor n greater than 2^{160}. If this does not work, go back to Step 2.
5. Check the MOV and anomalous condition for C. If this does not hold, go back to Step 2.
6. Pick a random point on the elliptic curve and raise it to the cofactor of n power in order to get G. If G is the point at infinity, try again.

Finally set $P = (q, \text{representation}, a, b, n, G, \text{seed})$.

Val$(t, q, \text{representation}, a, b, n, G, \text{seed})$:
1. Check that q is an odd prime or a power of 2 of appropriate size. In the latter case, check that the field representation choice is valid.
2. Check that a, b, x_G, y_G (where $G = (x_G, y_G)$) lie in $\mathbf{F}_q$.
3. Check that seed certifies a and b by generating c again and checking that $\frac{a^3}{b^2} = c$ or $b = c$ depending on the field type.
4. For q prime, check that $4a^3 + 27b^2 \bmod q \neq 0$. For q a power of two, check that $b \neq 0$. Check that G lies in the elliptic curve. Check that n is a prime greater than both 2^{160} and $4\sqrt{q}$. Check that $nG = \mathcal{O}$, the neutral element. Check the MOV and anomalous condition.

Gen$(q, \text{representation}, a, b, n, G)$: pick an integer d in $[1, n-1]$, compute $Q = dG$. Output $(K_p, K_s) = (Q, d)$.

Sig$(q, \text{representation}, a, b, n, G, d, M)$: pick k in $[1, n-1]$ at random and compute $(x_1, y_1) = kG$, $r = \overline{x_1} \bmod n$, and $s = \frac{H(M)+dr}{k} \bmod n$. (Here $\overline{x_1}$ is simply a standard way to convert a field element x_1 into an integer.) If $r = 0$ or $s = 0$, try again. Output the signature $\sigma = (r, s)$

Ver$(q, \text{representation}, a, b, n, G, Q, M, r, s)$: check that $Q \neq \mathcal{O}$, $Q \in C$, and $nQ = \mathcal{O}$. Check that r and s are in $[1, n-1]$ and that $r = \overline{x_1} \bmod n$ for $(x_1, y_1) = u_1 G + u_2 Q$, $u_1 = \frac{H(M)}{s} \bmod n$, and $u_2 = \frac{r}{s} \bmod n$.

The signature is a pair of integers. The public key is a point on a curve. So the standard should define a standard way for representing an integer, a point, and therefore a field element. In addition we need a standard way to represent the domain parameters: the field representation, the curve definition, etc. ANSI X9.62 [3] extensively defines all this.

To illustrate, we take the example with a 192-bit prime q from [3, Sect. J.3.1, p. 152]. This example is also called "Curve P-192" in FIPS 186 [6] and `secp192r1` in SEC2 [1]. We consider a domain parameter P defined by

$q = 6277101735386680763835789423207666416083908700390324961279$

$a = \texttt{ffffffff ffffffff ffffffff fffffffe ffffffff fffffffc}$

$b = \texttt{64210519 e59c80e7 0fa7e9ab 72243049 feb8deec c146b9b1}$

$$n = 6277101735386680763835789423176059013767194773182842284081$$
$$G = 03\ 188da80e\ b03090f6\ 7cbf20eb\ 43a18800\ f4ff0afd\ 82ff1012$$
$$seed = 3045ae6f\ c8422f64\ ed579528\ d38120ea\ e12196d5$$

(note that the leading "03" of G means that y_G is odd and that the remaining represents x_G, and that a, b, and G are in hexadecimal notations).[4] We can easily decompress G and compute the y coordinate. We obtain

$$y_G = 1740503322936220314048575522802194103640234889827386650641.$$

Note that the validation algorithm checks that the j-invariant comes from the seed. We consider a secret and public key defined by

$$d = 651056770906015076056810763456358567190100156695615665659$$
$$Q = 02\ 62b12d60\ 690cdcf3\ 30babab6\ e69763b4\ 71f994dd$$

(note that the leading "02" of Q means that y_Q is even).

3.2   Trusting Elliptic Curves

As shown in Koblitz [15], trust in elliptic curves is subject to many property checks. They are necessary due to the existence of weak elliptic curves, e.g. curves of trace one [18,22].

The use of the seed in the domain parameters should ensure the confidence that the elliptic curve was randomly — and therefore not maliciously — selected. It was shown to be necessary in the case of DSA due to possible malicious choice of p and q prime domain parameters (see [23]).

As mentioned in [24], the seed in ECDSA does not perform a good job in the characteristic two case since we can first select an elliptic curve then choose the finite field representation which validates it. It was proposed to tweak SetUp (and Val accordingly) as follows in the same spirit (i.e. the elliptic curve up to an isomorphism only is generated from the seed and not the a and b domain parameters).

Curves over $\mathbf{F}_q$ with $q > 3$ prime:
1. Choose a prime $q > 3$ and consider $\mathbf{F}_q$.
2. Generate a random bit string c and bit from seed and q.
3. Translate c into a field element.
4. Select arbitrarily a and b such that $a^3/b^2 \equiv c \pmod{q}$ and $\left(\frac{b}{q}\right) = (-1)^{bit}$, and take the elliptic curve defined by a, b, q.

Curves over $\mathbf{F}_q$ of characteristic 2:
1. Choose q a power of 2 and consider $\mathbf{F}_q$. We choose a representation of $\mathbf{F}_q$ (i.e. an irreducible polynomial).
2. Generate a random bit string c and bit from seed, q, and the field representation choice.

---

[4] Note that $q = 2^{192} - 2^{64} - 1$.

3. Translate c into a field element and call it b.
4. Select arbitrarily a such that $\text{Tr}(a) = \text{bit}$ and take the elliptic curve defined over $\mathbf{F}_q$ by a, b, q.[5]

3.3   Subgroup Integrity

There is actually no integrity protection for G. The attacker can actually replace G by a random power of Q. In this case she knows the discrete logarithm of Q in this basis and can forge signatures which will pass the Ver test for any message.

More precisely, following the model which is depicted on Fig. 3, the adversary performs a domain parameter shifting attack as follows.

1. Intercept the domain parameters P and extract G, n, and necessary materials in order to perform computations in the elliptic curve.
2. Get K_p and extract Q.
3. Pick an arbitrary $d' \in \mathbf{Z}_n^*$ and construct P' from P in which G is replaced by $G' = (d'^{-1} \bmod n).Q$.
4. Send P' to the verifier.
5. Forge signatures by using the Sig algorithm with d replaced by d'.

Note that no oracle call is made to the signer.

As a trivial example an attacker who intercepts P and Q can forge a domain parameter P' by replacing G by Q. The attacker can thus forge signatures for the public key Q with domain parameter P' by taking a secret key set to $d' = 1$. Making other examples with less trivial d' is quite straightforward.

This attack tells us that G must be protected by specific means. For instance random selection can be demonstrated by generating it from the seed.

3.4   Elliptic Curve Integrity

The integrity of the elliptic curve up to an isomorphism (more precisely with a fixed j-invariant) may also be problematic. Indeed, in the prime case, if an attacker is given $P = (q, a, b, n, G, \text{seed})$ and Q from a signer, she can try to forge a consistent $P' = (q, a', b', n, G, \text{seed})$ with $a' = au^4 \bmod q$ and $b' = bu^6 \bmod q$ and such that G and Q still lie in the elliptic curve defined by P' and that she knows the discrete logarithm in basis G. When G and Q are fully specified, this is not possible since (a', b') must be the unique solution of

$$y_G^2 - x_G^3 = a'x_G + b'$$
$$y_Q^2 - x_Q^3 = a'x_Q + b'$$

which is (a, b). When G and Q are specified with point compression, only their x coordinates are given together with one bit of the y coordinate. The attacker can thus for instance try to find u such that Q suddenly becomes equal to $2.G$

---

[5] Here $\text{Tr}(a)$ denotes $a + a^2 + a^4 + a^8 + \cdots + a^{\frac{q}{2}}$.

in the new curve. By using the expression of the x coordinate of $2.G$ we obtain the equation

$$x_Q = \frac{(3x_G^2 + au^4)^2}{4(x_G^3 + au^4 x_G + bu^6)} - 2x_G \tag{1}$$

which is a polynomial equation in u^2 of degree 3. It is thus likely to lead to at least one solution! More generally, one can try to solve $(d'.G)_1 = x_Q$ for a small integer d' where $d'.G$ stands for the computation in the new curve defined by the unknown u and $(d'.G)_1$ is its x coordinate.

More precisely, following the model which is depicted on Fig. 3, in the prime field case with point compression, the adversary performs a domain parameter shifting attack as follows.

1. Intercept the domain parameters P and extract q, a, b, G.
2. Get K_p and extract Q.
3. Solve Eq. (1) in u and set $d' = 2$. If there is no solution, increment d' and solve $(d'.G)_1 = x_Q$ until it has solutions.
4. Compute $a' = au^4 \bmod q$ and $b' = bu^6 \bmod q$.
5. Construct P' from P in which a and b are replaced by a' and b' respectively.
6. Send P' to the verifier.
7. Forge signatures by using the Sig algorithm with d replaced by d'.

Note that no oracle call is made to the signer.

Similar observations hold in the characteristic two case.

We illustrate the attack with our domain parameters example.

An attacker who intercepts P and the public key Q needs to solve Eq. (1) modulo q. This leads to two solutions

$u_1 = 2311343351391405937345224687072661594069562839099830631902$

$u_2 = 3965758383995274826490564736135004822014345861290494329377.$

The first solution $u = u_1$ leads to

$a' = $ 24f70108 7a05f49c 67119ba6 bba22c93 697a5cc8 5f936eb5

$b' = $ 31a2b88a dd0b97c0 fdf876b3 e505cc3b 22378efb 5a6d4eb7.

So the attacker can forge a domain parameter P' from P where a and b are replaced by a' and b' respectively. Since both elliptic curves have the same j-invariant the new one will pass the validation algorithm with the same seed.

On this new curve the y coordinate of G decompresses as

$y_G' = 1116315358594314146689456472165634567792857267210838842217$

and we can check that the x coordinate of $2.G$ is equal to x_Q and that its y coordinate is even on this new elliptic curve. So $2.G = Q$ on this elliptic curve. The attacker can thus forge signatures for the public key Q with domain parameter P' by taking a secret key set to $d' = 2$.

This attack tells us that we must have a stronger link than what [24] suggested between the domain parameters and the public key, e.g. generate a and b from the seed.

4 Conclusion

We have formalized the notion of digital signature schemes with domain parameters. We formulated security requirements. We demonstrated that ECDSA does not satisfy the domain parameter integrity condition due to the lack of validation procedure for the subgroup generator G domain parameter and elliptic curve a and b domain parameters and that the fix which was proposed in [24] is not sufficient. Finally, we propose an appropriate way to update the scheme in one of the two following ways.

1. Really generate a, b, G from the seed at random.
2. Forget about DSSDP and make sure that P is authenticated together with K_p by the certificate authority.

Acknowledgments. The work presented in this paper was supported (in part) by the National Competence Center in Research on Mobile Information and Communication Systems (NCCR-MICS), a center supported by the Swiss National Science Foundation under grant number 5005-67322.

References

1. SEC 2: Recommended Elliptic Curve Cryptography Domain Parameters. v1.0, Certicom Research, 2000.
2. ANSI X9.30. Public Key Cryptography for the Financial Services Industry: Part 1: The Digital Signature Algorithm (DSA). American National Standard Institute. American Bankers Association. 1997.
3. ANSI X9.62. Public Key Cryptography for the Financial Services Industry: The Elliptic Curve Digital Signature Algorithm (ECDSA). American National Standard Institute. American Bankers Association. 1998.
4. ISO/IEC 14888. Information Technology — Security Techniques — Digital Signatures with Appendix. ISO/IEC, Geneva, Switzerland, 1998.
5. Secure Hash Standard. *Federal Information Processing Standard* publication #180-1. U.S. Department of Commerce, National Institute of Standards and Technology, 1995.
6. Digital Signature Standard (DSS). *Federal Information Processing Standards* publication #186-2. U.S. Department of Commerce, National Institute of Standards and Technology, 2000.
7. D. Bleichenbacher. Generating ElGamal Signatures without Knowing the Secret Key. In *Advances in Cryptology EUROCRYPT'96*, Zaragoza, Spain, Lecture Notes in Computer Science 1070, pp. 10–18, Springer-Verlag, 1996.
8. W. Diffie, M. E. Hellman. New Directions in Cryptography. *IEEE Transactions on Information Theory*, vol. IT-22, pp. 644–654, 1976.
9. T. ElGamal. Cryptography and Logarithms over Finite Fields. PhD Thesis, Stanford University, 1984.
10. T. ElGamal. A Public-key Cryptosystem and a Signature Scheme based on Discrete Logarithms. In *Advances in Cryptology CRYPTO'84*, Santa Barbara, California, U.S.A., Lecture Notes in Computer Science 196, pp. 10–18, Springer-Verlag, 1985.

11. T. ElGamal. A Public-key Cryptosystem and a Signature Scheme based on Discrete Logarithms. *IEEE Transactions on Information Theory*, vol. IT-31, pp. 469–472, 1985.
12. S. Goldwasser, S. Micali, R.L. Rivest. A "Paradoxical" Solution to the Signature Problem. In *Advances in Cryptology CRYPTO'84*, Santa Barbara, California, U.S.A., Lecture Notes in Computer Science 196, pp. 467, Springer-Verlag, 1985.
13. S. Goldwasser, S. Micali, R.L. Rivest. A Digital Signature Scheme Secure against Adaptive Chosen-Message Attacks. *SIAM Journal on Computing*, vol. 17, pp. 281–308, 1988.
14. R. Housley, W. Ford, W. Polk, D. Solo. Internet X.509 Public Key Infrastructure Certificate and CRL Profile. Internet Standard. RFC 2459, 1999.
15. N. Koblitz. CM-Curves with good Cryptographic Properties. In *Advances in Cryptology CRYPTO'91*, Santa Barbara, California, U.S.A., Lecture Notes in Computer Science 576, pp. 279–287, Springer-Verlag, 1992.
16. A. Menezes, N. Smart. Security of Signature Schemes in a Multi-User Setting. To appear in Designs, Codes and Cryptography.
17. R. C. Merkle. Secure Communications over Insecure Channels. *Communications of the ACM*, vol. 21, pp. 294–299, 1978.
18. J. Monnerat. Computation of the Discrete Logarithm on Elliptic Curves of Trace One — Tutorial. Technical report EPFL/IC/2002/49, EPFL, 2002.
19. R. L. Rivest, A. Shamir and L. M. Adleman. A Method for Obtaining Digital Signatures and Public-key Cryptosystem. In *Communications of the ACM*, vol. 21, pp. 120–126, 1978.
20. C. P. Schnorr. Efficient Identification and Signature for Smart Cards. In *Advances in Cryptology CRYPTO'89*, Santa Barbara, California, U.S.A., Lecture Notes in Computer Science 435, pp. 235–251, Springer-Verlag, 1990.
21. C. P. Schnorr. Efficient Identification and Signature for Smart Cards. *Journal of Cryptology*, vol. 4, pp. 161–174, 1991.
22. N. P. Smart. The Discrete Logarithm Problem on Elliptic Curves of Trace One. *Journal of Cryptology*, vol. 12, pp. 193–196, 1999.
23. S. Vaudenay. Hidden Collisions on DSS. In *Advances in Cryptology CRYPTO'96*, Santa Barbara, California, U.S.A., Lecture Notes in Computer Science 1109, pp. 83–88, Springer-Verlag, 1996.
24. S. Vaudenay. The Security of DSA and ECDSA — Bypassing the Standard Elliptic Curve Certification Scheme. In *Public Key Cryptography'03*, Miami, Florida, USA, Lecture Notes in Computer Science 2567, pp. 309–323, Springer-Verlag, 2003.

Generic Construction of Certificateless Signature*

Dae Hyun Yum and Pil Joong Lee**

IS Lab., Dept. of Electronic and Electrical Eng., POSTECH, Republic of Korea
{dhyum, pjl}@postech.ac.kr
http://islab.postech.ac.kr

Abstract. To provide the binding between a user and his public key, traditional digital signature schemes use certificates that are signed by a trusted third party. While Shamir's identity-based signature scheme can dispense with certificates, the key escrow of a user's private key is inherent in the identity-based signature scheme. In Asiacrypt 2003, a new digital signature paradigm called the certificateless signature was introduced. The certificateless signature eliminates the need for certificates and does not suffer from the inherent key escrow problem. In this paper, we provide a generic secure construction of a certificateless signature. We also present an extended construction whose trust level is the same as that of a traditional public key signature scheme.

Keywords: Certificateless signature, identity-based signature, public-key signature.

1 Introduction

PUBLIC KEY SIGNATURE AND IDENTITY-BASED SIGNATURE. A digital signature is one of the most important security primitives in modern cryptography. In a traditional public key signature scheme, methods to guarantee the authenticity of a public key are required, since the public key of the signer is actually a type of random string. To provide the binding between a signer and his public key, the traditional public key signature uses a certificate that is a digitally signed statement issued by the CA (Certification Authority). The need for public key infrastructure supporting certificates is considered the main difficulty in the deployment and management of public key signature schemes. While Shamir's identity-based signature scheme can dispense with certificates, the key escrow of a user's private key is inherent in the identity-based signature scheme [15]; a trusted third party called the PKG (Private Key Generator) manages the generation and distribution of the users' private keys.

---

* This research was supported by University IT Research Center Project and the Brain Korea 21 Project.

** (on leave at KT Research Center)

H. Wang et al. (Eds.): ACISP 2004, LNCS 3108, pp. 200–211, 2004.

CERTIFICATELESS SIGNATURE. In Asiacrypt 2003, the certificateless signature was proposed [1]. A certificateless signature scheme does not require the use of certificates and yet does not have the inherent key escrow problem of the identity-based signature scheme. Unlike the PKG in an identity-based signature scheme, the KGC (Key Generating Center) in a certificateless signature scheme does not have access to the user's private key. The KGC derives a partial private key from the user's identity and the master key. The user then combines the partial private key with some secret information to generate the actual private signing key. The system is not identity-based, because the public key is no longer computable from a user identity. However, no authentication of the public key is necessary and no certificate is required.

OUR CONTRIBUTION. In this paper, we provide the generic secure construction of the certificateless signature scheme. While previous constructions are built from bilinear mappings that are implemented using Weil and Tate pairings on elliptic curves, our construction is built from general primitives: a public key signature scheme and an identity-based signature scheme. In addition, we present the extended construction that achieves trust level 3 in the hierarchy of [10].

RELATED WORK. In parallel with this work, we researched on the secure construction of certificateless encryption [16]. However, we could not extend the construction of certificateless encryption to the trust level 3.

2   Identity-Based Signature and Certificateless Signature

In this section, we review the definitions and security notions of identity-based signature schemes [6,8,12,15] and certificateless signature schemes [1].

2.1   Identity-Based Signature

Definition 1. *An identity-based signature scheme is a 4-tuple of polynomial time algorithms* (IB_Gen, IB_Ext, IB_Sign, IB_Vrfy) *such that:*

- IB_Gen, *the master key and parameter generation algorithm, is a probabilistic algorithm that takes as input a security parameter 1^k. It returns a master key $IBSK^*$ and a parameter list params.*
- IB_Ext, *the signing key issuance algorithm, is a deterministic algorithm that takes as input a user identity id and a master key $IBSK^*$. It returns the user id's private signing key $IBSK_{id}$.*
- IB_Sign, *the signing algorithm, is a probabilistic algorithm that takes as input a message M, a parameter list params, and a signing key $IBSK_{id}$.* IB_Sign$_{params}^{IBSK_{id}}(M)$ *returns a signature α.*
- IB_Vrfy, *the verification algorithm, is a deterministic algorithm that takes as input a message M, a user identity id, a parameter list params, and a signature α.* IB_Vrfy$_{params}(M, id, \alpha)$ *returns a bit b, where $b = 1$ means that the signature is accepted.*

In an identity-based signature scheme, IB_Gen and IB_Ext are performed by the PKG. A secret key $IBSK_{id}$ is given to a user id by the PKG through a secure channel. If IB_Vrfy$_{params}(M, id, \alpha) = 1$, we say that α is a valid signature of M by the user id. We require that all signatures output by IB_Sign$_{params}^{IBSK_{id}}(\cdot)$ are accepted as valid by IB_Vrfy$_{params}(\cdot, id, \cdot)$.

For security analysis, we define a key exposure oracle $O_{Exp}^{IB}(\cdot)$ that returns a private signing key $IBSK_{id}$ on input id. We also give the adversary access to a signing oracle $O_{Sign}^{IB}(\cdot, \cdot)$ that returns IB_Sign$_{params}^{IBSK_{id}}(M)$ on input (M, id). The security goal of an identity-based signature scheme is existential unforgeability. This means that any PPT (probabilistic polynomial time) adversary A should have a negligible probability of generating a valid signature of a new message given access to the key exposure oracle $O_{Exp}^{IB}(\cdot)$ and the signing oracle $O_{Sign}^{IB}(\cdot, \cdot)$. Naturally, A is considered successful if it forges a valid signature α of M by a user id where id was not queried to the key exposure oracle $O_{Exp}^{IB}(\cdot)$ and (M, id) was not queried to the signing oracle $O_{Sign}^{IB}(\cdot, \cdot)$.

Definition 2. *Let Π_{IB} be an identity-based signature scheme. For any adversary A, we may perform the following experiment:*

$$(IBSK^*, params) \leftarrow \text{IB\_Gen}(1^k);$$
$$(M, id, \alpha) \leftarrow A^{O_{Exp}^{IB}(\cdot), O_{Sign}^{IB}(\cdot, \cdot)}(params).$$

We say that A succeeds if IB_Vrfy$_{params}(M, id, \alpha) = 1$, *$id$ was never submitted to the key exposure oracle $O_{Exp}^{IB}(\cdot)$, and (M, id) was never submitted to the signing oracle $O_{Sign}^{IB}(\cdot, \cdot)$. Denote the probability of A's success by $\text{Succ}_{A, \Pi_{IB}}(k)$. If for any PPT A, the success probability $\text{Succ}_{A, \Pi_{IB}}(k)$ is negligible, we say that Π_{IB} is secure; that is, existentially unforgeable against chosen-message attacks.*

2.2   Certificateless Signature

Definition 3. *A certificateless signature scheme is a 7-tuple of polynomial time algorithms (CL_Gen, CL_Ext_Partial_Pri_Key, CL_Set_Sec_Val, CL_Set_Pri_Key, CL_Set_Pub_Key, CL_Sign, CL_Vrfy) such that:*

- CL_Gen, *the master key and parameter generation algorithm, is a probabilistic algorithm that takes as input a security parameter 1^k. It returns a master key $CLSK^*$ and a parameter list params.*
- CL_Ext_Partial_Pri_Key, *the partial private key issuance algorithm, is a deterministic algorithm that takes as input a user identity id, a parameter list params, and a master key $CLSK^*$. It returns the user id's partial private key CLD_{id}.*
- CL_Set_Sec_Val, *the secret value setup algorithm, is a probabilistic algorithm that takes as input a parameter list params and a user identity id. It returns the user id's secret value CLS_{id}.*
- CL_Set_Pri_Key, *the signing key generation algorithm, is a deterministic algorithm that takes as input a parameter list params, the user id's partial*

private key CLD_{id}, and the user id's secret value CLS_{id}. It returns the user id's private signing key $CLSK_{id}$.

- CL_Set_Pub_Key, *the verification key generation algorithm, is a deterministic algorithm that takes as input a parameter list params, a user identity id, and the user id's secret value CLS_{id}. It returns the user id's public verification key $CLPK_{id}$.*
- CL_Sign, *the signing algorithm, is a probabilistic algorithm that takes as input a message M, a user identity id, a parameter list params, and the user id's private signing key $CLSK_{id}$. CL_Sign$_{params}^{CLSK_{id}}(M)$ returns a signature α.*
- CL_Vrfy, *the verification algorithm, is a deterministic algorithm that takes as input a parameter list params, the public verification key $CLPK_{id}$, a message M, a user identity id, and a signature α. CL_Vrfy$_{params}^{CLPK_{id}}(M, id, \alpha)$ returns a bit b, where $b = 1$ means that the signature is accepted.*

In a certificateless signature scheme, CL_Gen and CL_Ext_Partial_Pri_Key are performed by a KGC. A partial private key CLD_{id} is given to a user id by the KGC through a secure channel. Since CL_Set_Sec_Val, CL_Set_Pri_Key, and CL_Set_Pub_Key are executed by a user, the key escrow of the user's private key is not inherent in a certificateless signature scheme. We require that all signatures output by CL_Sign$_{params}^{CLSK_{id}}(\cdot)$ are accepted as valid by CL_Vrfy$_{params}^{CLPK_{id}}(\cdot, id, \cdot)$.

For security analysis, we extend the model of an identity-based signature scheme to allow an adversary to extract partial private keys, or private keys, or both, for identities of his choice. We must also consider the ability of the adversary to replace the public key of any entity with a value of his choice, because there is no certificate in a certificateless signature scheme. Five oracles can be accessed by the adversary. The first is a partial private key exposure oracle $O_{Exp\_Partial}^{CL}(\cdot)$ that returns CLD_{id} on input a user identity id. The second is a private key exposure oracle $O_{Exp\_Pri}^{CL}(\cdot)$ that returns $CLSK_{id}$ on input a user identity id if id's public key has not been replaced. The third is a public key broadcast oracle $O_{Bro\_Pub}^{CL}(\cdot)$ that returns $CLPK_{id}$ on input a user identity id. The fourth is a public key replacement oracle $O_{Rep\_Pub}^{CL}(\cdot, \cdot)$ that replaces the public key $CLPK_{id}$ for a user id with $CLPK'_{id}$ on input $(id, CLPK'_{id})$. The fifth is a signing oracle $O_{Sign}^{CL}(\cdot, \cdot)$ that returns CL_Sign$_{params}^{CLSK_{id}}(M)$ on input (M, id).

The security of a certificateless signature scheme is against two different types of adversaries. The Type I adversary A_I has no access to the master key, but may replace public keys, extract partial private and private keys, and make signing queries. When A_I has replaced the public key of a user id and requests the user id's signature, we accept that the signing oracle's answer will be incorrect. We adopt this behavior of the signing oracle because we will construct certificateless signature schemes based on general primitives and do without any additional assumptions, such as the random oracle model [5]. However, we assume that the signing oracle's answer is correct, if A_I additionally submits the replaced public key $(CLPK'_{id})$ and the corresponding secret information $(CLS'_{id}$ or $CLSK'_{id})$ to the signing oracle.[1] The Type II adversary A_{II} equipped with the master

---

[1] This model was used in [9,13].

key models a dishonest KGC and can generate partial private keys by himself. However, A_{II} is not allowed to replace public keys.

Definition 4. *Let Π_{CL} be a certificateless signature scheme. For any adversary A, we may perform the following experiment:*

$$(CLSK^*, params) \leftarrow \mathsf{CL\_Gen}(1^k);$$
$$(M, id, \alpha) \leftarrow A^{O_1(\cdot), O_2(\cdot), O^{CL}_{Exp\_Pri}, O^{CL}_{Bro\_Pub}, O^{CL}_{Sign}(\cdot, \cdot)}(params, h).$$

where $h = \perp$, $O_1(\cdot) = O^{CL}_{Exp\_Partial}(\cdot)$, $O_2(\cdot) = O^{CL}_{Rep\_Pub}(\cdot, \cdot)$ for A_I and $h = CLSK^*$, $O_1(\cdot) = O_2(\cdot) = \perp$ for A_{II}. We say that A succeeds if $\mathsf{CL\_Vrfy}^{CLPK_{id}}_{params}(M, id, \alpha) = 1$ and A has followed the adversarial constraints. Denote the probability of A's success by $\mathsf{Succ}_{A, \Pi_{CL}}(k)$. If for any PPT A, the success probability $\mathsf{Succ}_{A, \Pi_{CL}}(k)$ is negligible, we say that Π_{CL} is secure; that is existentially unforgeable against chosen-message attacks.

If (M, id_{ch}, α) is the output of the adversary A_I, the identity id_{ch} cannot be submitted to the partial private key exposure oracle $O^{CL}_{Exp\_Partial}(\cdot)$; $CLD_{id_{ch}}$ is securely given to the user id_{ch} by definition and can be deleted after generating the private signing key. However, A_I is allowed to replace the public key of id_{ch}. The exposure of $CLD_{id_{ch}}$ can be treated by the Type II adversary A_{II} who is equipped with the master key $CLSK^*$. For other restrictions on the two types of adversaries and security notions, refer to [1].

3   Generic Construction of Certificateless Signature

3.1   Generic Secure Construction

We provide the generic secure construction of certificateless signature based on public key signature and identity-based signature. Let $\Pi_{PK} = (\mathsf{PK\_Gen}, \mathsf{PK\_Sign}, \mathsf{PK\_Vrfy})$ be a public key signature scheme that is secure in the sense of [11] and $\Pi_{IB} = (\mathsf{IB\_Gen}, \mathsf{IB\_Ext}, \mathsf{IB\_Sign}, \mathsf{IB\_Vrfy})$ be a secure identity-based signature scheme. To avoid the key escrow problem of Π_{IB}, we will use the idea of sequential double signing. A secure certificateless signature scheme $\Psi_{CL} = (\mathsf{CL\_Gen}, \mathsf{CL\_Ext\_Partial\_Pri\_Key}, \mathsf{CL\_Set\_Sec\_Val}, \mathsf{CL\_Set\_Pri\_Key}, \mathsf{CL\_Set\_Pub\_Key}, \mathsf{CL\_Sign}, \mathsf{CL\_Vrfy})$ can be constructed as in Table 1.

3.2   Security Analysis

The security of Ψ_{CL} in Table 1 can be proved by the security of Π_{PK} and Π_{IB}. If there is a Type I attacker A_I who can break Ψ_{CL}, we can construct the adversary A' against Π_{IB}. If there is a Type II attacker A_{II}, we can construct the adversary A'' against Π_{PK}.

Theorem 1. *Ψ_{CL} is a secure certificateless signature scheme if Π_{PK} and Π_{IB} are existentially unforgeable against chosen-message attacks.*

Table 1. Generic construction of certificateless signature.

$\mathsf{CL\_Gen}(1^k)$
  $(IBSK^{\square}, params) \leftarrow \mathsf{IB\_Gen}(1^k);$
  $CLSK^{\square} \leftarrow IBSK^{\square};$
  Return $(CLSK^{\square}, params)$

$\mathsf{CL\_Ext\_Partial\_Pri\_Key}(id, params, CLSK^{\square})$
  $IBSK_{id} \leftarrow \mathsf{IB\_Ext}(id, params, CLSK^{\square});$
  $CLD_{id} \leftarrow IBSK_{id};$
  Return CLD_{id}

$\mathsf{CL\_Set\_Pri\_Key}(params, CLD_{id}, CLS_{id})$
  Parse CLS_{id} as $(pk_{id}, sk_{id});$
  $CLSK_{id} \leftarrow (CLD_{id}, sk_{id});$
  Return $CLSK_{id}$

$\mathsf{CL\_Sign}(M, id, params, CLSK_{id})$
  Parse $CLSK_{id}$ as $(CLD_{id}, sk_{id});$
  $\alpha \leftarrow \mathsf{PK\_Sign}_{sk_{id}}(M);$
  $\beta \leftarrow \mathsf{IB\_Sign}_{params}^{CLSK_{id}}(\alpha, id);$
  Return $\langle \alpha, \beta \rangle$

$\mathsf{CL\_Set\_Sec\_Val}(params, id)$
  $(pk_{id}, sk_{id}) \leftarrow \mathsf{PK\_Gen}(1^k);$
  $CLS_{id} \leftarrow (pk_{id}, sk_{id});$
  Return CLS_{id}

$\mathsf{CL\_Set\_Pub\_Key}(params, id, CLS_{id})$
  Parse CLS_{id} as $(pk_{id}, sk_{id});$
  $CLPK_{id} \leftarrow pk_{id};$
  Return $CLPK_{id}$

$\mathsf{CL\_Vrfy}(params, CLPK_{id}, M, id, \langle \alpha, \beta \rangle)$
  $b_1 \leftarrow \mathsf{IB\_Vrfy}_{params}(\alpha, id, \beta);$
  $b_2 \leftarrow \mathsf{PK\_Vrfy}_{CLPK_{id}}(M, \alpha);$
  $b \leftarrow b_1 \& b_2;$ // bitwise AND
  Return b

Proof. (Sketch) Let A_I be a Type I attacker who can break Ψ_{CL}. Suppose that A_I has a success probability ϵ and runs in time t. We show how to construct from A_I an adversary A' against Π_{IB}. At the beginning, A' is given by a Π_{IB} challenger a parameter list *params* and two oracles: the key exposure oracle $\mathsf{O}^{\mathsf{IB}}_{\mathsf{Exp}}(\cdot)$ and the signing oracle $\mathsf{O}^{\mathsf{IB}}_{\mathsf{Sign}}(\cdot, \cdot)$. Let $\Pi_{PK} = (\mathsf{PK\_Gen}, \mathsf{PK\_Sign}, \mathsf{PK\_Vrfy})$ be a secure public key signature scheme that is chosen by A'. Then Ψ_{CL} is well-defined from Π_{IB} and Π_{PK}. To run A_I, A' simulates the $\mathsf{CL\_Gen}(1^k)$ by supplying A_I with *params*. A' keeps a list $L = \{(id, IBSK_{id}, pk_{id}, sk_{id})\}$ where $IBSK_{id}$ is the output of $\mathsf{O}^{\mathsf{IB}}_{\mathsf{Exp}}(\cdot)$ and (pk_{id}, sk_{id}) is an output of $\mathsf{PK\_Gen}(1^k)$. The list L need not be made in advance and is computed according to the A_I's queries. A' responds to A_I's oracle queries as follows.

- Partial private key exposure oracle $\mathsf{O}^{\mathsf{CL}}_{\mathsf{Exp\_Partial}}(\cdot)$ queries: Suppose that the request is on a user identity id.
  1. When the list L contains $(id, IBSK_{id}, pk_{id}, sk_{id})$, A' checks to determine whether $IBSK_{id} = \perp$ or not. If $IBSK_{id} \neq \perp$, A' returns $CLD_{id} = IBSK_{id}$ to A_I. If $IBSK_{id} = \perp$, A' sends id to the Π_{IB} key exposure oracle $\mathsf{O}^{\mathsf{IB}}_{\mathsf{Exp}}(\cdot)$ and obtains $IBSK_{id}$. A' writes $IBSK_{id}$ in the list L and returns $CLD_{id} = IBSK_{id}$ to A_I.
  2. When the list L does not contain $(id, IBSK_{id}, pk_{id}, sk_{id})$, A' sends id to the Π_{IB} key exposure oracle $\mathsf{O}^{\mathsf{IB}}_{\mathsf{Exp}}(\cdot)$ and obtains $IBSK_{id}$. A' sets $pk_{id} = sk_{id} = \perp$. The element $(id, IBSK_{id}, pk_{id}, sk_{id})$ is added to the list L. A' returns $CLD_{id} = IBSK_{id}$ to A_I.

- Private key exposure oracle $O^{CL}_{Exp\_Pri}(\cdot)$ queries: Suppose that the request is on a user identity id.
  1. When the list L contains $(id, IBSK_{id}, pk_{id}, sk_{id})$, A' checks $IBSK_{id} = \bot$ and $pk_{id} = \bot$. If $IBSK_{id} = \bot$, A' sets $IBSK_{id} = O^{IB}_{Exp}(id)$. If $pk_{id} = \bot$, A' runs PK_Gen(1^k) to obtain (pk_{id}, sk_{id}) and saves these values in the list L. A' returns $CLSK_{id} = (IBSK_{id}, sk_{id})$.
  2. When the list L does not contain $(id, IBSK_{id}, pk_{id}, sk_{id})$, A' adds the element $(id, IBSK_{id}, pk_{id}, sk_{id})$ to the list L by sending id to the Π_{ID} key exposure oracle $O^{IB}_{Exp}(\cdot)$ and running PK_Gen(1^k). A' returns $CLSK_{id} = (IBSK_{id}, sk_{id})$.
- Public key broadcast oracle $O^{CL}_{Bro\_Pub}(\cdot)$ queries: Suppose that the request is on a user identity id.
  1. When the list L contains $(id, IBSK_{id}, pk_{id}, sk_{id})$, A' checks to determine whether $pk_{id} = \bot$ or not. If $pk_{id} \neq \bot$, A' returns $CLPK_{id} = pk_{id}$. Otherwise, A' runs PK_Gen(1^k) and obtains (pk_{id}, sk_{id}). A' saves (pk_{id}, sk_{id}) in the list L and returns $CLPK_{id} = pk_{id}$.
  2. When the list L does not contain $(id, IBSK_{id}, pk_{id}, sk_{id})$, A' sets $IBSK_{id} = \bot$ and runs PK_Gen(1^k) to obtain (pk_{id}, sk_{id}). A' adds $(id, IBSK_{id}, pk_{id}, sk_{id})$ to the list L and returns $CLPK_{id} = pk_{id}$.
- Public key replacement oracle $O^{CL}_{Rep\_Pub}(\cdot, \cdot)$ queries: Suppose that A_I asks with an input $(id, CLPK_{id})$.
  1. When the list L contains $(id, IBSK_{id}, pk_{id}, sk_{id})$, A' sets $pk_{id} = CLPK_{id}$ and $sk_{id} = \bot$.
  2. When the list L does not contain $(id, IBSK_{id}, pk_{id}, sk_{id})$, A' sets $IBSK_{id} = \bot$, $pk_{id} = CLPK_{id}$, $sk_{id} = \bot$ and adds the element $(id, IBSK_{id}, pk_{id}, sk_{id})$ to the list L.
- Signing oracle $O^{CL}_{Sign}(\cdot, \cdot)$ queries: Suppose that A_I asks with an input (M, id).
  1. When the list L contains $(id, IBSK_{id}, pk_{id}, sk_{id})$, A' checks to determine whether $pk_{id} = \bot$ or not. If $pk_{id} = \bot$, A' runs PK_Gen(1^k) to get (pk_{id}, sk_{id}) and saves these values in the list L.
     a) A' checks whether $sk_{id} = \bot$ or not. If $sk_{id} = \bot$, i.e., the public key for the user id has been replaced by A_I, A' returns a random signature $\langle \alpha, \beta \rangle$.
     b) A' computes $\alpha = \text{PK\_Sign}_{sk_{id}}(M)$. A' checks whether $IBSK_{id} = \bot$ or not. If $IBSK_{id} = \bot$, A' sends (α, id) to the Π_{IB} signing oracle $O^{IB}_{Sign}(\cdot, \cdot)$. Let β be the output of $O^{IB}_{Sign}(\alpha, id)$. A' returns $\langle \alpha, \beta \rangle$ to A_I. If $IBSK_{id} \neq \bot$, A' computes $\beta = \text{IB\_Sign}^{IBSK_{id}}_{params}(\alpha, id)$. A' returns $\langle \alpha, \beta \rangle$ to A_I.
  2. When the list L does not contain $(id, IBSK_{id}, pk_{id}, sk_{id})$, A' sets $IBSK_{id} = \bot$ and runs PK_Gen(1^k) to obtain (pk_{id}, sk_{id}). A' adds $(id, IBSK_{id}, pk_{id}, sk_{id})$ to the list L and computes $\alpha = \text{PK\_Sign}_{sk_{id}}(M)$. A' sends (α, id) to the Π_{IB} signing oracle $O^{IB}_{Sign}(\cdot, \cdot)$. Let β be the output of $O^{IB}_{Sign}(\alpha, id)$. A' returns $\langle \alpha, \beta \rangle$ to A_I.

When the Type I attacker A_I outputs $(M, id, \langle \alpha, \beta \rangle)$, A' outputs (α, id, β) to the Π_{IB} challenger. Since the A_I's view is identical to its view in the real attack, the success probability of A' is also ϵ and A' runs in time $O(time(t))$.

Let A_{II} be a Type II attacker who can break Ψ_{CL}. Suppose that A_{II} has a success probability ϵ, runs in time t, and makes queries on l users, i.e., $(id_1, id_2, \cdots, id_l)$. We show how to construct from A_{II} an adversary A'' against Π_{PK}. At the beginning, A'' is given by a Π_{PK} challenger a public key pk and the signing oracle $O_{\mathsf{Sign}}^{\mathsf{PK}}(\cdot)$. Let $\Pi_{IB} = (\mathsf{IB\_Gen}, \mathsf{IB\_Ext}, \mathsf{IB\_Sign}, \mathsf{IB\_Vrfy})$ be a secure identity-based signature scheme that is chosen by A''. Then Ψ_{CL} is well-defined from Π_{PK} and Π_{IB}. To simulate $\mathsf{CL\_Gen}(1^k)$, A'' runs $\mathsf{IB\_Gen}(1^k)$ to obtain $(IBSK^*, params)$ and sets $CLSK^* = IBSK^*$. A'' gives $(params, CLSK^*)$ to A_{II} since A_{II} has access to the master key. As before, A'' keeps a list $L = \{(id, IBSK_{id}, pk_{id}, sk_{id})\}$ where $IBSK_{id}$ is the output of $\mathsf{IB\_Ext}(id, params, IBSK^*)$ and (pk_{id}, sk_{id}) is an output of $\mathsf{PK\_Gen}(1^k)$. A'' chooses a random index $j \in \{1, \cdots, l\}$ and sets $IBSK_{id_j} = \mathsf{IB\_Ext}(id_j, params, IBSK^*)$, $pk_{id_j} = pk$, $sk_{id_j} = \bot$. The element $(id_j, IBSK_{id_j}, pk_{id_j}, sk_{id_j})$ is added to the list L. The remainder of the list L is computed according to the A_{II}'s queries. A'' responds to A_{II}'s oracle queries as follows.

- Private key exposure oracle $O_{\mathsf{Exp\_Pri}}^{\mathsf{CL}}(\cdot)$ queries: Suppose that the request is on a user identity id. If $id = id_j$, A'' aborts.
    1. When the list L contains $(id, IBSK_{id}, pk_{id}, sk_{id})$, A'' checks $IBSK_{id} = \bot$ and $pk_{id} = \bot$. If $IBSK_{id} = \bot$, A'' sets $IBSK_{id} = \mathsf{IB\_Ext}(id, params, IBSK^*)$. If $pk_{id} = \bot$, A'' runs $\mathsf{PK\_Gen}(1^k)$ to obtain (pk_{id}, sk_{id}) and saves these values in the list L. A'' returns $CLSK_{id} = (IBSK_{id}, sk_{id})$.
    2. When the list L does not contain $(id, IBSK_{id}, pk_{id}, sk_{id})$, A'' adds the element $(id, IBSK_{id}, pk_{id}, sk_{id})$ to the list L by setting $IBSK_{id} = \mathsf{IB\_Ext}(id, params, IBSK^*)$ and running $\mathsf{PK\_Gen}(1^k)$. A'' returns $CLSK_{id} = (IBSK_{id}, sk_{id})$.
- Public key broadcast oracle $O_{\mathsf{Bro\_Pub}}^{\mathsf{CL}}(\cdot)$ queries: Suppose that the request is on a user identity id.
    1. When the list L contains $(id, IBSK_{id}, pk_{id}, sk_{id})$, A'' checks to determine whether $pk_{id} = \bot$ or not. If $pk_{id} \neq \bot$, A'' returns $CLPK_{id} = pk_{id}$. Otherwise, A'' runs $\mathsf{PK\_Gen}(1^k)$ and obtains (pk_{id}, sk_{id}). A'' saves (pk_{id}, sk_{id}) in the list L and returns $CLPK_{id} = pk_{id}$.
    2. When the list L does not contain $(id, IBSK_{id}, pk_{id}, sk_{id})$, A'' sets $IBSK_{id} = \bot$ and runs $\mathsf{PK\_Gen}(1^k)$ to obtain (pk_{id}, sk_{id}). A'' adds $(id, IBSK_{id}, pk_{id}, sk_{id})$ to the list L and returns $CLPK_{id} = pk_{id}$.
- Signing oracle $O_{\mathsf{Sign}}^{\mathsf{CL}}(\cdot, \cdot)$ queries: Suppose that A_{II} asks with an input (M, id).
    1. When the list L contains $(id, IBSK_{id}, pk_{id}, sk_{id})$, A'' checks to determine whether $IBSK_{id} = \bot$ and $pk_{id} = \bot$. If $IBSK_{id} = \bot$, A'' sets $IBSK_{id} = \mathsf{IB\_Ext}(id, params, IBSK^*)$. If $pk_{id} = \bot$, A'' runs $\mathsf{PK\_Gen}(1^k)$ to get (pk_{id}, sk_{id}) and saves these values in the list L. Now, A'' checks to see whether $sk_{id} = \bot$ or not.

a) If $sk_{id} = \bot$, A'' sends M to the Π_{PK} signing oracle $\mathsf{O}^{\mathsf{PK}}_{\mathsf{Sign}}(\cdot)$. Let α be the output of $\mathsf{O}^{\mathsf{PK}}_{\mathsf{Sign}}(M)$. A'' computes $\beta = \mathsf{IB\_Sign}^{IBSK_{id}}_{params}(\alpha)$. A'' returns $\langle \alpha, \beta \rangle$ to A_{II}.

b) Otherwise, A'' computes $\alpha = \mathsf{PK\_Sign}_{sk_{id}}(M)$ and $\beta = \mathsf{IB\_Sign}^{IBSK_{id}}_{params}(\alpha, id)$. A'' returns $\langle \alpha, \beta \rangle$ to A_{II}.

2. When the list L does not contain $(id,\ IBSK_{id},\ pk_{id},\ sk_{id})$, A'' sets $IBSK_{id} = \mathsf{IB\_Ext}(id, params, IBSK^*)$ and runs $\mathsf{PK\_Gen}(1^k)$ to obtain $(pk_{id},\ sk_{id})$. A'' adds $(id,\ IBSK_{id},\ pk_{id},\ sk_{id})$ to the list L. A'' computes $\alpha = \mathsf{PK\_Sign}_{sk_{id}}(M)$ and $\beta = \mathsf{IB\_Sign}^{IBSK_{id}}_{params}(\alpha, id)$. A'' returns $\langle \alpha, \beta \rangle$ to A_{II}.

When the Type II attacker A_{II} outputs $(M, id, \langle \alpha, \beta \rangle)$, A'' outputs (M, α) to the Π_{PK} challenger. If A'' does not abort during simulation, the A_{II}'s view is identical to its view in the real attack. Since the index j is chosen randomly, the probability that A'' does not abort during simulation is $1/l$. Hence, the success probability of A'' is at least ϵ/l and A'' runs in time $O(time(t))$.   Q.E.D. □

3.3   Extended Construction

The public key cryptosystem can be classified into three trust levels according to the trust assumption of the TTP (Trusted Third Party) [10]:

- At level 1, the TTP knows (or can easily compute) the users' private keys and therefore can impersonate any user at any time without being detected.
- At level 2, the TTP does not know (or cannot easily compute) the users' private keys. Nevertheless, the TTP can still impersonate a user by generating a false public key (or a false certificate).
- At level 3, the TTP does not know (or cannot easily compute) the users' private keys. Moreover, it can be proved that the TTP generates false public keys of users if it does so.

In a traditional public key signature scheme, if the CA forges certificates, the CA can be identified as having misbehaved through the existence of two valid certificates for the same identity. However, a false public key can be created by the KGC without being detected in the certificateless signature scheme Ψ_{CL}, since a new public key can be created by both the legitimate user and the KGC. While the traditional public key signature achieves trust level 3, the certificateless signature reaches only trust level 2.

At this point, our question is how the certificateless signature can achieve trust level 3. In other words, can we prevent the dishonest KGC from issuing two valid partial private keys for one user? We can use a simple technique to bind a user identity id and his public key $CLPK_{id}$, that was employed in [1].[2]

---

[2] This binding technique cannot raise a certificateless encryption scheme to trust level 3 as opposed to the claim in [1]. In a signature scheme, the existence of two different, working public keys for a single user can be proved by the corresponding two valid signatures; a digital signature is universally verifiable with the corresponding

Table 2. Generic construction of certificateless signature of trust level 3.

$\mathsf{CL\_Gen}(1^k)$
 $(IBSK^{\square}, params) \leftarrow \mathsf{IB\_Gen}(1^k);$
 $CLSK^{\square} \leftarrow IBSK^{\square};$
 Return $(CLSK^{\square}, params)$

$\mathsf{CL\_Set\_Sec\_Val}(params, id)$
 $(pk_{id}, sk_{id}) \leftarrow \mathsf{PK\_Gen}(1^k);$
 $CLS_{id} \leftarrow (pk_{id}, sk_{id});$
 Return CLS_{id}

$\mathsf{CL\_Set\_Pub\_Key}(params, id, CLS_{id})$
 Parse CLS_{id} as $(pk_{id}, sk_{id});$
 $CLPK_{id} \leftarrow pk_{id};$
 Return $CLPK_{id}$

$\mathsf{CL\_Ext\_Partial\_Pri\_Key}(id, CLPK_{id}, params, CLSK^{\square})$
 $IBSK_{id} \leftarrow \mathsf{IB\_Ext}(id||CLPK_{id}, params, CLSK^{\square});$
 $CLD_{id} \leftarrow IBSK_{id};$
 Return CLD_{id}

$\mathsf{CL\_Set\_Pri\_Key}(params, CLD_{id}, CLS_{id})$
 Parse CLS_{id} as $(pk_{id}, sk_{id});$
 $CLSK_{id} \leftarrow (CLD_{id}, sk_{id});$
 Return $CLSK_{id}$

$\mathsf{CL\_Sign}(M, id, params, CLSK_{id})$
 Parse $CLSK_{id}$ as $(CLD_{id}, sk_{id});$
 $\alpha \leftarrow \mathsf{PK\_Sign}_{sk_{id}}(M);$
 $\beta \leftarrow \mathsf{IB\_Sign}_{params}^{CLSK_{id}}(\alpha, id||CLPK_{id});$
 Return $\langle \alpha, \beta \rangle$

$\mathsf{CL\_Vrfy}(params, CLPK_{id}, M, id, \langle \alpha, \beta \rangle)$
 $b_1 \leftarrow \mathsf{IB\_Vrfy}_{params}(\alpha, id||CLPK_{id}, \beta);$
 $b_2 \leftarrow \mathsf{PK\_Vrfy}_{CLPK_{id}}(M, \alpha);$
 $b \leftarrow b_1 \& b_2;$
 Return b

public key. However, two ciphertexts do not guarantee the validity of the two public keys in an encryption scheme; without the corresponding private keys, we cannot check whether the ciphertexts are correct or not. To guarantee the existence of two different, working public encryption keys for a single user, the private keys or the partial private keys must be presented (or provided in a zero knowledge manner) in a certificateless encryption scheme. Note that we do not expect the dishonest KGC to reveal this information.

This technique reduces the degree of trust that users need to have in the KGC and raises the certificateless signature to trust level 3. A minor drawback of this technique is that the input of CL_Ext_Partial_Pri_Key includes $CLPK_{id}$ and hence, CL_Set_Pub_Key should be executed before the KGC runs CL_Ext_Partial_Pri_Key.

Let $\Pi_{PK} = (\text{PK\_Gen}, \text{PK\_Sign}, \text{PK\_Vrfy})$ be a secure public key signature scheme and $\Pi_{IB} = (\text{IB\_Gen}, \text{IB\_Ext}, \text{IB\_Sign}, \text{IB\_Vrfy})$ be a secure identity-based signature scheme. The construction of a trust level 3 certificateless signature scheme $\Lambda_{CL} = (\text{CL\_Gen}, \text{CL\_Ext\_Partial\_Pri\_Key}, \text{CL\_Set\_Sec\_Val}, \text{CL\_Set\_Pri\_Key}, \text{CL\_Set\_Pub\_Key}, \text{CL\_Sign}, \text{CL\_Vrfy})$ is shown in Table 2. Note that the existence of two different, working public keys for a single user will identity the KGC as having misbehaved in issuing both corresponding partial private keys, since the underlying Π_{IB} is a secure identity-based signature scheme and only the KGC knows the master key $IBSK^*$.

4   Concluding Remarks

A certificateless signature is a new digital signature paradigm that simplifies the public key infrastructure. A certificateless signature retains the efficiency of Shamir's identity-based signature while it does not suffer from the inherent private key escrow problem. We provided a generic secure construction of a certificateless signature in a more general manner. Moreover, the extended construction achieves trust level 3, the same level as is enjoyed in a traditional signature scheme.

Acknowledgment. The authors would like to thank Yong Ho Hwang for his help in preparing the final version of this paper.

References

1. S. S. Al-Riyami and K. G. Peterson, "Certificateless public key cryptography," Asiacrypt 2003, LNCS Vol. 2894, pp. 452-474, 2003.
2. M. Bellare, A. Desai, D. Jokipii, and P. Rogaway, "A concrete security treatment of symmetric encryption: analysis of the DES modes of operation," FOCS 1997, IEEE, 1997.
3. D. Boneh and M. Franklin, "Identity based encryption from the Weil pairing," Crypto 2001, LNCS Vol. 2139, pp. 213-229, 2001.
4. D. Boneh and M. Franklin, "Identity based encryption from the Weil pairing," SIAM J. of Computing, Vol. 32, No. 3, pp. 586-615, 2003.
5. M. Bellare and P. Rogaway, "Random oracles are practical: a paradigm for designing efficient protocols," 1st ACM Conf. on Computer and Communications Security, pp. 62-73, 1993.
6. J. C. Cha and J. H. Cheon, "An identity-based signature from gap Diffie-Hellman groups," PKC 2003, LNCS Vol. 2567, pp. 18-30, 2003.
7. L. C. Guillou and J. J. Quisquater, "A practical zero-knowledge protocol fitted to security microprocessor minimizing both transmission and memory," Eurocrypt 1988, LNCS Vol. 330, pp. 123-128, 1988.

8. L. C. Guillou and J. J. Quisquater "A "paradoxical" identity-based signature scheme resulting from zero-knowledge," Crypto 1988, LNCS Vol. 403, pp. 216-231, 1988.
9. C. Gentry, "Certificate-based encryption and the certificate revocation problem," Eurocrypt 2003, LNCS Vol. 2656, pp. 272-293, 2003.
10. M. Girault, "Self-certified public keys," Eurocrypt 1991, LNCS Vol. 547, pp. 490-497, 1992.
11. S. Goldwasswer, S. Micali, and R. Rivest, "A digital signature scheme secure against adaptive chosen-message attacks," SIAM J. Computing, Vol 7, No 2, pp. 281-308, 1988.
12. F. Hess, "Efficient identity based signature schemes based on pairings," SAC 2002, LNCS Vol. 2595, pp. 310-324, 2003.
13. G. Kang, J. H. Park, and S. G. Hahn "A certificate-based signature scheme," CT-RSA 2004, LNCS Vol. 2964, pp. 99-111, 2004.
14. K. G. Paterson, "ID-based signatures from pairings on elliptic curves," Electronics Letters Vol. 38 (18), pp. 1025-1026, 2002.
15. A. Shamir, "Identity-based cryptosystems and signature schemes," Crypto 1984, LNCS Vol. 196, pp. 47-53, 1984.
16. D. H. Yum and P. J. Lee, "Generic construction of certificateless encryption," The 2004 International Conference on Computational Science and its Applications, Assisi (Perugia, Italy), May 14 - May 17, 2004.

A Generalization of PGV-Hash Functions and Security Analysis in Black-Box Model[*]

Wonil Lee[1], Mridul Nandi[2], Palash Sarkar[2], Donghoon Chang[1], Sangjin Lee[1], and Kouichi Sakurai[3]

[1] Center for Information and Security Technologies
Korea University, Seoul, Korea
{wonil, dhchang, sangjin}@cist.korea.ac.kr
[2] Applied Statistics Unit, Indian Statistical Institute, Kolkata, India
{mridul_r,palash}@isical.ac.in
[3] Dept. of Computer Science and Communication Engineering,
Kyushu University, Fukuoka, Japan
sakurai@csce.kyushu-u.ac.jp

Abstract. In [1] it was proved that 20 out of 64 PGV-hash functions [2] based on block cipher are collision resistant and one-way-secure in black-box model of the underlying block cipher. Here, we generalize the definition of PGV-hash function into a hash family and prove that besides the previous 20 hash functions we have 22 more collision resistant and one-way secure hash families. As all these 42 families are keyed hash families, these become target collision resistant also. All these 42 hash families have tight upper and lower bounds on (target) collision resistant and one-way-ness.

1 Introduction

Brief History. Preneel, Govaerts, and Vandewalle [2] considered the 64 basic ways to construct a (collision-resistant) hash function $H : (\{0,1\}^n)^* \to \{0,1\}^n$ from a block cipher $E : \{0,1\}^n \times \{0,1\}^n \to \{0,1\}^n$. They regarded 12 of these 64 schemes as secure, though no proofs or formal claims were given. After that Black, Rogaway, and Shrimpton [1] presented a more proof-centric look at the schemes from PGV, providing both upper and lower bounds for each. They proved that, in the black box model of block cipher, 12 of 64 compression functions are CRHFs (Collision Resistant Hash Function) and 20 of 64 extended hash functions are CRHFs.

---

[*] The first author was partly supported by the grant M02-2003-000-20834-0 from Korea Science and Engineering Foundation, and also supported by the 21st Century COE Program "Reconstruction of Social Infrastructure Related to Information Science and Electrical Engineering" of the Graduate School of Information Science and Electrical Engineering, Kyushu Univ., Japan. The second and fifth authors were supported (in part) by the Ministry of Information & Communications, Korea, under the Information Technology Research Center (ITRC) Support Program.

H. Wang et al. (Eds.): ACISP 2004, LNCS 3108, pp. 212–223, 2004.
© Springer-Verlag Berlin Heidelberg 2004

Motivation of Our paper. The examples of most popular collision resistant hash functions are MD5 and SHA-1. For those hash function one can not exactly analyze the security. But the security of collision resistant or one-way for PGV hash functions can be analyzed under the assumption that the underlying block cipher is black-box i.e. random permutation. But the security of other notions like target collision resistant can not be analyzed as it needs a family of hash functions instead of single hash function. Beside that it seemed that more PGV hash function would become secure if we change the original definition of PGV hash function. So, we generalize the definition of PGV hash function into a PGV hash family and we will prove some security notions like target collision resistant, collision resistant and one-way.

General Definition of PGV-hash family. Let $0 \leq l < n$ and $E : \{0,1\}^n \times \{0,1\}^n \to \{0,1\}^n$ be a block cipher. If $l = 0$ let $\{0,1\}^0 = \{\epsilon\}$, where ϵ is the empty string. Using the block cipher E, we want to construct a compression function family $\mathcal{F} = \{f^k\}_{k \in \{0,1\}^l}$, $f^k : \{0,1\}^n \times \{0,1\}^{n-l} \to \{0,1\}^n$.

Let $h_0, v \in \{0,1\}^n$ be fixed values. We define the 64 ways to construct a *(block-cipher-based) compression function family* $\mathcal{F} = \{f^k\}_{k \in \{0,1\}^l}$ in the following manner: for each $k \in \{0,1\}^l$, $f^k(h,m) = E_a(b) \oplus c$, where $a, b, c \in \{h, (m\|k), h \oplus (m\|k), v\}$. Note that $|h| = n$ and $|m| = n - l$. Then we can define the *extended hash family* $\mathcal{H} = \{H^k\}_{k \in \{0,1\}^l}$ from the compression function family $\mathcal{F} = \{f^k\}_{k \in \{0,1\}^l}$ as follows: for each $k \in \{0,1\}^l$, $H^k : (\{0,1\}^{n-l})^* \to \{0,1\}^n$ is defined by

> **function** $H^k(m_1 \cdots m_t)$
> **for** $i \leftarrow 1$ **to** t **do** $h_i \leftarrow f^k(h_{i-1}, m_i)$
> **return** h_t

Note that the key k of extended hash family is equal to the key of compression function family. If $l = 0$ then $\mathcal{F} = \{f^k\}_{k \in \{0,1\}^0} = \{f^\epsilon\}$ is a singleton set and this corresponds to the original definition of PGV [2]. In this case, we denote this $\mathcal{F}$ as just f without superscript ϵ. We call this f a *(block-cipher-based) compression function*. Similarly, we denote $\mathcal{H}$ as H without superscript ϵ. And we call this H an *extended hash function*.

Our Results. For $0 < l < n$, the definitions and securities of the 64 schemes are summarized in Figures 1 and 2, In this paper, we fix E1 = $\{1, ..., 20\}$, E2 = $\{21, 22, 26, 28\}$, E3= $\{23, 24, 25, 31, 34, 35\}$, E4= $\{27, 29, 30, 32, 33, 36\}$, and E5 = $\{37, ..., 42\}$. Here, the numbers are corresponding to the numbers in the first column of Figures 1 and 2. And E6 is the set of remaining extended hash families which are not represented in the first column of Figures 1 and 2. So |E6| = 22. This classification is based on some property of hash family which is used to prove the security. A high-level summary of our findings is given by Table 1. The adversarial model (and the meaning of q) will be described momentarily.

Table 1. The $l = 0$ is analyzed in [1] . The case $l > 0$ is analyzed in this paper

Extended Hash Families $l = 0$	(Target) Collision Bound	Inversion Bound
E1 (20 schemes)	$\Theta(q^2/2^n)$	$\Theta(q/2^n)$ or $\Theta(q^2/2^n)$
E2/E3/E4/E5/E6 (44 schemes)	$\Theta(1)$	–
Extended Hash Families $l > 0$	(Target) Collision Bound	Inversion Bound
E1 (20 schemes)	$\Theta(q^2/2^n)$	$\Theta(q/2^l)$ or $\Theta(q/2^n)$ or $\Theta(q^2/2^n)$
E2 (4 schemes)	$\Theta(q/2^l)$	$\Theta(q/2^l)$
E3/E4/E5 (18 schemes)	$\Theta(q^2/2^l)$	$\Theta(q/2^l)$ or $\Theta(q^2/2^l)$ or $\Theta(q/2^n)$
E6 (22 schemes)	$\Theta(1)$	–

Black Box Model. Our security model is the one dating to Shannon [6] and used for works like [3,4,5]. An adversary $\mathcal{A}$ is given access to oracles E and E^{-1} where E is a random block cipher $E : \{0,1\}^n \times \{0,1\}^n \to \{0,1\}^n$ and E^{-1} is its inverse. That is, each key $a \in \{0,1\}^n$ names a randomly-selected permutation $E_a = E(a, \cdot)$ on $\{0,1\}^n$, and the adversary is given oracles E and E^{-1}. The latter, on input (a, y), returns the point x such that $E_a(x) = y$. See [1] for more details and discussions about black-box model.

In these PGV hash function families, we do not use any mask key unlike [7,10,12,13,16]. We prove the target collision resistance of these hash families under black box model and it will be more efficient in key size compare to the results in [7,10,12,13,16] wherein the mask keys are used.

Conventions. We follow the similar conventions as in [1]. Note that these conventions are important to make the discussion easy and to prove the security. Firstly, an adversary does not ask any oracle query in which the response is already known. Secondly, if M is one of the output(s) produced by an adversary, then the adversary should make necessary E/E^{-1} queries to compute $H^k(M)$ during the whole query process. These assumptions are all without loss of generality in that an adversary $\mathcal{A}$ not obeying these conventions can easily be modified to obtain an adversary $\mathcal{A}'$ having similar computational complexity that obeys these conventions and has the same advantage as $\mathcal{A}$. From now on, we always assume $E : \{0,1\}^n \times \{0,1\}^n \to \{0,1\}^n$ is a random block cipher, i.e., for each $a \in \{0,1\}^n$, $E_a(\cdot)$ is a random permutation. We fix some $h_0, v \in \{0,1\}^n$.

2   Preliminaries

We write $x \xleftarrow{R} S$ for the experiment of choosing a random element from the finite set S and calling it x.

Collision Resistance, Target Collision Resistance and Inversion Resistance of Hash function family ($0 < l < n$). To quantify the collision resistance and target collision resistance of a (block-cipher-based) hash function family $\{H^k\}_{k \in \{0,1\}^l}$, we consider random block cipher E. An adversary $\mathcal{A}$ is given oracles for $E(\cdot, \cdot)$ and $E^{-1}(\cdot, \cdot)$. Then, the adversary $\mathcal{A}^{E,E^{-1}}$ for collision resistance plays the following game called *Coll*.

ı	ȷ	$h_i =$	(T)CR LB	(T)CR UB	IR LB	IR UB
	1	$E_{x_i}(x_i) \oplus v$	1	1	–	–
22	2	$E_{h_{i-1}}(x_i) \oplus v$	$q/2^{l+1}$	$2q/2^{l+1}-1$	$q/2^{l+1}$	$q/2^{l-1}$
13	3	$E_{w_i}(x_i) \oplus v$	$.3q(q-1)/2^n$	$q^2/2^{n-1}$	$q/2^l$	$q/2^{l-1}$
	4	$E_v(x_i) \oplus v$	1	1	–	–
	5	$E_{x_i}(x_i) \oplus x_i$	1	1	–	–
1	6	$E_{h_{i-1}}(x_i) \oplus x_i$	$.3q(q-1)/2^n$	$q(q+1)/2^n$	$.4q/2^n$	$2q/2^n$
9	7	$E_{w_i}(x_i) \oplus x_i$	$.3q(q-1)/2^n$	$q(q+1)/2^n$	$.4q/2^n$	$2q/2^n$
	8	$E_v(x_i) \oplus x_i$	1	1	–	–
	9	$E_{x_i}(x_i) \oplus h_{i-1}$	1	1	–	–
21	10	$E_{h_{i-1}}(x_i) \oplus h_{i-1}$	$q/2^{l+1}$	$2q/2^{l+1}-1$	$q/2^{l+1}$	$q/2^{l-1}$
11	11	$E_{w_i}(x_i) \oplus h_{i-1}$	$.3q(q-1)/2^n$	$q(q+1)/2^n$	$.4q/2^n$	$2q/2^n$
	12	$E_v(x_i) \oplus h_{i-1}$	1	1	–	–
	13	$E_{x_i}(x_i) \oplus w_i$	1	1	–	–
3	14	$E_{h_{i-1}}(x_i) \oplus w_i$	$.3q(q-1)/2^n$	$q(q+1)/2^n$	$.4q/2^n$	$2q/2^n$
14	15	$E_{w_i}(x_i) \oplus w_i$	$.3q(q-1)/2^n$	$q^2/2^{n-1}$	$q/2^l$	$q/2^{l-1}$
	16	$E_v(x_i) \oplus w_i$	1	1	–	–
15	17	$E_{x_i}(h_{i-1}) \oplus v$	$.3q(q-1)/2^n$	$q^2/2^{n-1}$	$.15q^2/2^n$	$9(q+3)^2/2^n$
	18	$E_{h_{i-1}}(h_{i-1}) \oplus v$	1	1	–	–
16	19	$E_{w_i}(h_{i-1}) \oplus v$	$.3q(q-1)/2^n$	$q^2/2^{n-1}$	$q/2^l$	$q/2^{l-1}$
	20	$E_v(h_{i-1}) \oplus v$	1	1	–	–
17	21	$E_{x_i}(h_{i-1}) \oplus x_i$	$.3q(q-1)/2^n$	$q^2/2^{n-1}$	$.15q^2/2^n$	$9(q+3)^2/2^n$
23	22	$E_{h_{i-1}}(h_{i-1}) \oplus x_i$	$.3q(q-1)/2^l$	$q^2/2^{l-1}$	$q/2^l$	$q/2^{l-1}$
12	23	$E_{w_i}(h_{i-1}) \oplus x_i$	$.3q(q-1)/2^n$	$q(q+1)/2^n$	$.4q/2^n$	$2q/2^n$
35	24	$E_v(h_{i-1}) \oplus x_i$	$.3q(q-1)/2^{l-1}$	$q^2/2^{l-1}$	$.15q^2/2^l$	$q^2/2^{l-1}$
5	25	$E_{m_i}(h_{i-1}) \oplus h_{i-1}$	$.3q(q-1)/2^n$	$q(q+1)/2^n$	$.4q/2^n$	$2q/2^n$
	26	$E_{h_{i-1}}(h_{i-1}) \oplus h_{i-1}$	1	1	–	–
10	27	$E_{w_i}(h_{i-1}) \oplus h_{i-1}$	$.3q(q-1)/2^n$	$q(q+1)/2^n$	$.4q/2^n$	$2q/2^n$
	28	$E_v(h_{i-1}) \oplus h_{i-1}$	1	1	–	–
7	29	$E_{x_i}(h_{i-1}) \oplus w_i$	$.3q(q-1)/2^n$	$q(q+1)/2^n$	$.4q/2^n$	$2q/2^n$
24	30	$E_{h_{i-1}}(h_{i-1}) \oplus w_i$	$.3q(q-1)/2^l$	$q^2/2^{l-1}$	$q/2^l$	$q/2^{l-1}$
18	31	$E_{w_i}(h_{i-1}) \oplus w_i$	$.3q(q-1)/2^n$	$q^2/2^{n-1}$	$q/2^l$	$q/2^{l-1}$
25	32	$E_v(h_{i-1}) \oplus w_i$	$.3q(q-1)/2^{l-1}$	$q^2/2^{l-1}$	$q/2^l$	$q/2^{l-1}$

Fig. 1. Summary of results about 64 extended hash families. Column 1 is our number $\imath$ for the function family (We write $\mathcal{F}_i$ for the compression function family and $\mathcal{H}_i$ for its induced extended hash family). Column 2 is the number from [2]. Column 3 defines $f_k(h_{i-1}, m_i)$ for some $k \in \{0,1\}^l$. We write x_i for $(m_i\|k)$ and w_i for $x_i \oplus h_{i-1}$. Columns 4 and 5 give our (target) collision resistance bounds. Columns 6 and 7 give our inversion resistance bounds.

1. $\mathcal{A}^{E,E^{-1}}$ is given a key k which is chosen uniformly at random from $\{0,1\}^l$.
2. $\mathcal{A}^{E,E^{-1}}$ has to find M, M' such that $M \neq M'$ but $H_k(M) = H_k(M')$.

The adversary $\mathcal{A}^{E,E^{-1}} = (\mathcal{A}_{guess}, \mathcal{A}_{find}(\cdot,\cdot))$ for target collision resistance plays the following game called $TColl$.

1. $\mathcal{A}_{guess}$ commits to an M.

i	j	$h_i =$	(T)CR LB	(T)CR UB	IR LB	IR UB
19	33	$E_{x_i}(w_i)\oplus v$	$.3q(q-1)/2^n$	$q^2/2^{n-1}$	$.15q^2/2^n$	$9(q+3)^2/2^n$
26	34	$E_{h_{i-1}}(w_i)\oplus v$	$q/2^{l+1}$	$2q/2^{l+1}-1$	$q/2^{l+1}$	$q/2^{l-1}$
38	35	$E_{w_i}(w_i)\oplus v$	$.3q(q-1)/2^l$	$q^2/2^{l-1}$	$q/2^n$	$q/2^{n-1}$
37	36	$E_v(w_i)\oplus v$	$.3q(q-1)/2^{l-1}$	$q^2/2^{l-1}$	$.15q^2/2^l$	$q^2/2^{l-1}$
20	37	$E_{x_i}(w_i)\oplus x_i$	$.3q(q-1)/2^n$	$q^2/2^{n-1}$	$.15q^2/2^n$	$9(q+3)^2/2^n$
4	38	$E_{h_{i-1}}(w_i)\oplus x_i$	$.3q(q-1)/2^n$	$q(q+1)/2^n$	$.4q/2^n$	$2q/2^n$
27	39	$E_{w_i}(w_i)\oplus x_i$	$.3q(q-1)/2^l$	$q^2/2^{l-1}$	$q/2^l$	$q/2^{l-1}$
36	40	$E_v(w_i)\oplus x_i$	$.3q(q-1)/2^{l-1}$	$q^2/2^{l-1}$	$.15q^2/2^l$	$q^2/2^{l-1}$
8	41	$E_{x_i}(w_i)\oplus h_{i-1}$	$.3q(q-1)/2^n$	$q(q+1)/2^n$	$.4q/2^n$	$2q/2^n$
28	42	$E_{h_{i-1}}(w_i)\oplus h_{i-1}$	$q/2^{l+1}$	$2q/2^{l+1}-1$	$q/2^{l+1}$	$q/2^{l-1}$
29	43	$E_{w_i}(w_i)\oplus h_{i-1}$	$.3q(q-1)/2^l$	$q^2/2^{l-1}$	$q/2^l$	$q/2^{l-1}$
30	44	$E_v(w_i)\oplus h_{i-1}$	$.3q(q-1)/2^{l-1}$	$q^2/2^{l-1}$	$q/2^l$	$q/2^{l-1}$
6	45	$E_{x_i}(w_i)\oplus w_i$	$.3q(q-1)/2^n$	$q(q+1)/2^n$	$.4q/2^n$	$2q/2^n$
2	46	$E_{h_{i-1}}(w_i)\oplus w_i$	$.3q(q-1)/2^n$	$q(q+1)/2^n$	$.4q/2^n$	$2q/2^n$
39	47	$E_{w_i}(w_i)\oplus w_i$	$.3q(q-1)/2^l$	$q^2/2^{l-1}$	$q/2^n$	$q/2^{n-1}$
40	48	$E_v(w_i)\oplus w_i$	$.3q(q-1)/2^{l-1}$	$q^2/2^{l-1}$	$q/2^n$	$q/2^{n-1}$
	49	$E_{x_i}(v)\oplus v$	1	1	–	–
	50	$E_{h_{i-1}}(v)\oplus v$	1	1	–	–
41	51	$E_{w_i}(v)\oplus v$	$.3q(q-1)/2^l$	$q^2/2^{l-1}$	$q/2^n$	$q/2^{n-1}$
	52	$E_v(v)\oplus v$	1	1	–	–
	53	$E_{x_i}(v)\oplus x_i$	1	1	–	–
31	54	$E_{h_{i-1}}(v)\oplus x_i$	$.3q(q-1)/2^l$	$q^2/2^{l-1}$	$q/2^l$	$q/2^{l-1}$
32	55	$E_{w_i}(v)\oplus x_i$	$.3q(q-1)/2^l$	$q^2/2^{l-1}$	$q/2^l$	$q/2^{l-1}$
	56	$E_v(v)\oplus x_i$	1	1	–	–
	57	$E_{x_i}(v)\oplus h_{i-1}$	1	1	–	–
	58	$E_{h_{i-1}}(v)\oplus h_{i-1}$	1	1	–	–
33	59	$E_{w_i}(v)\oplus h_{i-1}$	$.3q(q-1)/2^l$	$q^2/2^{l-1}$	$q/2^l$	$q/2^{l-1}$
	60	$E_v(v)\oplus h_{i-1}$	1	1	–	–
	61	$E_{x_i}(v)\oplus w_i$	1	1	–	–
34	62	$E_{h_{i-1}}(v)\oplus w_i$	$.3q(q-1)/2^l$	$q^2/2^{l-1}$	$q/2^l$	$q/2^{l-1}$
42	63	$E_{w_i}(v)\oplus w_i$	$.3q(q-1)/2^l$	$q^2/2^{l-1}$	$q/2^n$	$q/2^{n-1}$
	64	$E_v(v)\oplus w_i$	1	1	–	–

Fig. 2. Summary of results about 64 extended hash families, continued.

2. A key k is chosen uniformly at random from $\{0,1\}^l$.
3. $\mathcal{A}_{find}(M,k)$ has to find M' such that $M \neq M'$ but $H_k(M) = H_k(M')$.

The adversary $\mathcal{A}^{E,E^{-1}}$ for inversion resistance plays the following game called *Inv*.

1. A key k is chosen uniformly at random from $\{0,1\}^l$.
2. h^* is chosen uniformly at random from the range $\{0,1\}^n$.
3. $\mathcal{A}^{E,E^{-1}}$ has to find M such that $H^k(M) = h^*$.

Definition 1. *(Collision resistance, target collision resistance, and inversion resistance of an extended hash family $\mathcal{H}$')* Let $\mathcal{H} = \{H^k\}_{k \in \{0,1\}^l}$ be a block-cipher-based extended hash family, where $H^k : (\{0,1\}^{n-l})^* \to \{0,1\}^n$. Then the advantage of $\mathcal{A}$ with respect to (target) collision resistance and inversion resistance are the the following real numbers.

$$\mathbf{Adv}_{\mathcal{H}}^{Coll}(\mathcal{A}) = Pr[k \xleftarrow{R} \{0,1\}^l; M, M' \leftarrow \mathcal{A}^{E,E^{-1}} :$$
$$M \neq M' \ \& \ H^k(M) = H^k(M')]$$

$$\mathbf{Adv}_{\mathcal{H}}^{TColl}(\mathcal{A}) = Pr[M \leftarrow \mathcal{A}_{guess}^{E,E^{-1}}; k \xleftarrow{R} \{0,1\}^l; M' \leftarrow \mathcal{A}_{find}^{E,E^{-1}}(M,k) :$$
$$M \neq M' \ \& \ H^k(M) = H^k(M')]$$

$$\mathbf{Adv}_{\mathcal{H}}^{Inv}(\mathcal{A}) = Pr[k \xleftarrow{R} \{0,1\}^l; h^* \xleftarrow{R} \{0,1\}^n; M \leftarrow \mathcal{A}^{E,E^{-1}} : H^k(M) = h^*]$$

Similarly we can define advantage for compression functions (for details see [15]). If $\mathcal{A}$ is an adversary and $\mathbf{Adv}_Y^{XXX}(\mathcal{A})$ is a measure of adversarial advantage already defined then we write $\mathbf{Adv}_Y^{XXX}(q)$ to mean the maximal value of $\mathbf{Adv}_Y^{XXX}(\mathcal{A})$ over all adversaries $\mathcal{A}$ that use queries bounded by the number q.

3   (Target) Collision Resistance of Extended Hash Family

In this section we will analyze the security of $\mathcal{H}_\imath$ for each $\imath \in [1, 42]$ defined in Section 1 in the notion of (target) collision resistant. We consider any adversary $\mathcal{A}$ with respect to Coll. i.e. after having random key k he will try to find a collision pair (M_1, M_2) for $H_\imath^k$ i.e. $M_1 \neq M_2$, $H_\imath^k(M_1) = H_\imath^k(M_2)$. For that he will make some E/E^{-1} queries. *Transcript* of $\mathcal{A}$ is defined by the sequence of query-response quadruples $\{(s_i, x_i, y_i, \sigma_i)\}_{1 \leq i \leq q}$ where q is the maximum number of queries made by adversary, $s_i, x_i, y_i \in \{0,1\}^n$ and $\sigma_i = +1$ (in case of E-query) or -1 (in case of E^{-1}-query) and for all i, $E_{s_i}(x_i) = y_i$. $(s_i, x_i, y_i, \sigma_i)$ will be called by i^{th} query-response quadruple (or q-r quadruple). In this section we fix some key k and v. Note that, if $\sigma_i = +1$ (resp. -1) then y (resp. x) is a random string as we assume that the block-cipher $E_s(\cdot)$ is a random permutation.

Proposition 1. *For fixed $x, y \in \{0,1\}^n$ and $A \subseteq \{0,1\}^n$, $Pr[y_i = y] \leq \frac{1}{2^n - i + 1}$ and $Pr[y_i \in A] \leq \frac{|A|}{2^n - i + 1}$ whenever $\sigma_i = +1$. Similarly, if $\sigma_i = -1$ then $Pr[x_i = x] \leq \frac{1}{2^n - i + 1}$ and $Pr[x_i \in A] \leq \frac{|A|}{2^n - i + 1}$*

Here we fix any arbitrary hash family $\mathcal{H}_\imath$ for $\imath \in [1, 42]$. In this section $V := \{0,1\}^n$ is called *vertex set* and $L := \{0,1\}^{n-l}$ is called *label set*. A triple $(h_1, h_2, m) \in V \times V \times L$ (or a pair $(h_1, h_2) \in V \times V$) is called a *labeled arc* (or an *arc* only). We also say (h_1, h_2, m) is an arc (h_1, h_2) with label m or m is a label of the arc (h_1, h_2) and we use the notation $h_1 \to_m h_2$. Now given a triple $\tau = (s, x, y)$ where, $s, x, y \in V$ define a set of labeled arcs $A(\tau)$ by the following set :

$$A(\tau) = \{(h_1, h_2, m) \in V \times V \times L : f^k(h_1, m) = h_2 \Leftrightarrow E_s(x) = y\}.$$

For example, in case of $\mathcal{H}_{21}$, $f^k_{21}(h_1, m) := E_{h_1}(m||k) \oplus h_1$. So, $(f^k(h_1, m) = h_2 \Leftrightarrow E_s(x) = y) \Longleftrightarrow (E_{h_1}(m||k) \oplus h_1 = h_2 \Leftrightarrow E_s(x) = y) \Longleftrightarrow (h_1 = s, h_2 = y \oplus h_1 = y \oplus s, m||k = x)$. Hence, $A(\tau) = \{(s, s \oplus y, x[L])\}$ if $x[R] = k$ otherwise it is an empty set. If $x \in \{0,1\}^n$ and $0 \le l < n$, $x = x[L]||x[R]$, where $|x[L]| = n - l$ and $|x[R]| = l$.

Given a set of labeled arcs A we define induced arc set $A' = \{(h_1, h_2) : \exists m \in L, (h_1, h_2, m) \in A\}$. For a set of triple(s) $\tau = \{\tau_1 = (s_1, x_1, y_1), \dots, \tau_a = (s_a, x_a, y_a)\}$ we can define *labeled arc set* $A(\tau) = \bigcup_{i=1}^{a} A(\tau_i)$. It can be easily checked that $A'(\tau) = \bigcup_{i=1}^{a} A'(\tau_i)$. Every member of $A(\tau)$ (or $A'(\tau)$) will be called an *labeled arc* (or *arc*) *corresponding* to the set of triple(s) τ. Given a transcript $\{(s_i, x_i, y_i, \sigma_i)\}_{1 \le i \le q}$ of an adversary $\mathcal{A}$ let $\tau[i]$ denote the set of triples $\{\tau_1 = (s_1, x_1, y_1), \dots, \tau_i = (s_i, x_i, y_i)\}$. For each i we have a labeled directed graph $T_i = T(\tau[i]) = (V, A(\tau[i]))$ and a directed graph $T'_i = (V, A'(\tau[i]))$. Define $T_0 = (V, \emptyset)$. Given a path $P = (h_1, h_2, \dots, h_p)$ from h_1 to h_p in T_i, $M = m_1||\dots||m_{p-1}$ is called a label of P if m_i is a label of (h_i, h_{i-1}) for each i. So we have a picture like $(h_1 \rightarrow_{m_1} h_2 \rightarrow_{m_2} \dots \rightarrow_{m_{p-1}} h_p)$ in T_i.

Observation 1 : By our conventions the adversary can compute $f^k_i(h_1, m) = h_2$ after i^{th} query iff for some $j \le i$, $E_{s_j}(x_j) = y_j \Rightarrow f^k_i(h_1, m) = h_2$ and hence $(h_1, h_2, m) \in A(\tau[i])$. Similarly, adversary can compute $H^k_i(m_1||\dots||m_a)$ after i^{th} query iff $h_0 \rightarrow_{m_1} h_1 \rightarrow_{m_2} \dots \rightarrow_{m_a} h_a$ is a path in $A(\tau[i])$ and $H^k_i(m_1||\dots||m_a) = h_a$.

Definition 2. *For each hash function and $0 \le i \le q$*

1. *When $\imath \in E1$, $E2$ or $E4$, h in T_i is **old** if $deg(h) \ge 1$ in T_i or $h = h_0$.*
2. *When $\imath \in E2$ or $E4$, h in T_i is **old** if $h = h_0$ or there exists h_1, $deg(h_1) \ge 1$ in T_i and $h[R] = h_1[R]$.*

*Remaining all other vertices are known as **new** vertices. Denote the set of all* old *vertices in T_i by O_i.*

The next Proposition will be used in the security analysis. It gives an upper bound on $|O_i|$ and describes the structure of the set of labeled arcs $A(\tau_i)$ and $A'(\tau_i)$ which will be useful to prove the upper bound of the advantage. Here we skip the proofs of all results. One can see the proofs in [15].

Proposition 2. *If $A(\tau_i)$ is not empty then we have,*

1. *For $\imath \in E1$ or $E2$, $A(\tau_i)$ is a singleton and $|O_i| \le 2i + 1$.*
2. *For $\imath \in E3$, $A'(\tau_i) = \{(h_1, h_2) : h_2[R] = u\}$ where, h_1 and u are fixed depending only on j and τ_i. So, the graph of the $A'(\tau_i)$ looks like an outward directed star and $|A'(\tau_i)| = 2^{n-l} = |A(\tau_i)|$ and hence $|O_i| \le (2i+1)2^{n-l}$.*
3. *For $\imath \in E4$, $A'(\tau_i) = \{(h, h \oplus a) : h[R] = u\}$ where, a and u are fixed depending only on j and τ_i. So, the graph of the $A'(\tau_i)$ consists of 2^{n-l} parallel arcs and $|A'(\tau_i)| = 2^{n-l} = |A(\tau_i)|$ and hence $|O_i| \le (2i+1)2^{n-l}$.*
4. *For $\imath \in E5$, $A'(\tau_i) = \{(h_1, h_2) : h_1[R] = u\}$ where, h_2 and u are fixed depending only on j and τ_i. So, the graph of the $A'(\tau_i)$ looks like an inward directed star and $|A'(\tau_i)| = 2^{n-l} = |A(\tau_i)|$ and hence $|O_i| \le (2i+1)2^{n-l}$.*

Moreover, for each $(h_1, h_2) \in A'(\tau_i)$, *there exists unique* m *such that* $h_1 \to_m h_2$.
For the hash families E3, E4 and E5 if $h_1[R] = h_2[R]$ *then* $h_1 \in O_i \Rightarrow h_2 \in O_i \forall i$.

Definition 3. *For each* $1 \le i \le q$ *we define some events.*

1. C_i : *adversary gets a collision after* i^{th} *query.*
2. $PathColl_i$: $\exists$ *two paths* P_1 *and* P_2 *(not necessarily distinct) from* h_0 *to some* h^* *in* T_i *such that* P_1 *and* P_2 *have two different labels.*
3. $Succ_i$: $\exists$ *an arc* $(h, h') \in A'(\tau_i)$ *where both* h *and* h' *are old vertices in* T_{i-1}.

Proposition 3. *The event* $PathColl_i$ *is equivalent to* C_i. *For E1, E2, E3, and E4 hash families, the event* $(C_i \mid \neg C_{i-1})$ *necessarily implies* $Succ_i$. *For E5,* C_i *necessarily implies* $Succ_{i'}$ *for some* $i' \le i$.

Observation 2: In E5, $C_q \Rightarrow \bigcup_{i=1}^{q} Succ_i$ by above Proposition 3. So we have $\Pr[\mathcal{A}$ gets a collision$] \le \sum_{i=1}^{q} \Pr[Succ_i]$. In other hash families by above Proposition 3, $\Pr[\mathcal{A}$ gets a collision$] \le \sum_{i=1}^{q} \Pr[C_i | \neg C_{i-1}] \le \sum_{i=1}^{q} \Pr[Succ_i]$. So it is enough to have an upper bound of $\Pr[Succ_i]$ in all hash functions.

Theorem 1. *For each* $1 \le i \le q$ *we have*

1. *For E1 hash family,* $\Pr[Succ_i] \le (2i - 1)/2^{n-1}$
2. *For E2 hash family,* $\Pr[Succ_i] \le 2/(2^{l+1} - 1)$ *if* $q \le 2^{n-l-1}$.
3. *For E3,E4 or E5 hash families,* $\Pr[Succ_i] \le (2i - 1)/2^{l-1}$.

So we have the following theorem using Observation 2.

Theorem 2.   *1.* $\mathbf{Adv}_{\mathcal{H}_\imath}^{C\,oll}(q) \le q^2/2^{n-1}$ *for* $\imath \in E1$
2. $\mathbf{Adv}_{\mathcal{H}_\imath}^{C\,oll}(q) \le 2q/(2^{l+1} - 1)$ *for all* $q \le 2^{n-l-1}$ *and* $\imath \in E2$.
3. $\mathbf{Adv}_{\mathcal{H}_\imath}^{C\,oll}(q) \le q^2/2^{l-1}$ *for* $\imath \in E3$, $E4$ *or* $E5$.

By the following theorem the upper bound of advantage for E1 hash family can also be obtained from that of corresponding hash function presented in [1].

Theorem 3. *For all* $\imath \in [1, 42]$, $\mathbf{Adv}_{\mathcal{H}_\imath}^{C\,oll}(q) \le \mathbf{Adv}_{H_\imath}^{C\,oll}(q)$

In [1] we know the followings :

1. For $\imath \in [1, 12]$, $\mathbf{Adv}_{H_\imath}^{Coll}(q) \le q(q + 1)/2^n$
2. For $\imath \in [13, 20]$, $\mathbf{Adv}_{H_\imath}^{Coll}(q) \le 3q(q + 1)/2^n$

So, we can conclude from Theorem 2 and 3 that,

Corollary 1. *For* $\imath \in [1, 12]$, $\mathbf{Adv}_{\mathcal{H}_\imath}^{T\,C\,oll}(q) \le \mathbf{Adv}_{\mathcal{H}_\imath}^{C\,oll}(q) \le q(q + 1)/2^n$.
For $\imath = [13, 20]$, $\mathbf{Adv}_{\mathcal{H}_\imath}^{T\,C\,oll}(q) \le \mathbf{Adv}_{\mathcal{H}_\imath}^{C\,oll}(q) \le q^2/2^{n-1}$.

4   Some Attacks in Target Collision Resistant Game

The idea of attack : Here we will give a generic attack for all $\mathcal{H}_j$ for the game TColl (See Section 2). Commit $M_1 = (m_1||\ldots||m_q)$. we will describe later how these m_i's will be chosen. Then given random key k compute $\mathcal{H}_j^k(M_1)$ by using q many queries. We will obtain $h_1,\ldots h_q$ and $\mathcal{H}_j^k(M_1) = h_q$ where, $h_0 \to_{m_1} h_1 \to_{m_2} \ldots h_{q-1} \to_{m_q} h_q$. If we get one such $i < i'$ such that $h_i = h_{i'}$ then define $M_2 = m_1||\ldots||m_i||m_{i'+1}||\ldots m_q$. So, M_1 and M_2 will be a collision pair. Roughly h_i's are random string and the probability of success will be probability for birthday collision of h_i's which is $o(q^2/2^n)$. We will choose m_i's such that the key for each query (i.e. s_i's) are different.

Choice of m_i's : If key of block cipher E is w in the definition of compression function then choose $m_i = 0$. So each w_i will be different as h_i's are different otherwise we get a collision. If key is h or m then choose $m_i = i$ and hence keys are different. If key is v then choose m_i's so that inputs of compression functions are different. In this case we will study the lower bound separately.

Theorem 4. $\mathbf{Adv}_{\mathcal{H}_i}^{C \circ 11}(q) \geq \mathbf{Adv}_{\mathcal{H}_i}^{TC \circ 11}(q) \geq \frac{0.3q(q-1)}{2^n}$ *for each* $i \in [1, 42]$ *whenever key of E is not v in the definition of compression function.*

For hash family E3/E4/E5 we can have better attack with lower bound $o(\frac{q^2}{2^l})$ if we just check whether $h_i[R] = h_{i'}[R]$ for $i < i'$. Construction of M_2 is given below where $h_i[R] = h_{i'}[R]$ for $i < i'$:

1. E3 : In E2 family if $h \to_m h'$ then $(h \oplus (a||0)) \to_{m\oplus a} (h' \oplus (a||0))$. So, define $M_2 = m_1||\ldots||m_{i'}||(m_{i+1} \oplus a)||\ldots||m_{i'} \oplus a||m_{i+1}||\ldots||m_q$. Here, $a = h_i[R] \oplus h_{i'}[R]$. This will give collision because $\mathcal{H}_j(m_1||\ldots||m_{i'}||(m_{i+1} \oplus a)||\ldots||(m_{i'} \oplus a) = h_i$.
2. E4 : By Proposition 2 we have some $m'_{i'}$ such that $h_{i'-1} \to_{m'_{i'}} h_{i'}$. So define $M_2 = m_1||\ldots||m_{i-1}||m'_{i'}||\ldots||m_q$. This will give a collision.
3. E5 : This case is very similar to E4 so we skip this.

Theorem 5. *Let* $i \in$ *E3 or E4 or E5. If v is not the key of E in the definition for compression function then* $\mathbf{Adv}_{\mathcal{H}_i}^{C \circ 11}(q) \geq \mathbf{Adv}_{\mathcal{H}_i}^{TC \circ 11}(q) \geq \frac{0.3q(q-1)}{2^l}$. *In other cases* $\mathbf{Adv}_{\mathcal{H}_i}^{C \circ 11}(q) \geq \mathbf{Adv}_{\mathcal{H}_i}^{TC \circ 11}(q) \geq \frac{0.3q(q-1)}{2^{l-1}}$.

Attack for E2 Hash Family : We will consider $\mathcal{H}_{21}$ hash family from E2. Other cases are similar. Fix some integer $a > 0$ such that $(a+1)(a+2)/2+a+1 \geq q$. Let $m_1,\ldots m_a \in_R \{0,1\}^{n-l}$. Commit $M_1 = m_1||\ldots||m_a$ where m_i's are chosen like above (to make the keys different and note that in E2 there is no hash function with key v). Then given random key k compute $\mathcal{H}_{21}(M_1)$ using a queries (we have to do it by our convention). We will obtain $h_0, h_1 \ldots, h_a = \mathcal{H}_{21}(M_1)$. If $h_i = h_{i'}$ for some $i < i'$ then $M_2 = m_1||\ldots m_i||m_{j+1}||m_a$. Output M_2. Otherwise run the loop below for $q - a$ many times.

For $i, j = 0$ to a ($j \neq i+1$, $i \leq j$)

Compute $E_{h_i}^{-1}(h_i \oplus h_j) = x$

If $x[R] = k$ then $M_2 = m_1||\ldots||m_i||m_{j+1}$ and output M_2.

Theorem 6. *For each $\imath \in E2$, $\mathbf{Adv}_{\mathcal{H}_\imath}^{\mathrm{C\,oll}}(q) \geq \mathbf{Adv}_{\mathcal{H}_\imath}^{\mathrm{TC\,oll}}(q) \geq \cdot 3a(a+1)/2^n + (q-a)/2^l$ for integer $a > 0$ such that $(a+1)(a+2)/2 + a + 1 \geq q$.*

Proposition 4. $1 - \prod_{i=1}^{q}(1 - \frac{i}{2^a}) \geq \frac{\cdot 3q(q-1)}{2^a}$ *for any integer a.*

Proof. It is given in [1] so we skip the proof.   ∎

5   Inversion Resistance of Extended Hash Family

5.1   Upper Bound

In the Inv game a random key k and a random h^* will be given where, $h^* \in \{0,1\}^n$. Then he will try to compute M in case of extended hash function or h, m in case of compression function such that $H_\imath^k(M) = h^*$ or $f_\imath^k(h, m) = h^*$. If he finds that then we will say that adversary wins. As we study in black-box model adversary can query E/E^{-1} similar to other games like Coll or TColl. So, adversary has a transcript or sequence of query-response quadruples $\{(s_i, x_i, y_i, \sigma_i)\}_{1 \leq i \leq q}$.

Theorem 7. $\mathbf{Adv}_{\mathcal{H}_\imath}^{\mathrm{Inv}}(q) \leq \mathbf{Adv}_{\mathcal{F}_\imath}^{\mathrm{Inv}}(q)$ *for each $\imath \in [1, 42]$.*

Now we will first study the security analysis of inversion resistance of compression functions. It can be easily observed that, for $\imath \in \{15, 17, 19, 20, 35, 36, 37\}$, the compression functions are not inversion resistance-secure. All other compression functions are inversion resistance-secure.

Theorem 8. $\mathbf{Adv}_{\mathcal{F}_\imath}^{\mathrm{Inv}}(q) \leq q/2^{l-1}$ *for $\imath \in [21, 34]$ or $\imath \in \{13, 14, 16, 18\}$.*

Theorem 9. $\mathbf{Adv}_{\mathcal{F}_\imath}^{\mathrm{Inv}}(q) \leq q/2^{n-1}$ *for $\imath \in [38, 42]$ or $[1, 12]$.*

For other cases $\imath \in \{35, 36, 37\}$ we can use the same technique used in proving the upper bound for Coll game. By the discussion made in beginning of the section we can have the following theorem.

Theorem 10. $\mathbf{Adv}_{\mathcal{H}_\imath}^{\mathrm{Inv}}(q) \leq q^2/2^{l-1}$ *for $\imath \in [35, 37]$ and* $\mathbf{Adv}_{\mathcal{H}_\imath}^{\mathrm{Inv}}(q) \leq \mathbf{Adv}_{H_\imath}^{\mathrm{Inv}}(q) \leq 9(q+3)^2/2^n$ *for $\imath \in \{15, 17, 19, 20\}$.*

5.2   Some Attacks in Inv Game for Lower Bound

Attack 1 : When $\imath \in \{15, 17, 19, 20, 35, 36, 37\}$ i.e. when the corresponding compression functions are not inversion resistance-secure we can perform meet-in-the-middle-attack. Idea of the attack is presented in [1]. Given h_0 and h^* we compute two sets F and B such that $h \to h_1$ for every $h_1 \in F$ and $h_2 \to h^*$ for every $h_2 \in B$. Note we can construct B as the compression functions are not inversion resistance-secure. If we get an element in $F \cap B$ say h then we have an inverse element of h^*. More precisely, if $h_0 \to_{m_1} h \to_{m_2} h^*$ for some m_1 and m_2 then $m_1 \| m_2$ will be an inverse element of h^*. So we have the following lower bound which is similar to the bound given in [1] and hence we skip the proof.

Theorem 11. $\mathbf{Adv}_{\mathcal{H}_\imath}^{\mathrm{Inv}}(q) \geq (0.15)q^2/2^n$ *for* $\imath \in \{15, 17, 19, 20\}$ *and* $\mathbf{Adv}_{\mathcal{H}_\imath}^{\mathrm{Inv}}(q) \geq (0.15)q^2/2^l$ *for* $\imath \in [35, 37]$.

Attack 2 : The attacking algorithm is same as the generic attack for target collision resistance described in Section 4. We choose $m_1, \cdots, m_q$ and then compute $h_1, \cdots, h_q$ and finally we will look for some h_i such that $h_i = h^*$ (for $\imath \in [38, 42]$ or $[1, 12]$) or $h_i[R] = h^*[R]$ (for $\imath \in [21, 34]$). One can prove it exactly but this will be same as the proof for collision attack so we skip the details.

Theorem 12. $\mathbf{Adv}_{\mathcal{H}_\imath}^{\mathrm{Inv}}(q) \geq q/2^{l+1}$ *for* $\imath \in [21, 34]$ *and* $\mathbf{Adv}_{\mathcal{H}_\imath}^{\mathrm{Inv}}(q) \geq q/2^n$ *for* $\imath \in [38, 42]$ *or* $[1, 12]$.

6   Conclusion

In this paper we first generalized the definition of PGV-hash functions into a PGV-hash families. In the new definitions we have more secure hash family (42 hash families) with respect to collision resistant and one-wayness. Unlike previous definitions ours is a keyed family so we can study other security notions like target collision resistant. In fact all these 42 hash families become target collision resistant. As AES is considered to be a good candidate for a block cipher, we can implement these hash families using AES. Because of our results, the only attacks for these hash families should be based on some internal weakness of AES. In other words, these hash families can be practically constructed using AES. The proof techniques used here are natural and apply directly to the security notions. So one can also study these proof techniques to get better ideas about using the black box model.

References

1. J. Black, P. Rogaway, and T. Shrimpton. *Black-box analysis of the block-cipher-based hash function constructions from PGV*, Advances in Cryptology - Crypto'02, Lecture Notes in Computer Science, Vol. 2442, Springer-Verlag, pp. 320-335, 2002.
2. B. Preneel, R. Govaerts, and J. Vandewalle. *Hash functions based on block ciphers:A synthetic approach*, Advances in Cryptology-CRYPTO'93, LNCS, Springer-Verlag, pp. 368-378, 1994.

3. S. Even, and Y. Mansour. *A construction of a cipher from a single pseudorandom permutation*, Advances in Cryptology-ASIACRYPT'91, LNCS 739, Springer-Verlag, pp. 210-224, 1992.

4. J. Kilian, and P. Rogaway. *How to protect DES against exhaustive key search*, Journal of Cryptology, 14(1):17-35, 2001, Earlier version in CRYPTO' 96.

5. R. Winternitz. *A secure one-way hash function built from DES*, In Proceedings of the IEEE Symposium on Information Security and Privacy, pp. 88-90, IEEE Press, 1984

6. C. Shannon. *Communication theory of secrecy systems*, Bell Systems Technical Journal, 28(4): pp. 656-715, 1949.

7. M. Bellare and P. Rogaway. *Collision-resistant hashing: towards making UOWHFs practical*, Advances in Cryptology - Crypto'97, Lecture Notes in Computer Science, Vol. 1294, Springer-Verlag, pp. 470-484, 1997.

8. I. B. Damgard. *A design principle for hash functions*, Advances in Cryptology - Crypto'89, Lecture Notes in Computer Sciences, Vol. 435, Springer-Verlag, pp. 416-427, 1989.

9. R. Merkle. *One way hash functions and DES*, Advances in Cryptology - Crypto'89, Lecture Notes in Computer Sciences, Vol. 435, Springer-Verlag, pp. 428-446, 1989.

10. I. Mironov. *Hash functions: from Merkle-Damgard to Shoup*, Advances in Cryptology - Eurocrypt'01, Lecture Notes in Computer Science, Vol. 2045, Springer-Verlag, pp 166-181, 2001

11. M. Naor and M. Yung. *Universal one-way hash functions and their cryptographic applications*, Proceedings of the Twenty First Annual ACM Symposium on Theory of Computing, ACM Press, pp 33-43, 1989.

12. P. Sarkar. *Construction of UOWHF: Tree Hashing Revisited*, Cryptology ePrint Archive, http://eprint.iacr.org/2002/058.

13. V. Shoup. *A composition theorem for universal one-way hash functions*. Advances in Cryptology - Eurocrypt'00, Lecture Notes in Computer Science, Vol. 1807, Springer-Verlag, pp 445-452, 2000.

14. D. Simon. *Finding collisions on a one-way street: can secure hash functions be based on general assumptions?*, Advances in Cryptology - Eurocrypt'98, Lecture Notes in Computer Science, Vol. 1403, Springer-Verlag, pp 334-345, 1998.

15. W. Lee, M. Nandi,P. Sarkar, D. Chang, S. Lee and K. Sakurai *A Generalization of PGV-Hash Functions and Security Analysis in Black-Box Model*, http://eprint.iacr.org/2004/069/

16. W. Lee, D. Chang , S. Lee, S. Sung and M. Nandi *New parallel domain extenders of UOWHF*, Advances in Crptology-Asiacrypt'03.

How to Re-use Round Function in Super-Pseudorandom Permutation

Tetsu Iwata and Kaoru Kurosawa

Department of Computer and Information Sciences,
Ibaraki University
4–12–1 Nakanarusawa, Hitachi, Ibaraki 316-8511, Japan
{iwata, kurosawa}@cis.ibaraki.ac.jp

Abstract. It is known that a super-pseudorandom permutation can be obtained from a pseudorandom function f and two universal hash functions, h and $h^{\square}$. It is a four round Feistel permutation denoted by $\phi(h_k, f, f, h^{\square}_{k'})$. In this paper, we show how to re-use the round function f in this construction. We show that (1) the same key can be used for both h and $h^{\square}$, and (2) the key for h and $h^{\square}$ can be derived from f. As a result, our construction requires only f as a key, while it preserves computational efficiency and security. Also, we derive a similar result for a five MISTY-type permutation.

1 Introduction

1.1 Background

It is ideal that a block cipher is indistinguishable from a random permutation. Luby and Rackoff provided formal definitions for the pseudorandomness and the super-pseudorandomness of block ciphers [9]. A block cipher is said to be pseudorandom if it is indistinguishable from a random permutation against adversaries with chosen plaintext attack. It is said to be super-pseudorandom if it is indistinguishable from a random permutation against adversaries with chosen plaintext and chosen ciphertext attacks.

1.2 Feistel Permutation

Let $\phi(f_1, f_2, f_3)$ denote the three round Feistel permutation such that the i-th round function is f_i. Similarly, let $\phi(f_1, f_2, f_3, f_4)$ denote the four round Feistel permutation.

Luby-Rackoff construction [9]. Suppose that each f_i is a pseudorandom function. Then Luby and Rackoff proved that $\phi(f_1, f_2, f_3)$ is a pseudorandom permutation and $\phi(f_1, f_2, f_3, f_4)$ is a super-pseudorandom permutation [9]. We call them Luby-Rackoff constructions.

Since then a considerable amount of research has been done focusing on the following question: Can we obtain *more efficient* construction of super-pseudorandom permutation than Luby and Rackoff's one? [5,10,15,17,18,19,20,

H. Wang et al. (Eds.): ACISP 2004, LNCS 3108, pp. 224–235, 2004.

24,25,26,28,29,30,31,35]. In this paper, for the efficiency, we consider the key and computation time.

The key of $\phi(f_1, f_2, f_3, f_4)$ is f_1, f_2, f_3, and f_4, and it requires four invocations of pseudorandom functions to compute its output.

Patarin construction [20]. Patarin showed that $\phi(f \circ \xi \circ f, f, f)$ is pseudorandom and $\phi(f \circ \xi \circ f, f, f, f)$ is super-pseudorandom, where ξ is, for example, a rotation of one bit [20]. The construction $\phi(f \circ \xi \circ f, f, f, f)$ requires only f as a key, while it requires five invocations of pseudorandom functions to compute its output. Thus, it requires only f as the key, but it is less efficient than Luby-Rackoff construction from a viewpoint of computation time.

Lucks construction [10]. Among others, Lucks is the first who noticed that a random function f_i can be replaced with a universal hash function h. Lucks showed that $\phi(h_k, f_2, f_3)$ is pseudorandom if h is an almost XOR universal (AXU) hash function [10]. This construction requires k (a key for h), f_2 and f_3 as a key. A universal hash function is a much weaker primitive than a pseudorandom function, and generally, hash functions can be processed much faster than pseudorandom functions.

PRS construction [24]. Patel, Ramzan and Sundaram [24] next introduced a notion of *bi-symmetric* AXU hash functions. Then they showed that $\phi(h_k, f, f, h'_{k'})$ is super-pseudorandom if h and h' are bi-symmetric AXU hash functions. We call it PRS construction. PRS construction is efficient from a viewpoint of computation time, since it requires only two pseudorandom functions and two hashes. This construction requires k, k' (keys for h and h'), and f as a key, which is more than Patarin construction.

Other related works. Naor-Reingold [15] showed an efficient way to improve Luby-Rackoff construction. They showed that $h'_{k'} \circ \phi(f_1, f_2) \circ h_k$ is a super-pseudorandom permutation if h and h' are pairwise independent permutations over $\{0, 1\}^{2n}$. The construction requires k, k', f_1, and f_2 as a key. We call it NR construction.

Next, Maurer [13] further improved NR construction, and showed that $h_{a,b}^{-1} \circ \phi(f, f) \circ h_{a,b}$ is super-pseudorandom if h is a linear polynomial $h_{a,b}(x) = ax + b$ over $GF(q^2)$, where a and b are defined by $a = (f(\text{Const}_1)\|f(\text{Const}_2))$ and $b = (f(\text{Const}_3)\|f(\text{Const}_4))$ for some fixed constant $\text{Const}_1, \ldots, \text{Const}_4$. This construction requires only f as a key, and also efficient from a viewpoint of computation time; two hashes over $GF(q^2)$ and two pseudorandom functions. We call it Maurer construction.

Other efficient constructions can be found in: Pieprzyk [26], Patel, Ramzan and Sundaram [25], and Iwata and Kurosawa [5]. See also reference in [15].

Another important area of research is to increase the number of rounds to obtain a better security bound. These line of results can be found in: Patarin [21,22,23] and Maurer and Pietrzak [14].

Vaudenay showed how to use this theory in practice and amplify the randomness [33].

1.3   MISTY-Type Permutation

Let $\psi(p_1, p_2, p_3, p_4, p_5)$ denote the five round MISTY-type permutation [11,12], where each p_i is a permutation.

GM construction [2]. Gilbert and Minier showed that $\psi(p_1, p_2, p_3, p_4, p_5)$ is a super-pseudorandom permutation if each p_i is a (super-pseudo)random permutation [2]. We call it GM construction. This construction requires $p_1, \ldots, p_5$ as a key, and it requires five invocations of (super-pseudo)random permutations to compute its output.

IYK construction [7]. Iwata et al. showed that $\psi(h_k, g, p, p^{-1}, {h'_{k'}}^{-1})$ is a super-pseudorandom permutation, where h is an XOR universal permutation, g is an orthomorphism, p is a (super-pseudo)random permutation, and h' is a uniform XOR universal permutation. We call it IYK construction. IYK construction is efficient from a viewpoint of computation time, since it requires only two (super-pseudo)random permutations and two hashes (g is a fixed permutation). The construction requires k, k', and p as a key.

Other construction. Other construction of super-pseudorandom permutation based on MISTY-type permutation can be found in [8].

1.4   Our Contribution

For Feistel permutation, it seems that the previous construction is either inefficient in computation time, but requires only one pseudorandom function as a key (Patarin construction), or efficient in computation time, but requires keys for a pseudorandom function and universal hash functions (PRS construction).

In this paper, we show how to re-use round function in Feistel permutation and MISTY-type permutation.

We first improve PRS construction $\phi(h_k, f, f, h'_{k'})$ in two ways: (1) First, we allow the same key to be used in h and h', and (2) secondly, we derive the key for h and h' from f. As a result, our construction requires only f as a key, and its computational time is as efficient as PRS construction. We also identify the general requirements on h and h'. Compared to Maurer construction, we do not restrict h and h' to be a linear polynomial $ax + b$, and these hash functions are defined on $\{0, 1\}^n$ instead of $\mathrm{GF}(q^2)$, which allows further efficient constructions.

For example, let $h_k(x) = k \cdot (k + x)$ and $h'_k(x) = c \cdot k \cdot (k + x)$, where addition and multiplication are over $\mathrm{GF}(2^n)$ and $c \in \mathrm{GF}(2^n)$ is a constant such that $c \neq 0, 1$. Further let $k = f(\mathtt{Const})$, where $\mathtt{Const}$ is an arbitrarily n-bit constant (for example, $\mathtt{Const} = 0^n$). We prove that $\phi(h_k, f, f, h'_k)$ is super-pseudorandom.

We next consider MISTY-type permutation. IYK construction $\psi(h_k, g, p, p^{-1}, {h'_{k'}}^{-1})$ is efficient in computation time, but requires k, k', and p as a key. We improve IYK construction in two ways: (1) First, we allow the same key to be used in h and h', and (2) secondly, we derive the key for h and h' from p. Then, our construction requires only p as a key, and its computational time is as efficient as IYK construction. As was done in Feistel permutation, we identify the general requirements on h and h'.

As a concrete example, let $h_{k_1,k_2}(x) = c_1 \cdot (k_1 \vee 0^{n-1}1) \cdot x + c_2 \cdot k_2$ and $h'_{k_1,k_2}(x) = c_3 \cdot (k_1 \vee 0^{n-1}1)^{-1} \cdot x + c_4 \cdot k_2$, where addition, multiplication and inversion are over $GF(2^n)$, and $c_1, \ldots, c_4 \in GF(2^n)$ are constants such that: (1) $c_1, c_3 \neq 0$, (2) $c_2 \neq 0, 1$, (3) $c_4 \neq 0$, and (4) $c_2 \oplus c_4 \neq 0, 1$. For example c_i is the n-bit binary representation of i. The bitwise-or is done so that h and h' become permutations. Further let $k_1 = p(\text{Const}_1)$ and $k_2 = p(\text{Const}_2)$, where Const_1 and Const_2 are arbitrarily distinct n-bit constants. We prove that $\psi(h_{k_1,k_2}, g, p, p^{-1}, h'_{k_1,k_2}{}^{-1})$ is super-pseudorandom.

An example of application of our constructions is to design block cipher modes of operations for disc sector encryption [16,3,4]. That is, if we use an n-bit block cipher as f and p, then $\phi(h_k, f, f, h'_k)$ and $\psi(h_{k_1,k_2}, g, p, p^{-1}, h'_{k_1,k_2}{}^{-1})$ can be considered as a new block cipher whose block length is $2n$.

2   Preliminaries

2.1   Notation

For $x \in \{0,1\}^{2n}$, x_L denotes the first (left) n bits of x and x_R denotes the last (right) n bits of x. That is, $x = (x_L, x_R)$. We denote by F_n the set of all functions from $\{0,1\}^n$ to $\{0,1\}^n$. Similarly, we denote by P_{2n} the set of all permutations over $\{0,1\}^{2n}$, and denote by P_n the set of all permutations over $\{0,1\}^n$. For two functions f and g, $g \circ f$ denotes the function $x \mapsto g(f(x))$. For a set S, $s \overset{R}{\leftarrow} S$ denotes the process of picking an element s from S uniformly at random.

2.2   Feistel Permutation

Definition 1 (The basic Feistel permutation). *For any function $f \in F_n$, define the basic Feistel permutation $\phi_f \in P_{2n}$ as $\phi_f(x_L, x_R) \overset{\text{def}}{=} (f(x_L) \oplus x_R, x_L)$.*

Note that it is a permutation since $\phi_f^{-1}(x_L, x_R) = (x_R, f(x_R) \oplus x_L)$.

Definition 2 (The r round Feistel permutation). *Let $r \geq 1$ be an integer. For $f_1, \ldots, f_r \in F_n$, define the r round Feistel permutation $\phi(f_1, \ldots, f_r) \in P_{2n}$ as $\phi(f_1, \ldots, f_r) \overset{\text{def}}{=} \phi_{f_r} \circ \cdots \circ \phi_{f_1}$.*

2.3   MISTY-Type Permutation [11,12]

Definition 3 (The basic MISTY-type permutation). *For any permutation $p \in P_n$, define the basic MISTY-type permutation $M_p \in P_{2n}$ as $M_p(x) \overset{\text{def}}{=} (x_R, p(x_L) \oplus x_R)$.*

Note that it is a permutation since $M_p^{-1}(x) = (p^{-1}(x_L \oplus x_R), x_L)$.

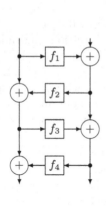

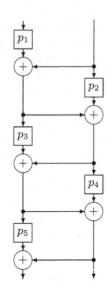

Fig. 1. Feistel permutation   **Fig. 2.** MISTY-type permutation

Definition 4 (The r round MISTY-type permutation). *Let $r \geq 1$ be an integer. For $p_1, \ldots, p_r \in P_n$, define the r round MISTY-type permutation $\psi(p_1, \ldots, p_r) \in P_{2n}$ as $\psi(p_1, \ldots, p_r) \overset{\text{def}}{=} \rho \circ M_{p_r} \circ \cdots \circ M_{p_1}$, where $\rho(x_L, x_R) = (x_R, x_L)$ for $x \in \{0, 1\}^{2n}$.*

ρ is added for illustrational simplicity.

See Fig. 1 (the four round Feistel permutation) and Fig. 2 (the five round MISTY-type permutation) for illustrations. Note that p_i in Fig. 2 is a permutation whereas f_i in Fig. 1 is a function. For simplicity, the left and right swaps are omitted.

2.4   Super-Pseudorandomness

Let Φ be a family of permutation over $\{0, 1\}^{2n}$. Intuitively, we say that Φ is super-pseudorandom if it is indistinguishable from P_{2n}, where the adversary is allowed adaptive chosen plaintext and chosen ciphertext attacks.

Our adaptive adversary $\mathcal{A}$ is an algorithm that has black-box access to two oracles, the forward direction of the permutation and the backward direction of the permutation.

The computational power of $\mathcal{A}$ is unlimited, but the total number of oracle calls is limited to a parameter q. After making at most q queries to the oracles, $\mathcal{A}$ outputs a bit.

Definition 5 (Advantage, sprp). *Let Φ be a family of permutations over $\{0, 1\}^{2n}$. For an adversary $\mathcal{A}$, we define the advantage of $\mathcal{A}$ as*

$$\mathbf{Adv}_{\Phi}^{\text{sprp}}(\mathcal{A}) \overset{\text{def}}{=} \left| \Pr\left(\phi \overset{R}{\leftarrow} \Phi : \mathcal{A}^{\phi, \phi^{-1}} = 1 \right) - \Pr\left(R \overset{R}{\leftarrow} P_{2n} : \mathcal{A}^{R, R^{-1}} = 1 \right) \right| .$$

The notation $\mathcal{A}^{\phi,\phi^{-1}}$ indicates $\mathcal{A}$ with an oracle which, in response to a query $(+, x)$, returns $y \leftarrow \phi(x)$, and in response to a query $(-, y)$, returns $x \leftarrow \phi^{-1}(y)$. The notation $\mathcal{A}^{R,R^{-1}}$ indicates $\mathcal{A}$ with an oracle which, in response to a query $(+, x)$, returns $y \leftarrow R(x)$, and in response to a query $(-, y)$, returns $x \leftarrow R^{-1}(y)$.

We say that Φ is a super-pseudorandom permutation family if $\mathbf{Adv}_{\Phi}^{\mathrm{sprp}}(\mathcal{A})$ is sufficiently small for any adversary $\mathcal{A}$ which makes at most q queries.

3 Construction Based on Feistel Permutation

3.1 Universal Hash Functions

Let $h, h' : K \times \{0,1\}^n \to \{0,1\}^n$ be two (keyed) hash functions such that for each $k \in K$, $h(k, \cdot) \in F_n$ and $h'(k, \cdot) \in F_n$. We write $h_k(\cdot)$ for $h(k, \cdot)$ and $h'_k(\cdot)$ for $h'(k, \cdot)$. Suppose that h and h' satisfy the following conditions for sufficiently small $\epsilon_1, \ldots, \epsilon_5$.

C1. $K = \{0,1\}^{\kappa}$. Define $l \stackrel{\mathrm{def}}{=} \lceil \kappa/n \rceil$.
C2. For any element $x \in \{0,1\}^n$ and any element $y \in \{0,1\}^n$, $\Pr(k \stackrel{R}{\leftarrow} K : h_k(x) = y) \leq \epsilon_1$ and $\Pr(k \stackrel{R}{\leftarrow} K : h'_k(x) = y) \leq \epsilon_2$.
C3. For any two distinct elements $x, x' \in \{0,1\}^n$ and any element $y \in \{0,1\}^n$, $\Pr(k \stackrel{R}{\leftarrow} K : h_k(x) \oplus h_k(x') = y) \leq \epsilon_3$ and $\Pr(k \stackrel{R}{\leftarrow} K : h'_k(x) \oplus h'_k(x') = y) \leq \epsilon_4$.
C4. For any elements $x, x' \in \{0,1\}^n$ (not necessarily distinct) and any element $y \in \{0,1\}^n$, $\Pr(k \stackrel{R}{\leftarrow} K : h_k(x) \oplus h'_k(x') = y) \leq \epsilon_5$.

C1 says that the key spaces of h and h' are $\{0,1\}^{\kappa}$. C2 and C3 are standard definitions follow from those given in [1,15,24,27,34]. C2 says that h and h' are almost uniformly distributed. C3 says that h and h' are almost XOR universal hash functions. C4 is a new condition. We note that this condition is defined for a pair of hash functions. We also note that the same key k is used for both h and h'. We show an example.

For $k \in K = \{0,1\}^n$, let $h_k(x) = k \cdot (k + x)$ and $h'_k(x) = c \cdot k \cdot (k + x)$, where addition and multiplication are over $\mathrm{GF}(2^n)$ and $c \in \mathrm{GF}(2^n)$ is a constant such that $c \neq 0, 1$.

Then it is easy to see that h and h' satisfy C1,...,C4 with $\epsilon_1 = \epsilon_2 = 2/2^n$, $\epsilon_3 = \epsilon_4 = 1/2^n$, and $\epsilon_5 = 2/2^n$. The last one follows since for any elements $x, x' \in \{0,1\}^n$ (not necessarily distinct) and any element $y \in \{0,1\}^n$, there exist at most two solutions for

$$k \cdot (k + x) + c \cdot k \cdot (k + x') = y .$$

3.2 Construction and Theorem

Let $h, h' : K \times \{0,1\}^n \to \{0,1\}^n$ be two hash functions which satisfy C1,...,C4 for some sufficiently small $\epsilon_1, \ldots, \epsilon_5$. Let $f \in F_n$ be a random function, k be the

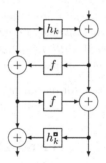

Fig. 3. Our construction. h, $h^\square$ satisfy C1,...,C4 and $f \in F_n$ is a random function. Note that k is the first κ bits of $f(\text{Const}_1),\dots,f(\text{Const}_l)$.

first κ bits of $f(\text{Const}_1),\dots,f(\text{Const}_l)$, and let k be the key of h and h', where $\text{Const}_1,\dots,\text{Const}_l$ are some fixed and distinct n-bit constants. For example Const_j is the n-bit binary representation of j.

Now we construct our four round Feistel permutation as:

$$\phi \overset{\text{def}}{=} \phi(h_k, f, f, h'_k),$$

where k is the first κ bits of $f(\text{Const}_1),\dots,f(\text{Const}_l)$. See Fig. 3.

Let $\Phi = \{\phi = \phi(h_k, f, f, h'_k) \mid f \in F_n\}$ and $R \in P_{2n}$ be a random permutation.

Then we obtain the following theorem (A proof is in the full version [6]).

Theorem 1. *For any adversary $\mathcal{A}$ that makes at most q queries in total,*

$$\mathbf{Adv}^{\text{sprp}}_{\Phi}(\mathcal{A}) \leq 2\epsilon q^2 - \epsilon q + 2\epsilon q l + \frac{q(q-1)}{2^{2n+1}},$$

where $\epsilon \overset{\text{def}}{=} \max\{\epsilon_1,\dots,\epsilon_5\}$.

Therefore, $\Phi = \{\phi = \phi(h_k, f, f, h'_k) \mid f \in F_n\}$ is a super-pseudorandom permutation family if ϵ is sufficiently small.

We obtain the following corollary.

Corollary 1. *Suppose that the example in Sec. 3.1 is used as h and h'. Then for any adversary $\mathcal{A}$ that makes at most q queries in total,*

$$\mathbf{Adv}^{\text{sprp}}_{\Phi}(\mathcal{A}) \leq \frac{4q^2}{2^n} + \frac{2q}{2^n} + \frac{q(q-1)}{2^{2n+1}}.$$

Proof. Let $\kappa = n$, $l = 1$, and $\epsilon = 2/2^n$ in Theorem 1.

Remark 1. Theorem 1 assumes that f is a random function. It is straight forward to prove that ϕ is a super-pseudorandom permutation even if f is a pseudorandom function, by using a standard hybrid argument. For example, see [9].

4   Construction Based on MISTY-Type Permutation

4.1   Universal Hash Functions

Let $h, h' : K \times \{0,1\}^n \rightarrow \{0,1\}^n$ be two (keyed) hash functions such that for each $k \in K$, $h(k, \cdot) \in P_n$ and $h'(k, \cdot) \in P_n$. We write $h_k(\cdot)$ for $h(k, \cdot)$ and $h'_k(\cdot)$ for $h'(k, \cdot)$. Suppose that h and h' satisfy the following conditions for sufficiently small $\epsilon_1, \ldots, \epsilon_9$.

C1. $K = \{(k_1, \ldots, k_l) \mid k_i \in \{0,1\}^n$ and $k_i \neq k_j$ for $1 \leq i < j \leq l\}$. In what follows, $k \xleftarrow{R} K$ means $k = (k_1, \ldots, k_l)$, where $k_i \neq k_j$. Note that $\#K = (2^n)!/(2^n - l)!$.

C2. For any element $x \in \{0,1\}^n$ and any element $y \in \{0,1\}^n$, $\Pr(k \xleftarrow{R} K : h_k(x) = y) \leq \epsilon_1$ and $\Pr(k \xleftarrow{R} K : h'_k(x) = y) \leq \epsilon_2$.

C3. For any two distinct elements $x, x' \in \{0,1\}^n$ and any element $y \in \{0,1\}^n$, $\Pr(k \xleftarrow{R} K : h_k(x) \oplus h_k(x') = y) \leq \epsilon_3$ and $\Pr(k \xleftarrow{R} K : h'_k(x) \oplus h'_k(x') = y) \leq \epsilon_4$.

C4. For any element $x \in \{0,1\}^n$, any element $y \in \{0,1\}^n$, and any $1 \leq i \leq l$, $\Pr(k \xleftarrow{R} K : h_k(x) \oplus k_i = y) \leq \epsilon_5$.

C5. For any two elements $x, x' \in \{0,1\}^n$ (not necessarily distinct), any element $y \in \{0,1\}^n$, and any $1 \leq i \leq l$, $\Pr(k \xleftarrow{R} K : h_k(x) \oplus h'_k(x') \oplus k_i = y) \leq \epsilon_6$.

C6. For any two distinct elements $x, x' \in \{0,1\}^n$, any two distinct elements $x'', x''' \in \{0,1\}^n$ and any element $y \in \{0,1\}^n$, $\Pr(k \xleftarrow{R} K : h_k(x) \oplus h_k(x') \oplus h'_k(x'') \oplus h'_k(x''') = y) \leq \epsilon_7$.

C7. For any two elements $x, x' \in \{0,1\}^n$ (not necessarily distinct) and any element $y \in \{0,1\}^n$, $\Pr(k \xleftarrow{R} K : h_k(x) \oplus h'_k(x') = y) \leq \epsilon_8$.

C8. For any two distinct elements $x, x' \in \{0,1\}^n$, any element $x'' \in \{0,1\}^n$, and any element $y \in \{0,1\}^n$, $\Pr(k \xleftarrow{R} K : h_k(x) \oplus h_k(x') \oplus h'_k(x'') = y) \leq \epsilon_9$.

C2 and C3 are standard definitions follow from those given in [1,15,24,27,34]. C4,...,C8 are new conditions. We show an example.

Let $l = 2$ in C1. For $k = (k_1, k_2) \in K$, let $h_k(x) = c_1 \cdot (k_1 \vee 0^{n-1}1) \cdot x + c_2 \cdot k_2$ and $h'_k(x) = c_3 \cdot (k_1 \vee 0^{n-1}1)^{-1} \cdot x + c_4 \cdot k_2$, where addition, multiplication and inversion are over $GF(2^n)$, and $c_1, \ldots, c_4 \in GF(2^n)$ are constants such that: (1) $c_1, c_3 \neq 0$, (2) $c_2 \neq 0, 1$, (3) $c_4 \neq 0$, and (4) $c_2 \oplus c_4 \neq 0, 1$. For example c_i is the n-bit binary representation of i. We note that bitwise-or is done so that h and h' become permutations.

Then it is easy to see that h and h' satisfy all of C1,...,C8 with $\epsilon_1 = \epsilon_2 = 1/(2^n - 1)$, $\epsilon_3 = \epsilon_4 = 2/(2^n - 1)$, $\epsilon_5 = \epsilon_6 = 1/(2^n - 1)$, $\epsilon_7 = 4/(2^n - 1)$, and $\epsilon_8 = \epsilon_9 = 1/(2^n - 1)$. ϵ_7 follows since for any two distinct elements $x, x' \in \{0,1\}^n$, any two distinct elements $x'', x''' \in \{0,1\}^n$ and any element $y \in \{0,1\}^n$, there exist at most two solutions s for

$$c_1 \cdot s \cdot x + c_1 \cdot s \cdot x' + c_3 \cdot s^{-1} \cdot x'' + c_3 \cdot s^{-1} \cdot x''' = y ,$$

and for each s, there are at most two k_1 which satisfies $s = k_1 \vee 0^{n-1}1$.

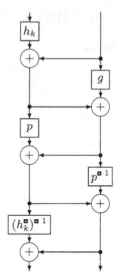

Fig. 4. Our construction. h, $h^\square$ satisfy C1,...,C8, $p \in P_n$ is a random permutation, and g is an orthomorphism. Note that $k = (p(\text{Const}_1), \ldots, p(\text{Const}_l))$, and $h_k(\cdot), h_k^\square(\cdot) \in P_n$.

4.2   Orthomorphism

A permutation g over $\{0,1\}^n$ is an orthomorphism if $x \mapsto g(x) \oplus x$ is also a permutation over $\{0,1\}^n$. That is, g is an orthomorphism if for any two distinct elements $x, x' \in \{0,1\}^n$, $g(x) \oplus x \neq g(x') \oplus x'$.

For example, let $g(x) = c \cdot x$ over $\text{GF}(2^n)$, where c is a fixed constant such that $c \neq 0, 1$. Then this g is an orthomorphism. Other examples can be found in [32].

Orthomorphisms are used in the analysis of the Lai-Massey scheme by Vaudenay [32] and also used in [7] with the name of XOR-distinct permutation.

4.3   Construction and Theorem

Let $h, h' : K \times \{0,1\}^n \to \{0,1\}^n$ be two hash functions which satisfy C1,...,C8 for some sufficiently small $\epsilon_1, \ldots, \epsilon_9$. Let $p \in P_n$ be a random permutation, $k = (k_1, \ldots, k_l) = (p(\text{Const}_1), \ldots, p(\text{Const}_l))$ be the key of h and h', where $\text{Const}_1, \ldots, \text{Const}_l$ are some fixed and distinct n-bit constants. Let g be an orthomorphism.

Now we construct our five round MISTY-type permutation as:

$$\psi \stackrel{\text{def}}{=} \psi(h_k, g, p, p^{-1}, h_k'^{-1}),$$

where $k = (p(\text{Const}_1), \ldots, p(\text{Const}_l))$. Note that $p^{-1} \in P_n$ and $h_k'^{-1} \in P_n$, and $p^{-1}(y)$ is the unique string x such that $p(x) = y$, and $h_k'^{-1}(y)$ is the unique string x such that $h_k'(x) = y$.

Let $\Psi = \{\psi = \psi(h_k, g, p, p^{-1}, {h'_k}^{-1}) \mid p \in P_n\}$ and $R \in P_{2n}$ be a random permutation.

Then we obtain the following theorem (A proof is in the full version [6]).

Theorem 2. *For any adversary $\mathcal{A}$ that makes at most q queries in total,*

$$\mathbf{Adv}_{\Psi}^{\mathrm{sprp}}(\mathcal{A}) \leq 4\epsilon q^2 - 2\epsilon q + 4\epsilon q l \ ,$$

where $\epsilon \overset{\mathrm{def}}{=} \max\{\epsilon_1, \ldots, \epsilon_9\}$.

Therefore $\Psi = \{\psi = \psi(h_k, g, p, p^{-1}, {h'_k}^{-1}) \mid p \in P_n\}$ is a super-pseudorandom permutation family if ϵ is sufficiently small.

We obtain the following corollary.

Corollary 2. *Suppose that the example in Sec. 4.1 is used as h and h'. Then for any adversary $\mathcal{A}$ that makes at most q queries in total,*

$$\mathbf{Adv}_{\Psi}^{\mathrm{sprp}}(\mathcal{A}) \leq \frac{16q^2}{2^n - 1} + \frac{24q}{2^n - 1} \ .$$

Proof. Let $l = 2$ and $\epsilon = 4/(2^n - 1)$ in Theorem 2.

Remark 2. Theorem 2 assumes that p is a random permutation. It is straight forward to prove that ψ is a super-pseudorandom permutation even if p is a super-pseudorandom permutation, by using a standard hybrid argument. See [9].

References

1. J. L. Carter and M. N. Wegman. Universal classes of hash functions. *J. Comput. Syst. Sci.,* vol. 18, no. 2, pp. 143–154, 1979.
2. H. Gilbert and M. Minier. New results on the pseudorandomness of some block cipher constructions. *Fast Software Encryption, FSE 2001, LNCS 2355,* pp. 248–266, Springer-Verlag.
3. S. Halevi and P. Rogaway. A tweakable enciphering mode. *Advances in Cryptology — CRYPTO 2003, LNCS 2729,* pp. 482–499, Springer-Verlag, 2003.
4. S. Halevi and P. Rogaway. A parallelizable enciphering mode. *Topics in Cryptology — CT-RSA 2004, LNCS 2964,* pp. 292–304, Springer-Verlag, 2004.
5. T. Iwata and K. Kurosawa. On the universal hash functions in Luby-Rackoff cipher. *Information Security and Cryptology — ICISC 2002, LNCS 2587,* pp. 226–236, Springer-Verlag.
6. T. Iwata and K. Kurosawa. How to re-use round function in super-pseudorandom permutation. A full version of this paper. Available from the author. 2004.
7. T. Iwata, T. Yoshino, and K. Kurosawa. Non-cryptographic primitive for pseudorandom permutation. *Fast Software Encryption, FSE 2002, LNCS 2365,* pp. 149–163, Springer-Verlag.
8. T. Iwata, T. Yoshino, T. Yuasa and K. Kurosawa. Round security and super-pseudorandomness of MISTY type structure. *Fast Software Encryption, FSE 2001, LNCS 2355,* pp. 233–247, Springer-Verlag.

234   T. Iwata and K. Kurosawa

9. M. Luby and C. Rackoff. How to construct pseudorandom permutations from pseudorandom functions. *SIAM J. Comput.*, vol. 17, no. 2, pp. 373–386, April 1988.
10. S. Lucks. Faster Luby-Rackoff ciphers. *Fast Software Encryption, FSE '96, LNCS 1039*, pp. 189–203, Springer-Verlag.
11. M. Matsui. New structure of block ciphers with provable security against differential and linear cryptanalysis. *Fast Software Encryption, FSE '96, LNCS 1039*, pp. 206–218, Springer-Verlag.
12. M. Matsui. New block encryption algorithm MISTY. *Fast Software Encryption, FSE '97, LNCS 1267*, pp. 54–68, Springer-Verlag.
13. U. M. Maurer. Indistinguishability of random systems. *Advances in Cryptology — EUROCRYPT 2002, LNCS 2332*, pp. 110–132, Springer-Verlag, 2002.
14. U. M. Maurer and K. Pietrzak. The security of many-round Luby-Rackoff pseudorandom permutations. *Advances in Cryptology — EUROCRYPT 2003, LNCS 2656*, pp. 544–561, Springer-Verlag, 2003.
15. M. Naor and O. Reingold. On the construction of pseudorandom permutations: Luby-Rackoff revised. *J. Cryptology*, vol. 12, no. 1, pp. 29–66, Springer-Verlag, 1999.
16. M. Naor and O. Reingold. A pseudo-random encryption mode. IEEE Computer Society, Security in Storage Working Group (SISWG). Available at http://siswg.org/, 2002.
17. Y. Ohnishi. A study on data security. Master's Thesis (in Japanese), Tohoku University, 1988.
18. J. Patarin. Pseudorandom permutations based on the DES scheme. *Proceedings of EUROCODE '90, LNCS 514*, pp. 193–204, Springer-Verlag, 1990.
19. J. Patarin. New results of pseudorandom permutation generators based on the DES scheme. *Advances in Cryptology — CRYPTO '91, LNCS 576*, pp. 301–312, Springer-Verlag, 1991.
20. J. Patarin. How to construct pseudorandom and super pseudorandom permutations from one single pseudorandom function. *Advances in Cryptology — EUROCRYPT '92, LNCS 658*, pp. 256–266, Springer-Verlag, 1992.
21. J. Patarin. Improved security bounds for pseudorandom permutations. *Proceedings of 4-th ACM Conference on Computer and Communications Security, ACM CCS '97*, pp. 142–150, 1997.
22. J. Patarin. About Feistel schemes with six (or more) rounds. *Fast Software Encryption, FSE '98, LNCS 1372*, pp. 103–121, Springer-Verlag, 1998.
23. J. Patarin. Luby-Rackoff: 7 rounds are enough for $2^{n(1-\varepsilon)}$ security. *Advances in Cryptology — CRYPTO 2003, LNCS 2729*, pp. 513–529, Springer-Verlag, 2003.
24. S. Patel, Z. Ramzan and G. Sundaram. Towards making Luby-Rackoff ciphers optimal and practical. *Fast Software Encryption, FSE '99, LNCS 1636*, pp. 171–185, Springer-Verlag, 1999.
25. S. Patel, Z. Ramzan and G. Sundaram. Luby-Rackoff ciphers: Why XOR is not so exclusive. *Selected Areas in Cryptography, SAC 2002, LNCS 2595*, pp. 271–290, Springer-Verlag.
26. J. Pieprzyk. How to construct pseudorandom permutations from single pseudorandom functions. *Advances in Cryptology — EUROCRYPT '90, LNCS 473*, pp. 140–150, Springer-Verlag, 1990.
27. Z. Ramzan and L. Reyzin. On the round security of symmetric-key cryptographic primitives. *Advances in Cryptology — CRYPTO 2000, LNCS 1880*, pp. 376–393, Springer-Verlag, 2000.

28. R. A. Rueppel. On the security of Schnorr's pseudorandom generator. *Advances in Cryptology — EUROCRYPT '89, LNCS 434,* pp. 423–428, Springer-Verlag, 1989.

29. B. Sadeghiyan and J. Pieprezyk. On necessary and sufficient conditions for the construction of super pseudorandom permutations. *Advances in Cryptology — ASIACRYPT '91, LNCS 739,* pp. 194–209, Springer-Verlag, 1991.

30. B. Sadeghiyan and J. Pieprezyk. A construction of super pseudorandom permutations from a single pseudorandom function. *Advances in Cryptology — EUROCRYPT '92, LNCS 658,* pp. 267–284, Springer-Verlag, 1992.

31. C. P. Schnorr. On the construction of random number generators and random function generators. *Advances in Cryptology — EUROCRYPT '88, LNCS 330,* pp. 225–232, Springer-Verlag, 1988.

32. S. Vaudenay. On the Lai-Massey scheme. *Advances in Cryptology — ASIACRYPT '99, LNCS 1716,* pp. 9–19, Springer-Verlag, 2000.

33. S. Vaudenay. Decorrelation: A theory for block cipher security. *J. Cryptology,* vol. 16, no. 4, pp. 249–286, 2003.

34. M. N. Wegman and J. L. Carter. New hash functions and their use in authentication and set equality. *J. Comput. Syst. Sci.,* vol. 22, no. 3, pp. 265–279, 1981.

35. Y. Zheng, T. Matsumoto, and H. Imai. Impossibility and optimality results on constructing pseudorandom permutations. *Advances in Cryptology — EUROCRYPT '89, LNCS 434,* pp. 412–422, Springer-Verlag, 1990.

How to Remove MAC from DHIES

Kaoru Kurosawa[1] and Toshihiko Matsuo[2]

[1] Ibaraki University,
4-12-1 Nakanarusawa, Hitachi, Ibaraki, 316-8511, Japan
kurosawa@cis.ibaraki.ac.jp
[2] Tokyo Institute of Technology,
2-12-1 Ookayama, Meguro-ku, Tokyo, 152-8552, Japan
tossy@crypt.ss.titech.ac.jp

Abstract. In this paper, we show that MAC can be eliminated from DHIES if the underlying symmetric-key encryption scheme is secure in the sense of IND-CCA. Further, ElGamal encryption part of DHIES *without MAC* is generalized to Half-Recovery (HR) schemes. Dependent-RSA encryption scheme [12] and Blum-Goldwasser encryption scheme [6] can be used as an HR scheme, for exmaple. Our construction also offers the first secure public-key encryption schemes with *no redundancy* in the *standard model*.

Keywords: DHIES, hybrid encryption scheme.

1 Introduction

DHIES (formerly named as DHAES) is a hybrid encryption scheme based on ElGamal encryption scheme [1,2]. It is in the draft standards of IEEE P1636a and ANSI X9.63 [1,3].

Abdalla et al. proved that DHIES is secure in the sense of IND-CCA (security against chosen ciphertext attack) under the Oracle Diffie-Hellman assumption (ODH assumption) in the standard model [2]. It requires a symmetric encryption scheme which is secure in the sense of IND-CPA (security against chosen plaintext attack) and a message authentication code (MAC) which is secure against chosen message attack.

In this paper, we show that MAC can be eliminated from DHIES if the underlying symmetric-key encryption scheme is more secure, *i.e.* secure in the sense of IND-CCA instead of IND-CPA. Hence the size of our ciphertexts becomes smaller. As the underlying symmetric encryption scheme, we can use the recently proposed modes, CMC mode [9] or EME mode [10]. They are both length preserving and still secure in the sense of IND-CCA.

Further, we generalize ElGamal encryption part of DHIES to Half-Recovery (HR) schemes. Dependent RSA encryption scheme [12] and Blum-Goldwasser encryption scheme [6] can be used as an HR scheme, for example. Similarly, ODH assumption is generalized to OHR assumption.

We then prove that such a generalized class of DHIES *without MAC* is secure in the sense of IND-CCA under the ODH assumption in the standard model. A

H. Wang et al. (Eds.): ACISP 2004, LNCS 3108, pp. 236–247, 2004.

cost is that the underlying symmetric-key encryption scheme must be secure in the sense of IND-CCA.

On the other hand, Desai [8] showed a symmetric-key encryption scheme which is secure in the sense of IND-CCA with *no redundancy*, where *no redundancy* means that every string is accepted as a valid ciphertext. Hence it has a smaller ciphertext expansion. Phan and Pointcheval showed a public-key encryption scheme which is secure in the sense of IND-CCA with *no redundancy* by using a random permutation [11]. They also applied it into the random oracle model [5]. However, the model of random permutation is very strong. The random oracle model is very strong, too.

Now our construction offers the first public-key encryption schemes which are secure in the sense of IND-CCA with *no redundancy* in the *standard model* if the CMC mode [9] or EME mode [10] is used as the underlying symmetric-key encryption scheme.

2   Preliminaries

We adopt a standard notation with respect to probabilistic algorithms and sets. If $A(\cdot, \cdot, \cdots)$ is a probabilistic algorithm, then $x \xleftarrow{R} A(x_1, x_2, \cdots)$ denotes the experiment of running A on input $x_1, x_2, \cdots$ and letting x be the outcome. We sometimes write $x = A(x_1, x_2, \cdots, r)$, where r is a random input. If S is a set, $x \xleftarrow{R} S$ denotes the experiment of choosing $x \in S$ at random. If G is a probability distribution on a set S, $x \xleftarrow{R} G$ denotes the experiment of choosing $x \in S$ according to G.

$|S|$ denotes the cardinality of S if S is a set. $|m|$ denotes the bit length of m if m is a string o a number.

2.1   Public-Key Encryption Scheme (PE)

A public-key encryption scheme PE is a three tuple of algorithms $(\mathcal{K}_p, \mathcal{E}_p, \mathcal{D}_p)$. The key generation algorithm $\mathcal{K}_p$ generates a pair $(pk, sk) \xleftarrow{R} \mathcal{K}_p$, where pk is a public key and sk is a secret key. The encryption algorithm $\mathcal{E}_p$ takes a public key pk and a plaintext m, then returns a ciphertext $c \xleftarrow{R} \mathcal{E}_p(pk, m)$. The decryption algorithm $\mathcal{D}_p$ takes a secret key sk and a ciphertext c, then returns $m/reject = \mathcal{D}_p(sk, c)$.

The security against chosen plaintext attack is defined as follows. We imagine a probabilistic polynomial time adversary $A = (A_1, A_2)$ that runs in two stages. In the "find" stage, A_1 takes a public key pk and returns a pair of equal length messages m_0 and m_1. It also retains some state information *state*. In the "guess" stage, let $b \xleftarrow{R} \{0,1\}$. A_2 is given a random (challenge) ciphertext c of m_b together with *state*. A_2 finally outputs a bit $\tilde{b}$. That is, we consider the following experiment.

$$(pk, sk) \xleftarrow{R} \mathcal{K}_p, \ (m_0, m_1, state) \xleftarrow{R} A_1(pk), \ b \xleftarrow{R} \{0,1\}, \ c \xleftarrow{R} \mathcal{E}_p(pk, m_b),$$

$$\tilde{b} \xleftarrow{R} A_2(pk, c, state).$$

The adversary A wins if $\tilde{b} = b$. The public-key encryption scheme PE is secure in the sense of IND-CPA if $|\Pr(\tilde{b} = b) - 1/2|$ is negligible.

The security against chosen ciphertext attack IND-CCA is defined similarly. The difference is that the adversary A is given access to a decryption oracle $\mathcal{D}_p(sk,)$ where A cannot query the challenge ciphertext c itself in the guess stage.

Definition 1. *Let* PE $= (\mathcal{K}_p, \mathcal{E}_p, \mathcal{D}_p)$ *be a public-key encryption scheme and let A be an adversary. Define the IND-CCA advantage of A as follows.*

$$\mathsf{Adv}_{\mathsf{PE}}^{cca}(A) = 2[\Pr(\tilde{b} = b) - 1/2]. \tag{1}$$

For any t, q_d and μ, define

$$\mathsf{Adv}_{\mathsf{PE}}^{cca}(t, q_d, \mu) = \max_A \mathsf{Adv}_{\mathsf{PE}}^{cca}(A)$$

where the maximum is over all A which runs in time t and makes at most q_d queries to the decryption oracle, and the total bit-length of queries is at most μ.

2.2　Symmetric-Key Encryption Scheme (SE)

A symmetric-key encryption scheme is a three tuple of algorithms SE $= (\mathcal{K}_s, \mathcal{E}_s, \mathcal{D}_s)$. The key generation algorithm $\mathcal{K}_s$ generates a key $k \xleftarrow{R} \mathcal{K}_s$. The encryption algorithm $\mathcal{E}_s$ takes a key k and a plaintext m, and returns a ciphertext $c \xleftarrow{R} \mathcal{E}_s(k, m)$. The decryption algorithm $\mathcal{D}_s$ takes a key k and a ciphertext c, then returns $m/reject = \mathcal{D}_s(k, c)$.

The security is defined similarly to Sec.2.1. The difference is that the adversary A can query to the encryption oracle $\mathcal{E}_s(k, \cdot)$ at most q_e times in the definition of IND-CPA. In addition that, A can query to the decryption oracle $\mathcal{D}_s(k, \cdot)$ at most q_d times in the definition of IND-CCA.

Definition 2. *Let* SE $= (\mathcal{K}_s, \mathcal{E}_s, \mathcal{D}_s)$ *be a symmetric-key encryption scheme and let A be an adversary. Define the IND-CCA advantage of A as follows.*

$$\mathsf{Adv}_{\mathsf{SE}}^{cca}(A) = 2[\Pr(\tilde{b} = b) - 1/2]. \tag{2}$$

For any t, q_e, q_d and μ, define

$$\mathsf{Adv}_{\mathsf{SE}}^{cca}(t, q_e, q_d, \mu) = \max_A \mathsf{Adv}_{\mathsf{SE}}^{cca}(A)$$

where the maximum is over all A which runs in time t, makes at most q_e queries to the encryption oracle and at most q_d queries to the decryption oracle, and the total bit-length of queries is at most μ.

We say that a SE is length preserving if $|\mathcal{E}_s(k, m)| = |m|$. In a length preserving SE, adversaries A is not allowed to query m_0 and m_1 to the encryption oracle, where (m_0, m_1) is the output of A in the find stage. A is also disallowed to make a query which can be answered trivially.

The CMC mode [9] and the EME mode [10] are length preserving. They are secure in the sense of IND-CCA if the underlying block cipher is a strong pseudorandom permutation (for example, AES [14] can be used).

(Remark) Halevi and Rogaway proved that the CMC mode and the EME mode are IND-CCA in the left-or-right sense [10,9]. However, we can easily derive that they are IND-CCA in the find-then-guess sense.

2.3 Message Authentication Code (MAC)

A message authentication code MAC is a three tuple of algorithms $(\mathcal{K}_a, \mathcal{T}_a, \mathcal{V}_a)$. The key generation algorithm $\mathcal{K}_a$ generates a key $k \xleftarrow{R} \mathcal{K}_a$. The message authentication algorithm $\mathcal{T}_a$ takes a key k and a plaintext m, then returns a tag $\tau \xleftarrow{R} \mathcal{T}_a(k, m)$. The verification algorithm $\mathcal{V}_a$ takes a key k and (m, τ), then returns 1 (means "accept") or 0 (means "reject").

The security against chosen message attack is defined as follows. We imagine a probabilistic polynomial time adversary A. It is given access to an message authentication oracle $\mathcal{T}_a(k, \cdot)$ which returns a tag τ on receiving a query m from the adversary A. It is also given access to an verification oracle $\mathcal{V}_a(k, \cdot)$ which returns "accept" or "reject" on receiving a message-tag pair (m, τ) from A. Finally, A outputs a forged plaintext-tag pair (m', τ') which is not previously obtained via a query to the oracle $\mathcal{T}_a(k, \cdot)$. That is, we consider the following experiment.

$$k \xleftarrow{R} \mathcal{K}_a, \ (m', \tau') \xleftarrow{R} A^{\mathcal{T}_a(k, \cdot), \mathcal{V}_a(k, \cdot)}$$

The adversary success forging if $\mathcal{V}_a(k, m', \tau') = 1$. The message authentication code MAC is secure in the sense of UNF-CMA if $\Pr(\mathcal{V}_a(k, m', \tau') = 1)$ is negligible.

Definition 3. *Let* MAC $= (\mathcal{K}_a, \mathcal{T}_a, \mathcal{V}_a)$ *be a message authentication code and let A be an adversary. Define the UNF-CMA advantage of A as follows.*

$$\text{Adv}_{\text{MAC}}^{cma}(A) = \Pr(\mathcal{V}_a(k, m', \tau') = 1). \tag{3}$$

For any t, q_a, q_v, μ and ν, define

$$\text{Adv}_{\text{MAC}}^{cma}(t, q_a, \mu, q_v, \nu) = \max_A \text{Adv}_{\text{MAC}}^{cma}(A)$$

where the maximum is over all A which runs in time t, makes at most q_a queries to the message authentication oracle the sum of whose length is at most μ, and makes at most q_v queries to the verification oracle the sum of whose length is at most ν.

3   DHIES

DHIES [3,1] is a hybrid encryption scheme which consists of ElGamal encryption scheme, a symmetric-key encryption scheme $\mathsf{SE} = (\mathcal{K}_s, \mathcal{E}_s, \mathcal{D}_s)$ and a message authentication scheme MAC.

Let G_q be a finite Abelian group of order q, where q is a prime. G_q can be constructed as a subgroup of Z_p^*, where p is a large prime. It can also be obtained from elliptic curves.

Let $H : G_q \to \{0,1\}^{l+\rho}$ be a hash function, where l is the length of keys of the SE and ρ is the length of keys of the MAC.

Key Generation. Choose a generator g of G_q at random. Choose $z \in Z_q$ at random and let $h = g^z$. The public key is (p, q, g, h) and the secret key is z.

Encryption. Given a message m, choose $r \in Z_q$ at random and compute $K = H(h^r)$. Parse K as $K_1 \| K_2$. Compute

$$u = g^r, \ e \stackrel{R}{\leftarrow} \mathcal{E}_s(K_1, m), \ \tau = \mathcal{T}_a(K_2, e),$$

where $\mathcal{T}_a(K_2, \cdot)$ is a tag generation algorithm of the MAC. The ciphertext is (u, e, τ).

Decryption. To decrypt a ciphertext $c = (u, e, \tau)$, compute $K_1 \| K_2 = H(u^z)$ and $m = \mathcal{D}_s(K_1, e)$. Check whether τ equals to $\mathcal{T}_a(K_2, e)$ or not. If it passes the check then output m, else output a reject symbol.

The Decisional Diffie-Hellman (DDH) assumption claims that a randomly generated (g, g^x, g^y, g^{xy}) and (g, g^x, g^y, r) are indistinguishable, where $r \stackrel{R}{\leftarrow} G_q$. The Oracle Diffie-Hellman (ODH) assumption claims that a randomly generated $(g, g^x, g^y, H(g^{xy}))$ and (g, g^x, g^y, r), where $r \stackrel{R}{\leftarrow} \{0,1\}^{l+\rho}$, are computationally indistinguishable even if a distinguisher D is given access to an oracle $\mathcal{H}_x$ where $\mathcal{H}_x$ returns $H(u^x)$ for a query u. In this definition, D is not allowed to query g^y to $\mathcal{H}_x$ if (g, g^x, g^y, v) is the input to D.

Abdalla et al. proved that DHIES is IND-CCA under the ODH assumption if the SE is IND-CPA and the MAC is UNF-CMA [2].

4   Extension of DHIES

In this section, we show that MAC can be eliminated from DHIES if the underlying symmetric-key encryption scheme is more secure, *i.e.* secure in the sense of IND-CCA instead of IND-CPA. Hence the size of our ciphertexts becomes smaller. As the underlying symmetric encryption scheme, we can use the recently proposed modes, CMC mode [9] or EME mode [10]. They are length preserving and still secure in the sense of IND-CCA.

Further, we generalize ElGamal encryption part of DHIES to a Half-Recovery (HR) scheme. Dependent RSA encryption scheme [12] and Blum-Goldwasser encryption scheme [6] can be used as an HR scheme, for example. Similarly, ODH assumption is generalized to OHR assumption.

We then prove that such a generalized class of DHIES *without MAC* is secure in the sense of IND-CCA under the ODH assumption in the standard model. A cost is that the underlying symmetric-key encryption scheme must be secure in the sense of IND-CCA.

4.1 Half Recovery Schemes

In a Half-Recovery (HR) scheme, (1) one can compute a valid (x, y) randomly from a base public key bp, and (2) one can compute y from x and a base secret key bs. For a hash function H, the Oracle-HR (OHR) assumption claims that $H(y)$ looks random independently of x even if a distinguisher D is given access to an oracle which returns $H(y^*)$ for a query x^*, where (x^*, y^*) is a valid pair.

Formally, a half-recovery scheme HR is a three tuple of algorithms $(\mathcal{BK}, \mathcal{BE}, \mathcal{BR})$ as follows.

- The base-key generation algorithm $\mathcal{BK}$ generates a pair $(bp, bs) \xleftarrow{R} \mathcal{BK}$, where bp is a base public key and bs is a base secret key.
- The base-encryption algorithm $\mathcal{BE}$ takes bp and returns a *valid pair* $(x, y) \xleftarrow{R} \mathcal{BE}(bp)$, where $x \in X$ and $y \in Y$. We require that x is uniformly distributed on X.
- The base-recovery algorithm $\mathcal{BR}$ takes bs and x, then returns y such that (x, y) is a valid pair. We require that y is uniquely determined from (bs, x).

Let $H : Y \rightarrow \{0, 1\}^l$ be a hash function. Define the Oracle-HR (OHR) assumption as follows: $U_0 = (bp, x, H(y))$ and $U_1 = (bp, x, r)$ are computationally indistinguishable, where $r \xleftarrow{R} \{0, 1\}^l$, even if a distinguisher D is given access to an oracle $\mathcal{H}_{bs}$ which returns $H(y^*)$ for a query x^*, where (x^*, y^*) is a valid pair. In this definition, D is not allowed to query x to $\mathcal{H}_{bs}$ if (bp, x, v) is the input to D. Formally,

Definition 4. *For a distinguisher D, consider the following experiment.*

$$(bp, bs) \xleftarrow{R} \mathcal{BK}, (x, y) \xleftarrow{R} \mathcal{BE}(bp), r \xleftarrow{R} \{0, 1\}^l.$$

Set $U_0 = (bp, x, H(y))$ and $U_1 = (bp, x, r)$. Define the OHR advantage of D as

$$\mathsf{Adv}_{\mathsf{HR}}^{ohr}(D) = 2|\Pr(D^{\mathcal{H}_{bs}}(U_0) = 1) - \Pr(D^{\mathcal{H}_{bs}}(U_1) = 1)|,$$

where $\mathcal{H}_{bs}$ is an oracle which returns $H(y^*)$ for a query x^*, where (x^*, y^*) is a valid pair. D is not allowed to query x to $\mathcal{H}_{bs}$ if $(bp, x, *)$ is the input to D.

For any t and q_d, define

$$\mathsf{Adv}_{\mathsf{HR}}^{ohr}(t, q_d) = \max_D \mathsf{Adv}_{\mathsf{HR}}^{ohr}(D)$$

where the maximum is over all D which runs in time t, makes at most q_d to its oracle.

4.2   Proposed Hybrid Encryption

Let $\mathsf{HR} = (\mathcal{BK}, \mathcal{BE}, \mathcal{BR})$ be a half-recovery scheme and $\mathsf{SE} = (\mathcal{K}_s, \mathcal{E}_s, \mathcal{D}_s)$ be a symmetric-key encryption scheme. Let $H : Y \to \{0,1\}^l$ be a hash function, where l is the key length of the SE. We then propose a hybrid encryption scheme HE as follows.

Key Generation. Let $(bp, bs) \overset{R}{\leftarrow} \mathcal{BK}$. The public key is bp and the secret key is bs.

Encryption. To encrypt a message m, compute

$$(x, y) \overset{R}{\leftarrow} \mathcal{BE}(bp), \ \ K = H(y), \ \ e \overset{R}{\leftarrow} \mathcal{E}_s(K, m).$$

The ciphertext is (x, e).

Decryption. To decrypt a ciphertext (x, e), compute

$$y = \mathcal{BR}(bs, x), \ \ K = H(y), \ \ m = \mathcal{D}_s(K, e),$$

and output m.

4.3   Security

We show that our HE is IND-CCA under the OHR assumption if the SE is IND-CCA.

Theorem 1. *For a security parameter ℓ, suppose that $|X| \geq |X_{min}|$. Let HE be the proposed hybrid encryption scheme and let SE be a symmetric-key encryption scheme. Then for any numbers t, q_d and μ,*

$$\mathsf{Adv}^{cca}_{\mathsf{HE}}(t, q_d, \mu) \leq \mathsf{Adv}^{ohr}_{\mathsf{HR}}(t', q_d) + \mathsf{Adv}^{cca}_{\mathsf{SE}}(t', 0, q_d, \mu) + 2q_d/|X_{min}|, \qquad (4)$$

where $t' = t + poly(\mu)$.

Proof. Let $A = (A_1, A_2)$ be an adversary who breaks the HE in the sense of IND-CCA. We consider a distinguisher D who breaks the OHR assumption using A as follows.

   D takes $U_0 = (bp, x^*, H(y^*))$ or $U_1 = (bp, x^*, r^*)$ as input, where (x^*, y^*) is a valid pair and $r^* \overset{R}{\leftarrow} \{0,1\}^l$. D can query to the oracle $\mathcal{H}_{bs}$, where $\mathcal{H}_{bs}$ returns $H(y)$ for a query x such that (x, y) is a valid pair. Denote the input to D as (bp, x^*, K^*), where $K^* = H(y^*)$ or r^*.

   D runs A on input bp. If A queries a ciphertext $c = (x, e)$ to the decryption oracle, then D first computes m as follows.

- If $x = x^*$, then let $m = \mathcal{D}_s(K^*, e)$.
- If $x \neq x^*$, then D queries x to the oracle $\mathcal{H}_{bs}$ which returns $H(y)$. Let $K = H(y)$ and compute $m = \mathcal{D}_s(K, e)$.

D next returns m to A.

At the end of the find stage, A_1 outputs a pair of messages m_0 and m_1. D then chooses $b = 0$ or 1 at random and computes $e^* \overset{R}{\leftarrow} \mathcal{E}_s(K^*, m_b)$. In the guess stage, D gives $c^* = (x^*, e^*)$ to A_2. A_2 finally outputs a bit $\tilde{b}$. D outputs 1 if $b = \tilde{b}$, and 0 otherwise. D then stops.

Case U_0. Suppose that the input to D is $U_0 = (bp, x^*, H(y^*))$. In this case, c^* is a valid ciphertext and D simulates the environment of A perfectly. Hence from eq. (1), we have

$$\Pr(D(U_0) = 1) = \frac{1}{2}\mathsf{Adv}_{\mathsf{HE}}^{cca}(A) + \frac{1}{2}. \tag{5}$$

Case U_1. Suppose that the input to D is $U_0 = (bp, x^*, r^*)$. We show that there exists an adversary B who attacks the SE in the sense of IND-CCA such that

$$\Pr(D(U_1) = 1) \leq \frac{1}{2}\mathsf{Adv}_{\mathsf{SE}}^{cca}(B) + \frac{1}{2} + \frac{q_d}{|X_{min}|}, \tag{6}$$

where B uses A as a subroutine. We consider an adversary $B = (B_1, B_2)$ for SE as follows.

In the find stage,
B_1 first generates (bp, bs) by running the key generation algorithm of the HE. B_1 next runs A_1 on input bp.
If A_1 queries to the decryption oracle, then B_1 runs the decryption algorithm of PE using the secret key bs.
If A_1 outputs (m_0, m_1) at the end of the find stage, then B_1 outputs the same (m_0, m_1).

In the guess stage,
B_2 is given a challenge ciphertext e^* such that $e^* \overset{R}{\leftarrow} \mathcal{E}_s(K^*, m_b)$, where $K^* \overset{R}{\leftarrow} \{0,1\}^l$ and $b \overset{R}{\leftarrow} \{0,1\}$.
B_2 runs A_2 on input $c^* = (x^*, e^*)$.
If A_2 queries a ciphertext $c = (x, e)$ to the decryption oracle, then B_2 behaves as follows.

- If $x \neq x^*$, then B_2 runs the decryption algorithm of the HE using the secret key bs.
- If $x = x^*$, then B_2 queries e to the decryption oracle $\mathcal{D}_s(K^*, \cdot)$ of the SE.

A_2 finally outputs a bit $\tilde{b}$, then B_2 outputs the same bit $\tilde{b}$. B then stops.

Now let Success be the event that B_2 outputs $\tilde{b}$ such that $\tilde{b} = b$. Then from eq. (2), we have

$$\Pr(\mathsf{Success}) = \frac{1}{2}\mathsf{Adv}_{\mathsf{SE}}^{cca}(B) + \frac{1}{2}.$$

On the other hand, let Good be the event that x^* has never been queried in the find stage. Then we can see that B behaves exactly in the same way as D does if Good occurs. Therefore,

$$\Pr(D(U_1) = 1 \mid \mathsf{Good}) = \Pr(\mathsf{Success} \mid \mathsf{Good}).$$

Hence

$$\Pr(D(U_1) = 1 \wedge \mathsf{Good}) = \Pr(\mathsf{Success} \wedge \mathsf{Good})$$

because x^* is randomly chosen. Now

$$
\begin{aligned}
\Pr(D(U_1) = 1) &= \Pr(D(U_1) = 1 \wedge \mathsf{Good}) + \Pr(D(U_1) = 1 \wedge \neg\mathsf{Good}) \\
&= \Pr(\mathsf{Success} \wedge \mathsf{Good}) + \Pr(D(U_1) = 1 \wedge \neg\mathsf{Good}) \\
&\leq \Pr(\mathsf{Success}) + \Pr(\neg\mathsf{Good}) \\
&\leq \left(\frac{1}{2} \mathsf{Adv}_{\mathsf{SE}}^{cca}(B) + \frac{1}{2} \right) + \frac{q_d}{|X_{min}|}
\end{aligned}
$$

because x^* is uniformly distributed on X.

Now from eq. (5) and eq. (6), we obtain that

$$\Pr(D(U_1) = 1) - \Pr(D(U_0) = 1) \leq \frac{1}{2} \mathsf{Adv}_{\mathsf{SE}}^{cca}(B) + \frac{q_d}{|X_{min}|} - \frac{1}{2} \mathsf{Adv}_{\mathsf{HE}}^{cca}(A).$$

Therefore,

$$
\begin{aligned}
\mathsf{Adv}_{\mathsf{HE}}^{cca}(A) &\leq 2(\Pr(D(U_0) = 1) - \Pr(D(U_1) = 1)) + \mathsf{Adv}_{\mathsf{SE}}^{cca}(B) + \frac{2q_d}{|X_{min}|} \\
&\leq 2|\Pr(D(U_0) = 1) - \Pr(D(U_1) = 1)| + \mathsf{Adv}_{\mathsf{SE}}^{cca}(B) + \frac{2q_d}{|X_{min}|} \\
&= \mathsf{Adv}_{\mathsf{HR}}^{ohr}(D) + \mathsf{Adv}_{\mathsf{SE}}^{cca}(B) + \frac{2q_d}{|X_{min}|}.
\end{aligned}
$$

Suppose that the arbitrary adversary A runs in time t and queries to the decryption oracle q_d times, and that the total bit-length of queries is μ. Since both of B and D can simulate in time $t' = t + poly(\mu)$, we obtain that

$$\mathsf{Adv}_{\mathsf{HE}}^{cca}(t, q_d, \mu) \leq \mathsf{Adv}_{\mathsf{HR}}^{ohr}(t', q_d) + \mathsf{Adv}_{\mathsf{SE}}^{cca}(t', 0, q_d, \mu) + \frac{2q_d}{|X_{min}|}.$$

5   Applications

5.1   Improvement of DHIES

The HR scheme related to DHIES is described as follows. Let g be a generator of G_q, where G_q is a finite group of prime order q. The base-key generation algorithm $\mathcal{BK}$ generates $bp = (g, \lambda(= g^i))$ and $bs = i$, where $i \xleftarrow{R} Z_q$. The base-encryption algorithm $\mathcal{BE}$ takes bp and returns $(g^w, \lambda^w) \xleftarrow{R} \mathcal{BE}(bp)$, where $w \xleftarrow{R} Z_q$. The base-recovery algorithm $\mathcal{BR}$ returns $\mathcal{BR}(i, g^w) = (g^w)^i = \lambda^w$. It is easy to see that the OHR assumption is equivalent to the ODH assumption.

Our hybrid encryption scheme is described as follows.

Key Generation. Generate $g \in G_q$ at random and choose $i \in Z_q$ at random. Compute $\lambda = g^i$. The public key is (p, q, g, λ) and the secret key is i.

Encryption. To encrypt a message m, choose $w \in Z_q$ at random, and compute

$$x = g^w, \ y = \lambda^w, K = H(y), \ e \xleftarrow{R} \mathcal{E}_s(K, m).$$

The ciphertext is (x, e).

Decryption. To decrypt a ciphertext (x, e), compute

$$y = x^i, K = H(y), \ m = \mathcal{D}_s(K, e)$$

and outputs m.

From Theorem 1, this scheme is IND-CCA under the ODH assumption if the SE is IND-CCA. (On the other hand, the SE is IND-CPA in DHIES.)

The size of our ciphertexts is smaller than that of DHIES because a MAC is not used in our scheme. For comparison, suppose that G_q is a subgroup of Z_p^* and the SE is length preserving. Then the size of our ciphertexts is $|p| + |m|$ while that of DHIES is $|p| + |m| + |\tau|$, where τ is a tag of the MAC. See Table 1.

Table 1. The proposed construction and DHIES

	size of ciphertext	MAC	SE
DHIES	$|p| + |m| + |\tau|$	Needed	IND-CPA
Proposal	$|p| + |m|$	No use	IND-CCA

5.2 Application to Dependent-RSA

The HR scheme related to Dependent-RSA encryption scheme [12] is described as follows. Let (N, e) be a public key and d be the secret key of RSA. The base-key generation algorithm $\mathcal{BK}$ generates $bp = (N, e)$ and $bs = d$ The base-encryption algorithm $\mathcal{BE}$ takes bp and returns $(w^e, (w + 1)^e) \bmod N$ where $w \xleftarrow{R} Z_N^*$. The base-recovery algorithm $\mathcal{BR}$ returns $\mathcal{BR}(d, w^e) = ((w^e)^d + 1)^e \bmod N$.

The OHR assumption is that $(N, e, w^e, H((w + 1)^e))$ and (N, e, w^e, r) are indistinguishable, where $r \xleftarrow{R} \{0, 1\}^l$, even if a distinguisher D is given access to an oracle $\mathcal{H}_d$ which returns $H((u + 1)^e)$ for a query u^e.

The related hybrid encryption scheme will be given in the final paper.

5.3 Application to Blum-Goldwasser

The HR scheme related to Blum-Goldwasser encryption scheme [6] is described as follows. Let p, q be two large primes such that $p = q = 3 \bmod 4$, and let $N = pq$. The base-key generation algorithm $\mathcal{BK}$ generates $bp = N$ and $bs = (p, q)$. The base-encryption algorithm $\mathcal{BE}$ takes bp and returns (x, y) as follows. Let

$w \xleftarrow{R} Z_N^*$ and $x_0 = w^2 \bmod N$. For $i = 1, \cdots, t$, let $x_i = x_{i-1}^2 \bmod N$ and y_i be the least significant bit of x_i. Finally, let $x = x_t^2 \bmod N$ and $y = (y_1, \cdots, y_t)$. The base-recovery algorithm returns $\mathcal{BR}((p, q), x) = y$.

The OHR assumption is that for $t > l$, $(N, x, H(y_1, \cdots, y_t))$ and $(N, x, r_1, \cdots, r_l)$ are indistinguishable, where $(r_1, \cdots, r_l) \xleftarrow{R} \{0, 1\}^l$, even if a distinguisher D is given access to an oracle $\mathcal{H}_{p,q}$ which returns $H(y^*)$ for a query x^*, where $y^* = \mathcal{BR}((p, q), x^*)$.

The related hybrid encryption scheme will be given in the final paper.

6   Discussion

6.1   On the Security of Symmetric-Key Encryption

The proposed scheme is not secure in the sense of IND-CCA if the underlying symmetric-key encryption scheme is not secure in the sense of IND-CCA in general.

It is easy to show such an example by using counter mode [4]. The counter mode is a block-cipher based symmetric-key encryption scheme which is secure in the sense of IND-CPA, but not secure in the sense of IND-CCA.

6.2   Relationship to KEM

Shoup formalized the notion of a key encapsulation mechanism (KEM) for hybrid encryption schemes [13]. A key encapsulation scheme (KEM) works just like a public-key encryption scheme, except that the encryption algorithm takes no input other than the recipient's public key. Instead, the encryption algorithm generates a pair (K, ψ), where K is a key of SE and ψ is an encryption of K.

Now our notion of HR schemes together with the OHR assumption provides a general framework to construct a secure KEM. In fact, a part of the proposed scheme can be seen as a KEM, where $K = H(y)$ and $\psi = x$.

Recently, Cramer and Shoup derived an inequation similar to eq.(4) [7, Theorem 5]. However, they overlooked the last term $2q_d/|X_{min}|$.

6.3   No Redundancy

Desai [8] showed a symmetric-key encryption scheme which is secure in the sense of IND-CCA with *no redundancy*, where *no redundancy* means that every string is accepted as a valid ciphertext. Hence it has a smaller ciphertext expansion. Phan and Pointcheval showed a public-key encryption scheme which is secure in the sense of IND-CCA with *no redundancy* by using a random permutation [11]. They also applied it into the random oracle model [5]. However, the model of random permutation is very strong. The random oracle model is very strong, too.

Now it is easy to see that our construction offers the first public-key encryption schemes which are secure in the sense of IND-CCA with *no redundancy* in the *standard model* if the CMC mode [9] or EME mode [10] is used as the underlying symmetric-key encryption scheme.

References

1. M. Abdalla, M. Bellare and P. Rogaway, DHAES: an encryption scheme based on the Diffie-Hellman problem. Submission to IEEE P1363, 1998
2. M. Abdalla, M. Bellare and P. Rogaway, "The oracle Diffie-Hellman assumption and an analysis of DHIES ", In *Topics in Cryptology - CT-RSA'01, Lecture Notes in Computer Science* LNCS 2020, pages 143-158. Springer-Verlag, 2001.
3. American National Standards Institute (ANSI) X9.F1 subcommittee. ANSI X9.63 Public key cryptography for the Financial Services Industry: Elliptic curve key agreement and key transport schemes, 1998. Working draft version 2.0.
4. M. Bellare, A. Desai, E. Jokipii and P. Rogaway, "A concrete security treatment of secret-key encryption: Analysis of the DES modes of operation ", In *Proc. of the 38th Annual Symposium on Foundations of Computer Science - FOCS'97*, pages 394-403. IEEE, 1997. Current version available at URL of first author.
5. M. Bellare and P. Rogaway, "Random oracles are practical: A paradigm for designing efficient protocols ", In *ACM Conference on Computer and Communications Security 1993* pages 62-73, 1993.
6. M. Blum and S. Goldwasser, "An efficient probabilistic public key encryption scheme which hides all partial information ", In *Advances in Cryptology - CRYPTO'84, Lecture Notes in Computer Science* LNCS 196, pages 289-302. Springer-Verlag, 1985.
7. R. Cramer and V. Shoup, "Design and analysis of practical public-key encryption schemes secure against adaptive chosen ciphertext attack ", SIAM J. Comput. 33, no. 1, 167–226 (electronic), 2003
8. A. Desai, "New paradigms for constructing symmetric encryption schemes secure against chosen-ciphertext attack ", In *Advances in Cryptology - CRYPTO'00, Lecture Notes in Computer Science* LNCS 1880, pages 394-412. Springer-Verlag, 2000.
9. S. Halevi and P. Rogaway, "A tweakable enciphering mode ", In *Advances in Cryptology - CRYPTO'03, Lecture Notes in Computer Science* LNCS 2729, pages 482-499. Springer-Verlag, 2003.
10. S. Halevi and P. Rogaway, "A parallelizable enciphering mode ", CT-RSA 2004, pp.292-304, 2004
11. D. Phan and D. Pointcheval, "Chosen-ciphertext security without redundancy ", In *Advances in Cryptology - ASIACRYPT'03, Lecture Notes in Computer Science* LNCS 2894, pages 1-18. Springer-Verlag, 2003.
12. D. Pointcheval, "New public key cryptosystems based on the Dependent-RSA problems ", In *Advances in Cryptology - EUROCRYPT'99, Lecture Notes in Computer Science* LNCS 1592, pages 239-254. Springer-Verlag, 1999.
13. V. Shoup, "Using hash functions as a hedge against chosen ciphertext attack ", In *Advances in Cryptology - EUROCRYPT'00, Lecture Notes in Computer Science* LNCS 1807, pages 275-288. Springer-Verlag, 2000.
14. U.S. Department of Commerce/National Bureau of Standards, National Technical Information Service, Springfield, Virginia. FIPS 197. *Advanced Encryption Standard*. Federal Information Processing Standards Publication 197, 2001.

Symmetric Key Authentication Services Revisited

Bruno Crispo, Bogdan C. Popescu, and Andrew S. Tanenbaum

Vrije Universiteit, Amsterdam
{crispo,bpopescu,ast}@cs.vu.nl

Abstract. Most of the symmetric key authentication schemes deployed today are based on principles introduced by Needham and Schroeder [15] more than twenty years ago. However, since then, the computing environment has evolved from a LAN-based client-server world to include new paradigms, including wide area networks, peer-to-peer networks, mobile ad-hoc networks and ubiquitous computing. Also, there are new threats, including viruses, worms and denial of service attacks.
In this paper we review existing symmetric key authentication protocols in the light of these changes, and propose a authentication infrastructure design specifically tailored to address the latest developments in the distributed computing landscape. The key element in our design is placing the authentication server off-line, which greatly strengthens the security of its cryptographic material and shields it from denial of service attacks. Although the authentication server is not accessible on-line, our scheme can handle a dynamic client population, as well as critical issues such as re-issuing of keys and revocation.

1 Introduction

Authentication is the foundation of most security services. The LAN-based, client-server-centric distributed computing environment of the mid 80's and early 90's was the golden age of authentication protocols based on symmetric key cryptography [15,16,13]. However, the distributed computing landscape has changed in the past few years: migration to wide area networks (WAN), peer to peer (P2P), mobile ad-hoc networks (MANET), and ubiquitous computing are just the major paradigm shifts. Authentication protocols based on public key cryptography are deemed to be better suited for this new environment, so recently they have been overshadowing the older symmetric key-based designs. Nevertheless, public key cryptography has its limitations: it is slower and requires larger keys than symmetric key cryptography, and involves CPU-intensive computations, which make it unsuitable for small, battery powered devices. Furthermore, developments in quantum computing may bring an end to some public key cryptosystems [18] (however, this is an unlikely scenario at least in the near future).

Given the fact that PKIs are by no means the "silver bullet" that solves all the problems related to authentication in distributed systems, it seems worth exploring whether protocols based on symmetric key encryption can be re-engineered

H. Wang et al. (Eds.): ACISP 2004, LNCS 3108, pp. 248–261, 2004.
© Springer-Verlag Berlin Heidelberg 2004

to be made more secure and reliable and constitute a viable alternative in all the cases where authentication rather than non-repudiation is the requirement. In this paper we examine symmetric key authentication protocols in this new light, point out the limitations of current designs, and propose an authentication infrastructure which overcomes these limitations, and is better suited for the reshaped distributed computing environment. The pivotal point in our design is placing the trusted authentication authority off-line, which removes the vulnerabilities present in existing protocols, in particular their exposure to hacking and denial of service (DoS) attacks. Although clients can no longer directly access the authentication server, our infrastructure can still handle a dynamic client population, with the condition that the maximum size of this population is known in advance. To the best of our knowledge, this is the first symmetric key authentication infrastructure that is based on an *off-line* trusted third party (TTP) *and* supports a dynamic client population.

The rest of the paper is organized as follows: in Section 2 we elaborate on the motivation for this paper, and in Section 3 we look at related work, focusing on protocols that allow the authentication server to be placed off-line. Following this, in Section 4 we describe the proposed authentication infrastructure, in Section 5 we look at key update and revocation issues, and in Section 6 we briefly describe our prototype implementation and a number of performance measurements we have done on it. We conclude in Section 7.

2   Motivation for a New Design

Most symmetric key authentication protocols derive from the seminal work of Needham and Schroeder [15,16]. The goal of the protocol is to allow two principals, A and B, to authenticate each other and establish a secure communication channel. A trusted authentication server AS shares a long term symmetric key with each principal and is capable of generating and sending "good" session keys on the request of these principals.

There are two main reasons why we believe symmetric key authentication services require an update: first, the state of the art implementations in this area [13,4,10] are based upon ten year old designs, with clear limitations. Second, the past few years have brought a number of major technological advances, but to our knowledge, no new symmetric key authentication technique based on these advances has yet been proposed.

2.1   New Developments in Distributed Computing

The distributed computing landscape has been more or less reshaped in the past years by a number of technological advances. Table 1 lists the major paradigm shifts, points out their consequences, and explains why existing symmetric key authentication infrastructures are not well suited to handle them.

Table 1. New developments in the distributed computing landscape

New paradigm	Consequences	Limitations of existing symmetric key authentication infrastructures
Migration to WAN	Network latency and bandwidth display great variability. DoS attacks are much more frequent and harder to prevent.	They were designed assuming "almost" synchronous LAN communication. Possible DoS attacks were not directly addressed in their design.
Personal computing devices (i.e., PDA's, laptops, smart-phones, etc.)	Users possess powerful **personal** computing devices. Such devices can generate good random numbers and symmetric keys. They have enough memory to store millions of keys. Users do not share these devices.	They were designed for a world consisting of shared workstations, where the only piece of information a user could securely carry around was a short password.
Peer-to-peer	User to user interaction becomes a lot more frequent.	Needham-Schroeder schemes mostly deal with the client-server model.
MANET	User devices may be portable and equipped with wireless adapters. Continuous connectivity cannot be assumed in a wireless network environment	They require an on-line authentication server, reachable by all parties.

2.2 Vulnerabilities in Traditional Symmetric Key Authentication Infrastructures

Existing symmetric key authentication infrastructures require the participation of the TTP not only during the authentication phase, but also for generating the session key. Thus, the TTP is actively involved every time any two clients need to establish a secure connection. This leads to the following shortcomings:

- The AS is a **single point of failure** because when the AS is out of service users cannot independently establish a new secure session. This makes it a particularly attractive target for DoS attacks.
- The AS is a performance **bottleneck**, since all the users need to contact the server for each new session they want to establish.
- Session keys are generated and distributed by the AS upon request. This means the AS server must be on-line. As a consequence the AS is an **highly sensitive target** since compromising the AS would result in a possible compromise of all the subsequent private communications among all users registered with that particular AS. Furthermore key material is **continuously exposed** since the AS needs to be online.

Our authentication infrastructure overcomes these limitations, and at the same time is better suited for the re-shaped distributed computing landscape. The pivotal point in our design is placing the AS server off-line - this reduces the risk of compromising the AS's cryptographic material, shields it from DoS attacks, and makes the infrastructure more appropriate for environments such as MANET, where continuous network connectivity cannot be assumed.

3   Related Work

As we already mentioned, most of the existing symmetric key authentication infrastructures [13,4,10] suffer from the limitations pointed out in Section 2, which stem from the need for the AS to be always on-line. However, the idea of redefining the role of the AS by decoupling the initial authentication of principals from the subsequent use of their session keys is not completely new, and a number of protocols aiming at this have already been proposed. The Neuman-Stubblebine [17] and KSL [12] protocols are two examples. Both these protocols allow session keys generated in an initial exchange involving the AS to be re-used in subsequent sessions, which do not involve the AS. As a result, the load on the AS can be greatly reduced, which overcomes some of the limitations mentioned earlier. However, in both these protocols the emphasis is on the use of nonces versus timestamps for freshness purposes, rather than re-designing the role of the AS. Furthermore, both these protocols are vulnerable to the attack described in [9], due to the way they re-use old session keys in the repeated authentication part of the protocol. Another drawback of both these protocols is that they are asymmetric: although the keys generated for the first session can be reused, only the initiator of the first exchange can start subsequent sessions.

In [11] Kao and Chow propose a protocol allowing re-using of session keys that is resistant to the attack described in [9]. This protocol is also symmetric, and provides a better solution compared to the previous ones. However, it still requires the two clients to contact the AS server for the first secure session they want to establish; although the traffic towards the AS is greatly reduced, the server still needs to be on-line, and thus subject to the security threats mentioned earlier.

A similar solution has been proposed by Boyd [6,7]. His protocol introduces a novel way to provide freshness by random input generated by users and a long term shared key distributed initially by the server. The protocol relies on the security property of *keyed hash functions* used as a basic primitive to generate fresh session keys. In detail, this protocol is as follows:

(1) $A \longrightarrow AS$: A, B
(2) $AS \longrightarrow A$: $\{A, B, K_S\}_{K_{AAS}}, \{A, B, K_S\}_{K_{BAS}}$
(3) $A \longrightarrow B$: $A, B, \{A, B, K_S\}_{K_{BAS}}, N_A$
(4) $B \longrightarrow A$: $[N_A]_{K_{AB}}, N_B$
(5) $A \longrightarrow B$: $[N_B]_{K_{AB}}$

where $K_{AB} = f(K_S, N_A, N_B)$ and f is an agreed-upon keyed hash function. $[M]_K$ is a transformation that only provides integrity (e.g. MAC). Once two clients run the above protocol, they can subsequently re-authenticate without contacting the server, by producing a new authenticated and fresh session key by completing the following protocol:

(1) A $\longrightarrow$ B: A, B, N'_A
(2) B $\longrightarrow$ A: $[N'_A]_{K'_{AB}}, N'_B$
(3) A $\longrightarrow$ B: $[N'_B]_{K'_{AB}}$

where $K'_{AB} = f(K_S, N'_A, N'_B)$. The fact that K'_{AB} depends on both N'_A and N'_B provides an association between message 2 and 3, thus preventing oracle session attacks [5]. The protocol is symmetric, since either A or B can initiate it. What it is still unsatisfactory here is that no specific expiration date is set for the long term secret K_S, leading to the possibility of cryptanalytic attacks. Despite this, [6] is the first to acknowledge that re-usable session keys do not come for free, since they require revocation mechanisms (to guard against possible key compromise), but does not propose any specific mechanism to address the revocation problem.

4   A Symmetric Key Authentication Framework Based on Offline TTPs

We propose a symmetric key authentication framework based on an **off-line** TTP. Most importantly, our framework can accommodate a dynamic client population and specifically addresses the problems of key update and revocation. Our system model consists of the following entities:

- A trusted **Authentication Server** (AS). The authentication server is responsible with registering clients - associating a number of attributes (names for example) to a cryptographic identity (in this case a set of symmetric keys). The AS is a key element in our security infrastructure, and its compromise is a catastrophic event. In order to strengthen its security and to shield it from DoS attacks, the AS is not accessible on-line.
- The **clients** - a number of computing devices interacting with each other. These include both human users and a variety of electronic services. Based on the peer-to-peer paradigm, we assume that any random pair of clients may want to interact (and authenticate each other). Clients may use a great variety of computing platforms - ranging from personal digital assistants and smart phones to high end application servers. We assume each client has a reasonably powerful CPU capable of performing symmetric cryptographic operations, a reasonably large amount of memory (both volatile and non volatile) and a network connection. However, our system does not require continuous network connectivity.
- A number of **infrastructure directories**. These are semi-trusted entities, in the sense that their compromise will not lead to a security breach, but may result in denial of service. Their purpose is to guarantee availability and they work more or less like caches.

Before a client can start using the authentication infrastructure, it has to go through a registration phase, which requires a secure physical channel between the client and the AS. By no means is this registration step specific only to our framework; in any authentication protocol based on TTPs there is an implicit registration phase, when a new client establishes a shared master secret with the AS by out-of-band means.

During the registration phase, the AS presumably checks the client's identity much in the same way as a Certification Authority would do it in a PKI. After verifying its credentials, the AS issues the client an endorsement, in the form of the *client authentication database*, which the client can use to authenticate itself to other clients. This endorsement is only valid for a limited period of time (in the order of months, even years). After this endorsement expires, the client needs to contact the AS again in order to obtain new authentication material - we call this step *key update*. The AS can also render a client's endorsement unusable before its natural expiration - we call is step *key revocation*.

The idea is to have every client in the realm share a secure *certified* symmetric key with every other *potential* client at registration time. Since identity information and issue/expiration times cannot be known in advance for future clients, this information needs to be explicitly exchanged during the authentication phase by the two clients involved, which results in a slightly modified authentication protocol.

In detail, the registration phase works as follows: assuming the maximum client population size N is known in advance, the AS starts with a *potential client key list* of N symmetric keys. When a new client A wants to register, the AS takes the next unused key K_I in the list and passes it to the client over the secure registration channel (K_I now becomes the *master client key* for A). The AS then updates its client records (shown in Figure 1) by associating $A's$ identity to the corresponding index I in the key list, the client's registration time - T_{issue_I}, and the time after which the client's registration expires - T_{expire_I}. The AS then generates for A an *introduction certificates database* consisting of $N-1$ (SIK_{IJ}, IC_{IJ}) tuples, for $J \in \{0, .., N-1\}$ and $J \neq I$, with SIK_{IJ} - the *secure introduction key* being a random symmetric key, and IC_{IJ} - $I's$ *introduction certificate* to J - of the form $\{SIK_{IJ}, I, J, SHA\text{-}1(Name_A), T_{issue_I}, T_{expire_I}\}_{K_J}$. The introduction certificates database can then be passed to the client by means of the same secure channel. Thus, the registration phase for client A is as follows:

(1) A $\longrightarrow$ AS: $Name_A$

(2) AS $\longrightarrow$ A: $I, K_I, T_{issue_I}, T_{expire_I}, (SIK_{IJ}, IC_{IJ})_{J \in \{0,..,N\}, J \neq I}$

Alternatively, $A's$ authentication database can be encrypted under K_I and placed on the untrusted directories, so that A can download it when needed. As an optimization, the AS can even encrypt individual rows in the database (that is individual (SIK_{IJ}, IC_{IJ}) pairs); in this way, A can only download the introduction certificates it needs during the authentication phase (however, if the size of the authentication database is too large, this may expose the master client key to cryptanalytic attacks).

For the authentication phase, consider a client A that wants to establish a secure session with a client B. We assume both A and B have registered with the AS, and they have been assigned the client indices I and J respectively. The protocol is as follows:

B. Crispo, B.C. Popescu, and A.S. Tanenbaum

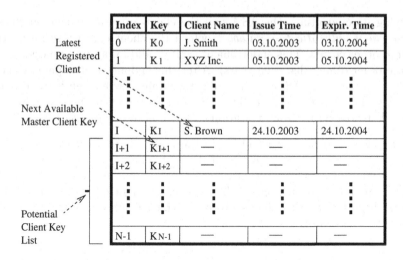

Fig. 1. AS client records

(1) A $\longrightarrow$ B: I, N_A
(2) B $\longrightarrow$ A: J, N_B, IC_{JI}
(3) A $\longrightarrow$ B: $\{Name_A, N_B\}_{K_{AB}}, IC_{IJ}$
(4) B $\longrightarrow$ A: $\{Name_B, N_A\}_{K_{AB}}$

In the above protocol, $K_{AB} = f(SIK_{IJ}, SIK_{JI}, N_A, N_B)$. We assume that initially A and B are complete strangers (they do not know each other's client indices). In steps (3) and (4) of the protocol, A and B exchange their names, protected under the shared secret (so no attacker can infer the identities of the authenticating parties). Before producing any cipher-text, both A and B decrypt IC_{JI} and IC_{IJ} respectively, and check that the expiration time in these certificates has not already passed; this prevents the usage of old (potentially compromised) ICs. Also, both parties must compute the *SHA-1* digest of the other party's name and make sure it matches the digest in the *IC*.

5   Key Update and Revocation

Our authentication scheme makes clients' transactions independent from the AS, which can now be placed off-line. The price we have to pay for this is lack of freshness: in our protocol SIKs are not freshly generated for each session but instead pre-distributed by means of an authentication database. However, because of possible cryptanalytic attacks, symmetric keys can only be used for a limited time, after which they should be discarded and replaced with fresh cryptographic material; furthermore, when exceptional events occur, keys may also need to be revoked. In this section we show how the scheme we propose can be modified in order to allow efficient key update and revocation.

5.1 Key Update

When a client registers, it receives from the AS a symmetric master client key and an authentication database. To prevent key compromise due to cryptanalytic attacks, the AS also sets a limit on how long the client is allowed to use this key material. This time limit is expressed through the T_{expire} value present in each IC. All the clients in the realm are required to reject an IC for which the T_{expire} has passed (this has the additional benefit of giving the AS certain control over the client). A client whose T_{expire} has passed needs to contact the AS to get new keys (key update).

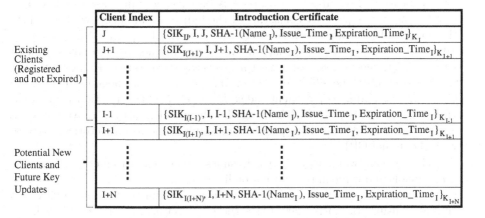

Fig. 2. The client IC database after a key update. It is assumed the client performing the update is assigned the new client index I, and the index of the earliest registered client not yet expired is J. N is the maximum number of clients in the realm.

One property that needs to be enforced here is *locality*: a key update should only affect the client that performs it, and none of the other clients. This is essential if we want to achieve our goal of keeping the AS off-line.

For the sake of simplicity, let us assume the client master key lifetime is the same for all clients (however, the key update mechanism is more or less the same, even if client key lifetime is not the same for all clients, only the formula for calculating the total memory requirements will change). If N is the maximum number of clients in the realm, the locality property can be achieved by requiring clients to store an authentication database consisting of at most $2 * N$ ICs. Key update works as depicted in Figure 2: when contacted by client A for a key update, the AS creates a new database consisting of ICs for all the other clients not expired at that moment (at most N) **and** N extra ICs, for the next N consecutive keys in the potential clients key list. The AS needs to ensure it always has at least N unused entries in this list, by generating new keys when it drops below this threshold. In this way, client A is guaranteed to have an IC for every other non-expired client in the realm. Furthermore, should new clients register, or existing clients perform the key update, they will be assigned one of the next N unused client master keys, for which A is also given an IC. Since there can be at most N clients, and the master client key lifetime is the same for all of them, there can be at most N new client master keys issued until $A's$ key will expire again, so A is guaranteed to have ICs for every new client master key to be issued. In this way, clients only need to contact the AS for key updates, and the locality property is achieved.

5.2   Key Revocation

The revocation mechanism we propose is based on certificate revocation lists (*CRL*): the AS keeps a list consisting of the indices of all clients whose authentication databases have been revoked, and periodically pushes this list to the infrastructure directories. Because the directories are not trusted not to tamper with this list, clients need a mechanisms to verify its integrity. To facilitate this, the AS computes one *CRL authentication code* for each client (and potential client) in the realm. For a client index I, the CRL authentication code is the *HMAC-SHA-1* [14] of the CRL using the client master key K_I. All the CRL authentication codes are then pushed to the infrastructure directories, together with the actual CRL.

When a client wants to verify the freshness of a given introduction certificate, it first needs to download the revocation list from the closest directory. The client then requests the CRL authenticator code corresponding to its client index, and verifies it using its master key. Once the CRL verification has succeeded, the client can proceed with validating the IC, by verifying that the client index in the IC is not present in the revocation list.

We can see that in this case revocation is more expensive than in a traditional PKI: for each CRL, the AS needs to generate a number of CRL authenticator codes linear to the number of clients; for traditional PKIs the CRL only needs to be signed once. This workload can be reduced if the infrastructure directories are trusted to correctly disseminate revocation information, in which case, the AS does not need to generate any CRL authenticator codes, (but clients need to establish secure channels with the directories when downloading the revocation list).

Key revocation also has implications on size of the client introduction certificates database. In the previous section, we showed that in order to ensure that a client only needs to contact the AS for registration or key update, it needs an IC database with at most $2 * N$ entries. When calculating this, we assumed N to be the maximum number of clients in the realm, so during a key lifetime, at most N key updates could occur. However, if clients can revoke their keys before expiration time, the total number of key issued can be larger than the number of clients (some clients may be issued more than one key during a key lifetime interval). Assuming that P is the probability that a client master key is revoked before expire, the new maximum size for the client IC database becomes $(2 + P) * N$.

It is worth noticing that although revocation significantly increases the AS workload, it does not require it to be on-line (it only needs an unidirectional network connection to the directories in order to periodically push the revocation information); furthermore, the tasks of credential issuing and revocation can be separated, as suggested in [2]. By introducing a separate revocation authority, we can even have the AS disconnected from the network (since it does not even need to push the revocation information to directories), which would greatly increase its security.

6   Performance Evaluation

We are in the advanced stages of building a prototype implementation for our authentication infrastructure, and we plan to experimentally deploy it at the Vrije Universiteit campus in Amsterdam. Our prototype consists of an Authentication Server and a client credential management library.

The Authentication Server is a stand-alone application that manages the master client key list, generates the IC database for client registration and credentials update, and manages credentials revocation. Its C source code consists of about two thousand lines of code. At initialization, the AS administrator needs to specify the maximum expected client population size, as well as the maximum expected revocation rate. Based on these values, the server generates a master client key list. During normal server operation, this list is stored in memory; the server also writes it on disk (as a binary file), protected under a password, so it can survive potential server crashes. The command line interface allows the AS administrator to register new clients, update existing clients' credentials and revoke issued credentials. In the case of client registration and credentials update, the output of the operation is a file storing the newly generated client authentication database; in the case of credentials revocation, the output is a binary file consisting of the (updated) CRL, together with CRL authentication codes for all the master client keys. The output file then needs to be transferred to the target system (the client's computer/PDA in the case of the authentication database, the revocation directory for the CRL) by some secure out-of-band mechanism (for example stored on a ZIP-drive, CD-ROM, memory stick). Consistent with our goal of keeping the AS server strictly off-line, we do not provide any support for transferring results via regular network connections.

We are currently developing the credentials management library, which will provide application programmers with an interface similar to the BSD Socket Interface. The library is initialized with the name of the authentication database file (possibly password-protected) obtained by the user from the AS server. After this, connecting our secure sockets involves executing the authentication protocol described in Section 4, with the shared key obtained at the end of the protocol being used to protect the future data traffic between the two endpoints. In addition to the regular connection information (the other party's network address, transport protocol, etc.), our secure sockets also store the authenticated name of the client at the other end. Two potential applications we have in mind are de-centralized ICQ-like chat services (users can authenticate each other without the need for a trusted-online server as it is in existing such applications), and one-to-one authentication for PDAs.

Finally, we have performed a number of experiments to measure the performance of our implementation; these were performed on a AMD Duron 750MHz 64K cache system, with 196MB RAM, running Linux Mandrake 9.1. Our code was compiled using the GNU C compiler, version 3.2.2. For the remaining of this section, we assume that all credentials are issued with the same lifetime, and the revocation probability (for that lifetime) is 0.1 (this later number is based on the results published in [3]). According to the formula derived in the previous section, this leads to an authentication database size of $2.1 * N$ entries per client, where N is the maximum expected client population size. We used the AES algorithm [1] for encrypting the ICs and for the authentication protocol. In both cases the key size was 128 bits.

The first experiment evaluates the performance of the AS server implementation. We measured the amount of time required to initialize the server (generating the master client key list) and to generate one client authentication database, for various maximum expected client population sizes. Figure 2 summarizes the results.

Table 2. AS server performance measurements

Number of master keys	AS initialization time	Generating one client database
1000	0.01 sec	0.04 sec.
10000	0.04 sec	0.32 sec.
100000	0.34 sec	2.97 sec.
1000000	3.36 sec	30.5 sec.
2000000	6.61 sec	59.8 sec.
5000000	16.55 sec	150.1 sec.

Not surprisingly, the amount of time needed for initialization and authentication database generation grows linearly with the maximum expected number of clients. The time to initialize the server (generating the client master key list) is by all means negligible. For the client authentication database generation, we can see that even for very large expected client populations (in the order of millions), the the time required is less than two minutes. We assume this is acceptable, considering that client registration and credentials update are rare events (once a year), and they anyway involve some sort of human to human interaction (in order to transfer the authentication database from the off-line AS server to the client system) which is much more time-consuming.

The second experiment compares our authentication protocol with public-key based SSL [8]. Our protocol is implemented in C using the OpenSSL Crypto library; we compare it with the protocol implemented by the OpenSSL SSL library (with the *AES128-SHA:RC4-MD5:DES-CBC-SHA:RC4-SHA* cipher suites enabled); the two authenticating end-points are processes running on the same host (the 750MHZ AMD Duron described earlier), so that network latency does not influence the experiment. For our protocol we have the two parties store their entire authentication database in memory. For SSL we use the "server and client authentication" option, and the public key algorithm is RSA with 1024 bit keys. The results, shown in Table 3, were obtained after running each type of authentication session for 10000 times and taking the average.

Table 3. SSV vs. our protocol - performance comparison

Authentication Protocol	Duration
our protocol - 1000 entries per client database	0.37 msec.
our protocol - 10000 entries per client database	0.38 msec.
our protocol - 100000 entries per client database	0.38 msec.
our protocol - 1000000 entries per client database	0.38 msec.
SSL - 1024 bit RSA keys (client and server authentication)	11.6 msec.

Not surprisingly, the size of the authentication database has little influence on the performance of the protocol, since the entire database is stored in memory. We can see that our authentication protocol is an order of magnitude faster than SSL. We expect the relative speedup to be even more significant on PDAs, normally equipped with less powerful CPUs. Besides the speedup, probably the biggest advantage of our protocol is that the symmetric key cryptographic operations it involves are much less CPU-intensive than the public key cryptographic operations needed by SSL, which is a great advantage for battery-powered PDAs.

Finally, another factor that should be taken into account when evaluating our architecture, is size of the client authentication database, which grows linearly with the maximum expected client population size. As shown in Table 4, the size of one *(SIK, IC)* database entry is 96B. Given that the number of entries in a client database is $2.1 * N$, where N is the maximum expected client population size, we can see that this database size grows linearly from 96KB for an authentication realm of thousand clients to 96MB for a million clients realm.

For efficiency and security reasons, clients should be able to store their entire authentication database in memory; considering the above numbers we can conclude that, at least for today's PDAs, our authentication infrastructure could scale up to authentication realms of at most hundred thousand clients (so the database size does not exceed 10MB).

7 Conclusion and Future Work

In this paper we have presented a symmetric key authentication infrastructure based on an off-line TTP. Because the TTP is off-line, it is shielded from both hacking and DoS attacks; the fact that authentication does not depend on continuous network connectivity makes our scheme particularly suited for MANET

260 B. Crispo, B.C. Popescu, and A.S. Tanenbaum

Table 4. Authentication database entry size

Entry Format:
(SIK, $\{SIK, Index_{src}, Index_{dest}, \text{SHA-1}(Name), T_{issue}, T_{expire}\}_{Key_{client}}$)

Field	Size
SIK	16B
$Index_{src}$	4B
$Index_{dest}$	4B
SHA-1($Name$)	20B
T_{issue}	4B
T_{expire}	4B
SHA-1 over above fields	20B

Total IC size	72B
Total after encryption in CBC mode	80B (5 blocks)
Grand total (encrypted IC + SIK)	96B

environments. Our authentication architecture can support a dynamic client population, with the condition that the maximum size of this population is known in advance. We are able to achieve this by trading memory for flexibility under the assumption that large storage devices are becoming a commodity in today's computing environment.

The scheme presented in this paper works for a single security domain, under the jurisdiction of a single authentication server. As future work we would like to expand our scheme to the case of multiple domains and we are now working on the details of these extensions.

Acknowledgments. This paper was inspired by Roger Needham, who, during an earlier discussion, raised the question what the Needham-Schroeder protocol would be if it were to be designed nowadays. We would like to give special thanks to Jacco de Leeuw for the prototype implementation. We also thank Jan Mark Wams, Bogdan Warinschi, Manuel Leone, and Melanie Rieback for reading and commenting earlier drafts of this paper, and to all the anonymous referees for their helpful comments.

References

1. Advanced Encryption Standard. FIPS 197, NIST, US Dept. of Commerce, Washington D. C. November 2001.
2. Lampson B., Abadi M., Burrows M., and Wobber E. Authentication in Distributed Systems: Theory and Practice. *ACM Trans. on Computer Systems*, 10(4):265–310, Nov. 1992.
3. S. Berkovits, S. Chokhani, J.A. Furlong, J.A. Geiter, and J.C. Guild. Public Key Infrastructure Study: Final Report. Produced by the MITRE Corporation for NIST, 1994.
4. R. Bird, I. Gopal, A. Herzberg, P. Janson, S. Kutten, R. Molva, and M. Yung. The KryptoKnight Family of Light-Weight Protocols for Authentication and Key Distribution. *IEEE/ACM Trans. on Networking*, vol. 3(1):31–41, 1995.

5. R. Bird, I. Gopal, A. Herzberg, P. Janson, S. Kutten, R. Molva, and M. Yung. Systematic Design of a Family of Attack-Resistant Authentication Protocols. *IEEE J. on Selected Areas in Communication*, 11(5):679–693, June 1999.

6. C. Boyd. A Class of Flexible and Efficient Key Management Protocols. In *Proc. 9th IEEE Computer Security Foundation Workshop*, 1996.

7. C. Boyd. A Framework for Design of Key Establishment Protocols. In *Proc. First Australasian Conf. on Information Security and Privacy*, pages 146–157, June 1996.

8. A. Freier, P. Karlton, and P. Kocher. The SSL Protocol Version 3.0. Internet Draft (expired), Nov. 1996.

9. T. Hwang, N.Y. Lee, C.M. Li, M.Y. Ko, and Y.H. Chen. Two attacks on Neuman-Stubblebine Authentication Protocols. *Information Processing Letters*, 55:103–107, 1995.

10. ISO/IEC. *ISO/IEC 9798-2 - Information Technology - Security techniques - Entity Authentication - Part2: Mechanisms using symmetric encipherment algorithms*, 1999.

11. I.L. Kao and R. Chow. An Efficient and Secure Authentication Protocol Using Uncertified Keys. *ACM Operating System Review*, 29(3):14–21, 1995.

12. A. Kehne, J. Schonwalder, and H. Langendolfer. A Nonce-Based Protocol for Multiple Authentication. *ACM Operating System Review*, 26(4):84–89, 1992.

13. J.T. Kohl and B.C. Neuman. The Kerberos Network Authentication Service (Version 5). Technical report, IETF Network Working Group, 1993. Internet Request for Comments RFC-1510.

14. H. Krawczyk, M. Bellare, and R. Canetti. RFC 2104 - HMAC: Keyed-Hashing for Message Authentication. Internet RFC 2104, Feb. 1997.

15. R.M. Needham and M.D. Schroeder. Using Encryption for Authentication in Large Networks of Computers. *Commun. of the ACM*, 21(12):993–999, 1978.

16. R.M. Needham and M.D. Schroeder. Authentication Revisited. *ACM Operating System Review*, 21(7):7–7, 1987.

17. B. Clifford Neuman and S.G. Stubblebine. A Note on the Use of Timestamps as Nonces. *ACM Operating System Review*, 27(2), 1993.

18. P. W. Shor. Algorithms for quantum computation: Discrete logarithms and factoring. In *Proc. of the 35th Annual IEEE Symp. on the Foundations of Computer Science*, pages 124–134, 1994.

Improvements to the Point Halving Algorithm

Brian King[1]* and Ben Rubin[2]

[1] Purdue School of Engineering
Indiana Univ. Purdue Univ at Indianapolis
briking@iupui.edu
[2] Department of Computer Science
Indiana Univ. Purdue Univ at Indianapolis
brubin@iupui.edu

Abstract. The focus of this paper is on elliptic curves defined over $GF(2^n)$. Here we provide enhancements to the elliptic curve point halving algorithm that was introduced in [13]. We discuss a new field square root algorithm which provides significant improvement over other field square root algorithms. We describe techniques to improve performance. Lastly, we develop an improved version of the elliptic curve half for curves with cofactor of 4.

1 Introduction

In [12,17], Koblitz and Miller independently proposed to use elliptic curves over a finite field to implement cryptographic primitives. The benefits for utilizing elliptic curves as a public key primitive are well recognized: smaller bandwidth, smaller keysize and faster computations, in particular a faster key exchange and signature generation.

As computing becomes more pervasive, small lightweight devices (by a lightweight device we are referring to a device that is constrained either by limited memory, limited bandwidth, and/or limited computing power) will be asked to perform necessary cryptographic computations needed to participate in today's networked society: Authentication protocols, encryption methods, key exchange methods, etc. All of these protocols will need to be supported by lightweight devices. Consequently algorithms need to be developed that provide suitable improvements.

As we have noted Elliptic Curve Cryptography (ECC) will most likely be an essential cryptographic tool for lightweight devices. A significant amount of research has been devoted towards developing improved computational techniques. In this paper, we will focus on elliptic curves which are defined over the binary field $GF(2^n)$. An essential reference for ECC defined over binary fields would be [8], as well as [5].

There are several approaches towards developing efficient elliptic curve cryptosystem. Some focus on selecting elliptic curves which provide a rich algebraic

---

* This work has been supported by a grant provided by The Lily Endowment and the Indiana University Pervasive Technology Labs

structure that enhances the performance, an example would be a Koblitz curve. Others build fields for which there are very efficient field arithmetic, and define the elliptic curve over this field. In [13], Knudsen introduced the *halving point coordinates* and the halving a point algorithm, which is the focus of this paper. Here we describe enhancements to the algorithm, new field arithmetic algorithms that will enable improvements, and we develop and a new version of the halving algorithm for elliptic curves with cofactor 4. We benchmark all of our results to provide the reader tangible results of our improvements.

2   Background in Elliptic Curve Arithmetic

For the finite field $GF(2^n)$, the standard equation or Weierstrass equation for a non supersingular elliptic curve is:

$$y^2 + xy = x^3 + a_2 x^2 + a_6 \qquad (1)$$

where $a_2, a_6 \in GF(2^n)$, $a_6 \neq 0$. The points $P = (x,y)$, where $x,y \in GF(2^n)$, that satisfy the equation, together with the point $\mathcal{O}$, called the point of infinity, form an additive abelian group E. Thus

$$E = \{(x,y) \in GF(2^n) \times GF(2^n) : y^2 + xy = x^3 + a_2 x^2 + a_6\} \cup \{\mathcal{O}\}.$$

An addition can be defined on E, due to space limitations we refer the reader to a source like [5] for the definition of addition of point belonging to E. The "add" operation (compute $P_1 + P_2$ where $P_1 \neq \pm P_2$) requires 2 field multiplications, 1 square, and 1 inverse. The "double" operation (compute $2P$) requires 2 field multiplications, 1 square, and 1 inverse.

The *Fundamental theorem of finite abelian groups* states that every finite abelian group is isomorphic to the direct product of cyclic groups of order equal to some prime to a power (see [4]). Thus there exist primes $p_1, ..., p_k$ (not necessarily distinct) and positive powers $e_1, ..., e_k$ such that the elliptic curve E is isomorphic to $\mathbf{Z}_{p_1^{e_1}} \times \mathbf{Z}_{p_2^{e_2}} \times \cdots \times \mathbf{Z}_{p_k^{e_k}}$ (where $\mathbf{Z}_{p_i^{e_i}}$ represents the residue system of integers mod $p_i^{e_i}$). In cryptographic applications the curve E is chosen so that it has a subgroup of large prime order. In fact E, when defined over $GF(2^n)$, is usually chosen so that E is isomorphic to $\mathbf{Z}_p \times \mathbf{Z}_2$ or $\mathbf{Z}_p \times \mathbf{Z}_4$. In the former case the curve will be said to have a cofactor of 2 and in the latter case the curve will have cofactor of 4. All elliptic curves defined over binary fields that are contained in the WAP/WTLS list of elliptic curves and NIST list [19] of recommended curves have cofactors equal to 2 or 4.

An essential calculation is to compute the scalar multiple of a point $k \cdot P$ where $P \in E$ belonging to the subgroup of large prime order and k is the secret key. There are several methods that one can use to compute kP. For a good overview see [5,8].

2.1   NIST Recommended Curves in $GF(2^n)$

In July 1999, NIST released a list [19] of recommended (but not necessarily required) curves to use for elliptic curve cryptography when dealing with federal
agencies. Today many of these curve have been adopted by standards organizations. Our interest is in those curves which are defined over the binary field
$GF(2^n)$. The curves listed are: K-163, B-163, K-233, B-233, K-283, B-283, K-
409, B-409,K-571, and B-571 where the K-*** refers to a Koblitz curve whose
Weierstrass equation (1) where $a_6 = 1$ and $a_2 \in \{0, 1\}$, and B-*** refer to a
"random curve" whose Weierstrass equation where $a_6 \neq 1$ and $a_2 = 1$.

3   Galois Field Arithmetic – Squares, Square Roots, and the Trace Function

Computing a Square

   If one utilizes a normal basis to represent a field element then a field element
can be squared by performing a circular shift. However most implementations
utilize a polynomial basis.

   To compute a square, one usually does the following: if $\mu = \mu_{n-1}x^{n-1} + \cdots +
\mu_1 x + \mu_0$ then $\mu^2 = \mu_{n-1}x^{2n-2} + \mu_{n-2}x^{2n-4} + \cdots + \mu_1 x^2 + \mu_0$. Thus one can
"insert zeros" in the bitstring $\mu_{n-1} \ldots \mu_1 \mu_0$, and construct $\mu_{n-1} 0 \ldots 0 \mu_1 0 \mu_0$
which is equivalent to μ^2 and then call the modular reduction algorithm. Thus
the computational cost would reflect the time to insert zeros and the time that
the reduction algorithm takes.

   In [10,11] as well as [9] an alternate method is presented which utilizes the
representation of field elements in terms of odd polynomial parts and even
polynomial parts. Due to space limitation we omit details and refer the reader
to these sources. However we do benchmark the performance of this algorithm.

Computing a Square Root

   If one uses a normal basis to represent elements in $GF(2^n)$, then one can
compute a square root by performing a circular shift. However, ECC is typically
implemented using a polynomial basis.

IEEE P1363. The IEEE P1363 Public key cryptography working group [20]
created an appendix which described how to perform most of the algebraic and
number-theoretic operations to implement public-key cryptography. In particular they described how to perform needed algebraic operations. For $\zeta \in GF(2^n)$,
the square root of ζ can be calculated as: $\sqrt{\zeta} = \zeta^{n-1}$ (see [20]).
Knudsen. A required calculation in the halving a point algorithm is the square
root. In [13], Knudsen described a method to compute square roots as follows.
For $\zeta \in GF(2^n)$, one can represent ζ as $\zeta = \xi_0 + \xi_1 x + \cdots + \xi_{n-1}x^{n-1}$, using the
polynomial basis. Then the square root of ζ is:

$$\sqrt{\zeta} = \sum_{\substack{i=0 \\ i\,even}}^{n-1} \xi_i x^{i/2} + \sqrt{x} \sum_{\substack{i=0 \\ i\,odd}}^{n-1} \xi_i x^{(i-1)/2}$$

This is a significant improvement on the IEEE P1363 method.

Computing the Square Root Using Odd and Even Part of the Field Element. Here we outline the method, unfortuately due to space limitations we must limit the details of our discussion, for a more detailed discussion of computing square roots using this technique we refer the reader to [10] (a similar method was discussed in [9]). Let $\zeta = \mu^2$, our goal is to compute μ. We assume n is odd and we let L denote $\frac{n-1}{2}$. Let $\zeta = (\xi_{L+L}, \dots, \xi_{L+1}, \xi_L, \dots, \xi_0)$. Let $\mathcal{O} = (\xi_{L+L-1}, \dots, \xi_3, , \xi_1)_O$ and let $\mathcal{E} = (\xi_{L+L}, \dots, \xi_2, \xi_0)_E$, so that $\zeta = \mathcal{O} + \mathcal{E}$. [1] Our goal is to compute $\mathcal{A}$ and $\mathcal{B}$, where $\mu = x^{L+1}\mathcal{B} + \mathcal{A}$ (here $\mathcal{A}$ represents the low $L+1$ monomial terms of μ and represents the high monomial terms of μ). That is, we start with ζ, and express $\zeta = \mathcal{O} + \mathcal{E}$. From $\mathcal{O}$, our goal will be to compute $\mathcal{B}$. Once we have $\mathcal{B}$, we compute $\mathcal{A}$. Then $\sqrt{\zeta} = \mathcal{B}x^{L+1} + \mathcal{A}$. In our notation $x^k \cdot C$ is the result of performing the appropriate left shift of C and C/x^k is the result of performing the appropriate right shift of C.

We have successfully derived a square root algorithm for all finite fields in the NIST list of curves [19], except for the field $GF(2^{571})$. We will now describe this approach for fields which have a trinomial as a generating polynomial (this is NOT a requirement, but does simplify the procedure)

We denote the generating polynomial as $x^n + x^m + 1$ and we will assume that $2m \leq n - 1$, this assumption allows us to demonstrate this computations in few steps. This assumption can be removed, the consequence is that the computation will take more steps, each step is comparable to steps we illustrate.

Computing Square Roots When Modulus Is $x^n + x^m + 1$ Where $m = 2I + 1$ Odd. To compute the square root of ζ we utilize the derivation of the square given in [10]. Let $\mathcal{O}$ denote the odd part of ζ. By recalling the derivation of the square as given in [10], we have $\mathcal{O} = \mathcal{B} + (\frac{\mathcal{B}}{x^{n-m}})_O$. Performing a right shift of $\mathcal{O}$ of suitable number of I bits (i.e. divide by x^{2I}) will shift out the term $(\frac{\mathcal{B}}{x^{n-m}})_O$, the result is equivalent to performing a right shift of $\mathcal{B}$ by I bits. The consequence will be that we now have the high $(n-m)/2$ bits of $\mathcal{B}$, since $(n-1)/2 > (m-1)/2$ we have recovered more than half of the bits of $\mathcal{B}$. To compute the remaining bits of $\mathcal{B}$ we perform a right shift by a suitable number of bits of the known high bits of $\mathcal{B}$, and then add this to $\mathcal{O}$ the result will be the remaining lower bits of $\mathcal{B}$. (This computation of $\mathcal{B}$ takes two steps due to our assumption that $2m \leq n-1$). Once $\mathcal{B}$ is known we can calculate $\mathcal{A}$ by $\mathcal{A} = \mathcal{E} + x^m(\frac{\mathcal{B}}{x^{n-m}})_O + (x^m\mathcal{B})_E$.

To illustrate the computations to compute the square root, consider the field $GF(2^{409})$ with the generating polynomial $x^{409} + x^{87} + 1$. This represents the underlying field for one of the curves in the NIST list of elliptic curves [19]. Let $\zeta = \mathcal{O} + \mathcal{E}$. To compute $\sqrt{\zeta}$ we compute $\mathcal{A}$ and $\mathcal{B}$. $\mathcal{B} = \mathcal{O} + (\frac{\mathcal{O}}{x^{322}})_O$ and $\mathcal{A} = \mathcal{E} + x^{87}(\frac{\mathcal{B}}{x^{322}})_O + (x^{87}\mathcal{B})_E$. Then $\sqrt{\zeta} = \mathcal{B}x^{L+1} + \mathcal{A}$.

Computing Square Roots When the Modulus Is $x^n + x^m + 1$ Where $m = 2I$ Even. To compute the square root of ζ we utilize the derivation of the

---

[1] Here we use (*bitstring*)$_O$ to represent the odd polynomial constructed from the terms of *bitstring* and (*bitstring*)$_E$ to represent the even polynomial constructed from the terms of *bitstring*.

square given in [10]. Utilizing the derivation of the square as given in [10], the odd part $\mathcal{O}$ of ζ, satisfies $\mathcal{O} = \mathcal{B} + (x^m \mathcal{B})_O$. Again we perform a series of additions of $\mathcal{O}$ with shifts of $\mathcal{O}$ to compute $\mathcal{B}$. However since $2m \leq n-1$, the number of terms in $(x^m \mathcal{B})_O$ exceeds L, so we will have to perform at least two additions (and most possibly more). Consequently $\mathcal{B} = \mathcal{O} + (x^m \mathcal{O})_O + (x^{2m} \mathcal{O})_O + \cdots + (x^{km} \mathcal{O})_O$ where integer k is the smallest positive integer satisfying $(k+1) \geq n$ (which is equivalent to $(k+1)I > L$). Once $\mathcal{B}$ is computed we compute $\mathcal{A}$ as
$$\mathcal{A} = \mathcal{E} + x^m \left(\frac{\mathcal{B}}{x^{n-m}}\right)_E + \left(\frac{\mathcal{B}}{x^{n-m}}\right)_E.$$
To illustrate the computations to compute the square root, consider the field $GF(2^{233})$ with the generating polynomial $x^{233} + x^{74} + 1$. This represents the underlying field for K-233 and B-233 curve in the NIST list of elliptic curves [19]. Let $\zeta = \mathcal{O} + \mathcal{E}$. To compute $\sqrt{\zeta}$ we compute $\mathcal{A}$ and $\mathcal{B}$. Here $\mathcal{B} = \mathcal{O} + (x^{74}\mathcal{O})_O + (x^{148}\mathcal{O})_O + (x^{222}\mathcal{O})_O$ and $\mathcal{A} = \mathcal{E} + x^{74}(\frac{\mathcal{B}}{x^{159}})_E + (\frac{\mathcal{B}}{x^{159}})_E$.

Trace Function

The trace function is a homomorphic mapping of $GF(2^n)$ onto $\{0, 1\}$. In [20], the trace of an element $\alpha \in GF(2^n)$, denoted by $Tr(\alpha)$ can be computed as $Tr(\alpha) = \sum_{i=0}^{n-1} \alpha^{2^i}$. For more information concerning the $Tr()$ operator and its importance see [14]. It can be shown that $Tr()$ is a linear operator which returns a 0 or a 1 and satisfies that $Tr(\alpha^2) = Tr(\alpha)$. In $GF(2^n)$, where n is odd (which is true for all binary fields that we are interested in), then $Tr(1) = 1$ (this can easily be derived). Consequently for all $\alpha \in GF(2^n)$ with $Tr(\alpha) = 0$ we have $Tr(\alpha + 1) = 1$ and vice versa. For a given $b \in GF(2^n)$, the quadratic equation $\lambda^2 + \lambda = b$ in $GF(2^n)$ has a solution if and only if $Tr(b) = 0$ [14]. Observe that if λ is a solution to the above quadratic equation, then $\lambda + 1$ is also a solution, and $Tr(\lambda + 1) = Tr(\lambda) + 1$. Hence whenever n is odd, which we always will assume, for each solvable quadratic equation there is a solution with trace 1 and a solution with trace 0. The computation $Tr(\alpha) = \sum_{i=0}^{n-1} \alpha^{2^i}$ as suggested in [20] is significant. In reality the trace function can be computed *extremely efficiently*. We have precomputed the requirement for field elements to have trace 0 for all binary fields that are used to define an elliptic curve in the NIST list, see Table 1. For each binary field used in the NIST list of elliptic curve we have explored the necessary and sufficient condition for a field element to have trace 0. We summarize our work in *Table 1* given in the following Theorem. Relevant to the implementations in this paper are the fields $GF(2^{233})$ and $GF(2^{409})$. In $GF(2^{233})$ for $\mu \in GF(2^{233})$, $\mu = \mu_0 + \mu_1 x + \cdots + \mu_{232} x^{232}$ $Tr(\mu) = 0$ iff $\mu_0 = \mu_{159}$. In $GF(2^{409})$ for $\mu \in GF(2^{409})$, $\mu = \mu_0 + \mu_1 x + \cdots + \mu_{408} x^{408}$ $Tr(\mu) = 0$ iff $\mu_0 = 0$.

Theorem 1. *For a NIST elliptic curve $K - ***, B - ***$ which is defined over a binary field $GF(2^n)$, the necessary and sufficient conditions for a field element $\mu \in GF(2^n)$ to have trace 0 is provided in table below.*

3.1   Solving for λ Where $\lambda^2 + \lambda = b$

As we noted above the necessary and sufficient condition for $\lambda^2 + \lambda = b$ to have a solution is that $Tr(b) = 0$. Since n is odd if ζ is a solution where $Tr(\zeta) = 0$ then

Table 1.

Curve types	Generating polynomial	condition for $\mu \in GF(2^n)$ to satisfy $Trace(\mu) = 0$
K-163, B-163	$p(t) = t^{163} + t^7 + t^6 + t^3 + 1$	$\mu_0 = \mu_{157}$
K-233, B-233	$p(t) = t^{233} + t^{74} + 1$	$\mu_0 = \mu_{159}$
K-283, B-283	$p(t) = t^{283} + t^{12} + t^7 + t^5 + 1$	$\mu_0 = \mu_{277}$
K-409, B-409	$p(t) = t^{409} + t^{87} + 1$	$\mu_0 = 0$
K-571, B-571	$p(t) = t^{571} + t^{10} + t^5 + t^2 + 1$	$\mu_0 + \mu_{561} + \mu_{569} = 0$

$\zeta + 1$ is also a solution where $Tr(\zeta + 1) = 1$. Thus each solvable equation has two solutions, one with trace 0, and the other with trace 1. It is trivial to show that half of the elements $\beta \in GF(2^n)$ provide a solvable equation $\lambda^2 + \lambda = \beta$ and for all $\alpha \in GF(2^n)$ there is a $b \in GF(2^n)$ such that $\alpha^2 + \alpha = b$.

How do we compute a solution to such a quadratic equation? In [5,20], a method to compute the solution, described as computing the *halftrace*, $\lambda = \sum_{j=0}^{(n-1)/2} b^{2^{2j}}$. In [13] Knudsen described an alternative, and is based on the following observation. If $\lambda_1^2 + \lambda_1 = b_1$ and $\lambda_2^2 + \lambda_2 = b_2$ then $(\lambda_1 + \lambda_2)^2 + (\lambda_1 + \lambda_2) = b_1 + b_2$. Thus if there exists a set $\mathcal{A}$ of trace zero elements which forms a basis for all trace zero elements, then one can precompute λ_α where for all $\alpha \in \mathcal{A}$ we have $\lambda_\alpha^2 + \lambda_\alpha = \alpha$. Then one can use these precomputed values to solve any *solvable* quadratic.

We now summarize the time it takes to perform the required field operations. All computations were performed on a Toshiba 380 MHz laptop.

	$GF(2^{233})$	$GF(2^{409})$
Addition	$0.52\mu s$	$0.78 \ \mu s$
Comb Multiply	$106.76\mu s$	$228.13 \ \mu s$
Shift Multiply	$267.90\mu s$	$648.21\mu s$
Square	$2.58\mu s$	$4.27\mu s$
Square Root (P1363)	$2093.31 \ \mu s$	$1935.19\mu s$
Square Root (Knudsen)	$41.91 \ \mu s$	$60.92\mu s$
Improved Square Root (Odd/Even)	$7.66\mu s$	$10.39\mu s$
Inverse	$849.25 \ \mu s$	$2188.77\mu s$
Halftrace	$656.53 \ \mu s$	$1904.76 \ \mu s$
Improved solve (halftrace)	$44.51 \ \mu s$	$70.24\mu s$
Trace check (P1363)	$715.94 \ \mu s$	$2020.42\mu s$
Improved Trace check	$0.18 \ \mu s$	$0.16\mu s$
Elliptic Curve Arithmetic	B-233	B-409
EC Double:	$1107.40\mu s$	$2831.09\mu s$
EC Add:	$1069.55\mu s$	$2636.56 \ \mu s$
EC half a point	$170.47\mu s$	$321.61\mu s$

All software was written in C. For the elliptic curve arithmetic operations we used our most optimal field operation. The field operations were developed following some of the methods described here, as well as algorithms described in [8]. Although our goal was to develop very efficient field implementations, we did not spend an inordinate amount of time on the code. Let us focus of the field $GF(2^{233})$, the best field multiply is about $1/8^{th}$ of a field inversion. The square is $1/50^{th}$ of the best field multiply. The performances of the three square root functions speak for themselves. The square root (odd/even) was three times the square. (We believe, that with more care this can be reduced, further.) The halftrace is the quadratic solve, and by precomputing the solutions of a basis of trace zero elements we were able to achieve a "solve" that is approximately 45% of a multiplication. As noted the trace check can be done very fast. Some of the formula listed in the P1363 document (halftrace and trace check, later projective points), were not the optimal algorithm.

In terms of elliptic curve arithmetic, we will focus on timings given for B-233. Both the EC add and EC double can be measure by the 2M+I (two field multiplications plus one inverse). The EC half was very efficient (here the input is a point in half coordinates and the out put is a point in halving coordinates). An EC Half is approximately 1.6 M (field multiplication), see below for relevant information on EC Half.

4   ECC and Halving a Point

4.1   Halving a Point

In [13], Knudsen introduced the concept of halving a point in elliptic curve over $GF(2^n)$ to compute the scalar multiple kP. [2] Knudsen described how to compute $\frac{1}{2}P$ given a point $P = (x, y) \in E$, where P is a double of some point. At the heart of this computation is the representation of a point. Rather that representing a point $P = (x, y) \in E$, Knudsen represented P as $P = (x, \lambda_P)$ where $\lambda_p = x + \frac{y}{x}$, which we refer to as *halving coordinates*. Observe that given x and λ_P then y can be computed since $y = x(x + \lambda_P)$.
Let $Q = (u, \lambda_Q) = \frac{1}{2}P$ where $P = (x, \lambda_P)$. Then λ_Q can be determined by solving:

$$\lambda_Q^2 + \lambda_Q = a_2 + x. \qquad (2)$$

Once one solves for λ_Q, u can be determined by computing

$$u = \sqrt{u^2} = \sqrt{x(\lambda_Q + 1) + y} = \sqrt{x(\lambda_Q + \lambda_P + x + 1)}. \qquad (3)$$

Observe that $Tr(a_2 + x)$ must equal 0, which is true if and only if P is the double of some point, an observation that is used in both [23,22].

Although the primary focus of Knudsen's work was with curves with cofactor of 2, he did not limit his work to only such curves. His formula concerning halving

---

[2] Independently, Schroepel [21] also developed the method of halving a point to perform cryptographic computations on an elliptic curve.

a point can be modified to handle curves with cofactor 2^L, $L \geq 2$. Of course many of the NIST curves possess cofactors of 4. The reasoning for focusing primarily on curves of cofactor 2 is as follows: given the equation $\lambda_q^2 + \lambda_Q = a_2 + x$ there will be two solutions, a λ_Q and $\lambda_Q + 1$, as computed by (2). If an elliptic curve E has cofactor 2, then when one computes u as described by (3), it follows that for one of the values $\{\lambda_Q, \lambda_Q + 1\}$, the corresponding u will satisfy $Tr(u) = 1$ and for the other λ-value the corresponding u will satisfy $Tr(u) = 0$. Thus it is easy to determine which of the points is the valid half of P, (valid in the sense that one of the halves belongs to this subgroup of prime order and the other belongs to the coset). A method to compute the scalar multiple of a point is given in [13]. We include it in the extended version of this paper. This method will utilize the "Point halving algorithm" and an "EC add" which will add a point given in halving coordinates with a point given in affine coordinates. The resulting point is in affine coordinates. Any addition formula which would output points in halving point coordinates would require an inverse to compute λ. Hence such an EC add would require two inverses, which defeats the benefit of the halving a point algorithm. Consequently any efficient algorithm which computes kP will parse the key k (i.e. visit) from the low bits to the high bits.

4.2 Elliptic Curve with Cofactors > 2

Knudsen did not limit his work to elliptic curves with cofactor 2. In fact he provided a brief outline of how to apply the halving a point algorithm to elliptic curve which are isomorphic to $\mathbf{Z}_p \times \mathbf{Z}_{2^k}$. Again G denotes a prime subgroup of E. Let $P = (x_P, \lambda_P) \in G$. Integral to our work (as well as to summarize the cost of Knudsen's algorithm) will be the following algorithms.

Algorithm 1

SOLVE(s)
    if $Tr(s) \neq 0$
        return **No solution**
    let ζ be one of the solutions to
        $w^2 + w = s$
    return ζ

HALF$(P = (x_P, \lambda_P))$
    if $Tr(x_P + a_2) \neq 0$
        return **No half point**
    $\lambda_Q = \mathbf{SOLVE}(x_P + a_2)$
    $u_Q = \sqrt{x_P(\lambda_Q + \lambda_P + x_P + 1)}$
    return (u_Q, λ_Q)

To half a point P, given in halving coordinates, where P belongs to G, and where the elliptic curve has a cofactor of 2^j, would require to run the **HALF** algorithm j times. As we shall soon demonstrate this can be improved upon. To put this cost into perspective, the task of computing the scalar multiple of a point P, i.e. compute kP when the curve has cofactor 4 using the halving a point algorithm is equivalent to computing a scalar multiple aP where a is twice the length of k but has the same hamming weight as k.

5   A Method of Halving a Point for Curves with Cofactor 4

Although we state this for curves with a cofactor of 4, we point out that by using a simple modification, we can adapt this method for curves with cofactors of 2^j, where $j > 2$. Let $T_2 \in E$ denote a point of order 2. Thus $T_2 = (0, \sqrt{a_6})$.

Suppose E is an elliptic with a cofactor of 4. Let $P = (x, \lambda) \in G$, and suppose we compute $P_1 = (x_1, \lambda_1) = \textbf{Half}(P)$. We note that either P_1 is equal to $\frac{1}{2}P$ or $\frac{1}{2}P + T_2$. Unfortunately we cannot distinguish between the two points. Our modified version of halving a point for curves with cofactor of 4 says we accept an answer as long as the point has a half. Thus the trace of the x-coordinate will have to equal $Tr(a_2)$ (which is zero for curves with cofactor 4). The method we are advocating is that after computing the "Half", we do not consider it to be an error if the answer belongs to the set $\{\frac{1}{2}P, \frac{1}{2}P + T_2\}$. We make the following modification, if P does belong to G, then when we compute λ_1 (in **Solve**$(a_2 + x_P)$ of Algorithm 1) rather than always return a λ-solution of trace 0, we return a λ-solution with trace 0 if coin is a *heads* and trace 1 if coin is a *tails*. That is, the coin flip determines the trace value of λ. Then the possibility of an error is $1/2$. We will denote the "Half" function which places a coin flip in the "Solve" equation by **Half**.

We now need to discuss how to compute the correct scalar multiple kP. Adopting the same terminology as [13], we will use T_{2^i} to denote a point of minimal 2^i torsion (i.e. a point of order 2^i). Let $P = (x_p + \lambda_P)$ and suppose we know that $P \in G$. Now let $P_1 = \textbf{Half}(P) = (x_1, \lambda_1)$, then $\lambda_1^2 + \lambda = a_2 + x_P$, $x_1 = \sqrt{x_P(\lambda_1 + \lambda_P + x_P + 1)}$. Again either $P_1 = \frac{1}{2}P$ or $\frac{1}{2}P + T_2$.

Now suppose we compute $P_2 = (x_2, \lambda_2) = \textbf{Half}(P_2)$ then $\lambda_2^2 + \lambda_2 = a_2 + x_1$ and $x_2 = \sqrt{x_1(\lambda_2 + \lambda_1 + x_1 + 1)}$. Now either $P_2 = \frac{1}{2}P_1$ or $P_2 = \frac{1}{2}P_1 + T_2$. Since either $P_1 = \frac{1}{2}P$ or $P_1 = \frac{1}{2}P + T_2$, we have one of four possibilities $P_2 = \frac{1}{4}P$ or $P_2 = \frac{1}{4}P_1 + T_{2^2}$, $P_2 = \frac{1}{4}P + T_{2^2}$ or $P_2 = \frac{1}{4}P_1 + 3T_{2^2}$ (this follows from the fact that $2T_{2^2} = T_2$ and $T_{2^2} + T_2 = 3T_{2^2}$). Since E has cofactor 4, both T_{2^2} and $3T_{2^2}$ do NOT have halves, thus the x-coordinate for $\frac{1}{4}P_1 + T_{2^2}$, and $\frac{1}{4}P_1 + 3T_{2^2}$ have a trace value $\neq$ to $Tr(a_2)$. If this is true we have detected that P_1 was of the form $\frac{1}{2}P + T_2$. However if the trace of the x coordinate is equal to $Tr(a_2)$ then P_1 was equal to $\frac{1}{2}P$. In the case that the trace of the x coordinate is equal to $Tr(a_2)$, we know that since $P_1 = \frac{1}{2}P$ we have $P_2 \in \{\frac{1}{2^2}P, \frac{1}{2^2}P + T_2\}$. And so we are satisfied with P_2. However if the trace of the x coordinate does not equal $Tr(a_2)$, Then we will need to modify P_2. Our goal is to compute P_2 where x_2 satisfies $Tr(x_2) = Tr(a_2)$, so that P_2 is either $\frac{1}{4}P$ or $\frac{1}{4}P + T_2$ (and we can implicitly assume that since P_2 possesses the correct properties that the adjusted P_1, although not physically calculated, is correct).

Suppose $Tr(x_2) \neq Tr(a_2)$ then we know $P_1 = \frac{1}{2}P + T_2$. Let us use $\overline{\lambda_1}$ and $\overline{x_1}$ for the correct coordinates for P_1. Then $\overline{\lambda_1} = \lambda + 1$ and

$$\overline{x_1} = \sqrt{x_P(\overline{\lambda_1} + \lambda_P + x_P + 1)}$$
$$= \sqrt{x_P(\lambda_1 + 1 + \lambda_P + x_P + 1)}$$

$$= x_1 + \sqrt{x_p}.$$

We can precompute and store τ where τ is the solution to $\tau^2 + \tau = \sqrt{a_2}$. Reminder a_2 is the elliptic curve parameter.

Now to compute $\overline{\lambda_2}$, which is the solution to $\lambda^2 + \lambda = a_2 + \overline{x_1}$. Since $a_2 + \overline{x_1} = a_2 + x_1 + \sqrt{x_P} = a_2 + x_1 + \sqrt{x_P + a_2} + \sqrt{a_2}$, we see that a solution is $\lambda_2 + \sqrt{\lambda_1} + \tau$. i.e. $\overline{\lambda_2} = \lambda_2 + \sqrt{\lambda_1} + \tau$ or $\lambda_2 + \sqrt{\lambda_1} + \tau + 1$. Observe that we do NOT need to compute the **Solve** equation when we detect an error. Now we compute $\overline{x_2}$.

$$\overline{x_2} = \sqrt{\overline{x_1}(\overline{\lambda_1} + \overline{\lambda_2} + \overline{x_1} + 1)}$$

$$= \sqrt{(x_1 + \sqrt{x_P})(\lambda_1 + 1 + \overline{\lambda_2} + x_1 + \sqrt{x_P} + 1)}$$

$$= \sqrt{(x_1 + \lambda_1 + \sqrt{\lambda_1} + \sqrt{a_2})(\lambda_1 + 1 + \lambda_2 + \sqrt{\lambda_1} + \tau + x_1 + \sqrt{x_P} + 1)}$$

$$= \sqrt{(x_1 + \lambda_1 + \sqrt{\lambda_1} + \sqrt{a_2})(\lambda_2 + x_1 + \tau + \sqrt{a_2})}$$

Above we used the fact that $\lambda_1 + \sqrt{\lambda_1} = \sqrt{x_P} + \sqrt{a_2}$. Thus we can compute $\overline{\lambda_2}$ and $\overline{x_2}$ by computing 1 square root and 1 multiplication (we can amortize the cost of solving for τ and computing $\sqrt{a_2}$ since it can be precomputed). We will treat the square root calculation as free. We know that when we compute a **Half**(), we will perform a coin flip in our choice of a λ during **Solve**, so we will have 50 % of making an incorrect choice. Hence we should expect an error only half of the time. Thus we will have to perform the error correction on an average of $N/2$ times where N is the length of the key.

Once one has parsed through the entire key, errors in the accumulator may have taken place. In some cases one has added a $\frac{1}{2}P_1$ and in other cases one has added $\frac{1}{2}P_1 + T_2$. Thus when all the computations are completed, if we made an even number of errors, the T_2 term will not be present in the final sum, but if we made an odd number of errors then the sum is equal to the correct value plus T_2. We can determine if sum is correct by computing **Half**(sum) $= (u, \lambda)$. If $Tr(u) \neq Tr(a_2)$, then **Half**(sum) cannot be halved and so we need to add T_2 to sum to get the correct sum. Otherwise sum is not in error.

Algorithm 2 Algorithm to Compute kP Where $P \in G$ and E Has Cofactor 4

$Input\ Key = k\ where\ k = k_{N-1}k_{N-2}\ldots k_1 k_0 = k_{N-1}\frac{1}{2^{N-1}}k_{N-2}\frac{1}{2^{N-2}}\ldots k_1\frac{1}{2}k_0$
$\quad and\ P = (x, y) \in G$
$Output\ Q = kP$
$\quad Precompute\ \tau = \textbf{Solve}(\sqrt{a_2})$
$\quad Let\ Q = (x, \lambda)\ where\ x_1 = x\ and\ \lambda_1 = x + y/x$
$\quad A = \mathcal{O}$
$\quad for\ i = 0\ to\ N - 1$
$\quad\quad if\ k_i = 1$
$\quad\quad\quad A = A + Q$

$$T = (x_T, \lambda_T) = \mathbf{Half}(Q)$$
$$if(Tr(x_T) \neq Tr(a_2)$$
$$x_T = \sqrt{(x_Q + \lambda_Q + \sqrt{\lambda_Q} + \sqrt{a_2})(\lambda_T + x_Q + \tau + \sqrt{a_2})}$$
$$\lambda_T = \lambda_T + \sqrt{\lambda_Q} + \tau$$
$$Q = T$$
$$x_3 = x_Q$$
$$y_3 = x_3(x_3 + \lambda_Q)$$
$$(u, \lambda) = \mathbf{Half}(Q)$$
$$if\ Tr(u) \neq Tr(a_2)$$
$$(x_3, y_3) = (x_3, y_3) + (0, \sqrt{a_6})$$
$$output\ (x_3, y_3)$$

The expected cost of computing kP on a curve with cofactor 4, using the modified version of halving a point is $\frac{N}{2}$ *EC Adds* + $\frac{N}{2}$ *Errors* + N **Halfs** which is approximately $\frac{N}{2}$ *EC Adds* + $\frac{N}{2}$ M + $N \cdot (1.6M)$ where N is the length of the key. Knudsen's algorithm would have cost $\frac{N}{2}$ *EC Adds* + $N \cdot (3.2M)$. Our algorithm would provide an improvement of $N \cdot (1.1M)$.

6   Further Implementation Options, Improvements, Timings, and Analysis

6.1   Montgomery Representation

An alternative to an affine representation and projective point representation is a Montgomery representation. This is based on an idea by Montgomery [18]. This is that the x coordinate can be computed from the x coordinates of Q_1, Q_2 and $Q_1 + Q_2$. When computing the scalar multiple kP one computes by parsing the key from left to right [8]. As described in [8], given the jth Montgomery point $(lP, (l+1)P)$ if the $j+1^{st}$ left most bit is one compute $(2lP, 2l+1)P$ else compute $(2l+1)P, (2l+2)P$. The cost of computing kP is approximately $N \cdot (6M)$ where N is the length of the key (here we are ignoring the non repetitive steps, as well as those field operations that are not time-consuming).

6.2   Projective Point Coordinates

The use of projective point arithmetic on an elliptic curve to compute kP is such that in projective point elliptic curve arithmetic one delays the computation of a field inverse until the very end of the process of computing kP. By doing so one will naturally see a rise in the number of required field multiplications. That is, one inverse will take place during the computation of the key kP, whereas in the affine method, one inverse takes place for each "add" function invoked (and as well, for each "double" function invoked). There are several different projective point representations to consider, see [1,16,6,20,15]. In [2] Al-Doud, et. al. introduced a new projective point formula. They utilize the same relationship between affine point (x', y') and projective point (x, y, z) as [15], that is $x' = \frac{x}{z}$

and $y' = \frac{y}{z^2}$. However by rearranging the field operations they were able to reduce the number of field multiplications that are needed to perform an elliptic curve add. The formula for the EC double is the same as Lopez & Dahab. The number of field multiplications and field squares for an add is 9 and 5, respectively. If one measures efficiency by requiring the least number of field multiplications then the Al-Doud, et. al. method is the most efficient projective point EC add.

The method that we use to compute kP when using the halving point algorithm is a right to left parsing of the key. Thus we cannot utilize any windowing technique. However this does not stop us from utilizing projective point coordinates for the EC addition. The improvement will be seen below. Whenever field inversion is substantially slower than field multiplication, one would want to use projective point for addition. By *substantially slower*, we mean that since the "EC add" for a halving point algorithm requires 3 multiplications and 1 inverse, if $I > 7M$ then one should use projective points. Suppose $P_1 = (x_1, \lambda_1)$ in halving coordinates and $P_2 = (x_2, y_2, z_2)$ then let $y_1 = x_1 \cdot (x_1 + \lambda_1)$. If we use the projective point representation given by Al-Doud,et. al. [2], then our EC projective point addition will require 10 M and 5 S (here S = squares). If a **Half** is approximately $1.6M$, then the cost of computing kP is $N \cdot 1.6M + \frac{N}{2}10M = 6.6M$. (Here we are ignoring the non repetitive steps, as well as those field operations that are not time-consuming).

6.3   Timings

	B-233	K-233	B-409	K-409
EC kP:	$387733.52\mu s$	$373746.16\mu s$	$1695977.67\mu s$	$1655505.52\mu s$
EC kP (with window)	$330636.24\mu s$	$314822.92\mu s$	$1455938.14\mu s$	$1391918.27\mu s$
EC kP using Montgomery	$149517.27\mu s$	$149875.47\mu s$	$558344.51\mu s$	$558967.63\mu s$
EC kP half and add		$83616.41\mu s$	$81853.34\mu s$	$445781.66\mu s$	$485328.14\mu s$
EC kP half and projective add	$55757.76\mu s$		$212315.53\mu s$	

We make the following observations concerning the timings. Again, all computations were performed on a Toshiba 380 MHz laptop. The windowed implementation of the scalar multiple simply precomputed the first 15 multiples of P and we computed kP parsing the key from right to left four bits at a time. The curves B-233 and B-409 have cofactors of 2. The curves K-233 and K-409 have cofactors of 4. There is an anomaly between the timings on B-233 and K-233. That is the random key generated for K-233 must have had a smaller hamming weight than the key B-233. As expected the EC half with projective point add performed the best. We did not implement the EC half with projective point addition for the curves with cofactor 4. All the EC half methods out performed the Montgomery method. These timings confirm some of the timing observations made in [7].

6.4 NAF

It is well known that if one uses a *nonadjacent form* or NAF for the key, then because the hamming weight of the key has been reduced, the time to compute kP will decrease as well. The Montgomery method of computing kP cannot utilize the NAF form of the key to improve performance. Knudsen pointed out that by expressing the key k in *nonadjacent form* NAF, one can improve efficiency significantly. Although we have written the key k as $k = k_{N-1}\frac{1}{2^{N-1}}k_{N-2}\frac{1}{2^{N-2}}\ldots k_1\frac{1}{2} + k_0$, we can still express it in NAF form. That is any bit sequence of consecutive ones like 1111 can be manipulated. Suppose 1111 represents $\frac{1}{2^j} + \frac{1}{2^{j-1}} + \frac{1}{2^{j-2}} + \frac{1}{2^{j-3}}$ which is equal to $\frac{1}{2^j}(1 + 2 + 2^2 + 2^3) = \frac{1}{2^j}(-1 + 2^4) = -1000(1)$ where the latter one represents a carry bit that needs to be added to the bit position prior to 1111. In [3] it was established that the expected number of nonzero values of a key of length N written in NAF form is $\frac{N}{3}$.

Suppose we approximate the cost of **Half** as $1.6M$, where M represents the time to perform a multiplication, then the time to compute kP for a curve of cofactor 2 is approximately $N \cdot 1.6M + \frac{10}{3} \cdot 10M$ assuming we use a projective point addition [2]. For curves which have a cofactor 4, then we approximate the cost as approximately $N \cdot 1.6M + \frac{N}{2}M + \frac{N}{3} \cdot 10M$ assuming we use a projective point addition [2]. We now summarize the effect of using NAF form with three methods of computing the scalar multiple.

	Curve with cofactor 2	Curve with cofactor 4
Montgomery Method	$6NM$	$6NM$
Projective point method [2] using a key in NAF form	$8NM$	$8NM$
EC point halving with projective point add using a key in NAF form	$4.93NM$	$5.43NM$

Here we ignore those computations that are done once (or as setup). We also are only measuring field multiplications (since none of the methods use a field inversion more than once). We did not implement the EC half algorithm using the NAF form for the key. The timings as discussed above do confirm this analysis.

7 Conclusion

We have demonstrated that the halving the point algorithm will provide a significant performance improvement when computing kP over other algorithms. Here we have described some new algorithms that support this improvement, as well as provided some important implementation considerations. First, we see that computing a square root is no way near as intensive as a field multiplication. This is especially true when the modulus is a trinomial (although not a requirement). We also demonstrated that the trace check is very efficient, in particular we provided the trace check for all fields in the NIST list of elliptic curves. We have also made the observation that one can utilize projective points within the point-halving algorithm. This allows us to limit the use of a field inversion. Lastly we have developed a new version of the point halving algorithm for curves with cofactor 4. The improvement is significant.

References

1. Agnew, G., R. Mullin, S. Vanstone, "On the development of a fast elliptic curve processor chip", In *Advances in Cryptology - Crypto '91*, Springer-Verlag, 1991, pp 482-487.
2. E. Al-Daoud, R. Mahmod, M. Rushdan, and A. Kilicman . "A New Addition Formula for Elliptic Curves over $GF(2^n)$". *IEEE Transactions on Computers.* 51(8): 972-975 (2002)
3. S. Arno and F. Wheeler. "Signed Digit Representations of Minimal Hamming Weight". In *IEEE Transactions on Computers.* 42(8), 1993, p. 1007-1009.
4. E. Bach and J. Shalit. *Algorithmic Number Theory* MIT Press, Cambridge, 1996.
5. I.F. Blake, Nigel Smart, and G. Seroussi, *Elliptic Curves in Cryptography.* London Mathematical Society Lecture Note Series. Cambridge University Press, 1999.
6. D. V. Chudnovsky and G. V. Chudnovsky. "Sequences of numbers generated by addition in formal groups and new primality and factorization tests." In *Adv. in Appl. Math.* 7 (1986) 385–434.
7. K. Fong, D. Hankerson, J. Lopez, A. Menezes, and M. Tucker. "Performance comparisons of elliptic curve systems in software". The 5th Workshop on Elliptic Curve Cryptography (ECC 2001).
   http://www.cacr.math.uwaterloo.ca/conferences/2001/ecc/hankerson.pdf
8. Darrel Hankerson, Julio Lopez Hernandez and Alfred Menezes. "Software Implementation of Elliptic Curve Cryptography over Binary Fields". In *CHES 2000.* p. 1-24.
9. D. Hankerson, S. Vanstone, and A. Menezes. "A Guide to Elliptic Curve Cryptography." Jan. 2004
10. B. King "A method to compute squares and square roots in $GF(2^n)$".
    http://www.engr.iupui.edu/~briking/papers/sqr.ps
11. B. King. "An Improved Implementation of Elliptic Curves over $GF(2^n)$ when Using Projective Point Arithmetic." *Selected Areas in Cryptography 2001.* pg. 134-150
12. Neal Koblitz, *Elliptic curve cryptosystems*, Mathematics of Computation, Vol. 48, No. 177, 1987, 203-209.
13. E. Knudsen. "Elliptic Scalar Multiplication Using Point Halving". In *Advances in Cryptology - ASIACRYPT '99.* LNCS Vol. 1716, Springer, 1999, p. 135-149
14. R. Lidl and H. Niederreiter. *Finite Fields*, Second edition, Cambridge University Press, 1997.
15. Julio Lopez and Ricardo Dahab. "Improved Algorithms for Elliptic Curve Arithmetic in GF(2n)". In *Selected Areas in Cryptography '98, SAC'98.* LNCS 1556, Springer, 1999, p. 201-212
16. Alfred Menezes,*Elliptic Curve Public Key Cryptosystems*, Kluwer Academic Publishers, 1993.
17. Victor S. Miller, "Use of Elliptic Curves in Cryptography", In *Advances in Cryptology CRYPTO 1985*,Springer-Verlag, New York, 1985, pp 417-42
18. Montgomery, P. L. "Speeding the Pollard and elliptic curve methods of factorization". *Mathematics of Computation* 48, 177 (1987), 243-264.

19. NIST, *Recommended elliptic curves for federal use,* http://www.nist.gov
20. *IEEE P1363 Appendix A.* http://www.grouper.org/groups/1363
21. Rich Schroeppel. "Elliptic Curves: Twice as Fast!". In *Rump session of CRYPTO 2000.*
22. G. Seroussi. "Compact Representation of Elliptic Curve Points over F_{2^n}", *HP Labs Technical Reports,* `http://www.hpl.hp.com/techreports/98/HPL-98-94R1.html`, pg. 1-6.
23. N. P. Smart. A note on the x-coordinate of points on an elliptic curve in characteristic two. Information Processing Letters, 80:261–263, October 2001
24. *WTLS Specification,* http://www.wapforum.org

Theoretical Analysis of XL over Small Fields

Bo-Yin Yang[1] and Jiun-Ming Chen[2]

[1] Department of Mathematics, Tamkang University, Tamsui, Taiwan; by@moscito.org
[2] Chinese Data Security Inc. & National Taiwan U., Taipei, jmchen@math.ntu.edu.tw

Abstract. XL was first introduced to solve determined or overdetermined systems of equations over a finite field as an "algebraic attack" against multivariate cryptosystems. There has been a steady stream of announcements of cryptanalysis of primitives by such attacks, including stream ciphers (e.g. Toyocrypt), PKC's, and more controversially block ciphers (AES/Rijndael and Serpent).

Prior discussions of XL are usually heavy in simulations, which are of course valuable but we would like more attention to theory, because theory and simulations must validate each other, and there are some nuances not easily discerned from simulations. More effort was made in this direction of recent, but much of it was restricted to a large base field of size q, which is usually equal to 2^k. By conducting an analysis of XL variants in general, we try to derive rigorous "termination conditions", minimal degree requirements for reliable, successful operation of XL and its relatives, hence better security estimates. Our work is applicable to small q, in particular the significant $q = 2$ case.

Armed with this analysis, we reexamine previously announced results. We conclude that XL and variants represent a theoretical advance that is especially significant over small fields (in particular over $GF(2)$). However, its applicability and efficacy are occasionally overestimated slightly. We discuss possible future research directions. Much remains to be done.

Keywords: XL, finite field, multivariate cryptography, system of quadratic equations, algebraic attack.

1 Introducing the XL Family of Algorithms

XL is loosely descended from the relinearization ([15]) of Shamir and Kipnis. [8] implied that relinearization is superseded by XL which will always succeed if relinearization does. We will herein discuss only XL and its variants.

Goal: Find one solution to the system of m quadratic equations $\ell_1(\mathbf{x}) = \ell_2(\mathbf{x}) = \cdots = \ell_m(\mathbf{x}) = 0$ in n variables $\mathbf{x} = (x_1, x_2, \ldots, x_n)$ over the base field $K = GF(q)$. We will also use the following notations: The degree of a monomial $\mathbf{x}^\mathbf{b} = x_1^{b_1} x_2^{b_2} \cdots x_n^{b_n}$, is denoted $|\mathbf{b}| = \sum_i b_i$. The set $\mathcal{T} = \mathcal{T}^{(D)}$ comprises all monomials of total degree $\leq D$. It has $T = T^{(D)}$ elements.

1.1 Basic Procedures of XL

XL only operates on determined or over-determined systems, i.e. $n \leq m$. With more variables than equations, we must guess at enough variables so as to have at least as many equations as variables. XL at degree D then proceeds as follows:

H. Wang et al. (Eds.): ACISP 2004, LNCS 3108, pp. 277–288, 2004.
© Springer-Verlag Berlin Heidelberg 2004

1. "X" means to eXtend or multiply. Take all $\mathbf{x^b} \in \mathcal{T}^{(D-2)}$ (i.e., all monomials of degree $\leq D - 2$), and generate a set of equations $\mathbf{x^b}\ell_i(\mathbf{x}) = 0$. The system of equations will be collectively termed $\mathcal{R} = \mathcal{R}^{(D)}$.

2. "L" means to Linearize. Run an elimination on the system of $R = mT^{(D-2)}$ equations $\mathcal{R} = \mathcal{R}^{(D)}$, treating each monomial $\mathbf{x^b} \in \mathcal{T}^{(D)}$ as a variable. Enough equations must be independent to resolve the system. Because the system $\mathcal{R}$ is homogeneous in the variables (monomials) of $\mathcal{T}$, if there is a solution, then the number of independent equations (which we will denote I as opposed to $Free$ as in some earlier works) cannot exceed $T - 1$, and is usually exactly $T - 1$ if there is a unique solution. It was noted in [8] that I need not be as high as $T - 1$. It suffices to be able to eliminate enough monomials to express 1 as a linear combination of powers of x_1 (or any other variable). Thus the *termination condition*, which ensures *reliable* resolution of the system, is $I = T - \min(D, q - 1)$. This was first noted in [10].

3. *Solve the last remaining variable (usually x_1 as above), and recursively solve for the other variables as needed.* The time cost of XL is hence $C_{\mathrm{XL}} = E(T, R)$, where $E(N, M)$ is *the cost elimination on N variables and M equations.*
   Courtois *et al* often uses $(7/64) T^{2.8}$ for $E(T, R)$ under Strassen's Blocking Elimination Algorithm when the field is $\mathrm{GF}(2)$. We believe that an adjustment is needed. The best all-around elimination algorithm in the literature is [3], where the versatile D. J. Bernstein describes GGE, or the "Generalized Gaussian Elimination", a general way to compute what he termed a *quasi-inverse* to a non-square matrix. Via GGE we can solve an equation (his algorithm "S") or find a suitable basis of the kernel of a matrix, essentially a reduced echelon form (algorithm "N"). If the cost of multiplying two $N \times N$ matrices is $\sim \alpha N^\omega$, and $\gamma = 7\alpha/(2^\omega - 4)$ then the time cost of GGE is given by

$$E_S(N, M) = \frac{2\alpha(1 + \gamma)}{(2^\omega - 2)} M^{\omega-1} N + \frac{\alpha M^\omega}{(2^\omega - 1)}; \tag{1}$$

$$E_N(N, M) = \frac{2\alpha(2 + \gamma)}{(2^\omega - 2)} M^{\omega-2} N^2 + \frac{4\alpha\gamma}{7} M^{\omega-1} N + \frac{\alpha M^\omega}{(2^\omega - 1)}. \tag{2}$$

With $\alpha = 7/64$ we get $E_S(T, R) = 0.76 T R^{1.8} + 0.023 R^{2.8}$. This likely represents a better estimate than $(7/64)T^{2.8}$, *because Strassen's original algorithm has a large probability of failure particularly in $\mathrm{GF}(2)$, and even the later Bunch-Hopcroft ([2]) version can work only for square matrices.*

Note: We need to decide on D before the algorithm is run, hence this study.

[8] assumed D_0, *the minimum D needed for XL to work*, to be not far removed from what makes $R > T$, and hence obtained the heuristic of $D_0 \sim n/\sqrt{m}$, and [10] repeated this estimate for $\mathrm{GF}(2)$. Over $\mathrm{GF}(2)$ XL will work with most dimensions, but for a large q it was found that $D_0 = 2^n$ for $m = n$; and[1] $D_0 = n = m - 1$ when $n = m - 1$. [8] claimed that when $n \leq m - 2$, "it is likely" that $D_0 \approx \sqrt{n}$ because D_0 "drops abruptly when $m - n$ increases", although [7] verified that for larger dimensions, "$m - n$ *may need to be yet higher*". So XL sometimes work less smoothly, which led to FXL ([8]). We seek to understand the behavior of D_0 (hence XL and variants) better.

---

[1] The formula below may be off by one equation, i.e. the authors may have meant m.

1.2 The XL' Variant

XL' operates like XL ([10]), except that we try to eliminate down to r equations that involves only monomials in r of the variables, say $x_1, \ldots, x_r$, then solve the remaining system by brute-force substitution. If T' is the number of degree $\leq D$ monomials in r variables, then we require $T - I$ to be at most $T' - r$ instead of D. Hopefully we can run with a smaller D, and q^r is relatively small. The time complexity is then bounded by

$$C_{\text{XL'}} = E(T, R) + q^r T' D / \left(1 - \tfrac{1}{q}\right). \qquad (3)$$

Note that we must test degree-D polynomials with r variables and up to $\binom{r+D}{D}$ terms, and there is a $1/q$ probability for any polynomial to vanish on random inputs. *We will discuss the behavior of XL' in the next section more accurately.*

1.3 The XL2 Variant: New Equations from Old?

Let $\mathcal{T}_i'$ be the set of monomials that when multiplied by x_i will still be in $\mathcal{T} = \mathcal{T}^{(D)}$, and T' be their number. I.e. $T' = |\mathcal{T}_i'|$, where $\mathcal{T}_i' = \{\mathbf{x}^{\mathbf{b}} : x_i \mathbf{x}^{\mathbf{b}} \in \mathcal{T}\}$. If $T > I$, $C \equiv T' + I - T > 0$, then we can try to generate more useful equations:

1. Starting from the equations $\mathcal{R} = \mathcal{R}^{(D)}$, we eliminate monomials not in $\mathcal{T}_1'$ first. We are then left with relations $\mathcal{R}_1$, which gives each monomial in $\mathcal{T} \setminus \mathcal{T}_1'$ as a linear combination of monomials in $\mathcal{T}_1$, plus C equations $\mathcal{R}_1'$ with terms only in $\mathcal{T}_1'$.
2. Repeat for $\mathcal{T}_2$ to get the equations $\mathcal{R}_2$ and $\mathcal{R}_2'$ (we should also have $|\mathcal{R}_2'| = C$).
3. For each $\ell \in \mathcal{R}_1'$, use $\mathcal{R}_2$ to write every monomial in $\mathcal{T} \setminus \mathcal{T}_2'$ in the equation $x_1 \ell = 0$ in terms of those in $\mathcal{T}_2$. Do the converse for each $x_2 \ell$, $\ell \in \mathcal{R}_2'$.

We get $2C$ new equations. [10], which proposed XL2 over GF(2) only, suggests that most of these $2C$ equations will be linearly independent, because they are somehow built out of all the equations. It was also remarked that XL2 can be repeated as needed for more equations and eventually a solution. The attacker can also run XL2 using more variables, as in adding $(x_3 \mathcal{R}_3')$, and so on.

1.4 Other Relatives of XL: FXL, XFL, XLF, and XSL

FXL and XFL: The "F" here means to "fix" ([8]). f variables are guessed at random in the hope that the degree D_0 needed for XL will decrease. After guessing at each variable, XL is run and tested for a valid solution. In [7], it was proposed that the R equations be generated and an elimination be run on them as far as it can go *before* guessing at the variables. It is named *improved FXL*, but we think that *XFL* suits better. For large (m, n) these are not very useful (cf. Sec. 3) in cutting down the operating degree D, but may be useful in removing excess solutions.

XLF: In [7] the authors proposed a variation, trying to use the Frobenius relations $x^q = x$ to advantage when $q = 2^k$, by considering $(x_i^2), (x_i^4), \ldots, (x_i^{2^{k-1}})$ as new independent variables, replicating all R equations k times by repeatly squaring them, and using the equivalence of identical monomials as extra equations. The variant is called XLF, for "field" or "Frobenius equations".

XSL: Not a true XL relative, this is a related linearization-based method designed to work on *overdefined systems of sparse quadratic equations that characterize certain block ciphers.* [9] suggested that it may be possible to break AES using XSL and thereby raised a storm of controversy. Occasionally we see amazingly low numbers given for this attack based on applying XSL to structural equations discovered by Murphy and Robshaw ([17]) in AES, but in contrast to the general public, few researchers appear to believe that AES has been broken. We mention XSL only because its final stage or the "T'-method" resembles XL2.

We omit detailed discussions for FXL/XFL/XLF because for small fields like GF(2), they do not appreciably increase speed or applicability compared to original XL.

2   Termination Behavior for XL – A Combinatorial Study

We discuss when XL can be expected to terminate using combinatorial technique. We first prove an easy lemma about T in general. The combinatorial notation $[u]\,p$ will denote "the coefficient of term u in the expansion of p". E.g. $[x^2](1+x)^4 = 6$.

Lemma 1 (Number of Monomials up to a Given Degree).

$$T = T^{(D)} = [t^D]\frac{(1+t+t^2+\cdots+t^{q-1})^n}{1-t} = [t^D]\frac{(1-t^q)^n}{(1-t)^{n+1}} \qquad (4)$$

Proof. Consider the product $\prod_{i=1}^{n}(1+x_i+x_i^2+\cdots x_i^{q-1}) = \prod_{i=1}^{n}[(1-x_i^q)/(1-x_i)]$. This generates all possible monomials, exactly once each. Set every x_i be equal to t in this expression, and clearly the coefficient of t^D counts the monomials of degree exactly D. As $(a_0 + a_1 t + a_2 t^2 + \cdots + a_D t^D + \cdots)(1 + t + t^2 + \cdots + t^D + \cdots)$ has as its D-th degree coefficient $(a_0 + \cdots + a_D)$, we have derived $T^{(D)}$ henceforth. □

Lemma 1 unites as useful corollaries the special cases of large D (i.e. $D > q$) where $T = \binom{n+D}{D}$ as first given in [8], and $q = 2$ when $T = \sum_{i=0}^{D}\binom{n}{i}$ as in [10]. $R^{(D)} = mT^{(D-2)}$ and hence is given by $m[t^{D-2}]\left((1-t^q)^n/(1-t)^{n+1}\right)$.

We want to know how many independent equations there are in the general case, when dependencies abound among the equations. Denote by $[f]$ the equation $f(\mathbf{x}) = 0$, and assume that $\ell_i(\mathbf{x}) = \sum_{j \le k} a_{ijk}x_j x_k + \sum_j b_{ij}x_j + c_i$, then

$$\sum_{j\le k} a_{ijk}[x_j x_k \ell_{i'}] + \sum_j b_{ij}[x_j \ell_{i'}] + c_i\,[\ell_{i'}] = \sum_{j\le k} a_{i'jk}[x_j x_k \ell_i] + \sum_j b_{i'j}[x_j \ell_i] + c_{i'}\,[\ell_i],$$

I.e. $[\ell_i \ell_j]$ appears as two different linear combinations of the equations. And there will be dependencies among the dependencies, so it is not so obvious that we can compute the number of free equations under reasonable conditions.

Theorem 1. *The number of independent XL equations over* GF(2) *is bound by*

$$T - I \ge [t^D]\left(\frac{1}{1-t}\left(\frac{1-t^q}{1-t}\right)^n \left(\frac{1-t^2}{1-t^{2q}}\right)^m\right), \text{ for all } D < D_{reg}, \qquad (5)$$

where D_{reg} is the "degree of regularity" defined by

$$D_{reg} = \min\{D : [t^D]\,((1-t)^{-n-1}\,(1-t^q)^n\,(1-t^2)^m\,(1-t^{2q})^{-m}) \leq 0\}. \quad (6)$$

If there are no extra dependencies, the bound would be an equality. For this to happen, no $\ell_i(\mathbf{x}) - \alpha$ can be non-trivially factorizable for any ℓ_i and $\alpha \in \mathrm{GF}(q)$, and the ℓ_i's must contain enough degree-2 monomials so make $\deg \ell_i \mathbf{x}^{\mathbf{b}} = |\mathbf{b}| + 2$ for any $\mathbf{b}$ and any i. These conditions being met, the minimum D for XL to operate reliably is

$$D_0 = \min\left\{D : [t^D]\,\frac{1}{1-t}\left(\frac{1-t^q}{1-t}\right)^n\left(\frac{1-t^2}{1-t^{2q}}\right)^m \leq \min(D, q-1)\right\}. \quad (7)$$

Proof. Linear subspaces of $\mathrm{span}\,\mathcal{T}^{(\mathcal{D})}$ (a.k.a. degree $\leq D$ polynomials in $x_1, \ldots, x_n$) form a partially ordered set. In fact, the intersection and the algebraic sum ($U + V \equiv \{\mathbf{u}+\mathbf{v} : \mathbf{u} \in U, \mathbf{v} \in V\}$) fulfill requirements for the infimum and supremum operations of a *modular lattice* with the dimension as the rank function, which in plainer language means that for any subspaces U and V, we have

$$\dim U + \dim V = \dim(U + V) + \dim(U \cap V). \quad (8)$$

Eq. 8 implies (among other things) a form of the Principle of Inclusion-Exclusion ([19]), one which states that if $A_1, \ldots A_k$ are subspaces of $\mathrm{span}\,\mathcal{T}^{(D)}$, then

$$\dim\left(\sum_{i=1}^{k} A_i\right) = \sum_{j=1}^{k}(-1)^{j-1}\left(\sum_{1 \leq i_1 < \cdots < i_j \leq k} \dim(A_{i_1} \cap \cdots \cap A_{i_j})\right). \quad (9)$$

Let A_i be the set comprising all polynomials of degree $\leq D$ that is divisible by ℓ_i. So $\mathrm{span}\,\mathcal{R}^{(D)} = \sum_{i=1}^{m} A_i$ and $I = \dim\mathrm{span}\,\mathcal{R}^{(D)}$, and we need to compute $\dim A_i$, $\dim A_i \cap A_j$, and in general $\dim A_{i_1} \cap \cdots \cap A_{i_j}$. We first find the dimension of $A_i = \mathrm{span}\,\{\mathbf{x}^{\mathbf{b}}\ell_i : |\mathbf{b}| \leq D - 2\} = \ell_i\,\mathrm{span}\,(\mathcal{T}^{(D-2)})$. We would have $\dim A_i = T^{(D-2)}$ *were there not $f(\mathbf{x})[\ell_i(\mathbf{x})]$ of degree $\leq D$ that are identically zero.* Since ℓ_i is assumed not to factor, $f(\mathbf{x})[\ell_i(\mathbf{x})]$ vanishes iff $f(\mathbf{x})$ is divisible by $(\ell_i(\mathbf{x}))^{q-1} - 1$, hence we have a 1-to-1 correspondence of A_i with a quotient space of $\mathrm{span}\,\mathcal{T}^{(D-2)}$ by $\{f(\mathbf{x}) : \deg f \leq D - 2, (\ell_i^{q-1} - 1)|f\} = (\ell_i^{q-1} - 1)\,\mathrm{span}\,\mathcal{T}^{(D-2q)}$. Ergo,

$$\dim A_i = \dim \ell_i\,\mathrm{span}\,(\mathcal{T}^{(D-2)}) = T^{(D-2)} - \dim\left((\ell_i^{q-1} - 1)\,\mathrm{span}\,(\mathcal{T}^{(D-2q)})\right).$$

So $\dim A_i$ would be $T^{(D-2)} - T^{(D-2q)}$ *except for that* $(\ell_i^{q-1} - 1)\,\mathrm{span}\,(\mathcal{T}^{(D-2q)}) = \{(\ell_i^{q-1} - 1)g(\mathbf{x}) : \deg g \leq D - 2q\}$, is not in bijective correspondence with $\mathrm{span}\,(\mathcal{T}^{(D-2q)})$ because we have to discount (or quotient out) all g such that $(\ell_i^{q-1} - 1)g(\mathbf{x}) = 0$. Under the conditions the theorem, this means $\ell_i|g$, so we must recompensate to get

$$\dim A_i = T^{(D-2)} - T^{(D-2q)} + \dim\left(\ell_i\,\mathrm{span}\,(\mathcal{T}^{(D-2q-2)})\right).$$

By the same reasoning, we must deduct $T^{(D-4q)}$, add $T^{(D-4q-2)}$, and so on, repeating until we hit zero. If we let $p(t) = (1-t)^{-n-1}(1-t^q)^n$, then $T^{(D)} = [t^D]p(t)$ and

$$
\begin{aligned}
\dim A_i &= [t^{D\square 2}]p - [t^{D\square 2q}]p + [t^{D\square 2q\square 2}]p - [t^{D\square 4q}]p + [t^{D\square 4q\square 2}]p - + - + \cdots \\
&= [t^D]\left((t^2 - t^{2q})\,p/(1-t^{2q})\right).
\end{aligned}
\tag{10}
$$

Similarly, $\quad \dim\left((\ell_i^{q\square 1} - 1)\mathrm{span}\,\mathcal{T}^{(D\square 2q)}\right) = [t^D]\left(t^{2q}(1-t^2)\,p/(1-t^{2q})\right).$ $\quad$ (11)

What is $\dim A_i \cap A_j = \dim\left(\ell_i\ell_j\,\mathrm{span}\,\mathcal{T}^{(D-4)}\right)$? $\ell_i(\ell_i^{q-1} - 1) = \ell_j(\ell_j^{q-1} - 1) = 0$, so any $(\ell_i^{q-1} - 1)g_1(\mathbf{x}) + (\ell_j^{q-1} - 1)g_2(\mathbf{x})$ vanishes when multiplied by $\ell_i\ell_j$. Hence

$$
A_i \cap A_j \cong \mathrm{span}\,\mathcal{T}^{(D-4)}\left((\ell_i^{q-1} - 1)\,\mathrm{span}\,\mathcal{T}^{(D-2q-2)} + (\ell_j^{q-1} - 1)\,\mathrm{span}\,\mathcal{T}^{(D-2q-2)}\right).
$$

So $\dim A_i \cap A_j$ should be $T^{(D-4)}$ minus the dimension of the subspace spanned by multiples of $(\ell_i(\mathbf{x})^{q-1} - 1)$ and $(\ell_j(\mathbf{x})^{q-1} - 1)$ that are of degree $\leq D - 4$, and

$$
\begin{aligned}
\dim A_i \cap A_j &= T^{(D-4)} - \dim\left((\ell_i^{q-1} - 1)\,\mathrm{span}\,\mathcal{T}^{(D-2q-2)}\right) \\
&- \dim\left((\ell_j^{q-1} - 1)\mathrm{span}\,\mathcal{T}^{(D-2q-2)}\right) + \dim\left((\ell_i^{q-1} - 1)(\ell_j^{q-1} - 1)\,\mathrm{span}\,\mathcal{T}^{(D-4q)}\right),
\end{aligned}
$$

again via Eq. 8, and $\dim\left((\ell_i^{q-1} - 1)(\ell_j^{q-1} - 1)\,\mathrm{span}\,\mathcal{T}^{(D-4q)}\right)$ via the same reasoning is found to be $T^{(D-4q)}$ minus

$$
\dim\left(\ell_i\mathrm{span}\,\mathcal{T}^{(D-4q-2)}\right) + \dim\left(\ell_j\,\mathrm{span}\,\mathcal{T}^{(D-4q-2)}\right) - \dim\left(\ell_i\ell_j\mathrm{span}\,\mathcal{T}^{(D-4q-4)}\right).
$$

I.e., if $\dim A_i \cap A_j = [t^D]f(t)$, then it is also equal to

$$
[t^D]\left((t^4 p) - 2\left(\frac{t^{2q+2}(1 - t^2)}{1 - t^{2q}}p\right) + (t^{4q}p) - 2\left(\frac{t^{4q}(t^2 - t^{2q})}{1 - t^{2q}}p\right) + (t^{4q}f(t))\right),
$$

which routinely simplifies to $[t^D]f(t) = \dim A_i \cap A_j = [t^D]\left((t^2 - t^{2q})^2 p/(1 - t^{2q})^2\right)$. The same Inclusion-Exclusion manuever assisted by mathematical induction shows that

$$
\dim\left(A_{i_1} \cap \cdots \cap A_{i_j}\right) = [t^D]\left(\left(\frac{t^2 - t^{2q}}{1 - t^{2q}}\right)^j p\right); \quad \text{in fact, we have also} \tag{12}
$$

$$
\dim\left(\prod_{k=1}^{j}(\ell_{i_k}^{q-1} - 1) \cdot \mathrm{span}\,\mathcal{T}^{(D-2jq)}\right) = [t^D]\left(\left(\frac{t^{2q} - t^{2q+2}}{1 - t^{2q}}\right)^j p\right). \tag{13}
$$

To see that this is so, we apply Eq. 8 two more times in succession on

$$
\dim\left(A_{i_1} \cap \cdots \cap A_{i_j}\right) = T^{(D-2j))} - \dim\left(\sum_{k=1}^{j}(\ell_{i_k}^{q-1} - 1)\,\mathrm{span}\,\mathcal{T}^{(D-2(q+j-1))}\right).
$$

and we verify Eqs. 12 and 13 as consistent. Substituting Eq. 12, we finally get

$$T - I = [t^D] \left(p \sum_{k=0}^{m} (-1)^k \binom{m}{k} (t^2 - t^{2q})^k / (1 - t^{2q})^k \right) = [t^D] \left(p \left(1 - \frac{t^2 - t^{2q}}{1 - t^{2q}} \right)^m \right)$$

$$= [t^D] \left((1 - t)^{\square \, n\square \, 1} (1 - t^q)^n \, (1 - t^2)^m \, (1 - t^{2q})^{\square \, m} \right).$$

That's Eq. 5. Any other dependency will make I smaller. Clearly, this cannot hold when the right hand side goes non-positive, which also indicates that XL will terminate. $\square$

Corollary 1. *When applying XL over the field* GF(2) *at degree* $D < D_{reg}$, *then*

$$T - I = [t^D] \left((1 - t)^{-1} (1 + t)^n (1 + t^2)^{-m} \right). \tag{14}$$

XL will usually terminate if the RHS$\leq$ 0, with a unique solution if $T - I = 1$.

Note: Eq. 14 is consistent with the partial results (i.e. for $D \leq 5$) of [10].

Corollary 2. *The degree of regularity (the maximum degree of in the elimination stage) of the Gröbner algorithm* $\mathbf{F_5}/\mathbf{2}$ *is no lower than XL's degree of regularity over* GF(2).

Proof. The degree of regularity for $\mathbf{F_5}/\mathbf{2}$ ([12,13]) is given (according to [1]):

$$D_{reg}^{F_5/2} = \min \left\{ D : [t^D] \left(\frac{(1+t)^n}{(1+t^2)^m} \right) \leq 0 \right\}. \tag{15}$$

$D_{reg}^{F_5/2}$ is the degree of the first non-positive coefficient in $(1+t)^n(1+t^2)^{-m}$. Compare this to Eq. 6, where our $D_{reg}^{\mathrm{XL}/2}$ is the degree of the first non-positive coefficient in $(1 + t)^n (1 + t^2)^{-m}(1 - t)^{-1}$, or the lowest degree up to which the coefficients sum up non-positive in $(1 + t)^n (1 + t^2)^{-m}$. We see that $D_{reg}^{F_5/2} \leq D_{reg}^{\mathrm{XL}/2}$. Actually,

$$D_{reg}^{\mathrm{XL}/2} \gtrsim D_{reg}^{F_5/2} \sim 0.900m + O(m^{\frac{1}{3}}), \tag{16}$$

via the same kind of asymptotic argument in [1]. *Note that the operation of both* $\mathbf{F_5}/\mathbf{2}$ *and* XL/2 *are hinged on the sparse system solving stage, so we cannot conclude that* $\mathbf{F_5}/\mathbf{2}$ *is faster even though it will have a smaller* D_0. $\square$

Corollary 3. *XL' (cf. Sec. 1.2) applied over* GF(2) *will operate when the* $T - I \leq \sum_{i=0}^{D} \binom{r}{D} - r$ *(cf. Eq. 5). This reduces to Theorem 1 if $r = 1$, as expected.*

The large q case differs sufficiently from small q that all further XL discussions on large fields probably belongs to another paper ([21]). But merely setting $t^q = 0$ we get:

Corollary 4 (Large q case). *For large q and $D < D_{reg}$, we have*

1. *If $q > D$, then $T - I = [t^D] \left((1 - t)^{m-n-1} (1 - t^2)^m \right) \geq 0$.*
2. *D_{reg} (resp. D_0) is the least D such that the RHS above ≤ 0 (resp. $\leq \min(D, q-1)$).*

3. *If* $\max(2q, D_0) > D \geq q$, *then* $T - I = [t^D]\left((1-t)^{m-n-1}(1 - nt^q)(1-t^2)^m\right)$.

Theorem 1 carries over nicely to higher-order equations with little change.

Theorem 2 (Non-Quadratic Equations). *If* $\deg \ell_i = d_i$ *instead of 2, then*

$$T - I = [t^D]\left(\left(\frac{(1-t^q)^n}{(1-t)^{n+1}}\right)\prod_{i=1}^{m}\left(\frac{(1-t^{d_i})}{(1-t^{d_i q})}\right)\right), \quad \text{for all } D < D_{reg}. \quad (17)$$

assuming no extra dependencies. Just as in Theorem 1, D_{reg} is the smallest D for which the left side of Eq. 17 is non-positive. In particular, if $\deg \ell_i = k$ *for all i, then*

$$T - I = [t^D]\left(\frac{1}{1-t}\left(\frac{1-t^q}{1-t}\right)^n\left(\frac{1-t^k}{1-t^{kq}}\right)^m\right), \quad \text{for all } D < D_{reg}. \quad (18)$$

The proof carries so well, in fact, that we can see that *if for example one of the ℓ_i is a product of two factors of degree k and k', then the corresponding factor in Eq. 17 becomes* $\left(1 - \left((t^k - t^{kq})(t^{k'} - t^{k'q})\right)/\left((1-t^{kq})(1-t^{k'q})\right)\right)$.

This theorem governs the behavior of XL when used for generalized or higher-order correlation attacks such as in [5,6], which is an application of Eq. 18 with $k = 3$.

3   Looking at Earlier Claims and Results over GF(2)

Enough theory! We turn to some practical assessment of XL over GF(2). An interesting tidbit from Eqs. 14 and 16 is that when $m = n$ (in fact whenever $m/n \to \beta$, a constant), we do not have $D_0 \approx n/\sqrt{m}$ as postulated by [10]; instead, Eq. 16 gives $D_0 \sim cn$, where $c \approx 0.09$ for $m = n$. Let us back this up by plotting up to around 2000:

The D_0 vs. m graph is a straight line with a linear correlation coefficient of around 0.9999. This precludes the ratio $\mu = T/R$ at $D = D_0$ from being proximate to 1. It apparently decreases to 0 inversely to an increasing m, which will be proved in Prop. 1.

[4] claims to break HFE ([18]) challenge 1 ($n = m = 80$). This is a "generalized algebraic attack", not via XL over GF(2). In [10] the authors were more cautious, allowing that for $m = n$ XL may turn out to be always somewhat slower than brute-force search. Using Eq. 6, $D_0 = 12$ for $m = n = 80$. The number of operations (by the Bernstein formula) is $\approx 2^{177}$ ($\approx 2^{154}$ substitutions), well above brute-force search.

All is not completely lost for XL. Solving sparse equations (cf. related texts, e.g. [11]) is easier than in general. If there are N variables, M rows, but only t terms in each row, an optimistic bound for a time cost is $E_L = tMN(c_0 + c_1 \lg N)$. The constants c_0 and c_1 for the best case are usually around 10 and $1/10$ respectively (and can be several times more). This get us a complexity of around 2^{84} substitutions, which is much better.

Let us justify somewhat the assessment of [5] of exponential running time for XL.

Proposition 1. *For $m = n \to \infty$, XL runs in exponential time ($\sim 2^{7n/8}$) over GF(2).*

Proof. If $m \to \infty$ while $\frac{D}{m} \to \alpha \approx 0.09$, then $\frac{R}{T} = \frac{m\binom{m}{D-2}}{\binom{m}{D}} \to \frac{m}{(\frac{1}{\alpha}-1)^2} \approx \frac{m}{100}$, and

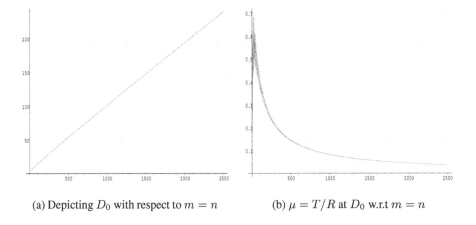

(a) Depicting D_0 with respect to $m = n$ (b) $\mu = T/R$ at D_0 w.r.t $m = n$

Fig. 1. Behavior of XL over $GF(2)$ when $m = n$

$$T \sim \sum_{j=0}^{\alpha n} \binom{n}{j} \sim \binom{n}{\alpha n} \sim \sqrt{\frac{1}{2\pi\alpha(1-\alpha)}} \left(\alpha^{-\alpha}(1-\alpha)^{-(1-\alpha)}\right)^n ,$$

using the optimistic (Lanczos) bound above, the time cost is at most polynomial times $\left(\alpha^{-2\alpha}(1-\alpha)^{-2(1-\alpha)}\right)^n$. If $\alpha \approx 0.09$ then $C_{XL/2} \sim 2^{7m/8} \cdot$ (rational in m).   □

This means that XL over $GF(2)$ *will eventually be a little better than brute-force.*

To show that in fact, decreasing n by fixing variables does not do much when $q = 2$, we let $m - n$ be 10, 25, and 50, and plot three D_0-vs.-m graphs using Eq. 14:

One is hard-pressed to see the difference in the three lines in Fig. 2(a)! For any fixed $m - n$, D_0/m approaches the same constant as $m \to \infty$. Hence as a speed improvement of XL, XFL/FXL are lacking. Obviously, they may have other useful traits.

Does things change much if we instead make m/n a fixed ratio? It seems not, see Fig. 2(b): Although the slopes are different, D_0/n still seems to approach a limit.

We are yet to understand all of the interesting behavior in XL, even asymptotically for large m *and* n, *because the coefficients of generating functions are hard enough to estimate, let alone the sign-change point. We leave some for a later work ([22]).*

4   XL2 (and XL') over Smaller Fields

One problem with the methods of XL' and XL2 is that they really require general and not sparse matrix methods. However, Strassen-like methods can still be used. Therefore, over $GF(2)$, XL2 and XL' may show good advantage, a small advantage or no advantage compared to running just XL with well-designed sparse-like algorithms (even though we are not sure how sparse matrices mesh with $GF(2)$), depending on how well everything can be optimized, and the exact comparison is still up in the air.

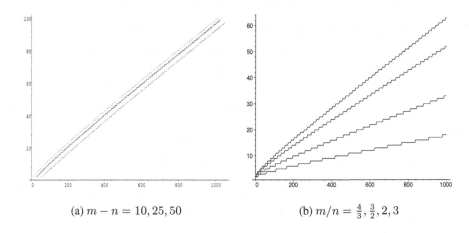

(a) $m - n = 10, 25, 50$ (b) $m/n = \frac{4}{3}, \frac{3}{2}, 2, 3$

Fig. 2. Behavior of D_0 in XL over $GF(2)$ for fixed $m - n$ and m/n

That said, it is likely possible to inject some extra insight. The authors of [10] seem to consider XL' inferior to XL2, so we aim to have some meaningful discussion about XL2 for both $GF(2)$ (for which XL2 had originally been designed) and larger fields where formerly only heuristics are available, viz. the following observations about XL2. While we believe these to be correct (tested only for small dimensions), the discussions above may not constitute mathematically rigorous proofs.

1. For large q, i.e. $q > D$, every $\mathcal{T}'_j$ is the same, in fact it is exactly $\mathcal{T}^{(D-1)}$. So XL2 can simultanenously apply to any subset of one, two or many variables, because $\mathcal{R}_1 = \mathcal{R}_2 = \cdots = \hat{\mathcal{R}}$, $\mathcal{R}'_1 = \mathcal{R}'_2 = \cdots = \mathcal{R}'$, so by multiplying the C relations $\mathcal{R}'$ by every variable x_i we can maximize the return from XL2, saving a little time.
2. It is not necessarily true that if $I - (T - T') = C > 0$ we will be able to run XL2. The reason is that for any j, all the monomials in $\mathcal{T} \setminus \mathcal{T}'_j$ are at the top degree D. Not all of the I independent equations have those terms.
   Let us illustrate with an example. For large q, we take $m = 11$, $n = 7$, and $D = 3$. Now we have $11 \times (7 + 1) = 88$ equations in XL, all of them independent and $\binom{7+2}{3} = 84$ cubic monomials. It seems as if we should be able to run XL2. Not so, because *only 77 of the equations actually have cubic terms*.
3. We can expand on the preceding discussion a little to find when XL2 can be run for larger q. There are $R^{(D)} - R^{(D-1)}$ equations at the top degree. There are usually $R^{(D)} - I^{(D)}$ dependencies, i.e. linear relations between equations, but we need to eliminate the $I^{(D-1)}$ independent equations from those, so there are

$$(R^{(D)} - R^{(D-1)}) - (R^{(D)} - I^{(D)} - I^{(D-1)}) = I^{(D)} - (R^{(D-1)} - I^{(D-1)})$$

independent equations involving the top-degreed monomials, of which there are $T^{(D)} - T^{(D-1)}$. So the condition we seek is: for $q > D$, XL2 operates if:

$$D < T^{(D)} - I^{(D)} < T^{(D-1)} - (R^{(D-1)} - I^{(D-1)}). \tag{19}$$

The term between the parenthesis is our correction to [10] for the large q case. For small q, the behavior is too complex for us to analyze it completely up to now. However, we can do things case-by-case. E.g., we diagnose for the HFE challenge ($m = 80$, $n = 80$, $q = 2$) case, that XL2 runs at $D = 11$, saving only one degree.

4. For $D \geq q > 2$ we can still run XL2. Here, $\mathcal{T}_j'$ generically comprises all monomials of degree less than D (i.e. every monomial in $\mathcal{T}^{(D-1)}$), plus all degree-D monomials where the exponent of x_j is exactly $q - 1$. So

$$T' = [t^D] \frac{(1 - t^q)^{n-1}}{(1 - t)^n} \left(\frac{t(1 - t^q)}{1 - t} + t^{q-1} \right).$$

5. Generally speaking, running XL2 on *all* independent variables x_i is equivalent to running XL at one degree higher, regardless of q. How so? Multiply each original XL equation in $\mathcal{R}$ by x_1. This new set of equations (we write $x_1\mathcal{R}$ for short) have only monomials in $x_1\mathcal{T} = \{x_1 p : p \in \mathcal{T}\}$. Run an elimination on $x_1\mathcal{R}$ to write every monomial in $x_1\mathcal{T} \setminus \mathcal{T}$ in terms of $x_1\mathcal{T} \cap \mathcal{T} = x_1\mathcal{T}_1'$. These can be bijectively mapped to the equations $x_1\mathcal{R}_1$, and the remaining C equations with only $x_1\mathcal{T}_1'$ monomials correspond similarly to the equations $x_1\mathcal{R}_1'$. Further substitution with relations of x_2 may simplify the equations but does not add new ones.

So, running XL2 with x_i effectively includes equations $x_i\mathcal{R}$ at one degree higher. Running it with every variable will consequently raise the degree of XL by 1.

5 Conclusion

XL is clearly an intriguing idea, one that due to its simplicity has the potential to join Gröbner bases methods ([12,13]) as a premier equation-solving method. Especially over $GF(2)$, when the objections of [16] seem inapplicable, XL may and should do well. On the other hand, its theory is still woefully incomplete. Even to implement a solver for large m and n for the simple field of $GF(2)$ still poses a challenge, due to its space requirements, so we do not know yet the final form of XL. In this, we are reminded of the 2^{63} bytes storage requirement that was suggested in [5]. Clearly some breakthrough in the form of less unwieldy space management techniques needs to be found, as witness the amount of sparse matrix algebra used by Faugère for $F_5/2$ ([12]).

Our misgivings aside, we sincerely hoped to have shed some light on the subject. Generating functions provide a relatively easy way to check if any particular combinations of dimensions will be an operative case for any XL variant. Much remains to be done. Even if behavior of coefficients in generating function can be asymptotically determined, an actual optimization with an obvious space-time tradeoff will still be hard.

Still, we do hope to see a practically useful XL solver at some point.

Acknowledgements. We thank everyone who supported us or made helpful suggestions or comments during the work leading to this manuscript. The first author would especially like to thank (a) his friend and mentor, Dr. Yeong-Nan Yeh of the Institute of Mathematics, Academia Sinica (Taipei) for his support and encouragement; and (b) his ever-tolerant Ping.

References

1. M. Bardet, J.-C. Faugère, and B. Salvy, *Complexity of Gröbner Basis Computations for Regular Overdetermined Systems*, INRIA RR. No. 5049 and private communication.
2. J. R. Bunch and J. E. Hopcroft, *Triangular Factorizations and Inversion by Fast Matrix Multiplication*, Math. Computations, 24 (1974), pp. 231–236.
3. D. Bernstein, *Matrix Inversion Made Difficult*, preprint, stated to be superseded by a yet unpublished version, available at http://cr.yp.to.
4. N. Courtois, *The Security of Hidden Field Equations (HFE)*, CT-RSA 2001, LNCS v. 2020, pp. 266–281.
5. N. Courtois, *Higher-Order Correlation Attacks, XL Algorithm and Cryptanalysis of Toyocrypt*, ICISC '02, LNCS v. 2587, pp. 182–199.
6. N. Courtois, *Fast Algebraic Attacks on Stream Ciphers with Linear Feedback*, CRYPTO'03, LNCS v. 2729, pp. 176-194.
7. N. Courtois, *Algebraic Attacks over* $GF(2^k)$, *Cryptanalysis of HFE Challenge 2 and SFLASH^{v2}*, proc. PKC 2004, LNCS v. 2947, pp. 201-217.
8. N. Courtois, A. Klimov, J. Patarin, and A. Shamir, *Efficient Algorithms for Solving Overdefined Systems of Multivariate Polynomial Equations*, EUROCRYPT 2000, LNCS v. 1807, pp. 392–407.
9. N. Courtois and J. Pieprzyk, *Cryptanalysis of Block Ciphers with Overdefined Systems of Equations*, ASIACRYPT 2002, LNCS v. 2501, pp. 267–287.
10. N. Courtois and J. Patarin, *About the XL Algorithm over GF(2)*, CT-RSA 2003, LNCS v. 2612, pp. 141–157.
11. I. S. Duff, A. M. Erismann, and J. K. Reid, *Direct Methods for Sparse Matrices*, published by Oxford Science Publications, 1986.
12. J.-C. Faugère, *A New Efficient Algorithm for Computing Gröbner Bases without Reduction to Zero (F5)*, Proceedings of ISSAC 2002, pp. 75-83, ACM Press 2002.
13. J.-C. Faugère and A. Joux, *Algebraic Cryptanalysis of Hidden Field Equations (HFE) Cryptosystems Using Gröbner Bases*, CRYPTO 2003, LNCS v. 2729, pp. 44-60.
14. M. Garey and D. Johnson, *Computers and Intractability, A Guide to the Theory of NP-completeness*, 1979, p. 251.
15. A. Kipnis and A. Shamir, *Cryptanalysis of the HFE Public Key Cryptosystem by Relinearization*, CRYPTO'99, LNCS v. 1666, pp. 19–30.
16. T. Moh, *On The Method of XL and Its Inefficiency Against TTM*, available at http://eprint.iacr.org/2001/047
17. S. Murphy and M. Robshaw, *Essential Algebraic Structures Within the AES*, CRYPTO 2002, LNCS v. 2442, pp. 1–16.
18. J. Patarin, *Hidden Fields Equations (HFE) and Isomorphisms of Polynomials (IP): Two New Families of Asymmetric Algorithms*, EUROCRYPT'96, LNCS v. 1070, pp. 33–48.
19. R. Stanley, *Enumerative Combinatorics*, vol. 1, second printing 1996; vol. 2 in 1999. Both published by Cambridge University Press, Cambridge.
20. V. Strassen, *Gaussian Elimination is not Optimal*, Numer. Math. 13 (1969) pp. 354-356.
21. B.-Y. Yang and J.-M. Chen, *All in the XL Family: Theory and Practice*, preprint.
22. B.-Y. Yang and J.-M. Chen, *Asymptotic Behavior for XL and Friends*, preprint.

A New Method for Securing Elliptic Scalar Multiplication Against Side-Channel Attacks

Chae Hoon Lim

Dept. of Internet Engineering, Sejong University
98 Gunja-Dong, Kwangjin-Gu, Seoul, 143-747, KOREA
chlim@sejong.ac.kr

Abstract. This paper presents a new method for elliptic scalar multiplication with protection against side-channel attacks. We first point out some potential security flaws often overlooked in most previous algorithms and then present a simple ±1-signed encoding scheme that can be used to enhance the security and performance of existing algorithms. In particular, we propose and analyze concrete signed binary and window algorithms based on the proposed ±1-signed encoding. The security of window-family algorithms against a DPA-style attack is also discussed with some possible countermeasures.

1 Introduction

Side channel attacks make use of some side channel information leaked from improper implementations, such as timing and power consumption measurements, to reveal the secret key involved [12,13]. In particular, simple and differential power analysis (referred to as SPA and DPA, respectively) have been demonstrated to be very powerful attacks for most straightforward implementations of symmetric and public key ciphers [17,22,21,30,23]. The timing and power analysis attacks are particularly effective and proven successful in attacking smart cards or other dedicated embedded systems storing the secret key. As elliptic curve systems are gaining increasing popularity for implementations on smart cards and other portable devices, greater research effort has been made to secure ECC implementations against SPA and DPA attacks [2,26,5,11,10,16,9].

In this paper, we present a simple and efficient method for securing elliptic scalar multiplication against power analysis attacks. We first examine some previously proposed algorithms for SPA-resistant scalar multiplication and point out some potential security flaws overlooked in these algorithms. A simple signed encoding scheme is then presented, which allows arbitrary odd integers to be encoded only using two bit values $\{-1, +1\}$. Since the encoding scheme produces constant length ±1-encoded values with the most significant bit always equal to one, it allows us to achieve uniform execution behavior in the signed binary and window algorithms without using any dummy addition and without worrying about the operations involving the point at infinity. It also reduces the storage requirement in the ordinary window algorithm. We present concrete signed binary and window algorithms based on the ±1-signed encoding and provide detailed analysis on their security and performance.

H. Wang et al. (Eds.): ACISP 2004, LNCS 3108, pp. 289–300, 2004.

2   Scalar Multiplication and SPA/DPA Resistance

2.1   Resistance Against SPA Attacks

Let $P = (x, y)$ be a point of prime order n on an elliptic curve. The main computational task in elliptic curve cryptosystems is to compute an integer multiple of a given point, $Q = dP$, where d is an integer less than n. Let $d = d_{k-1} \cdots d_1 d_0$ be the binary representation of d. The standard double-and-add binary algorithm computes $Q = dP$ by first setting $Q = O$ and then repeating, for i running from $k - 1$ down to 0, point doubling $Q \leftarrow 2Q$ (performed always) and point addition $Q \leftarrow Q + P$ (performed only if $d_i = 1$). However, this binary algorithm is particularly vulnerable to the timing and SPA attacks, since point addition and doubling consume quite different computational resources and point addition is performed only if $d_i = 1$.

Simple side-channel attacks, such as simple power analysis and timing attacks, can be prevented by using computational algorithms with uniform execution behavior independently of the value of key bits. The research work on this area has been advanced in the following three directions:

1) *Modifying existing algorithms* : The most common way to achieve uniform execution behavior is to modify existing algorithms appropriately, e.g., by inserting some dummy operations or using some encoding schemes [2,6,18, 19,28]. Our work also belongs to this category. Of course, we can make use of an algorithm already having such property, such as the Montgomery ladder algorithm for computing elliptic scalar multiplication [15,26,9].

2) *Randomizing scalar multiplication* : This approach tries to randomize a scalar multiplication algorithm itself by incorporating some random decision in each processing step and thus make the algorithm behave at random from instance to instance [24,3,31,7]. It is more generic in the sense that it can also provide some protection against the DPA attack. Such randomized algorithms are not much efficient at the present and may have some potential security flaws overlooked (e.g., see [25]), but appear to be a good alternative worth further research.

3) *Alternative elliptic curve parameterizations* : This approach concentrates on achieving computational uniformity in lower level elliptic operations by devising a unified formula for point addition and doubling [16,10,1]. Use of such unified formulas may be more desirable from the standpoint of computational uniformity, but it is certainly less efficient than using distinct formulas for point addition and doubling. Moreover, most proposed formulas are based on the special form of curves and thus cannot be used for most elliptic curves recommended in international standards.

2.2   Resistance Against DPA Attacks

Differential power analysis usually makes use of correlation between power consumption and specific key-dependent bits appearing at known steps of the computation [2]. It requires a number of power traces with dependencies on the data being processed by the same secret key, and uses some sophisticated statistical analysis techniques to remove the random noise effect, thereby obtaining a strong power signal from noise-like power traces. The DPA attack may even be applied to SPA-resistant scalar multiplication algorithms unless some randomness is introduced during the computation.

A number of randomization techniques have been proposed as countermeasures against the DPA attack, which can be used to enhance a SPA-resistant algorithm to be DPA-resistant [2,11] (see also [26] for some analysis on the methods in [2]). We may use randomized algorithms with SPA/DPA resistance, as mentioned before, but they are not much efficient yet and cannot be used with existing fast algorithms. It is thus more preferable to use a SPA-resistant algorithm with some randomization technique. Point randomization in projective coordinates [2] and elliptic curve randomization in affine coordinates [10] are two most popular countermeasures against the DPA attack, due to their efficiency.

On the other hand, it has been recently shown that implementations of RSA exponentiation with window-family algorithms could be susceptible to the DPA attack using just a single power trace [30]. The key idea of the window algorithm is to reuse the same precomputed value whenever the same secret key bits appear in a moving window, showing a clear dependence of secret key bits on precomputed values. So, the DPA technique can be used to differentiate repeated use of the same precomputed value in different windows, where the sub-power traces for multiplications by different fixed values within a single modular exponentiation take the place of the usual DPA power traces for multiple executions of modular exponentiations with different bases. This DPA attack only requires a single execution of modular exponentiation as in the SPA attack and thus cannot be defended by the randomization techniques developed for protection against the ordinary DPA attack. A possible countermeasure is to use a randomized scalar multiplication algorithm such as the one presented in [31]. As another but simpler possible countermeasure, we will present in Sect.5 a technique based on the randomization of fixed values using some internal random variables within the point addition operation.

3   Analysis of Existing SPA-Resistant Algorithms

Recall that we want to compute the scalar multiplication $Q = dP$ for a k-bit scalar d represented in binary as $d = d_{k-1} \cdots d_1 d_0$. The SPA-resistant binary algorithm presented in [2] uses dummy additions to achieve uniform execution behavior, i.e., point addition is performed always independently of the value of d_i, but the computation result is thrown away if $d_i = 0$. The algorithms BL and BR described below correspond to the SPA-resistant versions of the left-to-right and right-to-left binary algorithms respectively, directly taken from [2,9] for our further discussion.

Due to the use of dummy additions, these algorithms contains key-dependent point assignment operations. But such point assignment operations depending on key bits may be a potential weakness against SPA/DPA attacks (see [8] for a possible attack) and thus thus would be desirable to avoid whenever possible.

Algorithm BL : Binary L-R	**Algorithm BR** : Binary R-L
Input : d, P	Input : d, P
Output : $Q = dP$	Output : $Q = dP$

1: $Q[0] := P$	1: $Q[0] := P, Q[1] := O$
2: for $i = k - 2$ to 0 step -1	2: for $i = 0$ to $k - 1$ step $+1$
3: $\quad Q[0] := 2Q[0]$	3: $\quad Q[2] := Q[0] + Q[1]$
4: $\quad Q[1] := Q[0] + P$	4: $\quad Q[0] := 2Q[0]$
5: $\quad Q[0] := Q[d_i]$	5: $\quad Q[1] := Q[1 + d_i]$
6: return $Q[0]$	6: return $Q[1]$

In addition, the algorithm BL assumes that the most significant bit of d, d_{k-1}, equals 1. This assumption may also be problematic, since this already leaks one bit information on the secret key. Note that the assumption of $d_{k-1} = 1$ implies that we always set $d_{k-1} = 1$ or we always begin to process from the first nonzero bit of d by skipping any leading zeros in d. In either case, the effective bit-length of the secret key is reduced by one bit or more, since SPA immediately reveals how many point additions are performed in a given scalar multiplication. In the latter case, the effective key length can be shown to be reduced by almost two bits on average (taken over random d). We thus need a special treatment of the leading zeros in d to protect the effective key length (This weakness of course can be easily fixed by adding the order n of P to d as used in our proposed algorithms in Sect. 4).

The algorithm BR also has a potential security flaw if special care is not taken for the operation with the point at infinity O. Suppose that point addition with O is implemented just by point assignment as usual. Then, it is easy to see that all the least significant bits of d before the first nonzero bit appearing can be revealed by SPA due to the dummy addition in the case of $d_i = 0$. This reveals about two bits of the secret key on average as in the algorithm BL. Therefore, it is essential that the addition with O should be implemented to be indistinguishable from other point additions in resource usage.

Note that similar problems exist in the well-known Montgomery ladder algorithm [20,15,26,9].

The left-to-right binary algorithm can be easily extended to the fixed/sliding window algorithm using some precomputation. It is more difficult to protect the window method against power analysis attacks, since we have to consider the repeated use of the same fixed precomputed table in addition. A number of techniques based on randomized windows or new encoding schemes of the scalar value have been proposed as SPA/DPA countermeasures for the window method [18,16,19,6,28,29]. They are in general more complex and less efficient than the ordinary fixed window algorithm and still have some problems related with the reuse of the same precomputed values.

4   The Proposed Scalar Multiplication Algorithms

4.1 ± 1-Signed Encoding and Unified Point Addition/Subtraction

First note that the scalar value d in $Q = dP$ can always be made odd by adding the order n of P if d is even, since $nP = O$. Let us denote -1 by $\hat{1}$. It is easy to see that an odd integer d can be encoded only using $+1$ and -1 just by replacing every substring $0^a 1$ in the binary representation of d with the bit string $1\hat{1}^a$ of equivalent value, where 0^a means a consecutive 0's. For example, $1011001 = 11\hat{1}111\hat{1}$. This encoding process is simple enough to be carried out in real-time, but there exists a much simpler way to do this.

Let $\hat{d}$ be an l-bit ± 1-signed encoding of a k-bit odd integer d, where $l \geq k$. For notational purpose, let us rename $\hat{1}$ as 0 in $\hat{d}$ by regarding the bit 0 in $\hat{d}$ as having the value of -1. Then we can easily see that $\hat{d}$ can be obtained by $\hat{d} = \text{ROR}(l, d, 1) = \sum_{i=0}^{l-1} \hat{d}_i 2^i$, where $\text{ROR}(l, d, 1)$ denotes rotation of the l-bit integer d (with as many leading zeros as necessary) to the right by one bit position. Note that the most significant bit (msb) of $\hat{d}$ is always one since d is odd and that $\hat{d}$ can take arbitrary length greater than or equal to k. We can thus always encode a k-bit odd integer d as a $(k+1)$-bit value $\hat{d}$ with $\hat{d}_k = 1$. This constant length encoding with the nonzero msb allows us to eliminate the intriguing problem associated with the point at infinity. For example, for the 7-bit integer $d = 1011001$, we can verify that $\hat{d} = 11\hat{1}111\hat{1} \rightarrow 1101100 = \text{ROR}(7, d, 1)$ as a 7-bit encoding, and $\hat{d} = 1\hat{1}1\hat{1}111\hat{1} \rightarrow 10101100 = \text{ROR}(8, d, 1)$ as an 8-bit encoding.

In our proposed algorithms based on the ± 1-signed encoding, either point addition or point subtraction is performed, depending on the value of each scanned bit d_i. Therefore, it is essential for SPA resistance that point addition and subtraction should be implemented as an identical code, so that they cannot be distinguished by timing or power consumption measurements. Note that point subtraction requires just one more field addition/subtraction than point addition since for $P = (x, y)$, $-P = (x, y + x)$ in $\text{GF}(2^m)$ and $-P = (x, -y)$ for $\text{GF}(p)$. We may always compute this point negation and use the right point depending on the operation required.[1] Hereafter the following notation will be used for generalized elliptic addition and doubling:

$$\text{ECADD}(P, Q, s) = \begin{cases} P - Q & \text{if } s = 0, \\ P + Q & \text{if } s = 1, \end{cases}$$

$$\text{ECDBL}(Q, w) = 2^w Q.$$

---

[1] This is in fact using dummy operations for SPA-resistance and thus may be considered problematic as discussed in the previous section. But the dummy operation (field addition/subtraction) in this case is almost negligible in resource usage in the overall scalar multiplication (even point addition/subtraction) and if necessary, we may embed this dummy operation deeper into the calculation process up to the coordinate level. For example, a unified implementation in $\text{GF}(p)$ can be done only by swapping two intermediate variables during the calculation (see the addition formulas in Sect.5).

4.2   The Proposed SPA-Resistant Signed Binary Algorithm

The signed versions of Algorithms BR and BL are depicted below as Algorithms SBR and SBL, respectively.

Algorithm SBL : Signed BL	Algorithm SBR : Signed BR
Input : d, P, n	Input : d, P, n
Output : $Q = dP$	Output : $Q = dP$
1: if d is even, $d := d + n$	1: if d is even, $d := d + n$
2: $d := \text{ROR}(k + 1, d, 1)$	2: $d := \text{ROR}(k + 1, d, 1)$
3: $Q := P$	3: $Q := O,\ T := P$
4: for $i = k - 1$ to 0 step -1	4: for $i = 0$ to $k - 1$ step $+1$
5: $Q := \text{ECDBL}(Q, 1)$	5: $Q := \text{ECADD}(Q, T, d_i)$
6: $Q := \text{ECADD}(Q, P, d_i)$	6: $T := \text{ECDBL}(T, 1)$
7: return Q	7: return Q

In the fist two steps of the algorithms, the scalar d is first made odd by adding n if d is even, and then ± 1-sign encoded to $\hat{d} = \text{ROR}(k + 1, d, 1) = \sum_{i=0}^{k} \hat{d}_i 2^i$.[2] Due to the possibility of 1-bit expansion in d by the addition of n, we always regard the scalar d prior to encoding as a $(k + 1)$-bit odd integer, irrespective of its parity. So the encoded scalar $\hat{d}$ is assumed to be always $k + 1$ bits long. The computation of $Q = dP$ is now performed by the double-and-add-always method either from left to right or vice versa, where each bit $\hat{d}_i$, having the value of $+1$ or -1, is used as a sign bit to determine whether to perform point addition or subtraction in the addition step.

The proposed signed binary algorithms have several advantages over the unsigned versions. First, they do not use dummy additions or point assignment operations to achieve uniform execution behavior, so they can be more robust against the SPA attack. The use of dummy additions may break SPA resistance by telling that some computing result is ignored and not used at the next step or intermediate values from different locations are loaded into the same variable (e.g., see [8]). Second, there is no need to special treatment of the addition with the point at infinity, as in the unsigned binary and Montgomery algorithms. This is because we always have the most significant bit of the encoded scalar equal to one (in Algorithm SBL) and because we do not use any dummy addition (in Algorithm SBR). Note that the 1-bit expansion due to the encoding actually does not increase the computing complexity, compared to the unsigned binary algorithms, since the unsigned binary algorithms should also have the same number of iterations in the for-loop for the security reason we noted before. Finally, our proposed algorithms require less temporary point variables than the

---

[2] The first step of adjusting the secret key d may leak the parity bit of d with a straightforward implementation. So we may use dummy operation to alleviate the problem or modify the key generation algorithm to always produce $(k + 1)$-bit odd secret keys with similar techniques.

unsigned binary versions. Algorithm SBL (SBR, resp.) uses just one (two, resp.) point variable, while the unsigned counterpart uses two (three, resp.).

It is also possible to modify the Montgomery algorithm to work with the ± 1-signed encoding. The resulting advantage is that the signed Montgomery algorithm does not require the special treatment of the point at infinity (or leading zeros) at the beginning of the algorithm.

4.3   The Proposed SPA-Resistant Signed Window Algorithm

Algorithm SBL can be easily extended to a fixed window algorithm. Let w be the window size in bits and $t = \lceil (k+1)/w \rceil$. Compute $r = k + 1 \bmod w$ and if $r = 0$, then set $r = w$. Encode a given scalar d using the ± 1-signed encoding and represent the result in base $b = 2^w$ as

$$\hat{d} = \mathrm{ROR}(k+1, d, 1) = \sum_{i=0}^{k} \hat{d}_i 2^i = \sum_{j=0}^{t-1} \hat{e}_j b^j$$

where $\hat{e}_0 = \hat{d}_{r-1}\hat{d}_{r-2}\cdots\hat{d}_0$ and $\hat{e}_i = \hat{d}_{iw+r-1}\hat{d}_{iw+r-2}\cdots\hat{d}_{(i-1)w+r}$ for $1 \leq i \leq t-1$. The scalar multiplication $Q = dP$ can then be performed by processing each signed digit $\hat{e}_i$ from left to right using the repeated-double-and-add algorithm, as depicted in Algorithm SW below.

> **Algorithm SW** : Fixed Signed Window Algorithm
>
>   Input : d, P, n
>   Output : $Q = dP$
>
>   1: if d is even, $d := d + n$
>   2: $d := \mathrm{ROR}(k+1, d, 1)$
>   3: $r := k + 1 \bmod w$; if $r = 0$, set $r := w$
>   4: $T[j] := (2j + 1)P \ (0 \leq j < 2^{w-1})$
>   5: $j := d_{k-1}d_{k-2}\cdots d_{k-w+1}$
>   6: $Q := T[j]$
>   7: for $i = k - w$ to $r + w - 1$ step $-w$
>   8: $Q := \mathrm{ECDBL}(Q, w)$
>   9: $j := d_{i-1}d_{i-2}\cdots d_{i-w+1} \oplus d'_i d'_i \cdots d'_i$
> 10: $Q := \mathrm{ECADD}(Q, T[j], d_i)$
> 11: $Q := \mathrm{ECDBL}(Q, r)$
> 12: $j := d_{r-2}d_{r-3}\cdots d_0 \oplus d'_i d'_i \cdots d'_i$
> 13: $Q := \mathrm{ECADD}(Q, T[j], d_{r-1})$
> 14: return Q

Note that each encoded digit $\hat{e}_i$ can take only an odd integer in $\{\pm 1, \pm 3, \cdots, \pm(2^w - 1)\}$. Therefore, it suffices to precompute and store only odd multiples of P, $T[j] = (2j + 1)P$ for $0 \leq j < 2^{w-1}$, and thus the storage required for precomputed points can be reduced by half, compared to the ordinary unsigned window algorithm. For example, the following shows the precomputed table for $w = 3$ and how to access the table entry corresponding to the encoded digit $\hat{e}_i$.

$$T[0] = P, \quad T[1] = 3P, \quad T[2] = 5P, \quad T[3] = 7P$$

$$\hat{e}_i = \begin{array}{llll} 000 & \to & -7 & \to & -T[3], & 100 & \to & +1 & \to & +T[0] \\ 001 & \to & -5 & \to & -T[2], & 101 & \to & +3 & \to & +T[1] \\ 010 & \to & -3 & \to & -T[1], & 110 & \to & +5 & \to & +T[2] \\ 011 & \to & -1 & \to & -T[0], & 111 & \to & +7 & \to & +T[3] \end{array}$$

It can be seen in the above example that the most significant bit of $\hat{e}_i$ can be used as the sign bit and the table index j can be computed by XORing the remaining bits of $\hat{e}_i$ with the same number of repetitions of 1's complement of the sign bit (steps 9 and 12 in Algorithm SW).

Algorithm SW clearly achieves a constant sequence of point additions and doublings without using any dummy operation. Assuming a unified point addition and subtraction, we only need to care about a DPA-style attack due to the repeated use of fixed precomputed points depending on the windowed key bits (steps 10 and 13). The security of the algorithm against this kind of attack will be discussed in more details in the next section.

5   Enhancing Security Against DPA Attacks

Let us consider the security of the proposed algorithms against the DPA attack. Among various randomization techniques proposed as DPA countermeasures, we concentrate on the point randomization technique in projective coordinates in two reasons; the projective representation is a preferred choice for internal computation in most software implementations, and it may cause some security problem that should be addressed in window-family algorithms. Of course, the randomization technique in affine coordinates can be used without any problem encountered in projective coordinates if all computations are done in affine coordinates.

We assumed before that all fixed points used in the addition step, i..e., the fixed point P in Algorithm SBL and the precomputed points $T[j]$'s in Algorithm SW, are assumed to be represented in affine coordinates, irrespective of the coordinates used for internal computation. This means that for DPA resistance we only randomize the initial point variables entering the for-loop, i.e., Q in step 3 of Algorithm SBL, T in step 3 of Algorithm SBR and $T[j]$ in step 6 of Algorithm SW. We therefore need some justification for this.

We first note that the fixed point P added to Q in Algorithm SBL has no correlation with the secret key, under the assumption of our unified implementation of point addition and doubling. So the fixed, known value of P is of no help to the DPA attack, as far as an initial randomization on Q is done for each run of the algorithm. However, the situation is quite different for the window-family algorithm due to the repeated use of the same precomputed point for the same windowed key bits, as discussed in Sect.2. The correlation between a block of secret key bits and the corresponding precomputed points may be smartly analyzed using some DPA technique to identify the secret key [30]. It is not clear how much effective such a DPA-style attack is on elliptic scalar multiplication, since elliptic addition does not have so strong correlation with a fixed point as modular multiplication with a fixed multiplicand. However, we want to take some countermeasures anyway. A randomized algorithm such as the one proposed in [31] may be a possible countermeasure. In this paper, we consider an internal randomization technique as a simpler countermeasure that can be used with the fixed window algorithm.

Let us examine the following point addition formula to compute $(X_1, Y_1, Z_1) + (x_2, y_2, 1) = (X_3, Y_3, Z_3)$ in elliptic curves over $GF(p)$ with the change of variables $x = X/Z^2$ and $y = Y/Z^3$ [32]:

$$T_1 = \underline{y_2 Z_1^3}, \quad T_2 = \underline{x_2 Z_1^2},$$
$$A = Y_1 + T_1, \quad B = Y_1 - T_1, \quad C = X_1 + T_2, \quad D = X_1 - T_2,$$
$$Z_3 = DZ_1, \quad X_3 = B^2 - CD^2, \quad 2Y_3 = B(CD^2 - 2X_3) - AD^3.$$

The DPA-style attack utilizes the side-channel information leaked from the underlined field multiplications by fixed elements, which may allow correlation analysis between different point additions and corresponding windowed key bits. We thus want to randomize these multiplications to break the correlation between key and data. Our idea is to mask the fixed elements with some internal random variables, as shown in the following modified addition formula.

$$T_0 = \underline{(y_2 + Z_1)Z_1} - Z_1^2, \quad T_1 = \underline{T_0 Z_1^2}, \quad T_2 = \underline{(x_2 + T_0)Z_1^2} - T_1,$$
$$A = Y_1 + T_1, \quad B = Y_1 - T_1, \quad C = X_1 + T_2, \quad D = X_1 - T_2,$$
$$Z_3 = DZ_1, \quad X_3 = B^2 - CD^2, \quad 2Y_3 = B(CD^2 - 2X_3) - AD^3.$$

This modification is obtained almost for free, only costing 4 additional field additions. Note that the projective point (X_1, Y_1, Z_1), corresponding to Q in Algorithm SW, can be assumed to be a random point varying in each addition step of the algorithm due to the initial randomization and thus the masking variables Z_1 and T_0 can be assumed to vary at random in each point addition. Therefore, the underlined field multiplications now cannot be used to tell whether different point additions are associated with the same precomputed point.

The same internal randomization technique can be used for point additions in elliptic curves over $GF(2^m)$. Here is a modified addition formula to compute the point addition $(X_1, Y_1, Z_1) + (x_2, y_2, 1) = (X_3, Y_3, Z_3)$ in projective coordinates using the change of variables $x = X/Z$ and $y = Y/Z^2$ [14], where we used one more field squaring compared to the original addition formula:

$$T_1 = \underline{(x_2 + Z_1)Z_1} + Z_1^2, \quad A = X_1 + T_1, \quad B = AZ_1, \quad Z_3 = B^2,$$
$$C = A^2(B + aZ_1^2), \quad T_2 = \underline{(y_2 + A^2)Z_1^2} + Z_3, \quad D = Y_1 + T_2, \quad E = BD,$$
$$X_3 = D^2 + C + E, \quad T_3 = \underline{(y_2 + Z_3)Z_3} + Z_3^2, \quad F = X_3 + T_3,$$
$$T_4 = \underline{(x_2 + F)Z_3} + FZ_3, \quad G = X_3 + T_4, \quad Y_3 = EG + FZ_3.$$

We note that the above internal randomization technique only aims at making it difficult to distinguish between point additions with different fixed points. It is of no use if it is possible to distinguish between data accesses to different locations as used in the second-order DPA attack by Okeya and Sakurai [27]. But also note that the same authors confessed in [28] that the reality of the second-order DPA attack is controversial. If such an attack is demonstrated to be realizable, it would be almost impossible to protect DPA attacks in a software algorithm level.

6   Performance Comparison

The complexity of the proposed signed window algorithm with window size w for computing $Q = dP$ for a k-bit scalar d can be shown to be $(\lceil \frac{k+1}{w} \rceil + 2^{w-1} - 2)A + (w(\lceil \frac{k+1}{w} \rceil - 1) + 1)D$, including precomputation, where A and D denote the complexity of point addition/subtraction and point doubling, respectively. Its performance varies, depending on the window size typically determined according to the storage available. For example, under the resource-restricted environment, such as smart card implementations, we may take the window size of 2. Even with this minimum window size, the number of point additions can be reduced by half only using one additional precomputed point, compared to the binary algorithm. On the other hand, in the memory-rich environment, we can take optimal window sizes depending on the bit-length of d for best performances ($w = 5$ for typical parameters of 160-bit ECC).

The fastest known algorithm for SPA-resistant elliptic scalar multiplication in elliptic curves over $GF(2^m)$ is the binary algorithm using the Montgomery ladder [2]. Since it is already one of the fastest algorithms for scalar multiplication in $GF(2^m)$, our proposed algorithm will be somewhat slower than the Montgomery algorithm. However, in the case of elliptic curves over $GF(p)$, the Montgomery ladder algorithm is only slightly faster than the binary algorithm. Therefore, our proposed method will provide much better performances even with small window sizes.

7   Conclusion

We have presented improved algorithms for securing elliptic scalar multiplication against side-channel attacks. We first discussed some potential security flaws often overlooked in most previous algorithms, largely due to the improper handling of leading zeros and/or the point at infinity. We then proposed a simple ±1-signed encoding scheme and its application to the binary and window algorithms for SPA-resistant scalar multiplication. Our proposed algorithms do not suffer from the security flaw discussed and do not use any dummy operations to achieve SPA resistance. An efficient randomization technique, using some random variables within the point addition operation, has also been proposed as a possible countermeasure against a DPA-style attack on the window-family algorithm.

References

1. E.Brier and M.Joye, Weierstraß elliptic curves and side-channel attacks, *Public Key Cryptography - PKC 2002*, LNCS 2274, Springer-Verlag, 2002, pp.335-345.
2. J.Coron, Resistance against differential power analysis for elliptic curve cryptosystems, *Cryptographic hardware and embedded systems - CHES'99*, LNCS 1717, Springer-Verlag, 1999, pp.292-302.
3. C.Clavier and M.Joye, Universal exponentiation algorithm - A first step towards provanle SPA-resistance, *Cryptographic hardware and embedded systems - CHES 2001*, LNCS 2162, Springer-Verlag, 2001, pp.300-308.
4. L.Goubin, A refined power-analysis attack on elliptic curve cryptosystems, *IPKC 2003*, LNCS 2567, 2003, pp.199-211.
5. M.A.Hasan, Power analysis attacks and algorithmic approaches to their countermeasures for Koblitz curve cryptosystems, *IEEE Trans. Computers*, 50(10), Oct. 2001, pp.1071-1083.
6. Y.Hitchcock and P.Montague, A new elliptic curve scalar multiplication algorithm to resist simple power analysis, *Information Security and Privacy - ACISP 2002*, LNCS 2384, Springer-Verlag, 2002, pp.214-225.
7. J.C.Ha and S.J.Moon, Randomized signed-scalar mulitplication of ECC to resist power attacks, *Cryptographic hardware and embedded systems - CHES 2002*, LNCS 2523, Springer-Verlag, 2003, pp.551-563.
8. T.Itoh, T.Izu and M.Takenaka, Address-bit differential power analysis of cryptographic schemes OK-ECDH and OK-ECDSA, *Cryptographic hardware and embedded systems - CHES 2002*, LNCS 2523, Springer-Verlag, 2003, pp.129-143.
9. T.Izu and T.Takagi, A fast parallel elliptic curve multiplication resistant against side channel attacks, *Public Key Cryptography-PKC 2002*, LNCS 2274, Springer-Verlag, 2002, pp.280-296.
10. M.Joye and Quisquater, Hessian elliptic curves and side-channel attacks, *Cryptographic hardware and embedded systems - CHES 2001*, LNCS 2162, Springer-Verlag, 2001, pp.402-410.
11. M.Joye and C.Tymen, Protections against differential analysis for elliptic curve cryptography - An algebraic approach, *Cryptographic hardware and embedded systems - CHES 2001*, LNCS 2162, Springer-Verlag, 2001, pp.377-390.
12. C.Kocher, Timing attacks on implementations of Diffie-Hellman, RSA, DSS, and other systems, *Advances in Cryptology - Crypto'96*, LNCS 1109, Springer-Verlag, 1996, pp.104-113.
13. C.Kocher, J.Jaffe and B.Jun, Differential power analysis, *Advances in Cryptology - Crypto'99*, LNCS 1666, Springer-Verlag, 1999, pp.288-397.
14. J.Lopez and R.Dahab, Improved algorithms for elliptic curve arithmetic in $GF(2^m)$, *Selected Areas in Cryptography - SAC'98*, LNCS 1556, Springer-Verlag, 1999, pp.201-212.
15. J.Lopez and R.Dahab, Fast multiplication on elliptic curves over $GF(2^m)$ without precomputation, *Cryptographic hardware and embedded systems - CHES'99*, LNCS 1717, Springer-Verlag, 1999, pp.316-327.
16. P.Liardet and N.Smart, Preventing SPA/DPA in ECC systems using the Jacobi form, *Cryptographic hardware and embedded systems - CHES 2001*, LNCS 2162, Springer-Verlag, 2001, pp.391-401.
17. R.Mayer-Sommer, Smartly analyzing the simplicity and the power of simple power analysis on smartcards, *Cryptographic hardware and embedded systems - CHES 2000*, LNCS 1965, Springer-Verlag, 2000, pp.78-92.

18. B.Möller, Securing elliptic curve point multiplication against side-channel attacks, *Information Security - ISC 2001*, LNCS 2200, Springer-Verlag, 2001, pp.324-334.
19. B.Möller, Parallelizable elliptic curve point multiplication method with resistance against side-channel attacks, *Information Security - ISC 2002*, LNCS 2433, Springer-Verlag, 2002, pp.402-413.
20. P.L.Montgomery, Speeding the Pollard and elliptic curve methods of factorizations, *Math.Comp.*, vol.48, 1987, pp.243-264.
21. T.S.Messerges, E.A.Dabbish and R.H.Sloan, Power analysis attacks of modular exponentiation in smart cards, *Cryptographic hardware and embedded systems - CHES'99*, LNCS 1717, Springer-Verlag, 1999, pp.144-157.
22. T.S.Messerges, E.A.Dabbish and R.H.Sloan, Examining smart-card security under the threat of power analysis attacks, *IEEE Trans. Computers*, 51(5), May 2002, pp.541552.
23. R.Novak, SPA-based adaptive chosen-ciphertext attack on RSA implementation, *Public Key Cryptography - PKC 2002*, LNCS 2274, Springer-Verlag, 2002, pp.252-262.
24. E.Oswald and M.Aigner, Radomized addition-subtraction chains as a countermeasure against power attacks, *Cryptographic hardware and embedded systems - CHES 2001*, LNCS 2162, Springer-Verlag, 2001, pp.39-50.
25. K.Okeya and D.-G.Han, Side channel attack on Ha-Moon's countermeasure of randomized signed scalar multiplication, *Progress in Cryptology - Incrypt 2003*, LNCS 2904, Springer-Verlag, 2003, pp.334-348.
26. K.Okeya and K.Sakurai, Power analysis breaks elliptic curve cryptosystems even secure against the timing attack, *Progress in Cryptology - Indocrypt 2000*, LNCS 1977, Springer-Verlag, 2000, pp.178-190.
27. K.Okeya and K.Sakurai, A second-order DPA attack breaks a window-method based countermeasure against side channel attacks, *Information Security Conference (ISC 2002)*, LNCS 2433, Springer-Verlag, 2002, pp.389-401.
28. K.Okeya and T.Takagi, The width-w NAF method provides small memory and fast scalar multiplications secure against side channel attacks, *CT-RSA 2003*, LNCS 2612, Springer-Verlag, 2002, pp.328-343.
29. K.Okeya and T.Takagi, A more flexible countermeasure against side channle attacks using window method, *Cryptographic hardware and embedded systems - CHES 2003*, LNCS 2779, pp.397-410.
30. C.D.Walter, Sliding windows succumbs to big mac attack, *Cryptographic hardware and embedded systems - CHES 2001*, LNCS 2162, Springer-Verlag, 2001, pp.286-299.
31. C.D.Walter, Mist: an efficient, randomized exponentiation algorithm for resisting power analysis, *Topics in Cryptology - CT-RSA 2002*, LNCS 2271, Springer-Verlag, 2002, pp.53-66.
32. IEEE P1363, Standard specification for public key cryptography, 2000.

A Mobile Agent System Providing Offer Privacy

Ming Yao, Matt Henricksen, Greg Maitland, Ernest Foo, and Ed Dawson

Information Security Research Centre
Queensland University of Technology
Brisbane, QLD, 4000, Australia
{m.yao, m.henricksen, g.maitland, e.foo, e.dawson}@qut.edu.au
http://www.isrc.qut.edu.au

Abstract. In a shopping mobile agent scenario where the agent, on behalf of its owner, collects prices (offers) from vendors' servers, offer privacy is one of the major security concerns. In this paper, we propose a framework to achieve offer privacy. The framework can be implemented in an e-market environment where an e-market manager plays the role of authority. Based on the framework, a "hash chained group signature" scheme that employs a group signature scheme and a chaining relationship is proposed. The offer privacy can be reversed, with the assistance of the e-market manager, when a server's identity needs to be revealed.

1 Introduction

Mobile agents are software entities that move code, data and state to remote hosts. The benefits offered by mobile agents unfold in areas where it is advantageous to move computation processes over a network to the source of data instead of vice versa. They have great potential for electronic commerce applications.

One example of the use of mobile agents in electronic commerce is the shopping mobile agent [6]. The agent, on behalf of the buyer, travels the Internet in order to buy a specific product at the most convenient price. The agent migrates to multiple servers, collects price quotes and is free to choose its next move dynamically based on the data it acquired from the past journey. The agent finally returns to the buyer with the offers of all the vendors. The buyer then gathers all the prices and chooses the best offer.

However, there are two major security concerns with respect to this scenario:

- *Offer Integrity:* The integrity of the offers from previously visited servers carried by the agent needs to be protected along the agent's journey. Servers may try to delete, replace, or invalidate commitments to the agent, such as the offers that have been collected by the agent.
- *Offer Privacy:* One of the fundamental requirements in a fair and sound electronic commerce environment is maintaining the secrecy of the losing vendors while revealing only the winning vendor to the buyer.

In this paper, we focus on the *offer privacy* issue in mobile agent systems. Assume n servers will be included in the agent's itinerary. We define *"offer*

H. Wang et al. (Eds.): ACISP 2004, LNCS 3108, pp. 301–312, 2004.

privacy" as follows: *If a mobile agent visits a sequence of servers S_1, S_2, ..., S_n $(1 \leq i \leq n)$, none of the identities of the honest servers traversed by an agent can be traced from the contents of the offers o_1, o_2, ..., o_n.* The definition stresses that only the *honest* server will be provided offer privacy. In the case of dispute, the dishonest server(s) should be detectable and traceable. There are other situations where offer privacy needs to be revoked; for example, in the shopping agent application, when the buyer has chosen the winner. To revoke the offer privacy, in this paper, we use a trusted third party as the mediator to disclose the identity of an intended server.

The complexity of providing "offer privacy" stems from the fact that the collected offers will be returned and displayed to the originator for it to choose the winner. However the losing servers may want to remain anonymous from the other servers and the originator as well.

Contribution. In this paper, we propose a framework that attempts to preserve "offer privacy" for mobile agent systems. To demonstrate the viability of the framework, we also propose a protocol that provides offer privacy. The offers collected by the agent and returned to the originator cannot be tampered with undetectably. To achieve the aforementioned properties, a group signature scheme with a chaining relationship embedded is used to solve the problems described above.

Organisation. The rest of the paper is organised as follows: Section 2 briefly describes some related work. We discuss some attacks and other security properties regarding "offer privacy" protecting mobile systems in Section 3. Section 4 describes a framework for achieving "offer privacy". Section 5 describes a new "hash chained group signature" scheme to demonstrate the framework. Section 6 concludes the paper.

For ease of reading, the notations used in the paper are listed in Table 1. (An extended version of this paper is available upon request from the authors.)

2   Related Work

The group digital signature is a technique used to provide anonymity to the signer. It extends the traditional digital signature concept to a multi-party setting. The group signature scheme, first introduced by Chaum and van Heijst [5], allows any member of a group to digitally sign a document on behalf of the entire group. The group digital signature is generated in a manner such that a verifier can confirm that it came from the group, but does not know which individual in the group signed the document. The protocol allows for the identity of the signer to be discovered, in case of disputes, by a designated group manager who has some auxiliary information.

There are five steps involved in a group signature scheme: SETUP, JOIN, SIGN, VERIFY and OPEN [1]. A number of security properties that a group signature scheme must satisfy are [2]: *unforgeability, conditional signer anonymity, undeniable signer identity, unlinkability, security against framing attacks* and *coalition resistance.* For more details, we refer the readers to the papers [1][2].

Table 1. Notations used in this paper ($0 \leq i \leq n$ unless i is indicated)

Model Notations	Meaning
$\prod$	An agent's code.
$S_0 = S_{n+1}$	ID of the originator (the buyer).
$S_i, 1 \leq i \leq n$	ID of server i.
I_{EG}	ID of the e-market gateway.
o_0	A token issued by S_0 to identify the agent instance on return. It can be regarded as a dummy offer and is only known to the originator.
$o_i, 1 \leq i \leq n$	An offer from S_i.
εo_i	An encrypted offer of server S_i.
O_i	An encapsulated offer (cryptographically protected o_i) from S_i. It is an element of the append-only container carried by the agent.
$O_0, \cdots, O_n$	An ordered chain of encapsulated offers from servers $S_0, \cdots, S_n$.
Cryptographic Notations	Meaning
r_i	A random number generated by S_i.
$\mathbb{Z}_q$	The integers modulo q is the set of integers $\{0, 1, \cdots, q-1\}$.
$E_{y_o}(m)$	A message m asymmetrically encrypted with the public key of S_0. The encryption scheme is probabilistic such as ElGamal.
$H(m)$	A one-way collision-free hash function.
$\mathcal{Y}$	The group public key.
$\mathsf{SIGN}(m_i)$	The group signature of S_i on the message m_i.
$\mathsf{VERIFY}()$	The verification process of a group signature.
$\mathsf{OPEN}()$	The identity revealing process of a group member.
$\mathsf{Sig}_x(\mathrm{m})$	A regular digital signature on the message m with a private key x.
$\mathsf{Ver}_y(\mathrm{s, m}) =$ true or false	Verification of the signature s on the message m. It is true when $\mathrm{Sig}_x(\mathrm{m})= \mathrm{s}$; false otherwise.

3 Security Objectives

"Offer privacy" can be attained by hiding the identity of the server, and the relationship to its data from the other servers and the originator. To practically implement a secure "offer privacy" mobile agent system, there are some other objectives that need to be accomplished as well:

- *Offer integrity is assured.* Prevention of offer tampering is one of the most important goals to achieve in a mobile agent application. However an "offer privacy" mobile agent system is more vulnerable to offer integrity threats: since the ownership of the offer is obscured, attackers are provided more incentive to replace, modify or delete the offers from the agent.
- *Offer creator is non-repudiable.* After committing to the offer o_i, the offer creator cannot later deny the fact that it had made that offer.
- *Offer privacy is revokable.* There are two situations where the ownership of an offer needs to be revealed: (1) when the winning offer is chosen, the winner needs to be revealed; (2) when an attack is detected, the attacker needs to be identified.

4   A Framework for Providing Offer Privacy

In this section, a framework is presented that supports the incorporation of cryptographic tools and collaboration of participants to achieve offer privacy and other attributes found in Section 3 for mobile agent systems. A group signature scheme is utilised to provide offer privacy. A hash chaining relation is also employed to attain offer integrity.

The framework can be implemented in an e-market environment where an e-market manager as an authority can play the role of the group manager.

4.1   Participants and an Electronic Market

The participants in our framework include: (1) a buyer (the originator), (2) a number of vendors' servers, and (3) a trusted third party. When the winning offer is chosen or a malicious server needs to be identified, the trusted third party serves as an authority to revoke the offer privacy. As we employ a group signature scheme in our framework, the trusted third party can also play the role of the group manager to generate the group's public key, and issue membership certificates to the participant servers.

Note that all mobile agents enter and leave through the "e-market gateway". Without the e-market gateway, it is inevitable that the originator knows who are the first and the last servers, as it will send the agent to S_1 and and receive it from S_n. This hides the identities of S_i and S_n from the originator such that none of the participant servers is visible to the originator.

4.2   How It Works

The framework uses a group signature scheme and the hash chaining relationship, as well as cryptographic techniques such as "pseudonyms" and "single hop verification".

Pseudonyms. Pseudonyms of servers in our framework serve as credentials such that the holders of the pseudonyms can enjoy anonymity while being recognised as legitimate servers. A pseudonym should possess the following properties:

- *Publicly verifiable.* Anyone is able to determine whether a pseudonym's owner is a valid server by verifying the pseudonym, while not gaining extra information about the server's identity.
- *Forgery resistent.* No one, including the pseudonym's holder, can forge a pseudonym for a legitimate server.

In our framework, to generate a pseudonym for a server, an authority (e-market manager) must sign a token d_i that is unique to the server. Let I_i denote S_i's identity, then d_i is essentially a randomised identity I_i by a random number u_i.

Let x_T denote the private key of the e-market manager and y_T be the corresponding public key. Assume a pseudonym is generated and distributed via a secure and authenticated channel. The resulting pseudonym of S_i is $D_i = Sig_{x_T}(d_i)$. S_i can check whether D_i is formed correctly by performing $Ver_{y_T}(D_i) \overset{?}{=}$ true.

The pseudonyms can be generated offline, hence this scheme does not impact the overall performance of the framework. If a pseudonym is revealed or compromised, the holder of the pseudonym needs to obtain a new one for its future use.

Single hop verification. At each server, verification is conducted, which is referred to as "single hop verification". The verification consists of checking the correctness of the group signatures on each offer using the group public key, and validating the chaining relationship.

The benefit of "single hop verification" is that the malicious server can be identified immediately at the *next* server, if the malicious server has launched an attack. We will explain why this result can be achieved in Section 5.2.

Now let us discuss how the framework functions. Assume that there are m servers in the e-market, and the agent chooses n out of m to visit. Before the agent is dispatched to the vendors' servers, the e-market needs to be configured. The configuration of the system consists of:

- setting up the group signature scheme by conducting SETUP and JOIN procedures through the e-market manager. The e-market manager generates the group public key $\mathcal{Y}$. Participant servers gain their membership private keys and membership certificates; and
- the e-market manager granting pseudonyms $\{D_1, \cdots, D_m\}$ to participant servers.

Then the shopping agent starts to collect offers from the servers. In general, the system model of shopping agents is: each offer is signed using the server's membership secret key. The resulting signed offer $O_i = \text{SIGN}(S_i$'s offer$)$ is the encapsulated offer of S_i. The hash chaining mechanism linking the previous server's offer and the next server's pseudonym is embedded in the signed offer.

The concept of the chaining relationship was proposed in a number of schemes such as [6]. At any site, the online shopping mobile agent collects data from the server and appends it to the data from previously visited servers. Each site, in its turn, must provide a short proof of the agent computation (a group signature in our framework) that is stored in the agent. The main idea is to cryptographically link each proof with the one computed at the previous site. This establishes a *chaining relationship* between proofs, and makes it impossible to modify an intermediate proof without modifying all the subsequent ones. The originator eventually verifies the integrity of the "chain" of cryptographic proofs to detect any integrity violations.

A node in the hash chaining relationship is expressed as: $h_i = H(O_{i-1}, D_{i+1})$. Each entry of the chain depends on some of the previous and succeeding members, therefore, any illegitimate change in O_{i-1} and/or D_{i+1} invalidates the chaining relationship.

When the agent moves to the next server, carrying all the offers collected from previously visited servers, "single hop verification" is conducted to detect any violation of offer privacy and offer integrity. To verify the correctness of S_i's group signature O_i, the VERIFY(O_i) process is invoked.

When the shopping agent finishes its task, it returns to the originator. The originator then chooses the winner and requests the e-market manager to reveal the winner, where OPEN(O_c) $(1 \leq c \leq i)$ is conducted if the winner is S_c.

5   A New Scheme to Achieve Offer Privacy

In section 4, we described a conceptual framework for providing "offer privacy" to mobile agent systems. In this section, we propose a "hashed chained group scheme" to demonstrate the framework.

5.1   Hash Chained Group Signature Scheme

We elaborate the proposed scheme in five stages: **Setup, Initialisation, Execution, Migration** and **Completion**.

Stage 1 – Setup
This stage is to set up the group public key $\mathcal{Y}$, and membership private keys and membership certificates for participant servers. Pseudonyms are also generated and distributed to the members.

After the system has been setup, the agent will be dispatched from the originator (the user) to the e-market gateway. The e-market gateway serves as a well-known entry into and out of the e-market. It also provides a dummy offer to the agent.

Note that in the proposed framework and scheme, though the originator and the e-market gateway are the active participants in our framework, they are not members of the group and do not have group membership keys. Here we want to point out that, in order to retain consistency within the chaining relationship, the originator and e-market gateway use a regular signature scheme to generate dummy offers (see below). Since there are two signature schemes coexisting in our framework, we elaborate the proposed scheme at different stages in Fig. 1, Fig. 2 and Fig. 3 accordingly.

In the following, we assume that the public keys of the originator, e-market gateway, and the e-market manager are published beforehand and available to all the servers.

Stage 2 – Initialisation
The originator S_0 initialises the protocol in Fig. 1 by randomly generating r_0 for use in probabilistic encryption and also a secret token o_0. It encrypts o_0 and r_0 with its own public key, to produce εo_0.

Next, it initialises a chaining relationship. The originator computes the hash value h_0, the anchor value of the chaining relationship, by applying $H()$ over εo_0 and the identity I_{EG} of the e-market gateway.

Finally, the originator signs the encryption, the hash value h_0 and I_{EG}, and sends it with the agent to the e-market manager, as offer O_0.

S_0	E-market gateway (EG)
$r_0 \in_R \mathbb{Z}_q$	
$\varepsilon o_0 = E_{y_0}\{o_0, r_0\}$	
$h_0 = H(\varepsilon o_0, I_{EG})$	
$O_0 = Sig_{x_0}(\varepsilon o_0, h_0, I_{EG})$	
$\xrightarrow{\Pi, \langle O_0 \rangle}$	
	$Ver_{y_0}(O_0, (\varepsilon o_0, h_0, I_{EG}))$

Fig. 1. Hash chained group signature scheme: $S_0 \to$ E-market gateway (EG)

Stage 3 – Execution
This stage consists of the agent's execution at both the e-market gateway and all the vendors' servers.

At the E-market Gateway (EG)
Upon receiving the agent and its data, the e-market gateway retrieves the originator's public key y_0 and verifies the signature on O_0. If the verification is successful, the e-market gateway looks into the agent's (the buyer's) requests and searches for the potential service providers. The e-market gateway, providing directory services to the buyers, can randomly select one server from the candidates to be the first visited server S_1.

In Fig. 2, before the e-market gateway dispatches the agent, it requests S_1's pseudonym D_1. The e-market gateway needs to check the validity of D_1 using the e-market manager's public key. If D_1 is a valid pseudonym, the gateway constructs a dummy offer εo_{EG} by encrypting εo_0 and a random number r_{EG} using y_0. Next, the e-market gateway constructs the hash value h_{EG} and the encapsulated offer O_{EG}.

Finally the e-market gateway sends the agent with the encapsulated offers O_0 and O_{EG} to the first server S_1.

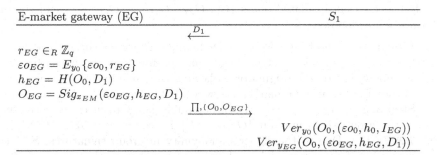

E-market gateway (EG)	S_1
	$\xleftarrow{D_1}$
$r_{EG} \in_R \mathbb{Z}_q$	
$\varepsilon o_{EG} = E_{y_0}\{\varepsilon o_0, r_{EG}\}$	
$h_{EG} = H(O_0, D_1)$	
$O_{EG} = Sig_{x_{EM}}(\varepsilon o_{EG}, h_{EG}, D_1)$	
$\xrightarrow{\Pi, \langle O_0, O_{EG} \rangle}$	
	$Ver_{y_0}(O_0, (\varepsilon o_0, h_0, I_{EG}))$
	$Ver_{y_{EG}}(O_0, (\varepsilon o_{EG}, h_{EG}, D_1))$

Fig. 2. Hash chained group signature scheme: e-market gateway (EG) $\to S_1$

O_{EG} can be viewed as a certificate to the agent from the e-market authority, in addition to obscuring the relationships between the originator and the first server, and the originator and the last server. This is because the e-market gateway can examine the authenticity of the agent (by some well established mechanisms such as authentication), in order to prevent a malicious agent from entering the e-market. If the verification succeeds, the e-market gateway issues O_{EG}.

At the Vendors' Servers $\{S_1, S_2, \cdots, S_n\}$.

From S_1 onwards, each server S_i performs the following steps:

- **Offer Encryption.** When the agent arrives at a server S_i, the server makes an offer o_i, and constructs εo_i by encrypting o_i and a random value r_i with the public key y_0 of the originator. Nobody other than the originator is able to view the offer.
- **Chaining Relationship.** Next S_i obtains the pseudonym D_{i+1} from S_{i+1} and validates D_{i+1}. S_1 and S_i ($1 < i \leq n$) extend the chaining relationship by computing slightly different values respectively. Server S_i computes h_i that contains the previous server's signed offer O_{i-1} and the next server's pseudonym D_{i+1}. Server S_1 includes a regular signature O_{EG} in h_1 instead of a group signature.
- **Offer Signing.** Before S_i transfers the agent and the collected data to S_{i+1}, S_i generates a group signature on the offer εo_i and the hash value h_i by computing $O_i = \texttt{SIGN}(\varepsilon o_i, h_i, D_{i+1})$.
  The agent exits from the e-market gateway upon the completion of the task. Hence the **last server** S_n will send the agent to the e-market gateway. S_n includes I_{EG} in its encapsulated offer O_n and h_n instead of a pseudonym.

At last, S_i sends the list of encapsulated offers $\{O_0, O_{EG}, O_1, O_2, \cdots, O_i\}$ to S_{i+1}.

Stage 4 – Migration

During the agent's migration, the "single hop verification" is enforced to detect any malicious actions in real time. A server must report any violation, otherwise it could be accused of having maliciously attacked other servers.

When the agent arrives at server S_{i+1} ($0 \leq i < n$), carrying a set of previously collected encapsulated offers $\{O_0, O_{EG}, O_1, \cdots, O_i\}$, S_{i+1} can conduct verification as follows:

- **Step 1.** S_{i+1} obtains O_0 from the chain and retrieves the originator's public key y_0. If $Ver_{y_0}(O_0) = \text{true}$, S_{i+1} can be sure that the agent has been genuinely sent by the originator. Following the same line of reasoning, S_{i+1} can verify O_{EG} using e-market gateway's public key y_{EG}.
- **Step 2.** S_{i+1} ($1 \leq i < n$) uses the group public key $\mathcal{Y}$ to check the correctness of the group signatures on $\{O_1, \cdots, O_i\}$ by conducting $\texttt{VERIFY}(O_1)$, $\cdots$, $\texttt{VERIFY}(O_i)$. Due to the signer's anonymity in group signatures, S_{i+1} can determine if O_i is signed by a legitimate member in the group. However S_{i+1} has no knowledge of who the signer is.

S_i $(1 \le i \le n)$	S_{i+1} $(1 \le i \le n)$
	$\xleftarrow{\quad D_{i+1} \quad}$

$r_i \in_R \mathbb{Z}_q$
$\varepsilon o_i = E_{y_0}\{o_i, r_i\}$

$h_1 = H(O_{EG}, D_2)$
$h_i = H(O_{i-1}, D_{i+1})$ $(1 < i < n)$
$h_n = H(O_{n-1}, I_{EG})$

$O_i = \mathtt{SIGN}(\varepsilon o_i, h_i, D_{i+1})$ $(1 \le i < n)$
$O_n = \mathtt{SIGN}(\varepsilon o_n, h_n, I_{EG})$

$$\xrightarrow{\quad \Pi, \{O_0, O_{EG}, O_1, ..., O_i\} \quad}$$

$Ver_{y_0}(O_0, (\varepsilon o_0, h_0, I_{EG}))$
$Ver_{y_{EG}}(O_0, (\varepsilon o_{EG}, h_{EG}, D_1))$
$\mathtt{VERIFY}(O_j)$ $(1 \le j \le i)$

Fig. 3. Hash chained group signature scheme: $S_i \to S_{i+1}$ $(1 \le i \le n)$

- **Step 3.** S_{i+1} extracts h_i and D_{i+1} from the data chain. S_{i+1} first checks whether D_{i+1} is its genuine pseudonym. If the verification is successful, S_{i+1} then computes $h'_i = H(O_{i-1}, D_{i+1})$ (when $i = 0$, S_1 checks h_{EG} and O_{EG}) and checks if the equation $h'_i = h_i$ is satisfied. h_i serves two purposes. First, it links the previous offer (contained in the group signature) with the current offer. Therefore O_{i-1} cannot be modified without modifying O_i as well. In fact, even server S_{i-1} cannot modify its own offer later without invalidating the chain at O_i. Secondly, the pseudonym of the next server guarantees that no one other than S_{i+1} can append the next offer.

As such, S_{i+1} can recursively verify all the signatures carried by the agent. Note the last server S_n will be verified by the originator by repeating the steps above. If all the verifications are successful, S_{i+1} ensures that no data integrity violation has occurred. We will discuss these issues in the *dispute* phase below.

Stage 5 – Completion
After the agent has finished its journey, it returns to the e-market gateway with the collected data $\{O_0, O_{EG}, O_1, O_2, \cdots, O_n\}$. The e-market gateway sends the agent and its data back to the originator via a secure channel. The originator does not know who the last server is.

Choose Winner
The originator first conducts a verification process by repeating steps 1–3 of stage 4 above. The originator also verifies the integrity of the token o_0. This is to check whether the instance of the returned agent is the same as that of the originator sent in the beginning of the protocol.

If the originator succeeds in verification, it obtains each of $\{\varepsilon o_1, \cdots, \varepsilon o_n\}$ from the data chain and decrypts them to gain the entire list of offers $\{o_1, o_2, ...o_n\}$.

The originator is able to select the best offer. However the originator does not know the real identity of the winning server S_c, though it can obtain its pseudonym D_c from returned data chain. To reveal the winner's identity, the originator sends O_c with the entire collected data to the e-market manager.

Winner Announcement

Only the e-market manager knows the identities of all the participant servers and their corresponding pseudonyms. The e-market manager runs OPEN(O_j) procedure in the group signature scheme [1] to reveal the winner's identity I_j.

The e-market manager encrypts I_j using the originator's public key and sends the encrypted winner's identity to the originator.

After the winner is revealed, the e-market manager publishes $\{O_0, O_{EG}, O_1, \cdots, O_n\}$ to allow servers to complain if any of their offers are missing from the published list. As each server knows its signed offer O_i $(1 \leq i \leq n)$, it can check whether the encapsulated offer is published. If any visited server discovers that its encapsulated offer is missing, it can contact the e-market manager. The e-market manager will conduct a *dispute* process.

Dispute

Let S_m be the server disputing the transaction. The e-market manager performs the following steps:

- The e-market manager extracts $\{D_1, D_2, \cdots, D_n\}$ from the data chain and then searches for the corresponding identities $\{I_1, I_2, \cdots, I_n\}$.
- The e-market manager contacts the victim server S_m $(1 \leq m \leq n)$ and requests its received encapsulated offer $\{O_0, O_{EG}, O_1, O_2, \cdots, O_{m-1}\}$. The e-market manager checks whether O_{m-1} contains S_m's pseudonym. If O_{m-1} indeed includes D_m, S_{m-1} is the suspect malicious server, providing that the group signature scheme is secure and undeniable, and the pseudonyms have been correctly generated. Note that it is impossible for S_{m-1} to successfully include another server's pseudonym (a server's pseudonym may be known to the other servers after a few protocol runs). It will be discovered by S_m when it verifies the chaining relationship $h_{m-1} = H(O_{m-2}, D_m)$ for S_{m-1}.

5.2   Security Analysis

The proposed "hash chained group signature scheme" achieves "offer privacy". It defends against the known attacks discussed in Section 3.

Offer Privacy. The anonymity of the signature signer relies on the security of underlying group signature scheme, since this is what the "hash chained group signature" scheme is based upon.

Assuming that the chosen signature scheme is secure, the group signature signer's anonymity can be retained. If the encryption scheme is secure, no one other than S_0 can decrypt an encapsulated offer O_i. As the encryption and hashing in O_i are randomised, they leak no information about their contents, and resist dictionary attacks as well. Therefore, no one other than the originator S_0 can view the offer o_i.

In our proposed framework and protocol, both originator and servers possess some knowledge regarding the offers and the identities of previous/next servers respectively. However, it is impossible for either to determine the ownership of an offer.

Furthermore, if the signature scheme used in generating the pseudonyms is secure, there is no real possibility of extracting any server's identity, I_i, from $d_i = I_i + u_i$ where u_i is chosen from $\mathbb{Z}_q$ randomly. To determine I_i from d_i is as difficult as guessing the correct number at random.

Due to the arguments above, "offer privacy" is achieved in our proposed scheme, whereby nobody can determine who made a particular offer without the assistance of e-market authorities.

In addition, "offer privacy" is reversible since the e-market manager can reveal a server's identity as we discussed in Section 5.1. In our proposed scheme, if the group signature is secure against framing attacks, a server that has made an offer can repudiate that offer.

Single Hop Verification. The "single hop verification" described in Section 4.2 serves two purposes. First, if any incorrect signature and/or invalid chain link is detected at a server, the agent's computation can abort early, instead of having to finish the computation and detecting integrity violations when the agent returns to the originator. Second, each server can prove its honesty by truthfully verifying all the existing encapsulated offers and the chaining relationship and reporting any malicious action in real time. If an incorrect signature is found by S_{i+1}, S_i could be suspected of having altered the signature, simply because the violation is not reported before S_i, but is discovered by S_{i+1}. Therefore, if S_i wants to avoid this embarrassment or any other consequences, it must honestly perform the verification and report any violation.

Prevention of Known Attacks. The new scheme provides defense mechanisms against the following attacks:

1. *Modification, insertion and deletion attacks.* In these attacks, the malicious server modifies one (or more) existing offer(s), adds a fake offer, or delete a string of previously collected data. Because the new protocol includes the chaining relationship (discussed in Section 4.2), it can defend against these attacks.

2. *Truncation attack and stemming attack.* A truncation attack is a special cases of the deletion attack, in which all offers after the ith offer are deleted; this is called *truncation* at i [6]. A "stemming attack" may follow when the attacker appends fake offers after it truncates at i [6]. As we have discussed in Section 5, the e-market manager will publish all the offers collected by the agent. The victim servers can therefore complain that their offers are missing. The malicious server(s) can be identified in the *dispute* stage. The stemming attack following the "truncation attack" occurs when a malicious server truncates a string of previous collected offers, and then makes fake offers, signing them with the group

signature private key. Since the signatures on the fake offers are still recognised as valid group signatures, this attack cannot be detected inst! an! tly. However it can be discovered after all the offers are published. The malicious servers can be identified by following the same procedure as when identifying malicious servers in "truncation attack".

Defense against other attacks is described in the extended paper.

6   Conclusion

We have proposed a new framework to provide "offer privacy" to mobile agent systems. A "hash chained group signature" scheme is proposed to demonstrate the framework. The idea of the new scheme is to make use of group signatures and also generate pseudonyms for all the servers through the e-market manager. The new scheme can also adopt a chaining relationship to prevent some known attacks and therefore provide data integrity.

However the complexity of the proposed scheme relies heavily on the underlying group signature scheme. The efficiency decreases linearly in the number of servers as the mobile agent travels. This is due to the complex signature generation and verification of group signatures. In particular, verification processes take much computational power. Therefore, any more efficient group signature would greatly help increase the efficiency of the proposed scheme.

References

1. Ateniese, G., Camenisch, J., Joye, M. and Tsudik, G.: A practical and provably secure coalition resistant group signature scheme. Advances in Cryptology — CRYPTO 2000, Lecture Notes in Computer Science, Vol. 1880. Springer-Verlag, Berlin Heidelberg (2000), 255–270.
2. Camenisch, J. and Stadler, M.: Efficient group signature schemes for large groups. In: Kaliski, B. (ed.): Advances in Cryptology — CRYPTO '97 Proceedings, Santa Barbara, CA, Lecture Notes in Computer Science, Vol. 1294. Springer-Verlag, Berlin Heidelberg (1997), 410–424.
3. Camenisch, J. and Michels, M.: A Group Signature Scheme with Improved Efficiency. In Advances in Cryptology - ASIACRYPT '98. Lecture Notes in Computer Science, Vol. 1514. Springer-Verlag, Berlin Heidelberg (1998), 160–174.
4. Camenisch, J. and Michels, M.: Separability and Efficiency for Generic Group Signature Schemes (Extended Abstract). Advances in Cryptology—CRYPTO '99. Lecture Notes in Computer Science, Vol. 1666. Springer-Verlag, Berlin Heidelberg (1999), 413–430.
5. Chaum, D., Heijst, E. V.: Group signatures. In Advances in Cryptology - Eurocrypt '91. Lecture Notes in Computer Science, Vol. 547. Springer-Verlag, Berlin Heidelberg (1991) 257–265.
6. Yao, M., Foo, E., Peng, K., Dawson, E.: An Improved Forward Integrity Protocol for Mobile Agents. In Proceeding of the 4th International Workshop on Information Security Applications (WISA 2003), Jeju Island, Korea. Lecture Notes in Computer Science, Vol. 2908. Springer-Verlag, Berlin Heidelberg (2003), 272–285.

Identity-Based Strong Designated Verifier Signature Schemes

Willy Susilo[1], Fangguo Zhang[2], and Yi Mu[1]

[1] Centre for Information Security Research
School of Information Technology and Computer Science
University of Wollongong
Wollongong 2522, Australia
{wsusilo,ymu}@uow.edu.au
[2] Department of Electronics and Communication Engineering
Sun Yat-Sen University
Guangzhou 510275, P.R. China
isdzhfg@zsu.edu.cn

Abstract. In this paper, we propose an identity based strong designated verifier signature scheme. Firstly, we provide a generic construction of such schemes. We show that the generic construction satisfies all the requirements of identity based strong designated verifier signature schemes. However, the resulting scheme will not be very efficient, since it requires an additional identity based encryption scheme. Then, we proceed with a specially designed identity based strong designated verifier signature scheme, which has low communication and computational cost. We provide complete security proofs for our schemes.

1 Introduction

The notion of *undeniable signature* is proposed by Chaum and van Antwerpen [5] in 1989, to allow a signer to have complete control over her signature. In this scheme, the verification of the signer's signature requires the participation of the signer in an interactive protocol. The signer is able to reject invalid signatures, but she must not be able to deny valid signatures.

Motivated by the above problem, Jakobsson, Sako and Impagliazzo proposed a *designated verifier* signatures in [7]. This signature scheme is the first non-interactive undeniable signature scheme that transforms Chaum's scheme [4] into non-interactive verification using a designated verifier proof. In a designated verifier scheme, the signature provides authentication of a message without providing a non-repudiation property of traditional signatures. A designated verifier scheme can be used to convince a single third party, i.e. the designated verifier, and only the designated verifier who can be convinced about its validity or invalidity. This is due to the fact that the designated verifier can always create a signature intended for himself that is indistinguishable from an original signature. This scheme does not require any interaction with the presumed signer to verify the authenticity of the message. Following this idea, Galbraith and

H. Wang et al. (Eds.): ACISP 2004, LNCS 3108, pp. 313–324, 2004.

Mao proposed a non-interactive undeniable signature scheme in finite fields [6] in the multi-user setting to have *invisibility* and *anonymity*. In [9], Libert and Quisqater proposed an identity based undeniable signature scheme that can be regarded as identity based version of Galbraith-Mao's scheme using pairings.

In [10], Saeednia, Kremer and Markowitch proposed an extension of the above idea by formalizing the notion of *strong designated verifier scheme*. The notion of strong designated verifier itself is not new, and it has been introduced in [7]. However, it is noted in [10] that a stronger definition of strong designated verifier scheme is required, by having an additional property that anyone should be able to produce an identically distributed transcripts that are indistinguishable from the original protocol that is run between the signer and the verifier.

Our Contribution
In this paper, firstly we introduce the notion of Identity based (or ID-based, for short) strong designated verifier schemes. We also provide a generic construction of such schemes based on a combination of *any* ID-based signature schemes, *any* ID-based encryption scheme and *any* ID-based chameleon hash function. However, we will show that the resulting scheme is not very efficient (for example, compared to the *regular* strong designated verifier schemes in [10]) due to the ID-based encryption used in the conversion. Then, we proceed with our novel construction of ID-based strong designated verifier schemes that do not require any ID-based encryption scheme involved. The resulting scheme is very efficient and requires low communication and computational cost.

The rest of this paper is organized as follows. In section 2, we recall definitions of designated verifier proofs of [7] and the notion of strong designated verifier signature scheme of [10]. We proceed with the new notion of ID-based strong designated verifier schemes by introducing its model and security requirements. Then, we continue with some cryptographic tools that will be required in our construction. In section 3, we provide a general construction for ID-based strong designated verifier schemes. We show how to convert *any* ID-based signature scheme into ID-based strong designated verifier schemes. In section 4, we provide our secure and efficient construction of ID-based strong designated verifier scheme. Our scheme does not require any additional encryption scheme (c.f. [7]). Section 5 concludes the paper.

2   Designated Verifier Signature Schemes

The goal of designated verifier proofs is to allow an entity, Alice, to prove the validity of a statement Θ to a specific entity, Bob, in such a way that Bob is convinced about this fact but he cannot transfer this conviction to other third party. In [7], it is suggested that Alice should prove the statement "Θ is correct or I know Bob's secret key". Bob, who is aware that he has not generated the proof himself and also sure that Alice does not know his secret key will be convinced by this proof (i.e. the first part of the proof, namely Θ is correct), while no other verifier can decide which part of the disjunction is correct.

The notion of designated verifier proofs are given in [7], and they are formalized in [10] as follows.

Definition 1. Designated Verifier *[10]*
Let $P(A, B)$ be a protocol between Alice and Bob so that Alice can prove the correctness of statement Θ. Bob is said to be a designated verifier if he can produce identically distributed *transcripts that are* indistinguishable *from those of $P(A, B)$.*

Using a designated verifier proof (or scheme, respectively), any third party, other the verifier himself, cannot be convinced about the validity of the proof, because the verifier can always generate the proof by himself which is indistinguishable from the original proof. This way, even the signature is made publicly available, no one except the verifier will be convinced with the authenticity of the signature.

In some circumstances, any other third party can be convinced that the publicly available signature designated to a verifier is valid. For example, when the verifier is well known to be honest, any third party would trust that the verifier will not deviate from his prescribed protocol. In this case, we require a stronger notion of designated verifier proofs as defined in [7] and strengthen in [10] as follows.

Definition 2. Strong Designated Verifier *[10]*
Let $P(A, B)$ be a protocol for Alice to prove the correctness of statement Θ to a designated verifier, Bob. $P(A, B)$ is called to be a strong designated verifier proof if anyone other than Bob can produce identically distributed transcripts that are indistinguishable from those of $P(A, B)$ for everyone, except for Bob.

To achieve (strong) designated verifier proofs, the general assumption is the verifier, Bob, has constructed his public key and made it available publicly (with a certificate from the trusted authority to make sure the authenticity of the public key). That means, before a signature can be designated to Bob, he has to setup his public key accordingly. Without this setup, a signer cannot designate her signature to Bob. The aim of our work is to reduce this restriction by introducing ID-based (strong) designated verifier proofs. In our setting, Bob is not required to have his public key setup before a message-signature pair is designated to him. This way, the signer can always designate her signature to anyone in the system without the need of any interaction with the receiver beforehand. We only require to have the ID of the receiver published. In the following, we introduce the notion of ID-based designated verifier.

Definition 3. ID-Based Designated Verifier
Let $P(A, B)$ be a protocol for Alice to prove the truth of the statement Θ to Bob. In ID-based designated verifier proof, Alice can obtain Bob's ID from the system and use this information to show the correctness of Θ to Bob. Bob is said to be a designated verifier if he can produce identically distributed transcripts that are indistinguishable from those of $P(A, B)$.

We note that we have added the requirement of ID-based system that will allow Alice, as the signer or sender, respectively, to obtain Bob's ID in order to generate the designated proof. Bob, on the other hand, may have no knowledge that Alice would send an authenticated message to him, since he is not required to have a public key setup before Alice can send an authenticated message to him. We also extend this definition to an ID-based strong designated verifier proof as follows.

Definition 4. ID-Based Strong Designated Verifier
Let $P(A, B)$ be a protocol for Alice to prove the truth of the statement Θ to Bob. We require that Alice can just obtain Bob's ID from the system and use this information to show the correctness of Θ to Bob. $P(A, B)$ is said to be a strong designated verifier proof if anyone can produce identically distributed transcripts that are indistinguishable from those of $P(A, B)$ for everyone, except for Bob.

In an ID-based strong designated verifier scheme, there are three main algorithms.

- **Signature Generation.** A probabilistic algorithm that uses the signer's (or sender's, respectively) secret key, an ID of the designated verifier and a message m to generate a signature σ. That is, $\sigma \leftarrow \mathsf{IDSign}(\mathsf{ID}, SK, M)$.
- **Signature Verification.** A deterministic algorithm that receives a message m, a signature σ, and a secret key $\mathcal{S}_{\mathsf{ID}}$, that returns True if the signature is correct, or $\perp$ otherwise. That is, $\{True, \perp\} \leftarrow \mathsf{IDVerify}(\mathcal{S}_{\mathsf{ID}}, m, \sigma)$.
- **Transcript Simulation.** An algorithm that is run by the verifier to produce identically distributed transcripts that are indistinguishable from the original proof.

In addition to the above main algorithms, we also require the following.

- **Correctness.** We require that all signatures that are generated correctly by IDSign algorithm, will always pass the verification algorithm. That is,

$$Pr\left(True \leftarrow \mathsf{IDVerify}(\mathcal{S}_{\mathsf{ID}}, m, \mathsf{IDSign}(\mathsf{ID}, SK, m))\right) = 1.$$

- **Transcript Simulation Generation.** We require that the verifier, who holds the secret key $\mathcal{S}_{\mathsf{ID}}$ can always produce identically distributed transcripts that are indistinguishable from the original proof via the Transcript Simulation algorithm.

2.1   Cryptographic Tools

Throughout this paper, we will use the following cryptographic tools and notations to design our schemes.

Bilinear Pairing
Let $\mathbb{G}_1$ be a cyclic additive group generated by P, whose order is a prime q, and $\mathbb{G}_2$ be a cyclic multiplicative group with the same order q. Let $e : \mathbb{G}_1 \times \mathbb{G}_1 \to \mathbb{G}_2$ be a map with the following properties:

1. **Bilinearity:** $e(aP, bQ) = e(P, Q)^{ab}$ for all $P, Q \in G_1, a, b \in Z_q$
2. **Non-degeneracy:** There exists $P, Q \in G_1$ such that $e(P, Q) \neq 1$, in other words, the map does not send all pairs in $G_1 \times G_1$ to the identity in G_2;
3. **Computability:** There is an efficient algorithm to compute $e(P, Q)$ for all $P, Q \in G_1$.

In our setting of prime order groups, the **Non-degeneracy** is equivalent to $e(P, Q) \neq 1$ for all $P, Q \in G_1$. So, when P is a generator of G_1, $e(P, P)$ is a generator of G_2. Such a bilinear map is called a bilinear pairing (more exactly, called an admissible bilinear pairing).

Definition 5. Bilinear Diffie-Hellman (BDH) Problem
Given a randomly chosen $P \in G_1$, as well as aP, bP and cP (for unknown randomly chosen $a, b, c \in \mathbb{Z}_q$), compute $e(P, P)^{abc}$.

For the BDH problem to be hard, G_1 and G_2 must be chosen so that there is no known algorithm for efficiently solving the Diffie-Hellman problem in either G_1 or G_2. We note that if the BDH problem is hard for a pairing e, then it follows that e is non-degenerate.

Definition 6. Bilinear Diffie-Hellman Assumption
If $\mathcal{IG}$ is a BDH parameter generator, the advantage $\text{Adv}_{\mathcal{IG}}(\mathcal{A})$ that an algorithm $\mathcal{A}$ has in solving the BDH problem is defined to be the probability that the algorithm $\mathcal{A}$ outputs $e(P, P)^{abc}$ on inputs $G_1, G_2, e, P, aP, bP, cP$, where (G_1, G_2, e) is the output of $\mathcal{IG}$ for sufficiently large security parameter K, P is a random generator of G_1 and a, b, c are random elements of $\mathbb{Z}_q$. The BDH assumption is that $\text{Adv}_{\mathcal{IG}}(\mathcal{A})$ is negligible for all efficient algorithms $\mathcal{A}$.

Chameleon Hashing and ID-Based Chameleon Hashing
Chameleon hashing (or *trapdoor commitment*) is basically non-interactive commitment schemes as proposed by Brassard, Chaum and Crepeau [3]. The idea of chameleon hash functions was introduced and formalized in [8] in the construction of their chameleon signature schemes. The name "chameleon" refers to the ability of the owner of the trapdoor information to change the input to the function to any value of his choice without changing the resulting output.

The idea of chameleon hashing has been extended in [1] to construct an Identity-based chameleon hash. An ID-based chameleon hash scheme is defined by a family of efficiently computable algorithms (Setup, Extract, Hash, Forge) as follows.

- Setup: A probabilistic algorithm that is run by a trusted authority TA to generate a pair of keys $\mathcal{SK}$ and $\mathcal{PK}$ defining the scheme. TA publishes $\mathcal{PK}$ and keeps $\mathcal{SK}$ secret.
- Extract: A deterministic algorithm that accepts $\mathcal{SK}$ and an identity string ID and outputs the trapdoor information $\mathcal{T}$ associated with the identity ID.
- Hash: A probabilistic algorithm that accepts $\mathcal{PK}$, an identity string ID and a message m to produce a hash value h. For the rest of this paper, we also denote this hash by IDChameleonHash.

- **Forge**: An algorithm that, on input $\mathcal{PK}$, an identity string ID, the trapdoor information $\mathcal{T}$ associated with ID, a message m', and a hash value $h = \mathsf{IDChameleonHash}(\mathcal{PK}, \mathsf{ID}, m')$, outputs a sequence of random bits that correspond to a valid computation of $\mathsf{IDChameleonHash}(\mathcal{PK}, \mathsf{ID}, m')$ yielding a collision on the same target value h.

Related to this definition is the notion of *collision forgery* defined [1] as follows.

Definition 7. *A collision forgery strategy is a probabilistic algorithm that given identity string* ID, *a message m and random bits r, outputs another message m' and random bits r', where $m \neq m'$ and $r \neq r'$, such that*

$$\mathsf{IDChameleonHash}(\mathsf{ID}, m, r) = \mathsf{IDChameleonHash}(\mathsf{ID}, m', r')$$

with non-negligible probability.

A hashing scheme is said to be *secure against existential collision forgery by passive attacks* if no collision-forgery strategy against it exists.

ID-Based Encryption Schemes

The idea of ID-based encryption schemes is to allow two participants to share a shared key by only using their identities. Encryption can also be done by only using identities. The first practical construction of ID-based encryption schemes was proposed by Boneh and Franklin in [2] by applying pairing technique. This construction has fully satisfied the requirement of ID-based public key cryptosystems as proposed by Shamir [11].

In general, there are four algorithms in ID-based cryptosystem as follows.

- **Setup**. A deterministic algorithm that is run by a trusted authority to generate global system parameters and *master key*.
- **Extract**. A deterministic algorithm that is run by a trusted authority on inputting the *master key* together with an arbitrary bit string $\mathsf{ID} \in \{0,1\}^*$, to generate the user's private key $\mathcal{S}_{\mathsf{ID}}$. That is, $\mathcal{S}_{\mathsf{ID}} \leftarrow \mathsf{Extract}(\mathsf{ID})$.
- **Encrypt**. A probabilistic algorithm that encrypts a message under the public identity ID. That is, $C \leftarrow \mathsf{IDEncrypt}(m, \mathsf{ID})$.
- **Decrypt**. A deterministic algorithm that receives a ciphertext and a private key $\mathcal{S}_{\mathsf{ID}}$, to generate the corresponding plaintext. That is,

$$m \leftarrow \mathsf{IDDecrypt}(C, \mathcal{S}_{\mathsf{ID}}).$$

3   Generic Construction for ID-Based Strong Designated Verifier

In this section, we provide a generic construction for ID-based strong designated verifier scheme from *any* ID-based signature scheme. The idea is to combine *any* ID-based signature scheme with an ID-based chameleon hash function, together with an ID-based encryption scheme. We note that by combining any ID-based signature scheme with an ID-based chameleon hash function, we obtain an ID-based designated verifier scheme. To achieve a *strong* designated verifier, we combine it with an ID-based chameleon hash function.

Model

We assume there are two participants involved, namely the signer (or sender, respectively), Alice, and the designated verifier, Bob. We assume Alice has established an ID-based system setup where her public key, PK, is her public identity ID_A, and her secret key, SK, is $\mathcal{S}_{\mathsf{ID}_A}$, obtained from the Extract procedure. The signature scheme used by Alice is denoted by (Sign, Verify), where Sign is a deterministic signing algorithm to generate a signature, and Verify is a deterministic verification algorithm to verify the authenticity of the signature. The algorithm Sign receives a message m and Alice's secret key, $\mathcal{S}_{\mathsf{ID}}$, to produce a signature σ. The verification algorithm receives a signature and Alice's public identity, ID_A, to return *True* or $\perp$, that indicates the verification is successful or not, respectively.

Bob has published his identity, ID_B. As in any other ID based system, there exists a PKG (Private Key Generator) in the system.

The generic construction is illustrated as follows.

- **Signature Generation.**

$$\mathsf{IDSign}(\mathsf{ID}_B, SK, m) = \begin{cases} \tilde{m} = \mathsf{IDChameleonHash}(m, \mathsf{ID}_B, R); \\ \tilde{\sigma} = \mathsf{Sign}(\tilde{m}, SK); \\ \sigma = \mathsf{IDEncrypt}(\tilde{\sigma}). \end{cases}$$

In the above algorithm, SK, is Alice's secret key, which is $SK = \mathcal{S}_{\mathsf{ID}_A}$. The signature on a message m is (σ, R).

- **Signature Verification.**

$$\mathsf{IDVerify}(\mathcal{S}_{\mathsf{ID}_B}, m, \sigma) = \begin{cases} \hat{\sigma} \quad = \mathsf{IDDecrypt}(\sigma, \mathcal{S}_{\mathsf{ID}_B}); \\ (\tilde{\sigma}, R) \leftarrow \hat{\sigma}; \\ \tilde{m} \quad = \mathsf{IDChameleonHash}(m, \mathsf{ID}_B, R); \\ Result = \mathsf{Verify}(\tilde{m}, \tilde{\sigma}, PK). \end{cases}$$

In the above algorithm, $PK = \mathsf{ID}_A$. The result of the signature verification is either *True* or $\perp$.

- **Transcript Simulation.** The verifier can always generate identically distributed transcripts that are indistinguishable from the original proof, after he *extracts* his secret key $\mathcal{S}_{\mathsf{ID}}$ from the PKG. This is due to the Forge algorithm that is defined in the ID-based chameleon hash function.

Theorem 1. *The above generic construction will produce an ID-based strong designated verifier scheme.*

Proof (sketch). We need to show that the above construction will satisfy the requirements of ID-based strong designated verifier scheme as described in section 2.

- *Correctness.* It is easy to verify that all signatures generated by the above construction can always be verified correctly.
- *Transcript Simulation Generation.* An identically distributed transcript can always be produced after the *extract* algorithm is performed. This is due to the ID-based chameleon hash function construction.
- *The scheme is ID-based.* It is easy to see that the verifier does not need to generate his public key setup before the signer (or sender, respectively) can send an authenticated message to him.

$\diamond$

4   An Efficient ID-Based Strong Designated Verifier

The generic construction proposed in section 3 can be used to convert *any* ID-based signature scheme to an ID-based strong designated verifier scheme. However, the scheme requires an ID-based encryption scheme involved, and therefore it is not efficient. In this section, we provide an efficient scheme that satisfies all the requirements of ID-based strong designated verifier schemes. Unlike the generic construction proposed in 3, our scheme does not require any encryption involved. The scheme is based on bilinear pairing.

Setup
TA generates two groups $(\mathbb{G}_1, +)$ and $(\mathbb{G}_2, \cdot)$ of prime order q and a mapping pair $e : (\mathbb{G}_1, +)^2 \to (\mathbb{G}_2, \cdot)$, together with an arbitrary generator $P \in \mathbb{G}_1$. He also selects his secret key (or master key) $s \in \mathbb{Z}_q$ and set $P_{pub} = sP$, where s denotes the master key. Finally, two cryptographically strong hash functions are selected: $H_0 : \{0,1\}^* \to \mathbb{G}_1$ and $H_1 : \{0,1\}^* \to \mathbb{Z}_q$. The system parameters and their descriptions are $(\mathbb{G}_1, \mathbb{G}_2, e, q, P, P_{pub}, H_0)$.

Each user has his/her identity published. In this scenario, Alice has published her identity, ID_A, and Bob has published his identity, ID_B. Their secret key is defined by the Extract algorithm as follows.

$$\mathcal{S}_{\mathsf{ID}} = sH_0(\mathsf{ID}).$$

We note that this computation can be performed after a party received an authenticated message.

The scheme is illustrated as follows.

- **Signature Generation.**
  To sign a message m for Bob, Alice selects two random values $k \in \mathbb{Z}_q$ and $t \in \mathbb{Z}_q^*$, and computes

$$c = e(\mathsf{Q}_{\mathsf{ID}_B}, P)^k;$$
$$r = H_1(m, c);$$
$$T = t^{-1}kP - r\mathcal{S}_{\mathsf{ID}_A}.$$

The signature on a message m is (T, r, t).

– **Signature Verification.**
Knowing that a signature is sent by Alice, Bob may verify its validity by testing whether

$$H_1\left(m, (e(T, Q_{\mathsf{ID_B}})e\,(Q_{\mathsf{ID_A}}, \mathcal{S}_{\mathsf{ID_B}})^r)^t\right) \stackrel{?}{=} r$$

holds with equality.

We note that nobody else other than Bob can perform this verification because his secret key is involved in the verification process. As we will show later on, even Bob is willing to reveal his secret key, no other third party can be convinced by the validity of such signature because Bob is capable to generate the same transcripts in an indistinguishable way.

Theorem 2. *All correct signatures will pass the verification test.*

Proof (sketch). We will show the correctness of the verification test, as follows.

$$H_1\left(m, (e(T, Q_{\mathsf{ID_B}})e\,(Q_{\mathsf{ID_A}}, \mathcal{S}_{\mathsf{ID_B}})^r)^t\right) \stackrel{?}{=} r.$$

We know that

$$e(T, Q_{\mathsf{ID_B}})^t = e(t^{-1}kP - r\mathcal{S}_{\mathsf{ID_A}}, Q_{\mathsf{ID_B}})^t$$
$$= e(kP, Q_{\mathsf{ID_B}})e(Q_{\mathsf{ID_A}}, \mathcal{S}_{\mathsf{ID_B}})^{-rt}.$$

Hence, we obtain

$$(e(T, Q_{\mathsf{ID_B}})e\,(Q_{\mathsf{ID_A}}, \mathcal{S}_{\mathsf{ID_B}})^r)^t = e(kP, Q_{\mathsf{ID_B}})e(Q_{\mathsf{ID_A}}, \mathcal{S}_{\mathsf{ID_B}})^{-rt}e\,(Q_{\mathsf{ID_A}}, \mathcal{S}_{\mathsf{ID_B}})^{rt}$$
$$= e(kP, Q_{\mathsf{ID_B}}) = e(Q_{\mathsf{ID_B}}, kP) = e(Q_{\mathsf{ID_B}}, P)^k.$$

Therefore,

$$H_1\left(m, (e(T, Q_{\mathsf{ID_B}})e\,(Q_{\mathsf{ID_A}}, \mathcal{S}_{\mathsf{ID_B}})^r)^t\right) = H_1\left(m, e(Q_{\mathsf{ID_B}}, P)^k\right)$$
$$= H_1\left(m, c\right) = r.$$

$\diamond$

– **Transcript Simulation.**
To simulate the transcript, Bob selects two random numbers, $R \in \mathbb{G}_1$ and $a \in \mathbb{Z}_q^*$, and perform the following computations:
1. $c' = e(R, Q_{\mathsf{ID_B}})e(Q_{\mathsf{ID_A}}, \mathcal{S}_{\mathsf{ID_B}})^a$
2. $r' = H_1(m', c')$
3. $t' = (r')^{-1}a \pmod{p}$
4. $T' = (t')^{-1}R$

Theorem 3. *The transcript (T', r', t') is indistinguishable from the original proof, for a message $m' \neq m$.*

Proof. (sketch) We will see that the verification will hold with equality. The verification is as follows.

$$H_1\left(m',\left(e(T',Q_{\mathsf{ID}_B})e(Q_{\mathsf{ID}_A},\mathcal{S}_{\mathsf{ID}_B})^{r'}\right)^{t'}\right)\overset{?}{=}r'.$$

We know that

$$e(T',Q_{\mathsf{ID}_B})^{t'}=e((t')^{-1}R,Q_{\mathsf{ID}_B})^{t'}=e(R,Q_{\mathsf{ID}_B}).$$

Now, we have

$$
\begin{aligned}
\left(e(T',Q_{\mathsf{ID}_B})e(Q_{\mathsf{ID}_A},\mathcal{S}_{\mathsf{ID}_B})^{r'}\right)^{t'} &= e(T',Q_{\mathsf{ID}_B})^{t'}e(Q_{\mathsf{ID}_A},\mathcal{S}_{\mathsf{ID}_B})^{r't'}\\
&= e(R,Q_{\mathsf{ID}_B})e(Q_{\mathsf{ID}_A},\mathcal{S}_{\mathsf{ID}_B})^{r't'}\\
&= e(R,Q_{\mathsf{ID}_B})e(Q_{\mathsf{ID}_A},\mathcal{S}_{\mathsf{ID}_B})^{a}=c'.
\end{aligned}
$$

Hence, we have obtained

$$H_1(m',c')=r'$$

with equality. $\diamond$

Theorem 4. *Our ID-based strong designated verifier scheme satisfies all the requirements mentioned in section 2.*

4.1   Security Consideration

Theorem 5. *If a valid designated signature can be generated without the knowledge of the sender and the designated verifier's secret keys, then the BDH problem may be solved in polynomial time.*

Proof. Let us recall the BDH problem as follows. Given a randomly chosen $P \in \mathbb{G}_1$, as well as aP, bP and cP (for unknown randomly chosen $a, b, c \in \mathbb{Z}_q$), compute $e(P,P)^{abc}$. We assume there is a polynomial algorithm $\mathcal{A}$ that can generate a valid signature (T, r, t) for a message m and we will show how to use this algorithm to solve the BDH problem.

In our setting, we know the public information P_{pub}, ID_A and ID_B, where A denote the sender (or signer) and B is the designated verifier. Since P is a generator in $\mathbb{G}_1$, then we can rewrite these three parameters as

$$Q_{\mathsf{ID}_A}=aP \qquad Q_{\mathsf{ID}_B}=bP \qquad P_{pub}=cP$$

for $a, b, c \in \mathbb{Z}_q$. We also note that $\mathcal{S}_{\mathsf{ID}_A}=cQ_{\mathsf{ID}_A}=acP$ and $\mathcal{S}_{\mathsf{ID}_B}=cQ_{\mathsf{ID}_B}=bcP$

Now, suppose $\mathcal{A}$ can find with non-negligible probability a valid signature (T, r, t) on a message m. We can construct an algorithm $\mathcal{B}$ that uses $\mathcal{A}$ to solve the BDH problem as follows.

– Compute $\varsigma = e(T,Q_{\mathsf{ID}_B})$.

- Compute $v = (\varsigma \cdot e(Q_{ID_A}, S_{ID_B})^t)^t$
- Compute $\tau = \left(\frac{\varsigma}{v^{t-1}}\right)^{(-r)^{-1}}$.
- Output τ as the solution to the BDH problem.

The correctness of algorithm $\mathcal{B}$ is justified as follows.

$$\tau = \left(\frac{\varsigma}{v^{t-1}}\right)^{(-r)^{-1}}$$

$$= \left(\frac{e(T, Q_{ID_B})}{\left((e(T, Q_{ID_B})e(Q_{ID_A}, S_{ID_B})^r)^t\right)^{t-1}}\right)^{(-r)^{-1}}$$

$$= \left(\frac{e(T, Q_{ID_B})}{e(T, Q_{ID_B})e(Q_{ID_A}, S_{ID_B})^r}\right)^{(-r)^{-1}}$$

$$= e(Q_{ID_A}, S_{ID_B}) = e(aP, cQ_{ID_B}) = e(aP, cbP) = e(P, P)^{abc}.$$

The success probability of $\mathcal{B}$ is the same as $\mathcal{A}$, which means the BDH problem could be solved in polynomial time. Hence, it contradicts with the BDH assumption. Therefore, we have obtained the contradiction. $\diamond$

Theorem 6. *Our ID-based scheme is a designated verifier scheme.*

Proof. We need to show that the transcript simulated by the receiver are indistinguishable from those that he receives from the signer. That is, the distributions of

$$\sigma = (T, r, t) : \begin{cases} k \in \mathbb{Z}_q \\ t \in \mathbb{Z}_q^* \\ r = H_1(m, e(Q_{ID_B}, P)^k) \\ T = t^{-1}kP - rS_{ID_A} \end{cases}$$

and

$$\sigma' = (T', r', t') : \begin{cases} R \in \mathbb{G}_1 \\ a \in \mathbb{Z}_q^* \\ c' = e(R, Q_{ID_B})e(Q_{ID_A}, S_{ID_B})^a \\ r' = H_1(m', c') \\ t' = (r')^{-1}a \pmod{p} \\ T' = (t')^{-1}r \pmod{p} \end{cases}$$

are identical.

Let $(\hat{T}, \hat{r}, \hat{t})$ be a randomly chosen signature in the set of all valid designated signatures from the signer to the designated verifier. Then, we have

$$Pr_{\sigma}[(T, r, t) = (\hat{T}, \hat{r}, \hat{t})] = Pr_{k; t \neq 0} \left[\begin{array}{l} r = H_1(m, e(Q_{ID_B}, P)^k) = \hat{r} \\ t = \hat{t} \\ T = t^{-1}kP - rS_{ID_A} = \hat{T} \end{array} \right] = \frac{1}{q(q-1)}$$

and

$$Pr_{\sigma'}[(T,r,t) = (\hat{T},\hat{r},\hat{t})] = Pr_{R;a \neq 0} \begin{bmatrix} r = H_1(m, e(R, \mathsf{Q}_{\mathsf{ID}_B})e(\mathsf{Q}_{\mathsf{ID}_A}, \mathcal{S}_{\mathsf{ID}_B})^a) = \hat{r} \\ t = (r')^{-1}a \pmod{q} = \hat{t} \\ T = (r)^{-1}aR \pmod{q} = \hat{T} \end{bmatrix}$$

$$= \frac{1}{q(q-1)}$$

which have the same probability. This means that both distributions of probabilities are the same.   ◇

5   Conclusion

In this paper, we proposed an ID-based strong designated verifier signature scheme. Firstly, we introduced this notion and showed the required properties of such schemes. We constructed a generic construction for ID-based strong designated verifier signature schemes from *any* ID-based signature schemes, in conjunction with an ID-based chameleon hash function and an ID-based encryption scheme. However, the resulting scheme requires an encryption involved and hence, it is not efficient. We proceeded with an efficient ID-based strong designated verifier signature scheme based on pairings which does not require any encryption involved. We showed complete security proofs of our scheme.

References

1. G. Ateniese and B. de Medeiros. Identity-based Chameleon Hash and Applications. *Financial Cryptography 2004*, 2004 (to appear).
2. D. Boneh and M. Franklin. Identity-based encryption from the Weil pairing. *LNCS*, 2139:213+, 2001.
3. G. Brassard, D. Chaum, and C. Crépeau. Minimum Disclosure Proofs of Knowledge. *JCSS, 37(2)*, pages 156 – 189, 1988.
4. D. Chaum. Zero-knowledge undeniable signatures. *Adv in Cryptology - Eurocrypt '90*, pages 458–464, 1990.
5. D. Chaum and H. van Antwerpen. Undeniable signatures. *Adv in Cryptology - Crypto '89, LNCS 435*, pages 212–216, 1990.
6. S. Galbraith and W. Mao. Invisibility and Anynimity of Undeniable and Confirmer Signatures. *CT-RSA 2003, LNCS 2612*, pages 80 – 97, 2003.
7. M. Jakobsson, K. Sako, and R. Impagliazzo. Designated Verifier Proofs and Their Applications. *Adv in Cryptology - Eurocrypt '96, LNCS 1070*, pages 143 – 154, 1996.
8. H. Krawczyk and T. Rabin. Chameleon hashing and signatures. *Network and Dist System Security Symp, The Internet Society*, pages 143 – 154, 2000.
9. B. Libert and J. J. Quisquater. Identity based Undeniable Signatures. *Topics in Cryptology, CT-RSA 2004, LNCS 2964*, pages 112 – 125, 2004.
10. S. Saeednia, S. Kramer, and O. Markovitch. An Efficient Strong Designated Verifier Signature Scheme. *The 6th Intl Conf on Inf Security and Cryptology (ICISC 2003)*, pages 40 – 54, 2003.
11. A. Shamir. Identity-based cryptosystems and signature schemes. *Adv in Cryptology - Crypto '84, LNCS 196*, pages 47–53, 1985.

Linkable Spontaneous Anonymous Group Signature for Ad Hoc Groups

(Extended Abstract)

Joseph K. Liu[1], Victor K. Wei[1], and Duncan S. Wong[2*]

[1] Department of Information Engineering
The Chinese University of Hong Kong
Shatin, Hong Kong
{ksliu9,kwwei}@ie.cuhk.edu.hk
[2] Department of Computer Science
City University of Hong Kong
Kowloon, Hong Kong
duncan@cityu.edu.hk

Abstract. We present a linkable spontaneously anonymous group (LSAG) signature scheme (alternatively known as linkable ring signature scheme) satisfying the following three properties. (1) Anonymity, or signer indistinguishability. (2) Linkability: That two signatures by the same signer can be linked. (3) Spontaneity: No group secret, therefore no group manager or group secret sharing setup. We reduce the security of our scheme to well-known problems under the random oracle model. Using the scheme, we construct a new efficient one-round e-voting system which does not have a registration phase. We also present a new efficient reduction of famous rewind simulation lemma which only relies on elementary probability theory. Threshold extensions of our scheme are also presented.

1 Introduction

We present a 1-out-of-n group signature scheme which satisfy three properties: (1) Anonymity, or signer-indistinguishability. (2) Linkability: That two signatures by the same signer can be linked. (3) Spontaneity: No group secret, and thus no group manager or secret-sharing setup stage.

A 1-out-of-n group signature scheme allows any member of a group of n signers to generate a signature such that any public verifier can determine if the signature is generated by a group member. They are typically achieved by generating a group secret and then share it out using centralized methods (with group manager) or distributed methods (with a all-n-member secret sharing setup stage) [8,9,5,6].

---

* The work described in this paper was fully supported by a grant from CityU (Project No. 7200005).

H. Wang et al. (Eds.): ACISP 2004, LNCS 3108, pp. 325–335, 2004.

In Cramer, et al. [10] and Rivest, et al. [18] a new paradigm for achieving 1-out-of-n group signature is presented. Any single user/signer can conscript the public keys of $n-1$ other users to form a group of n members. Then a signature can be generated by that single signer which can be publicly verified to be signed by one of the n group members. But the group formation and the signature generation are both *spontaneous*, meaning that no participation or even knowledge of the other $n-1$ users are needed. The 1-out-of-n signature generated this way is also anonymous (signer indistinguishable). Furthermore the anonymity is unconditional (information-theoretic) and exculpable (signer anonymous even after subpoenaing all n secret keys and all communications transcripts). Rivest, et al. [18] formalized this kind of signature to be 'Ring Signature' because their construction of the signature forms a ring structure. Some other works in the literature also call this kind of signature (with the above properties) 'Ring Signature' although some of them may not have a ring structure for their construction. In alternative terminology, we call this kind of signature 'Spontaneous Anonymous Group (SAG) Signature' as they fulfill Spontaneity, Anonymity and Group properties regardless of the construction structure.

This paradigm of SAG signature schemes have found many applications where maximum or near maximum privacy protection is needed such as whistle blowing. It has also found applications in group signatures for *ad hoc groups* where group secret setup and maintenance are too expensive due to frequent membership joins and drops. This kind of structure raises new challenges for security issues as the instance of ad hoc groups are not dependent on any particular network infrastructure. For example, a group of users who spontaneously decide to communicate some sensitive data which do not involve any trusted third party for participation while privacy need to be preserved at the same time. SAG signatures are perfectly suited to such situation due to its spontaneity property. Additional works on this topic includes [1,3,4,20,19,15].

In this paper, we present linkable SAG (LSAG) signatures. Linkability means two signatures by the same actual signer can be identified as such, but the signer remains anonymous.

There are several applications of the new LSAG signatures. (1) Linked whistle-blowing. SAG signature can be used to leak secret information [18]. However, some media or journalists may not believe what the secret leaker tells and may think that he is telling lies. They may only believe two or three different sources with the same piece of information. In this case, SAG signature cannot be used as one cannot distinguish whether two different SAG signatures are generated by the same signer or not. Instead, LSAG should be used to allow people to verify that two given signatures are in fact generated by two distinct signers. (2) A new efficient e-voting system can be built upon LSAG signatures. This new e-voting system has efficiency advantage in eliminating one of three typical phases in e-voting systems. Typical e-voting systems have three major phases: Registration, Voting, Vote Opening and Tallying Phases. Our e-voting eliminates the Registration phase, and thus achieve great efficiency and user friendliness.

The tradeoff is in increased bandwidth requirements. We are going to discuss this in the later section of this paper.

1.1 Contributions

Our contributions consists of (1) the first linkable SAG (ring) signature. (2) application of this new paradigm. (3) a new efficient and accessible reduction of the forking lemma.

We add the property of linkability to ring signatures by presenting the first linkable ring signature scheme. In alternative terminology, our scheme is the first LSAG (Linkable Spontaneous Anonymous Group) signature scheme. Unlike the original ring signature which is exculpable, our scheme is culpable. We stress the distinction between this new feature and the feature of *claimability*. Claimability allows a signer to come forth on his own volition and claim responsibility by providing proof of having generated a given signature. This feature is easy to achieve in any of the current ring signature schemes by embedding some secret proof of knowledge. In general, culpability implies claimability but not vice versa.

Our scheme is proven existentially unforgeable against adaptive chosen-plaintext, adaptive chosen-public-key attackers provided DL is hard, under the random oracle model (ROM). Signer anonymity (resp. linkability) is reduced to DDH (resp. DL) under ROM.

We present an application of the new LSAG signature paradigm: an e-voting system without registration phase.

Additionally, we present a new efficient reduction of the forking lemma in rewind simulation. The reduction efficiency is four times better than that of heavy-row lemma [16] per rewind. Our reduction proof is the most accessible in the literature, relying only on the moment inequality from elementary probability theory.

We also present threshold versions of our LSAG signature.

(Organization)   The rest of the paper is organized as follows. Some related work is reviewed in Sec. 2. It is followed by the description of the security model of a LSAG signature scheme in Sec. 3. Our LSAG signature scheme is then described in Sec. 4 and the security analysis is given in Sec. 5. In Sec. 6, we construct an e-voting system using our LSAG signature schemes. The paper is concluded in Sec. 7.

2 Related Work

SAG Signatures. The Spontaneous Anonymous Group (SAG) Signature was presented by Cramer, et al. [10] and Rivest, et al. [18]. Later on, a separable and ID-based version were given by Abe, et al. [1] and Zhang, et al. [20] respectively. Threshold version have been proposed in [3,4,19,15] as well. All of these schemes are unlinkable.

E-voting Schemes. The first e-voting scheme was proposed by Chaum in [7]. Since then, there were many different e-voting models proposed. In general, an e-voting system consists of a group of voters, a Registry to specify the group of eligible voters, a Voting Center for collecting votes and a Tally to count votes. A voting event can be divided into three phases : Registration Phase, Voting Phase and Vote-Open Phase. In the Registration phase, the Registry may need to interact with voters to define the group of eligible voters. In the Voting phase, eligible voters send their votes to the Voting Center. In the Vote-Open phase, the Tally counts the votes and publishes the result.

In the long version of this paper [14], we provide a more detailed description on the common security definitions of an e-voting scheme and the classification of current e-voting schemes.

3   The Security Model

A (1-out-of-n) linkable spontaneous anonymous group (LSAG) signature scheme is a triple of algorithms $(\mathcal{G}, \mathcal{S}, \mathcal{V})$.

- $(\hat{s}, P) \leftarrow \mathcal{G}(1^k)$ is a probabilistic polynomial time algorithm which takes security parameter k and outputs private key $\hat{s}$ and public key P.
- $\sigma \leftarrow \mathcal{S}(1^k, \hat{s}, L, m)$ is a probabilistic polynomial time algorithm which takes as inputs security parameter k, private key $\hat{s}$, a list L of n public keys which includes the one corresponding to $\hat{s}$ and message m, produces a signature σ.
- $1/0 \leftarrow \mathcal{V}(1^k, L, m, \sigma)$ is a polynomial time algorithm which accepts as inputs security parameter k, a list L of n public keys, a message m and a signature σ, returns 1 or 0 for accept or reject, respectively. We require that for any message m, any $(\hat{s}, P)$ generated by $\mathcal{G}(1^k)$ and any L that includes P,

$$\mathcal{V}(1^k, L, m, \mathcal{S}(1^k, \hat{s}, L, m)) = 1.$$

We omit the denotation of the security parameter as an input of the algorithms in the rest of the paper.

3.1   Existential Unforgeability Against Adaptive Chosen-Plaintext, Adaptive Chosen-Public-Key Attackers

A secure LSAG signature scheme should be able to thwart signature forgery under certain security models. Under the model of adaptive chosen-plaintext attack, existential unforgeability [12] means that given the public keys of all group members but not any of the corresponding private keys, an adversary, who can even adaptively obtain valid signatures for any messages that he wishes, cannot forge a signature for any message m.

In this paper, we adopt the stronger model of adaptive chosen-plaintext attack for defining the existential unforgeability of a LSAG signature scheme. The following definition is similar to that of [1] which also captures the adaptive chosen public-key attack.

Definition 1 (Existential unforgeability against adaptive chosen plaintext, adaptive chosen-public-key attackers). *Let $\mathcal{SO}(L', m')$ be a signing oracle that accepts as inputs any public key list $L' = \{PK_1, \cdots, PK_{n'}\}$ and any message m', produces a signature σ' such that $\mathcal{V}(L', m', \sigma') = 1$. An LSAG signature scheme is* **existentially unforgeable** *(against adaptive chosen-plaintext and adaptive chosen public-key attackers) if, for any PPT (probabilistic polynomial-time) algorithm $\mathcal{A}$ with signing oracle $\mathcal{SO}$ such that $(L, m, \sigma) \leftarrow \mathcal{A}^{\mathcal{SO}}(L)$, for a list L of n public keys chosen by $\mathcal{A}$, its output satisfies $\mathcal{V}(L, m, \sigma) = 1$ only with negligible probability. Note that (L, m, σ) should not correspond to any query-response pair to the signing oracle.*

3.2   Signer Ambiguity

Signer ambiguity means that it is infeasible to identify which private key was actually used in generating a given LSAG signature. Formally,

Definition 2 (Signer Ambiguity). *An LSAG signature scheme is* **signer ambiguous** *if for any PPT algorithm E, on inputs of any message m, any list L of n public keys, any set of t private keys $\mathcal{D}_t = \{\hat{s}_1, \cdots, \hat{s}_t\} \subset L$, and any valid signature σ on L and m generated by user π, we have*

$$\Pr[E(m, L, \mathcal{D}_t, \sigma) \to \pi] \begin{cases} \in (\frac{1}{n-t} - \frac{1}{Q(k)}, \frac{1}{n-t} + \frac{1}{Q(k)}), \\ \quad \text{if } \hat{s}_\pi \notin \mathcal{D}_t \text{ and } 0 \le t < n - 1 \\ > 1 - \frac{1}{Q(k)}, \text{ o.w.} \end{cases}$$

for any polynomial $Q(k)$.

Remark: Note that this implies culpability. That is, the actual signer is able to prove to others that he is the actual signer by revealing his signing key.

The definition of signer ambiguity for LSAG signature scheme differs from that of other SAG signature schemes such as [18,1,3,19,15] in two aspects: (1) The former signer-ambiguity comes with culpability, and the later is signer-ambiguous with exculpability because the latter achieves the probability of finding out the actual signer to $1/n$, independent of t and whether the private key of the actual signer is included or not; (2) The signer-ambiguity is now reducible to a hard problem (to DDHP as we shall see soon) for the former while the latter case reduces to information-theoretic security.

3.3   Linkability

Two LSAG signatures with the same public key list L are *linked* if they are generated using the same private key. Formally,

Definition 3 (Linkability). *Let $L = \{P_1, \cdots, P_n\}$ be a list of n public keys. A LSAG signature scheme is* **linkable** *if there exists a PPT algorithm $\mathcal{F}_1$ which outputs $1/0$ with*

$$\Pr[\mathcal{F}_1(L, m_1, m_2, \sigma_1, \sigma_2) = 0 : \pi_1 = \pi_2] \le \epsilon(k)$$

and

$$\Pr[\mathcal{F}_1(L, m_1, m_2, \sigma_1, \sigma_2) = 1 : \pi_1 \neq \pi_2] \leq \epsilon(k)$$

for all sufficiently large k, any $\pi_1, \pi_2 \in \{1, \cdots, n\}$, any messages m_1, m_2 and any $\sigma_1 \leftarrow \mathcal{S}(\hat{s}_{\pi_1}, L, m_1)$, $\sigma_2 \leftarrow \mathcal{S}(\hat{s}_{\pi_2}, L, m_2)$. ϵ is some negligible function for sufficiently large k.

The algorithm $\mathcal{F}_1$ outputs 1 if it thinks the two signatures are linked, that is, are signed by the same group member. Otherwise, it outputs 0.

Remark: Note that linkability defined above requires that the list of public keys L is fixed while there is no additional requirement on the messages of the signatures. Any two LSAG signatures with different L cannot be linked.

4   A LSAG Signature Scheme

Let $G = \langle g \rangle$ be a group of prime order q such that the underlying discrete logarithm problem is intractable. Let $H_1 : \{0, 1\}^* \rightarrow \mathbb{Z}_q$ and $H_2 : \{0, 1\}^* \rightarrow G$ be some statistically independent cryptographic hash functions. For $i = 1, \cdots, n$, each user i has a distinct public key y_i and a private key x_i such that $y_i = g^{x_i}$. Let $L = \{y_1, \cdots, y_n\}$ be the list of n public keys.

4.1   Signature Generation

Given message $m \in \{0, 1\}^*$, list of public key $L = \{y_1, \cdots, y_n\}$, private key x_π corresponding to y_π $1 \leq \pi \leq n$, the following algorithm generates a LSAG signature.

1. Compute $h = H_2(L)$ and $\tilde{y} = h^{x_\pi}$.
2. Pick $u \in_R \mathbb{Z}_q$, and compute

$$c_{\pi+1} = H_1(L, \tilde{y}, m, g^u, h^u).$$

3. For $i = \pi+1, \cdots, n, 1, \cdots, \pi-1$, pick $s_i \in_R \mathbb{Z}_q$ and compute

$$c_{i+1} = H_1(L, \tilde{y}, m, g^{s_i} y_i^{c_i}, h^{s_i} \tilde{y}^{c_i}).$$

4. Compute $s_\pi = u - x_\pi c_\pi \bmod q$.

The signature is $\sigma_L(m) = (c_1, s_1, \cdots, s_n, \tilde{y})$.

Remarks: Other methods of generating h can be used, provided it is computable by the public verifier and that it does not damage security. We shall see examples in some of our applications.

4.2   Signature Verification

A public verifier checks a signature $\sigma_L(m) = (c_1, s_1, \cdots, s_n, \tilde{y})$ on a message m and a list of public keys L as follows.

1. Compute $h = H_2(L)$ and for $i = 1, \cdots, n$, compute $z_i' = g^{s_i} y_i^{c_i}$, $z_i'' = h^{s_i} \tilde{y}^{c_i}$ and then $c_{i+1} = H_1(L, \tilde{y}, m, z_i', z_i'')$ if $i \neq n$.
2. Check whether $c_1 \overset{?}{=} H_1(L, \tilde{y}, m, z_n', z_n'')$. If yes, accept. Otherwise, reject.

4.3   Linkability and Culpability

For a fixed list of public keys L, given two signatures associating with L, namely $\sigma'_L(m') = (c'_1, s'_1, \cdots, s'_n, \tilde{y}')$ and $\sigma''_L(m'') = (c''_1, s''_1, \cdots, s''_n, \tilde{y}'')$, where m' and m'' are some messages, a public verifier after verifying the signatures to be valid, checks if $\tilde{y}' = \tilde{y}''$. If the congruence holds, the verifier concludes that the signatures are created by the same signer. Otherwise, the verifier concludes that the signatures are generated by two different signers.

For a valid signature $\sigma_L(m) = (c_1, s_1, \cdots, s_n, \tilde{y})$ on some message m and some list of public keys L, an investigator subpoenas a private key x_i from user i. If x_i is the private key of some $y_i \in L$ (that is, $y_i = g^{x_i}$) and $\tilde{y} = H_2(L)^{x_i}$, then the investigator conducts that the authorship of the signature belongs to user i.

4.4   Threshold Extension

It is trivial to extend our 1-out-of-n LSAG signature to t-out-of-n threshold LSAG signature by using the linkable property. Each signer simply generates his own 1-out-of-n LSAG signature and concatenate together to form the t-out-of-n threshold LSAG signature. By linkability, verifier can ensure the signature is generated by t distinct signers.

5   Security Analysis

In this section, we analyze the security of our proposed scheme with the assumption that all the hash functions are distinct and behave like random oracles [2].

5.1   Security of Our LSAG Signature Scheme

We give security theorems of our LSAG signature.

Theorem 1 (Existential Unforgeability). *Our LSAG signature scheme is existentially unforgeable against adaptive chosen-plaintext and adaptive chosen public-key attackers provided the DLP (Discrete Logarithm Problem) is hard, under the random oracle model.*

Corollary 1. *Assume there exists a PPT algorithm $\mathcal{A}$ which makes at most q_H queries to random oracles H_1 and H_2 combined and at most q_S queries to signing oracle $\mathcal{SO}$ defined in Def. 1 such that*

$$\Pr[\mathcal{A}(L) \to (m, \sigma) : \mathcal{V}(L, m, \sigma) = 1] > \frac{1}{Q_1(k)}$$

for some polynomial Q_1 and sufficiently large k. Then, there exists a PPT algorithm which can solve the Discrete Logarithm Problem (DLP) with probability at least $(\frac{1}{n(q_H + nq_S)Q_1(k)})^2$ and expected running time no more than twice that of $\mathcal{A}$.

Theorem 2 (Signer Ambiguity). *Our LSAG signature is signer ambiguous provided DDHP (Decisinal Diffie-Hellman Problem) is hard, in the random oracle model.*

Theorem 3 (Linkability). *Our LSAG signature is linkable provided DLP is hard, in the random oracle model.*

Proofs of the Theorems are in the long version of this paper [14].

5.2   The ROS (Rewind-on-Success Lemma)

In the proof of the above theorems, we have used a new proof of the core lemma in rewind simulation. This is the literature's third such proofs, after the forking lemma [17] and the heavy-row lemma [16]. We call it the ROS (Rewind-on-Success) Lemma. Our proof is the most accessible of the three, relying on only the moment inequality from elementary probability theory. And our proof has the best simulation efficiency of the three. Details of the ROS Lemma will be addressed in the long version of this paper [14].

6   A New E-voting System Without Registration Phase

We present a new e-voting scheme without a registration phase. The scheme uses LSAG signatures.

Most e-voting schemes that appeared after the paper by [11] consists of three phases: Registration phase, Voting phase and Vote-Open phase. In the Registration phase, voters obtain untraceable blank ballots from one or more Registry. The untraceability is often achieved by using blind signature techniques. In the Voting phase, each voter casts its filled ballot, in encrypted/blinded form, to one or more Voting Centers. Some e-voting schemes require that all cast ballots (in blinded or encrypted form) be published so each voter can ensure his vote is included. Then one or more independent tallies opens the votes using deblinding parameters sent in by satisfied voters and compute the voting results.

Using LSAG signatures, we can construct a new e-voting system which contains only two phases: the Voting phase and the Vote Opening phase. There is no Registration phase. It is believed that the eliminating of one of three phases will result in large efficiency improvement.

Infrastructure assumptions: We have in mind a voter population where each voter has a published public key. There is a trustworthy list of all voters' public keys that can be downloaded from a reliable repository. For example, the list of all citizens' public keys published by the national government. Or the list of all voting members' public keys published by a society or a board. For the time being, we assume all voters have discrete log key pairs with the same discrete log parameters p, q, and g. The list of all voters' public keys is denoted L.

To initiate a voting event: To initiate a voting event, some messages are generated by reliable means. There are many centralized or distributed methods to do so. Then the messages are published. For simplicity, we consider a yes/no referendum. In this case, two messages M_{yes} and M_{no} are published.

Voting Phase: Each yes-voter send in a LSAG signature on message M_{yes} and public key list L. Each no-voter does same on message M_{no}.

Vote Opening Phase: It is a simple matter to count the yes-votes and the no-votes.

If anyone votes twice (or more), whether both times in the same column or otherwise, his votes will be linked and appropriate actions taken.

6.1 Discussions

The above represents the bare essence of an anonymous e-voting scheme based on LSAG signatures. The most striking distinction between this scheme and popular schemes in the literature is the lack of the Registration phase. Many details are left out. Here we discuss some of them.

Anonymous Channel and Bulletin Board. In order to ensure voter anonymity, the send-in of LSAG signatures should be via anonymous channels. Furthermore, We assume that once the LSAG signature is sent in to a voting center, it will be published to a public bulletin and that public information cannot be altered further.

Multiple Voting Events. The above scheme works for one voting. If there are future voting events, we will need to alter the value of $h = H_2(L)$ for each event. This can be accomplished by several methods. For example, using a different H_2 each event, or change to $h = H_2(L, eventlabel)$.

Vote-and-Go. In comparison to most e-voting schemes in the literature, our scheme has the *vote-and-go* feature. That is, the voters are not involved in the Vote-Opening Phase.

Receipt-freeness. A receipt-free e-voting system prevents a voter from claiming the authorship of a particular vote. This property deters vote-buying. The voter cannot provide evidence of compliance to vote buyers. Since the LSAG signature scheme is claimable, the e-voting system above is not receipt-free. Our systems can be modified to support receipt-freeness by using a tamper-resistant randomizer [13]. A built-in randomizer is responsible for generating all the random numbers for probabilistic functions carried out in the device. Users are only allowed to enter their vote choices and their devices do the rest without further intervention. This is a practical model and we omit the details due to the page limitation.

7 Conclusions

In this paper, we present the first LSAG signature scheme which simultaneously achieves linkability, spontaneity, and anonymity. All these properties of our scheme are proven secure under the random oracle model. Our scheme has many applications, especially where maximum or near maximum privacy protection, and impromptu linkup are desired or required.

An e-voting system based on our LSAG signature scheme is proposed. In the system, there is no registration phase and the voting phase is only one-round (that is, vote-and-go). The Tally is just a public bulletin so that everyone can do the counting.

Additionally, we present a new proof of the core lemma in rewind simulation. This is the literature's third such proofs, after the forking lemma [17] and the heavy-row lemma [16]. Our proof is the most accessible of the three, relying on only the moment inequality from elementary probability theory. And our proof has the best simulation efficiency of the three.

There are many interesting problems that are to be solved. For example, it is interesting to design a LSAG signature scheme which still maintains unconditional anonymity. In addition, LSAG signature schemes may also be constructed based on other hard problems such as factorization. To obtain more scalable e-voting systems, much shorter and more efficient LSAG signature schemes are to be devised.

References

1. M. Abe, M. Ohkubo, and K. Suzuki. 1-out-of-n signatures from a variety of keys. In *Proc. ASIACRYPT 2002*, pages 415–432. Springer-Verlag, 2002. LNCS Vol. 2501.
2. M. Bellare and P. Rogaway. Random oracles are practical: A paradigm for designing efficient protocols. In *Proc. 1st ACM Conference on Computer and Communications Security*, pages 62–73. ACM Press, 1993.
3. E. Bresson, J. Stern, and M. Szydlo. Threshold ring signatures and applications to ad-hoc groups. In *Proc. CRYPTO 2002*, pages 465–480. Springer-Verlag, 2002. LNCS Vol. 2442.
4. E. Bresson, J. Stern, and M. Szydlo. Threshold ring signatures and applications to ad-hoc groups. full version. http://www.di.ens.fr/~bresson, 2002.
5. J. Camenisch. Efficient and generalized group signatures. In *Proc. EUROCRYPT 97*, pages 465–479. Springer-Verlag, 1997. LNCS Vol. 1233.
6. J. Camenisch and M. Stadler. Efficient group signature schemes for large groups. In *Proc. CRYPTO 97*, pages 410–424. Springer-Verlag, 1997. LNCS Vol. 1294.
7. D. Chaum. Untraceable electronic mail, return addresses, and digital pseudonyms. *Communications of the ACM*, 24(2):84–88, February 1981.
8. D. Chaum and E. Van Heyst. Group signatures. In *Proc. EUROCRYPT 91*, pages 257–265. Springer-Verlag, 1991. LNCS Vol. 547.
9. L. Chen and T. Pedersen. New group signature schemes. In *Proc. EUROCRYPT 94*, pages 171–181. Springer-Verlag, 1994. LNCS Vol. 950.
10. R. Cramer, I. Damgård, and B. Schoenmakers. Proofs of partial knowledge and simplified design of witness hiding protocols. In *Proc. CRYPTO 94*, pages 174–187. Springer-Verlag, 1994. LNCS Vol. 839.
11. A. Fujioka, T. Okamoto, and K. Ohta. A practical secret voting scheme for large scale election. In *AUSCRYPT 91*, pages 244–260. Springer-Verlag, 1992. LNCS Vol. 718.

12. S. Goldwasser, S. Micali, and R. Rivest. A digital signature scheme secure against adaptive chosen-message attack. *SIAM J. Computing*, 17(2):281–308, April 1988.
13. B. Lee and K. Kim. Receipt-free electronic voting scheme with a tamper-resistant randomizer. In *Proc. ICISC 2002*, pages 389–406. Springer-Verlag, 2003. LNCS Vol. 2587.
14. J. K. Liu, V. K. Wei, and D. S. Wong. Linkable spontaneous anonymous group signature for ad hoc groups. Cryptology ePrint Archive, Report 2004/027, 2004. http://eprint.iacr.org/.
15. J. K. Liu, V. K. Wei, and D. S. Wong. A separable threshold ring signature scheme. In *ICISC 2003*, pages 12–26. Springer-Verlag, 2004. LNCS Vol. 2971.
16. K. Ohta and T. Okamoto. On concrete security treatment of signatures derived from identification. In *Proc. CRYPTO 98*, pages 354–369. Springer-Verlag, 1998. LNCS Vol. 1462.
17. D. Pointcheval and J. Stern. Security proofs for signature schemes. In *Proc. EUROCRYPT 96*, pages 387–398. Springer-Verlag, 1996. LNCS Vol. 1070.
18. R. Rivest, A. Shamir, and Y. Tauman. How to leak a secret. In *Proc. ASIACRYPT 2001*, pages 552–565. Springer-Verlag, 2001. LNCS Vol. 2248.
19. D. Wong, K. Fung, J. Liu, and V. Wei. On the RS-code construction of ring signature schemes and a threshold setting of RST. In *5th Intl. Conference on Information and Communication Security (ICICS 2003)*, pages 34–46. Springer-Verlag, 2003. LNCS Vol. 2836.
20. F. Zhang and K. Kim. ID-Based blind signature and ring signature from pairings. In *Proc. ASIACRYPT 2002*, pages 533–547. Springer-Verlag, 2002. LNCS Vol. 2501.

A Group Signature Scheme
with Efficient Membership Revocation
for Reasonable Groups

Toru Nakanishi and Yuji Sugiyama

Department of Communication Network Engineering,
Faculty of Engineering, Okayama University
3-1-1 Tsushima-naka, Okayama 700-8530, Japan
{nakanisi,sugiyama}@cne.okayama-u.ac.jp

Abstract. Though group signature schemes with efficient membership revocation were proposed, the previous schemes force a member to obtain a public membership information of $O(\ell_n N)$ bits, where ℓ_n is the length of the RSA modulus and N is the number of members joining and removed. In the scheme proposed in this paper, the public membership information has only K bits, where K is the number of members' joining. Then, for groups with a reasonable size that is comparable to the RSA modulus size (e.g., about 1000 members for 1024 bit RSA modulus), the public membership information is a single small value only, while the signing/verification also remains efficient.

Keywords. Group signature scheme, Membership revocation, Strong RSA assumption, Zero-knowledge proof of integer relations

1 Introduction

1.1 Backgrounds

A *group signature scheme* allows a group member to anonymously sign a message on behalf of a group, where, in addition, a membership manager (MM) and an opening manager (OM) participate. MM has the authority to add a user into the group, and OM has the authority to revoke the anonymity of a signature. Since the scheme allows us to anonymously verify user's ownership of some privilege, it is applied to various cryptographic protocols such as anonymous credential system [6]. On the other hand, various group signature schemes are also proposed [10,5,1,4,2,7,12], with the improvements of efficiency, security and convenience. The breakthrough is achieved in [5]. In this scheme, the efficiency of the public key and signatures is independent from the group size, and furthermore an entity's joining has no influence on other member. The followers [1,4,2,7,12] also have these good characteristics. In both the efficiency and the provably unforgeability, the state-of-the-art scheme is due to Ateniese et al. [1], followed by [2,7,12].

H. Wang et al. (Eds.): ACISP 2004, LNCS 3108, pp. 336–347, 2004.

The essential idea in this type of schemes is the use of the membership certificate. MM issues a membership certificate to the joining member, where the certificate is MM's digital signature. Then, the group signature is a non-interactive zero-knowledge proof of knowledge of this certificate. Since the group signature has no relation with the other members, this idea provides the above good characteristics. However, on the other hand, this idea prevents a member from being easily removed from the group, since it is hard to erase the issued membership certificate in the removed member's environment without physical device's help. One plausible solution is to reissue certificates of all the members except the removed one by changing MM's public key of the digital signature, as [2]. However, the loads of unrelated members are too large.

1.2 Previous Works

Recently, some schemes [4,2,7,12] deal with this problem of the membership revocation. However, in the first schemes [4,2], signing and/or verification requires a computation that is linear in the number of removed members.

In [7], an elegant approach using a dynamic accumulator is proposed, which is followed by [12] with the efficiency improvement. The accumulator allows MM to hash a large set of effective certificates into a short value. In the group signature, the signer has to prove that own certificate is accumulated into the short value. Therefore, signing/verification is efficient, since the computation is independent from the number of the joining and removed members. However, whenever making a signature, the signer has to modify a secret key for the accumulator. Though the modification is performed efficiently, it requires certificates of joining and removed members since the last time he signed. To obtain the certificates, the signer must fetch the certificates of all joining and removed members from a public directory with the list of the certificates, as pointed out in [2]. This is because fetching a part of the list can reveal the information to trace the signer. The fetched public membership information has $O(\ell_n N)$ bits, where ℓ_n is the length of the RSA modulus and N is the number of members joining and removed, since each certificate has about ℓ_n bits. This communication cost is vast, and therefore those schemes are not a complete solution for efficient membership revocation.

1.3 Our Contributions

In this paper, we propose a group signature scheme with efficient membership revocation, where the public membership information has only K bits, where K is the number of members' joining. The information is only a composition of the group, where each bit indicates that a member is joining but not removed. Namely, the information includes no certificate. Then, for reasonable groups with a size that is comparable to the RSA modulus size (e.g., less than about 1000 members for 1024 bit RSA modulus), the public membership information falls in a single value that is comparable to the modulus. Though the signing/verification in our scheme utilizes a zero-knowledge proof of knowledge w.r.t. this membership information for realizing the efficient revocation, this proof's cost has no dependency on the number of joining and removed members, due to the public membership information with the reasonable size. Therefore, the signing/verification remains efficient. Furthermore, at each revocation, MM only has to perform a simple bit operation and the signer needs no modification of own secret key. On the other hand, for larger groups, the proposed scheme requires the signing/verification cost related to $O(K/\ell_n)$. Note that, for such larger groups, the accumulator-based schemes also have a problem of enormous public information with the size $O(\ell_n N)$.

2   Model

We show a model of group signature scheme with membership revocation.

Definition 1. *A group signature scheme with membership revocation consists of the following procedures:*

Setup: *MM and OM generate the general public key and their secret keys.*

Join: *MM issues a membership certificate for a membership secret chosen by a user joining a group. In addition, MM authentically publishes a public membership information that reflects the current members in the group such that the joining user belongs to the group.*

Membership revocation: *MM authentically publishes the public membership information that reflects the current members in the group such that the removed user does not belong to the group. Note that OM, unrelated members and even the removed member do not participate in this procedure.*

Sign: *Given a message, a group member with a membership secret and its membership certificate generates the signature for the message w.r.t. the public key and public membership information.*

Verify: *A verifier checks whether a signature for a message is made by a member in the group w.r.t. the public key and public membership information.*

Open: *Given a signature, OM with his secret specifies the identity of the signer.*

Definition 2. *A secure group signature scheme with membership revocation satisfies the following properties:*

Unforgeability: *Only a member in the group, which is indicated by the public membership information, can generate a valid signature.*

Coalition-resistance: *Colluding members including removed members cannot generate a valid membership certificate that MM did not generate, even if the members adaptively obtained valid certificates from MM.*

Anonymity: *Given a signature, it is infeasible that anyone, except the signer and OM, identifies the signer.*

Unlinkability: *Given two signatures, it is infeasible that anyone, except the signers and OM, determines whether the signatures ware made by the same signer.*

No framing: *Even if MM, OM, and members collude, they cannot sign on behalf of a non-involved member.*

Traceability: *OM is always able to open a valid signature and identify the signer.*

3 Preliminaries

3.1 Assumptions and Notations

Our scheme is based on the strong RSA assumption and decisional Diffie-Hellman (DDH) assumption, as well as the state-of-the-art group signature scheme [1].

Assumption 1 (Strong RSA assumption) *Let $n = pq$ be an RSA modulus, and let G be a cyclic subgroup of $\mathcal{Z}_n^*$. Then, for all probabilistic polynomial-time algorithm $\mathcal{A}$, the probability that $\mathcal{A}$ on inputs n and $z \in G$ outputs $e \in \mathcal{Z}$ s.t. $e > 1$ and $u \in G$ satisfying $z = u^e$ (mod n) is negligible.*

Intuitively, the DDH assumption means the infeasibility to decide whether the discrete logs of two random elements in G to the random bases are the same. When $n = pq$ is an RSA modulus for safe primes p, q (i.e., $p = 2p'+1, q = 2q'+1$, and p, q, p', q' are prime), let $QR(n)$ be the set of quadratic residues modulo n, that is, the cyclic subgroup of $\mathcal{Z}_n^*$ generated by an element of order $p'q'$. As well as the scheme due to Ateniese et al., we assume that $QR(n)$ satisfies the above both assumptions.

Notations: Let $[a, a + d]$ be an integer interval of all integers int such that $a \leq int \leq a + d$, for an integer a and a positive integer d. We additionally use notation $[a, a+d)$ for all int such that $a \leq int < a+d$, and notation $(a, a+d)$ for all int such that $a < int < a + d$. Let $\in_R$ denote the uniform random selection.

3.2 Camenisch-Lysyanskaya Signature Scheme for Blocks of Messages

Our group signature scheme is based on the ordinary (not group) signature due to Camenisch and Lysyanskaya [8] under the strong RSA assumption, which is an extension from the signature used as a membership certificate in Ateniese et al.'s scheme [1].

Key generation: Let $\ell_n, \ell_m, \ell_s, \ell_e, \ell$ be security parameters s.t. $\ell_s \geq \ell_n+\ell_m+\ell$, $\ell_e \geq \ell_m + 2$ and ℓ is sufficiently large (e.g., 160). The secret key consists of safe primes p, q, and the public key consists of $n = pq$ of length ℓ_n and $a_1, \ldots, a_L, b, c \in_R QR(n)$, where L is the number of blocks.

Signing: Given messages $m_1, \ldots, m_L \in [0, 2^{\ell_m})$, choose $s \in_R [0, 2^{\ell_s})$ and a random prime e from $(2^{\ell_e-1}, 2^{\ell_e})$. Compute A s.t. $A = (a_1^{m_1} \cdots a_L^{m_L} b^s c)^{1/e}$. The signature is (s, e, A).

Verification: Given messages $m_1, \ldots, m_L \in [0, 2^{\ell_m})$ and the signature (s, e, A), check $A^e = a_1^{m_1} \cdots a_L^{m_L} b^s c$ and $e \in (2^{\ell_e-1}, 2^{\ell_e})$.

Remark 1. The unforgeability of this scheme means that, given signatures of messages, an adversary cannot forge a signature of new messages. On the other hand, it allows that, given a signature of messages, the adversary can compute another signature of the same messages. Namely, given a messages-signature tuple $(m_1, \ldots, m_L, s, e, A)$, we can compute another signature (s', e, A') for m_1, $\ldots, m_L$, by $s' = s + ke$ and $A' = Ab^k$ for $k \in \mathcal{Z}$, since $A'^e = (Ab^k)^e = a_1^{m_1} \cdots a_L^{m_L} b^s c b^{ke} = a_1^{m_1} \cdots a_L^{m_L} b^{s'} c$.

3.3   Commitment Scheme

A commitment scheme on $QR(n)$ is proposed by Damgård and Fujisaki [11],under the strong RSA assumption. The following is a slightly modified version due to Camenisch and Lysyanskaya [8].

Key generation: The public key consists of a secure RSA modulus n of length ℓ_n, h from $QR(n)$, and g from the group generated by h.
Commitment: For the public key, input x of length ℓ_x, and randomness $r \in \mathcal{Z}_n$, the commitment C is computed as $C = g^x h^r$.

3.4   Signatures of Knowledge

As main building blocks, we use signatures converted from honest-verifier zero-knowledge proofs of knowledge, which are called as signatures of knowledge. We abbreviate them as SPKs. The SPKs are denoted as

$$SPK\{(\alpha, \beta, \ldots) : R(\alpha, \beta, \ldots)\}(m),$$

which means the signature for message m by a signer with the secret knowledge $\alpha, \beta, \ldots$ satisfying the relation $R(\alpha, \beta, \ldots)$.

The proofs used in our scheme show the relations among secret representations of elements in $QR(n)$ with unknown order. The simple SPK proves the knowledge of a representation [11]. We furthermore use the SPK of representations with equal parts, SPK of a representation with parts in intervals [9], and SPK of a representation with a non-negative part [3].

SPK of representation: An SPK proving the knowledge of a representation of $C \in QR(n)$ to the bases $g_1, g_2, \ldots, g_t \in QR(n)$ on message m is denoted as

$$SPK\{(\alpha_1, \ldots, \alpha_t) : C = g_1^{\alpha_1} \cdots g_t^{\alpha_t}\}(m).$$

In this SPK (including the following SPKs), the assurance of $C \in QR(n)$ is required for the soundness, but verifiers who do not know the factorization of n cannot check whether an element of $\mathcal{Z}_n^*$ is a quadratic residue. Hence, instead the above SPK, we use

$$SPK\{(\alpha_1, \ldots, \alpha_t) : C^2 = (g_1^2)^{\alpha_1} \cdots (g_t^2)^{\alpha_t}\}(m),$$

for such verifiers, as [6]. Then, the soundness is ensured such that $(\alpha_1, \ldots, \alpha_t)$ satisfies $C^2 = (g_1^2)^{\alpha_1} \cdots (g_t^2)^{\alpha_t}$, but it does not necessarily imply $C = g_1^{\alpha_1} \cdots g_t^{\alpha_t}$.

SPK **of representations with equal parts:** An *SPK* proving the knowledge of representations of $C, C' \in QR(n)$ to the bases $g_1, \ldots, g_t \in QR(n)$ on message m, where the representations include equal values as parts, is denoted as

$$SPK\{(\alpha_1, \ldots, \alpha_u) : C = g_{i_1}^{\alpha_{j_1}} \cdots g_{i_v}^{\alpha_{j_v}} \wedge C' = g_{i'_1}^{\alpha_{j'_1}} \cdots g_{i'_{v'}}^{\alpha_{j'_{v'}}}\}(m),$$

where indices $i_1, \ldots i_v, i'_1, \ldots i'_{v'} \in \{1, \ldots, t\}$ refer to the bases $g_1, \ldots, g_t$, and indices $j_1, \ldots j_v, j'_1, \ldots j'_{v'} \in \{1, \ldots, u\}$ refer to the secrets $\alpha_1, \ldots, \alpha_u$. This *SPK* is easily obtained by the similar way to the *SPK* for groups with the known order (e.g., [9]).

SPK **of representation with parts in intervals:** An *SPK* proving the knowledge of a representation of $C \in QR(n)$ to the bases $g_1, \ldots, g_t \in QR(n)$ on message m, where the i-th part lies in an interval $[a, a + d]$, is denoted as

$$SPK\{(\alpha_1, \ldots, \alpha_t) : C = g_1^{\alpha_1} \cdots g_t^{\alpha_t} \wedge \alpha_i \in [a, a + d]\}(m).$$

For this *SPK*, two types are known. One is due to Boudot [3], where it is assured that the knowledge exactly lies in the interval. However, this *SPK* needs the computations of about 10 normal *SPK*s of a representation. Another type appears in [9] for example, where the integer the prover knows in fact lies in the narrower interval than the interval the proved knowledge lies in. However, its efficiency is comparable to that of the normal *SPK*, and this is why we use the later type. For $\alpha_i \in [a, a + d]$ in fact, this *SPK* proves the knowledge in $[a - 2^{\tilde{\ell}}d, a + 2^{\tilde{\ell}}d]$, where $\tilde{\ell}$ is a security parameter derived from the challenge size and from the security parameter controlling the statistical zero-knowledge-ness (in practice, $\tilde{\ell} \approx 160$). This *SPK* can be easily extended into the *SPK* for two or more knowledges in intervals, such as $SPK\{(\alpha, \beta) : C = g^{\alpha}h^{\beta} \wedge \alpha \in [a, a + d] \wedge \beta \in [a', a' + d']\}(m)$.

SPK **of representation with non-negative part:** An *SPK* proving the knowledge of a representation of $C \in QR(n)$ to the bases $g_1, \ldots, g_t \in QR(n)$ on message m, where the i-th part is not negative integer, is denoted as

$$SPK\{(\alpha_1, \ldots, \alpha_t) : C = g_1^{\alpha_1} \cdots g_t^{\alpha_t} \wedge \alpha_i \geq 0\}(m).$$

As for this, since we need to prove that the knowledge is exactly 0 and over, we adopt the *SPK* due to Boudot [3].

The interactive ones are denoted by substituting *PK* for *SPK*.

4   Proposed Scheme

4.1   Idea

The foundation is that a group signature is an *SPK* of a membership certificate issued by *MM*. For simplicity, in the following, we omit the mechanism to trace the signer. Ateniese et al. [1] propose the state-of-the-art group signature scheme that is most efficient and provably coalition-resistant against an adaptive adversary. In the registration, MM computes an ordinary signature on a secret x chosen by a joining member, denoted by $Sign(x)$, and MM issues the member $Sign(x)$ as the membership certificate. Then, the member can compute his group signature on message M, as $SPK\{(x,v) : v = Sign(x)\}(M)$.

As the extension, Camenisch and Lysyanskaya [8] propose an ordinary signature scheme shown in Section 3.2, together with a PK of the signature. In the scheme, the signer can sign two blocks of messages. Then, by an interactive protocol in [8], a receiver can obtain a signature from the signer, where one message x is known by only the receiver, but another message m is known by both. Let $Sign(x,m)$ denote the signature on x and m. In the PK shown in [8], the owner of the signature can prove the knowledge of the signature on the messages in the zero-knowledge fashion, such as $PK\{(x,m,v) : v = Sign(x,m)\}$.

Our scheme effectively utilizes the part m to be signed in the Camenisch-Lysyanskaya signature scheme for efficient membership revocation. Concretely, for the i-th member, $m = 2^{i-1}$ is signed, where only the i-th bit from the LSB of m is 1. Then, MM issues a joining member the signature on member's secret x and the message m, $Sign(x,m)$, as the membership certificate. As the public membership information, MM publishes $\tilde{m}$ satisfying that, for all j, the j-th bit is 1 iff the j-th member is joining and not removed. Then, i-th member's group signature consists of the SPK of the certificate, and SPK proving that a bit specified by m in the certificate (i.e., the i-th bit) is 1 in $\tilde{m}$. In fact, the predicate proved by the latter SPK is that $\tilde{m}_U$ and $\tilde{m}_L$ exist such that $\tilde{m} = \tilde{m}_U(2m)+m+\tilde{m}_L$ and $0 \leq \tilde{m}_L \leq m-1$. Since a removed member cannot prove this predicate as shown in Lemma 3 below, the membership revocation is accomplished. Namely, the group signature on message M is $SPK\{(x,m,v,\tilde{m}_U,\tilde{m}_L) : v = Sign(x,m) \wedge \tilde{m} = \tilde{m}_U(2m) + m + \tilde{m}_L \wedge 0 \leq \tilde{m}_L \leq m - 1\}(M)$. Note that removing the i-th member is only the computation of $\tilde{m} - 2^{i-1}$, and it is the very low cost.

Finally we mention the traceability. In the previous scheme, a group signature includes an ElGamal ciphertext of the certificate $v = Sign(x)$. The decryption leads to the signer's identity. On the other hand, in the Camenisch-Lysyanskaya signature as a certificate, the owner of a certificate $v = Sign(x,m)$ can compute different certificates of the same x, m. This is why the previous technique is not applied to our scheme. Thus, our group signature includes an ElGamal ciphertext of a_1^x for a public a_1, while the owner has to register the value with MM. The decryption of the ciphertext leads to the owner's identity.

4.2   Proposed Protocols

Setup: Let ℓ_n be a security parameter. Then, MM sets up the Camenisch-Lysyanskaya scheme, i.e., MM computes two $(\ell_n/2)$-bit safe primes p, q and $n = pq$, and chooses $a_1, a_2, b, c \in_R QR(n)$. Furthermore, he sets up the commitment scheme on $QR(n)$ to generate g and h. He publishes $(n, a_1, a_2, b, c, g, h)$ as the public key, and keeps (p, q) as the secret key. For the Camenisch-Lysyanskaya scheme, security parameters $\ell_x, \ell_m, \ell_e, \ell_s, \ell$ are set s.t. $\ell_s \geq \ell_n + \max(\ell_x, \ell_m) + \ell$ and $\ell_e \geq \max(\ell_x, \ell_m) + 2$. Additionally, we use a security parameter $\tilde{\ell}$ that is for SPK of intervals as shown in Section 3.4. To simplify the description, we introduce interval notations as follows: Define $\mathcal{S} = [0, 2^{\ell_s})$, $\mathcal{E} = (2^{\ell_e - 1}, 2^{\ell_e})$, $\mathcal{X} = [0, 2^{\ell_x})$, $\mathcal{M} = [0, 2^{\ell_m})$. Since the following protocols adopt the efficient SPK of the interval, we need to prepare the narrower intervals $\tilde{\mathcal{E}} = [2^{\ell_e - 1} + 2^{\ell_e - 2}, 2^{\ell_e - 1} + 2^{\ell_e - 2} + 2^{\ell_e - 3 - \tilde{\ell}}]$, $\tilde{\mathcal{X}} = [2^{\ell_x - 1}, 2^{\ell_x - 1} + 2^{\ell_x - 2 - \tilde{\ell}}]$, $\tilde{\mathcal{M}} = [2^{\ell_m - 1}, 2^{\ell_m - 1} + 2^{\ell_m - 2 - \tilde{\ell}}]$ of $\mathcal{E}, \mathcal{X}, \mathcal{M}$, respectively. If $x \in \tilde{\mathcal{X}} = [2^{\ell_x - 1}, 2^{\ell_x - 1} + 2^{\ell_x - 2 - \tilde{\ell}}]$ in fact, the knowledge proved by the SPK lies in expanded $[2^{\ell_x - 1} - 2^{\ell_x - 2 - \tilde{\ell}} 2^{\tilde{\ell}}, 2^{\ell_x - 1} + 2^{\ell_x - 2 - \tilde{\ell}} 2^{\tilde{\ell}}]$, that is, $[2^{\ell_x - 1} - 2^{\ell_x - 2}, 2^{\ell_x - 1} + 2^{\ell_x - 2}]$. Thus, it is confirmed that the knowledge lies in $[0, 2^{\ell_x}) = \mathcal{X}$. This is the same in case of $\mathcal{M}, \tilde{\mathcal{M}}$, and similar to the case of $\mathcal{E}, \tilde{\mathcal{E}}$. The initial public membership information $\tilde{m}$ is set as 0.

On the other hand, OM sets up the ElGamal encryption on $QR(n)$, i.e., OM chooses a secret key $x_{OM} \in_R \{0, 1\}^{\ell_n}$ and publishes the public key $y = g^{x_{OM}}$.

Join and membership revocation: We describe the join protocol for the i-th user ($1 \le i \le K$). We assume $K \le \ell_m - 2 - \tilde{\ell}$. This protocol is derived from the interactive protocol shown in [8], as mentioned in Section 4.1. In our scheme, the membership certificate is (s, e, A) s.t. $A^e = a_1^x a_2^{m + 2^{\ell_m - 1}} b^s c$, where $m = 2^{i-1}$, e is a prime from $\tilde{\mathcal{E}} \subset \mathcal{E}$ and $x \in \tilde{\mathcal{X}} \subset \mathcal{X}$ is the user's secret. Furthermore, note that $m + 2^{\ell_m - 1} \in \tilde{\mathcal{M}} \subset \mathcal{M}$. Thus, (s, e, A) is a Camenisch-Lysyanskaya signature on messages x and $m + 2^{\ell_m - 1}$. The detail protocol is as follows:

1. The joining user U sends MM $C = a_1^x$, where $x \in_R \tilde{\mathcal{X}}$. Next, U proves the knowledge of the secret by $PK\{\alpha : C = a_1^\alpha \wedge \alpha \in \mathcal{X}\}$.
   In this step, note that MM can check $C \in QR(n)$ and that squaring is not needed in the PK.
2. For the membership information $m = 2^{i-1}$, MM computes $A = (C a_2^{\dot{m}} b^s c)^{1/e}$, where $\dot{m} = m + 2^{\ell_m - 1}$, $s \in_R \mathcal{S}$, and e is a random prime from $\tilde{\mathcal{E}}$, and sends (s, e, A) to U. Then, note that $\dot{m} \in \tilde{\mathcal{M}}$.
3. U obtains the membership certificate (s, e, A) on the membership secret x and membership information m such that $A^e = a_1^x a_2^{m + 2^{\ell_m - 1}} b^s c$.
4. MM publishes the new public membership information $\tilde{m} = \tilde{m} + 2^{i-1}$.

On the other hand, the membership revocation is simple as follows: When the i-th user is removed from the group, MM publishes the new public membership information $\tilde{m} = \tilde{m} - 2^{i-1}$.

Sign and verify: As mentioned in Section 4.1, the group signature proves the knowledge of the membership certificate for the membership information m, and the knowledge $\tilde{m}_U$ and $\tilde{m}_L$ satisfying $\tilde{m} = \tilde{m}_U(2m) + m + \tilde{m}_L$ and $0 \le \tilde{m}_L \le m - 1$, which imply $\tilde{m} = \tilde{m}_U(2(\dot{m} - 2^{\ell_m - 1})) + (\dot{m} - 2^{\ell_m - 1}) + \tilde{m}_L$ and $0 \le \tilde{m}_L \le (\dot{m} - 2^{\ell_m - 1}) - 1$, for $\dot{m} = m + 2^{\ell_m - 1}$. The SPK needs squared bases, since verifiers except MM do not know the factorization of n, as discussed in Section 3.4. This is why the following SPK proves the knowledge of the membership certificate, by the knowledge $(x, \dot{m}, s, e, A)$ satisfying the quadratic equation $A^{2e} = a_1^{2x} a_2^{2\dot{m}} b^{2s} c^2$. Additionally, the SPK has to prove $x \in \mathcal{X}$, $\dot{m} \in \mathcal{M}$ and $e \in \mathcal{E}$. Furthermore, for the traceability, the group signature contains an

ElGamal ciphertext on a_1^{2x} and the SPK proves the correctness. The detail protocol is as follows:

1. Member U signing message M computes $C_A = g^w A, C_w = g^w h^{\tilde{w}}, C_{\dot{m}} = g^{\dot{m}} h^{w_{\dot{m}}}, C_{\tilde{m}_U} = g^{\tilde{m}_U} h^{w_{\tilde{m}_U}}, C_{\tilde{m}_L} = g^{\tilde{m}_L} h^{w_{\tilde{m}_L}}, T_1 = g^{w_e}$ and $T_2 = y^{w_e} a_1^x$, where $w, \tilde{w}, w_{\dot{m}}, w_{\tilde{m}_U}, w_{\tilde{m}_L}, w_e \in_R \mathcal{Z}_n$.
2. U computes the following SPK:

$$V = SPK\{(\alpha, \beta, \gamma, \delta, \epsilon, \zeta, \eta, \theta, \iota, \kappa, \lambda, \mu, \nu, \xi, o, \pi, \rho):$$
$$c^2 = (C_A{}^2)^\alpha (1/a_1^2)^\beta (1/a_2^2)^\gamma (1/b^2)^\delta (1/g^2)^\epsilon \wedge C_w^2 = (g^2)^\zeta (h^2)^\eta$$
$$\wedge 1 = (C_w^2)^\alpha (1/g^2)^\epsilon (1/h^2)^\theta$$
$$\wedge C_{\dot{m}}^2 = (g^2)^\gamma (h^2)^\iota \wedge C_{\tilde{m}_U}^2 = (g^2)^\kappa (h^2)^\lambda \wedge C_{\tilde{m}_L}^2 = (g^2)^\mu (h^2)^\nu$$
$$\wedge T_1^2 = (g^2)^\xi \wedge T_2^2 = (y^2)^\xi (a_1^2)^\beta$$
$$\wedge (C_{\tilde{m}_U}^4)^{2^{\ell_m-1}} (g^2)^{\tilde{m}+2^{\ell_m-1}} (1/C_{\dot{m}}^2)(1/C_{\tilde{m}_L}^2) = (C_{\tilde{m}_U}^4)^\gamma (h^2)^o$$
$$\wedge C_{\dot{m}}^2 (1/g^2)^{1+2^{\ell_m-1}} (1/C_{\tilde{m}_L}^2) = (g^2)^\pi (h^2)^\rho$$
$$\wedge \mu \geq 0 \wedge \pi \geq 0 \wedge \alpha \in \mathcal{E} \wedge \beta \in \mathcal{X} \wedge \gamma \in \mathcal{M}\}(M).$$

Then, the group signature is $(C_A, C_w, C_{\dot{m}}, C_{\tilde{m}_U}, C_{\tilde{m}_L}, T_1, T_2, V)$. The verification of the signature is the verification of V. Note that U is allowed to send a negative value such as $T_1 = -g^{w_e}$ or $T_2 = -y^{w_e} a_1^x$, since verifiers except MM cannot check the membership in $QR(n)$. Thus, squared ElGamal encryption (T_1^2, T_2^2) is used.

Open: OM computes $T_2^2/(T_1^2)^{x_{OM}} = (a_1^x)^2$ to decrypt the ElGamal ciphertext (T_1^2, T_2^2). The obtained $(a_1^x)^2$ is linkable to the member's identity. The correctness is proved by $PK\{\alpha : T_2^2/(a_1^x)^2 = (T_1^2)^\alpha \wedge y^2 = (g^2)^\alpha\}$.

5 Security

Our membership certificate is a Camenisch-Lysyanskaya signature, but is slightly modified. Though the original chooses a random prime e from $\mathcal{E} = (2^{\ell_e-1}, 2^{\ell_e})$, our scheme chooses it from the narrower $\tilde{\mathcal{E}} = [2^{\ell_e-1} + 2^{\ell_e-2}, 2^{\ell_e-1} + 2^{\ell_e-2} + 2^{\ell_e-3-\tilde{\ell}}]$. Furthermore, in the security proof, our scheme requires that a forger $\mathcal{F}$, who adaptively obtains regular signature $(s_i, e_i, A_i = (a_1^{x_i} a_2^{\dot{m}_i} b^{s_i} c)^{1/e_i})$ on chosen messages $x_i, \dot{m}$ from the signing oracle, tries to output a new tuple $(x, \dot{m}, s, e, A)$ satisfying the quadratic equation $A^{2e} = a_1^{2x} a_2^{2\dot{m}} b^{2s} c^2$, due to the squared predicates in SPK V. In the original, $\mathcal{F}$'s output $(x, \dot{m}, s, e, A)$ simply satisfies the regular equation $A^e = a_1^x a_2^{\dot{m}} b^s c$. However, these modifications do not affect the security proof in [8]. Thus, the following lemma holds:

Lemma 1. *Assume the strong RSA assumption. Consider an adversary allowed to adaptively query the signing oracle about a signature (s_i, e_i, A_i) on messages $x_i \in \mathcal{X}, \dot{m}_i \in \mathcal{M}$ such that $A_i^{e_i} = a_1^{x_i} a_2^{\dot{m}_i} b^{s_i} c$, $s_i \in_R \mathcal{S}$, and e_i is a random prime from $\tilde{\mathcal{E}}$. Then, it is infeasible that any adversary computes a signature (s, e, A) on new messages $x \in \mathcal{X}, \dot{m} \in \mathcal{M}$ such that $A^{2e} = a_1^{2x} a_2^{2\dot{m}} b^{2s} c^2$ and $e \in \mathcal{E}$.*

From this lemma, we can obtain the coalition-resistance by the similar proof as [8].

Theorem 1. *Under the strong RSA assumption, the proposed scheme is coalition-resistant for the adversary who adaptively obtains valid membership certificates from MM.*

Next, we prove the unforgeability, using the following two lemmas.

Lemma 2. *Assume the strong RSA assumption. Then, V is an SPK of knowledge $(x, \dot{m}, s, e, A, \tilde{m}_U, \tilde{m}_L, w_e)$ s.t. $A^{2e} = a_1^{2x} a_2^{2\dot{m}} b^{2s} c^2$, $e \in \mathcal{E}$, $x \in \mathcal{X}$, $\dot{m} \in \mathcal{M}$, $T_1^2 = (g^2)^{w_e}$, $T_2^2 = (y^2)^{w_e}(a_1^x)^2$, $\dot{m} = \tilde{m}_U(2(\dot{m} - 2^{\ell_m-1})) + (\dot{m} - 2^{\ell_m-1}) + \tilde{m}_L$ and $0 \le \tilde{m}_L \le (\dot{m} - 2^{\ell_m-1}) - 1$.*

Proof sketch. Only the soundness is discussed. By the similar way to [8], from the SPK V, we can extract the knowledge of $(x = \beta, \dot{m} = \gamma, s = \delta, e = \alpha, A = C_A/g^\varsigma, w_e = \xi)$ such that $A^{2e} = a_1^{2x} a_2^{2\dot{m}} b^{2s} c^2$, $e \in \mathcal{E}$, $x \in \mathcal{X}$, $\dot{m} \in \mathcal{M}$, $T_1^2 = (g^2)^{w_e}$ and $T_2^2 = (y^2)^{w_e}(a_1^2)^x$.

From the SPK for the predicates

$$C_{\dot{m}}^2 = (g^2)^\gamma (h^2)^\iota, C_{\tilde{m}_U}^2 = (g^2)^\kappa (h^2)^\lambda, C_{\tilde{m}_L}^2 = (g^2)^\mu (h^2)^\nu, \text{and}$$

$$(C_{\tilde{m}_U}^4)^{2^{\ell_m-1}}(g^2)^{\tilde{m}+2^{\ell_m-1}}(1/C_{\dot{m}}^2)(1/C_{\tilde{m}_L}^2) = (C_{\tilde{m}_U}^4)^\gamma (h^2)^o,$$

by substituting the first three equations for the left hand in the last equation, the left hand is equal to $(g^2)^{2\kappa 2^{\ell_m-1}+\tilde{m}+2^{\ell_m-1}-\gamma-\mu}(h^2)^{2\lambda 2^{\ell_m-1}-\iota-\nu}$. On the other hand, the right hand is equal to $(g^2)^{2\kappa\gamma}(h^2)^{2\lambda\gamma+o}$. Thus, we can obtain the equation $2\kappa 2^{\ell_m-1} + \tilde{m} + 2^{\ell_m-1} - \gamma - \mu = 2\kappa\gamma \pmod{p'q'}$. Then, from the RSA assumption, the equation holds as integer equation. Thus, $\tilde{m} = \kappa \cdot 2(\gamma - 2^{\ell_m-1}) + \gamma - 2^{\ell_m-1} + \mu$ holds, where $\gamma = \dot{m}$ and κ, μ corresponds to $\tilde{m}_U, \tilde{m}_L$, respectively.

Similarly, from the SPK for $C_{\dot{m}}^2(1/g^2)^{1+2^{\ell_m-1}}(1/C_{\tilde{m}_L}^2) = (g^2)^\pi (h^2)^\rho$, we can obtain $(g^2)^\gamma (h^2)^\iota (1/g^2)^{1+2^{\ell_m-1}}(1/((g^2)^\mu (h^2)^\nu)) = (g^2)^\pi (h^2)^\rho$. Then, from $(g^2)^{\gamma-1-2^{\ell_m-1}-\mu}(h^2)^{\iota-\nu} = (g^2)^\pi (h^2)^\rho$, $\gamma - 1 - 2^{\ell_m-1} - \mu = \pi$ holds as integer equation. Since the SPK V proves $\pi \ge 0$, the inequation $\gamma - 1 - 2^{\ell_m-1} - \mu \ge 0$ holds and thus $\mu \le \gamma - 2^{\ell_m-1} - 1$. Furthermore, the SPK proves $\mu \ge 0$, and finally we obtain $0 \le \mu \le \gamma - 2^{\ell_m-1} - 1$, that is, $0 \le \tilde{m}_L \le \dot{m} - 2^{\ell_m-1} - 1$. $\square$

Lemma 3. *Let $\tilde{m} = \sum_{j=0}^{K-1} 2^j \bar{m}_j$ for K, where $\bar{m}_j \in \{0,1\}$. Then, $\tilde{m}_U$ and $\tilde{m}_L$ exist s.t. $\tilde{m} = \tilde{m}_U 2^i + 2^{i-1} + \tilde{m}_L$ and $0 \le \tilde{m}_L \le 2^{i-1} - 1$ if and only if $\bar{m}_{i-1} = 1$.*

Proof. Since the if part is straightforward, we prove the only if part. Then, $\tilde{m}_U$ and $\tilde{m}_L$ exist s.t. $\tilde{m} = \tilde{m}_U 2^i + 2^{i-1} + \tilde{m}_L$ and $0 \le \tilde{m}_L \le 2^{i-1} - 1$. For the contradiction, assume $\bar{m}_{i-1} = 0$. Then, $\tilde{m} = \sum_{j=0}^{i-2} 2^j \bar{m}_j + \sum_{j=i}^{K-1} 2^j \bar{m}_j$, and thus $\tilde{m} = \sum_{j=0}^{i-2} 2^j \bar{m}_j + 2^i \sum_{j=0}^{K-i-1} 2^j \bar{m}_{j+i}$. Let $\hat{m}_U = \sum_{j=0}^{K-i-1} 2^j \bar{m}_{j+i}$, and $\hat{m}_L = \sum_{j=0}^{i-2} 2^j \bar{m}_j$. Then, $\tilde{m} = \hat{m}_U 2^i + \hat{m}_L$, and $0 \le \hat{m}_L \le 2^{i-1} - 1$. Set $D := \tilde{m}_U 2^i + 2^{i-1} + \tilde{m}_L - \tilde{m}$. Then, $D = (\tilde{m}_U - \hat{m}_U) 2^i + 2^{i-1} + \tilde{m}_L - \hat{m}_L$.

Consider the case of $\tilde{m}_U \geq \hat{m}_U$. Because of $\tilde{m}_U - \hat{m}_U \geq 0$ and $\tilde{m}_L \geq 0$, $(\tilde{m}_U - \hat{m}_U)2^i + 2^{i-1} + \tilde{m}_L \geq 2^{i-1}$ holds. Thus, because of $\hat{m}_L \leq 2^{i-1} - 1$, we can obtain $D > 0$, which contradicts $D = 0$, i.e., $\hat{m} = \hat{m}_U 2^i + 2^{i-1} + \hat{m}_L$.

Consider the case of $\tilde{m}_U < \hat{m}_U$. This implies $(\tilde{m}_U - \hat{m}_U)2^i - \hat{m}_L \leq -2^i$, because of $\hat{m}_L \geq 0$. Thus, $(\tilde{m}_U - \hat{m}_U)2^i + 2^{i-1} - \hat{m}_L \leq -2^{i-1}$ holds. Therefore, because of $\tilde{m}_L \leq 2^{i-1} - 1$, we can obtain $D < 0$, which also contradicts $D = 0$. Therefore, $\bar{m}_{i-1} = 1$ must hold.   □

Theorem 2. *Under the strong RSA assumption, the proposed scheme satisfies the unforgeability.*

Proof. For signing, the signer must know the certificate $(s, e \in \mathcal{E}, A)$ on $x \in \mathcal{X}, \dot{m} \in \mathcal{M}$ s.t. $A^{2e} = a_1^{2x} a_2^{2\dot{m}} b^{2s} c^2$, owing to $SPK\ V$, as stated by Lemma 2. On the other hand, from Theorem 1, such a certificate is unforgeable even if valid members collude. Therefore, before signing, the signer must have conducted the join protocol with MM, which implies that the signer is a member.

In the rest, we show that a removed member with the certificate w.r.t. $\dot{m} = 2^{i-1} + 2^{\ell_m - 1}$ cannot compute a valid $SPK\ V$. In the certificate generated by MM, $\dot{m} = 2^{i-1} + 2^{\ell_m - 1}$ is assured. On the other hand, $SPK\ V$ proves the knowledge of $(\tilde{m}_U, \tilde{m}_L)$ such that $\tilde{m} = \tilde{m}_U(2(\dot{m} - 2^{\ell_m - 1})) + (\dot{m} - 2^{\ell_m - 1}) + \tilde{m}_L$ and $0 \leq \tilde{m}_L \leq (\dot{m} - 2^{\ell_m - 1}) - 1$. By substituting $\dot{m}$, this implies the knowledge of $(\tilde{m}_U, \tilde{m}_L)$ such that $\tilde{m} = \tilde{m}_U(2 \cdot 2^{i-1}) + 2^{i-1} + \tilde{m}_L$ and $0 \leq \tilde{m}_L \leq 2^{i-1} - 1$. However, Lemma 3 claims that such a knowledge does not exist, if the i-th bit in $\dot{m}$ (i.e., $\bar{m}_{i-1}$) is 0, which implies that the member is removed. Therefore, the removed member cannot compute a valid $SPK\ V$.   □

Finally, we simply discuss the other requirements. Anonymity and unlinkability hold, because of the the zero-knowledge-ness of $SPK\ V$ and the secrecy of the ElGamal encryption and the commitment scheme, as well as the original group signature [1]. No framing is also satisfied, since the $SPK\ V$ proves the knowledge of x, which is kept secret for others (even MM), owing to the PK in the join protocol and the $SPK\ V$. Traceability is satisfied as follows: Since V proves that (T_1^2, T_2^2) is an ElGamal ciphertext of $(a_1^x)^2$, which is shown in Lemma 2, openning the group signature produces $(a_1^x)^2$. On the other hand, V proves the knowledge of the certificate A of the x, and the unforgeability of the A implies that the owner registered the a_1^x. Therefore, the $(a_1^x)^2$ is linkable to the owner.

6   Efficiency

The signing/verification cost of our scheme depends on ℓ_m, i.e., K that is the maximum number of members' joining. At first, consider the case of $\ell_m \approx \ell_n$. In this case, our scheme allows about 1000 members, if ℓ_n is standard 1024. Then, the exponent length is all comparable to ℓ_n, and signing and verification require 31 and 18 multi-exponentiations respectively, on such an exponent length. Note that, in the state-of-the-art scheme [1] with no revocation, signing and verification require 5 and 3 multi-exponentiations, respectively. In the accumulator-based scheme [7] with revocation, signing and verification require 14 and 8 multi-exponentiations, respectively. The accumulator-based scheme [12] is slightly better. However, the schemes based on the accumulator require the modification of signer's secret key whenever signing, and the size of public membership information is $O(\ell_n N)$, where N is the number of joining and removed members. On the other hand, our scheme needs no modification of signer's secret key, and the public membership information is only $\tilde{m}$ with the length $O(\ell_n)$. For example, consider the case of $N, K = 1000$ and $\ell_n = 1024$. Though the size of the public membership information in the accumulator-based schemes is about 100 KBytes, the size in our scheme is about 100 Bytes only.

Next, consider the case of $\ell_m \gg \ell_n$, namely much more members joining than ℓ_n. Then, the computation and communication costs of signing/verification in our scheme are $O(K/\ell_n)$. If $\ell_n = 1024$, the feasible number of members' joining is the order of 1000. For such larger groups, note that the accumulator-based schemes also have a serious problem: It suffers from the long public information. In case of $N = 10000$ and $\ell_n = 1024$, the size of the information amounts to more than 1 MBytes.

References

1. G. Ateniese, J. Camenisch, M. Joye, and G. Tsudik, "A practical and provably secure coalition-resistant group signature scheme," Proc. CRYPTO 2000, LNCS 1880, pp.255–270, Springer, 2000.
2. G. Ateniese, D. Song, and G. Tsudik, "Quasi-efficient revocation of group signatures," Proc. FC 2002, LNCS 2357, pp.183–197, Springer, 2003.
3. F. Boudot, "Efficient proofs that a committed number lies in an interval," Proc. EUROCRYPT 2000, LNCS 1807, pp.431–444, Springer, 2000.
4. E. Bresson and J. Stern, "Group signature scheme with efficient revocation," Proc. PKC 2001, LNCS 1992, pp.190–206, Springer, 2001.
5. J. Camenisch and M. Stadler, "Efficient group signature schemes for large groups," Proc. CRYPTO '97, LNCS 1294, pp.410–424, Springer, 1997.
6. J. Camenisch and A. Lysyanskaya, "An efficient system for non-transferable anonymous credentials with optional anonymity revocation," Proc. EUROCRYPT 2001, LNCS 2045, pp.93–118, Springer, 2001.
7. J. Camenisch and A. Lysyanskaya, "Dynamic accumulators and application to efficient revocation of anonymous credentials," Proc. CRYPTO 2002, LNCS 2442, pp.61–76, Springer, 2002.
8. J. Camenisch and A. Lysyanskaya, "A signature scheme with efficient protocols," Proc. SCN '02, LNCS 2576, Springer, 2002.
9. J. Camenisch and M. Michels, "Separability and efficiency for generic group signature schemes," Proc. CRYPTO '99, LNCS 1666, pp.413–430, Springer, 1999.
10. D. Chaum and E. van Heijst, "Group signatures," Proc. EUROCRYPT '91, LNCS 547, pp.241–246, Springer, 1991.
11. I. Damgård and E. Fujisaki, "A statistically-hiding integer commitment scheme based on groups with hidden order," Proc. ASIACRYPT 2002, LNCS 2501, pp.125–142, Springer, 2002.
12. G. Tsudik and S. Xu, "Accumulating composites and improved group signing," Proc. ASIACRYPT 2003, LNCS 2894, pp.269–286, Springer, 2003.

Convertible Nominative Signatures[*]

Zhenjie Huang[1,2] and Yumin Wang[1]

[1] State Key Laboratory of Integrated Service Networks,
Xidian University, Xi'an, Shaanxi, 710071, P. R. China,
zhj_huang@hotmail.com,
[2] Department of Computer Science, Zhangzhou Teachers College,
Zhangzhou, Fujian, 363000, P. R. China

Abstract. A feasible solution to prevent potential misuse of signatures is to put some restrictions on their verification. Therefore S.J.Kim, S.J.Park and D.H.Won introduced the nominative signature, in which only the nominee can verify and prove the validity of given signatures, and proposed a nominative signature scheme (called KPW scheme). In this paper, we first show that KPW scheme is not nominative because the nominator can also verify and prove the validity of given signatures. Then we extend the concept of nominative signature to the convertible nominative signature which has an additional property that the nominee can convert given nominative signatures into universally verifiable signatures. We give a formal definition for it and propose a practical scheme that implements it. The proposed scheme is secure, in which its unforgeability is the same as that of the Schnorr's signature scheme and its untransferability relies on the hardness of the Decision-Diffie-Hellman Problem.

Keywords: Digital signature, nominative signature, convertible, untransferable

1 Introduction

Digital signature is one of the most important techniques of modern cryptography, and has many applications in information security systems. Normal digital signatures have the property that anyone having a copy of the signature can check its validity using the corresponding public information. This "self-authenticating" property is necessarily required for some applications of digital signature such as official announcements and public-key certificates issued by some authorities. However, such signatures seem to provide too much authentication than necessary in many other applications, where a signed message is personally or commercially sensitive, for example as in a bill of tax, a bill of health, a writ of summons, etc. Thus it may be preferable to put some restrictions on this property to prevent potential misuse of signatures.

---

[*] This work is supported by the National Natural Science Foundation of China under Grant No.19931010 and the National Grand Fundamental Research 973 Program of China under Grant No. G1999035803.

H. Wang et al. (Eds.): ACISP 2004, LNCS 3108, pp. 348–357, 2004.
© Springer-Verlag Berlin Heidelberg 2004

To achieve this purpose, up to now, there are four kinds of signatures with different restrictions on authentication having been proposed: the undeniable signature, the directed signature, the designated confirmer signature and the nominative signature. The *undeniable signature* was introduced by D.Chaum and H.van Antwerpen [1] at Crypto'89, in which the signature cannot be verified without the help of the signer. In [2] J.Boyar et al. extended the concept of undeniable signature to the *convertible undeniable signature*. The *directed signature*, first proposed by C.H.Lim and P.J.Lee [3] at Auscrypto'92, and the *designated confirmer signature*, introduced by D.Chaum [4] at Eurocrypt'94, have a common property that the use of the signatures is controlled by two people: the signer and the designated people (the recipient in directed signature, the confirmer in designated confirmer signature). The *nominative signature*, first proposed by S.J.Kim, S.J.Park and D.H.Won [5], is the dual signature scheme of the undeniable signature, in which not the signer but only the recipient can control the use of signatures. H.U.Park and I.Y.Lee proposed a nominative proxy signature scheme in [6].

In [5], S.J.Kim et al. also proposed a nominative signature scheme, called KPW scheme. Unfortunately, we find that KPW scheme is not nominative. In this paper, we first show that in KPW scheme the nominator (the signer) can also verify and prove the validity of given signatures. Then we extend the concept of nominative signature to the *convertible nominative signature* which has an additional property that the nominee (the designated verifier) can convert given nominative signatures into universally verifiable signatures. We give a formal definition for it and propose a practical scheme that implements it. The proposed scheme is secure, in which its unforgeability is the same as that of the Schnorr's signature scheme and its untransferability relies on the hardness of the Decision-Diffie-Hellman Problem. The convertible nominative signature is fit for signing personally or commercially sensitive message and may be useful to the Internet community and Web-based systems community.

The paper is structured as follows. The preliminaries are given in next section, and in Section 3 we give a description and an analysis of KPW scheme. In Section 4, we extend the concept of nominative signature to the convertible nominative signature and give a formal definition for it. We propose a practical convertible nominative signature scheme in Section 5 with analyses of its security. The conclusions are given in Section 6.

2   Preliminaries

2.1   Cryptographic Setting

Let p, q be large primes that satisfy $q|p-1$, and g be an element in $\mathbf{Z}_p^*$ with order q. We assume that there exists no algorithm running in expected polynomial time which decides with non-negligible probability better than guessing whether two discrete logarithms are equal. Let $H : \{0,1\}^* \to \mathbf{Z}_q$ be a public secure hash function.

Hereafter, we will use the notation $a \in_R A$ to mean that a is randomly chose from A and use the symbol $||$ to mean concatenation.

2.2 Zero-Knowledge Proof Protocol

Here we give a description of a zero-knowledge proof protocol, which was proposed in [7] and will be used as a building block in our convertible nominative signature scheme.

Assume the prover knows the discrete logarithm x of $y = g^x$ and wants to allow the verifier to decide whether $\log_g y = \log_h z$ for given group elements h and z. The prover and the verifier execute the following protocol.

ZKP: **Proving the equality or inequality of two discrete logarithms**

1. The verifier chooses random numbers $u, v \in_R \mathbf{Z}_q^*$, computes

$$\alpha = g^u y^v \pmod{p},$$

and sends α to the prover.

2. The prover chooses random numbers $k, k', w \in_R \mathbf{Z}_q^*$, computes

$$r_g = g^k \pmod{p},$$
$$r_g' = g^{k'} \pmod{p},$$
$$r_h = h^k \pmod{p},$$
$$r_h' = h^{k'} \pmod{p},$$

and sends $(r_g, r_g', r_h, r_h', w)$ to the verifier.

3. The verifier sends (u, v) to the prover.
4. If $\alpha \neq g^u y^v \pmod{p}$ the prover halts, otherwise he computes

$$s = k - (v + w)x \pmod{q},$$
$$s' = k' - (v + w)k \pmod{q},$$

and sends (s, s') to the verifier.

5. The verifier first checks whether

$$r_g = g^s y^{v+w} \pmod{p},$$
$$r_g' = g^{s'} r_g^{v+w} \pmod{p},$$
$$r_h' = h^{s'} r_h^{v+w} \pmod{p},$$

and then concludes:

if $r_h = h^s r_h^{v+w} \pmod{p}$, then $\log_g y = \log_h z$,

if $r_h \neq h^s r_h^{v+w} \pmod{p}$, then $\log_g y \neq \log_h z$.

The following theorem was proved in [7].

Theorem 1. *The above protocol is zero-knowledge under the assumption that there exists no algorithm running in expected polynomial time which decides with non-negligible probability better than guessing whether two discrete logarithms are equal.*

2.3   Signature of Equality

Following signature of equality [8] will be used in our convertible nominative signature scheme to convert given nominative signatures into universally verifiable signatures.

A pair (c, s) satisfying $c = H(g||h||y||z||g^s y^c||h^s z^c||m)$ is *signature of equality* of the discrete logarithm of y with respect to the base g and the discrete logarithm of z with respect to the base h for the message m and is denoted by $SEQDL(g, h, y, z, m)$.

A $SEQDL(g, h, y, z, m)$ can only be computed if the secret key $x = \log_g y = \log_h z$ is known, by choosing $k \in_R \mathbf{Z}_q^*$, and computing c and s according to

$$c = H(g||h||y||z||g^k||h^k||m),$$

$$s = r - cx \pmod{q}.$$

This signature of equality can also prove the logarithms of two group elements with respect to two different bases are the same [8]. Signature of equality is non-interactive and transferable while the zero-knowledge proof protocol above is interactive and untransferable.

3   Analysis of KPW Nominative Signature Scheme

In this section, we give a description and an analysis of KPW scheme. One can easily obtain the definition of nominative signature by removing the **Conv** and the **UVer** from the definition of convertible nominative signature in Section 4.

3.1   KPW Scheme

The cryptographic setting is the same as above. The nominator and the nominee's public and secret key pairs are (y_s, x_s) and (y_v, x_v), where $y_* = g^{x_*} \pmod{p}$. The following description is taken from [5].
- **Signing**
1. The nominator (the signer) S chooses random numbers $r, R \in_R \mathbf{Z}_q^*$, computes

$$c = g^{R-r} \pmod{p},$$

$$C = y_v^R \pmod{p}.$$

2. Computes

$$e = H(y_v||c||C||m),$$

$$s = r - x_s e \pmod{q}.$$

then publishes the signature $\sigma_m = (y_v, c, C, s)$ on message m.

- **Verification**

The nominee (the designated verifier) V checks that signature (y_v, c, C, s) is a valid signature on m by verifying

$$e = H(y_v||c||C||m) \text{ and } (g^s y_s^e c)^{x_v} = C \pmod{p}.$$

- **Confirmation**

The nominee V proves to the third party that $(g^s y_s^e c)^{x_v} = C \pmod{p}$ and $g^{x_v} = y_v \pmod{p}$ via the zero-knowledge proof protocol in [1].

3.2   Analysis

In [5] the authors claim that their scheme satisfies:

1. Only the nominee can verify the nominator's signature, even the nominator can not verify the signature.

2. If necessary, only the nominee can prove to the third party that the signature was issued to him by the nominator and is valid, even the nominator can not prove that the signature is valid.

Unfortunately, we find that, in their scheme, the nominator (the signer) not only can verify but also can prove the validity of the given signatures to the third party.

1. Verification

Note that the verification equation of KPW scheme $(g^s y_s^e c)^{x_v} = C \pmod{p}$ is derived from the equation $g^s y_s^e c = g^R \pmod{p}$ and the nominator (the signer) knows the number R, so he can verify a signature via checking

$$e = H(y_v||c||y_v^R||m) \text{ and } g^s y_s^e c = g^R \pmod{p}.$$

2. Proving

The same as the analysis above, the nominator (signer) can confirm the third party via proving

$$e = H(y_v||c||C||m) \text{ and } \log_g(s^s y_s^e c) = \log_{y_v} C,$$

where $C = y_v^R \pmod{p}$.

In a word, the KPW scheme is not a nominative signature scheme but a directed signature scheme or a designated confirmer signature scheme.

4   Definition of Convertible Nominative Signature

Here, we extend the concept of nominative signature above to the convertible nominative signature with an additional property that the nominee can convert given nominative signatures into universally verifiable signatures.

Definition 1. A secure convertible nominative signature scheme, which involves two parties: the nominator (the signer) S and the nominee (the designated verifier) V, is a six-tuple ($\boldsymbol{KG}, \boldsymbol{Sig}, \boldsymbol{Ver}, \boldsymbol{Conf}, \boldsymbol{Conv}, \boldsymbol{UVer}$) such that the following hold.

• **KG** is a probabilistic polynomial-time key generation algorithm that takes security parameter 1^n, outputs a public and secret key pair (pk, sk).

• **Sig** is an (interactive) probabilistic polynomial-time signature generation algorithm, which takes input security parameter 1^n, message m, the nominee's public key pk_v and the nominator's public and secret key pair (pk_s, sk_s), outputs either "*False*" or a signature σ_m on message m. Let Σ_{σ_m} be the set of signatures σ_m on message m.

• **Ver** is a polynomial-time verification algorithm for the nominee, in which the nominee inputs security parameter 1^n, the nominator S's public key pk_s, his public and secret key pair (pk_v, sk_v), message m, and the presumed signature σ, outputs either 0 or 1. For all m, if $\sigma \in \Sigma_{\sigma_m}$,

$$Ver(1^n, m, \sigma, pk_s, pk_v, sk_v) = 1,$$

otherwise,

$$Ver(1^n, m, \sigma, pk_s, pk_v, sk_v) = 0.$$

• **Conf** is an interactive confirmation and disavowal proof protocol between the nominee V and the third party T, in which they jointly input security parameter 1^n, message m, the presumed signature σ of m, the nominator S's public key pk_s, and the nominee V's public key pk_v, the nominee V also inputs his secret key sk_v privately. They engage in the proof protocol and stop in polynomial-time. When they stop, the third party T outputs either 0 or 1. For all m, for any constant c, and for sufficiently large n, if $\sigma \in \Sigma_{\sigma_m}$,

$$\Pr[Conf(1^n, m, \sigma, pk_s, pk_v, sk_v) = 1] > 1 - n^{-c},$$

otherwise,

$$\Pr[Conf(1^n, m, \sigma, pk_s, pk_v, sk_v) = 0] > 1 - n^{-c}.$$

The probability is taken over the coin tosses of S, V, T, m and σ.

• **Conv** is a polynomial-time conversion algorithm for the nominee, which takes input security parameter 1^n, message m and a valid signature σ_m of m, the nominator S's public key pk_s, and the nominee V's public and secret key pair (pk_v, sk_v), outputs a receipt r_m which makes σ_m can be universally verified.

• **UVer** is a polynomial-time universally verification algorithm which takes input security parameter 1^n, the receipt r_m, message m and a signature σ, the nominator S's public key pk_s, and the nominee V's public key pk_v, outputs either 0 or 1. For all m and r_m, if $\sigma \in \Sigma_{\sigma_m}$,

$$UVer(1^n, m, \sigma, pk_s, pk_v, r_m) = 1,$$

otherwise,

$$UVer(1^n, m, \sigma, pk_s, pk_v, r_m) = 0.$$

• **Unforgeability**

Let F be a probabilistic polynomial-time forging algorithm which takes input security parameter 1^n, the nominator S's public key pk_s, the nominee V's public and secret key pair (pk_v, sk_v), can request and receive signatures of polynomial-many adaptively chosen messages m_i, can request the execution of **Conf** and **Conv** for polynomial-many adaptively chosen strings, and finally outputs a pair of string (m, σ) with $m \notin \{m_i\}$. For all such F, for any constant c, and for sufficiently large n, the probability that F outputs (m, σ) for which at least one of **Ver** or **Conf** outputs 1 is less than n^{-c}. That is

$$\mathbf{Pr}[(m, \sigma) \leftarrow F^{\textbf{Sig}, \textbf{Conf}, \textbf{Conv}}(1^n, pk_s, pk_v, sk_v) :$$
$$(\textbf{Ver}(1^n, m, \sigma, pk_s, pk_v, sk_v) = 1 \vee \textbf{Conf}(1^n, m, \sigma, pk_s, pk_v, sk_v) = 1)$$
$$\wedge \, m \notin \{m_i\}] < n^{-c}.$$

The probability is taken over the coin tosses of F, S, V, m and σ.

- **Verification Untransferability**

   Let A be a probabilistic polynomial-time attacking algorithm which takes input security parameter 1^n, the nominator S's public and secret key pair (pk_s, sk_s), the nominee V's public key pk_v, message m and the presumed signature σ of m, can request the execution of **Conf** and **Conv** for polynomial-many adaptively chosen strings, and finally outputs either 0 or 1. For all such A, for any constant c, and for sufficiently large n,

$$|\mathbf{Pr}[A^{\textbf{Conf}, \textbf{Conv}}(1^n, m, \sigma, pk_s, sk_s, pk_v) =$$
$$\textbf{Ver}(1^n, m, \sigma, pk_s, pk_v, sk_v)] - 1/2| < n^{-c}.$$

The probability is taken over the coin tosses of A, S, V, m and σ.

- **Confirmation and Disavowal Untransferability**

   Let $\textbf{Conf}_A$ be a probabilistic polynomial-time (interactive) proof protocol which takes input security parameter 1^n, the nominator S's public and secret key pair (pk_s, sk_s), the nominee V's public key pk_v, message m and the presumed signature σ of m and can request the execution of **Conf** and **Conv** for polynomial-many adaptively chosen strings, where $\textbf{Conf}_A$ can request execution of **Conf** on the given (m, σ) but cannot request execution of **Conv** on (m, σ). The attacker and the third party engage in the signature issuing protocol and stop in polynomial-time. When they stop, the third party T outputs either 0 or 1. For all such $\textbf{Conf}_A$, for any constant c, and for sufficiently large n,

$$|\mathbf{Pr}[\textbf{Conf}_A^{\textbf{Conf}, \textbf{Conv}}(1^n, m, \sigma, pk_s, sk_s, pk_v) =$$
$$\textbf{Ver}(1^n, m, \sigma, pk_s, pk_v, sk_v)] - 1/2| < n^{-c}.$$

The probability is taken over the coin tosses of $\textbf{Conf}_A, T, S, V, m$ and σ.

5   A Convertible Nominative Signature Scheme

5.1   The Proposed Scheme

The cryptographic setting is as above. Assume the nominator (the signer) S's secret key is x_s, the corresponding public key is $y_s = g^{x_s} \pmod{p}$, and the nominee (the designated verifier) V's secret key is x_v, where x_v is odd, and the corresponding public key is $y_v = g^{x_v} \pmod p$.

- **Signing**

1. The nominee chooses random numbers $R_1, R_2 \in_R \mathbf{Z}_q^*$, and computes

$$a = g^{R_1} \pmod p,$$

$$c = y_v^{R_2} \pmod p,$$

then sends (a, c) to the nominator.

2. The nominator chooses a random number $r \in_R \mathbf{Z}_q^*$, and computes

$$b = ag^{-r} \pmod p,$$

$$e = H(y_v||b||c||m),$$

$$s' = r - x_s e \pmod q,$$

then sends (e, b, s') to the nominee.

3. The nominee accepts if and only if

$$e = H(y_v||b||c||m) \text{ and } g^{s'} y_s^e \, b = a \pmod p.$$

If the nominee accepts, she computes

$$s = s' + R_2 - R_1 \pmod q,$$

and publishes the signature $\sigma_m = (b, c, s)$. Otherwise, she outputs *"False"*.

- **Verification**

Given the signature (b, c, s), the nominee computes $e = H(y_v||b||c||m)$, and checks whether

$$(g^s y_s^e \, b)^{x_v} = c \pmod p.$$

- **Confirmation and Disavowal**

The nominee V can confirm or disavow a signature $\sigma_m = (b, c, s)$ via proving $\log_d c = \log_g y_v \pmod p$ or $\log_d c \neq \log_g y_v \pmod p$ using the interactive protocol **ZKP** in Section 2, where $d = g^s y_s^e \, b \pmod p, e = H(y_v||b||c||m)$.

- **Selective Conversion**

When the nominee want to convert the signature $\sigma_m = (b, c, s)$ into a universally verifiable one, he computes

$$e = H(y_v||b||c||m),$$

$$d = g^s y_s^e \, b \pmod p,$$

$$(c', s') = SEQDL(d, g, c, y_v, \sigma_m),$$

and publishes the receipt $r_m = (c', s')$.

- **Universal Verification**

Anyone can verify the signature $\sigma_m = (b, c, s)$ with its receipt r_m by verifying the corresponding signature of equality $SEQDL$.

5.2   The Security

Here we discuss the security of the proposed scheme above.
  • **Completeness**
  The completeness can easily be proved as follows.

$$
\begin{aligned}
(g^s y_s^e \, b)^{x_v} &= (g^{s'+R_2-R_1} y_s^e a g^{-r})^{x_v} \\
&= (g^{r-x_s e + R_2 - R_1} g^{x_s e} g^{R_1} g^{-r})^{x_v} \\
&= (g^{R_2})^{x_v} \\
&= y_v^{R_2} \\
&= c \; (\mathrm{mod} \; p).
\end{aligned}
$$

  • **Unforgeability**
  According to the definition of unforgeability, the adversary knows only security parameter 1^n, the nominator S's public key pk_s, the nominee V's public and secret key pair (pk_v, sk_v). If an adversary can forge a signature (b, c, s) such that $(g^s y_s^e b)^{x_v} = c \; (\mathrm{mod} \; p), e = H(y_v||b||c||m)$, which equivalent to $g^s y_s^e b = g^{R_2} \; (\mathrm{mod} \; p)$, where b and R_2 are chosen by the adversary, then he can find an s satisfying $g^s y_s^e = g^{r'} \; (\mathrm{mod} \; p)$. In other words, he can forge a valid Schnorr's signature [9]. Therefore, the security of our scheme is the same as that of the Schnorr's signature scheme, and it is unforgeable.
  • **Verification Untransferability**
  To verify a signature, one needs to verify $(g^s y_s^e b)^{x_v} = c \; (\mathrm{mod} \; p)$ or $g^s y_s^e b = g^{R_2} \; (\mathrm{mod} \; p)$. To verify the first equation, one must know the nominee V's secret key x_v or can verify $\log_d c = \log_g y_v \; (\mathrm{mod} \; p)$. For the second equation, the g^{R_2} can not be derived from the nominator's view (a, b, c, r, e, s', s), and all information about g^{R_2} the adversary knew is $(g^{R_2})^{x_v} = c$, so, for the adversary, verifying the second equation is equivalent to verifying the first one. In a word, to verify a signature, the adversary needs to verify $\log_d c = \log_g y_v \; (\mathrm{mod} \; p)$, since he knows neither the nominee V's secret key x_v nor the nominee's view $View_v$. Thus, the adversary needs to solve the DDH problem. On the other hand, the nominee's confirmation and disavowal protocol is zero-knowledge and untransferable (Theorem 1.), therefore our scheme is verification untransferable under the assumption that any polynomial-time algorithm solves the DDH problem only with negligible probability.
  • **Confirmation and Disavowal Untransferability**
  The verification untransferability and the untransferability of zero-knowledge proof protocol **ZKP** guarantee the confirmation and disavowal untransferability.
  • **Zero-Knowledge**
  The properties of **ZKP** (Theorem 1.) guarantee that the confirmation or disavowal of our scheme are zero-knowledge and uncheatable.

6   Conclusion

A feasible solution to prevent potential misuse of signatures is to put some restrictions on their verification. In this paper, we first show that KPW scheme is not nominative because the nominator can also verify and prove the validity of given signatures. Then we extend the concept of nominative signature to the convertible nominative signature which has an additional property that the nominee can convert given nominative signatures into universally verifiable signatures. We give a formal definition for it and propose a practical scheme that implements it. The convertible nominative signature may be useful to the Internet community and Web-based systems community.

References

1. D. Chaum and H. Antwerpen, "Undeniable Signatures", *Advances in Cryptology - CRYPTO'89*, LNCS 435, pp.212-216, Springer-Verlag, 1989.
2. J. Boyar, D. Chaum, I. Damgard, and T. Pedersen, "Convertible Undeniable Signatures", *Advances in Cryptology - CYPTO'90*, LNCS 537, pp.189-205, Springer-Verlag, 1990.
3. C. H. Lim and P. J. Lee, "Modified Maurer-Yacobi's Scheme and its Applications", *Advances in Cryptology - AUSCRYPT'92*, LNCS 718, pp.308-323, Springer-Verlag, 1992.
4. D. Chaum, "Designated Confirmer Signatures", *Advances in Cryptology - EURO-CYPT'94*, LNCS 950, pp.86-91, Springer-Verlag, 1994.
5. S. J. Kim, S. J. Park, and D. H. Won, "Zero-knowledge Nominative Signatures", *Proc. of PragoCrypt'96, International Conference on the Theory and Applications of Cryptology*, pp.380-392.
6. H. U.Park, and I. Y. Lee, "A Digital Nominative Proxy Signature Scheme for Mobile Communication", *Proc. of ICICS'01*, LNCS 2229, pp.451-455, Springer-Verlag, 2001.
7. M. Michels, and M. Stadler, "Efficient Convertible Undeniable Signature Schemes", *Proc. of 4th annual workshop on selected areas in cryptography (SAC'97)*, 1997, pp.231-244.
8. J. Camenisch, "Efficient and Generalized Group Signatures", *Advances in Cryptology - EUROCRYPT'97*, LNCS 1233, pp.465-479, Springer-Verlag, 1997.
9. C. P. Schnorr, "Efficient Signature Generation for Smart Cards", *Journal of Cryptology*, 1991(4), pp.239-252.

Protocols with Security Proofs for Mobile Applications*

Yiu Shing Terry Tin, Harikrishna Vasanta, Colin Boyd**, and
Juan Manuel González Nieto

Information Security Research Centre,
Queensland University of Technology.
PO Box 2434, Brisbane, QLD 4001, Australia.
{t.tin,h.vasanta,c.boyd,j.gonzaleznieto}@qut.edu.au

Abstract. The Canetti-Krawczyk (CK) model is useful for building
reusable components that lead to rapid development of secure protocols,
especially for engineers working outside of the security community.
We work in the CK model and obtain a new secure authenticated key
transport protocol with three parties. This protocol is constructed with
two newly developed components in the CK model, thus extending the
power of the model.

Keywords: Provable security, secure key exchange, authenticator, mobile security.

1 Introduction

A proof of security has become an essential statement for structural correctness of
new key establishment protocols. The first provably secure protocol was proposed
by Bellare and Rogaway [7] in 1993 with a two-party example. In 1995 they
extended their work to a three-party server-based key distribution protocol [8].
A feature of proofs in this model is that they are long and difficult to read for
the non-specialist, making them more error-prone. Another shortcoming is that
a minor change in the protocol requires a complete revision of the proof. There
is no easy way to reuse fragments of security proof.

In 1998, Bellare, Canetti and Krawczyk [4] proposed a new model for provable security. The novelty of their work was its modular approach. This approach
uses layers for separated treatments for key exchange and authentication. In
comparison to the approach used in [8], this approach turns out to be easier
to understand because of its modularity. Moreover, it provides reusable building blocks for construction of new provably secure protocols. More precisely, a
module carrying a security proof can be reused for construction of new secure

---

* Full version of this paper is available at http://sky.fit.qut.edu.au/~boydc/
papers/.
** Supported by ARC Discovery Project DP0345775.

H. Wang et al. (Eds.): ACISP 2004, LNCS 3108, pp. 358–369, 2004.
© Springer-Verlag Berlin Heidelberg 2004

protocols with other modules in the model that have been proven secure independently. This work was later extended by Canetti and Krawczyk [9]; we refer to this model as the CK model in this paper.

Despite all advantages of the CK approach, there exists a limited number of modules in the different layers. With a limited number of reusable modules, the full power of the CK approach cannot be seen. By increasing the number of reusable modules, secure protocols with different requirements can easily be constructed.

1.1 Motivation

A typical mobile network involves a network operator and mobile users. With advances in mobile technologies, independent application service providers (ASPs) start providing services to the mobile users via their mobile devices. Mobile users make payments to their respective network operators where funds are later transferred to the appropriate ASP. These activities need cryptographic protection for security reasons. The typical methodology of achieving security for communications is to first establish a session key, then encrypt all subsequent messages using the session key. Establishment of secure session keys was never an easy task historically. With limited resources in mobile networking, it is even harder to perform the task appropriately.

When considering the interactions between the three parties, network operator, mobile user and application service provider, it is easy to see that neither a public key nor a symmetric key scheme alone is sufficient and efficient for establishing a session key between the parties. From the viewpoints of mobile users, it is preferable to choose from a list of ASPs, thus implying the passive status of the ASPs until a choice is made.

To solve this problem, let us assume that the network operator is trustworthy. Since users and the network operator share symmetric keys in modern mobile networks, symmetric key cryptography can be applied to this link. With sufficiently high computational power, public key cryptography can be used by the network operator and ASP. Lastly, the network operator generates the session key and sends it to the user. This is an important setting for the sake of simplicity and providing the choice of ASPs to mobile users. The choice of ASPs is important for protecting the privacy of the user with regards to privacy policy. Note that this setting implies that the session key is forwarded by the user to the ASP.

From our library of reusable modules, there exists no suitable modules in the CK approach to address this real life application. Furthermore, there exists no suitable protocol in the literature of secure protocols for this particular requirement. The lack of a suitable candidate is the main motivation for this paper.

1.2 Main Contributions

We regard the following as the main contributions of this paper:

- A new key distribution protocol for applications in mobile networks;
- A new non-interactive MT-authenticator which does not generate additional messages for authentication;
- Two new authenticated protocols with security proofs.

2   The Model

In the CK model the definition of security for key-exchange (KE) protocols follows the tradition of Bellare and Rogaway [6], and is based on a game played between the adversary and the parties $P_1, \ldots, P_n$. In this game, protocol π is modeled as a collection of n programs running at different parties $P_1, \ldots, P_n$. Each program is an interactive probabilistic polynomial-time (PPT) machine. Each invocation of π within a party is defined as a *session*, and each party may have multiple sessions running concurrently. The communications network is controlled by an adversary $\mathcal{A}$, also a PPT machine, which schedules and mediates all sessions between the parties. $\mathcal{A}$ may activate a party P_i in two ways.

1. By means of an establish-session(P_i, P_j, s) request, where P_j is another party with whom the key is to be established, and s is a session-id string which uniquely identifies a session between the participants. Note that session-id is chosen by the adversary, with the restriction that it has to be unique among all sessions between the two parties involved. This allows the delivery of messages to the right protocol instantiation within a party.
2. By means of an *incoming message* m with a specified sender P_j.

A restriction on how the adversary activates parties exists depending on which of the following two adversarial models is being considered.

- *Authenticated-links adversarial Model (AM)* defines an idealised adversary that is not allowed to generate, inject, modify, replay and deliver messages of its choice except if the message is purported to come from a corrupted party. Thus, an *AM–adversary* can only activate parties using incoming messages that were generated by other parties in π.
- *The Unauthenticated-links adversarial Model (UM)* is a more realistic model in which the adversary does not have the above restriction. Thus, a *UM–adversary* can fabricate messages and deliver any messages of its choice.

Upon activation, the parties do some computations, update their internal state, and may output messages which include the identity of the intended receiver. Two activated parties P_i and P_j are said to have a *matching session* if they have sessions whose session-ids are identical and they recognised each other as their respective communicating partner for the session. In addition to the activation of parties, $\mathcal{A}$ can perform the following actions:

1. $\mathcal{A}$ may *corrupt* a party P_i at will, by issuing the query corrupt(P_i), and learn the entire current state of P_i including long-term secrets, session internal states and session keys. From this point on, $\mathcal{A}$ may issue any message in which P_i is specified as the sender and play the role of P_i;

2. $\mathcal{A}$ may issue the query session-key(P_i, s), which returns the session key (if any) accepted by P_i during a given session s;
3. $\mathcal{A}$ may issue the query session-state(P_i, s), which returns all the internal state information of party P_i associated to a particular session s;
4. $\mathcal{A}$ may issue the query test-session(P_i, s). To respond to this query, a random bit $b \in_R \{0, 1\}$ is selected. If $b = 1$ then the session key is returned. Otherwise, return a random key chosen from the probability distribution of keys generated by the protocol. This query can only be issued to a session that has not been *exposed*, i.e. that has not been the subject of a session-state or session-key queries, and whose involved parties have not been corrupted.

During the game, the adversary performs a test-session query to a party and session of its choice. After that, the adversary is not allowed to expose the test-session. $\mathcal{A}$ may continue with its regular actions with the exception that no more test-session queries can be issued. Eventually $\mathcal{A}$ outputs a bit b' as its guess on whether the returned value is the session key or a random number, then halts. $\mathcal{A}$ wins the game if $b = b'$. The definition of security follows.

Definition 1. *A KE protocol π is called* SK-secure *without perfect forward secrecy in the AM if the following properties are satisfied for any AM-adversary $\mathcal{A}$.*

1. *If two uncorrupted parties complete matching sessions then they both output the same key;*
2. *The probability that $\mathcal{A}$ guesses correctly the bit b is no more than $\frac{1}{2}$ plus a negligible fraction in the security parameter.*

The definition of SK-secure protocols in the UM is done analogously. The SK-security is defined with or without forward secrecy. By distinguishing between the AM and the UM, Canetti and Krawczyk allow for a modular approach to the design of SK-secure protocols. Protocols that are SK-secure in the AM can be converted into SK-secure protocols in the UM by applying an *authenticator* to it. An authenticator is a protocol translator $\mathcal{C}$ that takes as input a protocol π and outputs another protocol $\pi' = \mathcal{C}(\pi)$, with the property that if π is SK-secure in the AM, then π' is SK-secure in the UM. Authenticators can be constructed by applying a *message transmission (MT) authenticator* to each of the messages of the input protocol. Bellare *et al.* [4] and Canetti and Krawczyk [9] provided three examples of MT-authenticators.

3   Definition of Security of Bi-encryption Scheme

In this section, we define the notion of security to deal with the case where symmetric and asymmetric encryption schemes are used for separate encryptions of an identical message. We describe security in terms of indistinguishability [11] under chosen plaintext attacks (IND-CPA) [5]. Let $\Pi = (\mathcal{K}, \mathcal{E}, \mathcal{D})$ be an encryption scheme which consists of a key generation algorithm $\mathcal{K}$, a probabilistic encryption algorithm $\mathcal{E}$ and a decryption algorithm $\mathcal{D}$. Let m_0 be a message and $m_1 \in_R \{0,1\}^{|m_0|}$. Let $\mathcal{A}_{\Pi}^{cpa,\mathcal{E}(\cdot)}$ be a polynomial time adversary against Π given access to the encryption oracle $\mathcal{E}(\cdot)$. Let κ be a security parameter. Security in the sense of IND-CPA entails that an adversary cannot distinguish a ciphertext $C \leftarrow \mathcal{E}(m_b)$ where $b \in_R \{0,1\}$ with probability "significantly" more than $\frac{1}{2}$.

Let $\Pi_1 = \{\mathcal{K}_1, \mathcal{E}_1, \mathcal{D}_1\}$ and $\Pi_2 = \{\mathcal{K}_2, \mathcal{E}_2, \mathcal{D}_2\}$ be respectively a symmetric and an asymmetric encryption scheme that satisfy indistinguishability under CPA. We define the bi-encryption algorithm $\mathcal{E}^*$ to be the execution of $\mathcal{E}_1$ and $\mathcal{E}_2$ such that on input a message m, it outputs two ciphertexts $C_1 \leftarrow \mathcal{E}_1(m), C_2 \leftarrow \mathcal{E}_2(m)$. We write $\{C_1, C_2\} \leftarrow \mathcal{E}^*(m)$ and refer to this particular setting as "Bi-encryption".

We denote the bi-encryption scheme $\Pi^* = \{\Pi_1, \Pi_2\}$. Let $\mathcal{A}_{\Pi^*}^{cpa,\mathcal{E}^*(\cdot)}$ be an adversary attacking Π^* with access to the bi-encryption oracle $\mathcal{E}^*(\cdot)$.

Definition 2 (Security Notion of Bi-encryption in IND-CPA). *We define the experiment of the attacking mode in the sense of IND-CPA:*

$$\begin{aligned}
&\text{Experiment } \mathbf{Exp}_{\Pi^*}^{cpa}(\mathcal{A}_{\Pi^*}^{cpa,\mathcal{E}^*(\cdot)}, b) \\
&\quad k \leftarrow \mathcal{K}_1(\kappa_1), (e,d) \leftarrow \mathcal{K}_2(\kappa_2) \\
&(m_0, m_1, s) \leftarrow \mathcal{A}_{\Pi^*}^{cpa,\mathcal{E}^*(\cdot)}(find, \kappa_1, \kappa_2, e) \\
&\quad\quad\quad \{C_1, C_2\} \leftarrow \mathcal{E}^*(m_b) \\
&\quad z \leftarrow \mathcal{A}_{\Pi^*}^{cpa,\mathcal{E}^*(\cdot)}(guess, \kappa_1, \kappa_2, C_1, C_2, s) \\
&\quad\quad\quad\quad\quad \textbf{Return } z
\end{aligned}$$

The advantage of the adversary is defined as follows:

$$\begin{aligned}
\mathbf{Adv}_{\Pi^*}^{cpa}(\mathcal{A}_{\Pi^*}^{cpa,\mathcal{E}^*(\cdot)}) = {}& \Pr[\mathbf{Exp}_{\Pi^*}^{cpa}(\mathcal{A}_{\Pi^*}^{cpa,\mathcal{E}^*(\cdot)}, 1) = 1] \\
& - \Pr[\mathbf{Exp}_{\Pi^*}^{cpa}(\mathcal{A}_{\Pi^*}^{cpa,\mathcal{E}^*(\cdot)}, 0) = 1]
\end{aligned}$$

The encryption scheme Π^* is said to be secure under CPA if the function $\mathbf{Adv}_{\Pi^*}^{cpa}(\mathcal{A}_{\Pi^*}^{cpa,\mathcal{E}^*(\cdot)})$ is negligible for every polynomial time adversary $\mathcal{A}_1$ in κ_1 and $\mathcal{A}_2$ in κ_2.

It is important to confirm that the notion of indistinguishability in encryption algorithms is strong enough to also imply security in the bi-encryption. This problem was addressed by Baudron, Pointcheval and Stern [2] and independently by Bellare, Boldyreva and Micali [3]. Note that the proof by the latter is based on a single public key encryption scheme using different keys.

Theorem 1 ([2]). *If the encryption schemes Π_1 and Π_2 are secure under CPA, then the encryption scheme Π^* is secure under CPA. More precisely:*

$$\mathbf{Adv}_{\Pi^*}^{cpa}(\mathcal{A}_{\Pi^*}^{cpa,\mathcal{E}^*(\cdot)}) \leq \mathbf{Adv}_{\Pi_1}^{cpa}(\mathcal{A}_{\Pi_1}^{cpa,\mathcal{E}_1(\cdot)}) + \mathbf{Adv}_{\Pi_2}^{cpa}(\mathcal{A}_{\Pi_2}^{cpa,\mathcal{E}_2(\cdot)}) \tag{1}$$

The actual result in [2] considers only asymmetric encryption schemes. However, their result is also applicable to any combination of symmetric and asymmetric encryption schemes as long as the equivalent notion of security is satisfied.

4   A New Protocol Secure in the AM

We propose a key distribution protocol in the AM where two parties use a trusted server for session key generation. This protocol uses both symmetric and asymmetric encryption. There is a need for this type of setting, particularly for business in mobile networks. We explain why.

The typical setting in mobile networks involves a network operator and users with a mobile device. A third player in mobile networks is the ASP which provides services to users and gets payment from users via the network operator. Typically, they do not share a long term secret key. Thus it is required to setup a secure communication channel between them before any sensitive data could be exchanged. The secure communication channel is constructed with a session key generated by the network operator given that both the users and the ASPs trust the former. The trust on the network operator is reasonable because the basic telecommunications services are provided by the network operator.

When determining the mechanism for setting up the session key, we consider two links: the link between the users and the network operator and the link between the network operator and the ASPs. Since users in mobile networks share a long term secret key with the network operator for basic telecommunications services, it is natural to use a symmetric key encryption scheme on this link. It is also the best choice for the users due to the constraints in computation of mobile devices. On the link between the network operator and the ASPs, we use an asymmetric key encryption scheme. We have two reasons for this decision. Firstly, it is reasonable to assume that both the network operator and the ASPs are capable of running computationally intensive algorithms. Secondly, it is difficult to securely distribute long term secret keys to all ASPs, thus limiting the use of symmetric encryption schemes on this link.

Let S be the network operator, U be the user and A be the ASP. The sequence of the communications link is: $U \to S \to U \to A$. Note that the link between the network operator and the ASPs has been broken down to two links where U relays messages from S to A. This setting allows the users to choose different ASPs based on their preferences.

Assume that U shares a long term secret key k_{US} with S. Let (e_X, d_X) be the public and private key of party X. The session key is encrypted with the long term secret key shared between U and S. On the link between A and S, public key cryptography is employed. Let $\sigma \leftarrow Sn(1^\kappa)$ be a session key generated by the key generator $Sn(1^\kappa)$ with security parameter κ. We denote $\mathcal{E}_k(m)$ be encryption of some message m under key k. Similarly, $\mathcal{D}_k(c)$ denotes decryption of some ciphertext c with key k. The protocol is shown in Figure 1.

Remark 1. We note the importance of the session identifier s. It is used to match concurrent sessions running by protocol participants, thus its value must be unique such that probability of the appearance of the same value twice is negligible. A practical implementation for uniqueness of the session identifier is to enforce contributions s_1, s_2 from both parties. Each party then knows that the session identifier is fresh and unique.

S	U	A
$\sigma \leftarrow Sn(1^{\kappa})$		
$\mu_U \leftarrow \mathcal{E}_{k_{US}}(\sigma)$		
$\mu_A \leftarrow \mathcal{E}_{e_A}(\sigma)$		

$$\xrightarrow{\quad A, s, \mu_U \quad}$$
$$\xrightarrow{\quad U, s, \mu_A \quad}$$

$$\xrightarrow{\quad U, s, \mu_A \quad}$$
$$\sigma' \leftarrow \mathcal{D}_{k_{US}}(\mu_U) \qquad \sigma'' \leftarrow \mathcal{D}_{d_A}(\mu_A)$$

Fig. 1. The Protocol 3PKD

Theorem 2. *Let Π_1 be the symmetric encryption scheme and Π_2 be the asymmetric encryption scheme used in protocol 3PKD. The protocol 3PKD is SK-secure in the authenticated links model (AM) if the encryption schemes Π_1 and Π_2 are secure under chosen plaintext attacks.*

Proof. Due to space limitations, the proof is excluded and appears in the full paper.

5 New Authenticator

5.1 A Non-interactive Signature Based MT-Authenticator

We propose a non-interactive signature-based MT-authenticator λ_{Sig}^{Time} that uses time stamps to provide freshness. In contrast to the original signature–based MT–authenticator of Bellare *et al.* [4], our new MT–authenticator results in only one message in the UM for every message to be authenticated.

Using time stamps for freshness requires synchronisation in time. In practice, maintaining perfect synchronisation is extremely expensive and is not commonly used for communications between clients and servers. Thus, we need to accept "loosely synchronised" times for the scheme to be practical. In addition, the time stamp is required to be unique. The uniqueness is maintained by the procedures for signature verification.

Time stamps could be in different formats, but we provide an abstract formulation for our needs. We assume that there exists a secure time server $\mathcal{TS}$ which we model as a universal time oracle available to all parties. All parties access this oracle whenever a time stamp is required. We also assume that there exists a boolean function $\mathcal{V}$ which returns *TRUE* or *FALSE* on input a time stamp Υ. If it returns *TRUE*, then the time stamp Υ is fresh. Otherwise, Υ is expired. Note that this function may make decisions based on some "looseness" in time if necessary.

Let $\mathcal{I}$ be an initialisation function which invokes, once for each party, the key generation algorithm of a signature scheme secure under chosen message attacks with security parameter κ. Let *Sig* and *Ver* denote the signing and verification algorithms. Let sk_i and pk_i be the private and public keys of a party P_i where all public keys pk_i are known by all other parties. Whenever P_i needs a time stamp, it requests the time oracle $\mathcal{TS}(\cdot)$ for a time value.

The MT-authenticator λ_{Sig}^{Time} is activated within some party P_i with an external request to send a unique message m to party P_j. Then λ_{Sig}^{Time} invokes a two-party protocol λ_S^T that proceeds as follows. Since λ_S^T involves only two parties, we use A and B for their identities. Party A sends 'signature:$Sig_A(m, \Upsilon_A, B)$' to B and outputs 'A sent message m to B'. When 'signature:$Sig_A(m, \Upsilon_A, B)$' arrives at party B, B accepts m if the signature is *successfully verified* as described below. If m is accepted by B, B outputs 'B received m from A'. This type of transmission is captured in Figure 2.

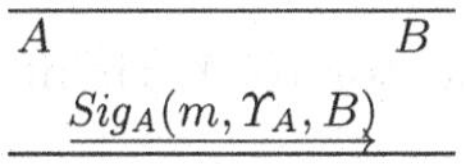

$$A \qquad\qquad\qquad B$$
$$\underline{\qquad Sig_A(m, \Upsilon_A, B) \qquad}$$

Fig. 2. Signature Based MT-authenticator using Time stamps

Remark 2. Our representation of the signature makes no assumption on its nature. In the case of a signature scheme with message recovery, only the signature is sent. In the case of a signature scheme with appendix, the messages signed and the signature are sent together.

For ensuring the security of λ_{Sig}^{Time}, B needs to maintain a list $\mathcal{L}$ of received and accepted messages by all instances run by B. Party B maintains this list with two operations, namely insertion and deletion of records. Let n be the maximum number of records in $\mathcal{L}$. A record $l_{i \in \{1,\ldots,n\}} = (m', \Upsilon_A')$ is added to $\mathcal{L}$ when m' is accepted by B such that B outputs 'B received m' from A'. The record l_i is removed from $\mathcal{L}$ when its associated time stamp Υ_A' has become invalid.

Upon receiving the message $Sig_A(m, \Upsilon_A, B)$ from A, party B proceeds to execute the signature verification procedures as follows. Firstly B recovers the data (m, Υ_A, B) from the signature and searches for an identical time stamp from its list of records $\mathcal{L}$. If an entry is found, then m is rejected. If not, B verifies the signature using the signature verification algorithm $Ver_{pk_A}(m, \Upsilon_A)$. If the signature is invalid, then m is rejected. Otherwise, B runs $\mathcal{V}$ to determine whether the time stamp is freshly generated. Party B only accepts m if $\mathcal{V}$ returns "TRUE".

Remark 3. Counters could be used to replace time stamps for freshness for our new MT-authenticator. Replacing time stamps with counters is straightforward [1] and the resultant MT-authenticator is also non-interactive. The security proof of λ_{Sig}^{Time} can easily be modified to suit the MT-authenticator that uses counters. The main difference in the proof is the mechanism used to verify freshness of messages.

Security Proof. We can show that the protocol λ_{Sig}^{Time} is a valid MT-authenticator which emulates an MT-protocol in the UM. An MT-protocol refers to the transmission of a single message flow while emulation follows the convention of Ballere, Canetti and Krawczyk [4]. Assume that the signature scheme is secure under adaptive chosen message attack in the convention of Goldwasser, Micali and Rivest [12] and is thus existentially non-forgeable.

Theorem 3. *Assume that the signature scheme in use is secure under adaptive chosen message attacks. Then protocol λ_{Sig}^{Time} emulates protocol MT.*

Proof. The proof follows the general technique in the security proof of an MT-authenticator using random nonces [4] and appears in the full paper.

5.2   From MT-Authenticator to Authenticator

Our new MT-authenticator λ_{Sig}^{Time} can be made into a full-fledged authenticator using Theorem 4 as follows.

Theorem 4 ([4]). *Let λ be an MT-authenticator such that λ emulates message transmission MT in unauthenticated networks, and let $\mathcal{C}_\lambda$ be a compiler constructed based on λ as described above. Then $\mathcal{C}_\lambda$ is an authenticator.*

Depending on the number of message flows in the AM, a full-fledged authenticator can be a combination of MT-authenticators. If there is a single message flow in the AM, a MT-authenticator is sufficient to be used as an authenticator. Otherwise, two or more MT-authenticators need to be combined for transforming different message flows in the AM. We stress that Theorem 4 implies authentication of a single message and puts no restriction on how the other messages of the same AM protocol are authenticated, thus is independent of the number of messages or participants.

A New Authenticator for Three Party Protocol. As an example for generating a full-fledged authenticator to transform a two-message AM protocol to a protocol secure in the UM, we recall a MAC-based MT-authenticator [9] and combine it with our signature-based MT-authenticator using time λ_{Sig}^{Time}. Other types of MT-authenticators exist, but the choice of λ_{MAC} is necessary to satisfy the unique requirements of the AM protocol of Figure 1. The MAC-based MT-authenticator is shown in Figure 3 and is referred to as λ_{MAC} hereafter.

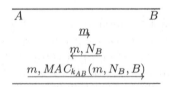

Fig. 3. MAC Based MT-authenticator

We combine the MT-authenticators λ_{MAC} and λ_{Sig}^{Time} for a secure transformation of protocol 3PKD. It is also applicable to other AM protocols with two message flows with the respective computational requirements. The full-fledged authenticator $\mathcal{C}_{\lambda_{Sig}^{Time}}^{\lambda_{MAC}}$ is illustrated in Figure 4.

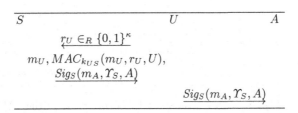

Fig. 4. A Full-fledged Authenticator derived from λ_{MAC} and λ_{Sig}^{Time}

Note the disappearance of the first message in $\mathcal{C}_{\lambda_{Sig}^{Time}}^{\lambda_{MAC}}$ from S to U. This message is not required as the MT-authenticator λ_{MAC} can be simplified to two message exchanges since the first message m from A to B is redundant.

6   Secure Protocols in the UM

In this section, we demonstrate the applications of our new modules in the CK model. First we show a secure three-party key transport protocol in the UM. Then we show an authenticated Diffie-Hellman key exchange.

6.1   An Authenticated Key Transport Protocol

Using $\mathcal{C}_{\lambda_{Sig}^{Time}}^{\lambda_{MAC}}$, we show that protocol 3PKD of Figure 1 can be compiled into a secure protocol in the UM. More precisely, we compile our new three-party key distribution protocol 3PKD of Figure 1 with $\mathcal{C}_{\lambda_{Sig}^{Time}}^{\lambda_{MAC}}$ to obtain a secure key distribution protocol in the UM. We denote by $\Upsilon_S \leftarrow \mathcal{TS}$ an action that S obtains a time from the time server to generate the time stamp. Let $a\|b$ be the concatenation of a and b. The resultant secure protocol following the above procedures is shown in Figure 5 and is named 3PKDUM.

The session identifier s in 3PKDUM is a simple concatenation of r_U and Υ_S. The ASP A gets assurance of freshness because the checking process ensures that no time stamp is accepted twice. Even though U does not check the freshness of Υ_S, and A cannot check the freshness of r_U, the combination of these values is unique. In practice, of course, only one copy of each value is required.

6.2   An Authenticated Diffie-Hellman Key Exchange Using Time Stamp

To further demonstrate the advantage of our new MT-authenticator, we construct an authenticator based solely on λ_{Sig}^{Time}. This authenticator is then applied

$$\begin{array}{ccc}
S & U & A
\end{array}$$

$$\xleftarrow{\quad r_U \in_R \{0,1\}^\kappa \quad}$$

$$\begin{aligned}
\sigma &\leftarrow Sn(1^k)\\
\mu_U &\leftarrow \mathcal{E}_{k_{US}}(\sigma)\\
\mu_A &\leftarrow \mathcal{E}_{e_A}(\sigma)\\
\Upsilon_S &\leftarrow \mathcal{TS}\\
s &= r_U \| \Upsilon_S
\end{aligned}$$

$$\xrightarrow{\quad A, s, \mu_U, MAC_{k_{US}}(A, s, \mu_U, r_U, U) \quad}$$
$$\xrightarrow{\quad Sig_S(U, s, \mu_A, \Upsilon_S, A) \quad}$$

$$\xrightarrow{\quad Sig_S(U, s, \mu_A, \Upsilon_S, A) \quad}$$

Fig. 5. A Key Transport Protocol Secure in the UM

to the ordinary Diffie-Hellman key exchange [10] to obtain an authenticated Diffie-Hellman key exchange in the UM. Assume that the session identifier s is known by A and B before the run of the protocol. Then we simply apply λ_{Sig}^{Time} to each of the messages of the Diffie-Hellman key exchange, then combine the results of these applications. Note that the ordinary Diffie-Hellman key exchange was proven SK-secure in the AM [9]. The authenticated Diffie-Hellman key exchange using time stamps is illustrated in Figure 6 and is named 2DHTUM.

$$\begin{array}{cc}
A & B
\end{array}$$

$$\begin{aligned}
\Upsilon_A &\leftarrow \mathcal{TS}\\
x &\in_R \mathbb{Z}_q \qquad\qquad y \in_R \mathbb{Z}_q
\end{aligned}$$

$$\xrightarrow{\quad Sig_{sk_A}(A, s, g^x, \Upsilon_A, B) \quad}$$
$$\Upsilon_B \leftarrow \mathcal{TS}$$
$$\xleftarrow{\quad Sig_{sk_B}(B, s, g^y, \Upsilon_B, A) \quad}$$
$$K' = (g^y)^x \qquad\qquad K = (g^x)^y$$

Fig. 6. Authenticated Diffie-Hellman Key Exchange using Time Stamps

It is worth noting that the message flows are not required to be sequential. That is, the protocol 2DHTUM is a one-round protocol. In comparison, the authenticated Diffie-Hellman key exchange [9] by applying the original signature based MT-authenticator in the CK model requires three rounds to complete.

7   Conclusion

In this paper, we defined a notion of security for encryptions of an identical message using one symmetric and one asymmetric encryption scheme. We then constructed a new three-party key transport protocol satisfying this notion of security in the AM.

We designed a new non-interactive MT-authenticator using time stamps from which a new authenticator was generated. This authenticator is used to translate AM protocols to secure protocols in the UM. We also discussed a variant of the MT-authenticator using counters.

From the new authenticator presented in this paper, we constructed a secure protocol 3PKDUM of Figure 5 as well as an authenticated Diffie-Hellman exchange of Figure 6.

References

1. Technical Committee ISO/IEC JTC 1. ISO/IEC DIS 11770-3 information technology - security techniques - key management - part 3: Mechanisms using asymmetric techniques. International Standard, 1996.
2. Olivier Baudron, David Pointcheval, and Jacques Stern. Extended notions of security for multicast public key cryptosystems. In *Proceedings of the 27th international Colloquium on Automata, Languages and Programming (ICALP '2000)*, volume 1853 of *LNCS*, pages 499–511. Springer-Verlag, July 2000.
3. M. Bellare, A. Boldyreva, and S. Micali. Public-key encryption in a multi-user setting: Security proofs and improvements. In *Advances in Cryptology – Eurocrypt 2000*, volume 1807 of *LNCS*, pages 259–274. Springer-Verlag, 2000. Full version at http://www-cse.ucsd.edu/users/mihir/papers/key-distribution.html.
4. M. Bellare, R. Canetti, and H. Krawczyk. A modular approach to the design and analysis of authentication and key exchange protocols. In *Proceedings of the 30th Annual Symposium on the Theory of Computing, ACM*, pages 412–428, 1998. Full version at http://www-cse.ucsd.edu/users/mihir/papers/modular.pdf.
5. M. Bellare, A. Desai, D. Pointcheval, and P. Rogaway. Relations among notions of security for public-key encryption schemes. In *Advances in Cryptology – Crypto 1998*, volume 1446 of *LNCS*, pages 26–45. Springer-Verlag, 1998.
6. M. Bellare and P. Rogaway. Random oracles are practical: A paradigm for designing efficient protocols. In *Proceedings of the First ACM Conference on Computer and Communications Security*, pages 62–73, 1993.
7. M. Bellare and P. Rogaway. Entity authentication and key distribution. In *Advances in Cryptology - Crypto 1993*, volume 773 of *LNCS*, pages 232–249. Springer-Verlag, 1994. Full version at http://www-cse.ucsd.edu/users/mihir/papers/eakd.pdf.
8. M. Bellare and P. Rogaway. Provably secure session key distribution - the three party case. In *Proceedings of the 27th ACM Symposium on the Theory of Computing*, pages 57–66, May 1995.
9. R. Canetti and H. Krawczyk. Analysis of key-exchange protocols and their use for building secure channels. In *Advances in Cryptology – Eurocrypt 2001*, volume 2045 of *LNCS*, pages 453–474. Springer-Verlag, 2001. Full version at http://eprint.iacr.org/2001/040.ps.
10. W. Diffie and M. Hellman. New directions in cryptography. *IEEE Transactions on Information Theory*, 22:644–654, 1976.
11. S. Goldwasser and S. Micali. Probabilistic encryption. *Journal of Computer and System Science*, 28(2):270–299, 1984.
12. S. Goldwasser, M. Sipser, and R. Rivest. A digital signature scheme secure against adaptive chosen-message attack. *SIAM Journal of Computing*, 17(2):281–308, 1988.

Secure Bilinear Diffie-Hellman Bits

Steven D. Galbraith[1], Herbie J. Hopkins[1], and Igor E. Shparlinski[2]

[1] Mathematics Department, Royal Holloway University of London
Egham, Surrey, TW20 0EX, UK
{Steven.Galbraith, H.J.Hopkins}@rhul.ac.uk
[2] Department of Computing, Macquarie University
Sydney, NSW 2109, Australia
igor@comp.mq.edu.au

Abstract. The Weil and Tate pairings are a popular new gadget in cryptography and have found many applications, including identity-based cryptography. In particular, the pairings have been used for key exchange protocols.

This paper studies the bit security of keys obtained using protocols based on pairings (that is, we show that obtaining certain bits of the common key is as hard as computing the entire key). These results give insight into how many "hard-core" bits can be obtained from key exchange using pairings.

The results are of practical importance. For instance, Scott and Barreto have recently used our results to justify the security of their compressed pairing technique.

1 Introduction

Let p be a prime and let $\mathbb{F}_p$ be the field of p elements, which we identify with the set $\{0, 1, \ldots, p - 1\}$. Let l be a prime which is coprime to p and define m to be the smallest positive integer such that $p^m \equiv 1 \pmod{l}$. [1] In this paper we consider a non-degenerate bilinear pairing

$$e : \mathbb{G}_1 \times \mathbb{G}_2 \longrightarrow \mathcal{G} \subseteq \mathbb{F}_{p^m}^*$$

where $\mathbb{G}_1$, $\mathbb{G}_2$ and $\mathcal{G}$ are cyclic groups of order l. The Weil and Tate pairings on subgroups of elliptic curves give rise to such pairings. One implementation which has $\mathbb{G}_1 = \mathbb{G}_2$ (given by Verheul [27]) is to take a supersingular elliptic curve E over $\mathbb{F}_p$ such that $l \| \#E(\mathbb{F}_p)$ and such that E has a suitable "distortion map" ψ (which is a non-$\mathbb{F}_p$-rational endomorphism on E). Let $\mathbb{G}_1 = \mathbb{G}_2$ be the unique subgroup of $E(\mathbb{F}_p)$ of order l. The pairing $e(P, Q)$ is defined to be the Weil (or Tate) pairing of P with $\psi(Q)$. For more details about pairings on elliptic curves and their applications see [3,7,8,15,16,19,20,21,27].

---

[1] Typical values of these parameters are $m = 2$, p a 512-bit prime and l a prime dividing $p + 1$ of at least 160 bits; or $m = 6$, $p \approx 2^{180}$ and $l \approx 2^{160}$. More generally we can replace p by a prime power.

H. Wang et al. (Eds.): ACISP 2004, LNCS 3108, pp. 370–378, 2004.
© Springer-Verlag Berlin Heidelberg 2004

Pairings have found many applications in cryptography including the tripartite key exchange protocol of Joux [15] (also see the variations by Al-Riyami and Paterson [1] and Verheul [27]) and the identity-based key exchange protocol of Smart [26]. These protocols enable a set of users to agree a random element K in the subgroup $\mathcal{G}$ of $\mathbb{F}_{p^m}^*$, and the "key" is then derived from K.

We recall the *tripartite Diffie-Hellman protocol* in the original formulation of Joux [15]: To set up the system, three communicating parties A, B and C choose suitable groups $\mathbb{G}_1$ and $\mathbb{G}_2$ of order l and points $P \in \mathbb{G}_1$ and $Q \in \mathbb{G}_2$ with $e(P,Q) \neq 1 \in \mathbb{F}_{p^m}^*$.

To create a common secret key, A, B and C choose secret numbers $a,b,c \in [0, l-1]$ and publish pairs

$$(aP, aQ), \qquad (bP, bQ), \qquad (cP, cQ).$$

Now each of them is able to compute the common key

$$K = e(P,Q)^{abc}.$$

For example, A can compute K as follows,

$$e(bP, cQ)^a = e(P, cQ)^{ab} = e(P,Q)^{abc} = K \in \mathbb{F}_{p^m}^*.$$

Note that K is an element of order l in $\mathbb{F}_{p^m}^*$.

Since p^m is very large (at least 1024 bits), and since K is an element of a smaller subgroup of order l, it makes sense to derive a key of about this size. One natural approach is to simply use a single component (or portion of it) of the representation of K in $\mathbb{F}_{p^m}$ as a vector space over $\mathbb{F}_p$. As is well known (see [18] Theorem 2.24) selecting a component can be described in terms of the trace. Hence, in this paper we consider the representation-independent framework of considering the trace of K with respect to $\mathbb{F}_{p^m}/\mathbb{F}_p$ to obtain an element of $\mathbb{F}_p$. We represent elements of $\mathbb{F}_p$ as integers in $[0, p-1]$ and obtain corresponding bitstrings in the usual way. We show that the trace is a secure key derivation function.

Note that the identity-based encryption scheme of Boneh and Franklin [3] is a hybrid scheme (key transport followed by symmetric encryption) and so our results shed light on the security in this case.

The use of part of the representation of K has been proposed by Scott and Barreto [24]. Our results show that there is no loss of security from using their technique.

The results follow from several recently established results [17,25] on the *hidden number problem with trace* in extension fields. Detailed surveys of bit security results and discussions of their meaning and importance are given in [9, 10]; several more recent results can be found in [4,5,6,11,12,13,14,17,23,25].

We obtain an almost complete analogue of the results of [6,11] for $m = 2$ (for example, for the elliptic curves used by Joux [15] and Verheul [27]) and much weaker, but nontrivial, results for $m \geq 3$. For example, in the case that $m = 2$ and p is a 512 bit prime, our results imply that, if the bilinear-Diffie-Hellman problem is hard, then the 128 most significant bits of the trace of K can be used to derive a secure key.

Finite fields of characteristic 2 or 3 are sometimes used in pairing-based systems. In these cases one can obtain a key by taking some components of the representation of the finite field element as a vector space over $\mathbb{F}_p$ $(p = 2, 3)$. Using linear algebra it is trivial to obtain very strong bit security results in these cases. The details are left to the reader.

Note that we allow all our constants to depend on m while p and l are growing parameters. Throughout the paper $\log z$ denotes the binary logarithm of $z > 0$.

2   Hidden Number Problem with Trace

We denote by

$$\mathrm{Tr}(z) = \sum_{i=0}^{m-1} z^{p^i} \quad \text{and} \quad \mathrm{Nm}(z) = \prod_{i=0}^{m-1} z^{p^i}$$

the *trace* and *norm* of $z \in \mathbb{F}_{p^m}$ to $\mathbb{F}_p$, see Section 2.3 of [18].

For an integer x we define

$$\|x\|_p = \min_{a \in \mathbb{Z}} |x - ap|$$

and for a given $k > 0$, we denote by $\mathrm{MSB}_{k,p}(x)$ any integer u, $0 \le u \le p-1$, such that

$$\|x - u\|_p \le p/2^{k+1}.$$

Roughly speaking, a value of $\mathrm{MSB}_{k,p}(x)$ gives the k most significant bits of the residue of x modulo p. Note that in the above definition k need not be an integer.

The *hidden number problem with trace* over a subgroup $\mathcal{G} \subseteq \mathbb{F}_{p^m}^*$ can be formulated as follows: Given r elements $t_1, \ldots, t_r \in \mathcal{G} \subseteq \mathbb{F}_{p^m}^*$, chosen independently and uniformly at random, and the values $\mathrm{MSB}_{k,p}\left(\mathrm{Tr}\left(\alpha t_i\right)\right)$ for $i = 1, \ldots, r$ and some $k > 0$, recover the number $\alpha \in \mathbb{F}_{p^m}$.

The case of $m = 1$ and $\mathcal{G} = \mathbb{F}_p^*$ corresponds to the hidden number problem introduced in [6] (for the case $\mathcal{G} \subset \mathbb{F}_p^*$ see [11]). The case of $m \ge 2$ is more difficult. Nevertheless in some special cases results of a comparable strength have been obtained in [17]. In other cases, an alternative method from [25] can be used, leading to weaker results.

The following statement is a partial case of Theorem 2 of [17].

We denote by $\mathcal{N}$ the set of $z \in \mathbb{F}_{p^m}$ with norm equal to 1, thus $|\mathcal{N}| = (p^m - 1)/(p - 1)$.

Lemma 1. *Let p be a sufficiently large prime number and let $\mathcal{G}$ be a subgroup of $\mathcal{N}$ of order l with $l \ge p^{(m-1)/2+\rho}$ for some fixed $\rho > 0$. Then for*

$$k = \left\lceil 2\sqrt{\log p} \right\rceil \quad \text{and} \quad r = \left\lceil 4(m+1)\sqrt{\log p} \right\rceil$$

there is a deterministic polynomial time algorithm $\mathcal{A}$ as follows. For any $\alpha \in \mathbb{F}_{p^m}$, if $t_1,\ldots,t_r$ are chosen uniformly and independently at random from $\mathcal{G}$ and if $u_i = \mathrm{MSB}_{k,p}(\mathrm{Tr}(\alpha t_i))$ for $i = 1,\ldots,r$, the output of $\mathcal{A}$ on the $2r$ values (t_i, u_i) satisfies

$$\Pr_{t_1,\ldots,t_r \in \mathcal{G}}[\mathcal{A}(t_1,\ldots,t_r;u_1,\ldots,u_r) = \alpha] \geq 1 - p^{-1}.$$

For smaller groups a weaker result is given by Theorem 1 of [25].

Lemma 2. *Let p be a sufficiently large prime number and let $\mathcal{G}$ be a subgroup of $\mathbb{F}_{p^m}^*$ of prime order l with $l \geq p^\rho$ for some fixed $\rho > 0$. Then for any $\varepsilon > 0$, let*

$$k = \lceil(1 - \rho/m + \varepsilon)\log p\rceil \qquad and \qquad r = \lceil 4m/\varepsilon\rceil$$

there is a deterministic polynomial time algorithm $\mathcal{A}$ as follows. For any $\alpha \in \mathbb{F}_{p^m}$, if $t_1,\ldots,t_r$ are chosen uniformly and independently at random from $\mathcal{G}$ and if $u_i = \mathrm{MSB}_{k,p}(\mathrm{Tr}(\alpha t_i))$ for $i = 1,\ldots,r$, the output of $\mathcal{A}$ on the $2r$ values (t_i, u_i) satisfies

$$\Pr_{t_1,\ldots,t_r \in \mathcal{G}}[\mathcal{A}(t_1,\ldots,t_r;u_1,\ldots,u_r) = \alpha] \geq 1 - p^{-1}.$$

3   Bit Security of Tripartite Diffie-Hellman

We have already described the tripartite Diffie-Hellman system of Joux. In that case an adversary sees $(P,Q),(aP,aQ),(bP,bQ)$ and (cP,cQ) and the key is derived from $\mathrm{Tr}(e(P,Q)^{abc}) \in \{0,1,\ldots,p-1\}$. Note that if distortion maps are used then $Q = \psi(P)$, see [27]. In this section we study the bit security of keys obtained in this way. Later in this section we discuss the bit security of keys obtained from the protocols of Al-Riyami and Paterson [1].

Let $\omega_1,\ldots,\omega_m$ be a fixed basis of $\mathbb{F}_{p^m}$ over $\mathbb{F}_p$ and let $\vartheta_1,\ldots,\vartheta_m$ be the dual basis, that is,

$$\mathrm{Tr}(\vartheta_j\omega_i) = \begin{cases} 0, & \text{if } i \neq j, \\ 1, & \text{if } i = j \end{cases}$$

see Section 2.3 of [18]. Then any element $\alpha \in \mathbb{F}_{p^m}$ can be represented in the basis $\omega_1,\ldots,\omega_m$ as

$$\alpha = \sum_{i=1}^{m} \mathrm{Tr}(\vartheta_i\alpha)\omega_i.$$

Hence, selecting a component of the representation of an element $\alpha \in \mathbb{F}_{p^m}$ with respect to some basis $\{\omega_i\}$ is equivalent to considering $\mathrm{Tr}(\vartheta\alpha)$ for a suitable element $\vartheta \in \mathbb{F}_{p^m}$.

We now assume that there is an algorithm which can provide some information about one of the components $\mathrm{Tr}(\vartheta_i e(P,Q)^{abc})$ of the above representation and show that it leads to an efficient algorithm to compute the whole value $e(P,Q)^{abc}$ and hence the key $\mathrm{Tr}(e(P,Q)^{abc})$. It follows that the partial information about one of the components is as hard as the whole key.

To make this precise, for every $k > 0$ we denote by $\mathcal{O}_k$ the oracle which, for some fixed $\vartheta \in \mathbb{F}_{p^m}^*$ and any $a, b, c \in [0, l-1]$, takes as input the pairs

$$(P, Q), \qquad (aP, aQ), \qquad (bP, bQ), \qquad (cP, cQ),$$

and outputs $\mathrm{MSB}_{k,p}\left(\mathrm{Tr}\left(\vartheta e(P, Q)^{abc}\right)\right)$.

We start with the case $m = 2$ for which we obtain a result of the same strength as those known for the classical two-party Diffie–Hellman scheme over $\mathbb{F}_p$, see [6,11]. Moreover, one can prove that there are infinitely many parameter choices to which our construction applies. Indeed, we know from [2] that there are infinitely many primes p such that $p + 1$ has a prime divisor $l \geq p^{0.677}$. These arguments can be easily adjusted to show that the same holds for primes in the arithmetic progression $p \equiv 2 \pmod{3}$. When $p \equiv 2 \pmod{3}$, the elliptic curve given by the Weierstrass equation $Y^2 = X^3 + 1$ has $\#E(\mathbb{F}_p) = p + 1$. Another infinite series of examples of $\#E(\mathbb{F}_p) = p + 1$ can be obtained with primes $p \equiv 3 \pmod{4}$ and the elliptic curve given by the Weierstrass equation $Y^2 = X^3 + X$, see [16].

Theorem 1. *Assume that p is an n-bit prime (for sufficiently large n) and l is the order of the groups $\mathbb{G}_1$ and $\mathbb{G}_2$ such that $l|(p + 1)$, $\gcd(l, p - 1) = 1$ and $l \geq p^{1/2+\rho}$ for some fixed $\rho > 0$. Then there exists a polynomial time algorithm which, given the pairs*

$$(P, Q), \qquad (aP, aQ), \qquad (bP, bQ), \qquad (cP, cQ)$$

for some $a, b, c \in \{0, \ldots, l-1\}$, makes $O(n^{1/2})$ calls of the oracle $\mathcal{O}_k$ with $k = \lceil 2n^{1/2} \rceil$ and computes $e(P, Q)^{abc}$ correctly with probability at least $1 - p^{-1}$.

Proof. The case when $ab = 0$ is trivial. In the general case choose a random $d \in \{0, \ldots, l-1\}$ and call the oracle $\mathcal{O}_k$ on the pairs

$$(P, Q), \qquad (aP, aQ), \qquad (bP, bQ), \qquad ((c+d)P, (c+d)Q)$$

(the points $(c+d)P$ and $(c+d)Q$ can be computed from the values of cP, cQ and d). Let $\alpha = \vartheta e(P, Q)^{abc}$ be the hidden number and let $t = e(P, Q)^{abd}$ which can be computed as $t = e(aP, bQ)^d$. The oracle returns

$$\mathrm{MSB}_{k,p}\left(\mathrm{Tr}(\vartheta e(P, Q)^{ab(c+d)})\right) = \mathrm{MSB}_{k,p}\left(\mathrm{Tr}(\alpha t)\right).$$

Since l is prime and $ab \not\equiv 0 \pmod{l}$ it follows that the "multipliers" t are uniformly and independently distributed in $\mathcal{G}$, when the shifts d are chosen uniformly and independently at random from $\{0, \ldots, l-1\}$. Now from Lemma 1 with $m = 2$ we derive the result. $\qquad\qquad\square$

Similarly, from Lemma 2 we derive:

Theorem 2. *Assume that p is an n-bit prime (for sufficiently large n) and l is the order of the groups $\mathbb{G}_1$ and $\mathbb{G}_2$ such that $l|(p^m - 1)$, $\gcd(l, p^i - 1) = 1$ for all*

$1 \leq i < m$, and $l \geq p^\rho$ for some fixed $\rho > 0$. Then, for any $\varepsilon > 0$, there exists a polynomial time algorithm which, given the pairs

$$(P, Q), \qquad (aP, aQ), \qquad (bP, bQ), \qquad (cP, cQ)$$

for some $a, b, c \in \{0, \ldots, l-1\}$, makes $O(\varepsilon^{-1})$ calls of the oracle $\mathcal{O}_k$ with $k = \lceil(1 - \rho/m + \varepsilon)n\rceil$ and computes $e(P, Q)^{abc}$ correctly with probability at least $1 - p^{-1}$.

We now consider the authenticated three party key agreement protocols of Al-Riyami and Paterson [1] (which are presented in the case $\mathbb{G}_1 = \mathbb{G}_2$). In this setting, users A, B and C have public keys aP, bP and cP and transmit ephemeral keys xP, yP and zP. We give details for the protocol TAK–3, which computes a shared key of the form

$$e(P, P)^{xyc + xzb + yza}.$$

If a bitstring is derived from this key using the trace then results analogous to Theorems 1 and 2 are obtained (with the same values of k).

Suppose $\mathcal{O}_k$ is an oracle which, on input $(P, aP, bP, cP, xP, yP, zP)$, outputs

$$\mathrm{MSB}_{k,p}(\mathrm{Tr}(\vartheta e(P, P)^{xyc + xzb + yza}))$$

and let $\alpha = \vartheta e(P, P)^{xyc + xzb + yza}$. Repeatedly choosing random w and calling $\mathcal{O}_k$ on $(P, aP, bP, cP, xP, yP, zP + wP)$ yields

$$\mathrm{MSB}_{k,p}(\mathrm{Tr}(\alpha t)) \qquad \text{where} \qquad t = e(xP, bP)^w e(yP, aP)^w.$$

It is straightforward to obtain analogues of of Theorems 1 and 2.

Al-Riyami and Paterson [1] also propose the protocol TAK–4, which is related to the MQV protocol. Our methods do not provide bit security results in this case, as the use of the hash function does not preserve algebraic relationships. It is an interesting open problem to give bit security results for this protocol.

4   Bit Security of Identity-Based Key Exchange

The first identity-based key exchange protocol is due to Sakai, Ohgishi and Kasahara [22], but we consider the protocol of Smart [26] as it has better security properties.

The trusted authority defines two groups $\mathbb{G}_1$ and $\mathbb{G}_2$, such that there is a suitable bilinear map as above. The authority chooses $P \in \mathbb{G}_2$ and a secret integer s, and publishes P and $P_{\mathrm{pub}} = sP$. The identities of users A and B give rise to points $Q_A, Q_B \in \mathbb{G}_1$ (see Boneh and Franklin [3] for details about identity-based cryptography using pairings) and the trusted authority gives them sQ_A and sQ_B respectively.

The key agreement protocol is as follows. User A chooses a random integer a and transmits $T_A = aP$ to B. Similarly, user B transmits $T_B = bP$ to A. Both users can compute the common key

$$K = e(aQ_B + bQ_A, P_{\mathrm{pub}})$$

for example user A computes $e(aQ_B, P_{\text{pub}})e(sQ_A, T_B)$. In practice, the key is derived from K using some key derivation function, which in this case we take to be the trace.

The bit security of this key-exchange protocol can be studied and results analogous to those above can be obtained. Suppose $\mathcal{O}_k$ is an oracle such that, for any $a, b, c \in [0, l-1]$, on input

$$(P, aP, bP, cP, Q_A, Q_B)$$

outputs $\text{MSB}_{k,p}(\text{Tr}(\vartheta e(aQ_B + bQ_A, cP)))$ for some fixed $\vartheta \in \mathbb{F}_{p^m}^*$. Let $\alpha = \vartheta e(aQ_B + bQ_A, P_{\text{pub}})$. Repeatedly choose random $d \in [0, l-1]$ and call the oracle $\mathcal{O}_k$ on

$$(P, T_A, T_B + dP, P_{\text{pub}}, Q_A, Q_B).$$

The oracle responses are of the form

$$\text{MSB}_{k,p}(\text{Tr}(\alpha t)) \quad \text{where} \quad t = e(Q_A, P_{\text{pub}})^d$$

and analogues of Theorems 1 and 2 are obtained.

5   Remarks

We remark that it would be valuable to extend our results (as well as the results of [4,5,6,11,12,14,17]) to case when the oracle works correctly only on a polynomially large fraction of all possible inputs. Unfortunately, at the moment it is not clear how to adjust the ideas of [6], underlying all further developments in this area, to work with such "unreliable" oracles.

It has been shown in [11] that for almost all primes p an analogue of Lemma 1 holds for subgroups $\mathcal{G} \in \mathbb{F}_p^*$ of cardinality $|\mathcal{G}| \geq p^\rho$, for any fixed $\rho > 0$. It is not immediately clear how to extend the underlying number theoretic techniques to extension fields, although this question definitely deserves further attention (see also the discussion in [25]).

Finally, we recall a different kind of bit security result (see [14]) concerning the value of the pairing $e(R, P)$ for an *unknown* point R, in case when $m = 1$ (although it is quite possible that the whole approach of [14] can be generalised to extension fields). In particular, if $l \geq p^{1/2+\rho}$ is a divisor of $p - 1$, where $\rho > 0$ is fixed, then an oracle producing about $(1 - \rho/5) \log p$ most significant bits of $e(R, P)$ for an *unknown* point $R \in \mathbb{G}_1$ and a *given* point $P \in \mathbb{G}_2$, can be used to construct a polynomial time algorithm to compute $e(R, P)$ exactly. It would be interesting to understand cryptographic implications of this result.

Acknowledgements. The authors are grateful to Kenny Paterson for several helpful comments.

References

1. S. Al-Riyami and K. G. Paterson, 'Tripartite Authenticated Key Agreement Protocols from Pairings', IMA Conference on Cryptography and Coding, *Lect. Notes in Comp. Sci.*, Springer-Verlag, Berlin, **2898** (2003), 332–359.
2. R. C. Baker and G. Harman, 'Shifted primes without large prime factors', *Acta Arithm.*, **83** (1998), 331–361.
3. D. Boneh and M. Franklin, 'Identity-based encryption from the Weil pairing', *SIAM J. Comp.*, **32** (2003), 586–615.
4. D. Boneh, S. Halevi and N. A. Howgrave-Graham, 'The modular inversion hidden number problem', *Proc. Asiacrypt'2001, Lect. Notes in Comp. Sci.*, Springer-Verlag, Berlin, **2248** (2001), 36–51.
5. D. Boneh and I. E. Shparlinski, 'On the unpredictability of bits of the elliptic curve Diffie–Hellman scheme', *Proc. Crypto'2001, Lect. Notes in Comp. Sci.*, Springer-Verlag, Berlin, **2139** (2001), 201–212.
6. D. Boneh and R. Venkatesan, 'Hardness of computing the most significant bits of secret keys in Diffie–Hellman and related schemes', *Proc. Crypto'1996, Lect. Notes in Comp. Sci.*, Springer-Verlag, Berlin, **1109** (1996), 129–142.
7. G. Frey and H.-G. Rück, 'A remark concerning m-divisibility and the discrete logarithm in the divisor class group of curves', *Math. Comp.*, **62** (1994), 865–874.
8. S. D. Galbraith, 'Supersingular curves in cryptography', *Proc. Asiacrypt'2001, Lect. Notes in Comp. Sci.*, Springer-Verlag, Berlin, **2248** (2001), 495–513.
9. M. Goldman, M. Näslund and A. Russell, 'Complexity bounds on general hard-core predicates', *J. Cryptology*, **14** (2001), 177–195.
10. M. I. González Vasco and M. Näslund, 'A survey of hard core functions', *Proc. Workshop on Cryptography and Computational Number Theory*, Singapore 1999, Birkhäuser, 2001, 227–256.
11. M. I. González Vasco and I. E. Shparlinski, 'On the security of Diffie–Hellman bits', *Proc. Workshop on Cryptography and Computational Number Theory*, Singapore 1999, Birkhäuser, 2001, 257–268.
12. M. I. González Vasco and I. E. Shparlinski, 'Security of the most significant bits of the Shamir message passing scheme', *Math. Comp.*, **71** (2002), 333–342.
13. J. Håstad and M. Näslund, 'The security of individual RSA and discrete log bits', *J. of the ACM*, (to appear).
14. N. A. Howgrave-Graham, P. Q. Nguyen and I. E. Shparlinski, 'Hidden number problem with hidden multipliers, timed-release crypto and noisy exponentiation', *Math. Comp.*, **72** (2003), 1473–1485.
15. A. Joux, 'A one round protocol for tripartite Diffie–Hellman', *Proc. ANTS-4, Lect. Notes in Comp. Sci.*, Springer-Verlag, Berlin, **1838** (2000), 385–393.
16. A. Joux, 'The Weil and Tate pairings as building blocks for public key cryptosystems', *Proc. ANTS-5, Lect. Notes in Comp. Sci.*, Springer-Verlag, Berlin, **2369** (2002), 20–32.
17. W.-C. W. Li, M. Näslund and I. E. Shparlinski, 'The hidden number problem with the trace and bit security of XTR and LUC', *Proc. Crypto'2002, Lect. Notes in Comp. Sci.*, Springer-Verlag, Berlin, **2442** (2002), 433-448.
18. R. Lidl and H. Niederreiter, *Finite fields*, Cambridge University Press, Cambridge, 1997.
19. V. Miller, 'Short programs for functions on curves', *Preprint*, 1986.
20. A. J. Menezes, T. Okamoto and S. A. Vanstone, 'Reducing elliptic curve logarithms to logarithms in a finite field', *IEEE Trans. Inf. Theory*, **39** (1993) 1639–1646.

21. K. Rubin and A. Silverberg, 'Supersingular abelian varieties in cryptology', *Proc. Crypto'2002, Lect. Notes in Comp. Sci.*, Springer-Verlag, Berlin, **2442** (2002) 336–353.

22. R. Sakai, K. Ohgishi and M. Kasahara, 'Cryptosystems based on pairing', Proc. of SCIS '00, Okinawa, Japan, 2000.

23. C. P. Schnorr, 'Security of almost all discrete log bits', *Electronic Colloq. on Comp. Compl.*, Univ. of Trier, **TR98-033** (1998), 1–13.

24. M. Scott and P. S. L. M. Barreto, 'Compressed pairings', Cryptology ePrint Archive, Report 2004/032.

25. I. E. Shparlinski, 'On the generalized hidden number problem and bit security of XTR', *Proc. AAECC-14, Lect. Notes in Comp. Sci.*, Springer-Verlag, Berlin, **2227** (2001), 268–277.

26. N. P. Smart, 'An identity based authenticated key agreement protocol based on the Weil pairing', *Electronics Letters*, **38** (2002), 630–632.

27. E. R. Verheul, 'Evidence that XTR is more secure than supersingular elliptic curve cryptosystems', *Proc. Eurocrypt'2001, Lect. Notes in Comp. Sci.*, Springer-Verlag, Berlin, **2045** (2001), 195–210.

Weak Property of Malleability in NTRUSign

SungJun Min[1]*, Go Yamamoto[2], and Kwangjo Kim[3]

[1] National Computerization Agency (NCA),
NCA Bldg, 77, Mugyo-Dong, Jung-Gu, Seoul, Korea,
sjmin@nca.or.kr
[2] NTT, Information Sharing Platform Laboratories,
1-1, Hikarinooka, Yokosuka, Kanagawa, Japan,
yamamo@isl.ntt.co.jp
[3] International Research center for Information Security (IRIS),
Information and Communications University (ICU),
119, Munjiro, Yuseong-Gu, Daejeon, 305-714, Korea,
kkj@icu.ac.kr

Abstract. A new type of signature scheme, called NTRUSign, based on solving the approximately closest vector problem in a NTRU lattice was proposed at CT-RSA'03. However no security proof against chosen messages attack has been made for this scheme. In this paper, we show that NTRUSign signature scheme contains the weakness of malleability. From this, one can derive new valid signatures from any previous message-signature pair which means that NTRUSign is not secure against strongly existential forgery. Finally, we propose a simple technique to avoid this flaw in NTRUSign scheme.

Keywords: NTRUSign, Digital Signature Scheme, Strong Existential Forgery, Malleability, Centered Norm

1 Introduction

Recently, Hoffstein *et al.* introduced a new type of authentication and digital signature scheme called NTRUSign [7] at CT-RSA'03. While traditional signature schemes are based on well-known hard problem such as factorization or discrete log problem, the hard problem underlying NTRUSign is to find the approximately shortest(or closest) vectors in a certain lattice, called NTRU lattice L_h^{NT}. In this scheme, the signer uses secret knowledge to find a point in the NTRU lattice close to the given point. He/She then exploits this approximate solution to the closest vector problem as his signature. One of the significant advantages is the fast operation: NTRU-based algorithms, for example, executes hundreds of times faster while providing the same security than competing algorithms such as RSA. In this paper, we claim that the NTRUSign signature scheme, however, does not contain one of important cryptographic properties

---

* This work was done while the author was with Information and Communications University(ICU).

H. Wang et al. (Eds.): ACISP 2004, LNCS 3108, pp. 379–390, 2004.
© Springer-Verlag Berlin Heidelberg 2004

that the signature scheme should guarantee, *non-malleability*. We first suggest a deterministic attack method how an attacker can generate new valid signatures from the previously signed message. Next, we propose a simple technique to avoid this attack.

History of NTRUSign scheme. Since the advent of NTRU encryption scheme based on a hard mathematical problem of finding short vectors in certain lattices in 1996, several related signature schemes such as NSS [10] and R-NSS [6] have been proposed. A fast authentication and digital signature scheme called NSS, based on the same underlying hard problem and using keys of the same form, was presented at Eurocrypt 2001 [10]. However, this scheme was broken by Mironov and Gentry *et al*, see [3,12]. In their Eurocrypt presentation, the authors of NSS sketched a revised version of NSS (called R-NSS) and published it in the preliminary cryptographic standard document EESS [18]. Although it seemed that R-NSS was significantly stronger than the initial version(NSS), it was proved that the key recovery attack could be mounted by Gentry and Szydlo [4]. The source of these weaknesses about NSS and R-NSS was an incomplete linking of the NSS method with the approximate closest vector problem in the NTRU lattice. In other words, the weaknesses of NSS and R-NSS arose from the fact that the signer did not possess a complete basis of short vectors for the NTRU lattice L_h^{NT}. Later on, Hoffstein *et al.* proposed a new NTRU based signature scheme called NTRUSign. Unlike the old signature schemes, the link in NTRUSign between the signature and the underlying approximate closest vector problem is clear and direct: the signer must solve an "approximate CVP problem" in the lattice *i.e.*, produce a lattice point that is sufficiently close to a message digest point. This paper, however, describes a weakness in NTRUSign: from any given message-signature pair, one can derive many different signatures of the same message, thus it is *malleable*.

Impact of malleability. If a signature scheme is malleable, we can derive another signature of the message from any message-signature pair. In this case, we cannot distinguish it from the original one generated by who knows the secret key, which can be in practice regarded as a forgery. Although such a weakness does not allow the attacker to change the message string, this forgery shows that the signature scheme cannot be used for all kinds of applications. For example, if one would like to apply it to electronic cash, finding a second valid signature for a given bill should be impossible. Also, an entity receiving the message-signature pairs (m, s) and (m, s') such that $s \neq s'$ at the same time, neither s nor s' will be accepted as a valid signature for the message m by him. If a legitimate signer wants to assert s as his/her own signature for the message m, then he/she should exhibit his/her private key, which is a negative property.

Our Contributions. In this paper, we show how a passive adversary observing only a valid message-signature pair can generate another signature on the same message. The main idea of this forgery is to use specific polynomials of which norm value is zero. Although this weakness might be overlooked for some applications, NTRUSign is not secure in the non-malleability sense against known message attack. The notion of this security is well described in [16]. Finally we propose a simple technique to avoid our proposed attack.

Organization. The rest of this paper is organized as follows: In Section 2, we briefly describe the NTRUSign signature scheme. We do not give all the technical and theoretical details for the functions used in the scheme. Only the general construction is described here.

In Section 3 we show how an attacker can forge an additional signature for a message previously signed using some specific polynomials, and then in Section 4, we introduce a simple method to avoid this weakness. Finally, we make concluding remarks in Section 5.

2   Description of NTRUSign Algorithm

In this section, we briefly describe NTRUSign digital signature scheme. As NTRU encryption scheme, basic operations take place in the quotient polynomial ring $R = \mathbb{Z}[x]/(x^N - 1)$, where N is the security parameter. A polynomial $a(x) \in R$ (shortly, a) can be presented by a vector $\mathbf{a}$ of its coefficients as follows:

$$\mathbf{a} = \sum_{i=0}^{N-1} a_i x^i = (a_0, a_1, \cdots, a_{N-1}).$$

For the sake of simplicity, we will use the same notation for the polynomial $a(x)$ and the vector $\mathbf{a}$. The product of two polynomials a and b in R is simply calculated by $a * b = c$, where the k-th coefficient c_k is

$$c_k = \sum_{i=0}^{k} a_i b_{k-i} + \sum_{i=k+1}^{N-1} a_i b_{N+k-i} = \sum_{i+j \equiv k \pmod{N}} a_i b_j.$$

In some steps, NTRUSign uses the quotient ring $R_q = \mathbb{Z}_q[x]/(x^N - 1)$, where the coefficients are reduced by modulo q, where q is typically a power of 2, for example 128. The multiplicative group of units in R_q is denoted by R_q^*. The inverse polynomial of $a \in R_q^*$ is denoted by a^{-1}. If a polynomial a has all coefficients chosen from the set $\{0, 1\}$, we call this a *binary* polynomial.

The security of NTRUSign scheme is based on the approximately closest vector problem in a certain lattice, called NTRU lattice. In this scheme, the signer can sign a message by demonstrating the ability to solve the approximately closest vector problem reasonably well for the point generated from a hashed message in a given space.

The basic idea is as follows: The signer's private key is a short basis for an NTRU lattice and his public key is a much longer basis for the same lattice. The signature on a digital document is a vector in the lattice with two properties:

- The signature is attached to the document being signed.
- The signature demonstrates an ability to solve a general closest vector problem in the lattice.

NTRUSign digital signature scheme works as follows:

System Parameters
1. N: a (prime) dimension.
2. q: a modulus.
3. d_f, d_g: key size parameters.
4. *NormBound*: a bound parameter of verification.

Key Generation
A signer creates his public key h and the corresponding private key $\{(f,g),(F,G)\}$ as follows:
1. Choose binary polynomials f and g with d_f 1's and d_g 1's, respectively.
2. Compute the public key $h \equiv f^{-1} * g \pmod q$.
3. Compute small polynomials (F,G) satisfying $f * G - g * F = q$.

Signing Step
A signer generates his signature s on the digital document D as follows:
1. Obtain the polynomials (m_1, m_2) mod q for the document D by using the public hash function.
2. Write

$$G * m_1 - F * m_2 = A + q * B,$$

$$-g * m_1 + f * m_2 = a + q * b,$$

where A and a have coefficients between $-q/2$ and $q/2$.
3. Compute polynomials s and t as

$$s \equiv f * B + F * b \pmod q,$$

$$t \equiv g * B + G * b \pmod q.$$

Here, a vector $(s,t) \in L_h^{NT}$ is very close to $m = (m_1, m_2)$.
4. The polynomial s is the signature on the digital document D for the public key h.

Verification Step
For a given signature s and document D, a verifier should do the following:
1. Hash the document D to recreate (m_1, m_2) mod q.
2. Using the signature s and public key h, compute the corresponding polynomial

$$t \equiv s * h \pmod q,$$

which becomes exactly the same as the polynomial $g * B + G * b \pmod q$. (Note that (s,t) is a point in the NTRU lattice L_h^{NT}.)

3. Compute the distance from (s,t) to (m_1, m_2) and verify that this value is smaller than the *NormBound* parameter. In other words, check that

$$\| s - m_1 \|^2 + \| t - m_2 \|^2 \leq NormBound^2,$$

where the norm($\| \cdot \|$) is a centered norm.

NTRUSign algorithm uses the centered norm concept instead of Euclidean norm in verification step to measure the size of an element $a \in R$.

Definition 1. *Let $a(x)$ be a polynomial in ring $R = \mathbb{Z}[x]/(x^N - 1)$. Then the centered norm of $a(x)$ is defined by*

$$\| a(x) \|^2 = \sum_{i=0}^{N-1}(a_i - \mu_a)^2 = \sum_{i=0}^{N-1}a_i{}^2 - \frac{1}{N}(\sum_{i=0}^{N-1}a_i)^2,$$

where $\mu_a = \dfrac{1}{N}\sum_{i=0}^{N-1}a_i$ is the average of the coefficients of $a(x)$.

The centered norm of an n-tuple $(a_1, a_2, \cdots, a_n)$ with $a_1, a_2, \cdots, a_n \in R$ can be defined by this formula

$$(\| (a_1, a_2, \cdots, a_n) \|)^2 = \| a_1 \|^2 + \| a_2 \|^2 + \cdots + \| a_n \|^2 .$$

Note that the signature on D is a vector (s,t) in NTRU lattice L_h^{NT}, which is very close to m. To solve an approximately closest vector problem in the lattice, a signer uses a "short basis" defined as below:

Definition 2. *A basis $\{(f,g),(F,G)\}$ is called a short basis in L_h^{NT} if*

$$\| f \|, \| g \| = O(\sqrt{N}), \text{ and } \| F \|, \| G \| = O(N).$$

The signing process of NTRUSign may be explained by the following matrix equation, which shows that the role of a signer is to find approximate solution about the closest vector problem by using his short basis $\{(f,g),(F,G)\}$:

$$(s\,t) = (B\,b)\begin{pmatrix} f & g \\ F & G \end{pmatrix} = \left\lfloor (m_1\ m_2)\begin{pmatrix} G/q & -g/q \\ -F/q & f/q \end{pmatrix}\right\rceil\begin{pmatrix} f & g \\ F & G \end{pmatrix}$$

$$= \left\lfloor (m_1\ m_2)\begin{pmatrix} f & g \\ F & G \end{pmatrix}^{-1}\right\rceil\begin{pmatrix} f & g \\ F & G \end{pmatrix}$$

A valid signature demonstrates that the signer knows a lattice point that is within *NormBound* of the message digest vector m. Clearly, the smaller that *NormBound* is set, the more difficult it will be for an attacker, without knowledge of the private key, to solve this problem. The designers recommend that the suggested parameters $(N, q, d_f, d_g, NormBound) = (251, 128, 73, 71, 300)$ offer security at least as strong as 1,024 bit RSA [8].

3   Weakness in NTRUSign

In this section we describe that the NTRUSign is strong existential forgeable, sometimes this notion is called as malleable. Strong existential forgeability for a given signature scheme means that one can create a message-signature pair that has never been observed by the signer [16]. A different signature for a once legitimately signed message can be regarded as a forgery. In practice, this forgery shows that the NTRUSign scheme cannot be used for all kinds of applications. For example, in electronic cash system, finding another valid signature for a given bill should be impossible. Thus the application area of this scheme is limited, because a digital signature scheme is selected according to both its security level and the context of use.

Now we will describe how we can generate a valid signature different from a previous valid signature for a given message. Remind that NTRUSign signature scheme uses the centered norm concept in verification step. The centered norm has quasi-multiplicative property, that is, $\| a(x) * b(x) \| \approx \| a(x) \| * \| b(x) \|$ for random polynomials $a(x)$ and $b(x)$ in R, which was well discussed in [9]. The properties of the centered norm will be employed to induce a new signature from a given signature without knowing the private key.

The following lemma describes the centered norm properties:

Lemma 1. *Let R be a quotient polynomial ring $R = \mathbb{Z}[x]/(x^N - 1)$. Then*

(i) In $R_q = \mathbb{Z}_q[x]/(x^N - 1)$, there exist exactly q polynomials $\alpha(x)$ such that $\| \alpha(x) \| = 0$.
(ii) If $\| \alpha(x) \| = 0$, then $\| \alpha(x) * \beta(x) \| = 0$ for every polynomial $\beta(x) \in R$.

Proof. (i) It is obvious that $\alpha_0 = \alpha_1 = \cdots = \alpha_{N-1}$ for $\alpha_i \in (-q/2, q/2]$ if and only if $\sum_{i=0}^{N-1} (a_i - \mu_a)^2 = 0$ where $\mu_a = \frac{1}{N} \sum_{i=0}^{N-1} a_i$, namely $\| a(x) \| = 0$.

(ii) From the result of (i) we can know that all coefficients of α are the same, say $\alpha = (\alpha_0, \alpha_0, \cdots, \alpha_0)$. Then, clearly the k-th coefficient of $\alpha * \beta$ is $\sum_{i=0}^{N-1}(\alpha_0 \beta_{k-i}) + \sum_{i=k+1}^{N-1}(\alpha_0 \beta_{N+k-i}) = \alpha_0(\beta_0 + \cdots + \beta_k + \beta_{k+1} + \beta_{N-1}) = \alpha_0 * \beta$, and so are the other coefficients of $\alpha * \beta$ the same. Again by applying to (i), we complete the proof of this lemma.   □

We call these q polynomials satisfying $\| \alpha(x) \| = 0$ *annihilating polynomial*. These annihilating polynomials makes the NTRUSign algorithm to be malleable.

Hoffstein *et al.* argued that forgery of a signature in NTRUSign is equivalent to solve an approximately closest vector problem in high dimension for the class of NTRU lattices. It seems to be true if we do not consider the stronger attack model. Historically, Goldwasser, Micali and Rivest [5] introduced the notion of existential forgery against chosen-message attack for public key signature scheme. This notion has become the *de facto* security definition for digital signature algorithm, against which all new signature algorithms are measured. In this scenario, an adversary with access to the public key of the scheme and to a signing oracle, should not be able to forge a valid signature for some new message or for a message of his choice(existential forgery and selective forgery, respectively). An even stronger requirement called the non-malleability, or strong unforgeability, also forbids an adversary to forge an additional signature for a message which might already have been signed by the oracle [16]. We can see more detail security notions for digital signature scheme and the relation between them in [5, 14].

Now we will show that one can easily generate a message-signature pair that has never been observed by the signer. To create additional valid signatures we use the following observations: Note that all coefficients of polynomials are reduced by modulo q.

Remark 1. Let α be an annihilating polynomial. Then $\| r + \alpha \| \approx \| r \|$ for randomly chosen polynomial $r \in R$.

If both "reduced form" and "not reduced form" of polynomial $r + \alpha$ are equal, then the centered norm values of $\| r \|$ and $\| r + \alpha \|$ are exactly the same. The differences between $\| r + \alpha \|$ and $\| r \|$ are caused from only the gap failure. The concepts of gapping and wrapping failure are presented in [15]. We have implemented the above remark with the suggested parameters 1,000 times for each α using Mathematica 4.2. It is clear that as the coefficients of annihilating polynomial gets smaller, the probability of having the same norm gets higher. When the coefficient of α is ± 1 or ± 2, our experiment shows that each probability which two centered norm values are exactly the same becomes 0.15 and 0.015 approximately. Figure 1 describes the distribution of distances between $\| r + \alpha \|$ and $\| r \|$ for random polynomial $r \in R$, where the x-axis denotes the integer coefficient α_i of an annihilating polynomial and y-axis denotes the average distance between $\| r + \alpha \|$ and $\| r \|$ for random polynomial r.

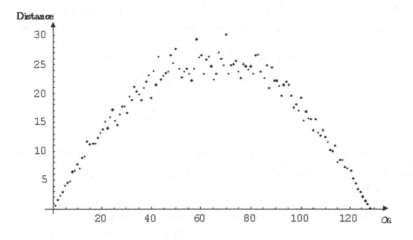

Fig. 1. Distance between $\| r + \alpha \|$ and $\| r \|$

We will see some results induced from the properties of an annihilating polynomial. For any polynomial $f = (f_0, f_1, \cdots, f_{N-1}) \in R$, $\mathcal{V}(f)$ denotes the sum of all coefficients of f modulus q, that is,

$$\mathcal{V}(f) = f(1) = \sum_{i=0}^{N-1} f_i \ (\mathrm{mod}\ q) \in \mathbb{Z}_q. \tag{1}$$

For any $f \in R$, the product $f * \alpha$ can be presented by $\mathcal{V}(f)\alpha$, where α is an annihilating polynomial (See the proof of Lemma 1.).

From (1) it is trivial that $\mathcal{V}$ has the following properties:

Lemma 2. *Let f and g be two polynomials in R.*

(i) $\mathcal{V}(f)\mathcal{V}(g) \equiv \mathcal{V}(f * g)$ (mod q).
(ii) $\mathcal{V}(f^{-1}) \equiv \mathcal{V}(f)^{-1}$ (mod q) if f has an inverse in R_q.

Proof. By definition of $\mathcal{V}$, we have

$$\mathcal{V}(f)\mathcal{V}(g) \equiv f(1)g(1) = (f * g)(1)$$
$$\equiv \mathcal{V}(f * g) \ (\mathrm{mod}\ q).$$

Obviously $\mathcal{V}(f^{-1})\mathcal{V}(f) \equiv \mathcal{V}(f^{-1} * f) \equiv \mathcal{V}(1) \equiv 1$ (mod q), hence $\mathcal{V}(f^{-1}) \equiv \mathcal{V}(f)^{-1}$ (mod q). □

Assume that one chooses two polynomial pair (f, g), where f has an inverse in R_q. If there exists somewhat small integer $\alpha_0 \in (-q/2, q/2]$ satisfying $\alpha_0 \mathcal{V}(f)^{-1}\mathcal{V}(g)$ (mod q) is also small, then we can know that both polynomial $\alpha = (\alpha_0, \alpha_0, \cdots, \alpha_0)$ and $(f^{-1} * g) * \alpha$ are annihilating polynomials with somewhat small coefficients from Lemma 2.

Remark 2. In the suggested parameters $(d_f, d_g) = (73, 71)$ given in [8], one has $\mathcal{V}(f) = -55$ and $\mathcal{V}(g) = -57$. In this case one can choose $\alpha = 8\sum_{i=0}^{N-1} x^i$ so that

$$h * \alpha \ (\mathrm{mod}\ q) = \mathcal{V}(h)\alpha = \mathcal{V}(f^{-1} * g) * \alpha$$
$$= \mathcal{V}(f)^{-1}\mathcal{V}(g) * \alpha$$
$$= -8 \sum_{i=0}^{N-1} x^i.$$

For a given signature $(s, t) \in L_h^{NT}$ generated under the suggested parameters, we take $s' = s + \alpha$ (mod q), where $\alpha = 8\sum_{i=0}^{N-1} x^i$. Then the corresponding signature pair t' is

$$t' = s' * h \ (\mathrm{mod}\ q) = s * h + \alpha * h \ (\mathrm{mod}\ q)$$
$$= t - 8 \sum_{i=0}^{N-1} x^i \ (\mathrm{mod}\ q).$$

At this time, we can expect that both $\parallel s - m_1 \parallel$ and $\parallel t - m_2 \parallel$ are small. Moreover, it is plausible that the small number of their coefficients are out of the range $(-64 + 8, 64 - 8]$. Form these reasons, the new lattice point $(s', t') = (s + 8\sum_{i=0}^{N-1} x^i, t - 8\sum_{i=0}^{N-1} x^i)$ will be another valid signature with high probability. Simply speaking, if one has $s - m_1$ without any coefficients greater than 56 and $t - m_2$ without any coefficients less than -55, then one can have the following equation exactly:

$$\parallel s' - m_1 \parallel^2 + \parallel t' - m_2 \parallel^2 = \parallel s - m_1 \parallel^2 + \parallel t - m_2 \parallel^2$$
$$\leq NormBound^2,$$

which means that (s', t') is always another valid signature.

A numerical experimental result shows that one has much more chance to succeed in the proposed attack: we examine a set P that consists of 128,000 elements from $\mathbb{Z}_{128}[x]/(x^{251} - 1)$ generated in such a way that all coefficients are randomly chosen from normal distribution with uniformly chosen means $\mu \in (-64, 64]$ and a fixed standard deviation $\sigma = \sqrt{NormBound^2/N} \approx 18.9$. For two sets

$$P' = \{s \in P \mid \parallel s \parallel^2 < 300^2\} \text{ and } P'' = \{s \in P' \mid \parallel s + 8\sum_{i=0}^{N-1} x^i \parallel^2 < 300^2\},$$

we obtained the result that the set P' consists of 20,650 distinct elements and that P' and P'' coincide exactly.

We implemented the full NTRUSign signature scheme as described in [8] and [17] with suggested parameters using GNU MP version 4.1.2. Our experiment illustrates that the proposed forgery s' almost always succeeds for given message document D and a valid signature s. Table 1 depicts the approximate probability that new pair $(s', t') = (s + \alpha, t + h * \alpha) \pmod q$ would be another signature for a given valid signature (s, t). In Table 1, note that α_i denotes the coefficient of an annihilating polynomial α and two sets A and B mean as follows:

$$A = \{(s, t) \in L_h^{NT} \mid (s, t) \text{ is a valid signature for given message } m\}$$

and

$$B = \{(s', t') \in L_h^{NT} \mid (s', t') \text{ is a valid forged signature for given message } m\},$$

respectively.

Remark 3. The EESS#1 standard introduces the centering method in the computation of centered norm [17,18]. This centering method means that if the center of t not reduced modulo q is near to $\frac{q}{2}$ or $-\frac{q}{2}$, then the coefficients of t are properly shifted before being reduced modulo q. Because this centering method removes any effect of wrapping, if we use this method, then our analysis always holds.

Table 1. Approximate forgery probability when $N = 251, q = 128$

α_i	$Success\ Prob(B|A)$
1	0.836
2	0.644
$\vdots$	$\vdots$
7	0.707
8	0.889
9	0.852
$\vdots$	$\vdots$
63	0.167
64	0.165

4   Repairing NTRUSign

In this section we present a simple way in order to avoid the weakness in the NTRUSign signature scheme. The strategy for repairing NTRUSign is to make the signing transformation one-to-one corresponding on a given secret key. It can be achieved by adding an annihilating polynomial in the signing step. Our idea is to make the most significant coefficient (*i.e.*, the coefficient of x^{N-1}) of the signature s obtained from the original NTRUSign to be zero. If the distance between the new signature s' computed by this process and the given point is not as close as to the expected distance (*i.e.*, $NormBound$), then we simply add the annihilating polynomial $\sum_{i=0}^{N-1} x^i$ to the signature s' until it becomes to a valid signature.

The repaired version of NTRUSign scheme is as follows:

Signing Signer generates his signature s' on the digital document D

INPUT: private key $\{(f,g),(F,G)\}$ and hashed message (m_1, m_2)
OUTPUT: valid signature s'

1. Obtain the signature s from the original NTRUSign.
2. Set $s' \longleftarrow s - s_{N-1} \sum_{i=0}^{N-1} x^i \pmod{q}$.
3. While $\| s' - m_1 \|^2 + \| t' - m_2 \|^2 > NormBound^2$ do the following:
   3.1. Set $s' \longleftarrow s' + \sum_{i=0}^{N-1} x^i \pmod{q}$.
4. Return(s').

Verifying Receiver verifies the signature s'

INPUT: signature s' and sender's public key h
OUTPUT: "Accept" or "Reject"

1. Compute $t' = s' * h \pmod{q}$.
2. If $\| s' - m_1 \|^2 + \| t' - m_2 \|^2 > NormBound^2$, then return("Reject").
3. While $s'_{N-1} \neq 0$:

   3.1. Set $s' \longleftarrow s' - \sum_{i=0}^{N-1} x^i \pmod{q}$.
   3.2. If $\| s' - m_1 \|^2 + \| t' - m_2 \|^2 \leq NormBound^2$, then return("Reject").
4. Return("Accept").

It is obvious that our modification does not degenerate the security of the original NTRUSign scheme. Actually two problems based on original NTRUSign and repaired NTRUSign are computationally equivalent. Although our proposed attack cannot be applied for repaired NTRUSign anymore, we do not know whether the repaired version of NTRUSign is non-malleable. It is an open problem to prove that the repaired NTRUSign is non-malleable signature scheme.

5   Concluding Remarks

In this paper we described a weakness of NTRUSign digital signature scheme that can cause significant problems in some real applications if one is not aware of it. We showed that NTRUSign signature scheme is not secure in terms of strongly existential forgeable, thus it is malleable. This notion allows an adversary to find new signatures for a message of his choice, given a signature for this message. This forgery requires a specific polynomial with small coefficient satisfying its norm value equal to zero. Even if this forgery does not admit an adversary to change the message, NTRUSign scheme cannot be used for all applications. We also proposed a simple technique to repair the scheme.

References

1. H. Cohen, *A course in computational algebraic number theory*, GTM 138, Springer-Verlag, 1993.
2. L. Granboulan, "How to repair ESIGN", SCN'02, LNCS, Vol.2576, Springer-Verlag, pp.234-240, 2003.
3. C. Gentry, J. Jonsson, J. Stern, and M. Szydlo, "Cryptanalysis of the NTRU Signature Scheme (NSS) from Eurocrypt '01" Advances in Cryptology-Asiacrypt '01, LNCS, Vol.2248, Springer-Verlag, pp.123-131, 2001.
4. C. Gentry and M. Szydlo, "Cryptanalysis of the Revised NTRU Signature Scheme", Advances in Cryptology-Eurocrypt '02, LNCS, Vol.2332, pp.299-320, Springer-Verlag, 2002.
5. S. Goldwasser, S. Micali, and R. Rivest, "A Digital Signature Scheme Secure Against Adaptive Chosen-Message Attacks", SIAM Journal of Computing, pp.281-308, 1998.
6. J. Hoffstein, J. Pipher, and J. Silverman, "Enhanced Encoding and Verification Methods for the NTRU Signature Scheme", NTRU Technical Note #017, 2001. Available from http://www.ntru.com.

7. J. Hoffstein, N. Graham, J. Pipher, J. Silverman, and W. Whyte, "NTRUSign: Digital Signatures Using the NTRU Lattice Preliminary Draft 2", Available from http://www.ntru.com.
8. J. Hoffstein, N. Graham, J. Pipher, J. Silverman, and W. Whyte, "NTRUSign: Digital Signatures Using the NTRU Lattice", CT-RSA'03, LNCS, Vol.2612, Springer-Verlag, pp.122-140, 2003.
9. J. Hoffstein, J. Pipher, and J. Silverman, "NTRU: A Ring-Based Public Key Cryptosystem", in Algorithmic Number Theory (ANTS III), LNCS, Vol.1423, Springer-Verlag, pp.267-288, 1998.
10. J. Hoffstein, J. Pipher, and J. Silverman, "NSS: An NTRU Lattice-Based Signature Scheme", Advanced in Cryptology-Eurocrypt '01, LNCS, Vol.2045, Springer-Verlag, pp.123-137, 2001.
11. A. Joux and G. Martinet, "Some Weaknesses in Quartz Signature Scheme", NESSIE public reports, NES/DOC/ENS/WP5/026/1, 2003.
12. I. Mironov, "A Note on Cryptanalysis of the Preliminary Version of the NTRU Signature Scheme", IACR preprint server, Available from http://eprint.iacr.org/2001/005/.
13. T. Okamoto, E. Fujisaki, and H. Morita, "TSH-ESIGN: Efficient Digital Signature Scheme Using Trisection Size Hash (Submission to P1363a)", 1998.
14. D. Pointcheval and J. Stern, "Security Proofs for Signature Schemes", Advances in Cryptology-Proceedings of Eurocrypt '96, LNCS, Vol.1070, Springer-Verlag, pp.387-398, 1996.
15. J. Silverman, "Wraps, Gaps and Lattice Constants" NTRU Technical Report #011, 2001, Available from http://www.ntru.com.
16. J. Stern, D. Pointcheval, J. Lee, and N. Smart, "Flaws in Applying Proof Methodologies to Signature Schemes", Advances in Cryptology-Crypto'02, LNCS, Vol.2442, Springer-Verlag, pp.93-110, 2002.
17. Consortium for Efficient Embedded Security. Efficient Embedded Security Standard (EESS)#1: Implementation Aspects of NTRUEncrypt and NTRUSign. Available from http:// www.ceesstandards.org.
18. Consortium for Efficient Embedded Security. Efficient Embedded Security Standard (EESS)#1: Draft 2.0. Previously on http://www. ceesstandards.org.

Information Security Risk Assessment, Aggregation, and Mitigation

Arjen Lenstra[1] and Tim Voss[2]

[1] Citigroup, Information Security Services
Technische Universiteit Eindhoven
1 North Gate Road, Mendham, NJ 07945-3104, USA
arjen.lenstra@citigroup.com
[2] Citigroup, Information Security Services
750 Washington Boulevard, 7th floor, Stamford, CT 06902, USA
tim.voss@citigroup.com

Abstract. As part of their compliance process with the Basel 2 operational risk management requirements, banks must define how they deal with information security risk management. In this paper we describe work in progress on a new quantitative model to assess and aggregate information security risks that is currently under development for deployment. We show how to find a risk mitigation strategy that is optimal with respect to the model used and the available budget.

Keywords: Risk management, risk assessment, risk aggregation, risk mitigation, Basel 2, multiple-choice knapsack problem

1 Introduction

Given the constantly changing vulnerabilities that may threaten the security of a company's data, how does the company decide where to spend its Information Security (IS) budget to limit as much as possible the damaging consequences of attacks? Traditionally, this decision-making process is mostly left to 'experienced' staff whose judgment, intuition, and taste is relied upon.

With the upcoming required compliance with the Basel 2 agreements, a stricter approach has to be adopted: banks must be able to quantify their operational risk, devise proper ways to contain it, and reserve an adequate budget to absorb potential damages. Since securing its data assets is part of a bank's operations, this applies to IS risk management as well.

In this paper we discuss the issues that need to be addressed to fulfil the IS risk management requirements and describe work in progress on the solution that is currently under development for deployment. It is generally recognized that subjectivity is inherent to any risk assessment methodology. Thus, there is no single 'a priori' correct way to approach this problem: the choice of a model and its various parameters can never be fully objective. An unrelated requirement is that the proposed solution must allow a user-friendly interface: our extremely varied world-wide user community of local security officers and

H. Wang et al. (Eds.): ACISP 2004, LNCS 3108, pp. 391–401, 2004.

business managers must be able and willing to use it and have confidence in the outcomes.

The formalization provided by our prototype solution and the underlying model choices, combined with its easy-to-use automated reporting mechanism, takes away some of the subjectivity of the IS risk management process. The resulting quantitative approach is consistent on a company-wide basis, leads to results that are optimal with respect to the model's quantification parameters, and meets the needs and expectations of local and global security and business staff. The work described in the present paper represents work in progress and our prototype may not be ready to meet all requirements for compliance with the new regulations. For instance, a conscious decision was made not to include temporal dependencies in the prototype model, in order to make it easier to access and understand by uninitiated users. At a later stage, and depending on our findings with the present approach, refinements may be proposed and implemented (cf. Remark 4.4).

The IS risk management model proposed in this paper is very similar to the familiar *Annual Loss Expectancy* (ALE) approach to risk management [3]. What is novel in our paper is that we argue why an ALE-like approach is the only alternative for our type of application. Another innovative aspect of our paper is the way we derive the optimal risk mitigation strategy.

In Section 2 the IS risk management problem that is addressed in this paper is described in more detail. Various approaches to risk assessment and aggregation are reviewed in Section 3 along with their pros and cons with respect to our IS risk management application. This leads, in Section 4, to our quantitative IS risk management model. In Section 5 it is shown how the IS risk can be optimally contained in our model by solving a multiple-choice knapsack problem.

2   IS Risk Management

Our goal is to quantify the corporation's total Information Security risk and to find the most cost-effective way to contain the risk. We reiterate the comment made above that risk management is subjective. Different subjective choices made in the design or parameters of the model may lead to different risk containment strategies that may all be optimal with respect to their respective models. The best one can aim for is consistency within the model, overall soundness of the model, and an on average high level of user acceptance and appreciation of the results.

More in detail, from an IS perspective the situation is as follows. The corporation relies on a number of business processes. Each business process is exposed to a certain *current IS risk*. As a consequence, the corporation is exposed to the combined current IS risks of its business processes: the *current aggregated IS risk*. Each business process uses a number of applications, where a single application may be used by more than one process. For each application any number of IS vulnerabilities may be identified, and for each such vulnerability any number of IS threats may exist that realize that vulnerability. The IS threats are responsible for the corporation's aggregated IS risk. For each threat there may be any number of action plans of varying costs and degrees of effectiveness to counter the threat. Realization of an action plan against a threat mitigates the current IS risks of all processes using the application that was affected by that threat to their *residual IS risks*. The question is how, given a certain fixed budget, the action plans should be selected in such a way that the combination of all mitigated risks, the *residual aggregated IS risk*, is minimized.

Identification of vulnerabilities, threats, and action plans is done on a per application basis by the process owners, all relevant subject matter experts, and if possible representatives from the audit, risk, and review department. Because different processes may share applications, these application data may already have been provided by another business. It is the responsibility of the various businesses to coordinate and consolidate their views on their shared applications (cf. Remark 4.3).

A vulnerability would be, for instance, unencrypted customer data sent over a public network. One of the threats affecting that vulnerability would be an eavesdropper on the network, and each type of encryption of the data (symmetric using a system-wide shared key or using a customer-specific shared key, asymmetric, etc.) corresponds to an action plan countering the threat.

An important restriction on the solution to the above problem is that it has to work in a highly non-uniform environment. Central management is required (to be able to share vulnerability and threat data about shared applications), but data about business processes and applications must be entered by the businesses in many different countries on almost all continents. Inevitably the data will be colored by different regulatory and cultural influences. It is probably impossible to design a solution that is totally oblivious of all such effects and that works irrespective of the level of expertise or commitment of the staff that enters the data. But the robustness of the solution is strongly supported by making it easy to teach, understand, and use. We believe that the latter is a *conditio sine qua non* for an effective IS risk management solution for any even moderately large company. First, however, we have to discuss what we mean by risk.

3   Risk Assessment and Aggregation

The two most common approaches to risk assessment are qualitative risk analysis and quantitative risk analysis. The qualitative approach identifies events affecting a process (cf. *threats*) and a variety of corresponding controls that may mitigate the effects of the events (cf. *action plans*). Based on the perceived relational model between events and controls the risks are assessed and a strategy is decided upon, where it is often helpful to associate subjective qualitative rankings (such as High, Medium, Low) to the severity of the events or the effectiveness of the controls. As a result, the qualitative approach is mostly intuitive. It has the advantage that no probability data of past events are needed and that it leads to a reasonable decision model more or less built from scratch.

A qualitative approach may be applicable in simple situations where a vague indication suffices. For our IS risk management application it is not suitable. Its lack of precision makes consistency unachievable and, more importantly, the coarse-grained categorization makes aggregation virtually impossible and meaningless: what overall ranking should one assign the aggregate of four events with rankings High, Medium, Medium, and Low? And is it better or worse than all Medium? As a consequence, selecting an adequate set of action plans remains guesswork without any claims of mathematical rigor or soundness.

The quantitative approach employs as much as possible the distribution functions underlying the events and defines risk as a certain function of the distribution function. For instance, the distribution functions may be used to calculate the *Annual Loss Expectancy* for a single event, which can then be defined as the risk of the event. This type of risk can easily be aggregated over any number of events using standard statistical techniques. This is a consequence of the well known statistical fact that the expected value of a sum of distributions equals the sum of the expected values, irrespective of the type and potential dependencies or correlations of the distributions involved. This observation is important in circumstances where the precise distribution functions are not known but where expected losses can be estimated, since only the expected values are needed. Combined with projected costs and estimated effectiveness of controls, and defining risk as the expected loss, the best decision with respect to the residual aggregate expected losses, and as far as allowed by a given budget, can then be found using analytic methods.

In many industries risk analysis entails more than just minimization, with respect to a budget, of the expected losses. Although it is certainly relevant to know the expected losses, for capital management purposes it is also important to have accurate insight into the variability of the losses and in the *Value at Risk* (VaR), the probability that the losses exceed a given amount. But this more general quantitative approach (i.e., using more than just expected loss values) is not applicable in all situations. In the first place, it may be hard to collect so many data that the distribution functions can accurately be determined. This is in particular the case for so-called *heavy-tailed distributions* where high impact events occur with a very low probability; these typically occur in Information Security. It is illustrated by the observation that different companies often select different distribution functions for the same types of events [1]. Furthermore, collecting enough data to determine the distribution function underlying the behavior of a certain IS threat is most likely impossible given the fast and constantly changing IS environment. From this point of view IS risk management is quite different from more traditional insurance and stock portfolio risk management.

An additional problem of general quantitative risk analysis is risk aggregation. Although loss variation and VaR can be determined per event based on its distribution function, aggregation of these and similar risk related quantities is much more difficult than aggregation of the expected losses. To mention some of the complications this type of risk aggregation runs into: it requires knowledge of the dependencies and correlations among the events, the problems are notoriously ill-conditioned (thereby requiring many more data points before anything can be said with any degree of reliability), and the results can be surprisingly counter-intuitive. To illustrate the latter point, examples have been published of identically distributed but independent events for which the aggregated VaR is larger than the sum of the individual VaRs [2]. Strange phenomena of this sort take place in particular when the distributions involved are heavy-tailed. As noted above, events to which this may apply are hard to recognize in practice and their precise distribution functions are, in practice, impossible to determine.

To summarize, the qualitative model is mostly intuitive, lacks any degree or claim of precision, but has proved to be a valuable tool. The finer points of risk analysis do not enter into the picture in the qualitative approach, with the pleasant side-effect that the intricacies and pitfalls of general aggregated risk analysis are also avoided. But it is not suitable for our application. The quantitative model, when supported by adequate amounts of data, lays greater claims to accurateness. Its mathematical underpinnings may inspire attempts to address more general risk questions. This carries the inherent danger that over-precise results are obtained and relied upon, while losing sight of the fact that the underlying distributions cannot be assessed with sufficient certainty. For general aggregated risk problems the analysis can easily be led astray by intuition. In particular the presence of hard-to-recognize and hard-to-pin-down heavy-tailed distributions makes any type of intuitive guesswork irresponsible. This implies that quantitative risk analysis in its full generality cannot be used for our IS risk management application. That leaves a single alternative for our application, namely the most simpleminded quantitative risk analysis where risk is defined as an expected loss value. As argued above, that approach does not require the actual event distributions or their interactions, reasonable estimates for the expected losses suffice, and aggregation is nothing but simple summation. This is further explored in the next section.

Obviously, our approach still requires risk quantification, which is admittedly a hard problem, but the degree to which it is needed is as small as can reasonably be expected for a quantitative approach.

4   IS Risk Management Model

The conclusion from Section 3 is that if we want to have a definition of IS risk that is workable in a rapidly changing environment and that allows meaningful aggregation, then IS risk must be defined as a simple expected value of some sort. This leads to the following slightly more formal approach to the setup described in Section 2.

Remark 4.1 The description below is not identical to the prototype that is actually implemented, but contains all relevant details. A desire for simplicity and backward compatibility with systems that are familiar to our user community has led to some choices that may be unexpected. They have no effect on the principle of the model. Once enough data are available for analysis, it will be investigated to what extent the 'incongruent' aspects of the prototype design adversely affect the outcome. This may lead to small adaptations in later versions.

The IS risk faced by a business process are due to a breach of either confidentiality, integrity, or availability. For each of these categories the user enters an estimated loss amount, denoted for business process p by $L_c(p)$, $L_i(p)$, and $L_a(p)$, respectively. It is assumed that $\max(L_c(p), L_i(p), L_a(p)) > 0$.

The likelihood that these losses are actually incurred depends on the threats against the process (or rather: the threats realizing the vulnerabilities identified in the applications used in the process, cf. Section 2). To estimate this likelihood, the user characterizes a threat t by selecting three *type of threat* choices:

- **Source of threat**, with two possible choices indicating if the threat comes from a party *external* (Source$(t) = 1$) or *internal* (Source$(t) = 0.8$) to the company.
- **Access required for the threat**, with two possible choices indicating if *remote* access (Access$(t) = 1$) suffices to realize the threat or if *local* access (Access$(t) = 0.6$) is required.
- **Skill level required for the threat**, with four possible choices indicating the least level of skill required to realize the threat:
  - unstructured nontechnical (Skill$(t) = 1$);
  - unstructured technical (Skill$(t) = 0.9$);
  - structured nontechnical (Skill$(t) = 0.75$);
  - structured technical (Skill$(t) = 0.25$).

  A hacker, for instance, would be 'unstructured technical', but a script kiddie would be 'unstructured nontechnical'.

The *current likelihood indicator* $P(t)$ of threat t is defined as

$$P(t) = \text{Source}(t) * \text{Access}(t) * \text{Skill}(t).$$

These four numeric values remain hidden for the user. A qualitative ranking of $P(t)$, however, is presented to the user: High if $P(t) \geq 0.6$, Low if $P(t) < 0.2$, and Medium otherwise. This is done for compatibility and consistency with another business reporting tool (cf. Remark 4.1). The user gets the option to change the qualitative ranking; if done so the hidden likelihood indicator is changed: if the user specifies High and $P(t) < 0.6$, then replace $P(t)$ by 0.6; if the user specifies Medium and $P(t) \geq 0.6$, then replace $P(t)$ by $0.6 - \epsilon$ for some small $\epsilon > 0$; if the user specifies Medium and $P(t) < 0.2$, then replace $P(t)$ by 0.2; if the user specifies Low and $P(t) \geq 0.2$, then replace $P(t)$ by $0.2 - \epsilon$.

Remark 4.2 The various values and formulas used in the calculation of the likelihood indicators are not crucial to the model. They were chosen because of their ease of use and because the resulting qualitative rankings are consistent with the business tool referred to that the user community is already familiar with. They are by no means the unique values and formulas that achieve these goals: additive versions can be made to work equally well and simple table look up would be just as effective. Our approach follows [5]. See also Remark 4.4.

To indicate what *type of loss* can be inflicted by a threat, the user enters three bits $T_c, T_i, T_a \in \{0, 1\}$, where $T_c = 1$ if and only if the threat may cause a breach in confidentiality (similar for T_i and T_a with respect to integrity and availability, respectively). Note that these bits depend just on the threat and not on the process they may affect (cf. Remark 4.1).

Remark 4.3 As indicated in Section 2, data about threats (as above) and action plans (as below) should be agreed upon by all businesses using that application. One business may originally have entered threat data and action plans for an application, but other businesses affected by the same threat may review the data provided and propose changes. It is the responsibility of all parties involved to come to an agreement on the proper values. A welcome side-result of this interaction is corporate-wide consistency of (and agreement on) the 'quantification' of the threats and action plans.

Given these values entered by the user, the *current IS risk indicator of process p with respect to threat t* is defined as

$$\mathcal{R}_{\mathrm{cur}}(p, t) = \max(T_c L_c(p), T_i L_i(p), T_a L_a(p)) P(t).$$

Denoting by $\mathcal{S}(p)$ the set of applications used in process p and by $\mathcal{T}(A)$ the set of threats affecting application A, the *current IS risk indicator of process p* is defined as

$$\mathcal{R}_{\mathrm{cur}}(p) = \sum_{A \in \mathcal{S}(p)} \sum_{t \in \mathcal{T}(A)} \mathcal{R}_{\mathrm{cur}}(p, t).$$

If $\mathcal{P}$ is the set of all business processes, the corporation's overall (quantitative) *current aggregated IS risk indicator* is defined as

$$\mathcal{R}_{\mathrm{cur}} = \sum_{p \in \mathcal{P}} \mathcal{R}_{\mathrm{cur}}(p).$$

For an action plan α countering a threat t, denote by t_α the residual threat, i.e., what remains of t after action plan α has been carried out. For each action plan α countering a threat t the user characterizes the residual threat t_α by entering the three type of threat values Source(t_α), Access(t_α), and Skill(t_α), similar to Source(t), Access(t), and Skill(t) above except that they now represent the values after action plan α has been carried out. This results in the *residual likelihood indicator*

$$P(t_\alpha) = \mathrm{Source}(t_\alpha) * \mathrm{Access}(t_\alpha) * \mathrm{Skill}(t_\alpha).$$

Obviously, for an action plan to be any good, is should be the case that $P(t_\alpha) < P(t)$; it is assumed that this condition holds for all threats t and action plans α under consideration. As above, and using the same calculations, the qualitative ranking of $P(t_\alpha)$ is presented to the user, who has the option to change it, which may change the value $P(t_\alpha)$. If the resulting $P(t_\alpha)$ happens to be larger than

$P(t)$, which may happen if the user manually changed $P(t)$ or $P(t_\alpha)$ values, $P(t_\alpha)$ is set to $P(t)$; action plans for which this happens do not have to be further considered. The user also enters the *projected expense* $w(\alpha)$ of action plan α.

The type of loss bits are, in the present model, not affected by the action plans (cf. Remark 4.1). Therefore, the *residual IS risk indicator of process p with respect to threat t after action plan α is carried out* is defined as

$$\mathcal{R}_{\text{res}}(p, t_\alpha) = \max(T_c L_c(p), T_i L_i(p), T_a L_a(p)) P(t_\alpha).$$

We assume that either zero or at most a single action plan can be carried out per threat, that action plans cannot be carried out partially, and that different threats have different action plans. It is easily seen that this is not a restriction. In situations were it makes sense to consider a fractional combination of one or more action plans countering a single threat, one simply enters the relevant fractional combination of action plans with their partial or cumulative effects (and expenses) as an alternative action plan.

An *allowed set of action plans* is a set of action plans that contains at most one action plan per threat. Let $\mathcal{A}$ be an allowed set of action plans and let $w(\mathcal{A}) = \sum_{\alpha \in \mathcal{A}} w(\alpha)$ be the projected expense of $\mathcal{A}$. The *residual IS risk indicator of process p with respect to threat t after the action plans in $\mathcal{A}$ are carried out* is defined as

$$\mathcal{R}_{\text{res}}(p, t, \mathcal{A}) = \begin{cases} \mathcal{R}_{\text{cur}}(p, t) & \text{if } \mathcal{A} \text{ does not contain an action plan countering threat } t \\ \mathcal{R}_{\text{res}}(p, t_\alpha) & \text{if } \mathcal{A} \text{ contains action plan } \alpha \text{ countering threat } t \end{cases}$$

and the *residual IS risk indicator of process p under allowed action plan set $\mathcal{A}$* is defined as

$$\mathcal{R}_{\text{res}}(p, \mathcal{A}) = \sum_{A \in \mathcal{S}(p)} \sum_{t \in \mathcal{T}(A)} \mathcal{R}_{\text{res}}(p, t, \mathcal{A}).$$

Finally, the corporation's (quantitative) *residual aggregated IS risk indicator after allowed action plan set $\mathcal{A}$* is defined as

$$\mathcal{R}_{\text{res}}(\mathcal{A}) = \sum_{p \in \mathcal{P}} \mathcal{R}_{\text{res}}(p, \mathcal{A}).$$

Optimal risk mitigation consists of finding an allowed action plan set $\mathcal{A}$ that minimizes $\mathcal{R}_{\text{res}}(\mathcal{A})$. This is trivially solved by determining for each threat t the action plan α that minimizes $P(t_\alpha)$ (in case of conflict, select one), and by defining $\mathcal{A}$ as the set of those action plans (which will be allowed due to the construction). A more interesting problem is how to find an allowed action plan set $\mathcal{A}$ that minimizes $\mathcal{R}_{\text{res}}(\mathcal{A})$ under a budgetary constraint $w(\mathcal{A}) \leq W$ on $\mathcal{A}$'s projected expense. That problem is addressed in the next section.

Remark 4.4 The current and residual aggregated IS risk indicators $\mathcal{R}_{\text{cur}}(p)$ and $\mathcal{R}_{\text{res}}(p, \mathcal{A})$ for a process p and allowed action plan set $\mathcal{A}$ must not and cannot be interpreted as the expected loss amount for p before and after $\mathcal{A}$. Any interpretation of that sort would at the very least require introduction of a temporal dependency in the model. This may be done, if required, at a later stage. Similarly, a threat's likelihood indicator $P(t)$ should not immediately be interpreted as the probability that the threat is realized. It requires more threat related data and fine-tuning of the above parameter choices before the likelihood of a threat's occurrence can reliably be estimated based on the type of threat values. It may also be the case that for a reasonably accurate estimate more threat characteristics are required.

However, we are not convinced that the disadvantage of the introduction of any extra complications (a steeper learning curve) would be outweighed by the potential advantages. At present the $P(t)$, $P(t_\alpha)$, $\mathcal{R}_{\mathrm{cur}}(p,t)$, $\mathcal{R}_{\mathrm{cur}}(p)$, $\mathcal{R}_{\mathrm{res}}(p,t_\alpha)$, $\mathcal{R}_{\mathrm{res}}(p,t,\mathcal{A})$, and $\mathcal{R}_{\mathrm{res}}(p,\mathcal{A})$ values by themselves are simply not intended to be meaningful. What is relevant is the consistency that is achieved by this approach and the fact that the relative values are meaningful. That allows us to interpret terms such as $\mathcal{R}_{\mathrm{cur}}(p,t)$ as expected values (of some value, up to an unknown and irrelevant constant scaling factor) and thereby to aggregate them into a quantitative IS risk indicator using simple summation, as in the definitions of $\mathcal{R}_{\mathrm{cur}}(p)$, $\mathcal{R}_{\mathrm{res}}(p,\mathcal{A})$, $\mathcal{R}_{\mathrm{cur}}$, and $\mathcal{R}_{\mathrm{res}}(\mathcal{A})$. It also allows us to find an optimal allowed set of action plans under a budgetary constraint, as described in the next section. Note that also the values $\mathcal{R}_{\mathrm{cur}}$ and $\mathcal{R}_{\mathrm{res}}(\mathcal{A})$ by themselves are hardly meaningful. What is meaningful is the quantity

$$\frac{100(\mathcal{R}_{\mathrm{cur}} - \mathcal{R}_{\mathrm{res}}(\mathcal{A}))}{\mathcal{R}_{\mathrm{cur}}}$$

because it gives the percentage how much 'better' the situation is after carrying out the action plans in $\mathcal{A}$, with 0% indicating no improvement and 100% that there is no residual aggregated IS risk left (since $\mathcal{R}_{\mathrm{res}}(\mathcal{A}) = 0$).

Remark 4.5 It may be tempting to include a weighting mechanism in the IS risks to account for 'relative importance' of the various business processes. However, this may be done only if the weights are not correlated to the loss indicator values, because a correlation would undermine the soundness of the aggregation method. If risk is no longer defined as the expected value of a linear function of a loss indicator (as would be the case if loss indicator correlated weights are included), risk aggregation can no longer be done by summation. Correct aggregation would require the distribution functions underlying the threats and their correlation behavior, leading to numerous complications and pitfalls (cf. Section 3 and [2]) and, if those can be solved and avoided, respectively, to considerably more involved definitions of $\mathcal{R}_{\mathrm{cur}}(p)$, $\mathcal{R}_{\mathrm{res}}(p,\mathcal{A})$, $\mathcal{R}_{\mathrm{cur}}$, and $\mathcal{R}_{\mathrm{res}}(\mathcal{A})$. Weights that reflect the relative importance of businesses may be used if they are independent of the amount of loss the businesses may incur due to IS failures. Obviously, this is only meaningful if the same set of weights is used in $\mathcal{R}_{\mathrm{cur}}$ and $\mathcal{R}_{\mathrm{res}}(\mathcal{A})$. Our current model does not use weights. Using weights would be one way to include a temporal dependency in the model.

5 Optimal Risk Mitigation and Multiple-Choice Knapsacks

With notation and definitions as in Section 4 the risk mitigation under budget constraint problem is as follows:

$$\text{minimize } \mathcal{R}_{\text{res}}(\mathcal{A})$$

$$\text{subject to the condition that } w(\mathcal{A}) \leq \mathcal{W}$$

$$\text{and that } \mathcal{A} \text{ is an allowed action plan set.}$$

This is a multiple-choice knapsack problem, as defined in [4]. For ease of reference we present the straightforward translation from the above formulation to the framework from [4].

Let k be the number of threats (counted over all applications) and let N_i be the set of action plans for the ith threat, $i = 1, 2, \ldots, k$. Each action plan $\alpha \in N_i$ has an *IS risk reduction indicator* $p_{i\alpha}$ ('profit' in [4]) and a *projected expense* $w_{i\alpha} = w(\alpha)$ ('weight' in [4]): if t is the ith threat, then

$$p_{i\alpha} = \sum_{\substack{\text{processes } p \text{ for} \\ \text{which } t \text{ affects an} \\ \text{application used by } p}} (\mathcal{R}_{\text{cur}}(p, t) - \mathcal{R}_{\text{res}}(p, t_\alpha)).$$

For $0 < i \leq k$ we include a default 'free' action plan α in N_i with $w(\alpha) = 0$ and $P(t) = P(t_\alpha)$ (and thus $p_{i\alpha} = 0$) for the ith threat t, corresponding to not doing anything against t. The multiple-choice knapsack problem equivalent to our risk mitigation under budget constraint problem may then be formulated as:

$$\max \sum_{i=1}^{k} \sum_{\alpha \in N_i} p_{i\alpha} x_{i\alpha}$$

$$\text{subject to } \sum_{i=1}^{k} \sum_{\alpha \in N_i} w_{i\alpha} x_{i\alpha} \leq \mathcal{W},$$

$$\sum_{\alpha \in N_i} x_{i\alpha} = 1, \quad i = 1, 2, \ldots, k,$$

$$x_{i\alpha} \in \{0, 1\}, \quad i = 1, 2, \ldots, k, \quad \alpha \in N_i.$$

To see the equivalence of both formulations, note that it amounts to switching the order of the summations: in Section 4 we summed over all threats affecting a process p to define $\mathcal{R}_{\text{cur}}(p)$ and $\mathcal{R}_{\text{res}}(p, \mathcal{A})$, in the alternative formulation we sum over all processes affected by the ith threat to define $p_{i\alpha}$. Without loss of generality it may be assumed that all coefficients $p_{i\alpha}$, $w_{i\alpha}$, and $\mathcal{W}$ are non-negative integers (if necessary after appropriate scaling).

Although problems of this sort are known to be NP-hard, they can be solved quickly in pseudo-polynomial time. In [4] a particularly efficient method is presented that finds the optimal solution for any fixed budget constraint W using dynamic programming. We refer to [4] for a detailed description. For our purposes it is interesting to know that the LP-relaxation of the problem leads to an almost linear time optimal solution if small variations are allowed in the budget constraint W. This follows by considering the sequence of weights encountered in the course of [4, Algorithm 1 *Greedy*], with respect to which the greedy solutions built so far are all optimal. Either way, finding the optimal spending strategy even for very large IS risk mitigation problems will be a matter of at most a few seconds.

6   Conclusion

We have presented an easy to use quantitative approach to IS risk management that allows a meaningful quantitative interpretation of the effect of risk mitigation and fast determination of the optimal risk mitigation strategy. The prototype model is sufficiently flexible that it allows fine-tuning and other more substantial refinements, if that is found to be desirable based on practical experience with the model. At this point in time the prototype's implementation is under development for imminent deployment on a world-wide scale.

Acknowledgments. We thank Carl Heybroeck, Satya Vithala, and Gary Word for their support and useful discussions.

References

1. Basel Committee's Risk Management Conference on Leading Edge Issues in Operational Risk Management, New York, May 29-30, 2003. Presentations available from www.newyorkfed.org/pihome/news/speeches/2003/con052903.html
2. P. Embrechts, A. McNeil, D. Straumann, *Correlation and dependence in risk management: properties and pitfalls*, August 1999; Chapter 7 in M.A.H. Dempster (ed.) *Risk Management, value at risk and beyond*, Cambridge University Press, January 2002
3. National institute of standards and technology, *Guideline for automatic data processing risk analysis*, FIPS PUB 65, August 1979
4. D. Pisinger, *A minimal algorithm for the multiple-choice knapsack problem*, Technical report 94/25, DIKU, University of Kopenhagen, Denmark; available from www.diku.dk/~pisinger
5. T.Voss, *A simple one-dimensional quantitative risk assessment model, v. 1.4*, internal Citigroup Information Security Office document, February 2002

A Weighted Graph Approach to Authorization Delegation and Conflict Resolution

Chun Ruan[1] and Vijay Varadharajan[1,2]

[1] School of Computing and Information Technology
University of Western Sydney, Penrith South DC, NSW 1797 Australia
{chun,vijay}@cit.uws.edu.au
[2] Department of Computing
Macquarie University, North Ryde, NSW 2109 Australia
vijay@ics.mq.edu.au

Abstract. Solving conflicts in authorization delegation has not been considerably explored by researchers. In [5] we proposed a graph based framework supporting authorization delegation and conflict resolution. We proposed a predecessor-take-precedence based conflict resolution method, which gives higher priorities to the predecessors along the delegation paths to achieve the well-controlled delegations. In this paper, we further extend the model to allow grantors to express degrees of certainties about their delegations and grants of authorizations. This expression of certainty gives subjects more flexibility on the control of their delegations of access rights. A new conflict resolution policy based on weighted lengths of authorization paths is proposed. This policy deals with the conflicts in a more flexible way in that not only the relationship of predecessor-successor but also the weights of authorizations are taken into consideration. Cyclic authorizations are allowed to further enhance the expressive flexibility, and the undesired situations caused by them can be avoided through the proposed conflict resolution method. The intuitive graph interpretation provides a formal basis for the underlying semantics of our model.

1 Introduction

Access control models provide a formalism and framework for specifying, analyzing and evaluating security policies that determine how access is granted and delegated among particular users. Various access control models have been published over the years [1,2,3,6]. Some are defined in terms of well known abstraction of subjects, objects and access rights and some in terms of roles, permissions and users. Some models are formulated in matrix form, some in the form of rules, some in graphs, while others use logic representation.

One of the key issues for an access control model is related to the authorization administration policy, which refers to the function of granting and revoking authorizations. Decentralized administration allows multiple subjects to have the privilege to grant and revoke authorizations, and the administration privilege can usually be delegated between subjects. It is rather flexible and apt

H. Wang et al. (Eds.): ACISP 2004, LNCS 3108, pp. 402–413, 2004.

to the particular requirements of individual subjects. Most commercial DBMSs adopt such decentralized authorization. Nevertheless, the authorizations become more difficult to manage. In particular, when both positive and negative authorizations are allowed, conflict problem becomes a crucial issue since multiple administrators greatly increase the chance of conflict and cyclic authorizations may lead to unexpected situations. However, despite its significance, the problem of handling conflicts in authorization delegations has not been considerably explored by researchers. We have observed that most current conflict resolution methods, such as *Negative (Positive)-takes-precedence*, *Strong-and-Weak*, *More specific-take-precedence*, and *Time-take-precedence*, seem limited when worked in decentralized administration (although they worked well in most centralized administration models). See more details in [5]. To solve this problem, we presented a graph based model and proposed a predecessor-take-precedence based conflict resolution policy in [5]. The idea is to trace the delegation paths explicitly, and give higher priorities to the predecessors whenever the grantors of conflicting authorizations fall in a path. The main advantage of this method is to enforce a well-controlled delegation model. The delegators do not lose control of the objects in that their authorization grants will override the delegates' grants whenever conflicts occur between them. In particular, assuming all the access rights on an object are first delegated from the owner of this object, the owner will always have the highest priority for this object and his/her authorizations can never be overridden.

In this paper, the graph based model (GBM for short) in [5] is extended to a weighted graph based model (WGBM for short) which allows grantors to express degrees of certainties about their authorization grants. In WGBM, each authorization is associated with a weight given by the grantor. The weight is a non-negative number, and a smaller number represents a higher certainty. In general, to resolve conflicts, the delegation path together with the weighted length of the path is considered, and the authorization on the path of the smaller length will win. This method can deal with the *comparable conflicts* in GBM(grantors of authorizations fall in a path) in a more flexible way, and reduce the amount of *incomparable conflicts* (grantors do not fall in a path). In fact, when all the certainties of authorizations are restricted to be positive and equal, WGBM is reduced to a model similar to GBM. When all the certainties of authorizations are 0, WGBM is reduced to a model in which every subject has the same priority. Furthermore, to further increase the expressive power, we remove the restriction in GBM that cyclic authorizations are not allowed. The unexpected situations caused by cyclic authorizations(for instance, a delegates to b, and b delegates to c, but c denies b) can be avoided using the proposed conflict resolution method, since we can give predecessors higher priorities than successors by assigning positive weight to each authorization. We give the formal description of the model. The intuitive graph interpretation provides a formal basis for the underlying semantics.

The paper is organized as follows. Section 2 describes some limitations of GBM. Section 3 presents the basic ideas to extend GBM. Section 4 presents the formal description of WGBM, while Section 5 concludes the paper with certain remarks.

2   Limitations

Recall that, in GBM, we allow for both positive and negative authorizations, and permit access rights to be delegated from one subject to another. So, for any access right on any object, there may be multiple administrators that can grant authorizations. Different to the previously proposed conflict resolution policies, we classify conflict authorizations into two categories namely *comparable* and *incomparable* conflicts. Consider the situation where a subject s_3 is granted two conflicting authorizations with respect to an access right r on an object o from subjects s_1 and s_2 respectively. We say that these two conflicting authorizations are comparable if s_2's administrative privilege for r on o is granted (or transitively granted) by s_1, or vice versa. In the first case we assign a higher priority to s_1's grant than s_2's grant to solve the conflict occurring over the subject s_3. On the other hand, if there is no grant connectivity relationship between s_1 and s_2, then this conflicting authorization is said to be incomparable. In GBM, we support multiple policies to solve incomparable conflicts to meet different user's requirements. For example, we may use the positive authorization to override the negative authorization or vice versa. We require that all the rights of an object be originally delegated from the owner of the object, so that the owner's authorization will take precedence over any other conflicting authorizations. This model is further extended to achieve more flexible delegation control in this paper.

We have observed that some limitations exist in GBM. First, in GBM, the delegates of an access right from the same delegator have the same priority, and hence their conflicting grants of authorizations are incomparable. This may not apply well in some applications, and may result in many incomparable conflicts. Let us revisit the example within the university framework. The Dean of a college creates a budget file and then delegates the "read" right to his/her subordinate Heads of Schools (HOS) and Directors of Centers (DC). The Heads of Schools and the Directors of Centers receive the same priority from the Dean and their conflicting grants to a specific staff would become incomparable, as shown in Figure 1. However, the Dean may wish to give the Heads of Schools higher priorities than Directors of Centers. As a result, their conflicting authorization grants become comparable.

Second, the comparable conflict resolution policy in GBM may be not general enough for some applications. Take the above university example again. Consider the situation where a specific staff receives a "read" from the Dean and a "not read" from his/her Head of School for the budget file, as shown in Figure 2. There may exist two possibilities: (1). The Dean is quite confident about his/her grant to the staff and would not want it to be overridden. This situation is well supported by GBM. (2). The Dean is not too sure about his/her grant to the staff and would not mind if it is overridden by a more confident grant from the Head of School. This situation could not be supported by GBM.

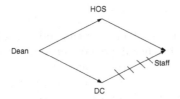

Fig. 1. An Incomparable Conflict

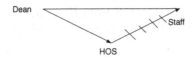

Fig. 2. A Comparable Conflict

Third, a subject can increase his/her relative priority by issuing a new authorization in GBM. Look at the example illustrated by Figure 3 and Figure 4. First, HOS1 and HOS2 have the same priority (Figure 3). After issuing a new authorization to HOS2, HOS1 has achieved a higher priority than HOS2 (Figure 4).

Finally, cyclic authorizations are prohibited in GBM to simplify the model. However, on the other hand, this may restrict the expressive power of the model as well. To improve all the above limitations, we propose a weighted graph based model.

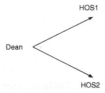

Fig. 3. HOS1 and HOS2 Have the Same Priority

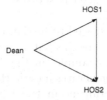

Fig. 4. HOS1 Has Higher Priority Than HOS2

3 Basic Idea

In general, the idea is that each grantor can add a weight to his/her authorization grant which expresses his/her degree of certainty about this grant. The weight is a non-negative integer, with the smaller number denoting the higher priority. Then, we can solve conflicts based on the weighted lengths of authorization paths, and let the authorization with the smaller weighted length override the others.

Let us see how it works for the above examples. In Figure 1, the Dean can assign weight 1 to the grant to HOS, and weight 2 to the grant to DC to distinguish the priorities of the two grants, as shown in Figure 5. In this way, the two conflicting grants on the staff from HOS and DC, with the same weight, become comparable, and the grant from HOS will override since it has a shorter weighted length of 2.

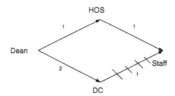

Fig. 5. Weighted Authorizations for Figure 1

In Figure 2, the Dean can assign weight 1 to the grant to HOS and weight 5 to the grant to the staff. Thus, when HOS assign weight 1 to his/her grant to the staff, this grant will override the Dean's (see Figure 6).

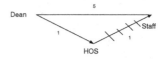

Fig. 6. Weighted Authorizations for Figure 2

In Figure 4, suppose the weights of grants from the Dean to HOS1 and HOS2 are both 1. An additional grant from HOS1 to HOS2 will not decrease the relative priority of HOS2 since the shortest weighted path from the Dean to it is not changed (see Figure 7).

Cyclic authorizations are allowed to further enhance the flexibility in authorization specification, and the unexpected situations can be avoided using our conflict resolution policy. For example, in Figure 5, if the Staff gives HOS an negative authorization which generates a cycle that is not desired, the grant will be overridden by the Dean's grant no matter what the weight of the authorization is. On the other hand, if the Staff grants DC a negative authorization with

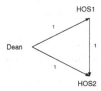

Fig. 7. Weighted Authorizations For Figure 4

weight 1, it makes a cycle as well. Although it is also overridden by the Dean's grant, it would become active when the Dean revokes the grant to DC.

In summary, WGBM has following properties. First, the shortest weighted length to a subject indicates the priority of the subject (See Figure 5). The lesser the value, the higher priority the subject has. Second, the priority of an authorization depends on not only the priority of the grantor but also the weight of the authorization assigned by the grantor. This means that an authorization from a grantor with higher priority could be overridden by an authorization from a grantor with lower priority, as is the case in Figure 6. This gives a grantor more flexibility to control his/her authorization delegations. Third, although weights are non-negative, a delegate's priority could be higher than its delegator's due to the possible multiple paths to it. For instance, in Figure 5, the Staff's priority is 2 which would be higher than DC if the grant from the Dean to DC is 3. Fourth, a delegator can grant a delegate the same priority as itself's by assigning 0 to the weight of the delegation. Finally, there are two extreme cases for this model. On one hand, when all the weights of authorization are 0, the model reduce to the situation where all the subjects have the same priority. In this case, the predecessors have no higher priorities than successors along the delegation path. All authorizations become incomparable. On the other hand, when all the authorizations have the same positive weight, the model reduces to a model similar to GBM, where predecessors have higher priority than successors on their authorization grants.

4   Formal Description of the Model

Let S be a finite set of subjects (users), O be a finite set of objects (files, relations), R be a finite set of access rights (e.g. read, write, select, etc.), and T be a finite set of grant types. Then we have the following definition for authorization.

Definition 1. (Authorization) *An* Authorization *is of the form* (s, o, t, r, g) : w, *where* $s \in S, o \in O, t \in T, r \in R, g \in S$, *and* w *is a non-negative integer.*

Intuitively, an authorization (s, o, t, r, g) : w states that grantor g has granted subject s the access right r on object o with grant type t; and the weight of this authorization is w. The lesser the weight, the higher priority it denotes. We consider three grant types: $T = \{*, +, -\}$, where

* : delegable, which means that the subject has been granted the administrative
    privilege of access right r.
+ : positive, which means that the subject has been granted the access right r.
− : negative, which means that the subject has been denied the access right r.

For example, $(user_1, file_1, +/-, read, user_2) : 3$ states that $user_1$ is granted
/ denied to "read" $file_1$ by $user_2$ with weight 3. $(user_1, file_1, *, read, user_2) : 1$
states that $user_1$ is granted by $user_2$ not only the capability to "read" $file_1$,
but also the capability to grant the "read" on $file_1$ to other subjects; and the
certainty weight for this grant is 1.

Definition 2. (Authorization State) *An authorization state, denoted by $\mathcal{A}$,
is the set of all authorizations at a given time.*

In order to formalize our approach effectively, we use a weighted digraph
to represent an authorization state as follows. We use three types of arcs to
represent three grant types, as shown in Figure 8.

Fig. 8. Arc types.

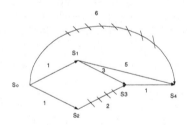

Fig. 9. $G_{F,R}$

For every object o and access right r, let $G_{o,r}$ represents all the authorizations
on o and r such that for each weighted authorization $(s, o, t, r, g) : w$, there is an
arc of type t from g to s in $G_{o,r}$ labelled with w. We can define a weight function
w which matches each arc in $G_{o,r}$ to its weight. That is, $w((g, s)) = w$. We can
also define an arc type function t which matches each arc to its type. That is,
$t((g, s)) = t$

Example 1. Suppose we have following authorizations: $(s_1, F, *, R, s_0) : 1$,
$(s_2, F, *, R, s_0) : 1$, $(s_3, F, -, R, s_2) : 2$, $(s_3, F, *, R, s_1) : 3$, $(s_4, F, *, R, s_3) : 1$,
$(s_4, F, -, R, s_0) : 6$, $(s_4, F, *, R, s_1) : 5$. Then the corresponding $G_{F,R}$ is shown in
Figure 9.

We say that an authorization state $\mathcal{A}$ is **delegation correct**, if for any subject s, object o and right r, s can grant r on o to other subjects if and only if s is the owner; or s has been granted r on o with delegatable type $*$, that is, $\exists g, (s, o, *, r, g) \in \mathcal{A}$. In our graph representation, this means that in $G_{o,r}$, only the owner or the vertices pointed to by at least one $*$ arc can have out-arcs, while the vertices pointed to only by $+$ or $-$ arcs must be terminal ones.

We say that two authorizations (s, o, t, r, g) and (s', o', t', r', g') are **contradictory** if $s = s', o = o', r = r', g = g', but\, t \neq t'$. The contradictory authorizations state that a grantor gives the same subject two different types of authorizations over the same object and access right. For example, authorizations $(s_2, F_1, *, R, s_1) : w_1, (s_2, F_1, +, R, s_1) : w_2$ and $(s_2, F_1, -, R, s_1) : w_3$ contradict each other. An authorization state $\mathcal{A}$ is **not contradictory** if for any a and a' in $\mathcal{A}$, a and a' are not contradictory. In our graph representation, this means that in any $G_{o,r}$ there is only one arc from each vertex to another. Note that one can still update his/her grants by revoking the previous grants first.

Definition 3. *(Consistent Authorization State) An authorization state is consistent if it is delegation correct and not contradictory.*

A path in $G_{o,r}$ is called a *delegation path* if every arc in the path is of type $*$. Then we have the following theorem about the graph property of the consistent authorization state:

Theorem 1. *Let $\mathcal{A}$ be a consistent state, then for any object o and access right r, $G_{o,r}$ in $\mathcal{A}$ is a simple rooted digraph, with the owner of the object s_o as the root. Furthermore, for each subject s in $G_{o,r}$, there is a path $(s_o, s_1, ..., s_k, s)$ to it where $(s_o, s_1, ..., s_k)$ is a delegation path when $k > 0$.*

Remember that in a simple graph there are no multiple arcs between each pair of vertices. Also in the rooted graph, from the root one can reach any vertex in the graph.

Proof. Since $\mathcal{A}$ is a consistent state, it is not contradictory, which means that $G_{o,r}$ in $\mathcal{A}$ is a simple digraph for any o and r. Next we prove for each subject s, there is a path $(s_o, s_1, ..., s_k, s)$ to it such that $(s_o, s_1, ..., s_k)$ is a delegation path when $k > 0$. Suppose $(s_o, s_1, ..., s_k, s)$ is the longest path to s, we prove by induction on k. When $k = 0$, it is obviously true, since at first, only the owner can grant. Suppose it is true when $k \leq n$. Then, when $k = n + 1$, there must exist a path $(s_o, s_1, ..., s_m, s_{m+1}, s)$ such that (s_m, s_{m+1}) is of type $*$, according to the definition of delegation correctness. Since $(s_o, s_1, ..., s_{n+1}, s)$ is the longest path to s, we have $m \leq n$, which means that there is a delegation path to s_m based on the induction hypothesis. This concludes the proof.

Definition 4. *(Conflicting Authorizations) Two authorizations (s, o, t, r, g) : w and (s', o', t', r', g') : w' in $\mathcal{A}$ are conflicting if $s = s'$, $o = o'$, $r = r'$, $t \neq t'$ and $g \neq g'$.*

From the definition, two authorizations are in conflict if they have the same subject, object and access right, but have different grant types and grantors. The reason we require $g \neq g'$ is that otherwise the two authorizations are contradictory, which is forbidden in a consistent state. In our graph $G_{o,r}$, this means that the conflicting arcs have the same terminal vertex but different initial vertices and arc types. Since there are three grant types in our model, three kinds of conflicts may arise, namely + and −, ∗ and −, + and ∗. Note that type ∗ and + are considered to be conflicting in that ∗ holds the administrative privilege on an access right while + does not.

Now we are in a position to define our conflict resolution method. First, we introduce the concept of *useful path*. Since the lower weight of an authorization denotes higher priority, we intend to find a shortest path to a subject in $G_{o,r}$. In addition, to keep the resulting state delegation correct, the selected path should be of the form $s_0, ..., s_k, s$, where $s_0, ..., s_k$ is a delegation path as well as a shortest path to s_k (to guarantee any arc in $s_0, ..., s_k$ will not be overridden). Thus we have the following definition:

Definition 5. *(Useful Path) Let $G_{o,r}$ be a weighted graph for any object o and access right r rooted at s_o; s be any vertex in $G_{o,r}$. Then a useful path to any vertex s is a path: $s_0, s_1, ..., s_k, s\,(k \geq 0)$, where $s_0, s_1,...,s_k$ is a delegation path as well as a shortest path to s_k when $k > 0$.*

From the definition, it is easy to see that any useful path in $G_{o,r}$ is from s_o. To solve the conflicts, only arcs on useful paths can compete with each other, and the arc in the shortest path will override the others.

Example 2. In Figure 9, (s_o, s_1) is the only useful path to s_1 and therefore is the shortest useful path to s_1. For the same reason, (s_o, s_2) is the shortest useful path to s_2. There are two paths to s_3, (s_o, s_1, s_3) and (s_o, s_2, s_3), and they are both useful paths with (s_o, s_2, s_3) being the shortest. Therefore (s_2, s_3) will override (s_1, s_3). There are four paths to s_4. (s_o, s_1, s_3, s_4) is not a useful path since (s_o, s_1, s_3) is not a shortest path to s_3. (s_o, s_2, s_3, s_4) is also not a useful path since (s_o, s_2, s_3) is not a delegation path $((s_2, s_3)$ is not of type ∗), although (s_o, s_2, s_3) is the shortest path to s_3. (s_o, s_1, s_4) and (s_o, s_4) are two useful paths to s_4 with the same shortest length 6.

Definition 6. *(Active Authorization) An authorization $(s, o, t, r, g) : w$ is active if the corresponding arc (g, s) in $G_{o,r}$ is in a shortest useful path to s. Otherwise it is inactive.*

Definition 7. *(Effective Authorization State) Let $\mathcal{A}$ be a consistent authorization state, then the subset of all of its active authorizations forms its* effective authorization state, *denoted by $Eff(\mathcal{A})$.*

Theorem 2. *Let $\mathcal{A}$ be a consistent authorization state, then its effective authorization state $Eff(\mathcal{A})$ is also consistent.*

Proof. Since $\mathcal{A}$ is consistent, it is not contradictory. Thus $Eff(\mathcal{A})$ is also not contradictory , since $Eff(\mathcal{A})$ is a subset of $\mathcal{A}$. On the other hand, according to the definition, an active arc is either from the root or from a subject that has an active delegatable in-arc to it, which follows that $Eff(\mathcal{A})$ is also delegation correct.

Please note that, an active path to a vertex s may be not the shortest path from s_o to s, but is the shortest useful path from s_o to s. Also, an active path to a vertex s may be not unique. That is, there may exist multiple active paths to a vertex s if they have the same shortest length. In addition, for each active path $s_o, ..., s_k, s, s_o, ..., s_k$ must be an active delegation path.

Example 3. The effective authorization state of Figure 9 is shown in Figure 10. There are two active paths to s_4, (s_o, s_1, s_4) and (s_o, s_4). Neither (s_o, s_1, s_4) nor (s_o, s_4) is the shortest path from s_o to s_4. In fact, (s_o, s_2, s_3, s_4) is the shortest path to s_4. However it is not a useful path to s_4 and therefore not an active path.

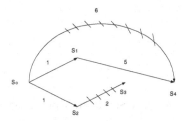

Fig. 10. Eff($G_{o,r}^w$) of Figure 9.

Inactive authorizations are not removed from the system. They are still kept in the system for the purpose of possible re-activation when the authorizations that cause them inactive are revoked. Conflicts may still exist in the effective state when two active paths have the same smallest weighted length, as is the case in Figure 10. In this case, we say these two conflicting authorizations are *incomparable*.

For incomparable conflicts, as in GBM, we support multiple strategies for resolving them. A user can select the appropriate strategy that best suits the needs of his/her application. For example, we can support the following three strategies according to the grant types of authorizations: Pessimistic, where the priority sequence is $- > + > *$; Optimistic, where the priority sequence is $* > + > -$; Any, where the priority sequence is $* = + = -$. This leads us to a similar situation where incomparable conflicts occur in GBM. We would not address this issue again, but just give the following definition of stable weighted authorization state.

Definition 8. *(Stable Authorization State) If an authorization state $\mathcal{A}$ is consistent, then the maximal consistent and conflict-free subset of $Eff(\mathcal{A})$ forms a stable authorization state of $\mathcal{A}$, denoted as stable($\mathcal{A}$).*

Example 4. Figure 11 and Figure 12 are two stable authorization states of Figure 10.

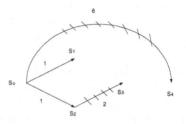

Fig. 11. One Stable State of $G_{o,r}$ in Figure 10

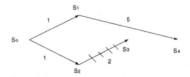

Fig. 12. Another Stable State of $G_{o,r}$ in Figure 10

Now we can define our access control policy. We use a 3-ary tuple (s, o, r) to denote an *access request* to the system, where $s \in S$, $o \in O$, $r \in R$. It states that a subject s requests to exercise access right r on object o. Then we have following access control policy.

Definition 9. (Access Control Policy) *Let $\mathcal{A}$ be an authorization state, (s, o, r) be an access request, P be a policy to resolve the incomparable conflicts on o, stable($\mathcal{A}, P$) be a stable state of $\mathcal{A}$ when applying P to o. We say that (s, o, r) is permitted if there exists some grantor g and some weight w such that $(s, o, *, r, g) : w$ or $(s, o, +, r, g) : w$ is in stable($\mathcal{A}, P$); (s, o, r) is denied if there is some grantor g and some weight w such that $(s, o, -, r, g) : w$ is in stable($\mathcal{A}, P$); otherwise, (s, o, r) is undecided.*

5   Conclusion

Authorization delegation and negative authorizations are two significant issues for a decentralized authorization model. In this paper, we proposed a flexible authorization model to deal with the problem of authorization delegation and conflict resolution. A conflict resolution method based on the shortest weighted length-take-precedence is proposed, which makes it possible for grantors to control their authorization grants in a very flexible way. The weighted graph representation provides a formal basis for the semantics of the model. For the future work, we would like to implement the prototype of the model. We also intend to apply the model in a parallel environment.

References

1. S. Castano, M. Fugini, G. Martella, and P. Samarati, *Database Security*. Addison-Wesley Publishing Company, 1995.
2. W. Essmayr, F. Kastner, S. Preishuber et al, Access controls for federated database environments-taxonomy of design choices. In *Joint IFIP TC 6 & 11 Working Conference on Communications and Multimedia Security Chapman & Hall*, Graz, Austria, pp 117-132, Septemper 1995.
3. S. Jajodia, P. Samarati, V.S. Subrahmanian, and E. Bertino, A unified framework for enforcing multiple access control policies. In *Proc. of ACM SIGMOD Conference on Management of Data*, pp 474-485, 1997.
4. T.F. Lunt, D.E. Denning, R.R. Scheel, M. Heckman, and W.R. Shockley, The SeaView security model. *IEEE Trans. on Software Engineering*, 16(6): 593-607, 1990.
5. C. Ruan and V. Varadharajan, Resolving conflicts in authorization delegations, 2002. *Proceedings of the 7th Australasian Conference on Information Security and Privacy*, pp 271-285, 2002.
6. R. Sandhu and P. Samarati, Access control: Principles and practice. *IEEE Communications*, 32(9):40-48, 1994.
7. M. Satyanarayanan, Interating security in a large distributed system. *ACM-TOCS*, vol.7, no.3, pp 247-280, Aug. 1989.

Authorization Mechanisms for Virtual Organizations in Distributed Computing Systems

Xi-Bin Zhao[1], Kwok-Yan Lam[2], Siu-Leung Chung[3], Ming Gu[2], and
Jia-Guang Sun[2]

[1] School of Comp Sci & Telecom Engrg, Jiangsu University, Zhenjiang, PR China
zxb@ujs.edu.cn
[2] School of Software, Tsinghua University, Beijing, PR China
{lamky, guming, sunjg}@tsinghua.edu.cn
[3] School of Business Administration, The Open University of Hong Kong
slchung@ouhk.edu.hk

Abstract. With the rapid development of the global information infrastructure, the use of virtual organization (VO) is gaining increasing importance as a model for building large-scale business information systems. The notion of VO is significant in that it could serve as a basic framework for implementing geographically distributed, cross-organizational application systems in a highly flexible manner. VO is generally composed of participants from different organizations driven by specific tasks. In order to control both participation and access to shared resources, authorization is essential in VO. However, authorization in VO is challenging because of the dynamic and distributed nature of VO; thus requiring mechanisms that are efficient, scalable and being able to handle complex access control policies. This paper analyzes the requirement of authorization services for VO and proposes the use of threshold scheme as a basic mechanism for implementing authorization services in large scale distributed computing systems. While pointing out the desirable features of threshold schemes for complex authorization policies, the paper also discusses the practical limitations of threshold schemes in such an environment. The main contribution of this paper is that it suggests a practical approach for deploying threshold closure, an optimal form of threshold schemes, for implementing authorization of VO. In essence, we suggest segregating the policy and mechanism aspects of threshold closure so that complex policies may be specified using threshold closure which are implemented conveniently using existing authentication-based enforcement mechanisms available in traditional security infrastructure.

Keywords: Authorization, Access Control, Distributed system security, Secure commercial applications

H. Wang et al. (Eds.): ACISP 2004, LNCS 3108, pp. 414–426, 2004.

1   Introduction

The pervasive growth of the global Internet has created significant impact on the design of distributed computing systems. Starting in the 80s as a platform for sharing data and expensive equipment in a local area environment, distributed computing systems of today typically cover wide geographic areas and are used as a model for organizing and implementing large-scale business applications. More notably, in recent years, the Grid Computing System (GCS) has emerged as a special form of distributed computing and is distinguished from conventional distributed computing systems by its focus on dynamic and larger-scale resource sharing over a wide geographical distribution [1]. In contrast to conventional distributed computing systems, GCS may be viewed as a sophisticated distributed computing system with high-level abstractions and services to facilitate large-scale sharing of resources in a dynamic manner.

Resource sharing in GCS is built on the VO model [1]. VO is an abstraction for designing distributed systems that aims to provide a flexible abstraction for implementing distributed systems with complex inter-process relationships. The objectives of GCS are to facilitate coordinated resource sharing and problem solving in dynamic, multi-institutional VO. A key requirement of VO is the ability to negotiate resource-sharing arrangements among a set of parties and then use the resulting resource pool for achieving some application objectives. The major issue in GCS is the provision of services and protocols that facilitate implementation of VO over a widely distributed environment.

The notion of VO has enabled GCS to support a wide variety of applications beyond scientific computing. In particular, recent development in e-commerce has made the concept of VO especially suitable for organizing and implementing distributed commercial applications. For example, e-commerce applications in the healthcare industry typically require large-scale sharing of resources (medical records, laboratory test results and expensive equipments) by participating organizations. The sharing is usually specific to certain tasks originated from business objectives that require close cooperation and coordination of a number of medical information systems and computing components.

The operation and functioning of a VO involves, firstly, the enrolment of participants and their resources and, secondly, the establishment of relationship among participants and resources within the VO in order to collaborate and to achieve the specific task. Thus the implementation and management of VO require that these two operations be carefully controlled and in accordance with the security policies of the VO. However, the tasks of specifying and enforcing the policies are challenging in that each participating organization may nominate a large number of users to access the shared resources and, for accountability and liability reasons typical in business applications, controlled access authorized by a group of users is required. Furthermore, in general, VO participants join and leave the VO in a dynamic manner. This paper analyzes the authorization requirements for VO management and introduces a new authorization service to meet such requirements.

In this paper, we adopt the GCS as a basic model for organizing VO, and the authorization issues of VO is addressed through the design of an authorization service for GCS. The rest of the paper is organized as follows. The characteristics of VO and the corresponding authorization issues will be discussed in Section 2. This is followed by a close investigation of the deficiency of existing Grid security infrastructure in addressing the authorization needs of VO. Section 4 presents the design of a new authorization service based on the concept of threshold closure, it also explains the advantages of threshold closure in meeting the authorization needs of VO. Section 5 describes the operation model and system architecture of the new authorization service. Section 6 concludes the discussion of this paper.

2 Authorization Issues of VO

The VO abstraction is especially suitable for implementing mission-specific applications initiated by special operations such as disease control, crisis management or law enforcement [2]. The accomplishment of such mission-specific operations typically requires close cooperation of multiple organizations. These organizations may or may not have prior working relationship and may not trust each other. The cooperation is driven by events and is established dynamically in response to the occurrence of the events. In general, sharing of resources in such circumstances is subjected to stringent control of the resource owner. These characteristics fit the profile of VO applications and the problem is preferably addressed using the VO abstraction.

To illustrate, we consider an application scenario in which Grid computing is a suitable approach. In this example, an epidemiological surveillance and control taskforce is established in response to the outbreak of Dengue Fever in Asia, a fatal disease transmitted by mosquitoes which can lead to clinical shock and death within 24 hours [3]. In order to monitor and control the spreading of the fever effectively, there are a number of key areas to be monitored closely. Among others, for example, it is important to keep track of hospitals' reports of suspicious cases for the Dengue symptoms, to retrieve immigration records of patients in recent weeks to determine the source of infection (whether the source is local or from overseas), to access to overseas data such as the DengueNet which is a global surveillance system for Dengue fever, to identify the residential and work addresses of patients with the Dengue symptoms and to study inspection reports from the environment authority on the hygienic conditions of the surrounding community of possible source of the disease.

It is obvious from this example that, in order to combat the disease more effectively and efficiently, close cooperation among a number of otherwise independent institutions is necessary. In this case, the immigration authority, the environment authority and the health authority, etc. Typically, some form of cross-institutional taskforce will be established for the special mission. The participating institutions are geographically distributed and independent of one another. Each of them may nominate a number of officers to join the taskforce.

The operation of the taskforce will require access to computer systems and data across the participating organizations. These organizations need to provide interconnectivity to facilitate the operation of the taskforce. For legislative reasons, these systems normally do not share information except for special situations in which authorization by top officials from the government administration is granted. The organizations participating in the taskforce may not trust one another previously and they may join and leave the taskforce dynamically depending on operational needs. The officers nominated to join the taskforce, hence authorized to access the shared resources, must be carefully managed in order to minimize risks of breaching legislative policies.

Therefore, VO management is a challenging task due to the complex characteristics of VO. Operations on a VO typically involves the following:

1. Registration of participants and their resources to form the VO.
2. Registration of shared resources by these participants so as to allow them to collaborate in order to achieve some specific tasks.
3. Nomination of users authorized to access the resources on behalf of the participants.
4. Specification of policies for controlling access to shared resources.
5. Enforcement of access control policies when users access resources during the course their work.

Within such a complex and distributed computing system, membership in a VO is "dynamic" as participants may join or leave any time. Hence, the relationship among participants and the access control policy are also changed frequently. Furthermore, sharing is usually conditional and, in various application scenarios, many restrictions are imposed. For example, in order to ensure accountability and liability protection, business application systems typical enforce dual control and separation of duties. In these cases, access to resources almost invariably requires that access be authorized by a group of approved users from different organizations.

Given this setting of the problem, there are mainly two specific authorization requirement of VO:

Expressive power. Authorization policies in GCS could be highly complex when there is a large number of participants and resources. For example, suppose there are 5 organizations participating in the VO and they nominated 20 users, say $P_1, P_2, P_3, P_4, \cdots, P_{20}$ to join the taskforce. Consider the situation that they need to access some clinical data about the Dengue virus for analysis, and the required data are stored in one particular node in the VO. In order to ensure organizational integrity, it requires that access is allowed only if any two users from different organizations make the access request together. Therefore, the access control policy will look like: "any two users P_i and P_j may access the shared data together, except when P_i and P_j belong to the same organization". Obviously, the problem will become more complex when the number of users is grows and when the security policies are more refined. Therefore, the authorization service is required to have the ability to describe such complex access policies.

Scalability. Because of the dynamic nature of VO, the access control rules are changing and expanding constantly. Therefore, the authorization service is required to have the ability to efficiently handle changes in access policies in a highly dynamic manner.

Due to the complex and dynamic nature of VO, the authorization issues are not straightforward if the authorization service is to be implemented in an efficient and effective manner. Firstly, the authorization service is required to have the ability to support such complex authorization policies. Secondly, the authorization service is required to have the ability to handle changes in policy rules in a highly dynamic manner.

Furthermore, from a practical point of view, the authorization service should be built on the existing security infrastructure of typical distributed computing systems. More specifically, security policies of most distributed computing systems are enforced through strong authentication and access control list at the resource manager. Thus it is highly desirable that the authorization service is implementable on top of this security infrastructure. For example, the Globus Security Infrastructure (GSI) is widely used for implementing VO among the GCS community. As the GSI is based on the use of public key infrastructure and PKI-based authentication, a practical authorization service should preferably be implementable using these basic mechanisms.

3   Authorization in the Grid Security Infrastructure

Authorization policy is important for controlling access to resources in GCS. GCS needs a flexible and scalable authorization service to support the management of complex VO structures.

Due to the dynamic nature of sharing relationships in VO, security solutions for GCS must allow applications to coordinate diverse access control policies and to operate securely in heterogeneous environments. VO may grow and shrink dynamically, acquiring resources when solving a problem and releasing them when they not needed. Grid security solutions need to provide mutual authentication that allows a user, the processes that comprise a user's computation, and the resources used by those processes, to verify each other's identity.

The GSI provides an implementation of security infrastructure in Globus that aims to meet the aforementioned requirements [4]. GSI provides a number of services for Grid applications, including mutual authentication and single sign-on. GSI is based on public key infrastructure, X.509 certificates, and the Secure Socket Layer (SSL) communication protocol. The GSI provides a delegation capability, by extending the standard SSL protocol, to simplify the security interface to the Grid user. The delegation function is implemented using a new entity called "proxy". A proxy is created to represent the user, within a time limit, in a Grid application. The proxy's private key is a short-term key, thus has a less stringent security requirement as the owner's private key. The use of short-term digital certificate for implementing security that aims to balance risk and efficiency is discussed in [5]. The proxy also serves as the basis of the single sign-on implemented by Globus which provides a mechanism by which a process can authenticate to its user proxy or another process.

Though the Globus Toolkit implemented GSI protocols and APIs to address Grid security needs, it focus primarily on authentication and message protection. In recent efforts of Globus, a Community Authorization Service (CAS) has been added to the Globus Toolkit [6,7]. CAS augments the existing local mechanisms provided via GSI and enables community policies to be enforced based on the user's GSI identity, which is constant across resources. The architecture of CAS is shown in Figure 1 which shows that ACL is used as the basic authorization mechanism of CAS in Globus Tookit.

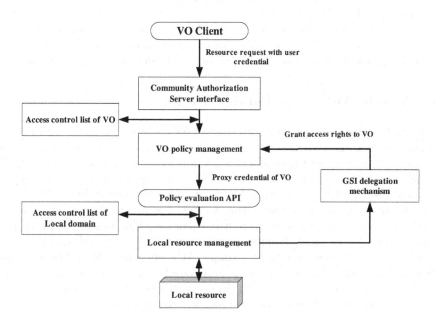

Fig. 1. The Globus Community Authorization Service Architecture

While the GSI offers a sophisticated security solution for implementing security in Grid applications, in order to support the kind of policies described in Section 2, the existing approach needs to be enhanced in order to support the authorization needs of VO efficiently. Access control list (ACL) is used widely as a means for describing authorization policies in GCS. It specifies the access rights a principal has on an object or resource. The limitations of ACL are obvious. Firstly, the expressive power of ACL is very restrictive, it can only directly express policies such as "who can do what" and is a lot more clumsy to express complex access policies such as "any three of the five officers can open the genetic analysis report of Dengue virus". In this case, the ACL needs to be generalized to include groups in addition to individuals, and the "3 out of 5" policy is implemented by a number of group access rules. Secondly, when authorization policies change, a large number of ACL operations are needed to update the policy descriptions. For example, if the "3 out of 5" rule is changed and become "3 out of 6", then a lot of ACL operations will be needed in order to ensure that the ACL remains consistent with the security policy. Some other shortcomings of ACL are described in [8].

Despite its simplicity, systems using ACL cannot efficiently handle complex access control policies such as those described above. Since ACL cannot express these policies easily, the security administrator needs to analyze these policies and decides to create groups in order to facilitate description of complex policies. Obviously, it is inefficient to maintain the ACL in this manner. Besides, in order to cope with policy changes, the designer needs to analyze the policy rules and the corresponding ACL frequently.

It is clear that the cost becomes huge when there is a large number of participants and resources. Thus, the authorization issues of VO are not straightforward even to implement such a simple policy in an efficient and effective manner.

4   A New Authorization Service for VO

As explained in Section 2, authorization of VO is not straightforward because of the complex and dynamic nature of authorization policies needed by VO. In this section, we present the design of a new authorization service for meeting the security and practical requirements of VO. In essence, our scheme adopts the use of threshold closure [9], which is an optimal collection of threshold schemes [10], as the basis of the authorization service. For practical considerations, we segregate the policy and mechanism aspects of threshold closure. With this approach, the complex and dynamic policies are specified by a threshold closure which allows the construction of a simple ACL efficiently. With the simplified ACL, enforcement of the policies may be achieved using the authentication-based mechanisms available from the GSI. In short, the new authorization service for VO proposed here will meet the following key requirements:

- Ability to represent complex and dynamic security policies efficiently.
- Can be implemented efficiently over existing security infrastructure of GCS.

ACL is one of the simplest approach for specifying authorization policies. Authorization of resource access is implemented by firstly specifying the identity of a user in the ACL maintained by the resource manager; and secondly requiring the user to authenticate himself/herself to the resource manager. Access is granted if the user's identity is listed in the ACL and the accessing party is the authentic user. ACL is simple to implement but usually inconvenient to use in real situations. Almost invariable, ACL is extended to include groups in addition to individual users. As such, the ACL is supplemented by some group membership mechanism.

Though ACL may support group access control in order to cater for more complex authorization policies, it is inefficient when describing security policies typical in commercial applications. For example, dual control and separation of duties are typical in business applications, and the security policies are typically of the form "access is allowed if any three of the five directors agree". In this connection, the threshold scheme was proposed for implementing access control [10]. With a (t, l) threshold scheme, a secret key needed for accessing the resource is split into l pieces such that any t (or more) of the l pieces are needed to reconstruct the secret, hence enabling access to the resource.

The beauty of the threshold scheme is that it is a simple mechanism for describing the "t out of l" authorization rules. More importantly, such rules can be directly implemented very efficiently using threshold cryptography [10]. Hence, a collection of threshold schemes may be used to efficiently implement the kind of security policies described in Section 2. The threshold scheme is attractive because it is computationally efficient and only involves the computation of a simple Lagrange interpolation. However, its expressive power is still very limited as it was proven that threshold schemes cannot express authorization policies in many cases [11]. For example, it cannot specify exactly which subset of participants is allowed to determine the secret and which is not. Therefore, the concept of access structure for representing complex secret sharing schemes was proposed by [12]. Unfortunately, access structures are difficult to implement. Furthermore, the use of threshold schemes will be tedious if the policies they represent are dynamic. For example, when more "t out of l" rules are added to the system, it is highly likely that the overall collection of threshold schemes are redundant, thus leading to serious security management problems [9].

To allow efficient implementation of access structures and at the same time address the security management issues of threshold schemes, threshold closure was proposed by [9] as an efficient and flexible approach to secret sharing. A threshold closure is an efficient approach for representing an access structure by specifying a collection of threshold schemes. Besides, a threshold closure is an optimal collection of threshold schemes such that it uses the minimum number of threshold schemes to represent the policy rules of the original collection of threshold schemes. Therefore, complex authorization policies may be represented using an access structure (with each authorized set in the access structure represented by a threshold scheme) which is then translated to a threshold closure which in turn can be implemented efficiently using an optimal collection of threshold schemes.

In distributed computing systems such as the GCS, the authorized sets represented in an access structure will be excessively large due to the complex authorization policies and the large number of potential participants/users. Therefore the threshold closure algorithm is attractive for effectiveness and efficiency reasons. To facilitate discussion of the new authorization service, we briefly recap the concept of threshold closure. A threshold closure, denoted as ε, is a collection of (t, S)-threshold schemes (S is a set of l users such that $0 < t \le |S|, S \subseteq P$ where P is the set of all potential participants/users), and satisfies the three conditions:

1. Redundant-free i.e. there do not exist two distinct $(t_1, S_1), (t_2, S_2) \in \varepsilon$ such that

$$S_1 \subseteq S_2 \text{ or } |S_1 \cap S_2| \ge \min\{t_1, t_2\}, t_1 \ne t_2.$$

2. Reduced i.e. there do not exist $(t, S_1), (t, S_2), \ldots, (t, S_m) \in \varepsilon$ such that

$$\bigcup_{i=1}^{m} [S_i]_t = [\bigcup_{i=1}^{m} S_i]_t.$$

where

$$[S]_t = \{S' : |S'| = t, S' \subseteq S\}.$$

3. Closed i.e. $\forall (t, S_1), (t, S_2), \ldots, (t, S_m) \in \varepsilon$ and $S'_1 \subseteq S_1, S'_2 \subseteq S_2, \ldots, S'_m \subseteq S_m$ ("=" cannot be held by all) if

$$\bigcup_{i=1}^{m} [S'_i]_t = [\bigcup_{i=1}^{m} S'_i]_t$$

then

$$(t, \bigcup_{i=1}^{m} S'_i) \in \varepsilon, \text{ or}$$

$$(t, \bigcup_{i=1}^{m} S'_i) \notin \varepsilon \text{ and } (\exists (t, S) \in \varepsilon) \bigcup_{i=1}^{m} S'_i \subset S.$$

It was proven in [9] that there exists a one-to-one correspondence between access structure Γ_0 and threshold closure ε. In addition, the $\min(\varepsilon)$ which is the minimal covering of threshold closure ε can be obtained. After implementing the algorithm of converting Γ_0 to ε, the number of the threshold schemes in the destination threshold closure is very much smaller than the number of the authorized sets in the access structure.

Besides, [9] also introduced four kinds of operation on Γ_0 and ε to allow authorization policies to be dynamically changed efficiently. The operations are:

1. Add (t, S) into ε.
2. Add S into Γ_0.
3. Delete (t, S) from ε.
4. Delete S from Γ.

The consistency between Γ_0 and ε can be maintained using these four operations. In fact, the authorization policies are changed frequently in real world scenarios. As such, the threshold closure also needs to be dynamic in order to correctly represent the access structure. By exploring these convenient operations, the threshold closure not only can expand and contract freely but also preserve its permanent consistency with the dynamic access structure. Therefore we can see that threshold closure has better efficiency and scalability while it keeps the high express power of other general access structure schemes.

To illustrate the advantages of threshold closure as an underlying mechanism for implementing authorization in VO, the following table compares the characteristics of the various schemes including ACL, threshold scheme, general access structure scheme and threshold closure.

Scheme	Easy to implement	Easy to manage	Performance efficiency	Good expressive power	Scalability
ACL	√	√	√		
Threshold Scheme	√	√			√
Genera Access Structure scheme				√	
Threshold closure	√	√	√	√	√

Albeit threshold closure is a desirable approach for specifying complex access control policies for scenarios described in Section 2, there are practical constraints when they are implemented in a distributed computing system. For example, it is impossible to revoke a group once the secret shares are distributed to the group members unless the secret is changed. However, this will mean reconstructing and re-distributing the secret for all groups - an effort which is not practical in a large scale distributed environment. Besides, the implementation of threshold cryptography cannot leverage on the existing security infrastructure typically available in distributed computing systems. For example, the GSI of Globus is a PKI-based security mechanism that relies on strong authentication and ACL. In order to implement threshold closure in such a system, an additional security infrastructure based on threshold cryptography will be needed. This will be a serious concern for security practitioners, thus they are unlike to adopt threshold closure for building a practical authorization service for GCS.

To this end, we address the implementation issues of threshold closure by segregating the policy and mechanism aspects of threshold schemes. We note that a threshold scheme is a simple security mechanism for enforcing a simple security policy of the form "access is allowed if any t or more out of l users make the request together". In other words, a threshold scheme implemented using threshold cryptography is both a security policy and a security mechanism. An access structure, however, is a complex security policy which is not easy to enforce due to the lack of suitable security mechanisms. The threshold closure was designed to be an efficient structure that represents the complex policies of an access structure using an optimal collection of threshold schemes. That means a threshold closure, like the threshold schemes, is both a security policy and a security mechanism.

To summarize, in this section, we analyzed various potential candidates for building the authorization service of VO. We concluded that threshold closure is a most suitable approach for use in this scenario. However, threshold closure cannot be implemented directly using threshold cryptography for practical reasons. We suggest that the new authorization service adopt the threshold closure as an approach for representing and managing authorization policies. However, the policies are not implemented using threshold cryptography. Instead, they are converted into an optimal collection of ACLs so that existing security infrastructure of distributed computing systems may be used to implement the enforcement mechanism.

5   System Architecture of the Authorization Service

With our new authorization service for VO, we adopt the threshold closure as a structure for representing and processing security policies while the enforcement is still achieved using the traditional ACL and authentication approaches. As explained, we acknowledge the effectiveness and efficiency of threshold closure for representing complex and dynamic security policies of VO. However, implementation of the security mechanism of threshold closure using threshold cryptography is undesirable in a GCS environment. Therefore, in our system, the authorization server uses a threshold closure for representing authorization policies so that they can be manipulated as the VO participants/users change. However, the threshold closure, which is a collection of threshold schemes, is not implemented directly using threshold cryptography. Instead, the collection of (t, l) policies are stored explicitly at the authorization server. If a group of users need to access a shared resource, they need to authenticate themselves to the authorization server which in turn will check against the optimal set of (t, l) rules before deciding if the access should be granted. Figure 2 below illustrates the authorization mechanism based on the new authorization service for VO.

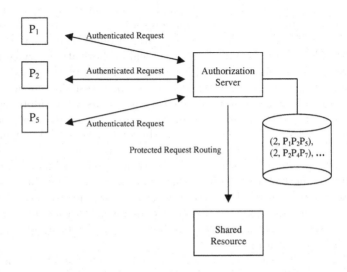

Fig. 2. The New Authorization Service for VO

In Figure 2, the authorization server maintains the authorization policy rules for each of the shared resource in the system. For each shared resource, the rules are represented by a collection of threshold schemes. In this example, the rules include $(2, P_1, P_2, P_5)$, $(2, P_2, P_4, P_7)$, ... However, each of these rules literally represents the policies such as "any 2 out of P_1, P_2 and P_5" rather than being a denotation of the corresponding threshold cryptographic systems. When some participants need to access a shared resource, they need to make an authenticated access request to the authorization server. The authorization server verifies their authenticity, then checks against the rules to decide if the access should be granted. In the example as shown in Figure 2, the participants are P_1, P_2, P_5 and they match some rule at the authorization server, thus access is granted. In this case, the authorization server route the access request to the corresponding resource manager M in a secure manner. The protection of the request routing mechanism may be achieved by facilitating the group P_1, P_2, P_5 and M to establish a shared session key - a function/protocol that is commonly available from security infrastructure of distributed computing systems.

The threshold closure approach has been implemented and we are convinced that this is a pragmatic approach for implementing an effective, scalable and efficient authorization service in a cost-efficient manner. This approach of authorization service for VO has the following advantages:

- It uses the rich expressive power of access structure and the scalability of threshold closure.
- It is implemented on simple and practical mechanisms available in typical security infrastructure e.g. ACL and strong authentication based on PKI.
- The operation model of the authorization server and request routing is typical in most contemporary web-based Internet applications. For example, the policy manager of most commercial single sign-on and privilege management infrastructures are implemented using this operation model.

6   Conclusion

With the rapid development of the global information infrastructure, the use of VO is gaining increasing importance as a model for building large-scale business information systems. VO is generally composed of participants from different organizations driven by specific tasks. In order to control both participation and access to shared resources, authorization is essential in VO. However, authorization in VO is challenging because of the dynamic and distributed nature of VO; thus requiring mechanisms that are efficient, scalable and being able to handle complex access control policies.

This paper analyzed the requirement of authorization services for VO and proposed the use of threshold closure as a basic mechanism for implementing authorization services in large scale distributed computing systems. While pointing out the desirable features of threshold closure for complex authorization policies, the paper also discussed the practical limitations of threshold closure in such an environment. The proposed approach of authorization service for VO makes use of the rich expressive power of access structure and the scalability of threshold closure and can be implemented on simple and practical mechanisms available in typical security infrastructure e.g. ACL and strong authentication based on PKI. Furthermore, the operation model of the authorization server and request routing is typical in most contemporary web-based Internet applications. For example, the policy manager of most commercial single sign-on and privilege management infrastructures are implemented using this operation model.

The main contribution of this paper is that it suggested a practical approach for deploying threshold closure, an optimal form of threshold schemes, for implementing authorization of VO. In essence, we suggested segregating the policy and mechanism aspects of threshold closure so that complex policies may be specified using threshold closure which are implemented conveniently using existing authentication-based enforcement mechanisms available in a traditional security infrastructure. The new authorization service for VO proposed here has ability to represent complex and dynamic security policies efficiently and can be implemented efficiently over existing security infrastructure of GCS.

Acknowledgements. This research was partly funded by the National 863 Plan (Projects Numbers: 2003AA148020), P. R. China and the Grid Security project of PrivyLink International Limited (Singapore).

References

1. I. Foster, C. Kesselman, S. Tuecke. "The anatomy of the grid: enabling scalable virtual organizations", *Int. J. Supercomputer Applications*, Vol. 15, Issue 3, 2001, pp. 200-222.
2. K.Y. Lam, X.B. Zhao, S.L. Chung, M. Gu, J.G. Sun. "Enhancing Grid Security Infrastructure to Support Mobile Computing Nodes", 4th International Workshop on Information Security Applications (WISA 2003), Jeju Island, Korea, August 25-27, 2003, Springer-Verlag LNCS, to appear.
3. "Dengue fever prevention and control", *Weekly Epidemiological Record*, Vol. 77 Issue 6, August 2002, pp. 41-48.
4. "Overview of the Grid Security Infrastructure" at http://www-fp.globus.org/security/overview.html.
5. J.Y. Zhou and K.Y. Lam. "Securing digital signatures for non-repudiation", *Journal of Computer Communications*, Vol. 22, No. 8, 1999, pp. 710–716.
6. K. Keahey, V. Welch, "Fine-Grain Authorization for Resource Management in the Grid Environment". *Proceedings of Grid2002 Workshop*, 2002.
7. L. Pearlman, V. Welch, I. Foster, C. Kesselman, S. Tuecke. "A Community Authorization Service for Group Collaboration". *Proceedings of the IEEE 3rd International Workshop on Policies for Distributed Systems and Networks*, 2002.
8. S.V. Nagaraj. "Access control in distributed object systems: problems with access control lists". *Enabling Technologies: Infrastructure for Collaborative Enterprises, 2001. WET ICE 2001. Proceedings. Tenth IEEE International Workshops*, 2001.
9. C.R. Zhang, K.Y. Lam, S. Jajodia. "Scalable threshold closure". *Theoretical Computer Science*, 226(1999) 185-206.
10. A. Shamir. "How to share a secret", *Communications of the ACM*, Vol 22, No 11, 1979, pp. 612-613.
11. J.C. Benaloh, J. Leichter. "Generalized secret sharing and monotone functions". *Advances in Cryptology-CRYPTO'88, Lecture Notes in Computer Science*, vol.403, Springer, Berlin, 1989, pp27-35.
12. M. Ito, A. Saito, T. Nishizeki. "Secret sharing scheme realizing general access structure". in Globecom'87, Tokyo, Japan, 1987, pp.99-102.

Unconditionally Secure Encryption Under Strong Attacks

Luke McAven[1], Rei Safavi-Naini[1], and Moti Yung[2]

[1] School of Information Technology and Computer Science, University of
Wollongong, Northfields Avenue, NSW 2522, Australia.
{lukemc,rei}@uow.edu.au
[2] Department of Computer Science, Columbia University, New York, NY 10027,
USA.
moti@cs.columbia.edu

Abstract. We develop a formalism for unconditionally secure single
sender single receiver encryption under strong attacks. We consider coping with adversarial goals assuring *secrecy* and *non–malleability*, combined with adversarial power similar to those used in computationally
secure systems: ciphertext only, chosen plaintext, and chosen ciphertext.
We relate the various security notions described, and give bounds on the
keysize for systems secure under the various security notions. In addition to defining systems with perfect secrecy, *a la* Shannon, we consider
weaker ϵ–secure systems.

1 Introduction

In various scenarios communicating parties cannot reliably know the computational power of their potential adversary. In this cases, unconditionally secure
(US) encryption schemes may be used to provide security independent of the resources available to subversive forces. The related US authentication schemes [5]
have been well studied, but unlike US authentication schemes, which can be key
efficient, US encryption schemes face an inefficient keysize limit [13]. US encryption schemes under multiple ciphertext only attacks, so–called *L–fold secrecy*,
were considered by [16]. However, stronger attacks, such as *chosen plaintext* and
chosen ciphertext attacks have been largely ignored. A natural line of theoretical
development for US encryption follows that of computationally secure encryption, through investigations of stronger adversaries [1,10].

Hanaoka *et al.* [9] consider an unconditionally secure analogy of public key
encryption systems, which they call Unconditionally Secure Asymmetric Encryption (USAE). In parallel with the development of public key cryptography,
they furthermore consider the goal of *non–malleability* (NM). They give an information theoretic definition of NM and construct a USAE that provides perfect
secrecy and perfect non–malleability.

We consider two–party encryption systems. We define two goals, secrecy and
non–malleability (NM), and consider three attacks, which taken pairwise give
notions of security. We show how some notions are related in a step towards

H. Wang et al. (Eds.): ACISP 2004, LNCS 3108, pp. 427–439, 2004.
© Springer-Verlag Berlin Heidelberg 2004

developing a comprehensive theory of US secrecy. We note that both [9] and [16] add authentication in their study of secrecy systems, while our work, instead, focuses on symmetric encryption systems (secrecy only).

In evaluating security with respect to the proposed notions we consider two types of systems, *perfect* and *ε–perfect*. The former follows Shannon [13], while the latter weakens security in favour of construction flexibility and efficiency.

We give keysizes bounds for systems with perfect secrecy under the various attacks. For ease of exposition, we include some small illustrative examples.

The paper is organised as follows. Section 2 contains basic definitions of unconditionally secure encryption. In section 3 we outline relevant goals and attacks. In section 4 we formally define the goals and security notions for secrecy. Section 5 describes the combinatorics of systems with perfect secrecy under various attacks. Section 6 contains some constructions with perfect secrecy. In section 7 we define NM. We give a view based, and entropy related, definition. We summarise our results in section 8.

2   Unconditionally Secure Encryption (USE)

We assume a single sender and a single receiver, with a common key. Such an encryption system is a tuple $E = (\mathcal{S}, \mathcal{M}, \mathcal{K}, \mathcal{E}, \mathcal{D})$. Each element of the tuple is a set: $\mathcal{S}$ of plaintext messages, $\mathcal{M}$ of ciphertexts (messages sent over the channel), $\mathcal{K}$ of keys, $\mathcal{E}$ of *encryption functions*, each function an injective mapping from $\mathcal{S}$ to $\mathcal{M}$, while $\mathcal{D}$ is the set of *decryption functions* which map from $\mathcal{M}$ to $\mathcal{S}$.

The sets $\mathcal{E}$ and $\mathcal{D}$ are indexed by elements of $\mathcal{K}$, that is E_k is the encryption function in $\mathcal{E}$ associated with the key k, and D_k is the decryption function in $\mathcal{D}$ associated with the key k. The encryption and decryption functions have the property that, $\forall s \in \mathcal{S}$, $m \in \mathcal{M}$, if $E_k(s) = m$ then $D_k(E_k(s)) = s$. This requires that $|\mathcal{M}| \geq |\mathcal{S}|$. We assume the functions in $\mathcal{E}$ and $\mathcal{D}$ are deterministic.

We assume an *a priori* probability distribution on the source states denoted by P_S, and also a probability distribution on the key space, both of which are publicly known. The probability distribution is a function $P_S : \mathcal{S} \to [0, 1]$ such that, $\sum_{s \in \mathcal{S}} P_S(s) = 1$, and $P_S(s) > 0, \forall s \in \mathcal{S}$. We represent by $\mathcal{M}(k)$ a subset of $\mathcal{M}$ generated by $E_k(s), \forall s \in \mathcal{S}$. A plaintext, ciphertext pair (s, m) is *valid* if there exists a key k for which $E_k(s) = m$.

The system works as follows:

1. *Key initialisation:* A trusted authority randomly chooses a key $k \in \mathcal{K}$, and gives it to the sender and receiver.
2. *Encryption:* For a plaintext s the sender transmits the ciphertext $m = E_k(s)$.
3. *Decryption:* The receiver calculates the plaintext as $s = D_k(m)$.

We record encryption rule E_k as a set $\{m_1, m_2, \ldots m_{\mathcal{S}}\} : E_k(s_i) = m_i$.

3   Notions of Security

We consider notions of security obtained by pairing a goal of security and an attack [3,12]. A **goal** represents what challenge the attacker is trying to solve.

We consider two properties of coping with the following two goals: confidentiality and non–malleability. Confidentiality copes with the aim of learning the plaintext corresponding to a given ciphertext challenge, while non–malleability copes with foiling the aim of "meaningfully" modifying the given ciphertext challenge, that is producing another ciphertext "related" to the first.

Attack models or simply attacks, consist of two stages represented by a pair of algorithms (A_1, A_2). Before attack execution a secret key is chosen, and remains a secret during the attack. At the end of Stage 1, the attacker outputs (i) a distribution on plaintexts and ciphertexts, and (ii) some state information passed onto Stage 2. Then a plaintext is chosen and encrypted under the secret key to form the *challenge ciphertext*. Defining success of the attacker in Stage 2, after receiving the challenge ciphertext and other outputs of Stage 1, depends of the security goal. The notions of security are defined by also taking into account the attacker's access to other resources, in our case an encryption or decryption oracle. Oracle access in general can be in either stage, with access in Stage 2 being called *adaptive* with respect to the challenge ciphertext [10]. Subsection 3.1 explains why in our setting all oracle access can be assumed to be in Stage 1.

We define the *knowledge set* $\mathcal{R}$ of an adversary to be the set of plaintexts, ciphertexts, and plaintext, ciphertext pairs obtained by interaction with oracles. We need not specify the stage of the attack the interaction occurs in.

We consider 3 attacks, described in the order of increased information, thus making the adversary increasingly more powerful. One may also define attacks where a mixture, possibly adaptive, of CP and CC queries are available.

Ciphertext only attack (COA_L) : This directly extends Shannon's perfect secrecy model (for $L = 1$), as in Stinson [16]. The adversary observes the output of an encryption oracle and obtains a set of L ciphertexts. As [16] did, we consider only the set, and not the order of ciphertexts.

Chosen plaintext attack (CPA_L) : The adversary has access to an encryption oracle, submits L plaintexts, and receives the associated ciphertexts.

Chosen ciphertext attack (CCA_L) : The adversary has access to a decryption oracle, submits L ciphertexts, and receives the corresponding plaintexts. If there is no plaintext corresponding to a particular ciphertext under the key used, the decryption oracle outputs $\perp$ for that ciphertext.

Let us define the *source view* and *advantage* of an adversary. Let $\mathcal{K}(\mathcal{R})$ denote the set of keys incident with $\mathcal{R}$.

Definition 1. *We say the* **source view** $P_{S,E}(\mathcal{R})$ *of an adversary, given the knowledge set $\mathcal{R}$, is the conditional probability distribution on the source states in $\mathcal{S} \setminus \mathcal{R}$. The source view is a probability distribution $P_{S,E}(\mathcal{R}) : \mathcal{S} \to [0,1]$ satisfying*

$$\sum_{\tilde{s} \in \mathcal{S}} P_{S,E}(\tilde{s}|\mathcal{R}) = 1 \quad and \quad P_{S,E}(\tilde{s}|m; \mathcal{R}) \geq 0, \forall \tilde{s} \in \{\mathcal{S} \setminus \mathcal{R}\} \ .$$

Definition 2. *The* **advantage** $\mathbf{Adv}_{\mathrm{E}}^{\mathrm{PS-ATT}}(\mathcal{R})$ *of an adversary with the knowledge set* $\mathcal{R}$ *is defined as*

$$\mathbf{Adv}_{\mathrm{E}}^{\mathrm{PS-ATT}}(R) = \max_{\tilde{s} \in \mathcal{S}} \left| \frac{P_{\mathcal{S} \backslash \mathcal{R}, \mathrm{E}}(\tilde{s} | m, \mathcal{R})}{P_{\mathcal{S} \backslash \mathcal{R}}(\tilde{s})} - 1 \right|.$$

In $\mathbf{Adv}_{\mathrm{E}}^{\mathrm{PS-ATT}}(\mathcal{R})$ we replace the superscript ATT by the attack, which in turn specifies the nature of the members of $\mathcal{R}$. We distinguish between the stage 1 knowledge set $\mathcal{R}$, and the stage 2 challenge ciphertext m.

The advantage is the difference in the probability of a source state relative to its original probability. The ratio emphasises that a small absolute difference may be significant if the associated $P_{\mathcal{S}}(\tilde{s})$ is small. No division by zero can arise in our definition, since, while the source view may be zero, the value of $P_{\mathcal{S} \backslash \mathcal{R}}(\tilde{s})$ is always non–zero if the space $\mathcal{S} \backslash \mathcal{R}$ still contains plaintext elements. If $\mathcal{S} \backslash \mathcal{R}$ is empty, the associations between all plaintexts and ciphertexts must have been established so this case is of no concern.

3.1 A Note on Adaptivity in Unconditional Security

The natures of unconditional (US) and computational security are fundamentally different. Computational security relies on adversaries having limited resources, so that while decryption will be eventually possible, the eventually is too long to be of practical use. US allows adversaries unlimited resources, particularly time.

The information theoretic, rather than complexity theoretic, basis of US also eliminates the distinction between adaptive and non–adaptive attacks. Many adaptive attacks assume queries are asked one by one, and most of the time they do not help. Since in our setting we consider the best case for the adversary in the querying process (i.e. the worst case) adaptivity does not help. Another issue of adaptivity is querying after the challenge is known (in a chosen–ciphertext attack); this issue is also taken care of by the above argument. In the computationally secure model it may be possible to eliminate significant portions of the key space by judiciously selecting which query to make on the basis of the previous queries. While the same is true for a sequence of queries against an unconditionally secure systems in general, in the worst case analysis of unconditionally secure systems, security is measured against the sequence that results in the highest advantage for the adversary. This means that in worst case analysis of encryption systems the term "chosen" refers not to the means of selection, rather it identifies that the adversary may choose to submit queries to an encryption or a decryption oracle.

4   Secrecy as a Goal

After defining perfect secrecy following the information theoretic approach pioneered and formalised by Shannon [14], we propose a less demanding goal of

ϵ–perfect secrecy. This is similar but allows weaker security with the aim of allowing more flexibility and efficient constructions. We use the terms *source view* and *advantage*, defined in section 3, to formalise these levels of secrecy.

Perfect secrecy (PS): The adversary aims to learn about the plaintext associated with ciphertext m. The system lacks PS if an adversary's source view, after observing m, with knowledge set $\mathcal{R}$, differs from the *a priori* view.

Definition 3. *An encryption system* E *provides* **perfect secrecy** *if*

$$\mathbf{Adv}_{\mathrm{E}}^{\mathrm{PS-ATT}} = \max_{m \in \mathcal{M}} \mathbf{Adv}_{\mathrm{E}}^{\mathrm{PS-ATT}}(m; \mathcal{R}) = 0 \ .$$

Shannon [13] proved this requirement is very demanding. He considered COA$_1$ and proved that systems that provide perfect secrecy, assuming adversaries observe one ciphertext, are equivalent to a *one–time–pad* with key length at least equal to the plaintext length.

Under this attack model, a single observed ciphertext, the view of the adversary is the conditional probability distribution $P_{\mathcal{S}}(s|m)$ defined by the expression

$$P_{\mathcal{S}}(s|m) = \frac{P(s,m)}{P_{\mathcal{M}}(m)} = \frac{P_{\mathcal{S}}(s) \sum_{k:s=D_k(m)} P_{\mathcal{K}}(k)}{\sum_{k:m \in \mathcal{M}(k)} P_{\mathcal{K}}(k) P_{\mathcal{S}}(D_k(m))} \ .$$

We see then that perfect secrecy is equivalent to satisfying,

$$\frac{\sum_{k:s=D_k(m)} P_{\mathcal{K}}(k)}{\sum_{k:m \in \mathcal{M}(k)} P_{\mathcal{K}}(k) P_{\mathcal{S}}(D_k(m))} = 1 \quad \forall s, m \ . \tag{1}$$

We illustrate this with two examples, one with perfect secrecy and one without.

An encryption system with perfect secrecy (C_1): Let $\mathcal{S} = \mathcal{M} = \{0, 1, 2\}$ and let $\mathcal{E} = \{E_1, E_2, E_3\}$ be defined by the sets $E_1 = \{0, 1, 2\}, E_2 = \{2, 0, 1\}$ and $E_3 = \{1, 2, 0\}$. Let the initial distribution be uniform in keys and source states, i.e. $P(k_i) = 1/3, \forall k_i \in \mathcal{K}$, and $P(s_i) = 1/3, \forall s_i \in \mathcal{S}$. Consider equation (1) for $m = s = 0$. The numerator allows the key k_1, so the top line is $P_{\mathcal{K}}(k_1) = 1/3$. The denominator is $P_{\mathcal{K}}(k_1) P_{\mathcal{S}}(0) + P_{\mathcal{K}}(k_2) P_{\mathcal{S}}(1) + P_{\mathcal{K}}(k_3) P_{\mathcal{S}}(2) = \frac{1}{3} \times \frac{1}{3} + \frac{1}{3} \times \frac{1}{3} + \frac{1}{3} \times \frac{1}{3} = \frac{1}{3}$. Since all s, m satisfy equation (1) the system has perfect secrecy [16, Ex. 1.1].

An encryption system without perfect secrecy: Consider a system defined by the key set $\mathcal{K} = \{k_1, k_3\}$, with the keys of C_1. We compare the *a priori* distribution and the adversaries *view*, again for $m = s = 0$, using equation (1). The numerator is now, $1/2$, since we have only two keys. The denominator is $P_{\mathcal{K}}(k_1) P_{\mathcal{S}}(0) + P_{\mathcal{K}}(k_3) P_{\mathcal{S}}(2) = \frac{1}{2} \times \frac{1}{3} + \frac{1}{2} \times \frac{1}{3} = \frac{1}{3}$. Thus the system does not have perfect secrecy, indeed this case has $P_{\mathcal{S}}(0) = \frac{1}{3}$ and $P_{\mathcal{S}}(0|0) = \frac{1}{2}$ so that the advantage is going to be at least $|\frac{3}{2} - 1| = \frac{1}{2}$.

Definition 4. *An encryption system* E *provides* ϵ–**perfect secrecy** *if*

$$\mathbf{Adv}_{\mathrm{E}}^{\mathrm{PS-ATT}} = \max_{m \in \mathcal{M}} \mathbf{Adv}_{\mathrm{E}}^{\mathrm{PS-ATT}}(m; R) \leq \epsilon \ .$$

In the example without perfect secrecy the advantage is $\frac{1}{2}$, as in the $m = s = 0$ case. That encryption system has $\frac{1}{2}$–perfect secrecy. The following theorem bounds the mutual information between the plaintext and the ciphertext.

Theorem 1. *For encryption systems with ϵPS against an attack* ATT *and with knowledge set* $\mathcal{R}$, *we have* $I(\mathcal{S}; \mathcal{M}|\mathcal{R}) \leq \log_2(1 + \epsilon)$.

Proof. Let $\mathbf{r}$ denote the variable for the adversaries information set (all plaintext, ciphertext, and plaintext, ciphertext pairs). Since $\log_2$ is an increasing function,

$$I(\mathcal{S}; \mathcal{M}|\mathcal{R}) = H(\mathcal{S}|\mathcal{R}) - H(\mathcal{S}|\mathcal{M}, \mathcal{R}) = \sum_{s \in S \backslash \mathcal{R}, m, \mathbf{r}} P(s, m|\mathbf{r}) \log_2 \frac{P(s|m, \mathbf{r})}{P(s|\mathbf{r})}$$

$$\leq \log_2 \max_{s,m} \frac{P(s|m, \mathbf{r})}{P(s|\mathbf{r})} .$$

The definition of ϵ–perfect secrecy implies $-\epsilon \leq \frac{P(s|m,\mathbf{r})}{P(s|\mathbf{r})} - 1 \leq \epsilon$. It follows that, for a US encryption system with ϵ–perfect secrecy, $I(\mathcal{S}; \mathcal{M}|\mathcal{R}) \leq \log_2(1 + \epsilon)$. □

Schemes with perfect secrecy meet the bound, that is $I(\mathcal{S}; \mathcal{M}) = 0$. For $\epsilon << 1$, we have $\log_2(1 + \epsilon) \approx \epsilon$ and $I(\mathcal{S}; \mathcal{M}) \leq \epsilon$.

4.1   Notions and Levels of Security

Notions of security are specified by combining a goal and an attack. We can pair secrecy with each of the attacks (COA_L,CPA_L,CCA_L) to obtain three notions of security for encryption systems. We may also consider two levels, PS and ϵPS. However since PS and ϵPS are related by setting $\epsilon = 0$ we represent the six notions using the ϵPS only.

Let $\mathbf{X_L}$ be a vector from $\mathcal{X}$, as in [2], with $|\mathbf{X_L}| = L$. So, for example, $\mathbf{M_L}$ is a ciphertext vector $\{m_1 \ldots m_L\}$ of L distinct elements of $\mathcal{M}$. The notions follow:

ϵ**PS–COA$_L$: ϵ–Perfect secrecy against ciphertext only attacks.**
The adversary observes L ciphertexts, $\mathbf{M_L}$, which includes a challenge ciphertext m. An encryption system is PS–COA$_L$ if

$$\max_{\mathbf{M_L} \in \mathcal{M}} \mathbf{Adv}_E^{\text{PS−COA}_L}(\mathbf{M_L}) \leq \epsilon.$$

ϵ**PS–CPA$_L$: ϵ–Perfect secrecy against chosen plaintext attacks.**
The adversary sends a plaintext vector S_L to the encryption oracle and receives the corresponding ciphertext vector in response. The adversaries source view should not change appreciably. This means

$$\max_{\mathbf{S_L}, \mathbf{M_L}, m \in \mathcal{M} \backslash \mathbf{M_L}} \mathbf{Adv}_E^{\text{PS−CPA}_L}(m; (\mathbf{S_L}, \mathbf{M_L})) \leq \epsilon .$$

We emphasise the need to consider all possible plaintext vectors $\mathbf{S_L}$ and all possible response ciphertext vectors $\mathbf{M_L}$ under all possible keys. The challenge ciphertext is m and, for secrecy, the adversary should not have a significantly changed source view given R, m.

ϵPS–CCA$_L$: ϵ–Perfect secrecy against chosen ciphertext attacks.

This is similar to ϵPS–CPA$_L$ but here the adversary has access to a decryption oracle. He chooses a ciphertexts vector from $\mathcal{M}$ and submits it to the decryption oracle. For each ciphertext the oracle either returns the corresponding plaintext, or outputs $\perp$. If $|\mathcal{M}| = |\mathcal{S}|$, an ϵPS–COA$_L$ query will always have a plaintext vector as the response. However, if $|\mathcal{M}| > |\mathcal{S}|$ not all ciphertexts are valid under a given key, so the response $\mathbf{R_L}$ will be a vector on $\{\mathcal{S}, \perp\}$.

An encryption system $\mathbf{E}$ is ϵPS–COA$_L$, if it satisfies the following.

$$\max_{\mathbf{M_L}, \mathbf{R_L}, m \in \mathcal{M} \backslash \mathbf{M_L}} \mathbf{Adv}_{\mathbf{E}}^{\mathrm{PS-COA_L}}(m; (\mathbf{M_L}, \mathbf{R_L})) \leq \epsilon .$$

We also define L–fold PS notions. If $L = 1$ the L–fold term is redundant. We explicitly define only L–fold PS–COA$_L$, which is equivalent to L–fold secrecy in [16]. The other L–fold PS notions are similarly defined.

Definition 5. *An encryption system satisfies the notion L–fold ϵPS–COA$_L$ if it is also ϵPS–COA$_{L'}$ for all $1 \leq L' < L$.*

We have the following relationships between these security notions.

Theorem 2. *For any encryption system (i) ϵPS–CCA$_L \implies \epsilon$PS–CPA$_L$, and (ii) if $|\mathcal{S}| = |\mathcal{M}|$ then ϵPS–CCA$_L \impliedby \epsilon$ PS–CPA$_L$ also.*

Proof. To prove (i), we note $\mathbf{Adv}_{\mathbf{E}}^{\mathrm{PS-CCA}}((\mathbf{M_L}, \mathbf{R_L})) \leq \mathbf{Adv}_{\mathbf{E}}^{\mathrm{PS-CPA}}((\mathbf{S_L}, \mathbf{M_L}))$. This is true because the set of pairs $(\mathbf{S_L}, \mathbf{M_L})$ generated through a CPA$_L$ attack is a subset of pairs $(\mathbf{M_L}, \mathbf{R_L})$ generated through a CCA$_L$ attack and so if the source view under CCA$_L$ is bounded by ϵ, it will be bounded by at least by the same amount under CPA$_L$.

To prove (ii), we note that if $|\mathcal{S}| = |\mathcal{M}|$, then an L–query $\mathbf{M_L}$ always results in a plaintext set S_L and so $\mathbf{Adv}_{\mathbf{E}}^{\mathrm{PS-CCA}}((\mathbf{M_L}, \mathbf{R_L})) = \mathbf{Adv}_{\mathbf{E}}^{\mathrm{PS-CPA}}((\mathbf{S_L}, \mathbf{M_L}))$. $\square$

Let us illustrate how chosen ciphertext may give distinct information from chosen plaintext. Consider a construction with $\mathcal{S} = \{0, 1, 2\}$, $\mathcal{M} = \{0, 1, 2, 3\}$. Choosing $|\mathcal{S}| \neq |\mathcal{M}|$ allows for the possibility of a distinction. Let the encryption rules be $E_1 = \{0, 1, 2\}, E_2 = \{2, 0, 1\}$ and $E_3 = \{1, 2, 3\}$.

Assume the adversary submits the ciphertext 3 to the decryption oracle. The response is from $\{2, \perp\}$. If the response is 2 the key is k_3, while if the response is $\perp$ one of the other two keys must be being used. This system is not CPA$_1$ since submitting 2 to an encryption oracle reveals which key is being used.

The following relationships are easy to prove (since no query is allowed).

Theorem 3. ϵPS–CCA$_0 \iff \epsilon$PS–CPA$_0 \iff \epsilon$PS–COA$_0$.

5 Combinatorics of Perfect Secrecy Systems

Here we consider the combinatorics of perfect secrecy systems. We assume uniform probability distributions on the key and source state spaces.

For an encryption system $E = (\mathcal{S}, \mathcal{M}, \mathcal{K}, \mathcal{E}, \mathcal{D})$ and a knowledge set $\mathcal{R}$, define the $\mathcal{R}$–reduced system, $E_R = (\mathcal{S}_R, \mathcal{M}_R, \mathcal{K}_R, \mathcal{E}_R, \mathcal{D}_R)$ as follows. We have $\mathcal{S}_R = \mathcal{S} \setminus \mathcal{R}$, $\mathcal{M}_R = \mathcal{M} \setminus \mathcal{R}$, $\mathcal{K}_R = \mathcal{K}(\mathcal{R})$, and the encryption and decryption functions associated with these keys are restricted to the $\mathcal{S}_R$ and $\mathcal{M}_R$.

Following [16] we give a bound on the key size of L–fold PS–COA$_L$ systems.

Theorem 4. *[16, Thm. 2.1] If a system is L–fold PS–COA$_L$ then* $|\mathcal{K}| \geq \binom{|\mathcal{S}|}{L}$.

In the case $|\mathcal{M}| = |\mathcal{S}|$ the security notions PS–CPA$_L$ and PS–CCA$_L$ are the same, see theorem 2. The lower bounds are therefore the same if $|\mathcal{M}| = |\mathcal{S}|$.

Theorem 5. *Let E provide L–fold PS–CPA$_1$. Then* $|\mathcal{K}_R| \geq |\mathcal{M}|(|\mathcal{S}| - 1)$.

Proof. For a plaintext s and its corresponding ciphertext m, we must have $P(s'|m', (s, m)) = P(s')$, $\forall s' \in \mathcal{S} \setminus \{s\}, \forall m' \in \mathcal{M} \setminus \{m\}$. So at least $|\mathcal{S}| - 1$ keys map different s to m' (one key for each s').

Moreover for each $m \in \mathcal{M}$ there must be at least one key mapping s to m. We show this as follows. Suppose there is a ciphertext $\hat{m}$ that no key can map s to $\hat{m}$. This means $P(s, \hat{m}) = 0$. Consider a valid pair (s', m'). We must have $P(s|\hat{m}, (s', m')) = P(s) \neq 0$ from the definition of PS–CPA$_1$. Rearranging this using the product rule we get $P(s, \hat{m}|(s', m')) = P(\hat{m}|(s', m'))P(s)$. This implies $P(s, \hat{m}) \neq 0$ which implies $P(s|\hat{m}) \neq 0$ also, contradicting our assumption.

Finally, $\mathcal{K}(m, s) \cap \mathcal{K}(m', s) = \emptyset, m \neq m'$.   □

Theorem 6. *An encryption system E is L–fold PS–CPA$_L$ if, given any S_L and response M_L, so $\mathcal{R} = (S_L, M_L)$, the $\mathcal{R}$–reduced system E_R is PS–COA$_0$.*

Proof. Recall the definition of PS–CPA$_L$ requires $P(s|m, (S_L, M_L)) = P(s)$ for all consistent parameters. Let $\mathcal{R} = (S_L, M_L)$. Then the $\mathcal{R}$–reduced encryption system must be PS–CCA$_0$ and so $|\mathcal{K}_R| \geq |\mathcal{S}| - L$.   □

Theorem 7. *If a system is L–fold PS–CPA$_L$ then*

$$|\mathcal{K}| \geq (|\mathcal{S}| - L)\frac{|\mathcal{M}|!}{(|\mathcal{M}| - L)!L!} .$$

We say an L–fold PS–CPA$_L$ system is optimal if it meets the bound above. Observe that if $L = 0$ the bound result is $|\mathcal{K}| \geq |\mathcal{S}|$, as for a PS–COA$_1$.

Theorem 8. *An encryption system is PS–CCA$_L$ if, given any M_L and any set R_L in return, the $\mathcal{R}$–reduced system is PS–COA$_1$.*

Theorem 9 (PS–CCA$_L$ bound). *If a system is PS–CCA$_L$ then*

$$|\mathcal{K}| \geq (|\mathcal{S}| - L)\frac{|\mathcal{M}|!}{(|\mathcal{S}| - L)!(|\mathcal{M}| - |\mathcal{S}|)!} .$$

If $|\mathcal{M}| = |\mathcal{S}|$ this expression reduces to that in theorem 7.

6 Constructions for Perfect Secrecy

L–fold **PS–COA$_L$**: Stinson [16] demonstrated how perpendicular arrays (PA's) [11] can be used to construct systems with perfect L–fold secrecy (PS–COA$_L$). More details on PA's and their application to secrecy and authentication are in [4]. Construction C$_1$, given earlier, is a PA construction.

Definition 6. *A **perpendicular array** $PA_\lambda(L,k,v)$ is a $\lambda \begin{pmatrix} v \\ L \end{pmatrix} \times k$ array A filled from the alphabet $\{1,\dots,v\}$ such that*

- *Every row of A contains k distinct symbols.*
- *For any L columns of A, and any L distinct symbols, there are exactly λ rows of A in which the L given symbols all occur in the given L columns.*

Theorem 10. *[16, Theorem 2.3] If there is a $PA_\lambda(L,k,v)$, $k \geq 2L - 1$, then there is a L–fold PS-COA$_L$ system with $|\mathcal{S}| = k, |\mathcal{M}| = v$ and $|\mathcal{K}| = \lambda \begin{pmatrix} v \\ L \end{pmatrix}$.*

One example of a PS–COA$_L$ system, for $1 \leq L \leq |\mathcal{S}|$, is given by taking the key set to be the set of all permutations of $\{0,\dots,|\mathcal{S}|-1\}$. This is equivalent to a one–time pad and is optimal for $L = |\mathcal{S}|$. Another construction, for PS–COA$_1$, is the set of $|\mathcal{S}|$ cyclic permutations on $\{0\dots|\mathcal{S}|-1\}$.

PS–CPA$_L$: Let C$_2$ be a system with $|\mathcal{S}| = |\mathcal{M}| = 3$ and encryption rules $E_1 = \{0,1,2\}, E_2 = \{0,2,1\}, E_3 = \{1,2,0\}, E_4 = \{1,0,2\}, E_5 = \{2,0,1\}$ and $E_6 = \{2,1,0\}$. The definition of PS–CPA$_1$ requires that, given any (plaintext,ciphertext) pair, any other ciphertext is associated with probability unchanged relative to the view before observing the pair. Above we see that for any (s,m) pair the number of valid keys is reduced to two. Each of the remaining (s',m') pairs occurs with equal probability. This system is an optimal PS–CPA$_1$.

7 Non–malleability as a Security Goal

Non–malleability in computational security is defined informally as [1,2,3,6,7,8]:

Definition 7 (Non–malleable). *An adversary is given an input ciphertext y of a plaintext x drawn from the message distribution, and must produce another ciphertext y' such that the corresponding plaintext x' has a relation R with x, that is $R(x,x')$ is true. A system is non–malleable if the likelihood of finding such a corresponding ciphertext is negligible.*

Bellare and Sahai [2] demonstrated the equivalence of NM with indistinguishibility when a special type of query, parallel chosen–ciphertext queries, is considered. In this attack the attacker is presented with a challenge ciphertext which is the encryption of one of two known plaintexts, s_1 or s_2, and is allowed to ask a vector query $\mathbf{m}^\ell$ of ℓ ciphertexts $(m_1, \cdots m_\ell)$, and receive the corresponding plaintext vector $\mathbf{s}^\ell = (s_1, \cdots s_\ell)$. The attacker will succeed if he has a success chance better than $1/2$ in determining which plaintext had been used for the encryption of the challenge ciphertext. As noted earlier, because of the worst case analysis we need not consider the order of presenting the challenge to the attacker and the formation of queries.

Following this approach we define NM to be the ability to obtain information about plaintexts, given a vector $(\mathbf{m}^\ell, \mathbf{r}^\ell)$ where $\mathbf{r}^\ell = \mathbf{s}^\ell$ if there is an encryption key incident with $\mathbf{m}^\ell$, and $\perp$ otherwise. We use the difference between the source views before and after the query to measure the leakage of information.

Definition 8. *The ℓ–non–malleability advantage for a ciphertext m' is*

$$\mathbf{Adv}_E^{NM_\ell-ATT}(m'; (\mathbf{m}^\ell, \mathbf{r}^\ell), \mathcal{R}) = \max_{s' \in S, s' \neq s} \left| \frac{P_{S,E}(s'|m', (\mathbf{m}^\ell, \mathbf{r}^\ell), \mathcal{R})}{P_{S,E}(s'|(\mathbf{m}^\ell, \mathbf{r}^\ell), \mathcal{R})} - 1 \right|.$$

Intuitively, an ℓ-non–malleable system requires that the source view be independent of the challenge m' conditional on the ℓ–query. That is the view evaluated in the reduced encryption system resulting from the query. This ensures that the challenge ciphertext is not related to any vector of of ℓ ciphertexts.

For the basic notion of NM we take the knowledge set $\mathcal{R}$ to be empty. We define ϵ–perfect non–malleability$_\ell$ of an encryption system (ϵPNM_ℓ) as:

Definition 9. *An encryption system is said to be ϵPNM_ℓ if*

$$\mathbf{Adv}_E^{NM_\ell-ATT}(m') = \max_{(\mathbf{m}^\ell, \mathbf{r}^\ell), m', m' \notin \mathbf{m}^\ell} \mathbf{Adv}_E^{NM_\ell-ATT}(m'; (\mathbf{m}^\ell, \mathbf{r}^\ell), \mathcal{R}) \leq \epsilon.$$

Here $\mathcal{R}$ is the knowledge set associated with the attack ATT.

Theorem 11. *For systems with ϵNM_ℓ, $I((S, M)|M^\ell, \mathcal{R}^\ell) \leq \log_2(1 + \epsilon)$.*

Proof. Using Jensen's inequality, to get from the second to third line, we have

$$I(S'; M'|R^\ell, M^\ell) = \sum_{r^\ell, m^\ell, m', s'} P(s', m'|\mathbf{m}^\ell, \mathbf{r}^\ell) \log_2 \frac{P(s', m'|(\mathbf{m}^\ell, \mathbf{r}^\ell))}{P(s'|m, s)P(m'|(\mathbf{m}^\ell, \mathbf{r}^\ell))}$$

$$= \sum P(s', m'|(\mathbf{m}^\ell, \mathbf{r}^\ell)) \log_2 \frac{P(s'|m', (\mathbf{m}^\ell, \mathbf{r}^\ell))}{P(s'|(\mathbf{m}^\ell, \mathbf{r}^\ell))}$$

$$\leq \log_2 \left[\sum P(s', m'|\mathbf{m}^\ell, \mathbf{r}^\ell) \frac{P(s'|m', \mathbf{m}^\ell, \mathbf{r}^\ell)}{P(s'|\mathbf{m}^\ell, \mathbf{r}^\ell)} \right]$$

The definition of ϵPNM gives $\frac{P(s'|m', \mathbf{m}^\ell, \mathbf{r}^\ell)}{P(s'|\mathbf{m}^\ell, \mathbf{s}^\ell)} < 1 + \epsilon$, implying $\frac{P(s'|m', \mathbf{m}^\ell, \mathbf{s}^\ell)}{P(s'|\mathbf{m}^\ell, \mathbf{s}^\ell)} < 1 + \epsilon$ so $I(S'; M'|S, M) \leq (1 + \epsilon)$. $\square$

When $\epsilon = 0$ we have perfect non–malleability, represented by the requirement

$$P(s'|m', (\mathbf{m}^\ell, \mathbf{r}^\ell)) = P(s'|(\mathbf{m}^\ell, \mathbf{r}^\ell)) \ \forall \text{ valid } (\mathbf{m}^\ell, \mathbf{r}^\ell), (m's')$$

or $H(\mathcal{S}'|\mathcal{M}',(\mathcal{M}^\ell,\mathcal{R}^\ell)) = H(\mathcal{S}'|(\mathcal{M}^\ell,\mathcal{R}^\ell))$, or $I((\mathcal{M}';\mathcal{S}'|(\mathcal{M}^\ell,\mathcal{R}^\ell)) = 0$. An special case of the latter with $\ell = 1$ is used to define perfect non–malleability in [9]. We call that *average NM*, or ANM, since it records average properties implied by the entropy measure, rather than the maximal approach to bound every system part taken in our NM definition. We represent this relationship in a theorem.

Theorem 12. $NM_1 \implies ANM$ but $ANM \not\implies NM_1$.

Proof. (sketch) We demonstrated how definition 9 implies $I((\mathcal{M}';\mathcal{S}'|(\mathcal{M},\mathcal{S})) = 0$, so NM $\implies$ ANM. The converse follows by examination of the entropy condition. If $H(X) = H(Y)$ then $\mathbb{E}(P_X) = \mathbb{E}(P_Y)$, however the probability of choosing different x using the variables x and y need not be the same.   □

The notions associated with NM are defined similarly to those for PS.

$\epsilon\mathbf{NM}_\ell\mathbf{-COA}_L$: ϵ**–Perfect NM_ℓ against ciphertext only attacks.**

The adversary observes L ciphertexts, $\mathbf{M_L}$ and so $\mathcal{R} = \mathbf{M_L}$. An encryption system is $NM_\ell\mathrm{-COA}_L$ if

$$\max_{\mathbf{M_L}\in\mathcal{M}} \mathbf{Adv}_{\mathrm{E}}^{\mathrm{NM}_\ell-\mathrm{COA_L}}(m';(\mathbf{m}^\ell,\mathbf{r}^\ell),\mathbf{M_L}) \leq \epsilon.$$

$\epsilon\mathbf{NM}_\ell\mathbf{-CPA}_L$: ϵ**–Perfect NM_ℓ against chosen plaintext attacks.**

The adversary submits L plaintexts to the encryption oracle and receives the corresponding ciphertexts in response. The attacker should not have an appreciably changed source view, thus

$$\max_{\mathbf{S_L},\mathbf{M_L},m\in\mathcal{M}\setminus\mathbf{M_L}} \mathbf{Adv}_{\mathrm{E}}^{\mathrm{NM}_\ell-\mathrm{CPA_L}}(m';(\mathbf{m}^\ell,\mathbf{r}^\ell),(\mathbf{S_L},\mathbf{M_L})) \leq \epsilon.$$

$\epsilon\mathbf{NM-CCA}_L$: ϵ**–Perfect NM against chosen ciphertext attacks.**

$$\max_{\mathbf{R_L},\mathbf{M_L},m\in\mathcal{M}\setminus\mathbf{M_L}} \mathbf{Adv}_{\mathrm{E}}^{\mathrm{NM}_\ell-\mathrm{CCA_L}}(m';(\mathbf{m}^\ell,\mathbf{r}^\ell),(\mathbf{R_L},\mathbf{M_L})) \leq \epsilon.$$

Definition 10. *An encryption system provides L–fold $\epsilon NM_\ell\mathrm{-COA}_L$ if it is also $\epsilon NM_\ell\mathrm{-COA}_{L'}$ for all $1 \leq L' < L$.*

We can relate PNM_1 to CPA_1. The notion PNM_1 considers secrecy within the reduced space consistent with $(\mathbf{m}^\ell,\mathbf{r}^\ell)$ and requires the source view in this space be independent of the challenge ciphertext. CPA_1 however requires the source view to be independent of the challenge ciphertext and the query and response. That is it requires neither the challenge nor the query have significant effect on the attacker's view of the source. This gives the following theorem.

Theorem 13. $PS\text{-}CPA_1 \implies PNM_1$ but $PNM_1 \not\implies PS\text{-}CPA_1$.

Proof. We begin with the defining relationships for PNM and CPA_1, which are, respectively, $P(s'|m',(m,s)) = P(s'|(m,s))$ and $P(s'|m',(m,s)) = P(s)$. These can be expressed in the form $P(x|y,z) = P(x)$ and $P(x|y,z) = P(x|y)$. If $P(x|y,z) = P(x)$ then x is independent of y and z so $P(x|y) = P(x)$ would hold and CPA_1 would imply PNM. If, however $P(x|y,z) = P(x|y)$ is the only requirement, x could well depend on y so that $P(x|y,z) = P(x|y) \neq P(x)$.   □

7.1   Illustrating Non–malleability

Consider C_1 given in section 4, and shown to have perfect secrecy. C_1 is also malleable. Informally, encryption key k_i corresponds to the ciphertext being related to the plaintext by a shift of $(i - 1) \mod 3$. Formally, we see observing any (s, m) pair gives a reduced system with keysize 1, which is not PS–COA$_1$.

By Theorem 13 we can use a PS–CPA$_1$ system to give an PNM system. C_2 in section (6) is PS–CPA$_1$. We can also identify it as an example of the NM (k, n)–One–Time USAE scheme of [9], with $k = 0, n = 1$ and $q = 3$. The $f_i(x)$ functions therein become constants between the single sender and the single receiver, who trust each other. The key is a pair $(f_1(x), f_2(x))$, where the dependence on x is unnecessary so that the pair is $(f_1 \in F_3, f_2 \in F_3^*)$. The keys encrypt a plaintext s according to the function $f_1 + sf_2$.

8   Summary

The description of perfect secrecy systems secure against multiple message observations was developed some time ago [16], building on the founding definitions of perfect secrecy [13]. We have extended the modelling of systems with unconditional security to include protection against chosen–plaintext and chosen–ciphertext attacks. We have defined goals of perfect secrecy and non–malleability. We have given some constructions and bounds for perfect secrecy systems.

References

1. M. Bellare, A. Desai, D. Pointcheveal & P. Rogaway 'Relations among notions of security for public–key encryption schemes.' *Crypto'98* LNCS **1462** (Springer–Verlag, Berlin, 1998) 26–45.
2. M. Bellare & A. Sahai 'Non–malleable encryption: Equivalence between two notions, and an indistinguishability–based characterisation.' *Crypto '99* LNCS **1666** (Springer–Verlag, Berlin, 1999).
3. M. Bellare, A. Desai, D. Pointcheveal & P. Rogaway 'Relations among notions of security for public–key encryption schemes.' 2001.
4. J. Bierbrauer & Y. Edel 'Theory of perpendicular arrays.' *J. Combin. Designs* **2**(6) (1994) 375–406.
5. Y. Desmedt, Y. Frankel & M. Yung 'Multi–receiver/multi–sender network security: efficient authenticated multicast/feedback.' *IEEE Infocom'92* (1992) 2045–54.
6. D. Dolev, C. Dwork & M. Naor 'Non–malleable cryptography.' *23rd STOC* ACM, (1991) 542–552.
7. D. Dolev, C. Dwork & M. Naor 'Non–malleable cryptography.' Technical Report CS95-27, Weizmann Institute of Science (1995).
8. D. Dolev, C. Dwork & M. Naor 'Non–malleable cryptography.' *SIAM J. Computing* **30**(2) (2000) 391–437.
9. G. Hanaoka, J. Shikata, Y. Hanaoka & H. Imai 'Unconditionally secure anonymous encryption and group authentication.' *Asiacrypt 2002*, LNCS **2501** (Springer–Verlag, Berlin, 2002) 81–99.

10. J. Katz & M. Yung 'Complete characterization of security notions for probabilistic private–key encryption.' *32nd STOC*, ACM (2000), 245–254.
11. R. C. Mullin, P. J. Schellenberg, G. H. J. van Rees & S. A. Vanstone 'On the construction of perpendicular arrays.' *Utilitas Math.* **18** (1980) 141–160.
12. M. Naor & M. Yung 'Public–key cryptosystems provably secure against chosen–ciphertext attacks.' *22nd STOC*, ACM (1990) 427–437.
13. C. E. Shannon 'A mathematical theory of communication.' *The Bell System Technical Journal* **27** (1948) 379–423.
14. C. E. Shannon 'Communication theory of secrecy systems.' *The Bell System Technical Journal* **28**(4) (1949) 656–715.
15. G.J. Simmons 'Authentication theory/coding theory.' *Crypto'84* LNCS **196** (Springer–Verlag, 1984) 411–31.
16. D. R. Stinson 'The combinatorics of authentication and secrecy codes.' *Journal of Cryptology* **2** (1990) 23–49.

ManTiCore: Encryption with Joint Cipher-State Authentication

Erik Anderson, Cheryl Beaver, Timothy Draelos, Richard Schroeppel, and
Mark Torgerson

Sandia National Laboratories** Albuquerque, NM 87185-0785
{weander, cbeaver, tjdrael, rschroe, mdtorge}@sandia.gov

Abstract. We describe a new mode of encryption with inexpensive
authentication, which uses information from the internal state of the
cipher to provide the authentication. Our algorithms have a number of
benefits: The encryption has properties similar to CBC mode, yet the
encipherment and authentication can be parallelized and/or pipelined;
The authentication overhead is minimal; The authentication process
remains resistant against some IV reuse. Our first construction is the
MTC4 encryption algorithm based on cryptographic hash functions
which supports variable block sizes up to twice the hash output length,
and variable key lengths. A proof of security is presented for MTC4. We
then generalize the construction to create the Cipher-State (CS) mode
of encryption that uses the internal state of any round-based block
cipher as an authenticator. We give a concrete example using AES as
the encryption primitive. We provide performance measurements for all
constructions.

Keywords: Encryption Mode, Inexpensive Authentication, Luby-
Rackoff, Feistel, Middletext, Hash, Cipher

1   Introduction

When choosing a cipher, its mode of operation, and method of authentication,
one needs to consider the security, speed, size, and functionality required by
the application. Data security schemes have typically relied on combining an
encryption step (with a mode of cipher operation) and a message authentication
mechanism. These separate processes lead to undesirable computational costs.

One would like to speed up the process by using information from the encryption step for authentication. Recent research has considered authenticated
encryption schemes that are more efficient than current standards and prac-
tices [10,11,22,23]. In particular, OCB [22] is parallelizable and offers CBC-like
authenticated encryption with only two extra block cipher invocations over that

** Sandia is a multiprogram laboratory operated by Sandia Corporation, a Lockheed
Martin Company, for the United States Department of Energy under Contract DE-
AC04-94AL85000.

H. Wang et al. (Eds.): ACISP 2004, LNCS 3108, pp. 440–453, 2004.
© Springer-Verlag Berlin Heidelberg 2004

needed for encipherment alone. CCM [23], as specified in NIST Draft Pub 800-38C, offers authenticated encryption with associated data (AEAD) for AES, which accommodates a combination of secret and non-secret data by authenticating all data and encrypting only secret data.

We strive to take a new and different approach - to examine using a cipher's internal state as inputs for an authentication mechanism. Our approach is also parallelizable, yet exhibits many of the practical benefits of CBC mode. The authentication adds minimal cost to the encryption process. The presented methods also offer security in the face of IV reuse, which, to our knowledge, existing authenticated encryption mechanisms do not. Finally, given the landscape of cryptographic algorithms, we have chosen to not pursue patents on these new algorithms so as not to contribute to the current patent minefield.

We examine block ciphers comprised of $2n$ rounds. The authentication tag is a function of the encryption state after n rounds. Our first construction, MTC4, is based on a four round Feistel network with cryptographic hash functions as round functions. Many of the components necessary for security can be added into the round functions because of the hash algorithm's ability to accept arbitrary length inputs. In Section 2.1, the MTC4 algorithm is shown to be secure with respect to both privacy and integrity, under general security assumptions.

Extensive research has been conducted on the security and construction of low round Feistel ciphers. In [15], Luby and Rackoff show how to construct $2n$-bit pseudorandom permutations using a Feistel network. Their constructions are secure against any adversary who has combined adaptive chosen plaintext and ciphertext attacks. In [12], Knudsen provides a nice survey and analysis of the security bounds for low round Feistel constructions. Much research has also been done finding practical instantiations of low round Feistel networks using cryptographic hashes as round functions. In [1,16], the authors examine three round ciphers, while Lim [14] looks at four round constructions. Naor and Reingold [18] and Patel, Ramzan, and Sundaram [19] examine replacing some of the hash functions used in the various rounds with less expensive function calls.

For our second construction, we show how to take an arbitrary round-based cipher and extend it to provide inexpensive authentication. As with the hash-based construction, the general version exhibits encryption properties similar to CBC mode, is parallelizable, and the authentication adds minimal overhead and provides security against some IV reuse. We use AES as a concrete example and have submitted the CS (Cipher State) mode to NIST as a proposed mode of operation for AES. We provide performance figures for the various constructions.

2 ManTiCore4

As its namesake implies, our construction, ManTiCore4 (MTC4), comprises a number of common elements. The basic cipher elements use cryptographic hash functions in a four-round Feistel network and can be viewed as a variant of [14]. One attractive feature is the ability of the hash to accept arbitrary sized inputs. This allows us to insert an IV, round counter, and block counters into the round inputs in a simple fashion. This construction can be used to create a block

442 E. Anderson et al.

cipher of any bit length up to twice the hash size. Of course, the hash may be truncated to produce shorter block sizes. The key size is adjustable and impacts performance only when the input block size of the hash function is exceeded.

Let H be a cryptographically strong hash function mapping arbitrary number of bits to h bits. Let K be a k-bit key and IV be a v-bit initialization vector. Let $M = m_1, m_2, \cdots, m_{2j}$ be the message to be encrypted, where each m_i is h bits in length. We assume the message M is padded with some suitable padding scheme, if necessary, so it is a multiple of $2h$ bits in length.

The following is the MTC4 algorithm, which is depicted in Figure 1.

MTC4
INPUT $(IV, M), K$
OUTPUT $(IV, C, AUTH)$
Set $CS \leftarrow 0$
For i from 1 to $2j - 1$ by 2 do
    Set $x \leftarrow m_i \oplus H(K, IV, 0, i, m_{i+1})$
    Set $y \leftarrow m_{i+1} \oplus H(K, IV, 1, i, x)$
    Set $CS \leftarrow CS \oplus x \oplus y$
    Set $c_{i+1} \leftarrow x \oplus H(K, IV, 2, i, y)$
    Set $c_i \leftarrow y \oplus H(K, IV, 3, i, c_{i+1})$
Set $AUTH = H(K, IV, 0, 0, CS)$
RETURN $(IV, C, AUTH)$

To enable a security proof, the fields presented to the hash must be aligned to ensure independence. Hence the sizes of the round and block counters must be consistent. At a minimum, we need 2 bits to represent the round number and $log_2(j)$ bits for the block number. Although cryptographic hash functions accept arbitrary-length inputs, typically they process a block of b bits at a time. For instance, SHA-1 [7] operates on 512-bit blocks and outputs 160 bits. From an efficiency standpoint, one should limit the parameter size so the arguments fit in one input block, that is $k + v + 2 + \log_2(j) + h \leq b$. Given that they do, the expected speed of MTC4-SHA-1 is on the order of the $160/512 * 1/2 = 5/32$ times as fast as SHA-1. The cost to authenticate the entire message is essentially that of having to hash only a single block of data. In addition, both the encryption and authentication for each message block can be computed in parallel, leaving a single hash of the combined pre-authenticators, CS, to complete the process.

2.1 Security Considerations

When viewed strictly as a block cipher, MTC4's security relies on the pseudorandomness of a four-round Feistel network. In MTC4 and like ciphers, the work to mount a key recovery attack, even given inputs and outputs of the round functions, is the minimum of 1) exhaustion of the key space or 2) inversion of the hash. So if $k \leq h$, the best method to recover the key is exhaustion. In practice, the inputs and outputs of the round function are not given to an adversary, so a non-exhaustive key recovery method is harder than inverting the hash directly.

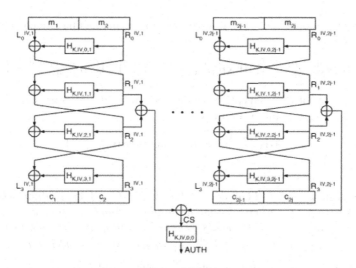

Fig. 1. MTC4

There are two notions of security to consider. The first is message privacy, which looks at the security of the encryption and decryption processes. The second is ciphertext integrity, which measures the ability to force an authentication. For notational purposes, we first provide a quick review of message privacy.

A symmetric scheme $\mathcal{SE} = (\mathcal{K}, E, D)$ consists of three algorithms, a key generation algorithm $\mathcal{K}(n)$ that takes a security parameter n and returns a random key K, and encryption and decryption algorithms E_K, D_K respectively. The encryption algorithm takes a message m and key K and returns a ciphertext $C \overset{R}{\leftarrow} E_K(m)$, either randomly or based on some predetermined state. The decryption algorithm D_K takes a ciphertext C and returns deterministically either a message m such that $(D_K \circ E_K)(m) = m$ or the symbol $\perp$, reflecting that C was not a valid ciphertext.

Definition (Indistinguishability of a Symmetric Encryption Scheme [5]). Let $b \overset{R}{\leftarrow} \{0,1\}$ and (m_0, m_1) denote two equal length plaintexts. Following [3], define the left-or-right encryption oracle $E_K(\mathcal{LR}(\cdot, \cdot, b))$, as the oracle taking queries of the form (m_0, m_1) and returning either $E_K(m_0)$ if $b = 0$ or $E_K(m_1)$ if $b = 1$. A symmetric encryption scheme is said to be secure against chosen-plaintext attacks if for any adversary A_{cpa} with oracle access to $E_K(\mathcal{LR}(\cdot, \cdot, b))$, denoted $A_{cpa}^{E_K(\mathcal{LR}(\cdot, \cdot, b))}$, the advantage in determining the correct value of b is negligible.

More formally, let $\mathcal{SE} = (\mathcal{K}, E, D)$ be a symmetric encryption scheme and consider the following experiment.

$$\mathbf{Exp}_{\mathcal{SE}, A_{cpa}}^{ind-cpa-b}$$

1. $K \overset{R}{\leftarrow} \mathcal{K}$

2. $d \leftarrow A_{cpa}^{E_K(\mathcal{LR}(\cdot, \cdot, b))}$

3. Return d

444   E. Anderson et al.

The advantage obtained by the adversary in distinguishing the correct value of b is defined as

$$\mathbf{Adv}_{\mathcal{SE},A_{\mathrm{cpa}}}^{\mathrm{ind-cpa}} := \left| \Pr[\mathbf{Exp}_{\mathcal{SE},A_{\mathrm{cpa}}}^{\mathrm{ind-cpa}-1} = 1] - \Pr[\mathbf{Exp}_{\mathcal{SE},A_{\mathrm{cpa}}}^{\mathrm{ind-cpa}-0} = 1] \right|.$$

The advantage of the encryption scheme $\mathcal{SE}$ over all adversaries A_{cpa} making q queries totaling $\leq \mu$ bits is defined as

$$\mathbf{Adv}_{\mathcal{SE}}^{\mathrm{ind-cpa}}(q, \mu) := \max_{A_{\mathrm{cpa}}} \{ \mathbf{Adv}_{\mathcal{SE},A_{\mathrm{cpa}}}^{\mathrm{ind-cpa}} \}.$$

Proposition 1. *Let MTC4 denote the ManTiCore4 encryption scheme with round function f, where f is a random function taking $n + |IV| + |BlockCounter| + 2$-bits to n-bits. Then for any q queries totaling $\leq \mu$ bits, the distinguishing advantage $\mathbf{Adv}_{MTC4}^{\mathrm{ind-cpa}}(q, \mu) = 0$ in the IND-CPA model.*

Proof: Let A_{cpa} be any distinguishing algorithm and Γ the set of all transcripts σ such that $A_{\mathrm{cpa}}(\sigma) = 1$. Let T_{MTC4} denote the transcript generated by A_{cpa} given oracle access to $MTC4$. The advantage may be rewritten as

$$\mathbf{Adv}_{MTC4,A_{\mathrm{cpa}}}^{\mathrm{ind-cpa}}(q, \mu) = \left| \Pr[\mathbf{Exp}_{MTC4,A_{\mathrm{cpa}}}^{\mathrm{ind-cpa}-1} = 1] - \Pr[\mathbf{Exp}_{MTC4,A_{\mathrm{cpa}}}^{\mathrm{ind-cpa}-0} = 1] \right|$$

$$= \left| \sum_{\sigma \in \Gamma} \left(\Pr{}_{MTC4}[T_{MTC4} = \sigma \mid b = 1] - \right. \right.$$

$$\left. \Pr{}_{MTC4}[T_{MTC4} = \sigma \mid b = 0] \right) \right|.$$

Notice that for each round in the encryption block, the IV/counter value pairs are unique. This implies the output of the each round, including the final authentication tag $AUTH$, are random. Therefore for every transcript σ,

$$\Pr{}_{MTC4}[T_{MTC4} = \sigma \mid b = 1] = \Pr{}_{MTC4}[T_{MTC4} = \sigma \mid b = 0]$$

$$= \frac{1}{2^{n\mu}} \cdot \frac{1}{2^{nq}}.$$

where q and μ are the number of different IV's and bits queried. Therefore it follows,

$$\mathbf{Adv}_{MTC4}^{\mathrm{ind-cpa}}(q, \mu) = 0. \qquad \square$$

Since MTC4's message security and authentication are integrated, one must be cautious that neither leaks enough information to allow an adversary to mount an attack. To ensure that tapping the internal state of the cipher does not compromise security, we need to show that the ciphertext integrity is protected.

Definition (Integrity Awareness [5]). Let $\mathcal{SE} = (\mathcal{K}, E, D)$ be a symmetric encryption scheme and A_{ctxt} an adversary with access to two oracles, E_K and V_K. The oracle V_K takes a ciphertext C and returns 1 if there is a plaintext m satisfying $E_K(m) = C$ and 0 otherwise. If after $C_1, \ldots, C_q$ oracle replies to E_K, A_{ctxt} can produce a ciphertext C different from C_i, $i = 1, \ldots, q$, satisfying

$V_K(C) = 1$, then we say A_{ctxt} was successful. The adversary's success is defined as

$$\mathbf{Adv}_{\mathcal{SE}, A_{\text{ctxt}}}^{\text{int}-\text{ctxt}} := \Pr[V_K(C) = 1].$$

The ciphertext integrity for the symmetric encryption scheme $\mathcal{SE}$ over all adversaries A_{ctxt} is defined as

$$\mathbf{Adv}_{\mathcal{SE}}^{\text{int}-\text{ctxt}}(q, \mu) := \max_{A_{\text{ctxt}}}\{\mathbf{Adv}_{\mathcal{SE}, A_{\text{ctxt}}}^{\text{int}-\text{ctxt}}\}.$$

Proposition 2. *Suppose MTC4 has round function f, where f is a random function taking $n + |IV| + |BlockCounter| + 2$ bits to n bits. Then for any q queries totaling $\leq \mu$ bits, the advantage in forging an authentication is*

$$\mathbf{Adv}_{MTC4}^{\text{ind}-\text{ctxt}}(q, \mu) = \frac{1}{2^n} + \frac{1}{2^n}\left(1 - \frac{1}{2^n}\right).$$

Proof: Let A_{ctxt} be any algorithm as defined in the Integrity Awareness model and let σ denote the transcript generated by A_{ctxt}'s plaintext query/ciphertext replies. We will use the word ciphertext loosely to define the ciphertext/authentication tag pair. We observe that the final integrity check query made by A_{ctxt} must satisfy one of the following four cases:

Case 1: A_{ctxt} queries a ciphertext using an IV that it has not seen before.
Case 2: A_{ctxt} queries a ciphertext/IV pair using a previously seen IV, but the ciphertext is longer than the one contained in σ.
Case 3: A_{ctxt} queries a ciphertext/IV pair that is either shorter or the same length as that contained in σ, but at least one of the ciphertext blocks is changed by A_{ctxt}.
Case 4: A_{ctxt} queries a truncated version of a ciphertext/IV pair contained in σ.

Recall the advantage A_{ctxt} achieves in forging an authentication is defined as

$$\mathbf{Adv}_{MTC4, A_{\text{ctxt}}}^{\text{int}-\text{ctxt}} := \Pr[V_K(C) = 1].$$

If we let Ψ denote the set of all ciphertext such that $V_K(C) = 1$, the above equation can be rewritten as

$$\mathbf{Adv}_{MTC4, A_{\text{ctxt}}}^{\text{int}-\text{ctxt}} = \sum_{\sigma} \Pr[\Psi \ni C \leftarrow A_{\text{ctxt}} \mid T_{MTC4} = \sigma] \cdot \Pr[T_{MTC4} = \sigma].$$

If we can show for arbitrary transcripts σ that A_{ctxt}'s advantage is bounded above by some negligible factor for each of the four cases, then our claim will follow. We now analyze each case separately.

Case 1 is straightforward since the authenticator has never seen an input with this type of IV. Hence $\Pr[\Psi \ni C \leftarrow A_{\text{ctxt}} \mid T_{MTC4} = \sigma] = 1/2^n$. In Case

2, the output of both $R_1^{IV,i_{new}}$ and $R_2^{IV,i_{new}}$ for each new counter value i_{new} is random, since they are both independent of the transcript σ. Algorithm A_{ctxt} may choose to keep the same authentication tag $Auth_{IV}$ in its final query or replace it with another. It is not difficult to show the best choice for A_{ctxt} is not to change $Auth_{IV}$. Therefore the probability of success is no larger than

$$\Pr[\Psi \ni C \leftarrow A_{ctxt} \mid T_{MTC4} = \sigma] \qquad (1)$$
$$\leq \Pr\big[CS_{new}^{IV} = CS_{old}^{IV} \text{ or } CS_{new}^{IV} \neq CS_{old}^{IV} \text{ and}$$
$$f\big(IV.0.0.CS_{new}^{IV}\big) = Auth_{IV} \mid T_{MTC4} = \sigma\big]$$
$$= \frac{1}{2^n} + \frac{1}{2^n}\Big(1 - \frac{1}{2^n}\Big).$$

For Case 3, there are two different types of attacks that A_{ctxt} may choose from. Without loss of generality, we will assume that only one ciphertext block is changed and all the rest remain untouched. Changing several ciphertext blocks does not give A_{ctxt} an advantage. Given this assumption, the two cases are:

(3.a) For some i, the left hand output $L_3^{IV,i}$ is changed, but the right hand $R_3^{IV,i}$ remains the same.
(3.b) For some i, the right hand output $R_3^{IV,i}$ is changed.

For case 3.a, observe the value $R_2^{IV,i}$ must be different from the original, since $L_3^{IV,i}$ has been modified. The output $f(IV.2.i.R_2^{IV,i})$ must be random and hence following Equation 1, A_{ctxt}'s success can be no larger than $1/2^n + 1/2^n(1 - 1/2^n)$. Case 3.b follows the same reasoning, except now the probability that $CS_{new}^{IV} = CS_{old}^{IV}$ is no longer $1/2^n$. In particular, we have

$$\Pr[CS_{new}^{IV} = CS_{old}^{IV} \mid T_{MTC4} = \sigma]$$
$$= \Pr[R_{2,new}^{IV,i} = R_{2,old}^{IV,i} \text{ and } R_{1,new}^{IV,i} = R_{1,old}^{IV,i} \text{ or}$$
$$R_{2,new}^{IV,i} \neq R_{2,old}^{IV,i} \text{ and } R_{2,new}^{IV,i} \oplus R_{1,new}^{IV,i} = R_{2,old}^{IV,i} \oplus R_{1,old}^{IV,i}]$$
$$= 0 + \frac{1}{2^n}\Big(1 - \frac{1}{2^n}\Big).$$

Therefore,

$$\Pr[\Psi \ni C \leftarrow A_{ctxt} \mid T_{MTC4} = \sigma] = \frac{1}{2^n}\Big(1 - \frac{1}{2^n}\Big) + \frac{1}{2^n}\Big(1 - \frac{1}{2^n}\Big(1 - \frac{1}{2^n}\Big)\Big).$$

For the fourth and final case, suppose A_{ctxt} returns a query to a truncated version of an IV with m_{IV} blocks. Let $m'_{IV} < m_{IV}$ denote the number of blocks in the truncated ciphertext. Since,

$$CS_{new}^{IV} = CS_{old}^{IV} \Leftrightarrow \sum_{i=m'_{IV}+1}^{m_{IV}} \left(f(IV.0.i.R_0^{IV,i}) \oplus f(IV.1.i.R_1^{IV,i}) \right.$$

$$\left. \oplus L_0^{IV,i} \oplus R_0^{IV,i} \right) = 0$$

and $T_{MTC4} = \sigma \Leftrightarrow$ for each IV and $i = 1, \dots, m_{IV}$

$$(L_0^{IV,i}, R_0^{IV,i}) \text{ input}$$

$$f(IV.0.i.R_0^{IV,i}) \oplus f(IV.2.i.R_2^{IV,i}) = L_0^{IV,i} \oplus R_3^{IV,i}$$

$$f(IV.1.i.R_1^{IV,i}) \oplus f(IV.3.i.R_3^{IV,i}) = R_0^{IV,i} \oplus L_3^{IV,i}$$

$$f(IV.0.0.CS^{IV}) = Auth_{IV}$$

are independent events, it follows that

$$\Pr[\Psi \ni C \leftarrow A_{\text{ctxt}} \mid T_{MTC4} = \sigma]$$

$$\leq \Pr[CS_{new}^{IV} = CS_{old}^{IV} \mid T_{MTC4} = \sigma] +$$

$$\Pr[CS_{new}^{IV} \neq CS_{old}^{IV} \text{ and}$$

$$f(IV.0.0.CS_{new}^{IV}) = Auth_{IV} \mid T_{MTC4} = \sigma]$$

$$= \frac{1}{2^n} + \frac{1}{2^n}\left(1 - \frac{1}{2^n}\right).$$

In each of the four cases, the probability that A_{ctxt} successfully returns an authenticated ciphertext after seeing an arbitrary transcript σ is bounded above by $1/2^n + 1/2^n(1 - 1/2^n)$. Therefore,

$$\mathbf{Adv}_{MTC4, A_{\text{ctxt}}}^{\text{int-ctxt}}(q, \mu)$$

$$= \sum_{\sigma} \Pr[\Psi \ni C \leftarrow A_{\text{ctxt}} \mid T_{MTC4} = \sigma] \cdot \Pr[T_{MTC4} = \sigma]$$

$$\leq \sum_{\sigma} \left(\frac{1}{2^n} + \frac{1}{2^n}\left(1 - \frac{1}{2^n}\right) \right) \cdot \Pr[T_{MTC4} = \sigma]$$

$$= \frac{1}{2^n} + \frac{1}{2^n}\left(1 - \frac{1}{2^n}\right).$$

Equality holds when A_{ctxt} chooses Case 2, 3.a, or 4 for its final query. Hence,

$$\mathbf{Adv}_{MTC4}^{\text{int-ctxt}}(q, \mu) = \frac{1}{2^n} + \frac{1}{2^n}\left(1 - \frac{1}{2^n}\right). \qquad \square$$

It is important to note that in each of the above propositions we assumed our cryptographic primitive was perfectly random. Similar security results follow whenever we assume our primitive is a pseudorandom function.

2.2   Initialization Vector Considerations

In a typical cipher design, the codebook mode of operation is undesirable, since repeats in plaintext give repeats in ciphertext. CBC mode overcomes this to some extent, since repeats in the plaintext do not generally produce repeats in the ciphertext. Further, if two identical messages have different IVs, then they encrypt to different values. However, given a repeated IV, if two messages agree on the first few blocks of plaintext, then CBC mode will return ciphertexts that agree in the same positions.

Because of the counters, MTC4 has some CBC-like properties. In particular, repeated plaintext blocks in the same message encrypt to different values, and given identical messages with different IVs, the correlation between the two ciphertexts is negligible. However, given a repeated IV, two messages that have identical plaintext blocks in identical positions will produce identical ciphertext in that position. This is a little weaker than what occurs in CBC mode.

The assumption of unique IVs, counters, nonces and the like are often used in cryptographic designs to allow proofs of security in various adversarial models. The fact that when IVs are repeated, plaintext blocks in equal positions give equal ciphertext implies that the cipher can be distinguished from random. This is also true of most cryptographic designs that rely on unique message nonces to attain the desired level of security. Unfortunately, many of these other designs also have easily exploited weaknesses whenever an IV is repeated. For instance, the authentication mechanisms of both XORMAC [4] and OCB [22] are trivially broken with a few messages processed with the same IV.

Since security under nonce reuse is difficult, the solution is often to insist the implementation never reuse nonces and so pass responsibility to the implementors. However, nonce reuse is a practical concern and may result from natural or malicious causes. This must be addressed widely from the management down through the hardware. For instance, if the particular hardware supporting an algorithm is rebooted often sequence numbers and the like simply start over.

Our goal is to offer a scheme that addresses a pragmatic set of system-wide security issues, including security under nonce reuse, that has measured degreadation in security when various suppositions are not met, rather than a more brittle approach where it is disastrous to reuse an IV. To this end, the inputs of our authentication designs are key dependent and never exposed. Even if an adversary has multiple messages processed with the same IV, the advantage in foiling the authentication mechanism is limited.

3   Cipher-State Mode of Encryption

MTC4 is a specific implementation of a Luby-Rackoff cipher using internal state for authentication. Here we examine a more general case and propose a simple method of adding authentication to any round-based block cipher as a mode of encryption. This provides a computationally low cost alternative to CBC mode, with stronger authentication properties. It is parallelizable, allowing faster execution. As with MTC4, the new idea is to tap into the middle of the encryption for authentication information. Of course, the security of the construction depends on the security of the underlying cipher. The algorithm uses a $2n$-round, d-bit block cipher, E. Half-way through each block encryption, the state (middletext) is tapped and non-commutatively mixed into a running pre-authenticator, CS. The final value of the pre-authenticator is passed through a one-way function and appended to the message. The one-way function may be either created from the cipher, E, or a cryptographically strong hash function, H.

We use a simple linear feedback shift register (LFSR) as a pseudo-random number generator (PRNG) to pre-whiten the plaintext. The ciphertext is post-whitened with the same parameter, R. Multiple steps of the PRNG and the authentication combining operation are easy to compute, facilitating parallelism. The polynomial selected for the authentication combiner and the PRNG is the lexicographically least primitive polynomial, $p(x)$, of degree d. (A polynomial is primitive when x has maximum order). For the CS algorithm with 128-bit AES, we use $p(x) = x^{128} + x^7 + x^2 + x + 1$.

The algorithm given below, CS for Cipher-State mode of encryption with efficient authentication, illustrates this construction.

CS

INPUT $(IV, M), K$
OUTPUT $(IV, C, AUTH)$
Set $CS \leftarrow 0$
Set $R \leftarrow E(K, IV \oplus K) \oplus K$
If $R = 0$, Set $R = K$
For i from 1 to j do
    Set $t \leftarrow E_{1-n}(K, m_i \oplus R)$
    Set $CS \leftarrow CS * x \pmod{p(x)} \oplus t$
    Set $c_i \leftarrow E_{(n+1)-2n}(K, t) \oplus R$
    Set $R \leftarrow R * x \pmod{p(x)}$
IF using E only, Set $AUTH = E(K, CS \oplus R) \oplus CS$
ELSE, Set $AUTH = H(K, CS, R)$
RETURN $(IV, C, AUTH)$

The block cipher is split into two roughly equal pieces, E_{1-n} and $E_{(n+1)-2n}$. E_{1-n} returns the middletext after completing half of the rounds. In the case of AES, this includes the initial XOR of the zeroth-round key, through five rounds of AES, finishing after the XOR of the fifth-round round key. The middletext is tapped to compute the running pre-authenticator. The second half of AES resumes with the middletext, starting with the S-box mapping of round 6, and continuing through round 10. Since the middletext is not altered, but merely tapped for authentication, the combined result of the two cipher halves is the same as an ordinary AES encryption of the plaintext $m_i \oplus R$. For the additional-round variants of AES, the extra rounds are divided evenly between the two halves. For definiteness, any odd round goes with the first half.

We propose that new ciphers should define this tap point. The location is somewhat arbitrary, but should be far enough away from the start and end of the encryption so that the middletext has no simple relationship to either plaintext or ciphertext. Placing the tap point near the middle of the cipher provides the maximum protection against the differential attack sketched below.

The non-commutative combining operation in the pre-authenticator, CS, is cheap to compute, simple to advance multiple steps, and results from separate computations are easy to combine. For both encryption and decryption, the authentication combiner and whitening PRNG can be easily adjusted for several kinds of parallelism: low-level parallelism where successive cipher blocks are parceled out; higher-level parallelism where larger chunks of the message are handled by different processors; and even pipelined chip architectures that process consecutive cipher blocks in consecutive clocks. The adjustments are straightforward for the more complex cases of pipelined hardware that intermixes processing for multiple messages, or when messages are broken into variable-sized pieces, or even when several kinds of parallelism are used together.

The IV is used to initialize the LFSR-PRNG for whitening the plaintext and concealing the raw ciphertext, and as an ingredient in the final message authenticator. Ideally, the IVs are unpredictable and cannot be influenced by an opponent. As with the MTC algorithms, nonrepeated IVs are preferred. However, the fact that the authentication mechanism is hidden from the adversary's view means that the method has a certain amount of resistance to IV reuse.

As a final note, the use of an involutional block cipher is not recommended with this scheme. We don't know of such ciphers in widespread use.

3.1   Security Considerations

One security concern with CS-AES is that it could somehow leak information from the middle of an encryption. We consider this below.

The authenticator value $AUTH$ is computed in a finalization step from the pre-authenticator value CS. This step is either a strong hash or a strong cipher, so we expect no detectable relationship between the pre-authenticator values and authenticator values.

In the strongest attack we know, we assume a long period of IV reuse for the attacker to make headway. (If the IV is changed even occasionally, the attacker has no prospect of collecting a statistically useful amount of message data.) Any attack based on finding weak correlations between middletext values of related messages is doomed, since weak correlations will be destroyed by the finalization step.The only useful datum for an attacker is that two messages have the same authenticator. From this, he guesses that the pre-authenticator values are also the same, and he tries to deduce a relationship between the messages. Two different single-block messages (with the same IV and same key) will have different middletexts and therefore differing pre-authenticator values. So, nontrivial collisions of single-block messages are impossible. (We can take this a step further: Take a multi-block message and vary one particular block within it, running through all possible values. Then the ciphertext and middletext will run through all values, and so will the pre-authenticator. So, two messages which match in all but one block will have differing pre-authenticators.)

For two-block messages, the attacker can try to engineer a pre-authenticator collision using differentials. (XOR-based differentials propagate transparently through the PRNG whitening step.) He uses a two-block differential (δ_1, δ_2), and hopes that the encryption of the two-block messages (P_1, P_2) and $(P_1 \oplus \delta_1, P_2 \oplus \delta_2)$ will produce compatible middletext differentials. The middletexts are (M_1, M_2) and (N_1, N_2). For a pre-authenticator collision, the equation $M_1 * x$ $(\mathrm{mod}\ p(x)) \oplus M_2 = N_1 * x\ (\mathrm{mod}\ p(x)) \oplus N_2$ must hold. This will happen if the second-block differential $M_2 \oplus N_2$ is a one-bit left shift of the first-block differential $M_1 \oplus N_1$. Also, the high-order-bit of the first-block differential is 0, so no carry occurs in the multiplication by x. The chance of a match is the square of the individual probabilities for the half-cipher differentials, which is comparable to the chance of a differential propagating through the full cipher. For a strong cipher, like AES, this is negligible.

4   Empirical Timing Results

To test performance, we chose Wei Dai's Crypto++ 5.1 C++ cryptographic library [6] as a common framework. The Crypto++ library uses Barreto's implementation of AES [2]. Future work will include optimizing our algorithms as well as utilizing Gladman's efficient AES implementations [9]. Test programs were compiled using Microsoft Visual C++ 7.1 and executed on a Dell Precision 340 computer with 2.53 GHz Pentium IV processor. 1024-byte messages were used. Table 1 provides comparative figures of the MTC4 algorithm and the CS-AES mode against core cryptographic primitives and the typical usage of AES in CBC mode for encryption with HMAC authentication [13].

Table 1. Performance comparison of cryptographic primitives, the MTC4 algorithm, and the CS mode of AES against the standard combined encryption/authentication algorithm of AES-CBC-HMAC.

Algorithm	MByte/Sec	Algorithm	MByte/Sec
SHA1	77	CS-AES-AES	61
MD5	239	CS-AES-SHA1	61
AES	69	CS-AES-MD5	61
MTC4-SHA1	14	AES-CBC-HMAC-SHA-1	32
MTC4-MD5	25	AES-CBC-HMAC-MD5	44

Our implementation of the MTC4 algorithm is limited by the speed of the primitives. Improvements on the hash primitives are worth investigating. One simple enhancement is to use only the compression functions of the hash algorithms (i.e., no byte-swapping or padding). The number of bytes used for the round and block counters in MTC4 were 1 and 4 respectively. The timing estimates presented in Section 2 suggest MTC4-SHA-1 and MTC4-MD5 should be approximately 6 and 8 times slower, respectively, than simply hashing the same message. Taking the authentication steps and extra XOR operations into account, these estimates are borne out.

The CS mode of encryption can run about as fast as the underlying cipher plus a small overhead for authentication in each round and at the end. In software, a significant fraction of the overhead is due to the mixing operation in the whitening parameter, R, and for the running authentication, A. The speed of this operation would be negligible in hardware. The MTC4 algorithm and the

452 E. Anderson et al.

CS mode of encryption are block-parallelizable, which will make implementations with a parallelization capability faster with no loss of security.

5 Conclusion

We take advantage of the internal state of a secure block cipher to provide secure authentication. In the MTC4 algorithm, the arbitrary input size and inherent strength of cryptographic hash functions allow for an extremely flexible round function for a Feistel cipher and a proof of security for privacy and integrity. We also present a Cipher-State mode of encryption that provides authentication from the internal state of a multi-round block cipher, such as AES. All of our algorithms provide an encryption mode with little overhead for authentication, resistance against IV reuse, positive CBC mode qualities, and opportunities for parallelization. Future work will include optimizing the performance of all of our algorithms and investigating hardware implmentations.

References

1. R. Anderson, E. Biham, "Two Practical and Provably Secure Block Ciphers: BEAR and LION," *Fast Software Encryption*, LNCS 1039, Springer-Verlag, 113-120, 1996.
2. P. Barreto, "The Block Cipher Rijndael," http://www.esat.kuleuven.ac.be/ ~rijmen/rijndael/.
3. M. Bellare, A. Desai, E. Jokipii, P. Rogaway, "A Concrete Security Treatment of Symmetric Encryption," *In FOCS '97*, IEEE, 394-403.
4. M. Bellare, R. Guerin, P. Rogaway, "XOR MACS: New Methods for Message Authentication using Finite Pseudorandom Functions," *CRYPTO 1995*, LNCS 963, Springer-Verlag, 1995.
5. M. Bellare, C. Namprempre, "Authenticated Encryption: Relations Among Notions and Analysis of the Generic Composition Paradigm," *ASIACRYPT 2000*, LNCS 1976, Springer-Verlag, 531-545, 2000.
6. W. Dai, "Crypto++ Library," http://www.eskimo.com/weidai/ cryptlib.html.
7. Department of Commerce/NIST, "Secure Hash Standard," FIPSPUB 180-1, 2001.
8. Department of Commerce/NIST, "Advanced Encryption Standard," FIPSPUB 197, 2001.
9. B. Gladman, "Implementations of AES (Rijndael) in C/C++ and Assembler," http://fp.gladman.plus.com/cryptography_technology/rijndael/.
10. V. D. Gligor, P. Donescu, "Fast Encryption and Authentication: XCBC Encryption and XECB Authentication Modes," *Fast Software Encryption (FSE)*, LNCS 2355, Springer-Verlag, 92-108, 2001.
11. C. Jutla, "Encryption Modes with Almost Free Message Integrity," *Advances in Cryptology - EUROCRYPT 2001*, LNCS 2045, Springer-Verlag, 2001.
12. L. Knudsen, "The Security of Feistel Ciphers with Six Rounds or Less," *J. of Cryptology*, Volume 15 # 3, 207-222, 2002.
13. H. Krawczyk, M. Bellare, R. Canetti, "HMAC: Keyed hashing for message authentication," Internet RFC 2104, February 1997.
14. C. H. Lim, "Message Encryption and Authentication Using One-Way Hash Functions," *Proc. of 3rd Annual Workshop on Selected Areas in Cryptology (SAC '96)*, Queens University, Kingston, Ontario, Canada, 117-131, 1996.

15. M. Luby, C. Rackoff, "How to Construct Pseudorandom Permutations from Pseudorandom Functions," *SIAM Journal of Computing*, 17: # 2, 373-386, 1988.
16. S. Lucks, "Faster Luby-Rackoff Ciphers," *FSE*, LNCS 1039, 189-203, 1996.
17. U. M. Maurer, "A Simplified and Generalized treatment of Luby-Rackoff Pseudorandom Permutation Generators," *EUROCRYPT 1992*, LNCS 658, 239-255, 1992.
18. M. Naor, O. Reingold, "On the Construction of Pseudo-Random Permutations: Luby-Rackoff revisited," *J. of Cryptology*, Volume 12 # 1, 29-66, 1999.
19. S. Patel, Z. Ramzan, G. S. Sundaram, "Towards Making Luby-Rackoff Ciphers Optimal and Practical," *Fast Software Encryption*, LNCS 1636, 171-185, 1999.
20. S. Patel, Z. Ramzan, G. S. Sundaram, "Sha-zam: A Block Cipher. Fast as DES, Secure as SHA," *Contribution for the Third-Generation Partnership Project (3GPP)*, December 6, 1999.
21. R. Rivest, "The MD5 message digest algorithm," IETF Network Working Group, RFC 1321, April 1992.
22. P. Rogaway, M. Bellare, J. Black, T. Krovetz, "OCB: A Block-Cipher Mode of Operation for Efficient Authenticated Encryption," *8th ACM Conf. on Computer and Communications Security*, ACM Press, 2001.
23. D. Whiting, R. Housley, N. Ferguson, "Counter with CBC-MAC (CCM)," June 2002. http://csrc.nist.gov/encryption/ modes/proposedmodes/

On Security of XTR Public Key Cryptosystems Against Side Channel Attacks

Dong-Guk Han[1]*, Jongin Lim[1]**, and Kouichi Sakurai[2]

[1] Center for Information and Security Technologies (CIST),
Korea University, Seoul, KOREA
{christa,jilim}@korea.ac.kr
[2] Department of Computer Science and Communication Engineering 6-10-1,
Hakozaki, Higashi-ku, Fukuoka, 812-8581, Japan,
sakurai@csce.kyushu-u.ac.jp

Abstract. The XTR public key system was introduced at Crypto 2000. It is regarded that XTR is suitable for a variety of environments, including low-end smart cards, and XTR is the excellent alternative to either RSA or ECC. In [LV00a,SL01], authors remarked that XTR single exponentiation (XTR-SE) is less susceptible than usual exponentiation routines to environmental attacks such as timing attacks and Differential Power Analysis (DPA). In this paper, however, we investigate the security of side channel attack (SCA) on XTR. This paper shows that XTR-SE is immune against simple power analysis under assumption that the order of the computation of XTR-SE is carefully considered. However, we show that XTR-SE is vulnerable to Data-bit DPA, Address-bit DPA, and doubling attack. Moreover, we propose countermeasures that prevent the proposed attacks. As the proposed countermeasure against doubling attack is very inefficient, a good countermeasure against doubling attack is actually necessary to maintain the advantage of efficiency of XTR.

Keywords: XTR Public Key Cryptosystem, Side Channel Attacks, SPA, Data-bit DPA, Address-bit DPA, doubling attack

1 Introduction

In general, it is well known that ECC is suitable for a variety of environments, including low-end smart cards and over-burdened web servers communicating with powerful PC clients. But XTR has some advantages such as its very faster parameter and key selection, small key sizes, and speed. Combined with its very easy programmability, this makes XTR an excellent public key system for a very wide variety of environments, ranging from smart cards to web serves.

---

* This work was done while the first author visits in Kyushu Univ. and was supported by the Korea Science and Engineering Foundation (KOSEF). (M07-2003-000-20123-0)
** This work was supported by the Ministry of Information & Communications, Korea, under the Information Technology Research Center (ITRC) Support Program.

H. Wang et al. (Eds.): ACISP 2004, LNCS 3108, pp. 454–465, 2004.

XTR single exponentiation (XTR-SE) [LV00a,SL01] has a rather unusual property that the two computations involved are very similar and take the same number of instructions. Thus, the instructions carried out in XTR-SE for the two different cases are very much alike. So, authors remarked that XTR-SE is less susceptible than usual exponentiation routines to environmental attacks such as timing attacks and Differential Power Analysis (DPA).

In this paper, we investigate the security of side channel attack (SCA) on XTR. Especially, we consider following four SCA : simple power analysis (SPA), data-bit differential power analysis (DDPA) proposed by Coron [Cor99], address-bit differential power analysis (ADPA) proposed by Itoh et al. [IIT02], and doubling attack proposed by Fouque et al. [FV03].

This paper shows that XTR-SE is immune against SPA under assumption that the order of the computation of XTR-SE is carefully considered. As the instructions performed during XTR-SE does not depend on the secret value being processed, the order of computation is flexible. Thus, if the order of computation of XTR-SE is not considered, XTR-SE could not be any more secure against SPA.

However, we will show that XTR-SE is vulnerable to DDPA, ADPA, and doubling attack and propose several countermeasures against the proposed attacks. First, we introduce two countermeasures against DDPA : randomization of the base element using field isomorphism and randomization of the private exponent. Also, we propose a countermeasure against ADPA by using random number. In the case of doubling attack, randomization of the base element using field isomorphism which is proposed to defeat DDPA could be used to break doubling attack. Note that the proposed attacks and countermeasures are naturally applicable to XTR-SE on the generalized extension field $GF(p^{6m})$ [Han02].

Thus, if we only deal with SPA, DDPA, ADPA, and doubling attack as the attack algorithm for XTR-SE, XTR-SE should be added following countermeasures : randomization of the base element using field isomorphism (DDPA and doubling attack) + randomized addressing (ADPA).

However, as the proposed countermeasure against doubling attack that is randomization of the base element using field isomorphism is very inefficient, a good countermeasure against doubling attack is actually necessary to maintain the advantage of efficiency of XTR. Construction of efficient countermeasures against doubling attack is an open question.

Note that we hope this first step towards side channel attack on XTR public key cryptosystems will be a motivating starting point for further research.

2   XTR Public Key System

2.1   Preliminaries

In this section, we review some of the results from [LV00a,SL01].

Definition 1. *The trace $Tr(h)$ over $GF(p^2)$ of $h \in GF(p^6)$ is the sum of the conjugates over $GF(p^2)$ of h, i.e., $Tr(h) = h + h^{p^2} + h^{p^4}$.*

In XTR, elements of $< g >$ are represented by their trace over $GF(p^2)$. Throughout this paper, c_n denotes $Tr(g^n) \in GF(p^2)$, for some fixed p and g. Efficient computation of c_n given c_1 is based on the following facts.

Corollary 1 ([LV00a,SL01]). *Let* c, c_{n-1}, c_n *and* c_{n+1} *be given.*

i. $c = c_1$.

ii. $c_{-n} = c_{np} = c_n^p$ *for* $n \in Z$.

iii. $c_n \in GF(p^2)$ *for* $n \in Z$.

iv. $c_{2n} = c_n^2 - 2c_n^p$ *takes two multiplications in* $GF(p)$.

v. $c_{n+2} = c * c_{n+1} - c^p * c_n + c_{n-1}$ *takes three multiplications in* $GF(p)$.

vi. $c_{2n-1} = c_{n-1} * c_n - c^p * c_n^p + c_{n+1}^p$ *takes three multiplications in* $GF(p)$.

vii. $c_{2n+1} = c_n * c_{n+1} - c * c_n^p + c_{n-1}^p$ *takes three multiplications in* $GF(p)$.

Let $S_n = (c_{n-1}, c_n, c_{n+1}) \in GF(p^2)^3$; thus $S_1 = (3, c_1, c_1^2 - 2c_1^p)$. The triple $S_{2n-1} = (c_{2(n-1)}, c_{2n-1}, c_{2n})$ can be computed from S_n and c_1 by applying Corollary 1 *iv* twice to compute $c_{2(n-1)}$ and c_{2n} based on $c_{(n-1)}$ and c_n, respectively, and by applying Corollary 1 *vi* to compute c_{2n-1} based on $S_n = (c_{n-1}, c_n, c_{n+1})$ and c_1. This takes seven multiplications in $GF(p)$. The triple S_{2n+1} can be computed in a similar manner from S_n and c_1 at the cost of seven multiplications in $GF(p)$ using Corollary 1 *vii*.

2.2   XTR Single Exponentiation

In XTR, the algorithm to compute $Tr(g^n)$ given $Tr(g)$ and $n \in Z$ is needed like the algorithm to compute g^n in public key system based on discrete logarithm problem. We call this algorithm as XTR single exponentiation (XTR-SE).

Notation: Define following three functions:

$$XTRDBL(c_n) := c_{2n},$$
$$XTR\_C_{n+2}(c_{n-1}, c_n, c_{n+1}, c) := c_{n+2},$$
$$XTR\_C_{2n-1}(c_{n-1}, c_n, c_{n+1}, c) := c_{2n-1},$$
$$XTR\_C_{2n+1}(c_{n-1}, c_n, c_{n+1}, c) := c_{2n+1}.$$

Note that $XTRDBL$, XTR_C_{n+2}, XTR_C_{2n-1}, and XTR_C_{2n+1} are defined by Corollary 1 *iv*, *v*, *vi*, and *vii*, respectively.

When $n > 2$, XTR-SE could be simplified as following Table 1.

The only difference between the two different cases in XTR-SE is the application of Corollary 1 *vi* if $m_j = 0$ and of Corollary 1 *vii* if $m_j = 1$. But, the two computations involved are very similar and take the same number of instructions. Thus, in [[LV00a], Remark 2.3.9] they claimed that XTR-SE is much less susceptible than exponentiation routines to environmental attacks such as timing attacks and Differential Power Analysis.

Table 1. XTR Single Exponentiation Algorithm (XTR-SE).

INPUT : c and n where $n > 2$
OUTPUT : $S_n = (c_{n-1}, c_n, c_{n+1})$

---

1. Compute initial values:
   1.1. $C[3] \leftarrow c$, $C[0] \leftarrow XTRDBL(C[3])$,
      $C[1] \leftarrow XTR\_C_{2n+1}(3, C[3], C[0], C[3])$,
      and $C[2] \leftarrow XTRDBL(C[0])$.
   1.2. If n is even, n replace $n - 1$.
      Let $n = 2m + 1$ and $m = \sum_{j=0}^{l} m_j 2^j$ with $m_j \in \{0, 1\}$ and $m_l = 1$.
2. for $j = l - 1$ downto 0
   2.1. $T[1] \leftarrow XTRDBL(C[m_j])$
   2.2. $T[2] \leftarrow XTRDBL(C[1 + m_j])$
   2.3. if $(m_j = 0)$ then
         $T[3] \leftarrow XTR\_C_{2n-1}(C[0], C[1], C[2], C[3])$
      if $(m_j = 1)$ then
         $T[3] \leftarrow XTR\_C_{2n+1}(C[0], C[1], C[2], C[3])$
   2.4. $C[0] \leftarrow T[1]$
   2.5. $C[1] \leftarrow T[3]$
   2.6. $C[2] \leftarrow T[2]$
3. If n is odd then
      return $(C[0], C[1], C[2])$,
   else $C[0] \leftarrow XTR\_C_{n+2}(C[0], C[1], C[2], C[3])$
      return $(C[1], C[2], C[0])$.

2.3 Toy Example

Let $n = 181$. Then $m = 90 = 2^6 + 2^4 + 2^3 + 2$, i.e, $(m_6, m_5, m_4, m_3, m_2, m_1, m_0) = (1, 0, 1, 1, 0, 1, 0)$. Given c and n, S_{181} could be computed as following Table 2.

3 Side Channel Attacks on XTR-SE

In 1998, Kocher described in a technical draft [KJJ98] SPA and DPA on DES. SPA only uses a single observed information, while DPA uses a lot of observed information together with statistic tools.

In 1999, Messerges et al. proposed a new powerful attack against the secret key cryptosystems, the address-bit DPA (ADPA), which analyzes a correlation between the secret information and addresses of registers [MDS99]. To distinguish from ADPA, we call general DPA as Data-bit DPA (DDPA).

In 2003, Fouque et al. proposed doubling attack against a classical implementation of the modular exponentiation or scalar multiplication in the ECC that only requires two queries to the device [FV03].

In this section, we investigate the security of side channel attack on XTR, especially SPA, DDPA, ADPA, and doubling attack are considered.

Table 2. Compute S_{181} given c.

j	m_j	k	$(C[0], C[1], C[2])$
6	1	1	(c_2, c_3, c_4)
5	0	2	(c_4, c_5, c_6)
4	1	5	(c_{10}, c_{11}, c_{12})
3	1	11	(c_{22}, c_{23}, c_{24})
2	0	22	(c_{44}, c_{45}, c_{46})
1	1	45	(c_{90}, c_{91}, c_{92})
0	0	90	$(c_{180}, c_{181}, c_{182})$

3.1 XTR-SE Is Secure Against SPA

The computation of the XTR-SE requires the computations repeatedly that $(XTRDBL, XTRDBL, XTR\_C_{2n-1})$ or $(XTRDBL, XTRDBL, XTR\_C_{2n+1})$ from $(C[0], C[1], C[2], C[3])$ depending on the value of each bit m_j. As XTR_C_{2n-1} and XTR_C_{2n+1} require same multiplications in $GF(p)$, these two operations are indistinguishable from the observation of the power consumption. This means that the instructions performed during XTR-SE does not depend on the secret value being processed. Thus, XTR-SE is resistant against SPA.

Caution: Since $XTRDBLs$ and XTR_C_{2n-1} (or XTR_C_{2n+1}) are independent, the order of computation is flexible. But the order of the computation is very important. For instance, assume that XTR-SE is implemented as following order $XTRDBL, XTRDBL$, and then XTR_C_{2n-1} if $m_j = 0$, and XTR_C_{2n+1}, $XTRDBL$, and then $XTRDBL$ if $m_j = 1$. Then, the order of the computation can be easily known to an attacker by SPA.

Thus, if the order of the computation of XTR-SE is not considered XTR-SE could not be any more secure against SPA.

Remark 1. Similar results could be found in the computation of the scalar multiplication on the Montgomery-form elliptic curves [OS00].

Remark 2. In step 3 in XTR-SE, a dummy XTR_C_{n+2} operation is needed when n is odd. Otherwise the least significant bit of n, i.e., n is even or not, could be revealed.

3.2 Data-Bit DPA Against XTR-SE

In this section, we describe a DDPA [Cor99] against an implementation of XTR-SE. DDPA on XTR-SE can be performed by noticing that at step j the processed $T[1]$ depends only on the first bits $(m_l, \ldots, m_j)$ of m. Now assume that we know how field elements are represented in memory $T[i]$ (or $C[i]$) during computation and select a particular bit of this representation. When $C[i]$ is processed to update $T[1]$, power consumption will be correlated to this specific bit of $C[i]$. No correlation will be observed with an element $C[i]$ not computed inside the card. To update $T[1]$, $C[0]$ is used when $m_j = 0$ and $C[1]$ is used when $m_j = 1$.

Thus, it is possible to successively recover the bits of the exponent by guessing which $C[i]$ are computed by the card.

3.3 Address-Bit DPA Against XTR-SE

The address-bit DPA was originally investigated by Messerges, Dabbish and Sloan [MDS99] and Itoh et al. extended the analysis to elliptic curve based cryptosystems [IIT02].

This paper extends the analysis to XTR-SE. Since XTR-SE has similar structure to the Montgomery form elliptic curves, the analysis technique proposed by Itoh et al. could be applicable to XTR-SE.

ADPA [IIT02] is successful if there is a close dependence between a secret value and addresses of accessed registers. Thus, if we could find correlations between address value and secret value then XTR-SE is also vulnerable to ADPA.

Following property shows that there are correlations between address value and secret value m_j in XTR-SE.

Property 1. In substep 2.1 and 2.2 in XTR-SE,

- When $m_j = 0$
  - To update $T[1]$ read address $C[0]$ and to update $T[2]$ read address $C[1]$.
- When $m_j = 1$
  - To update $T[1]$ read address $C[1]$ and to update $T[2]$ read address $C[2]$.

From Property 1, XTR-SE is not any more secure against ADPA.

3.4 Doubling Attack Against XTR-SE

In CHES 2003, Fouque et al. proposed the new attack against a classical implementation of the modular exponentiation or scalar multiplication in the ECC that only requires two queries to the device [FV03]. Their attack only works for the Left-to-Right implementation.

The main idea of the doubling attack is based on the fact that, even if an attacker could not know which computation is done by the device, he/she could at least detect when the device does twice the same operation. Namely, if the device computes $2 \cdot X$ and $2 \cdot Y$, the attacker could not guess the value of X or Y but he/she could check if $X = Y$.

First, consider an example. This example is the same as that described in section 2.3. Then we compare the sequence of operations when XTR-SE is used to compute $S_{180} = (c_{180}, c_{181}, c_{182})$ given c_1 and $\widetilde{S}_{180} = (c_{180 \cdot 2}, c_{181 \cdot 2}, c_{182 \cdot 2})$ given $\widetilde{c}_1 = c_2$. Note that $\widetilde{S}_v = (\widetilde{c}_{v-1}, \widetilde{c}_v, \widetilde{c}_{v+1}) = (c_{(v-1)t}, c_{(v)t}, c_{(v+1)t})$ if $\widetilde{c}_1 = c_t$.

From the table 3, we can see that $XTRDBL$ operation at $j = 5, 2$, and 0 to update $C[0]$ in the computation S_{181} is the same as the $XTRDBL$ operation at $6, 3$, and 1 to update $C[0]$ in the computation $\widetilde{S}_{181}$, respectively.

In XTR-SE, we can easily derive the following property.

Table 3. Compute S_{181} and $\widetilde{S}_{180}$ given c_1 and $\widetilde{c}_1 = c_2$, respectively.

j	m_j	k	Compute S_{181} given c_1 $(C[0], C[1], C[2])$	Compute $\widetilde{S}_{181}$ given $\widetilde{c}_1 = c_2$ $(C[0], C[1], C[2])$
6	1	1	(c_2, c_3, c_4)	$(\widetilde{c}_2, \widetilde{c}_3, \widetilde{c}_4) = (\boxed{c_{2\cdot 2}}, c_{3\cdot 2}, c_{4\cdot 2})$
5	0	2	$(\boxed{c_4}, c_5, c_6)$	$(\widetilde{c}_4, \widetilde{c}_5, \widetilde{c}_6) = (c_{4\cdot 2}, c_{5\cdot 2}, c_{6\cdot 2})$
4	1	5	(c_{10}, c_{11}, c_{12})	$(\widetilde{c}_{10}, \widetilde{c}_{11}, \widetilde{c}_{12}) = (c_{10\cdot 2}, c_{11\cdot 2}, c_{12\cdot 2})$
3	1	11	(c_{22}, c_{23}, c_{24})	$(\widetilde{c}_{22}, \widetilde{c}_{23}, \widetilde{c}_{24}) = (\boxed{c_{22\cdot 2}}, c_{23\cdot 2}, c_{24\cdot 2})$
2	0	22	$(\boxed{c_{44}}, c_{45}, c_{46})$	$(\widetilde{c}_{44}, \widetilde{c}_{45}, \widetilde{c}_{46}) = (c_{44\cdot 2}, c_{45\cdot 2}, c_{46\cdot 2})$
1	1	45	(c_{90}, c_{91}, c_{92})	$(\widetilde{c}_{90}, \widetilde{c}_{91}, \widetilde{c}_{92}) = (\boxed{c_{90\cdot 2}}, c_{91\cdot 2}, c_{92\cdot 2})$
0	0	90	$(\boxed{c_{180}}, c_{181}, c_{182})$	$(\widetilde{c}_{180}, \widetilde{c}_{181}, \widetilde{c}_{182}) = (c_{180\cdot 2}, c_{181\cdot 2}, c_{182\cdot 2})$

Property 2. $C[0]$ is updated as $c_{2k\cdot 1}$ (or $c_{2k\cdot v}$) in S_n (or $\widetilde{S}_n$ when $\widetilde{c}_1 = c_v$). If $m_i = 0$ then $k_i = 2 \cdot k_{i-1}$, where k_i denotes the value of k when index $j = i$. Thus, if $v = 2$ and $m_i = 0$ then $c_{2k_i \cdot 1} = c_{2k_{i-1}\cdot 2}$. If $m_i = 1$ then $k_i = 2 \cdot k_{i-1} + 1$. Thus, if $v = 2$ and $m_i = 1$ then $c_{2k_i\cdot 1} \neq c_{2k_{i-1}\cdot 2}$.

From the above property, $XTRDBL$ operation at rank j to update $C[0]$ in the computation S_n is the same as the $XTRDBL$ operation at rank $j + 1$ to update $C[0]$ in the computation $\widetilde{S}_n$ (when $\widetilde{c}_1 = c_2$) if and only if $m_j = 0$.

Therefore, with only two requests to the device, it is possible to recover all the bits of the secret value.

4 Countermeasures Against the Proposed Attacks

4.1 Countermeasures Against Data-Bit DPA

Many countermeasures against side channel attacks have been proposed. Okeya et al. classified them into several types such as fixed procedure type, randomized addition chains type, indistinguishable operations type, data randomization type, and so on [OT03]. Especially, to resist against DDPA randomized exponent methods contained in randomized addition chains type and the data randomization type are used.

Randomization of the Base Element Using Field Isomorphism. To randomize computing objects, we use field isomorphism. As $p \equiv 2 \bmod 3$, the zeros α and α^p of the polynomial $(X^3 - 1)/(X - 1) = X^2 + X + 1$ form an optimal normal basis for $GF(p^2)$ over $GF(p)$. An element $x \in GF(p^2)$ is represented as $x_1\alpha + x_2\alpha^2$ with $x_1, x_2 \in GF(p)$. Namely, $x \in GF(p)[X]/(X^2 + X + 1) \cong GF(p^2)$.

As we know, there is one and only one finite field $GF(p^2)$ up to isomorphism. So, if we find another quadratic monic irreducible polynomial $X^2 + a_1 X + a_0$ over $GF(p)$ then we can construct $GF(p)[X]/(X^2 + a_1 X + a_0)$ isomorphic to $GF(p^2)$. Thus, we obtain another representation for the element x using the roots of $X^2 + a_1 X + a_0$.

The field isomorphism method is described as follows:

- **Goal** : Compute S_n from given c and n.
  Note that c is represented as the element of $GF(p)[X]/(X^2 + X + 1)$.
- Step 1 : Choose randomly a quadratic monic irreducible polynomial $X^2 + a_1 X + a_0$ over $GF(p)$.
  Let ϕ denote an isomorphism from $GF(p)[X]/(X^2 + X + 1)$ to $GF(p)[X]/(X^2 + a_1 X + a_0)$.
- Step 2 : Represent c as an element $\phi(c) \in GF(p)[X]/(X^2 + a_1 X + a_0)$. Let $c' := \phi(c)$. Note that in this case basis conversion is needed.
- Step 3 : Compute $S_n' :=$ XTR-SE$(c', n) = (c_{n-1}', c_n', c_{n+1}')$.
- Step 4 : Go back to the original representation by representing S_n' as an element

$$S_n = (\phi^{-1}(c_{n-1}'), \phi^{-1}(c_n'), \phi^{-1}(c_{n+1}')) \in (GF(p)[X]/(X^2 + X + 1))^3.$$

Efficiency of the countermeasure: The efficiency of the countermeasure depends on the choice of the irreducible polynomial $X^2 + a_1 X + a_0$ and basis. To speed up XTR-SE, $x^2, xy, x^p, xz - yz^p$ for $x, y, z \in GF(p^2)$ should be efficient because these operations play an important role in XTR-SE. Table 4 shows the efficiency of basic operations in XTR and S_n for XTR [SL01] using optimal normal basis type I and XTR using random quadratic monic irreducible polynomial with polynomial basis. Note that the numbers in Table 4 denote the required number of multiplications in $GF(p)$.

Table 4. The costs of the basic operations in XTR.

	x^p	x^2	$x \cdot y$	$xz - yz^p$	Basis	Cost of S_n
XTR [SL01]	free	2	2.5	3	Optimal normal basis type I	$7 \log_2 n$
XTR	$1.3 \log_2 p$	4.6	6	$12 + 1.3 \log_2 p$	Polynomial basis	$(21.2 + 5.2 \log_2 p) \cdot \log_2 n$

Remark 3. In step 2 and 4, basis conversions are needed. In general, the cost of basis conversion is not negligible because square root calculation is required in the case of XTR. For instance, in step 2, to represent $c \in GF(p)[X]/(X^2 + X + 1)$ with normal basis as an element of $GF(p)[X]/(X^2 + a_1 X + a_0)$ with polynomial basis a root of $X^2 + X + 1$ should be represented with respect to normal basis of $GF(p)[X]/(X^2 + a_1 X + a_0)$. At that case, square root calculation is required. If two field bases which are changed between themselves are fixed and a root of $X^2 + X + 1$ is represented with respect to basis of $GF(p)[X]/(X^2 + a_1 X + a_0)$ then we could use the novel basis conversion method proposed by Kaliski and Yin [KY98]. But their method can not be directly applicable to the countermeasure using field isomorphism because in step 1 a quadratic irreducible polynomial $X^2 + a_1 X + a_0$ is randomly chosen. So, whenever a quadratic irreducible polynomial is randomly chosen we should do square root calculation to represent a root of $X^2 + X + 1$ with respect to basis of the randomly chosen field $GF(p)[X]/(X^2 + a_1 X + a_0)$.

Remark 4. In Table 4, we assume that squaring takes 80% of the complexity taken for multiplication in $GF(p)$. The result of the second low in the above table could be changed depending on the choice of basis and multiplication (squaring) method. However, if the basic operations such as $x^2, xy, x^p, xz - yz^p$ are overlooked in the construction of $GF(p^2)$, there is not any more advantage of speed on XTR. For example, the cost S_n of second low is 129 times slower than that of the first low in the above table in the case that p is 170-bit prime.

Remark 5. The field isomorphism method is originally proposed by Joye and Tymen to protect against DDPA for elliptic curve cryptography [JT01].

Randomization of the Private Exponent. The randomized exponent methods [Cor99] is well known countermeasure against DDPA.

The computation of S_n =XTR-SE(c, n) is done by the following algorithm:
1. Select a random number r.
2. Compute $n' = n + r \cdot q$.
3. Compute $S_n = $ XTR-SE(c, n'). Note that

XTR-SE$(c, n') = (c_{n'-1}, c_{n'}, c_{n'+1}) = (Tr(g^{n'-1}), Tr(g^{n'}), Tr(g^{n'+1}))$ $\overset{(*)}{=}$ $(Tr(g^{n-1}), Tr(g^n), Tr(g^{n+1})) = $ XTR-SE(c, n), where $c = Tr(g)$. $(*)$: as order of g is prime q.

Efficiency of the countermeasure: The effective key length may increase depending on the bit length of $r \cdot q$. In general, the recommended bit length of r is over 20 bits. Thus, required computing time become at least 1.2 times than that of without countermeasure.

4.2   Countermeasure Against Address-Bit DPA

Address-bit DPA is based on the relation between a secret value and addresses of the accessed registers. In order to resist ADPA, this relation should be hidden.

We use random number $r_{l-1}2^{l-1} + \cdots + r_12 + r_0$ where $r_i \in \{0, 1\}$. Define $[a]_3$ denote remainder of a modulo 3 for any $a \in Z$. For example, $[5]_3 = 2$.

Goal: Remove the relations described in Property 1.

- When $m_j = 0$ and $r_j = 0$,
   - To update $T[1]$, read address $C[0]$, and to update $T[2]$, read address $C[1]$.
- When $m_j = 0$ and $r_j = 1$,
   - To update $T[1]$, read address $C[1]$, and to update $T[2]$, read address $C[2]$.
- When $m_j = 1$ and $r_j = 0$,
   - To update $T[1]$, read address $C[1]$, and to update $T[2]$, read address $C[2]$.
- When $m_j = 1$ and $r_j = 1$,
   - To update $T[1]$, read address $C[0]$, and to update $T[2]$, read address $C[1]$.

If we could obtain above relations in XTR-SE, ADPA is infeasible to XTR-SE.

Efficiency of the countermeasure: The proposed countermeasure has almost no overhead for the protection, i.e., the processing speed is no slower than that without the countermeasure.

XTR-SE with countermeasure against ADPA
___

INPUT : c and n where $n > 2$

OUTPUT : S_n
___

1. Compute initial values:
   1.1. $C[3] \leftarrow c$,
       $C[[r_{l-1}(1 + m_{l-1})]_3] \leftarrow XTRDBL(C[3])$,
       $C[[1 + r_{l-1}(1 + m_{l-1})]_3] \leftarrow XTR\_C_{2n+1}(3, C[3], C[[1 + r_{l-1}(1 + m_{l-1})]_3], C[3])$,
       and $C[[2 + r_{l-1}(1 + m_{l-1})]_3] \leftarrow XTRDBL(C[[r_{l-1}(1 + m_{l-1})]_3])$.
   1.2. If n is even, n replace $n - 1$.
       Let $n = 2m + 1$ and $m = \sum_{j=0}^{l} m_j 2^j$ with $m_j \in \{0, 1\}$ and $m_l = 1$.
2. for $j = l - 1$ downto 0
   2.1. $T[1] \leftarrow XTRDBL(C[[m_j + r_j(1 + m_j)]_3])$
   2.2. $T[2] \leftarrow XTRDBL(C[[1 + m_j + r_j(1 + m_j)]_3])$
   2.3. if $(m_j = 0)$ then
       $T[3] \leftarrow XTR\_C_{2n-1}(C[[r_j(1 + m_j)]_3], C[[1 + r_j(1 + m_j)]_3], C[[2 + r_j(1 + m_j)]_3], C[3])$
       if $(m_j = 1)$ then
       $T[3] \leftarrow XTR\_C_{2n+1}(C[[r_j(1 + m_j)]_3], C[[1 + r_j(1 + m_j)]_3], C[[2 + r_j(1 + m_j)]_3], C[3])$
       If $(j = 0)$ go to step 3.
   2.4. $C[[r_{j-1}(1 + m_{j-1})]_3] \leftarrow T[1]$
   2.5. $C[[1 + r_{j-1}(1 + m_{j-1})]_3] \leftarrow T[3]$
   2.6. $C[[2 + r_{j-1}(1 + m_{j-1})]_3] \leftarrow T[2]$
3. Compute $C[0] \leftarrow XTR\_C_{n+2}(T[1], T[2], T[3], C[3])$.
   If n is odd then return $(T[1], T[3], T[2])$,
   else return $(T[3], T[2], C[0])$.
___

4.3   Countermeasure Against Doubling Attack

Since no attack as efficient as the doubling attack is known on the upward double-and-add (square-and-multiply) algorithm from the least to the most significant bit in ECC (RSA), this routine is recommended to the countermeasure against doubling attack.

But there is no upward algorithm in XTR. In the case of XTR, the method of randomization of the base element by using field isomorphism proposed at Section 4.1 could be used to break doubling attack.

Remark 6. As previously remarked the countermeasure using field isomorphism is not efficient. Construction of an efficient countermeasure against doubling attack is an open question.

5   Comparison Among XTR, ECC, and RSA

In this section, we compare XTR to ECC and RSA with countermeasures against SCA, such as SPA, DDPA, ADPA, and doubling attack.

In the case of ECC: Itoh et al. [IIT03] recommended the best combination countermeasures against SPA, DDPA, and ADPA from the security level and processing speed. The upward binary method could be used to defeat doubling attack. Thus, in ECC, upward binary method (i.e., from LSB) (doubling attack) + double-and-add-always method (SPA) + randomized projective coordinate (or randomized curve) (DDPA) + randomized addressing (ADPA) are needed to resist against SCA.

In the case of RSA: upward binary method (doubling attack) + square-and-multiply-always method (SPA) + randomization of the private exponent (DDPA) + randomized addressing (ADPA) are needed to resist against SCA.

In the case of XTR: XTR-SE + randomization of the base element using field isomorphism (DDPA and doubling attack) + randomized addressing (ADPA) are needed to resist against SCA. Note that XTR-SE does not need a countermeasure against SPA.

Efficiency: If the side channel attack is not considered, XTR is faster than 170-bit ECC and 1020-bit RSA in the signing (decrypting) step [LV00a].

We roughly compare the efficiency among ECC (170-bit), RSA (1020-bit), and XTR (170-bit) with the countermeasures against SCA. We ignore the cost for randomization or transformations required in the countermeasures such as randomized projective coordinate and randomized addressing because they are relatively small compared to basic operations, for instance, point addition or 1020-bit multiplication.

- **ECC:** 85 point additions are additionally required in the combination of countermeasures.
  - 85 ($= 170/2$) point additions are additionally required in double-and-add-always method.

  Thus, required computing time become at least 1.38 times than that of scalar multiplication without SCA countermeasures.

- **RSA:** 530 1020-bit multiplications and 20 squarings are additionally required in the combination of countermeasures.
  - 510 1020-bit multiplications are additionally required in square-and-multiply-always method.
  - 20 1020-bit multiplications and 20 squarings are additionally required in randomization of the private exponent if the bit length of random number r is 20 bits.

  Thus, required computing time become at least 1.41 times than that of single exponentiation without SCA countermeasures.

- **XTR:** The efficiency of XTR-SE with SCA countermeasures is at least 129 times slower (without considering the cost of basis conversion) than that of XTR-SE without that.

Thus, the comparison of efficiency among XTR, ECC, and RSA with SCA countermeasures may be meaningless if there is no efficient countermeasure against doubling attack.

References

[Cor99]   Coron, J.S., *Resistance against Differential Power Analysis for Elliptic Curve Cryptosystems*, Cryptographic Hardware and Embedded Systems (CHES'99), LNCS1717, (1999), 292-302.

[FV03]   Fouque, P.-A., Valette, F., *The Doubling Attack Why Upwards is better than Downwards*, Workshop on Cryptographic Hardware and Embedded Systems 2003 (CHES 2003), LNCS 2779, (2003), 269-280.

[Han02]   Han, D.-G., Yoon, K.S., Park, Y.-H., Kim, C.H., Lim, J., *Optimal Extension Fields for XTR*, Proceedings of Selected Areas in Cryptography 2002 (SAC 2002), LNCS 2595, (2002), 369-384.

[IIT02]   Itoh, K., Izu, T., Takenaka, M., *Address-bit Differential Power Analysis of Cryptographic Schemes OK-ECDH and OK-ECDSA*, Workshop on Cryptographic Hardware and Embedded Systems 2002 (CHES 2002), LNCS 2523, (2002), 129-143.

[IIT03]   Itoh, K., Izu, T., Takenaka, M., *A Practical Countermeasure against Address-bit Differential Power Analysis*, Workshop on Cryptographic Hardware and Embedded Systems 2003 (CHES 2003), LNCS 2779, (2003), 382-396.

[JT01]   Joye, M., Tymen, C., *Protections against differential analysis for elliptic curve cryptography: An algebraic approach*, Cryptographic Hardware and Embedded Systems (CHES'01), LNCS2162, (2001), 377-390.

[Koc96]   Kocher, C., *Timing Attacks on Implementations of Diffie-Hellman, RSA, DSS, and Other Systems*, Advances in Cryptology - CRYPTO '96, LNCS 1109, (1996), 104-113.

[KJJ98]   Kocher, P., Jaffe, J., Jun, B., *Introduction to Differential Power Analysis and Related Attacks*, 1998. http://www.cryptography.com/dpa/technical.

[KJJ99]   Kocher, C., Jaffe, J., Jun, B., *Differential Power Analysis*, Advances in Cryptology - CRYPTO '99, LNCS1666, (1999), 388-397.

[KY98]   Kaliski, B.S., Yin, Y.L., *Storage-Efficient Finite Field Basis Conversion*, Proceedings of SAC 98, LNCS1556 , (1998), 81-93.

[LV00a]   Lenstra, A.K., Verheul, E.R., *The XTR public key system*, Advances in Cryptology - CRYPTO '00, LNCS1880, (2000), 1-19. http://www.ecstr.com

[MDS99]   Messerges, T., Dabbish, E., Sloan, R., *Investigations of Power Analysis Attacks on Smartcards*, preprint, USENIX Workshop on Smartcard Technology, 1999.

[OS00]   Okeya, K., Sakurai, K., *Power Analysis Breaks Elliptic Curve Cryptosystems even Secure against the Timing Attack*, Progress in Cryptology - INDOCRYPT 2000, LNCS1977, (2000), 178-190.

[OT03]   Okeya, K., Takagi, T., *The Width-w NAF Method Provides Small Memory and Fast Elliptic Scalar Multiplications Secure against Side Channel Attacks*, Topics in Cryptology, The Cryptographers' Track at the RSA Conference 2003 (CT-RSA 2003), LNCS2612, (2003), 328-342.

[SL01]   Stam, M., Lenstra, A.K., *Speeding Up XTR*, Proceedings of Asiacrypt 2001, LNCS2248, (2001), 125-143. http://www.ecstr.com

On the Exact Flexibility of the Flexible Countermeasure Against Side Channel Attacks

Katsuyuki Okeya[1], Tsuyoshi Takagi[2], and Camille Vuillaume[2]

[1] Hitachi, Ltd., Systems Development Laboratory,
292, Yoshida-cho, Totsuka-ku, Yokohama, 244-0817, Japan
ka-okeya@sdl.hitachi.co.jp
[2] Technische Universität Darmstadt, Fachbereich Informatik,
Hochschulstr. 10, D-64283 Darmstadt, Germany
takagi@informatik.tu-darmstadt.de

Abstract. Although elliptic curve cryptosystems are attractive candidates for implementing cryptography in memory constrained environments, in this context, one has to care about side channel attacks, which allow to reveal secret parameters by observing side channel information. Okeya and Takagi presented a fast countermeasure against side channel attacks on elliptic curves and qualified it as "flexible", since the user has full control on the ratio between memory consumption and efficiency. In this paper, we present two weaknesses in their scheme. We repair one of the weaknesses with a better implementation of their countermeasure, and recommend an additional countermeasure for repairing the second. Finally, we describe the situations where the repaired scheme is indeed flexible, that is, when it shows greater efficiency without compromising security.

Keywords: Elliptic Curve Cryptosystems, Smartcard, Fractional Window, Side Channel Attacks, Flexibility, Discrete Logarithm Problem

1 Introduction

In a lot of cases, the embedded cryptography cannot make use of all available memory to optimize its efficiency due to hardware and software restrictions. Thus, developing software solutions that can take advantage of all available resources is important. However, side channel attacks (SCA) are a major threat for embedded cryptographic devices: the information leakage arisen from cryptographic operations may enable attackers to recover secret parameters stored on tamper-resistant locations [Koc96,KJJ99]. There are two different approaches to make use of the correlation between power consumption and the secret information. The first technique, called simple power analysis (SPA) is to directly identify the power signature of specific operations, and from the operation chain, retrieve the secret parameter [KJJ99]. The second technique, called differential power analysis, allows attackers to detect the smallest details related to the secret information in power samples thanks to a statistical tool [KJJ99].

H. Wang et al. (Eds.): ACISP 2004, LNCS 3108, pp. 466–477, 2004.

If no precaution is taken, SCA can break the discrete logarithm problem (DLP) on elliptic curve cryptosystems (ECC) [Cor99]. DPA resistance is generally achieved thanks to randomization techniques [Cor99,JT01]. Among the numerous SPA countermeasures, the method developed by Okeya and Takagi in [OT03a] is optimal in terms of computational cost and memory consumption. In [OT03b], they extended their idea in order to utilize all available memory for optimizing efficiency. This countermeasure, which will be referred as OT scheme in this paper, is not only an excellent method to easily adapt any specific hardware platform, but also of particular interest for highly functional devices, where free memory is a dynamic parameter which depends on the applications that are running at a given time. Currently, there is no other SPA countermeasure proposing this feature.

In this paper, we first analyze the security of OT scheme in the sense of both standard and side channel attacks. We present two weaknesses that slightly decrease its security. (1) To allow any choice for the size of the pre-computed table, OT scheme utilizes a degenerated width w pre-computed table where some points are missing. Avoiding scalars which are not compatible with the degenerated table decreases the computational cost of exhaustive searches. (2) In some cases, the length of the scalar recoded by OT scheme is related to a secret random choice; the knowledge of this choice further helps attackers. From point (1), we show how to enhance Shank's square-root attack BSGS. Concretely speaking, for 160-bit scalars and a table size of 3, it is possible to recover the secret scalar with about 2^{73} elliptic operations instead of 2^{80}.

Second, we explain how to repair OT scheme. We propose a new recoding strategy which is immune to length-variation attacks and, in the same time, is faster and requires less memory. To resist the "missing digit" weakness, we propose to extend the length of scalars and estimate the minimal length of a "secure" scalar. For instance, with 3 pre-computed points, to reach a security level equivalent to 160 bits with OT scheme, we recommend to use 174-bit scalars. For 5 pre-computed points only 167 bits are needed. The negative impact of longer scalars on the computational cost also depends on "external" parameters like the underlying field and the coordinate system. Typically, the choice of the coordinate system is determined by the type of SCA countermeasure that is deployed. Analyzing OT scheme alone and combined with several DPA and 2nd-order DPA countermeasures, we identify the cases where performances can be improved compared to [OT03a] without compromising security, in other words, where OT scheme is truly flexible.

2   OT Scheme: A Fast and Flexible Countermeasure Against Side Channel Attacks

In this section, we review OT scheme [OT03b], which combines the SPA-resistant w-NAF method [OT03a] with the principles of the fractional window [Möl03].

The purpose of the SPA-resistant w-NAF method is to recode the scalar so that the operation chain becomes always the same: the constant pattern detected by side channel measurements consists of w point doublings and one point addition [OT03a]. Among all SPA countermeasures based on an uniform operation pattern, the SPA resistant w-NAF is optimal [OT03a]: only $2^{w-1} - 1$ points are pre-computed, namely $[3]P, [5]P, \ldots, [2^w - 1]P$.

Algorithm 1: SPA resistant w-NAF recoding [OT03a]

INPUT: odd n-bit scalar d, width w;
OUTPUT: a $n + w - 1$-digit recoded scalar d_w;

---

1. $i \leftarrow 0$;
2. **while** $d \neq 1$ **do**
   2.1. $u \leftarrow (d \bmod 2^{w+1}) - 2^w$; $d_w[i] \leftarrow u$; $d_w[i+1] \leftarrow 0$; $\ldots$; $d_w[i + w - 1] \leftarrow 0$;
   2.2. $i \leftarrow i + w$; $d \leftarrow (d - u)/2^w$;
3. $d_w[i] \leftarrow 1$; $d_w[i+1] \leftarrow 0$; $\ldots$; $d_w[n + w - 2] \leftarrow 0$;
4. **return** d_w;

Okeya and Takagi proposed a more *flexible* variation of the SPA-resistant w-NAF [OT03b]. We call it OT scheme in this paper.

Definition 1 (Flexible). *We describe a scalar multiplication scheme as "flexible" when the number of pre-computed points can be freely chosen. Aside from the cost of pre-computations, the computational cost of the scalar multiplication decreases when the size of the pre-computed table increases.*

On the one hand, the size of the pre-computed table of the SPA-resistant w-NAF is discrete: it can only be a power of two. On the other hand, OT scheme allows to choose any number of pre-computed points, thus, it satisfies our criteria of flexibility.

To achieve SPA resistance, OT scheme randomizes the set of pre-computed points: the 2^{w-2} points $\{P, [3]P, \ldots, [2^{w-1} - 1]P\}$ are always pre-computed, and $k - 2^{w-2}$ points are picked in the set $\{[2^{w-1} + 1]P, \ldots, [2^w - 1]P\}$. In the following, we call B be the set of k integers b where $[b]P$ is pre-computed; then $w = \lceil \log_2(2k) \rceil$ and $p = k/2^{w-2} - 1$. Since the distribution of width w and width $w - 1$ substrings does not depends on the scalar d but only on random choices, we can expect that even though SCA reveals this distribution, attackers cannot derive the secret scalar from it.

It is noticeable that OT scheme can make use of a very wide range of table sizes. Therefore, it can easily adapt any specific hardware platform by utilizing all available memory. Besides, the free memory is in fact a dynamic parameter, especially for highly functional embedded devices. Thus, how much memory is available for cryptographic algorithms depends on individual situations.

Algorithm 2: Fractional Width Recoding [OT03b]

INPUT: odd scalar d, set B, probability p, upper width w;
OUTPUT: a $n + w - 1$-digit recoded scalar d_k;

1. $i \leftarrow 0$;
2. **while** $d \neq 1$ **do**
   2.1. $x \leftarrow \left(d \bmod 2^{w+1}\right) - 2^w$; $y \leftarrow (d \bmod 2^w) - 2^{w-1}$;
   2.2. **if** $|x| < 2^{w-1}$ **then**
       2.2.1 generate random number $0 \leq rand \leq 1$;
       2.2.2 **if** $rand < p$ **then** $u \leftarrow x$; $r \leftarrow w$; **else** $u \leftarrow y$; $r \leftarrow w - 1$;
   2.3. **else if** $|x| \in B$ **then** $u \leftarrow x$; $r \leftarrow w$; **else** $u \leftarrow y$; $r \leftarrow w - 1$;
   2.4. $d_k[i] \leftarrow u$; $d_k[i+1] \leftarrow 0$; $\ldots$;$d_k[i+r-1] \leftarrow 0$; $i \leftarrow i+r$; $d \leftarrow (d-u)/2^r$;
3. $d_k[i] \leftarrow 1$; $d_k[i+1] \leftarrow 0$; $\ldots$;$d_k[n+w-2] \leftarrow 0$;
4. **return** d_k;

---

3 Security Analysis of OT Scheme: SPA Resistance

Because the distribution of widths w and $w-1$ only depends on random choices, we could expect OT scheme to be immune to SPA attacks. But in fact, this is not the case. In this section, we describe two weaknesses which apply to the algorithms reviewed in section 2.

3.1 Reducing the Search Space Using Missing Digits

We first explain the case $k = 3$ and then discuss the general case. One may observe that, when $k = 3$, either ± 5 or ± 7 is missing in the recoded scalar. If a width 2 is detected by SPA, there are 4 possible digits (± 1 and ± 3). If a width 3 is detected, there are 6 possible digits (± 1, ± 3 and either ± 5 or ± 7). In total, there are $n/5$ width 3 and $n/5$ width 2 substrings. Finally, since the choice of B is unknown to the attacker, he/she has to try $5 \in B$ and $7 \in B$. Thus, SPA reduces the search space to $2 * 4^{n/5} * 6^{n/5}$ elements, where n is the bit length of the original scalar. A brute force attack has to search among 2^n candidates for an n-bit scalar. Thus, for $k = 3$, the ratio between the two search spaces is as follows:

$$\theta_3 = \frac{2^n}{2 * 4^{n/5} * 6^{n/5}} \approx \frac{1}{2} \cdot \exp\left(0.0575 * n\right) \tag{1}$$

For $n = 160$ bits, the new search space is about 5,000 times smaller.

Proposition 1. *SPA reduces the search space to $\#S = \#B \cdot 2^{(w-1)(1-p)\tilde{n}} \cdot (2k)^{p\tilde{n}}$ elements, where n is the bit length of the original scalar, the number of non-zero digits in the recoded scalar is $\tilde{n} = n/(w + p - 1)$ and the number of possible choices for B is $\#B = \frac{2^{w-2}!}{(2^{w-1}-k)!(k-2^{w-2})!}$.*

Proof. The attack strategy in the general case is the same: the attacker picks a candidate for B and performs an exhaustive search until he/she finds out the valid scalar. Choosing a candidate for B is equivalent to choosing $k - 2^{w-2}$ points among 2^{w-2}. Besides, there are 2^{w-1} possible points if a width $w - 1$ recoded substring is detected by SPA and $2k$ for a width w. Denote the number of non-zero digits in the recoded scalar by $\tilde{n} = n/(w+p-1)$. Then, there are on average $p \cdot \tilde{n}$ width w and $(1-p) \cdot \tilde{n}$ width $w-1$ recoded substrings. Therefore, the search space in the general case is: $\#S = \#B \cdot 2^{(w-1)(1-p)\tilde{n}} \cdot (2k)^{p\tilde{n}}$ □

Since $p = k/2^{w-2} - 1$, $\ln(2k) = (w-1)\ln 2 + \ln(1+p)$. And by definition, $(w-1)(1-p)\tilde{n} + wp\tilde{n} = n$. Therefore: $\#S = \#B \cdot \exp[n \cdot \ln 2 - p\tilde{n}(\ln 2 - \ln(1+p))]$. Hence, the ratio θ_k of the search spaces of the original and recoded scalars is:

$$\theta_k = 2^n/\#S = \exp\left[p\tilde{n}\left(\ln 2 - \ln(1+p)\right)\right]/\#B \tag{2}$$

$\theta_k \geq 1$ with equality if and only if k is a power of two (in this situation, OT scheme is reduced to the SPA-resistant w-NAF). Table 1 indicates that the search space reduction is not negligible if $k = 3$ is chosen, but not really important for other values. Furthermore, this weakness is a practical threat for OT scheme only if it is possible to make use of it in a square root attack against the DLP.

Table 1. Search space ratios for a bit length $n = 160$ bits and several k

k	3	5	6	7	9	10
θ_k	4977	81	120	18	2	3

3.2   Application to Square-Root Attacks

The fastest attacks against the DLP on ECC have a running time of $O(\sqrt{2^n})$, where n is the bit length of the secret scalar. Shank's baby step giant step (BSGS) belongs to this class of attacks. To find the scalar d verifying $Q = [d]P$, it executes two successive stages, called "baby steps" and "giant steps". During the baby steps, the pairs $(i, Q - [i]P)$ are computed for all i from 0 to $2^{n/2}$. If for some i, we obtain $Q - [i]P = \mathcal{O}$, then the algorithm returns i and terminates. If no such i has been found, the giant steps $[j * 2^{n/2}]P$ are computed for j from 1 to $2^{n/2}$. If, for some giant step, there is a baby step verifying $Q - [i]P = [j * 2^{n/2}]P$, then $Q = [i + j * 2^{n/2}]P$: the algorithm returns $i + j * 2^{n/2}$. In the worst case, $2^{n/2}$ points are stored (only during baby steps) and $2 * 2^{n/2}$ point additions are computed.

The idea of the enhanced attack is to search through the space of recoded scalars using side channel information: the positions of non-zero digits are known and we choose B at random. If the assumption on B is correct, a result will be found because BSGS is deterministic. If BSGS does not return any result, we have to change the assumption on B. Besides, we skip computations involving a scalar which is not compatible with B. For example, under the assumption that $7 \notin B$, we avoid scalars containing the digits ± 7. Algorithm 3 computes $[d]P$ for all candidates d compatible with the choice of B.

Proposition 2. *The memory requirements and the number of elliptic operations of algorithm 3 are on the same order as the number of candidates which are compatible with the choice of B.*

Proof. In step 2.2. of algorithm 3, the points $[2^j b]P$ are pre-computed. Step 2.2. is executed for each non-zero digit and each $b \in B$, that is $\tilde{n} * \#B$ times in total, where the number of non-zero digits can be expressed as $\tilde{n} = n/(p + w - 1)$. Therefore, the order of the computational cost and memory requirements of the pre-computations is only polynomial.

The strategy of this algorithm is to compute all valid candidates having j non-zero digits at the first j positions given by SPA and store them in the list $\mathcal{Q}$. Then, the valid candidates having $j + 1$ non-zero digits can be computed by adding/subtracting $[2^j b]P$ for all $b \in B$ to/from every point $Q \in \mathcal{Q}$. By construction, this algorithm computes all possible candidates in the last loop. The previous iterations in the loop do not change the order of the complexity: if the last step give us the $\#S'$ candidates and requires $\#S'$ point additions, the last but one step requires $\#S'/\#B$ point additions, the step before $\#S'/(2\#B*\#B)$, the step before $\#S'/((2\#B)^2 * \#B)$, etc... In fact, the total cost is:

$$\#S' + \frac{\#S'}{\#B} \sum_{i=0}^{\tilde{n}-1} \frac{1}{(2\#B)^i} < \#S' \left(1 + \frac{2}{2\#B - 1}\right) = O(\#S') \qquad (3)$$

$\square$

Proposition 3. *Using algorithm 3 for computing the baby steps and the giant steps, the order of the search space is quadratically reduced by BSGS: $\#S_{BSGS} = O(\sqrt{\#S})$, where $\#S$ is the size of the search space reduced with side channel information. The memory requirements and computational cost of BSGS are on the same order as $\#S_{BSGS}$.*

Proof. Recall that the reduced search space is $\#S = \#B\#S'$ where $\#S' = \exp(n \cdot \ln 2 - pn(\ln 2 - \ln(1 + p))/(p + w - 1))$, and $\#B$ does not depend on n but only on k. BSGS separates the scalar into two equal parts for baby steps and giant steps, therefore, for each of the two stages and for each assumption on $\#B$, the search is performed on a space which is quadratically reduced from $\#S'$ to $\sqrt{\#S'}$. The size of the search space is $\#S_{BSGS} = 2 * \#B\sqrt{\#S'}$. Because $\#B$ does not depend on n but only on k, the order of the search space is quadratically reduced. We proved that the memory requirements and the computational cost of algorithm 3 are on the same order as the size of its search space; in our situation, algorithm 3 is executed over $\sqrt{\#S'}$ elements, for each assumption on

$\#B$ and for both of the baby steps and giant steps, that is, $2\#B$ times in total. In fact, the number of points additions that are computed is:

$$2\#B\sqrt{\#S'}\left(1+\sum_{i=0}^{\tilde{n}-1}\frac{1}{\#B\,(2\#B)^i}\right) < \#S_{BSGS}\left(1+\frac{2}{2\#B-1}\right) = O(\#S_{BSGS})$$

(4)

In terms of memory, for each assumption on B, we have to store all candidates for both of baby steps and giant steps. In other words, the number of points that must be stored is $2\sqrt{\#S'} = O(\#S_{BSGS})$. □

Algorithm 3: Efficient computation of the candidates $[d]P$ compatible with B

INPUT: base point P, set of digits B, position of non-zero digits (NZD) in the scalar;
OUTPUT: computation of all candidates $[d]P$;

1. $\mathcal{Q} \leftarrow \{\mathcal{O}\};\ j \leftarrow 0;\ lbo \leftarrow$ position of the last but one NZD;
2. **while** $j \leq lbo$ **do**
    2.1. $\mathcal{R} \leftarrow \{\}$;
    2.2. **for all** $b \in B$ pre-compute $[2^j b]P$;
    2.3. **for all** $Q \in \mathcal{Q}$ and all $b \in B$ **do** $\mathcal{R} \leftarrow \mathcal{R} \cup \{Q + [2^j b]P, Q - [2^j b]P\}$;
    2.4. $\mathcal{Q} \leftarrow \mathcal{R};\ j \leftarrow$ position of the next NZD;
3. $\mathcal{R} \leftarrow \{\}$;
4. **for all** $b \in B$ pre-compute $[2^j b]P$;
5. **for all** $Q \in \mathcal{Q}$ and all $b \in B$ **do** $\mathcal{R} \leftarrow \mathcal{R} \cup \{Q + [2^j b]P\}$;
6. **return** $\mathcal{R}$;

We confirmed our theoretical work by practical implementation and could solve the DLP for small scalar lengths. Whether the same is applicable to Pollard's rho or lambda method is an open question. In [Tes01], Teske reviewed square-root attacks and their possible enhancements depending on the degree of knowledge of the attacker. BSGS may be customized for specific situations, whereas the probabilistic character of Pollard's methods makes them difficult to adapt to specific situations.

3.3   Attack on the Variation of Length

In the recoding algorithm presented in Algorithm 2, the length of the recoded scalar may be longer than n. In fact, it can be at most $n + w - 1$. The attacker can easily recover this information with SPA or timings.

Proposition 4. *The recoded scalar has a length of $n + w - 1$ if and only if $2^w - 3 \in B$.*

Proof. The bit length of d is decreased by $r \in \{w - 1, w\}$ after each iteration of algorithm 2. The recoded scalar has a length of $n + w - 1$ if and only if the following occurs: the sum of all chosen widths except the last is $n - 2$, and the last chosen width is w. With the terminal case $(d = 1)$, the total length is $n + w - 1$ and it is the greatest possible length. Just before the terminal case $(d = 1)$, the last but one d had two bits. Because d is always odd and its MSB is one, it can only be $d = 3$. Therefore, we have $x = 3 - 2^w$ in the last iteration, and $|x| = 2^w - 3 > 2^{w-1}$. Since the last width is w, $|x| \in B$.   □

An attacker may repeat SPA until he/she detects a $(n + w - 1)$-digit scalar. Then, he/she knows that $2^w - 3 \in B$. Then, one of the randomly chosen digits of B is revealed. This makes the work to guess B easier for the attacker, who can increase the efficiency of the previous attack.

4 Recommended Countermeasures

In this section, we recommend countermeasures against the previous attacks. First, we propose a new left-to-right recoding strategy which is immune to length-variation attacks and allows to recode the scalar on-the-fly. Second, we estimate the minimal bit length of the scalar in order to fully resist "missing digit" attacks, and determine the consequences of longer scalars on efficiency. Finally, we study the influence of the type of deployed SCA countermeasure on the efficiency of the scalar multiplication.

4.1 Avoiding Length Attacks: Left-to-Right Strategy

It is somehow unnatural to use a right-to-left recoding method and then a left-to-right multiplication scheme like in [OT03a] and [OT03b]. A full left-to-right strategy would have the advantage to save the memory necessary for converting the scalar into its new representation. Recoding the scalar from the most significant bit is possible, because there is no carry in algorithm 1. In fact, the operation $d \leftarrow d - u$ sets the w lower bits of d to zero and the $(w + 1)$th bit to one; the remaining bits of d are unchanged. Besides, $u \leftarrow (d \bmod 2^{w+1}) - 2^w$ corresponds to the extraction of the $w + 1$ least significant bits of d. If $d[w] = 1$, $u = d[2^{w-1} \to 1]||1$, and if $d[w] = 0$, $u = (d[2^{w-1} \to 1]||1) - 2^w$, where $d[i \to j]$ refers to the bit string extracted from d, starting from its jth bit and ending at the ith bit, $i > j$, and $||$ to the concatenation of two bit strings.

The "missing digit" attack described in section 3.1 is obviously applicable to right-to-left and left-to-right recoding strategies. However, the left-to-right strategy is immune to the attack on the variation of length since the number of point doublings computed in algorithm 5 is the same as the bit length of the scalar. Algorithm 5 nevertheless terminates with an exceptional procedure which generates substrings whose width can be $1, 2, \ldots, w - 1$, and this information is revealed by SPA. But the choice of each width is random (depending either on a random number or on the random choice of B), and the last width is chosen as the number of remaining bits. Therefore, the following proposition is true:

Algorithm 4: SPA resistant w-NAF scalar multiplication with on-the-fly recoding

---

INPUT: odd n-bit scalar d, base point P, with w, precomputed points $[u]P$;
OUTPUT: multiplied point $Q = [d]P$;

---

1. $i \leftarrow n$; $Q \leftarrow \mathcal{O}$;
2. **while** $i > w$ **do**
   2.1. $u \leftarrow d[i-1 \rightarrow i-w+1]\|1$; **if** $d[i] = 0$ **and** $i < n$ **then** $u \leftarrow u - 2^w$;
   2.2. $Q \leftarrow [2^w]Q$; $Q \leftarrow Q + [u]P$; $i \leftarrow i - w$;
3. $u \leftarrow d[i-1 \rightarrow 0]$; **if** $(d[i] = 0)$ **then** $u \leftarrow u - 2^i$; $Q \leftarrow [2^i]Q$; $Q \leftarrow Q + [u]P$;
4. **return** Q;

Algorithm 5: OT scalar multiplication with on-the-fly recoding

---

INPUT: odd scalar d, base point P, upper width w, probability p, pre-computed points
$[b]P$, $b \in B$;
OUTPUT: multiplied point $Q = [d]P$;

---

1. $i \leftarrow n$; $Q \leftarrow \mathcal{O}$;
2. **while** $i \geq w$ **do**
   2.1. $x \leftarrow d[i-1 \rightarrow i-w+1]\|1$; $y \leftarrow d[i-1 \rightarrow i-w+2]\|1$;
   2.2. **if** $d[i] = 0$ **and** $i < n$ **then** $x \leftarrow x - 2^w$; $y \leftarrow y - 2^{w-1}$;
   2.3. **if** $|x| < 2^{w-1}$ **then**
       2.3.1 generate random number $0 \leq rand \leq 1$;
       2.3.2 **if** $rand < p$ **then** $u \leftarrow x$; $r \leftarrow w$; **else** $u \leftarrow y$; $r \leftarrow w - 1$;
   2.4. **else if** $|x| \in B$ **then** $u \leftarrow x$; $r \leftarrow w$; **else** $u \leftarrow y$; $r \leftarrow w - 1$;
   2.5. $Q \leftarrow [2^r]Q$; $Q \leftarrow Q + [u]P$; $i \leftarrow i - r$;
3. $u \leftarrow d[i-1 \rightarrow 0]$; $r \leftarrow i$; **if** $(d[i] = 0)$ **then** $u \leftarrow u - 2^i$; $Q \leftarrow [2^r]Q$; $Q \leftarrow Q + [u]P$;
4. **return** Q;

Proposition 5. *The last width in algorithm 5 only depends on the random choices of the previous widths.*

Especially, the last width is independent from the scalar or secret parameters like B.

4.2   The Required Bit-Length

If $\#E$ is the order of the curve, then we can add $r\#E$ to the scalar d, where r is a random integer [Cor99]. This has no influence on the result of the scalar multiplication. Because d is on the order of $\#E$, we can extend the bit length of the scalar by that of r, and consequently, make attacks more difficult. In the following, we estimate how long the scalar must be so that the reduced search space has 2^n elements, where n is the bit length of the scalar. Denote by $n + n'$ the extended bit length of the scalar recoded by OT scheme, and

$\tilde{n} = (n + n')/(p + w - 1)$ the number of non-zero digits. Then, the size of the search space is: $\#S = \#B \cdot (2k)^{p\tilde{n}} * (2^{w-1})^{(1-p)\tilde{n}}$. We write $\#S = \exp(n \ln 2 + Q)$, where:

$$Q = \frac{(w - 1) n' \ln 2 + p (n + n') \ln (1 + p) + (p + w - 1) \ln \#B - pn \ln 2}{p + w - 1} \quad (5)$$

To match the desired security, Q must be positive; that is, the scalar must be extended at least by $n' = \alpha n - \beta$, where α and β, which depend on k only, are as follows:

$$\alpha = \frac{p(\ln 2 - \ln(1 + p))}{(w - 1) \ln 2 + p \ln(1 + p)} \quad \text{and} \quad \beta = \frac{(p + w - 1) \ln \#B}{(w - 1) \ln 2 + p \ln(1 + p)} \quad (6)$$

However, extending the scalar also increases the computational cost of the scalar multiplication, and fractional windows with extended scalars may become slower than integral windows with less pre-computed points. Table 2 presents theoretical costs (expressed in the number of field multiplications and using modified Jacobian coordinates) for a 160-bit scalar. Clearly, the additional computational cost makes fractional windows inefficient compared to smaller integral windows (corresponding to $k = 4$ and $k = 8$). But this analysis strongly depends on the relative cost of point additions (ECADD) and point doublings (ECDBL): if point additions are expensive compared to point doublings, the additional computational cost due to extended scalar may be affordable.

Table 2. Theoretical scalar multiplication cost, $n = 160$ bits

Table length	3	4	5	6	7	8	9	10
Add. bits	14	0	7	8	5	0	2	2
Standard	2049	1943	1916	1895	1881	1871	1878	1887
Extended	2217	1943	1992	1980	1933	1871	1898	1907

4.3 Influence of the Ratio ECADD/ECDBL

In the following, we analyze the influence of the ratio $\gamma = \text{ECADD/ECDBL}$ on the relative speed of fractional / integral windows, assuming the following approximations: we neglect the influence of pre-computations (which depend only on k) in cost estimations, and following the notations of section 4.2, to reach a sufficient security, the minimal extended bit length is $(1 + \alpha)n - \beta \approx (1 + \alpha)n$. The cost of the scalar multiplication using k pre-computed points and extended scalars, and that of the scalar multiplication using an integral width $w - 1$, are:

$$C_k = (1 + \alpha)(1 + \frac{\gamma}{p + w - 1})n \cdot \text{ECDBL} \quad \text{and} \quad C_{w-1} = (1 + \frac{\gamma}{w - 1})n \cdot \text{ECDBL} \quad (7)$$

If γ is big enough, we may have $C_{w-1} > C_k$. We determine the minimal ratio γ which satisfies $C_{w-1} > C_k$. Under our hypothesis, γ_{mini} depends on k only.

Table 3. Minimal ratio γ

k	3	5	6	7	9	10	11	12	13	14	15
γ_{mini}	1.42	6.32	2.13	0.72	19.54	8.42	4.71	2.84	1.71	0.95	0.41

4.4 Discussion on the Type of Countermeasure

The relative cost of point additions and doublings depends on the type of finite field (prime or binary) and the type of coordinates used for the point representation. The choice of the type of underlying field is done according to design criteria, whereas the choice of the coordinate system typically depends on the type of SCA countermeasure. In the following, for each possible field and different scenarios of SCA resistance, we verify whether OT scheme is efficient or not compared to smaller integral windows. On the one hand, SCA resistance only is needed in the frame of a secure implementation of the ECDSA signature algorithm since the scalar is blinded by a random number. On the other hand, combined SPA/DPA-resistance is necessary for ECDH. To promote OT scheme to DPA-resistance, one can randomize projective or Jacobian coordinates [Cor99]. Finally, since Okeya and Sakurai proposed a 2nd-order DPA against Möller's countermeasure [OS02b], we discuss the case where the scalar multiplication is resistant to 2nd-order DPA in addition to SPA and DPA, using the table randomization renewal method proposed by Okeya and Takagi [OT03a].

Table 4 summarizes the results of this analysis: table sizes which can be used in practical situations appear checked ($\checkmark$). The SPA-resistant w-NAF method can only use table sizes which are a power of two: 2, 4, 8 points ... For 160-bit scalars, storing one point in affine coordinates requires 40 bytes. Therefore, the available table sizes are 40, 120, 280 bytes. In the case of OT scheme, there are much more possibilities: one can choose 40, 80, 120, 200, 240, 280 bytes over binary fields, for instance. In the case of DPA or 2nd-order DPA countermeasures using randomized coordinates, the advantage of using OT scheme is even greater because one pre-computed point occupies 60 bytes.

Table 4. Efficient table sizes for several countermeasure classes

Field	Countermeasure	3	4	5	6	7	8	9	10	11	12	13	14	15
prime	SPA only	$\checkmark$	$\checkmark$		$\checkmark$	$\checkmark$							$\checkmark$	$\checkmark$
binary	SPA only	$\checkmark$	$\checkmark$		$\checkmark$	$\checkmark$	$\checkmark$					$\checkmark$	$\checkmark$	$\checkmark$
prime	coord. random.	$\checkmark$	$\checkmark$		$\checkmark$	$\checkmark$	$\checkmark$					$\checkmark$	$\checkmark$	$\checkmark$
binary	coord. random.	$\checkmark$	$\checkmark$		$\checkmark$	$\checkmark$	$\checkmark$				$\checkmark$	$\checkmark$	$\checkmark$	$\checkmark$
prime	random. renewal	$\checkmark$	$\checkmark$		$\checkmark$	$\checkmark$	$\checkmark$				$\checkmark$	$\checkmark$	$\checkmark$	$\checkmark$
binary	random. renewal	$\checkmark$	$\checkmark$		$\checkmark$	$\checkmark$	$\checkmark$				$\checkmark$	$\checkmark$	$\checkmark$	$\checkmark$

5 Conclusion

In this paper, we presented a comprehensive security analysis of the side channel attack countermeasure proposed by Okeya and Takagi in [OT03b]. Their countermeasure aims at utilizing all available memory to optimize the efficiency of the scalar multiplication while protecting against SPA. However, the security against side channel attacks provided by OT scheme is not as high as it was first expected. We improved its SPA-resistance with a new left-to-right strategy for the recoding stage and recommended an additional countermeasure to reach the expected security level. Nevertheless, due to the additional countermeasure, the flexibility of OT scheme is partially lost. We evaluated in which situations OT scheme indeed provides greater efficiency without compromising security, in the case of SPA resistance only and combined with DPA/SPA and 2nd-order DPA/SPA countermeasures.

References

[CMO98]   H. Cohen, A. Miyaji, and T. Ono. Efficient elliptic curve exponentiation using mixed coordinates. *ASIACRYPT'98, LNCS 1514*, pp 51–65, 1998.

[Cor99]   J. S. Coron. Resistance against differential power analysis for elliptic curve cryptosystems. *CHES'99, LNCS 1717*, pp 292–302, 1999.

[HHM01]   D. Hankerson, J. L. Hernandez, and A. Menezes. Software implementation of elliptic curve cryptography over binary fields. *CHES'00, LNCS 1965*, pp 1–24, 2001.

[JT01]   M. Joye and C. Tymen. Protections against differential analysis for elliptic curve cryptography. *CHES'01, LNCS 2162*, pp 377 – 390, 2001.

[KJJ99]   P. Kocher, J. Jaffe, and B. Jun. Differential power analysis. *CRYPTO'99, LNCS 1666*, pp 388–397, 1999.

[Koc96]   P. C. Kocher. Timing attacks on implementations of Diffie-Hellman, RSA, DSS, and other systems. *CRYPTO'96,LNCS 1109*, pp 104–113, 1996.

[Mes00]   T. Messerges. Using second-order power analysis to attack DPA resistant software. *CHES'00, LNCS 1965*, pp 238–251, 2000.

[Möl03]   B. Möller. Improved techniques for fast exponentiation. *ICISC'02, LNCS 2587*, pp 298–312, 2003.

[OS02b]   K. Okeya and K. Sakurai. A second-order DPA attack breaks a window-method based countermeasure against side channel attacks. *ISC'02, LNCS 2433*, pp 389–401, 2002.

[OT03a]   K. Okeya and T. Takagi. The width-w NAF method provides small memory and fast elliptic scalar multiplications secure against side channel attacks. *CTRSA'03, LNCS 2612*, pp 328–342, 2003.

[OT03b]   K. Okeya and T Takagi. A more flexible countermeasure against side channel attacks using window method. *CHES'03, LNCS 2779*, pp 397–410, 2003.

[Tes01]   E. Teske. Square-root algorithms for the discrete logarithm problem. In *Public Key Cryptography and Computational Number Theory*, pp 283–301. Walter de Gruyter, 2001.

Fault Attacks on Signature Schemes

Christophe Giraud[1] and Erik W. Knudsen[2]

[1] Oberthur Card Systems,
25, rue Auguste Blanche, 92 800 Puteaux, France.
c.giraud@oberthurcs.com
[2] Logos Smart Card A/S
Sorgenfrivej 18, DK-2800 Kgs. Lyngby, Denmark.
ewk@logossmartcard.com

Abstract. In 1996, Bao, Deng, Han, Jeng, Narasimhalu and Ngair presented bit-fault attacks on some signature schemes such as DSA, El Gamal and Schnorr signatures schemes. Unfortunately nowadays, their fault model is still very difficult to apply in practice. In this paper we extend Bao *et al.*'s attacks on the DSA, the ElGamal and the Schnorr signature by using a byte-fault model which is easier to put into practice. We also present byte-fault attacks on two other signature schemes: ECDSA and XTR-DSA. All these fault attacks are based on a common principle which allows us to obtain a 160-bit secret key by using 2300 faulty signatures on average.

Keywords: Fault Attack, Side-Channel Attack, Signature schemes, DSA, ECDSA, XTR-DSA, ElGamal signature, Schnorr signature, Smartcard.

1 Introduction

Nowadays, perturbation attacks provide a very efficient way to attack both symmetric and asymmetric cryptosystems. Since the publication in 1996 of the first paper [6] introducing the idea of fault attacks, dozens of papers dealing with this subject have been published.

In 1996, Boneh, DeMillo and Lipton succeeded theoretically in breaking the RSA (in both CRT and SFM mode), Fiat-Shamir and Schnorr authentication schemes [6]. Their attack on the RSA-CRT was improved shortly after by Lenstra [12].

In [3], Biham and Shamir introduced the concept of Differential Fault Analysis to attack symmetric cryptosystems such as DES.

Bao, Deng, Han, Jeng, Narasimhalu and Ngair presented in [1] fault attacks on many types of public-key cryptosystems such as ElGamal signature, Schnorr signature and DSA. In 2000, Dottax extended the Boa *et al.*'s attack on DSA to ECDSA and she also presented fault attacks on various other signature schemes [9].

Then, at CRYPTO 2000, Biehl, Meyer and Müller succeeded in breaking the elliptic curve scalar multiplication [2]. By disturbing one bit of the secret scalar

H. Wang et al. (Eds.): ACISP 2004, LNCS 3108, pp. 478–491, 2004.
© Springer-Verlag Berlin Heidelberg 2004

during the multiplication, they described a way to obtain information about this scalar. This attack was refined by Ciet and Joye in 2003 [8].

In [5,7,10,11,15,18], the AES was also attacked by DFA. The best known attack is Piret and Quisquater's [15] published at CHES 2003. With a byte-fault model, they succeeded in finding the secret key of an AES-128 by using only two faulty ciphertexts.

However, all of these fault attacks could be avoided by applying the appropriate countermeasure. It is commonly acknowledged that an attacker cannot reproduce the same error twice[1]. So by performing the cryptographic operation twice and by comparing if the two results are equal before sending the result out, we prevent fault attacks.

An ingenious fault attack, called *safe-error*, to bypass this kind of countermeasure was introduced in 2000 by Yen and Joye [19] and improved in 2001 by Yen, Kim, Lim and Moon [20]. They used the fact that to protect cryptographic algorithms against Single Power Analysis, an efficient countermeasure is to use dummy operations such as dummy multiplication for the RSA or dummy additions for the elliptic curve scalar multiplication. So, if we induce a fault during one of these dummy operations and by observing if the card sends the result out or not, we then obtain one bit of the secret key.

The researchers of the National University of Singapore (NUS) considered in [1] fault attacks on signature schemes such as ElGamal, Schnorr and DSA. By using a bit-fault model, they succeeded in recovering a Schnorr or a DSA secret key by using 160 couples (faulty signature, correct signature) and an ElGamal secret key by using 1024 couples. But nowadays, although a byte-fault model can be put into practice, a bit-fault model is rather difficult to obtain. So their fault model is still more theoretical than practical.

In this paper, we extend NUS attacks on the DSA and on the ElGamal and the Schnorr signatures by using a byte-fault model. Moreover, the NUS bit-fault attack on DSA can be adapted to two other signature schemes: ECDSA and XTR-DSA. Here we also describe how to break these two signature schemes by using byte-fault attack on the secret key.

Firstly, we explain why a byte-fault model is much easier to put into practice than a bit-fault model. Secondly, we describe the principle of our byte-fault attack before applying it to five signature schemes: the DSA, the XTR-DSA, the ECDSA, the ElGamal and the Schnorr signatures.

2   Byte-Fault Versus Bit-Fault

In [17], the authors claimed they succeeded in flipping the value of only one bit. A careful reader notices they attacked an old unprotected chip. Due to the numerous hardware countermeasures implemented in the latest smartcards, it is very difficult to change the value of only one bit of a memory cell. For example, encryption of memory forbids to change only one bit: if a bit is flipped into

---

[1] i.e. the attacker cannot induce the same error at the same step of two different executions of the same algorithm.

an encrypted memory, this modification impacts (at least) the whole byte after decryption. The parity checks are another example: if an attacker succeeds in flipping one bit in the memory, the parity checks will automatically correct this modification.

Moreover, flipping a single bit requires very sophisticated material and can only be achieved thanks to light or magnetic attacks. The impact of the disturbance must be limited to a precise part of a memory cell which is nearly impossible in practice: even if a single bit is targeted, the required energy to flip the bit will affect the rest of the memory cell.

Due to these reasons, we consider a bit-fault model too restrictive to put into practice and that a byte-fault model is a more realistic one. We have therefore studied fault attacks in this paper by supposing a byte-fault model feasible as does Blömer *et al.* in [4], in which a very interesting classification of the different fault models is done.

3   Byte-Fault Attacks on Signature Schemes

Fault Attacks offer the attacker plenty of possibilities to attack a cryptosystem. The ways to exploit a faulty result are very different from one algorithm to another. Here we focus on fault attacks applied to signature schemes.

Fault attacks on the ElGamal, the Schnorr signatures and on the DSA have only been studied once in [1]. Theoretically their attacks are very efficient but they are very difficult to apply from a practical point of view. In this section, we first describe the principle of our attack which remains the same through the different signature schemes we attack. Then we describe our byte-fault attack applied to the DSA and to two of its variants, the XTR-DSA and the ECDSA, before looking at the ElGamal and the Schnorr signature schemes.

3.1   Principle

The principle of our fault attack is to recover the 8-bit value of the random fault induced on the secret key during the signature. Once the value e of the error is discovered, we obtain information on one byte of the secret key.

Let us denote by a the secret key and by $\tilde{a}$ the corresponding faulty secret key. As the induced fault affects only one byte, say the ith, if we denote the value of this byte of a by a_i and the value of the ith byte of $\tilde{a}$ by $\tilde{a}_i$, we have:

$$a_i + e = \tilde{a}_i \tag{1}$$

with $a_i, \tilde{a}_i \in \{0, ..., 255\}$ and $e \in \{-255, ..., 255\}$ where $e = 0$ corresponds to not inflicting any error. From (1) we have:

$$e \in \{-a_i, ..., 255 - a_i\} \tag{2}$$

We will henceforth make two assumptions: the errors are uniformly distributed in this interval with probability $p = \frac{1}{256}$ and errors inflicted are mutually independent.

We want to deduce information on a_i by the e's observed. It follows from (2) that a sufficient condition for restricting a_i to n values is to observe e and e' with

$$e < e' : e' - e = 256 - n$$

in which case

$$-e \le a_i \le -e + (n-1)$$

For $1 \le n$ and series $(e(t))_{t\ge 1}$, $0 \le e(t) \le 255$ define the functions:

$$T_n := min\{t \ge 2 | \exists 1 \le r, s \le t : e(s) - e(r) \ge 256 - n\}$$

In Appendix A we prove the following theorem:

Theorem 1. *For any $1 \le n \le 255$ and for any $t \ge 2$ the probability of having found $e(s) - e(r) \ge 256 - n$ after t faulty signatures, which in turn limits a_i to at most n values, is*

$$P(T_n \le t) = 1 - (n+1)(1-np)^t + n(1-(n+1)p)^t$$
$$= 1 - (n+1)\left(\frac{256-n}{256}\right)^t + n\left(\frac{255-n}{256}\right)^t$$

The expected waiting time is given by

$$E[T_n] = \frac{2n+1}{n(n+1)p} = \frac{2n+1}{n(n+1)}256$$

For $n = 1,...,8$ the rounded value of the expected waiting time is $384, 213, 149, 115, 94, 79, 69, 60$ respectively. If we conduct the following attack on an m-byte key: *"for each byte stop inducing faults as soon as the number of possible values has been restricted to at most n"* the total number of possible keys will be bounded from above by n^m and the number of faulty signatures will on average be $mE[T_n]$. To get an idea of how many faults are required to recover a 20-byte secret key, with $115.2 * 20 = 2304$ faulty signatures a $256^{20} = 2^{160}$ key-space is reduced to at most $4^{20} = 2^{40}$ whereafter the right key can be found by exhaustive search.

Average number of faulty signatures required	Average number of keys left for a 20-byte secret key
7680	1
4267	2^{20}
2987	$3^{20} < 2^{32}$
2304	$4^{20} = 2^{40}$
1877	$5^{20} < 2^{47}$
1585	$6^{20} < 2^{52}$
1371	$7^{20} < 2^{57}$
1209	$8^{20} = 2^{60}$

3.2   DSA

Let us describe the signature of the DSA: firstly the signer chooses a 160-bit prime number q and a 1024-bit prime p such that q divides $p-1$. Then he chooses a positive integer g less than $p-1$ of order q modulo p. Finally he chooses a positive integer a less than $q-1$ and computes $A = g^a \bmod p$. His public key is $(p,\ q,\ g,\ A)$ and his secret key is a.

To sign a message m, the signer chooses a non-null random k less than $q-1$ and computes

$$\begin{cases} r = (g^k \bmod p) \bmod q \\ s = k^{-1}(h + a.r) \bmod q \end{cases} \tag{3}$$

where h is the hash of m obtained by using the SHA-1 algorithm. The signature of the message m is the couple $(r,\ s)$.

If we succeed in inducing a fault on a random byte of the secret key a during the computation of the signature, we obtain a faulty signature $(r,\ \widetilde{s})$ where $\widetilde{s} = k^{-1}(h + \widetilde{a}.r) \bmod q$. The attacker can compute

$$\begin{aligned} T &= g^{\widetilde{s}^{-1}.h \bmod q}.A^{\widetilde{s}^{-1}.r \bmod q} \bmod p \bmod q \\ &= g^{\widetilde{s}^{-1}(h+a.r) \bmod q} \bmod p \bmod q \end{aligned} \tag{4}$$

and

$$R_{i,j} = g^{\widetilde{s}^{-1}.r.e_{i,j} \bmod q} \bmod p \bmod q \tag{5}$$

where $e_{i,j} = 2^{8i} + j$ with $i \in \{0, ..., 19\}$ and $j \in \{0, ..., 255\}$.

Then we have from (4) and (5):

$$TR_{i,j} \equiv g^{k \frac{h+r(a+e_{i,j})}{h+r\widetilde{a}} \bmod q} \bmod p \bmod q \tag{6}$$

$$T/R_{i,j} \equiv g^{k \frac{h+r(a-e_{i,j})}{h+r\widetilde{a}} \bmod q} \bmod p \bmod q \tag{7}$$

If the fault has flipped the ith byte of a then $a - (2^{8i} + 256) < \widetilde{a} < a + (2^{8i} + 256)$. So we have two cases:

1. If $\widetilde{a} > a$, then we can find a couple $(i,\ j)$ such as $\widetilde{a} = a + e_{i,j}$ and so from (6) $TR_{i,j} \equiv r \bmod p \bmod q$.

2. If $\widetilde{a} < a$, then we can find a couple $(i,\ j)$ such as $\widetilde{a} = a - e_{i,j}$ and so from (7) $T/R_{i,j} \equiv r \bmod p \bmod q$.

So by iterating i and j and by testing if $TR_{i,j} \equiv r \bmod p \bmod q$ or $T/R_{i,j} \equiv r \bmod p \bmod q$, we deduce the value $e_{i,j}$ of the difference between a and $\widetilde{a}$.

By applying the method described in section 3.1 to the ith byte of a with $e = j$ if we are in the first case or $e = -j$ if we are in the second and by iterating this attack we obtain the value of the secret key a.

3.3   XTR-DSA

XTR has been introduced by Lenstra and Verheul in [14]. This public-key system is based on a method using the trace function to represent elements of a subgroup of a multiplicative group of a finite field. This system, called XTR for Efficient and Compact Trace Representation, works with order $p^2 - p + 1$ subgroups of the multiplicative group $GF(p^6)^*$.

Due to space constraints we do not explain in detail XTR and its cryptographic applications. For a full description of XTR and of XTR-DSA, the reader can refer to [13].

Denote by $(p, q, Tr(g), Tr(g^{a-1}), Tr(g^a), Tr(g^{a+1}))$ the public key[2] and by a the secret key of the signer where p is a 170-bit prime (equal to 2 mod 3), q a 160-bit integer which divides $p^2 - p + 1$, g an element of $GF(p^6)$ of order q and a a 160-bit integer.

To sign a message m, the signer chooses a random $k \in [2, q-3]$ and computes $Tr(g^k)$. Then he writes $Tr(g^k) = x_1\alpha + x_2\alpha^2$ where[3] $\alpha^2 + \alpha + 1 = 0$ and computes

$$\begin{cases} r = (x_1 + px_2) \bmod q, \\ s = k^{-1}(h + ar) \bmod q. \end{cases} \tag{8}$$

where $h = \text{SHA-1}(m)$. The signature of m is (r, s).

If we succeed in inducing a byte-fault on the secret key a during the computation of s, we obtain a faulty signature $(r, \widetilde{s})$ where $\widetilde{s} = k^{-1}(h + \widetilde{a}r) \bmod q$. The attacker can compute

$$\begin{cases} u^+_{1,i,j} = \widetilde{s}^{-1}(h + e_{i,j}.r) \bmod q \\ u_2 = r\widetilde{s}^{-1} \bmod q \end{cases} \tag{9}$$

where $e_{i,j} = 2^{8i} + j$ with $i \in \{0, ..., 19\}$ and $j \in \{0, ..., 255\}$.
He then applies the algorithm 2.4.8 of [14] to $Tr(g)$, $S_a(Tr(g)) = (Tr(g^{a-1}), Tr(g^a), Tr(g^{a+1}))$, $u^+_{1,i,j}$ and u_2 to compute

$$\begin{aligned} v^+_{i,j} &= Tr(g^{u^+_{1,i,j}} g^{au_2}) \\ &= Tr(g^{\widetilde{s}^{-1}(h + e_{i,j}r + ar)}) \\ &= Tr\left(g^{k \frac{h + (e_{i,j} + a)r}{h + \widetilde{a}r}}\right) \end{aligned} \tag{10}$$

The attacker can write:

$$v^+_{i,j} = \widetilde{x}^+_{1,i,j}\alpha + \widetilde{x}^+_{2,i,j}\alpha^2 \tag{11}$$

and then he computes

---

[2] $Tr(g^{a-1})$ and $Tr(g^{a+1})$ are not always included into the signer's public key but any verifier can reconstruct these two values from p, q, $Tr(g)$ and $Tr(g^a)$ as shown in subsection 5.5 of [13].

[3] α and α^p are the roots of the irreducible polynomial $X^2 + X + 1$ over $GF(p)$ and they form an optimal normal basis for $GF(p^2)$ over $GF(p)$.

$$\widetilde{r}_{i,j}^+ = (\widetilde{x}_{1,i,j}^+ + p\widetilde{x}_{2,i,j}^+) \bmod q \tag{12}$$

With the same method as describe above with $u_{1,i,j}^- = \widetilde{s}^{-1}(j - e_{i,j}r)$ instead of $u_{1,i,j}^+ = \widetilde{s}^{-1}(j + e_{i,j}r)$, we obtain

$$v_{i,j}^- = Tr(g^{\widetilde{s}^{-1}((h - e_{i,j}r) + ar)})$$
$$= Tr\left(g^{k\frac{h(a - e_{i,j})r}{h + \widetilde{a}r}}\right) \tag{13}$$

so the attacker can write:

$$v_{i,j}^- = \widetilde{x}_{1,i,j}^- \alpha + \widetilde{x}_{2,i,j}^- \alpha^2 \tag{14}$$

and then he computes

$$\widetilde{r}_{i,j}^- = (\widetilde{x}_{1,i,j}^- + p\widetilde{x}_{2,i,j}^-) \bmod q \tag{15}$$

If the fault has flipped the ith byte of a then $a - (2^{8i} + 256) < \widetilde{a} < a + (2^{8i} + 256)$. So we have two cases:

1. If $\widetilde{a} > a$, then we can find a couple (i, j) such as $\widetilde{a} = a + e_{i,j}$ and so from (10), $v_{i,j}^+ = Tr(g^k)$ and hence $\widetilde{r}_{i,j}^+ = r$

2. If $\widetilde{a} < a$, then we can find a couple (i, j) such as $\widetilde{a} = a - e_{i,j}$ and so from (13), $v_{i,j}^- = Tr(g^k)$ and hence $\widetilde{r}_{i,j}^- = r$

So by iterating i and j and by testing if $\widetilde{r}_{i,j}^+ = r$ or $\widetilde{r}_{i,j}^- = r$, we deduce the value $e_{i,j}$ of the difference between a and $\widetilde{a}$.

By applying the method described in section 3.1 to the ith byte with $e = j$ if we are in the first case or $e = -j$ if we are in the second and by iterating this attack we obtain the value of the secret key a.

3.4   ECDSA

A bit-fault attack on ECDSA has been described in [9]. With the same approach described previously, we extend this attack by using a byte-fault model.

Denote by (q, b_2, b_6, g, G, A) the signer's public key and by a his private key where q is a 160-bit prime, b_2 and $b_6 \in GF(q)$ the coefficients defining the elliptic curve, G a curve point generating a subgroup of order g and $A = aG$. To sign a message m, the signer generates a random u and computes the point $V = uG = (x_V, y_V)$. Then he converts x_V into an integer k. Finally he computes the two parts of the signature:

$$\begin{cases} r = k \bmod g, \\ s = u^{-1}(f + a.r) \bmod g. \end{cases} \tag{16}$$

where $f = \text{SHA-1}(m)$.

If we succeed in inducing a byte-fault on the secret key a during the computation of s, we obtain a faulty signature $(r, \tilde{s})$ where $\tilde{s} = u^{-1}(f + \tilde{a}r) \bmod g$, an attacker can compute

$$T = \tilde{s}^{-1}fG + \tilde{s}^{-1}rA \tag{17}$$

and

$$R_{i,j} = \tilde{s}^{-1}.r.e_{i,j}G \tag{18}$$

where $e_{i,j} = 2^{8i} + j$ with $i \in \{0, ..., 19\}$ and $j \in \{0, ..., 255\}$. From (17) and (18):

$$T + R_{i,j} = u\frac{f + r(a + e_{i,j})}{f + r\tilde{a}}G = (x_{i,j}^+, y_{i,j}^+) \tag{19}$$

$$T - R_{i,j} = u\frac{f + r(a - e_{i,j})}{f + r\tilde{a}}G = (x_{i,j}^-, y_{i,j}^-) \tag{20}$$

Then he converts $x_{i,j}^+$ (resp. $x_{i,j}^-$) into an integer $k_{i,j}^+$ (resp. $k_{i,j}^-$). If the fault has flipped the ith byte of a then $a - (2^{8i} + 256) < \tilde{a} < a + (2^{8i} + 256)$. So we have two cases:

1. If $\tilde{a} > a$, then we can find a couple (i, j) such as $\tilde{a} = a + e_{i,j}$ and so from (19), $T + R_{i,j} = uG$ and hence $k_{i,j}^+ \equiv r \bmod g$.

2. If $\tilde{a} < a$, then we can find a couple (i, j) such as $\tilde{a} = a - e_{i,j}$ and so from (20), $T - R_{i,j} = uG$ and hence $k_{i,j}^- \equiv r \bmod g$.

So by iterating i and j and by testing if $r \equiv k_{i,j}^+$ or $k_{i,j}^-$ $\bmod g$, we deduce the value $e_{i,j}$ of the difference between a and $\tilde{a}$.

By applying the method described in section 3.1 to the ith byte with $e = j$ if we are in the first case or $e = -j$ if we are in the second and by iterating this attack we obtain the value of the secret key a.

3.5   ElGamal and Schnorr Signature Schemes

Let us briefly describe the ElGamal signature: firstly the signer chooses a large prime p (let us say of 1024 bits), a positive random number g and another random number $a \in [1, p - 2]$. He then computes $A = g^a \bmod p$. His public key is (A, g, p) and his secret key is a.

To sign a message m, the signer chooses a random $k \in [1, p - 2]$ such as $\gcd(k, p - 1) = 1$ and computes

$$\begin{cases} r = g^k \bmod p \\ s = k^{-1}(h - a.r) \bmod (p - 1) \end{cases} \tag{21}$$

where h is the result of m through a hash function. The signature of the message m is the couple (r, s).

If an attacker succeeds in disturbing one byte of the secret key a during the computation of s, we obtain a faulty signature $(r, \tilde{s})$ where $\tilde{s} = k^{-1}(h - \tilde{a}.r) \bmod (p-1)$. The attacker can compute

$$
\begin{aligned}
T &= A^r . r^{\tilde{s}} \bmod p \\
&= g^{h+r(a-\tilde{a})} \bmod p
\end{aligned}
\tag{22}
$$

Let

$$
R_{i,j} = g^{r.e_{i,j}} \bmod p
\tag{23}
$$

where $e_{i,j} = 2^{8i} + j$ with $i \in \{0, ..., 127\}$ and $j \in \{0, ..., 255\}$. Then we have from (22) and (23):

$$
TR_{i,j} \equiv g^{h+r(a-\tilde{a}+e_{i,j})} \bmod p
\tag{24}
$$

$$
T/R_{i,j} \equiv g^{h+r(a-\tilde{a}-e_{i,j})} \bmod p
\tag{25}
$$

If the fault has flipped the ith byte of a then $a - (2^{8i} + 256) < \tilde{a} < a + (2^{8i} + 256)$. So we have two cases:

1. If $\tilde{a} > a$, then we can find a couple (i, j) such as $\tilde{a} = a + e_{i,j}$ and so from (24) $TR_{i,j} \equiv g^h \bmod p$.

2. If $\tilde{a} < a$, then we can find a couple (i, j) such as $\tilde{a} = a - e_{i,j}$ and so from (25) $T/R_{i,j} \equiv g^h \bmod p$.

So by iterating i and j and by testing if $TR_{i,j} \equiv g^h \bmod p$ or $T/R_{i,j} \equiv g^h \bmod p$, we deduce the value $e_{i,j}$ of the difference between a and $\tilde{a}$.

By applying the method described in section 3.1 to the ith byte of a with $e = j$ if we are in the first case or $e = -j$ if we are in the second and by iterating this attack we obtain the value of the secret key a.

This attack works exactly in the same way on the Schnorr signature scheme: with a faulty signature $(r, \tilde{s}) = (h(m\|g^k \bmod p), \tilde{a}r + k \bmod q)$, we apply the same method with $T = g^{\tilde{s}} A^{-r} \bmod p$ and $R = g^{r.e_{i,j}} \bmod p$. By testing if $h(m \| TR_{i,j} \bmod p) = r$ or $h(m \| T/R_{i,j} \bmod p) = r$, we deduce the value $e_{i,j}$ of the difference between a and $\tilde{a}$.

4   Conclusion

We have presented fault attacks on the most popular signature schemes. Our attacks are based on the fact that one random byte of the secret key of the signer is disturbed during the computation of the signature. This fault model is practical and with 2300 faulty signatures we can recover the whole value of the secret key in either DSA, ECDSA, XTR-DSA or Schnorr signature. This number increases to 50000 in the case of the El Gamal signature due to of the very large size of the secret key.

To protect signature schemes against this kind of fault attack, the signer must check that the secret value used during the computation of the signature has not been disturbed. To do so, he could verify his signature by using his public key and not return the signature if the verification is wrong. The signer could also add a CRC to the secret scalar: before sending the signature out, the signer computes the CRC of the secret scalar used for this signature (and so stored in RAM) and compares it with the CRC stored in the non-volatile memory.

References

1. F. Bao, R. Deng, Y. Han, A. Jeng, A. D. Narasimhalu, and T.-H. Ngair. Breaking Public Key Cryptosystems an Tamper Resistance Devices in the Presence of Transient Fault. In 5th *Security Protocols WorkShop*, volume 1361 of *LNCS*, pages 115–124. Springer-Verlag, 1997.
2. I. Biehl, B. Meyer, and V. Müller. Differential Fault Analysis on Elliptic Curve Cryptosystems. In M. Bellare, editor, *Advances in Cryptology – CRYPTO 2000*, volume 1880 of *LNCS*, pages 131–146. Springer-Verlag, 2000.
3. E. Biham and A. Shamir. Differential Fault Analysis of Secret Key Cryptosystem. In B.S. Kalisky Jr., editor, *Advances in Cryptology – CRYPTO '97*, volume 1294 of *LNCS*, pages 513–525. Springer-Verlag, 1997.
4. J. Blömer, M. Otto, and J.-P. Seifert. A New RSA-CRT Algorithm Secure Against Bellcore Attacks. In *ACM-CCS'03*. ACM Press, 2003.
5. J. Blömer and J.-P. Seifert. Fault based cryptanalysis of the Advanced Encryption Standard. In R.N. Wright, editor, *Financial Cryptography – FC 2003*, volume 2742 of *LNCS*. Springer-Verlag, 2003.
6. D. Boneh, R.A. DeMillo, and R.J. Lipton. On the Importance of Checking Cryptographic Protocols for Faults. In W. Fumy, editor, *Advances in Cryptology – EUROCRYPT '97*, volume 1233 of *LNCS*, pages 37–51. Springer-Verlag, 1997.
7. C.-N. Chen and S.-M. Yen. Differential Fault Analysis on AES Key Schedule and Some Countermeasures. In R. Safavi-Naini and J. Seberry, editors, *Information Security and Privacy - 8th Australasian Conference – ACISP 2003*, volume 2727 of *LNCS*, pages 118–129. Springer-Verlag, 2003.
8. M. Ciet and M. Joye. Elliptic Curve Cryptosystems in the Presence of Permanent and Transient Faults. In *Designs, Codes and Cryptography*, 2004. To appear.
9. E. Dottax. Fault Attacks on NESSIE Signature and Identification Schemes. Technical report, NESSIE, Available from `http://www.cosic.esat.kuleuven.ac.be/nessie/reports/phase2/SideChan_1.pdf`, October 2002.
10. P. Dusart, G. Letourneux, and O. Vivolo. Differential Fault Analysis on A.E.S. Cryptology ePrint Archive, Report 2003/010, 2003. `http://eprint.iacr.org/`.
11. C. Giraud. DFA on AES. Cryptology ePrint Archive, Report 2003/008, 2003. `http://eprint.iacr.org/`.
12. A.K. Lenstra. Memo on RSA Signature Generation in the Presence of Faults. Manuscript, 1996. Available from the author at `arjen.lenstra@citicorp.com`.
13. A.K. Lenstra and E.R. Verheul. An overview of the XTR public key system. In *Public Key Cryptography and Computational Number Theory Conference*, 2000.
14. A.K. Lenstra and E.R. Verheul. The XTR public key system. In M. Bellare, editor, *Advances in Cryptology – CRYPTO 2000*, volume 1880 of *LNCS*, pages 1–19. Springer-Verlag, 2000.

15. G. Piret and J.-J. Quisquater. A Differential Fault Attack Technique Against SPN Structures, with Application to the AES and KHAZAD. In C.D. Walter, Ç.K. Koç, and C. Paar, editors, *Cryptographic Hardware and Embedded Systems – CHES 2003*, volume 2779 of *LNCS*, pages 77–88. Springer-Verlag, 2003.
16. Wolfram Research.
    http://mathworld.wolfram.com/Inclusion-ExclusionPrinciple.html.
17. S. Skorobogatov and R. Anderson. Optical Fault Induction Attack. In B. Kaliski Jr., Ç.K. Koç, and C. Paar, editors, *Cryptographic Hardware and Embedded Systems – CHES 2002*, volume 2523 of *LNCS*, pages 2–12. Springer-Verlag, 2002.
18. S.-M. Yen and J.Z. Chen. A DFA on Rijndael. In A.H. Chan and V. Gligor, editors, *Information Security – ISC 2002*, volume 2433 of *LNCS*. Springer-Verlag, 2002.
19. S.-M. Yen and M. Joye. Checking before output may not be enough against fault-based cryptanalysis. *IEEE Transactions on Computers*, 49(9):967–970, 2000.
20. S.-M. Yen, S.-J. Kim, S.-G. Lim, and S.-J. Moon. A Countermeasure against one Physical Cryptanalysis May Benefit Another Attack. In K. Kim, editor, *Information Security and Cryptology – ICISC 2001*, volume 2288 of *LNCS*, pages 414–427. Springer-Verlag, 2001.

Appendix

A   Proof of Theorem 1

In the proof of both Theorem 1 and Lemma 1 we will use the Inclusion-Exclusion Principle [16]. Define $I_n = \{1, \cdots, n\}$ and let $I_k \subset I_n$ denote a subset on k elements. The Inclusion-Exclusion Principle states that for any sets $C_1, \cdots, C_n$ the following identities hold:

$$P(\bigcup_{k=1}^{n} C_k) = \sum_{k=1}^{n}(-1)^{k+1} \sum_{I_k \subset I_n} P(\bigcap_{i \in I_k} C_i)$$

$$P(\bigcap_{k=1}^{n} C_k) = \sum_{k=1}^{n}(-1)^{k+1} \sum_{I_k \subset I_n} P(\bigcup_{i \in I_k} C_i)$$

Theorem 1. *For any $1 \leq n \leq 255$ and for any $t \geq 2$ the probability of having found $e(s) - e(r) \geq 256 - n$ after t faulty signatures, which in turn limits a_i to at most n values, is*

$$P(T_n \leq t) = 1 - (n+1)(1 - np)^t + n(1 - (n+1)p)^t$$
$$= 1 - (n+1)\left(\frac{256-n}{256}\right)^t + n\left(\frac{255-n}{256}\right)^t$$

The expected waiting time is given by: $E[T] = \frac{2n+1}{n(n+1)p} = \frac{2n+1}{n(n+1)}256$.

Proof. Let $t \geq 2$ and $1 \leq n \leq \frac{1}{p} - 1 = 255$ be given. Put $a := a_i$ (to gain one indexing variable). For $1 \leq j \leq \frac{1}{p} = 256$ define events A_j: "with t faulty signatures we obtain an induced error which is equal to $-a + j - 1$" and for $1 \leq j \leq n$ define $C_j = A_j \cap \bigcup_{i=256-n+j}^{256} A_i$. C_j is the event that $-a + j - 1$ and one of $\{255-a-n+j,\cdots,255-a\}$ occurs, i.e. the event of observing $-a+j-1$ and one other error such that their difference is at least $256-n$, and we thus have $\{T_n \le t\} = \bigcup_{j=1}^{n} C_j$.

Define $I_n = \{1,\cdots,n\}$ and let $I_k \subset I_n$ denote a subset of size k. Applying the Inclusion-Exclusion Principle we have:

$$P(T_n \le t) = \sum_{k=1}^{n}(-1)^{k+1} \sum_{I_k \subset I_n} P(\bigcap_{j\in I_k} C_j)$$

Since all errors occur with equal probability we have

$$\forall I_k \subset I_n : P(\bigcap_{j\in I_k} A_j) = P(\bigcap_{j=1}^{j=k} A_j)$$
$$\forall I_k \subset I_n : P(\bigcup_{j\in I_k} A_j) = P(\bigcup_{j=1}^{j=k} A_j)$$

Denote the common probability of k intersections by p_k and k unions by q_k. Let $I_k^{(s)} \subset I_n$ denote a subset of size k with $max\{1 \le i \le n : i \in I_k\} = s$. In Lemma 1 we prove that

$$\forall 1 \le k \le s \le n : P(\bigcap_{i\in I_k^{(s)}} C_j) = \sum_{i=1}^{n-s+1}(-1)^{i+1}\binom{n-(s-1)}{i}p_{k+i}$$

Using this formula we get

$$P(T_n \le t) = \sum_{k=1}^{n}(-1)^{k+1}\sum_{I_k\subset I_n}P(\bigcap_{j\in I_k}C_j)$$
$$= \sum_{k=1}^{n}(-1)^{k+1}\sum_{s=k}^{n}\sum_{I_k^{(s)}\subset I_n}P(\bigcap_{j\in I_k^{(s)}}C_j)$$
$$= \sum_{k=1}^{n}\sum_{s=k}^{n}(-1)^{k+1}\sum_{I_k^{(s)}\subset I_n}\sum_{i=1}^{n-s+1}(-1)^{i+1}\binom{n-(s-1)}{i}p_{k+i}$$

The innermost sum is independent of $I_k^{(s)}$ for fixed s and so occurs $\binom{s-1}{k-1}$ times:

$$P(T_n \le t) = \sum_{k=1}^{n}\sum_{s=k}^{n}(-1)^{k+1}\sum_{i=1}^{n-s+1}(-1)^{i+1}\binom{n-(s-1)}{i}p_{k+i}\sum_{I_k^{(s)}\subset I_n}1$$
$$= \sum_{k=1}^{n}\sum_{s=k}^{n}\sum_{i=1}^{n-s+1}(-1)^{k+i}\binom{s-1}{k-1}\binom{n-(s-1)}{i}p_{k+i}$$

By afterwards changing the order of summation twice we get

$$P(T_n \le t) = \sum_{k=1}^{n}\sum_{i=1}^{n-k+1}(-1)^{k+i}p_{k+i}\sum_{s=k}^{n-i+1}\binom{s-1}{k-1}\binom{n-(s-1)}{i}$$
$$= \sum_{m=2}^{n+1}(-1)^{m}p_m\sum_{k=1}^{m-1}\sum_{s=k}^{n+k-(m-1)}\binom{s-1}{k-1}\binom{n-(s-1)}{m-k}$$

From the identity (cf. Lemma 1):

$$\forall 1 \le k \le n : \sum_{s=k}^{n+k-(m-1)}\binom{s-1}{k-1}\binom{n-(s-1)}{m-k} = \binom{n+1}{m}$$

it follows that

$$P(T_n \leq t) = \sum_{m=2}^{n+1}(-1)^m p_m \sum_{k=1}^{m-1}\binom{n+1}{m}$$

$$= \sum_{m=2}^{n+1}(-1)^m (m-1)\binom{n+1}{m}p_m$$

$$= (-1)^{n+1}np_{n+1} + \sum_{m=1}^{n}(-1)^{m+1}p_m(1-m)\binom{n+1}{m}$$

$$= -(-1)^{n+2}np_{n+1} + \sum_{m=1}^{n}(-1)^{m+1}p_m\left((n+1)\binom{n}{m}-n\binom{n+1}{m}\right)$$

$$= (n+1)\sum_{m=1}^{n}(-1)^{m+1}\binom{n}{m}p_m - n\sum_{m=1}^{n+1}(-1)^{m+1}\binom{n+1}{m}p_m$$

Since

$$\forall 0 \leq k : q_k = P(\bigcup_{j=1}^{k} A_j) = 1 - P(\bigcap_{j=1}^{k} A_j^c) = 1 - P(\forall s \leq t : e(s)$$

$$\notin \{-a, \cdots, -a+(k-1)\}) = 1 - (1-kp)^t$$

and by Lemma 1:

$$\forall 1 \leq k : q_k = \sum_{i=1}^{k}(-1)^{i+1}\binom{k}{i}p_i$$

the first statement in the theorem is obtained:

$$P(T_n \leq t) = (n+1)q_n - nq_{n+1}$$
$$= 1 - (n+1)(1-np)^t + n(1-(n+1)p)^t$$

Finally, using this result and the formula for a geometric sum the expected waiting time is derived:

$$E[T] = \sum_{t=1}^{\infty} tP(T=t)$$
$$= \sum_{t=1}^{\infty} P(T \geq t)$$
$$= \sum_{t=0}^{\infty} 1 - P(T \leq t)$$
$$= \sum_{t=0}^{\infty} (n+1)(1-np)^t - n(1-(n+1)p)^t$$
$$= \frac{n+1}{1-(1-np)} - \frac{n}{1-(1-(n+1)p)}$$
$$= \frac{2n+1}{n(n+1)p}$$
$$= \frac{2n+1}{n(n+1)}256$$

$\square$

Lemma 1. *The following identities hold:*

$$\forall 1 \leq k : q_k = \sum_{i=1}^{k}(-1)^{i+1}\binom{k}{i}p_i$$

$$\forall 1 \leq k \leq s \leq n : P(\bigcap_{i \in I_k^{(s)}} C_j) = \sum_{i=1}^{n-s+1}(-1)^{i+1}\binom{n-(s-1)}{i}p_{k+i}$$

$$\forall 1 \leq k \leq m-1 : \sum_{s=k}^{n+k-(m-1)}\binom{s-1}{k-1}\binom{n-(s-1)}{m-k} = \binom{n+1}{m}$$

Proof. To prove the first statement, we use the Inclusion-Exclusion Principle:

$$q_k = P(\bigcup_{i=1}^{k} A_i) = \sum_{i=1}^{k}(-1)^{i+1} \sum_{I_i \subset I_n} P(\bigcap_{j \in I_i} A_i)$$

$$= \sum_{i=1}^{k}(-1)^{i+1} \sum_{I_i \subset I_n} p_i = \sum_{i=1}^{k}(-1)^{i+1} \binom{n}{i} p_i$$

To prove the second statement, let n and $s \leq n$ be given. Reuse the definitions introduced in the proof of Theorem 1 and define furthermore sets

$$\forall 1 \leq j \leq n : B_j = A_{256-n+j}$$

With this notation $C_j = A_j \cap \bigcup_{i=j}^{n} B_j$ for all j, $1 \leq j \leq n$. For any $1 \leq s \leq n$ we have

$$\bigcap_{j \in I_k^{(s)}} C_j = \bigcap_{j \in I_k^{(s)}}(A_j \cap \bigcup_{i=j}^{n} B_i) = \bigcap_{j \in I_k^{(s)}} A_j \cap \bigcap_{j \in I_k^{(s)}}(\bigcup_{i=j}^{n} B_i)$$

$$= \bigcap_{j \in I_k^{(s)}} A_j \cap \bigcup_{i=s}^{n} B_i = \bigcup_{i=s}^{n}(B_i \cap \bigcap_{j \in I_k^{(s)}} A_j)$$

The probability of this event is independent of $I_k^{(s)}$ for fixed s. This is because all A_j's are defined in the same way. It therefore suffices to consider one of these, say $\bigcap_{j=1}^{k} C_j$. Using the Inclusion-Exclusion Principle and p_k defined in the proof of theorem 1 we get:

$$P(\bigcap_{j \in I_k^{(s)}} C_j) = P(\bigcap_{j=1}^{k} C_j) = P(\bigcup_{i=s}^{n}(B_i \cap \bigcap_{j=1}^{k} A_j))$$

$$= \sum_{i=1}^{n-s+1}(-1)^{i+1} \sum_{I_i \subset I_{n-s+1}} P(\bigcap_{m \in I_i} B_m \cap \bigcap_{j=1}^{k} A_j)$$

$$= \sum_{i=1}^{n-s+1}(-1)^{i+1} \sum_{I_i \subset I_{n-s+1}} p_{k+i}$$

$$= \sum_{i=1}^{n-s+1}(-1)^{i+1} \binom{n-(s-1)}{i} p_{k+i}$$

The third statement is merely a different way of counting subsets of size m in I_{n+1}. Use the notation $I_m = \{i_1, \cdots, i_m\}$ where $\forall 1 \leq j < k \leq m : i_j < i_k$ and let a k with $1 \leq k \leq m-1$ be given. The expression counts for each s with $k \leq s \leq n+k-(m-1)$ the number of sets I_m whose k'th element equals s:

$$\binom{n+1}{m} = |\{I_m \subset I_{n+1}\}| = |\bigcup_{s=k}^{n+k-(m-1)}\{I_m \subset I_{n+1} : i_k = s\}|$$

$$= \sum_{s=k}^{n+k-(m-1)} |\{I_m \subset I_{n+1} : i_k = s\}|$$

$$= \sum_{s=k}^{n+k-(m-1)} |\{I_{k-1} \subset \{1, \cdots, s-1\}\}||\{I_{(m-1)-(k-1)} \subset \{s+1, \cdots n+1\}\}|$$

$$= \sum_{s=k}^{n+k-(m-1)} \binom{s-1}{k-1}\binom{n-(s-1)}{m-k}$$

□

Author Index

Lecture Notes in Computer Science

For information about Vols. 1–3027

please contact your bookseller or Springer-Verlag

Vol. 3071: A. Omicini, P. Petta, J. Pitt (Eds.), Engineering Societies in the Agents World. XIII, 409 pages. 2004. (Subseries LNAI).

Vol. 3070: L. Rutkowski, J. Siekmann, R. Tadeusiewicz, L.A. Zadeh (Eds.), Artificial Intelligence and Soft Computing - ICAISC 2004. XXV, 1208 pages. 2004. (Subseries LNAI).

Vol. 3068: E. André, L. Dybkj{\}ae r, W. Minker, P. Heisterkamp (Eds.), Affective Dialogue Systems. XII, 324 pages. 2004. (Subseries LNAI).

Vol. 3067: M. Dastani, J. Dix, A. El Fallah-Seghrouchni (Eds.), Programming Multi-Agent Systems. X, 221 pages. 2004. (Subseries LNAI).

Vol. 3066: S. Tsumoto, R. Słowiński, J. Komorowski, J.W. Grzymała-Busse (Eds.), Rough Sets and Current Trends in Computing. XX, 853 pages. 2004. (Subseries LNAI).

Vol. 3065: A. Lomuscio, D. Nute (Eds.), Deontic Logic in Computer Science. X, 275 pages. 2004. (Subseries LNAI).

Vol. 3064: D. Bienstock, G. Nemhauser (Eds.), Integer Programming and Combinatorial Optimization. XI, 445 pages. 2004.

Vol. 3063: A. Llamosí, A. Strohmeier (Eds.), Reliable Software Technologies - Ada-Europe 2004. XIII, 333 pages. 2004.

Vol. 3062: J.L. Pfaltz, M. Nagl, B. Böhlen (Eds.), Applications of Graph Transformations with Industrial Relevance. XV, 500 pages. 2004.

Vol. 3061: F.F. Ramos, H. Unger, V. Larios (Eds.), Advanced Distributed Systems. VIII, 285 pages. 2004.

Vol. 3060: A.Y. Tawfik, S.D. Goodwin (Eds.), Advances in Artificial Intelligence. XIII, 582 pages. 2004. (Subseries LNAI).

Vol. 3059: C.C. Ribeiro, S.L. Martins (Eds.), Experimental and Efficient Algorithms. X, 586 pages. 2004.

Vol. 3058: N. Sebe, M.S. Lew, T.S. Huang (Eds.), Computer Vision in Human-Computer Interaction. X, 233 pages. 2004.

Vol. 3057: B. Jayaraman (Ed.), Practical Aspects of Declarative Languages. VIII, 255 pages. 2004.

Vol. 3056: H. Dai, R. Srikant, C. Zhang (Eds.), Advances in Knowledge Discovery and Data Mining. XIX, 713 pages. 2004. (Subseries LNAI).

Vol. 3055: H. Christiansen, M.-S. Hacid, T. Andreasen, H.L. Larsen (Eds.), Flexible Query Answering Systems. X, 500 pages. 2004. (Subseries LNAI).

Vol. 3054: I. Crnkovic, J.A. Stafford, H.W. Schmidt, K. Wallnau (Eds.), Component-Based Software Engineering. XI, 311 pages. 2004.

Vol. 3053: C. Bussler, J. Davies, D. Fensel, R. Studer (Eds.), The Semantic Web: Research and Applications. XIII, 490 pages. 2004.

Vol. 3052: W. Zimmermann, B. Thalheim (Eds.), Abstract State Machines 2004. Advances in Theory and Practice. XII, 235 pages. 2004.

Vol. 3051: R. Berghammer, B. Möller, G. Struth (Eds.), Relational and Kleene-Algebraic Methods in Computer Science. X, 279 pages. 2004.

Vol. 3050: J. Domingo-Ferrer, V. Torra (Eds.), Privacy in Statistical Databases. IX, 367 pages. 2004.

Vol. 3049: M. Bruynooghe, K.-K. Lau (Eds.), Program Development in Computational Logic. VIII, 539 pages. 2004.

Vol. 3047: F. Oquendo, B. Warboys, R. Morrison (Eds.), Software Architecture. X, 279 pages. 2004.

Vol. 3046: A. Laganà, M.L. Gavrilova, V. Kumar, Y. Mun, C.K. Tan, O. Gervasi (Eds.), Computational Science and Its Applications - ICCSA 2004. LIII, 1016 pages. 2004.

Vol. 3045: A. Laganà, M.L. Gavrilova, V. Kumar, Y. Mun, C.K. Tan, O. Gervasi (Eds.), Computational Science and Its Applications - ICCSA 2004. LIII, 1040 pages. 2004.

Vol. 3044: A. Laganà, M.L. Gavrilova, V. Kumar, Y. Mun, C.K. Tan, O. Gervasi (Eds.), Computational Science and Its Applications - ICCSA 2004. LIII, 1140 pages. 2004.

Vol. 3043: A. Laganà, M.L. Gavrilova, V. Kumar, Y. Mun, C.K. Tan, O. Gervasi (Eds.), Computational Science and Its Applications - ICCSA 2004. LIII, 1180 pages. 2004.

Vol. 3042: N. Mitrou, K. Kontovasilis, G.N. Rouskas, I. Iliadis, L. Merakos (Eds.), NETWORKING 2004, Networking Technologies, Services, and Protocols; Performance of Computer and Communication Networks; Mobile and Wireless Communications. XXXIII, 1519 pages. 2004.

Vol. 3040: R. Conejo, M. Urretavizcaya, J.-L. Pérez-de-la-Cruz (Eds.), Current Topics in Artificial Intelligence. XIV, 689 pages. 2004. (Subseries LNAI).

Vol. 3039: M. Bubak, G.D.v. Albada, P.M. Sloot, J.J. Dongarra (Eds.), Computational Science - ICCS 2004. LXVI, 1271 pages. 2004.

Vol. 3038: M. Bubak, G.D.v. Albada, P.M. Sloot, J.J. Dongarra (Eds.), Computational Science - ICCS 2004. LXVI, 1311 pages. 2004.

Vol. 3037: M. Bubak, G.D.v. Albada, P.M. Sloot, J.J. Dongarra (Eds.), Computational Science - ICCS 2004. LXVI, 745 pages. 2004.

Vol. 3036: M. Bubak, G.D.v. Albada, P.M. Sloot, J.J. Dongarra (Eds.), Computational Science - ICCS 2004. LXVI, 713 pages. 2004.

Vol. 3035: M.A. Wimmer (Ed.), Knowledge Management in Electronic Government. XII, 326 pages. 2004. (Subseries LNAI).

Vol. 3034: J. Favela, E. Menasalvas, E. Chávez (Eds.), Advances in Web Intelligence. XIII, 227 pages. 2004. (Subseries LNAI).

Vol. 3033: M. Li, X.-H. Sun, Q. Deng, J. Ni (Eds.), Grid and Cooperative Computing. XXXVIII, 1076 pages. 2004.

Vol. 3032: M. Li, X.-H. Sun, Q. Deng, J. Ni (Eds.), Grid and Cooperative Computing. XXXVII, 1112 pages. 2004.

Vol. 3031: A. Butz, A. Krüger, P. Olivier (Eds.), Smart Graphics. X, 165 pages. 2004.

Vol. 3030: P. Giorgini, B. Henderson-Sellers, M. Winikoff (Eds.), Agent-Oriented Information Systems. XIV, 207 pages. 2004. (Subseries LNAI).

Vol. 3029: B. Orchard, C. Yang, M. Ali (Eds.), Innovations in Applied Artificial Intelligence. XXI, 1272 pages. 2004. (Subseries LNAI).

Vol. 3028: D. Neuenschwander, Probabilistic and Statistical Methods in Cryptology. X, 158 pages. 2004.